Human Rights and Common Good

Works of John Finnis available from
Oxford University Press

Reason in Action
Collected Essays: Volume I

Intention and Identity
Collected Essays: Volume II

Human Rights and Common Good
Collected Essays: Volume III

Philosophy of Law
Collected Essays: Volume IV

Religion and Public Reasons
Collected Essays: Volume V

Natural Law and Natural Rights
Second Edition

Aquinas
Moral, Political, and Legal Theory

Nuclear Deterrence, Morality and Realism
with Joseph Boyle and Germain Grisez

HUMAN RIGHTS AND COMMON GOOD

Collected Essays: Volume III

John Finnis

OXFORD
UNIVERSITY PRESS

Great Clarendon Street, Oxford OX2 6DP

Oxford University Press is a department of the University of Oxford.
It furthers the University's objective of excellence in research, scholarship,
and education by publishing worldwide in

Oxford   New York

Auckland   Cape Town   Dar es Salaam   Hong Kong   Karachi
Kuala Lumpur   Madrid   Melbourne   Mexico City   Nairobi
New Delhi   Shanghai   Taipei   Toronto

With offices in

Argentina   Austria   Brazil   Chile   Czech Republic   France   Greece
Guatemala   Hungary   Italy   Japan   Poland   Portugal   Singapore
South Korea   Switzerland   Thailand   Turkey   Ukraine   Vietnam

Oxford is a registered trade mark of Oxford University Press
in the UK and in certain other countries

Published in the United States
by Oxford University Press Inc., New York

© J. M. Finnis, 2011

The moral rights of the author have been asserted

Crown Copyright material reproduced with the permission of the
Controller, HMSO (under the terms of the Click Use licence)

Database right Oxford University Press (maker)

First published 2011

All rights reserved. No part of this publication may be reproduced,
stored in a retrieval system, or transmitted, in any form or by any means,
without the prior permission in writing of Oxford University Press,
or as expressly permitted by law, or under terms agreed with the appropriate
reprographics rights organization. Enquiries concerning reproduction
outside the scope of the above should be sent to the Rights Department,
Oxford University Press, at the address above

You must not circulate this book in any other binding or cover
and you must impose the same condition on any acquirer

British Library Cataloguing in Publication Data

Data available

Library of Congress Cataloging in Publication Data

Data available

Typeset by Newgen Imaging Systems (P) Ltd, Chennai, India
Printed in Great Britain
on acid-free paper by
CPI Antony Rowe

ISBN 978–0–19–958007–1

1 3 5 7 9 10 8 6 4 2

PREFACE

The earliest of the essays collected in these five volumes dates from 1967, the latest from 2010. The chronological Bibliography of my publications, near the end of each volume, shows how the collected essays are distributed across the volumes. But each volume also contains some essays previously unpublished.

Many of the essays appear with new titles. When the change is substantial, the original published title is noted at the beginning of the essay; the original can of course always also be found in the Bibliography.

Revision of previously published work has been restricted to clarification. Where there seems need for substantive qualification or retraction, I have said so in an endnote to the essay or, occasionally, in a bracketed footnote. Unless the context otherwise indicates, square brackets signify an insertion made for this Collection. Endnotes to particular essays have also been used for some updating, especially of relevant law. In general, each essay speaks from the time of its writing, though the dates given in the Table of Contents are dates of publication (where applicable) not composition—which sometimes was one or two years earlier.

I have tried to group the selected essays by theme, both across and within the volumes. But there is a good deal of overlapping, and something of each volume's theme will be found in each of the other volumes. The Index, which like the Bibliography (but not the 'Other Works Cited') is common to all volumes, gives some further indication of this, though it aspires to completeness only as to names of persons. Each volume's own Introduction serves to amplify and explain that volume's title, and the bearing of its essays on that theme.

CONTENTS

List of Abbreviations   ix
The Cover Picture   xi

Introduction   1

Part One   *Human Rights and Common Good: General Theory*   17

1. Human Rights and Their Enforcement (1985)   19
2. Duties to Oneself in Kant (1987)   47
3. Rawls's *A Theory of Justice* (1973)   72
4. Distributive Justice and the Bottom Line (1979)   76
5. Limited Government (1996)   83
6. Virtue and the Constitution (2001)   107
7. Migration Rights (1992)   116
8. Boundaries (2003)   125
9. Nationality and Alienage (2007)   133

Part Two   *Justice and Punishment*   151

10. Hart's Philosophy of Punishment (1968)   153
11. The Restoration of Retribution (1972)   161
12. Retribution: Punishment's Formative Aim (1999)   167

Part Three   *War and Justice*   181

13. War and Peace in the Natural Law Tradition (1996)   183

Part Four   *Autonomy, Euthanasia, and Justice*   209

14. Euthanasia and Justice (1995)   211
15. Economics, Justice, and the Value of Life (1992)   242
16. Euthanasia and the Law (1998)   251

Part Five *Autonomy, IVF, Abortion, and Justice*   271

17. C.S. Lewis and Test-Tube Babies (1984)   273
18. The Rights and Wrongs of Abortion (1973)   282
19. Justice for Mother and Child (1993)   307

Part Six *Marriage, Justice, and the Common Good*   315

20. Marriage: A Basic and Exigent Good (2008)   317
21. Law, Morality, and 'Sexual Orientation' (1997)   334
22. Sex and Marriage: Some Myths and Reasons (1997)   353

Bibliography of the Works of John Finnis   389
Other Works Cited   401
Acknowledgements   409
Index   411

LIST OF ABBREVIATIONS

AAS	*Acta Apostolicae Sedis* (Rome)
AJJ	American Journal of Jurisprudence
AL	Joseph Raz, *The Authority of Law: Essays on Law and Morality* (OUP, 1979)
Aquinas	1998d: John Finnis, *Aquinas: Moral, Political and Legal Theory* (OUP)
CCC	*Catechism of the Catholic Church* (rev edn, 1997)
CDF	Congregation for the Doctrine of the Faith (of the Holy See)
CL	H.L.A. Hart, *The Concept of Law* [1961] (2nd edn, OUP, 1994)
CLR	Commonwealth Law Reports (of decisions of the High Court of Australia)
CUP	Cambridge: Cambridge University Press
ECtHR	European Court of Human Rights
FoE	1983b: John Finnis, *Fundamentals of Ethics* (OUP; Washington, DC: Georgetown University Press)
HUP	Cambridge, Mass.: Harvard University Press
In Eth.	Aquinas, *Sententia Libri Ethicorum* [Commentary on *NE*] (ed. Gauthier) (1969)
In Pol.	Aquinas, *Sententia Libri Politicorum* [Commentary on *Pol.* I to III.5]
LCL	Germain Grisez, *The Way of the Lord Jesus*, vol. 2 *Living a Christian Life* (Quincy: Franciscan Press, 1993)
LQR	Law Quarterly Review
MA	1991c: John Finnis, *Moral Absolutes: Tradition, Revision, and Truth* (Catholic University of America Press)
NDMR	1987g: John Finnis, Joseph Boyle, and Germain Grisez, *Nuclear Deterrence, Morality and Realism* (OUP)
NE	Aristotle, *Nicomachean Ethics*
NLNR	1980a: John Finnis, *Natural Law and Natural Rights* (2nd edn, OUP, 2011)
OUP	Oxford: Oxford University Press (including Clarendon Press)

Pol.	Aristotle, *Politics*
ScG	Aquinas, *Summa contra Gentiles* [A Summary against the Pagans] (c. 1259–65?)
Sent.	Aquinas, *Scriptum super Libros Sententiarum Petri Lombardiensis* [Commentary on the Sentences [Opinions or Positions of the Church Fathers] of Peter Lombard] (c. 1255)
ST	Aquinas, *Summa Theologiae* [A Summary of Theology] (c. 1265–73)
TJ	John Rawls, *A Theory of Justice* (HUP, 1971)
TRS	Ronald Dworkin, *Taking Rights Seriously* ([1977] rev edn with Reply to Critics) (HUP; London: Duckworth, 1978)

THE COVER PICTURE

Glen Osmond Mine 1845; watercolour by S.T. Gill, Adelaide 1845.

The first mineral discovery in South Australia was here, four miles south-east of the centre of Adelaide, in 1839. By 1841, ore was being lifted from a shaft a little further up the hill. Twenty tons sent back to England were found to be 75 per cent lead with 18 ounces of silver to the ton. The Glen Osmond Union Mining Company was formed in London in 1843–44, with paid-up capital of £30,000, to mine the land under a lease. The high rate of royalty demanded by the landowner, Mr Osmond Gilles, resulted in litigation and abandonment of the mine before the main lodes were reached. The mines up the hill were more productive, until most of those involved (and a large proportion of the colony's men) left for the goldfields in the neighbouring colony of Victoria in 1850–51. These Glen Osmond mines were the first mines in Australia, but by 1850 South Australia was producing 10 per cent of the world's copper, in the districts north and a little east of the Barossa Valley. But the Glen Osmond mines alone had been sufficient, even in the absence of royalties payable to the government, to bring the colony back from ruinous public and private poverty.

Osmond Gilles had come to Adelaide with the first Governor in 1836, as first Colonial Treasurer, having for many years been a merchant in Hamburg. This wealthy, difficult man, who served in public office in the colony for only a couple of years, was one of those responsible for encouraging the emigration of Germans to South Australia in the colony's first years (see 'The Cover Picture' in vol. II).

The picture is looking north-north-east, in or soon after summer. Within a few years, the slopes below the mines were planted with vineyards for red and white wines. On the brow of the hill above the mine, just out of this part of the picture, the artist (whose attitude to the indigenous inhabitants was always sympathetic) has depicted three Aboriginals, two with their backs to the mine, the other sitting, relaxed, looking out over the plain to the western sea.

INTRODUCTION

The reasons each of us has for choosing and acting are those intelligible goods which go to make up the flourishing of human persons and their communities. Though basically common to us all, those benefits of action—common goods, in a first sense of the phrase—can reasonably be brought about in many different ways and thus be elements of the flourishing of individuals in many different kinds of association. In each such association the actions of its members as members seeking to promote and benefit from it are actions envisaging a common good. A common good in this second sense of the phrase is in one way or another the benefit (whether as end or means or both) of so associating with other persons that their good purposes and one's own are advanced. The common good of a lecture audience is that by maintaining the conditions for undistracted audibility and so forth, the lecturer's immediate purposes in speaking and the audience's in listening (even if only to spot mistakes) are advanced. The common good of a political community (paradigmatically, a state) is vastly more ambitious and complex, and includes the upholding of the rights of all its members against threats of injustice from inside and outside the community.

Thus, this volume's essays on human rights and common good mark another step along the way from Volume I's explorations of practical reason's truth and normativity, via Volume II's studies of the persons at stake in intending and choosing, towards Volume IV's essays on law and the Rule of Law as normally vital conditions for the upholding of rights under threat, and Volume V's attention to the ultimate grounds for goodwill towards one's neighbours and oneself. Many of this volume's essays, beginning with the first, take our law and constitution as the frame for their pursuit of questions not about law but about what kinds of flourishing, and thus what kinds of rights, would appropriately be the object of legal protection, in our societies or, again, in any.

The headings for this volume's six parts mostly refer to justice. They do so because of an inter-definability acknowledged by Mill[1] as firmly as by the Roman jurists and Aquinas:[2] the object of the virtue of justice, and thus the source of the justness of just acts and arrangements, is that people all get what is theirs by right. Which is to say: that (to the extent measured by one's duties of justice) each person's *rights* are respected and promoted.

I. HUMAN RIGHTS AND COMMON GOOD: GENERAL THEORY

It is relatively easy to give a formal or conceptual account of human rights. Less easy, but vastly more important, is showing that human rights are not like unicorns, phlogiston, or taboos: of ethnographic interest only.

Human rights have the logic explored, in relation to legal rights, in essay IV.18 (1972b) and *NLNR* VIII.2–3, and in relation to moral rights, in essay 18. Though statements of them standardly take the two-term form '[Each person] has the [right to life]' or '[A, like everyone else] has the [right not to be tortured]', a specification of them that is sufficient to guide choice needs to be in three-term form. Such a specification will—to take the central case—identify not only the (classes of) persons who have the right, and the interest of theirs that they have the right to (respect for or promotion of), but also the persons who have that duty of respect or promotion of interest and the kind of choice (to act or forbear) that is required of them to fulfil that duty. ('Interest' is shorthand for an element in a person's well-being, in such persons' flourishing.) Thus: 'The state's government and legislature have the duty to prevent threats to the lives of persons within the state's jurisdiction', and so forth. The right may be that deleterious choices shall not be made, or that choices to assist shall be made, or both. It may require, as an ancillary aspect of its content, that officials or legislators exercise their constitutional powers to provide such assistance and to forestall and punish violations of the right whether by officials or others within the jurisdiction.

Equally straightforward is the conceptual mapping of *human* rights' place in modern discourse. It broadly tracks the conceptual map of what an earlier way of speaking called *natural* right(s). Gaius in the second century AD taught that neither state law nor communal convention can do away with natural rights.[3] Aquinas in the thirteenth century taught that

---

[1] e.g. *Utilitarianism*, ch. 5: 'Justice implies something which it is not only right to do, and wrong not to do, but which some individual person can claim from us as his moral right.'
[2] *ST* II–II q.58 a.1c quoting Justinian's *Digest* I.1.i.10 and *Institutes* I.1.1.
[3] *Digest* 43.18.2: *civilis ratio corrumpere naturalia iura non potest*. Likewise Gaius, *Institutes* II.65.

positive law, even written, definite, and clear, cannot make just, morally binding, or properly enforceable what is inherently repugnant to natural right.[4] So today Ronald Dworkin says that it is the mark of genuine rights that, morally, politically and (in well-ordered states) constitutionally, they prevail against legislation, executive authority, and judicial decisions erroneously failing to enforce them.[5] And Joseph Raz accounts for human rights as interests of individuals such that, in the prevailing conditions of internal social and political arrangements and international relations, any state government not only has a duty to respect and/or promote those individual interests as rights but also, in the event of default in such respect or promotion, is legitimately subject to rectificatory interference by other states or entities in the international community.[6]

Equally plainly, laws and decisions declaring and giving effect to human rights have the complexity characteristic of positive law. Some of them stand to the right in question as a simple application or deductive conclusion. More commonly they stand to the right in question as *determinationes*, that is, specifications and delimitations which when reasonable could nonetheless reasonably have been different, in some or many respects: think of rules about anonymity of defendants, or complainants, or witnesses, in criminal trials, as specifications of the right to a fair trial and the right to free speech.[7] Some rules—perhaps many—stand to the right they purport to enforce as more or less unsatisfactory would-be specifications which, on a better understanding of that or other rights, would be reversed or amended more or less extensively. Some fairly common features of declarations of human rights are juridically primitive, introducing deeply misleading concepts such as justified interferences with or violations of rights,[8] and crude formulations of the principles of such justifications.[9] Such infelicities are constantly magnified by more or less manifestly unreasonable judicial or legislative interpretations.[10] In all these ways, at least, what can be true of certain elemental human rights accurately defined is more or less clearly not true of many rights constitutionally, legislatively, or judicially declared to be human: that they are properly enforceable against anyone and everyone's conceptions of common good or public interest. Unjustly established legal human rights are 'human rights', not human rights

---

[4] *ST* II–II q.57 a.2c and ad 2; q.60 a.5.   [5] See essay 1, secs II and VII.
[6] Raz, 'Human Rights Without Foundations', secs 3 and 4.
[7] See *NLNR* VIII.5, X.7; and essay I.1 (2005a) at n. 3.
[8] See essay 1 at 40 and its endnote §.
[9] Notably: 'necessary in a democratic society for the protection of …'. See essay 1 at 40.
[10] See essay 1 at 39; for an illustration see the analysis in 2009e, sec. 1, of *R (Begum) v Denbigh High School Governors* [2006] UKHL 15, [2007] 1 AC 100. The analysis concludes: 'The conceptual slackness of human rights law-in-action is impressive.'

(except for purposes of intra-systemic discourse within that legal system). And the same can be said for rights which are legally declared, in a given jurisdiction, to be human rights but which there and in other places could just as well be different in their content, force, and effect.

But all this conceptual mapping or accounting leaves unaddressed, and squarely in play, the question whether anyone *truly* has such rights, truly has interests such that other persons and groups who (with or without claiming justification) violate them act immorally by doing so. Or are they yet another conventional *taboo*, a way of speaking, thinking, and feeling—perhaps one that the weak or sentimental employ to chain in mythic guilt the strong who would otherwise, and fittingly, be their masters? Or is the very idea of human rights an immoral or rationally groundless *speciesism*, arbitrarily favouring some human beings who in value or moral status are below some non-human animals? In face of all the manifold inequalities between human beings, how can there possibly be sufficient, or any, grounding for the claim that all members of the human race are *equally* entitled to these or any rights?

Human persons share a nature that is known by knowing the many and deeply varied objects that make sense of human acts; for it is those acts that reveal what human beings can do, and to know a being's capacities is to know its nature. Take Anscombe's example (essay II.3, at p. 71). It was not about pointing, as such; some other animals perhaps do this. It was about the act of pointing to a figure to distinguish its shape from its colour (and perhaps, I add, to compare the former with a battleship at Trafalgar, and the latter with maps of the British Empire). And about the act of attending to the pointer to understand the precise point being made about the figure, and then perhaps about the comparison or analogy. Both are intentional acts whose intended objects are twofold: intelligibilities (shape and colour, as concepts; and as analogies; and as what the pointer intended and meant); and the communicating of these to an audience (so to speak). Or take again the example deployed in *Natural Law and Natural Rights*: the story of Nathan's rebuke to King David by the parable of the rich man's covetous and devious appropriation of the poor man's ewe has as its object the drawing and communicating of an analogy, and the articulation of a moral, and the suasive educating of the audience's heart (willingness) as well as mind (intellect). Or again: Socrates' recounting to his jurors the true story of his perilous refusal to participate in a politically motivated liquidation of a tyranny's opponent ('the others went off to Salamis [to arrest the opponent] and I went home') has a similarly complex spiritual object, meant for and available to the understanding and the informed goodwill, and the intellectual conversion, of those of his jurors willing to make comprehending him one of their own objects; and Plato's objects in narrating that recounting share in some of Socrates' more ultimate purposes though not his immediate object, acquittal. A final example: Shakespeare's so-called 'Phoenix and Turtle' is the kind of spiritual object we call a poem, in which formality, linguistic and literary form, and allusion are put in service of meanings and here of double-meanings celebrating not merely the upper-level's abstract possibilities of interpersonal unity but also, in mourning, the concealed and secret lower-level's requiem and urn/poem burial of a wife and husband united despite parting by exile and then death.[11] The reflectively astounding multi-vocality and many-levelled complexity of the objects referred to in such an object—such objects as fidelity to marital commitment, faith in things not seen but reasonably believed and hoped in, political opposition, preservation of secrecy, secret sharing of secrets, and many more—gives us a way of grasping the *kind* of radically trans-material, spiritual objects of human action (the lovers', the poet's, the witnesses' and audiences', and one's own). And thus of grasping human capacities. And nature.

In doing so, one is enriching one's understanding of the basic elements in human flourishing, the basic goods that have made sense of one's reasonable actions since one first became able to understand them and the directiveness (normativity) they have for one's practical reasoning, deliberations, and choices. In each of these cases the good of knowledge and truth is instantiated and made more significant and directive, and in the three stories (each with stories within stories) truths about other basic human goods are conveyed—about friendship including political friendship, about practical reasonableness itself, and about marriage, for example. In every case one understands these goods as *good for me and anyone like me*. The at first indefinite extensional and intensional reference of 'anyone like me' is clarified, in reflection, as: 'any human person'.

For: reflection on the continuity of one's identity and life—through sleep, through traumatic unconsciousness, through the unrememberable eventfulness of one's infant life, through one's life in the womb and, as it may be, one's future life in senility and dementia (Shakespeare's 'second childishness')—makes evident that what is valuable for oneself is valuable and significant in a qualitatively similar way for any being with the same capacities as oneself. For all of us, those dynamic capacities were once only *radical*, and then by maturation and good health became active capacities, ready for actualization in actions made intelligible by their objects— mostly intended objects of the kinds just now recalled in exemplary

[11] See essay II.2 (2005c), sec. V; 2003e; essay I.1 (2005a), sec. V and Postscript.

form. So it is the sharing in radical dynamic capacities that is the basic unity of the human race or species and, by virtue of the true goodness and directiveness of the basic human goods, is the ground and foundation of the human rights which are specific objects of that directiveness in its interpersonal implications. What is fundamentally good (and bad) for me is fundamentally good (and bad) for you. 'You are the man.'[12] 'Go and do thou likewise.'[13]

Acts of meaning (say pointing, or poetic composition, or rigorous scientific reflection), like other intentional acts (say resolving to 'do likewise', or betraying, promising, or rescuing) are understood by those who choose to do them, and by intelligent participants and observers, as actions *of* an individual, a responsible person, author of and answerable for his or her conduct. They make manifest (even, though in an extended sense, when they are successful deceptions) the person, someone whose complete, non-fungible distinctness from other human persons the human baby begins to be aware of, and soon enough to understand, as the baby locks onto and follows *eyes* and learns to read them, that is to make inferences from them as if they were windows of the soul—intentionality, emotionality, sensitivity—of the person whose eyes they are. To that person his or her *own* individuality, responsibility (authorship), and subsisting identity is vastly more transparent. At the same time, the fact that other persons have the same *kind of*—and therefore thoroughly particular, non-replicably individual—transparent-to-self and partially self-shaped identity is as indubitable as if it were transparent rather than inferred. Despite their difference, each of these logically distinct kinds of knowledge of the person fits easily within our idea of the experienced and perceived. Together these ways of knowing oneself and others as not only intelligible but also intelligent, not only active but each a doer and maker, provide the stable factual basis for the practical norms centring on 'Do to others as you would wish them to do to you, and don't do to them...'. Such norms or principles, being about what is needed to instantiate the good of being reasonable and the good of friendship, are not inferred from their factual foundation, but rather take it as the matrix, so to speak, for the practical insight they articulate: that a way of relating personally and humanely to other persons is not only factually possible but also desirable, intelligent, and in itself incalculably superior to alternative ways of relating (such as sadistic harm-doing, or indifference to the baby

---

[12] The accusatory conclusion of Nathan's parable to the covetous royal killer, who acted against not only the good of life but also the good of marriage: 2 Samuel 12: 7; *NLNR* 106–7.
[13] The conclusion of the parable of the Good Samaritan: Luke 10: 30–7, v. 37.

in the snow alongside one's path).[14] So those principles' 'being about what is needed to instantiate the good of being reasonable ... etc.' turns out to mean: their being about what is needed to be a person who respects other persons, for their own sake, and sees the need to give to each of them their due, and indeed to (in ways involving all manner of prioritization and nothing merely sentimental) love—will the good of—these neighbours as oneself.

One's identity (as a person with interests that are truly intelligible goods) all the way back to one's beginning as a pre-implantation embryo[15] (with the radical capacities whose ultimate objects—those same intelligible goods—one now participates in and deliberately intends) is the ontological foundation of one's human rights, because it is the foundation of one's judgment that 'I matter' and of one's duties to respect and promote one's own good, and therefore of one's judgment that 'others matter' and of one's duties to other persons to respect and promote their good. For they too have such identities (all the way back, and all the way forward to the end of their lifetimes), such radical capacities, and intelligible forms of flourishing (and harm) of just the same kind as one's own. Just as immaturity and impairment do not, in one's own existence, extinguish the radical capacities dynamically oriented towards self-development and healing, so they do not in the lives of other human persons. *There* is the ontological unity of the human race, and radical equality of human persons which, taken with the truths about basic human goods, grounds the duties whose correlatives are human rights—duties *to*, responsibilities *for*, persons.

Where these duties are negative duties of respect (duties *not* to intentionally damage or destroy persons in basic aspects of their flourishing) they can be unconditional and exceptionless: 'absolute rights'. Where they are affirmative responsibilities to promote well-being, they must inevitably be conditional, relative, defeasible, and prioritized by rational criteria of responsibility such as parenthood, promise, inter-dependence, compensation and restitution, and so forth. Such criteria of priority in responsibility, in combination with other conditions of securing common good, are in play in shaping the reasonable specification of the obligations of membership in one or other of the communities, political and non-political, of which one is non-voluntarily or voluntarily a member. And many such obligations are correlative to rights. Thus, for example, the obligations of parents to their children are correlative to rights of those children to support, nurture, education, protection, and so forth, rights which in their

---

[14] On the character and reliability of our understanding of first practical (normative) principles, see e.g. essay I.1 (2005a), secs IV and V; essay I.9 (1987a); *NLNR* chs III and IV.
[15] See essay II.16 (1993a).

basic aspects, at least, can reasonably be called human. (On gross parental default, such obligations pass to surrogates specified by or under law, against whom the rights avail thereafter.) A legally tolerated practice of infanticide or incest might reasonably, in appropriate circumstances (now perhaps rare), be grounds for international intervention and regime change (even, perhaps, by force).

Understood as grounded in the truths about human make-up and well-being recalled briefly in the preceding five paragraphs, human rights are vindicated against general moral scepticism, and against the charge of speciesism. For they are predicated of all human persons not as members of the class 'our race/species', nor out of an emotional or arbitrary sympathy of like with like, but as beings each and all of whom have the *dignity* of having the at least radical capacity of participating in the human goods that are picked out in practical reason's first principles (first and foremost the good of human existence/life) and that make sense of all human intending. For dignity denotes a rank of being, and all beings of this rank have the *worth* that we reasonably predicate of beings and ways of being that participate (even if only radically) in those intelligible goods, participate in them (even the bodily and earthy goods) in the remarkable way I earlier called spiritual, and so when flourishing maturely participate in them intentionally and with intent that others of the same rank share such participation and flourishing. And the 'each' and 'all' in the preceding sentences demarcate the sense in which we all are basically equal and entitled to the concern and respect appropriate for human persons, and to the substantive human rights applicable to our state of maturity, health, and activated capacities. Differences of intelligence that are properly relevant to the distribution of educational opportunities and of occupational responsibilities are quite irrelevant to this dignity of the human over all that is subhuman, and to the human rights to equal concern and respect, life, and so forth.

It would in principle be reasonable to go no further in this sketch of answers to the challenges to the very idea of human rights. Any further questions about the foundations of the foundations I have pointed to might properly—and prudently—be remitted to Volume V. But without straying even momentarily beyond philosophy's bounds, it can be observed that ascribing the manifold intelligibilities of nature to sheer chance is a hypothesis far less plausible than the judgment (or if you like, the hypothesis) that they are to be ascribed to intelligence. Not to an intelligence immanent within nature, but to an intelligence transcending the nature that lies open to our experience and empirical investigation. But if to an intelligence, then also to a will capable of freely choosing *this* vast universal order of intelligible natures and laws-of-nature governed events rather than any of the infinitely many possible alternative orders, or than choosing to abstain altogether from such creating and sustaining. And if to intelligence, will, and freedom in willing, then to something somehow personal. Our finding ourselves persons in a universe where all other beings known to us by experience and observation are subpersonal is then complemented by the hypothesis of a supreme centre and height of personality, creative and governing of everything else, though without prejudice to the freedom of choice we know (from philosophically warrantable experience) we have. And fittingly there are two further, linked hypotheses which for many philosophers from Plato onwards are judgments, albeit variously conceived and expressed. (1) That our own free intending of benefits in choices and actions for the sake of ourselves and our communities is a kind of interpersonal partnership, albeit of unequals, in shaping nature and history: a cooperation, so to speak, in Providence. And (2) that our understanding of ourselves and so of other human persons as each ends in ourselves, not merely means to other ends, corresponds to the intention of the providential author and sustainer of the universe for each of us, an intention that ratifies our status.

Neither of these hypotheses or judgments is a mere Kantian postulation to save the phenomena of morality. Each is, rather, a sober reflection on what the structure of reality makes inferable once its remarkable uniting of matter with spirit, and of intelligibility with theoretical and practical intelligence, is held steadily in mind. And, as Nietzsche understood in (without sufficient reason) denying it, that inference is highly if not indispensably supportive of the thesis that human beings are of equal worth and bearers of true moral rights by virtue of their humanity.

Essays 1–6, and to some extent essay 9, all take the perspective customary in political philosophy. That is, they treat the political community, and the problems of justice that arise within it, as if it were the only political community in the world. Essays 7, 8, and to some extent 9, take some steps towards accommodating the reality that the world is divided up between many states, not to mention regions and resources that are still common to all.

Essay 1 was originally entitled 'A Bill of Rights for Britain? The Moral of Contemporary Jurisprudence', and approaches human rights from a juridical and specialized perspective. But it seems to me to deserve its place at the opening of the volume. For although it touches also on constitutional and institutional issues which are in themselves far from universal, it deals concretely with many of the main philosophical issues that bear on moral rights as conclusions from, rather than axioms among, ethical first principles. On the way from practical reason's first principles to such rights-affirming conclusions, let alone to constituent decisions about their enforcement by government and law, a number of important questions must be answered clearly—for instance, about the aggregatability of goods that utilitarianism assumes. Ronald Dworkin's and John Rawls's work, though in each case strongly shaped by methods and assumptions peculiar to its author, provided ample stimulus and opportunity for testing the theses of a new-classical moral and political theory that is neither liberal nor anti-liberal, but is opposed to taking liberalism either for granted or as framework.

Essay 2 seeks to get to the roots of Kant's political and legal theory. It makes no attempt to disguise the extent to which his positions anticipate contemporary liberal theses that have been employed with vast success in dismantling constitutional support for and acknowledgement of some fundamental truths about human well-being and children's rights. But it shows something very unwelcome to some members of its original audience: how plainly distant Kant was from sponsoring those theses as now meant and deployed. It touches, too, on fundamental weaknesses in Kant's understanding of practical reason which are a little more amply explored in my *Fundamentals of Ethics*, and are taken up again in relation to contemporary neo-Kantians in essay I.1 (2005a).

My own approach to paternalism in essay 2 lacks precision. As in *NLNR* VIII.6, state paternalism is not endorsed, though it is defended against the unsound objections of Rawls, Dworkin, and Richards; as in *NLNR* VIII.4, it is implicitly endorsed (subject to considerations of subsidiarity) in relation to children, as a matter of children's rights. But essay 2 fails to bring into view let alone to endorse (and it should be endorsed) the classical position about which I get clear in *Aquinas* VII.2–7 and heavily underline, against Hart, in essay IV.11 (2009b), secs III–IV: the coercive jurisdiction of the state's government and law is restricted to the upholding of justice and peace—of *public* good—and does not have as its proper object either the character or the other-worldly destiny of adult individuals so far as they are affected by their own choices and actions. Essay 5, sec. III from n. 30 to the end of the section, has the right distinctions in place but treats Aquinas as if his position resembled Aristotle's paternalism, whereas in truth that state paternalism is quite rejected, in principle, by Aquinas. It was only after writing essay 5 (1996a) that I came across or correctly understood the passages in Aquinas's published and until recently unpublished texts that, taken together, make his anti-paternalism clear (see *Aquinas* VII.2).

Of course, it is one thing to deny that state government and law have coercive jurisdiction over the truly private acts of consenting adults, and quite another to assert, as Dworkin and many others have, that state government and law should be neutral—and are required to be by people's right to equal concern and respect—about even the basic elements of human good and therefore about what is morally right or wrong besides injustice. (As if injustice itself could be identified without conceptions of harm dependent on conceptions of human goods! And as if governments and laws can be neutral about the good without incurring grave injustice to the many children whose parents are similarly neutral, mistaken, or negligent about true human good, or hostile to it.) Essay 6 sets out and illustrates some main aspects of the position that seems to me sound after the clarification achieved in 1996/7.

Essays 7–9 relate to the social conditions which are needed—as is argued in essays II.6 (2008b) and II.7 (2008a)—for a political community to have sufficient unity to be ruled without extensive resort to force and legislative and executive measures departing more or less widely from the Rule of Law. Essays 7 and 8 concern the holding of the state's territory. Whether treated as *imperium* (understood as territorial sovereignty) or *dominium* (territorial ownership), the relationships of the political community and its citizens with the territory it holds as its own are strongly analogous to legal property rights over land within that territory. Fundamental, in either case, is the right that non-citizens/non-owners shall enter only with permission, and the liberty, authority and ability to exclude them both in advance of, during, or after entry. The question whether this right of exclusion is itself a violation of human rights, a fundamental kind of injustice, or is rather a sound and just arrangement of human affairs and conducive to the protection and promotion of justice and human rights worldwide, is the question taken up in essays 7 and 8, each with slightly different starting points. The question's constitutional implications are the subject of essay 9, the last paragraph of which broaches an urgent and under-debated contemporary problem also discussed in essay II.7 (2008a), essay V.1 (2009c), sec. VII, essay V.4 (2006a), sec. VII, and essay 2009e, sec. 4, not to mention essay IV.11 (2009b), sec. IV.

II. JUSTICE AND PUNISHMENT

Rights, natural and human and then legal, are what just punishment vindicates. Just compensation, whether volunteered or lawfully assessed and ordered in judicial (including arbitral) proceedings, also vindicates rights. Often these two forms of vindication relate to the same conduct, which was both a crime (offence) and a civil wrong (tort/delict, breach of trust, or the like). Civil vindication concerns the rights of the victim, punitive vindication the rights of all members of the political community considered as law-abiding subjects of the same laws as the offender. Although the theory of punishment foreshadowed in essay 10 and set out in essay 11 is grounded (as essay 12, sec. II makes clear) in thoughts vigorously articulated by Aquinas, it must be said that the tradition, right down into the modern era,[16] is not at all firm, or even much interested, in making the distinction between penal and civil vindication of rights.

It is a distinction fundamental to distinguishing retribution from revenge and vengeance, and to locating retribution within a general account of the justice that is the primary object of state government and law. Ensuring that the advantages and disadvantages of social life are kept in a fair balance, as between the members of the political community, is a primary responsibility of government and law. Punishment is concerned—and defined by its concern—with the restoration of that balance when the offender's choices and chosen conduct have upset it by illicitly gaining the advantages of following his own preferences in defiance of restraints accepted by his fellow subjects. Of course, in most cases that illicit conduct is a violation of rights of his victims, and that violation entitles them (morally and by civil law) to compensation from him. But the law-abiding have the right that government and law nullify the advantage he gained by his lack—indeed, abandonment—of the self-restraint needed to respect the demands implicit in the law's definition of offences.

That is the root of the procedural distinctions institutionalized in modern legal systems. Victims have their civil actions in tort, and so forth, independently of prosecution, conviction, or sentencing for the crimes committed in the very same act or omission. That is as it should be, and does not entail that the sentencing process must never include orders of compensation to victims, or that the sentence must never include labour whose fruits enure to them to the extent specified by the sentencing court. Nor does the distinction entail that criminal proceedings against, say, young offenders may not have as their primary form and object the confronting of young offenders with the harms they have imposed on their victims, in the hope that reality may induce genuine apology, regret, repentance, and reform. But the distinction does entail that victims have no right to demand punishment tailored to their desires or sense of grievance, rather than what is due retributively to the community of the law-abiding. Is not the proper standing of the victims in the criminal court just their status as witnesses, especially to the offence's gravity, and, as it may be, as equal members of the community whose laws were flouted? As to civil

---

[16] See Hale's and Blackstone's conceptual problems: essay IV.8 (1967b), sec. I.

proceedings: these too should not be the arena for punishing the tortfeasor as an offender, in the manner of the republican and classical Roman law of, say, delictual theft. Can punitive damages payable to the plaintiff-victim be justified except as, in substance, compensation for an accompanying (parallel) tort in the nature of *injuria* or *hubris*, that is, as civil wrongs in the nature of contemptuous insult? Essay 12 takes the occasion to put such issues in the context of the deep questions raised and pressed by Nietzsche about the very nature of rights and common good—moral objects whose truth, along with all other moral truth, he treats with an infectious scorn that deserves some reply, if not a remedy.

III. WAR AND JUSTICE

The distinction just stressed in relation to punishment turns out to have a perhaps surprising relevance in the developing history of 'the just war tradition'. If retributive punishment is the responsibility of those who have the care of a community, and irreparable measures of punishment are a responsibility reserved to those who have the care of a political community (state),[17] war cannot be justified as a punitive measure. Essay 13 shows how this thought takes shape in the thesis that war is justified only as a matter of defence (self-defence or assistance to others in their self-defence). Of course, the term 'punitive' is used with many senses besides its strict sense correlative with retribution; military operations can be described as punitive when conducted within a framework of self-defensive war, where a military objective is selected for the deterrent effects that would result from attaining it. And it may be too quick to conclude, as essay 13 does, that the exclusion of retributive-punitive justifications for war entails— even apart from customary or treaty-based international positive law— the exclusion of all purposes of obtaining by self-help some otherwise unobtainable reparation/compensation for unjust damage. But those are details compared with the basic reframing of thought about the justice of war which that essay both reports and contextualizes, and in its own measure participates in.

IV. AUTONOMY, EUTHANASIA, AND JUSTICE

Germain Grisez and Joseph Boyle, with whom I wrote extensively on some foundational questions about justice in war (in our 1987 book *Nuclear Deterrence, Morality and Realism*), had earlier written a book arguing that

[17] See *Aquinas* 248–50.

suicide can be a private matter: *Life and Death with Liberty and Justice: A Contribution to the Euthanasia Debate* (1979). But the same cannot be said, they argued, of assisting suicide or of euthanasia in any of that slippery term's senses. Such interpersonal actions always involve issues that no government or law could justly regard as merely private and in need of no public scrutiny. Their book's argument also embraced public considerations of the kind that have deeply impressed the most thorough and competent commissions of inquiry in recent years: the unjust impact that the legalizing of assisting suicide and/or euthanasia would have on the poor and other disadvantaged and vulnerable sections of society. Those and similar considerations are explored in some detail in essay 16, which sets aside all questions about the morality of killing oneself or, even by request, another. That essay was written for a face-to-face debate with Ronald Dworkin, whose own views I had also considered in their legal setting, in essay 15.

Essay 14, a three-part sequence of contributions to a debate with John Harris, does consider those personal-ethical questions, but also shows their direct bearing on the justice issues: see especially the last three paragraphs of sec. IV of that essay. That was written in the mid-1990s. The line has been held, for the most part, in English-speaking lands, though the last act of the Appellate Committee of the House of Lords, in 2009, was to do what the Law Lords could to cross it, by a morally, constitutionally, and jurisprudentially lamentable argument from the 'right to private life' (see 2009i). The line is drawn, clearly and fully defensibly, in terms of *intention*: there should in our societies be no conduct chosen with intent to kill another human being. The conflicted judgments of the Law Lords in *Bland* (see essay II.19 (1993c)), authorizing such conduct provided it takes the form of an omission, are witnesses to the reality—the moral truth—of the line they crossed. Today it seems ever clearer that if the line is abandoned by authorizing assisting suicide and/or euthanasia, the resultant prejudicing of the rights of the vulnerable will be matched and reinforced by the impact on other basic elements of the common good.

For: the case for abandoning the line has two kinds of premise: autonomy and the avoidance of suffering. Both premises are inconsistent with restricting the authorization of assisting suicide and euthanasia to the dying. And as arguments for a limited permission, each premise is inconsistent with the other's rationale. Once the permission were granted (not just in a few, isolated states *ad experimentum*, but generally across our civilization), the two premises would reinforce each other in breaking down the restriction, in life if not in law. The sick and elderly—not least those of a people that had ceased (as has now become a settled pattern) both to reproduce itself and to maintain stably committed nuclear families, and that in its own country, close to home, confronted peoples mostly younger and expanding—would experience a now legally and culturally driven sense of duty to *make way for* 'the next generation', a disposition in many cases reinforced by despondency about the future of their own culture, land, and people. Their law, in the name of rights and autonomy, would in its rationale and effect have wounded, even lethally, their autonomy and their right to life. Or so it seems; for this is one of those factual *aestimationes* whose strategic significance for judgment I take up in the Introduction to Volume IV, near the end of sec. III, and in this volume explore throughout essay 16.

V. AUTONOMY, IVF, ABORTION, AND JUSTICE

The issues in this part are taken up in various ways in other volumes, especially essay I.16 (1998a) and essay II.17 (2000b). But sec. I of essay 19 explores the implications of taking rights seriously in relations between mother and child. Some of the implications will seem hard, as is not rarely found when what are taken to be human rights conflict with what are taken to be human rights, and a delimitation of these claims' just boundaries is required. Essay 18 is included as a memento of the first 'feminist' argument for abortion rights, Judith Jarvis Thomson's 'A Defense of Abortion' (1971). Surveying the literature only four or five years earlier (1970c), I had found few if any claims, let alone arguments, that abortion is a matter of right. Since 1971, most arguments for legal freedom to terminate pregnancy have been, like hers, an argument from and to a right. But within thirty years, they had mutated further, into the right Thomson disclaimed: to kill; to make sure that the baby is got dead (see essay I.16, sec. I). So this is another breach of the line hitherto held by our law against intending to kill (the innocent, at least). As I have said in essay II.13 (2001a) at n. 11 (p. 243) and in both the endnotes to the essay itself, essay 18 is opaque in its handling of the range of possible intentionalities in terminations of pregnancy. Its handling of what it means to frame these issues in terms of rights retains, I think, its value.

The then novel question of baby-making, by in vitro fertilization, as taken up in essay 17 (and in essay II.17 (2000b)), was something I had worked on, creatively albeit not single-handedly, for the committee documents I have sufficient reason, I think, to include in the Bibliography as 1983e, followed up in 1984c and 1987j. It involves the right to life and the right not to be enslaved, and foreshadows the important ways in which the rights of children and the basic human good of marriage are inter-defined and inter-dependent. The involvement of my own (and C.S. Lewis's) English university in lethal research on human embryos is a dark shadow on its present, and over its future and ours.

VI. MARRIAGE, JUSTICE, AND THE COMMON GOOD

Essay 21 is the short version published in 1997 of essay 1994b (itself published in two slightly different versions); it omits those parts of 1994b which concern the *ad hominem* matters explored at much greater length in 1994d ('"Shameless Acts" in Colorado'), an essay recording and reflecting on the abuse of history in constitutional contexts. The chronology is important for understanding why the issue of homosexual conduct is taken up in essay 5, too. For that was an issue peripheral to my interests and concerns before 1993, when I was invited by the Government of Colorado to testify in a court in Colorado about the state of the law in Europe about that issue, and was then asked to deal also with the unexpected testimony of Martha Nussbaum claiming that only Christianity had been concerned to condemn such conduct. Essay 2 in 1987 had touched upon the issue only to the rather slight extent that Kant did (and then in footnotes responding to objections). My real concern, from essay V.20 (1970b) to essay 20 here, has been with marriage, which I came belatedly to understand as a basic human good, and one damaged and contemned in many ways in the revolutions of normative thought in our time.[18] Damaged in so many ways that the emergence of 'gay rights', and their triumph over children's rights, is merely a consequence and manifestation of deeper misunderstandings and wider losses. The part played in these revolutions by false history is explored in essays 5 and 21, with repetition that I have allowed to stand, partly because there are also differences, and partly because the historical issue—our vision of where we stand in relation to a past that is *ours*—is so important. The historical issue is taken up again, in relation precisely to marriage and marital acts, in essay 22. That essay then pivots on the true history to *develop* truths once understood more securely but still with insufficient depth and coherence to sustain the tradition and the goods and rights it fostered. Essay 20 is the resultant synthesis.

[18] See the endnote to essay 20.

Part One
Human Rights and Common Good: General Theory

1

HUMAN RIGHTS AND THEIR ENFORCEMENT[*]

I

Many poor reasons are advanced for entrenching the European Convention on Human Rights in our law.[1]

After incorporating the Convention, it is said, we would no longer struggle to anticipate the developing *jurisprudence*[2] of the European Court of Human Rights [ECtHR]; no longer be embarrassed internationally by frequent declarations that we violate the rights progressively identified by that court; no longer be so immediately and regularly subject to the rule of a far-away tribunal of which we know little.

But after incorporation, just as today, the final arbiter would remain the ECtHR; nor would it reverse our highest courts less freely than they reverse the courts below them. Diplomatic embarrassments, then, would be little fewer—if anyone really thinks that fear of such pinpricks should determine our constitution and forms of life.[3] And is it apparent why anticipating European *jurisprudence* should be for our courts, rather than for Parliament?

---

[*] 1985a ('A Bill of Rights for Britain? The Moral of Contemporary Jurisprudence', the Maccabaean Lecture in Jurisprudence, at the British Academy, 30 October 1985).

[1] For a review of many arguments for and against incorporation and/or entrenchment of the Convention (or some similar instrument), and for a bibliography of the British political and legal discussions since 1968, see Zander, *A Bill of Rights?* Zander's study makes it clear that many consider the Convention unsatisfactory, but equally that there is no prospect of sufficient political support for any alternative instrument, imported or home-made.

[2] The scope, and dubious character, of these developments may be gathered from the dissenting judgments of Judge Sir Gerald Fitzmaurice in *Golder v United Kingdom* (1975) 1 EHRR 524 at 562–7 (paras 32–9); *National Union of Belgian Police v Belgium* (1975) 1 EHRR 578 at 601–6 (paras 1–11); *Ireland v United Kingdom* (1978) 2 EHRR 25 at 125–7 (paras 12–18); *Marckx v Belgium* (1979) 2 EHRR 330 at 366–77 (paras 6–31).

[3] Moreover, '...experience has shown that incorporation may not result in a drastic reduction in the number of applications submitted to and judgments given against an incorporating state': Andrews, 'The European Jurisprudence of Human Rights', at 487; see also Zander, *A Bill of Rights?*, 37, n. 31.

Equally poor, however, are many arguments against entrenchment of the Convention. Would conservative judges stymie Parliament's progressive initiatives (past or future) touching property, industrial relations, or education? I assume, but do not in this essay defend the assumption, that our constitution would be found sufficiently flexible to absorb a mutation in conceptions of parliamentary sovereignty, so that in accordance with solemn statutory provisions[4] the Bill of Rights would be enforced even against Acts of Parliament—at least against those not protected by special procedures of enactment (such as enhanced majorities, or approval by referendum) or by some politically unpalatable formula of derogation, such as 'notwithstanding the Bill of Rights'. I shall assume throughout, then, an incorporation with a measure of entrenchment and judicial review of legislation (for short, 'judicial review'). On this basis, I accept that judicial decisions might sometimes hinder some legislative goal. But governments whose main projects fell before the courts would in time contrive to secure enough sympathetic judges.

Nor would the reshaping of the legal profession, or at least of its cursus honorum, need heroic transplant surgery. As Ronald Dworkin's 1977 Maccabaean Lecture said: 'If law had a different place here, different people would have a place in the law'; 'men and women who would [now] never think of a legal career, because they want a career that will make a difference to social justice, will begin to think differently' about a legal career, and so the profession would change, 'as it did dramatically in the United States earlier in this century'.[5†]

Lacking in the debates on incorporation is any lively sense of the difference it would make, not simply to the practice of law (and the prosperity of lawyers), but to the national life in many matters outside the 'big politics' of wealth and poverty, and national security. Only in extraordinary circumstances would Parliament be looked to for the decisive public answer to questions such as the permissibility of the closed shop, the lawfulness of incest, abortion, and the artificially assisted generation of children by or

---

[4] Even the submerged and strangled tones of s. 2(4) of the European Communities Act 1972—a subsection carefully modelled on provisions (Acquisition of Land (Assessment of Compensation) Act 1919, s. 7(1)) authoritatively interpreted (*Ellen Street Estates Ltd v Minister of Health* [1934] 1 KB 590 (CA)) as incapable of affecting either the construction or the effect of future statutes—have been judicially regarded as perhaps capable of so affecting the 'construction' of post-1972 statutes that nothing short of

> an express positive statement in an Act...that a particular provision is intended to be made in breach of an obligation...under a Community treaty would justify an English court in construing that provision in a manner inconsistent with a Community treaty obligation...however wide a departure from the prima facie meaning of the language of the provision might be needed in order to achieve consistency. (*Garland v British Rail Engineering Ltd* [1983] 2 AC 751, [1982] 2 All ER 402 at 415d–e per Lord Diplock (obiter).)

[5] Dworkin, *A Matter of Principle*, 31 = 'Political Judges and the Rule of Law' at 285.

for single women,[6] the validity of polygamous or homosexual marriages, the legal protection of reputation, the admissibility of confessions or of evidence obtained fairly but in some way unlawfully, the convict's right to conduct business or litigation from his prison, the legality of single-sex sports and of motorcycling without a helmet... and many other issues of personal existence within politically ordered society. And all would be determined (and re-determined) by stylized manipulation of relatively few specialized terms, above all, perhaps, 'privacy', 'discrimination', and 'proportionality'. Legal learning would be *necessary* to participate in these litigious determinations; whether it would be *sufficient* to justify, authentically, the particular dispositions (either way) is for consideration.

Am I implying that the courts' dispositions would be worse than Parliament's? By no means. That is another poor objection to a justiciable bill of rights. True, the English-speaking North Atlantic courts which invalidate legislation under bills of rights have a record disfigured with unjust or malign and ill-reasoned decisions, overthrowing statutory protections against dismissal for joining a union (*Adair v US* 208 US 161 (1908)), against child labour (*Hammer v Dagenhart* 247 US 252 (1918)), against exploitation by excessive hours of work (*Lochner v New York* 198 US 45 (1905)), against being aborted for convenience (*Roe v Wade* 410 US 113 (1973)), and others. But legislatures, too, fail in justice, or promote injustice; anyone who thinks *Roe v Wade* unjust had better recall the priority of the UK Abortion Act 1967. And it is absurd to seek an 'overall balance' sheet, identifying possible worlds with and without judicial review of legislation as better and worse states of affairs all things considered.

'Judicial review is undemocratic': another unimpressive objection. It is put in two ways, asserting an (improper) reduction in the power, either (i) of the majority, or (ii) of individuals. Dworkin concedes the minor premise of the first (though not its major premise, that reducing the power of the majority is improper):

Any constraint on the power of a democratically elected legislature decreases the political power of the people who elected that legislature.... the argument that the present majority has no right to censor opinions is actually an argument for reducing the political power of any majority.... the majority's political power will be decreased by the constitutional protection of speech.[7]

---

[6] See *Report of the Committee of Inquiry into Human Fertilisation and Embryology* (Chairman: Dame Mary Warnock), Cmnd. 9314 (1984), para. 2.9.

[7] *A Matter of Principle*, 62. See also 111:

Once it is conceded that the question is only one of the common interest—that no question of distinct majority and minority interests arises—... the majority rather than some minority must in the end have the power to decide what is in *their* common interest (emphasis added).

But the concession, I think, was premature. Talk of the power of 'the majority', as 'the people who elected the legislature', needs clarification. Think of election time, with its absurd claims that the nation or the people (or the majority?) have voted for, say, a hung Parliament—when perhaps almost every voter wanted a clear majority for his party. And before one speaks of 'the power of a majority' within Parliament (or within the governing party or its inner circles), one might recall that in any deliberative body (of more than four) deciding issues by majority vote, the majority can be in the minority on a majority of the issues voted upon.[8] That possibility in no way depends upon tactical voting; when the varieties of tactical voting are recalled, the notion that determinations by majority are exercises of 'the power of the majority' (or of 'the people who elected the legislature') will be recognized as a hazardous equivocation on the adjectival term 'majority', transposed into the personified substantive supposed to 'have power'. I dwell on this, not to deny that majority voting fairly resolves many issues, but because indiscriminate use of the collective term, 'majority', foreshadows other confusions about collectivities, confusions more directly relevant to the notion of rights and thus to my theme.

Meanwhile, let the claim that judicial review is undemocratic be put in the second way, as by Judge Learned Hand in his 1958 Oliver Wendell Holmes lectures, *The Bill of Rights*:

Democracy supposes equality of political power, and if genuine political decisions are taken from the legislature and given to courts, then the political power of individual citizens, who elect legislators but not judges, is weakened, which is unfair.[9]

One reply to Hand is Dworkin's: while transfer of all political power to judges would be unfair, 'we are now considering only a small and special class of political decisions', of which only 'some' are assigned to courts.[10] But this reply will not do. As Dworkin elsewhere remarks, the issues entrusted to judges under a bill of rights are 'the most fundamental issues of morality',[11] and virtually all serious moral or political issues are justiciable constitutional issues.[12]

A better reply might be this: in a North Atlantic type of political order, the free citizen's power over judicial appointments is not less than his influence on legislation. Justice Roberts's 'switch in time', in December 1936, cannot be proved to have 'followed the election returns' of November;[13]

---

[8] Anscombe, 'On Frustration of the Majority by Fulfilment of the Majority's Will' at 128.
[9] Dworkin, *A Matter of Principle*, 27 = Proc Brit Acad 44: at 280. I quote Dworkin's clarifying transposition of the argument which Hand puts, rather opaquely, in his *The Bill of Rights*, 73.
[10] *A Matter of Principle*, 27.   [11] *Ibid.*, 70.   [12] See *TRS* 208.
[13] Cf. *Morehead v New York, ex rel. Tipaldo* 298 US 587 (1936) with *West Coast Hotel v Parrish* 300 US 379 (1937); Frankfurter, 'Mr Justice Roberts' at 313–15; Friedman and Israel (eds), *The Justices of the United States Supreme Court 1789–1969*, iii (1969), 2261–2.

but certainly, without his switch from principled opposition to the New Deal, the Supreme Court's nine would promptly—and to the satisfaction of many voters—have been afforced, to achieve the same result. The vulgar campaign to 'impeach Earl Warren' petered out, but may not have been quite barren. The campaign to secure that all new federal judges will oppose the *Roe v Wade* 'right to an abortion' seems to be going smoothly. There is no special public provision for these initiatives, but nothing antecedently unequal, or covert, or otherwise irregular about each citizen's opportunity to join them.

Perhaps you feel uneasy about this reply. Isn't there something distasteful, or even contrary to principle, about subjecting the judiciary to popular opinion? Doesn't this treat the judiciary as if it were a kind of legislature?

But here we have left the objection from democracy, and enter a more fruitful zone of reflection.

II

Your unease stems from an assumption: that the courts should offer a forum different in kind from the legislatures which we appropriately subject to popular election. And in some form, that constitutional assumption is surely reasonable. But in one version—some of whose terms are central to recent jurisprudential debate and have been taken up at the highest judicial level[14]—the assumption has been advanced as a premise for welcoming judicial enforcement of a bill of rights against Parliament. This version is sketched (though without explicitly concluding to a justiciable bill of rights) in the 1977 Maccabaean Lecture: judicial review offers each individual citizen

an independent forum of principle...in which his claims about what he is entitled to have will be steadily and seriously considered at his demand.[15]

Since then, this version of the constitutional principle, with the full conclusion about judicial review of legislation, has been set out in a paper entitled 'The Forum of Principle' (note the definite article). In a passage I have already quoted from, Dworkin says:

judicial review insures that the most fundamental issues of political morality will finally be set out and debated as issues of principle and not political power alone,

---

[14] *McLoughlin v O'Brian* [1983] 1 AC 410, [1982] 2 All ER 298 at 310 f–h, per Lord Scarman; *Emeh v Kensington AHA* [1985] QB 1012, [1984] 3 All ER 1044 at 1051 c–e, per Waller LJ. But cf. *TRS* 180.

[15] *A Matter of Principle*, 32 = Proc Brit Acad, lxiv at 287.

a transformation that cannot succeed, in any case not fully, within the legislature itself.[16]

So: the hierarchical division of powers and functions between institutions—legislatures and courts, the latter reviewing and in some measure controlling the former—is constitutionally appropriate because it corresponds to a division between the types of reason or justification characteristically employed in the respective types of constitutional institution. Courts justify their decisions by appeal to principle, and arguments of principle are defined as arguments about 'the rights of individuals'. Legislatures (it is said) justify their decisions in another way, in which principle plays a lesser role when it has a role at all.

The *form* of this strategy for explaining and justifying the constitutional division of responsibilities is rightly congenial to contemporary jurisprudence. For jurisprudence has progressed mainly by attending, not merely to the externals of structure, practices, or even feelings, but rather to the characteristic *reasons* people have for acting in the ways that go to constitute distinctive social phenomena, such as law and the various sorts of legal rule, standard, and institution. Jurisprudence attends to types of justifications for decision.

But I have not yet fully reported the proposed division. *Courts*, it is said, can be opposed to *legislatures* because *rights and principles* can be opposed to...what? Two candidates seem to be proposed for the missing final term in that four-term analogy.

The first candidate appears in the contrast I quoted, between issues or arguments of principle and issues or arguments of 'political power alone'.[17] And that reference to issues of political power takes its meaning from the context, identifying certain arguments and political decisions as unfair, and as denials of equal representation, because they 'count the majority's moral convictions about how other people should live' as the *ground* for political decision, and thus yield 'legislation that can be justified only by appealing to the majority's preferences about which of their fellow citizens are worthy of concern and respect',[18] that is, legislation that imposes 'constraints on liberty that can be justified only on the ground that the majority finds [such-and-such] distasteful, or disapproves the culture it generates'.[19]

---

[16] Ibid., 70.

[17] NB: what is in question is issues *of* political power, not the fact that issues will be decided *by* political power alone. Courts wield political power, and justiciable issues are decided by the brute facts of authoritative determination, majorities, and so forth—as litigants and counsel are keenly aware. The question is rather the 'internal' question, how the issues are framed and considered within the respective forums.

[18] Ibid., 68.   [19] Ibid. See also ibid., 67.

In all this there is a confusing ambiguity inimical to the main lines of its author's own jurisprudence. For that rests on a strict adherence to an 'internal' point of view, whereas the analyses just quoted, about 'issues of political power alone', saddle 'the majority' with a curiously 'external' argumentation.

From an 'internal' viewpoint, reasons are understood as reasons, not merely reported as psychological phenomena. Thus: the claim that there can be a right answer in a hard case is not confuted by the fact that well-informed and honest lawyers disagree about what that answer is. Very vigorously and effectively, Dworkin presses his argument that the correctness or otherwise of a legal answer to a legal question can be determined only by one who enters into the legal arguments and uses legal criteria to judge one answer better than another. From within the practice of legal argument, the disagreements noted by the external critic or sceptic are simply irrelevant.[20] Capitalizing on, and effectively explaining, the manifest failure of forty years' meta-ethical scepticism, Dworkin has urged a similar philosophical defence of the objectivity, or *truth*, of moral judgments. Arguments for the truth of a moral judgment are moral arguments; arguments against are going to have to be moral arguments.[21] In particular, the observation, external to the practice of moral reasoning, that some disagree with a moral argument or conclusion is simply no *ground* for denying that argument or conclusion.

But of course, if the fact of disagreement is normally no ground for the disagreement, nor is the fact of agreement a ground for agreeing. From an observer's 'external' viewpoint, the fact that I or we believe that p (is true) is an important fact, quite distinct from the fact (if fact it be) that p (is true). But in one's own thinking about whether or not p (is true), the fact that one thinks it is not in focus; save in the idiomatic sense in which 'I think' signals uncertainty, the assertion 'I think that p (is true)' is *transparent for*[22] the assertion 'p (is true)'.

So too: legislation enacted by majority vote, and imposing constraints on liberty, is characteristically justified not: 'only by appealing to the majority's [sc. of the citizenry's] preferences', nor: 'on the ground that the majority find' such-and-such deplorable, nor: by appeal to the '"rights" of the majority as such'.[23] Indeed, what the majority is believed to think does not, characteristically, figure much (let alone exclusively) in the grounds

---

[20] *A Matter of Principle*, 137–42; Dworkin, 'A Reply...' at 277–80.
[21] *A Matter of Principle*, 171–7. [22] See *FoE* 3, 23, 71.
[23] *TRS* 194. In some other contexts, Dworkin has clearly recognized and stated the distinction between reliance on the truth of p and reliance on the fact that one holds that p, or that the majority hold that p: *ibid.*, 123–4.

by which a voter justifies his vote, a vote which will help enact law only if more than a minority of voters happen to vote likewise. For the deliberating majority-voter, 'we find that such-and-such is deplorable' is transparent for 'such-and-such is deplorable'. (All this is clearer when one speaks not about that illusory collective, the personified majority and 'its preferences', but about the reasoning and action of the real individuals whose actions turn out to count as the majority deciding. But if you insist on speaking of the majority as subject, let us say that what the majority characteristically do is *express* their views about what is, say, deplorable; in doing so, they are *not* 'appealing to the majority's preferences'.)[24] Similarly, royal commissions, law reform commissioners, and participants in parliamentary debate about capital punishment, abortion, homosexual intercourse, reproductive surrogacy, police powers, and the like, rarely make serious appeal to the fact that their view commands majority support in the legislature, or give centrality to the claim or fact that their view is supported by a majority in the country.[25] (The political scientist, from a relatively external viewpoint, will rightly identify ways in which the outcome of legislative deliberations is affected by factors the debaters would not advance as good reasons for choosing that outcome. But he will do the same for the higher judiciary, and for the process of choosing its members. So the present consideration does neither, but remains, like Dworkin's, a jurisprudential consideration of the character of the arguments properly justificatory in the respective forums of deliberation and decision.)

So I return to the initial characterization of the constitutional division, between courts, as the forum in which issues are treated as issues of principle, and Parliament, as the forum in which they are treated, ultimately, as 'issues of political power alone'. I have argued that it is no division. Arguments of principle are the very stuff of many arguments proposed to and in legislatures, especially on the matters indicated in bills of rights.

III

Before considering the second and more interesting characterization of the proposed constitutional division, I want to point out a different but

---

[24] Cf. Dworkin in Cohen (ed.), 287–8.

[25] Appeals to the fact that a view is supported by 'most' people or 'few' people are, of course, common enough in these contexts; but usually they are merely intended (often pardonably) to exempt the speaker from supplying argument, in just the same manner as Dworkin's dismissal of 'platonism': see n. 36 below. As for MPs, each doubtless cares about his seat. But will he calculate what the majority of his constituency think? Or will he, more likely, be careful (if at all) about the views (if any) of a small minority, the floating voters?

very relevant neglect of transparency, and substitution of an external for an internal viewpoint.

Five articles of the European Convention (Arts 6, 8, 9, 10, and 11) provide that certain measures otherwise unjustifiable or a violation of rights can be justified if necessary for the protection of (inter alia) 'morals'. In dealing with these provisions, the ECtHR says it 'is not concerned with making any value-judgment as to the morality of'[26] any activities subjected to national laws 'for the protection of morals'. Accordingly, it treats the term 'morals' ('*la morale*') as referring to a mere fact about opinion widespread in a given community.[27]

Thus the Court interprets the Convention as if it embodied what I venture to call the cardinal error of the 1959 Maccabaean Lecture. The error—no slip or oversight but very deliberately embraced by Lord Devlin as the *right* position, at least for us[28]—consists in bracketing out the question of truth (here, moral truth). The proper justification of laws for protection of morals is thus not the vice of the prohibited conduct, nor its tendency to degrade, deprave, or corrupt and in these ways to *harm*, but rather the sheer fact that many *believe* the conduct vicious. The concern which Devlin thought capable of justifying legal prohibitions is not that individuals will thus harm and be harmed by their own conduct, but that society's morale and cohesion will suffer if deeply held moral *beliefs* widespread in that society are left to be flouted, unsupported by law.

Now this is an understandable concern, like that of minorities for their language, and of nations for their war effort. But if one substitutes it for the concern for truth, one does more than abandon, as Lord Devlin did, the doctrine of the old common lawyers: that besides the law of God (unavailable—as that Maccabaean Lecture stressed—to legal thought in a

---

[26] *Dudgeon v United Kingdom* (1981) 4 EHRR 149 at 165.
[27] *Handyside v United Kingdom* (1976) ECHR Ser. A, vol. 24, 22 (para. 48); *Dudgeon* at 163–6 ('moral standards obtaining in' the community (para. 46), the 'moral ethos or moral standards' of that society 'as a whole' (paras 47, 49), 'the moral climate' in that community (para. 57), 'the vital forces' of the country (para. 52)). See also *Sunday Times v United Kingdom* (1979) 2 EHRR 245 at 276 (para. 59) (morals a far less objective notion than the authority of the judiciary).
[28] Devlin, *The Enforcement of Morals*, 89:

> The State may claim on two grounds to legislate on matters of morals. The Platonic ideal is that the State exists to promote virtue among its citizens.... This is not acceptable to Anglo-American thought. It invests the State with power of determination between good and evil, destroys freedom of conscience and is the paved road to tyranny.... The alternative ground is that society may legislate to preserve itself.... What makes a society is a community of ideas... about the way its members should behave and govern their lives.... under the second theory the law-maker is not required to make any judgment about what is good and what is bad. The morals which he enforces are those ideas about right and wrong which are already accepted by the society for which he is legislating and which are necessary to preserve its integrity.

These statements, from a lecture given two and a half years after his Maccabaean Lecture, state more crisply ideas to be found *ibid.*, 5, 9, 10 = Proc Brit Acad, xlv (1959), 129–51 at 133, 137–40.

pluralist society), and the posited law of our land, there is a law of reason. One also denatures the modern bill of rights.

For a bill of rights purports to identify certain interests as truly fundamental aspects of human flourishing: to neglect or trespass on them really is unjust. A bill of rights purports to make a reasonable, a justified selection amongst competing conceptions of human flourishing and of justice, and to pick out one which, by its approximation to the truth about these matters, *warrants* the commitment made on its adoption. If that commitment is expected to help sustain morale and *esprit de corps*, it is precisely by its *appropriateness* as an identification of truly worthwhile grounds for individual and social choices, strivings, and self-restraints.

Just so, however, those who hold to moral standards enforced by legislation affecting, say, free speech, or 'privacy', very commonly rest their approval of such legislation on grounds quite other than the fact that they do hold those standards, or that they are in the majority, or that society coheres around those standards. A necessary premise of their case is that these are true standards, whose violation is per se harmful—harmful perhaps in the ways recognized by even the Williams Committee on Obscenity and Film Censorship: 'cultural pollution, moral deterioration and the undermining of human compassion...disregard for decency...a taste for the base, a contempt for restraint and responsibility...'[29]

Founding one's case thus, one need not support the defining of offences *in terms of* unspecified 'corruption of (public) morals', or even 'tendency to deprave and corrupt'. The European Convention has not hastened the desirable replacement of the rule in *Shaw's Case*.[30] But under the principles of the ECtHR's emerging jurisprudence, an incorporated Convention might well promote the undesirable elimination of even closely drafted laws against specifiable activities which do tend to deprave and corrupt.

A court's refusal to consider the truth of moral standards might, of course, be premised on grounds much narrower than Devlin's (which were addressed to citizen, court, and legislature alike). But however understandable the court's reluctance to venture beyond legal learning into an acknowledgement of moral standards (other than honesty, fidelity, respect for property, and due care), the refusal exacts a price: the court is bound to misconceive the significance of those other standards. Sometimes, though not, I think, in Devlin's work, the protestation that

---

[29] Cmnd. 7772 (1979), para. 6.73; see also paras 5.30, 6.76.
[30] *Shaw v DPP* [1962] AC 220; *Knuller v DPP* [1973] AC 435; Criminal Law Act 1977, s. 5(3). The judgments in *Shaw* can be seen as attempting a synthesis of Viscount Radcliffe's appeal, in *The Law and Its Compass*, 52–3, to the judge's 'fundamental assessment of human values and of the purposes of society' with Lord Devlin's appeal to the standards of the man in the jury box.

their truth is irrelevant is simply a sign that their falsity (or, at least: the falsity of the view that they are true) is being covertly presumed. Thus the ECtHR's disclaimer of 'any value judgment' as to the morality of a certain prohibited activity was followed, after a page or two, with the following value-judgment (central to the Judgment):

as compared with the era when that [impugned] legislation was enacted, there is now a better understanding, and in consequence an increased tolerance, of [the behaviour in question].[31]

Those who hold to the standards enforced by the law which the Court condemned may well demur: what the Court thought a better understanding is really a more restricted and superficial understanding, a misunderstanding (to say the least) of a whole domain of human integrity and well-being—so that the 'consequent' increase in tolerance thus may well have lacked the justification (and the justifying force) so casually ascribed to it by the Court's value-judgment.

IV

These reflections on judicial reluctance to give due weight to certain matters of principle may help assess the second, more well-known and beguiling characterization of the constitutional division: courts can properly review legislation because courts are the forum of principle, whereas legislatures, though not unconcerned with principle, are *the forum of policy*. Arguments of principle identify rights; arguments of policy assert that some decision or law will promote some conception of the general welfare, the public interest, the collective good. And a defining feature of rights is that they 'trump', prevail over, policies—not every policy, or every consideration of general welfare or collective good, but at least some. In any contest between principle and policy, that is, between right and collective good, the presumption, rebuttable but real, will favour the right.

Thus the moral-political primacy of rights grounds the constitutional supremacy of courts. Such a conception marries easily with one of the ECtHR's most significant doctrines: rights enumerated in the European Convention will be broadly construed, and broadened by implying unstated rights, whereas the limiting grounds mentioned in the Convention, such as health or morals, will be read narrowly, without expansion by implication, and allowed application only for 'pressing social need'.[32] The presumption, rebuttable but real, will favour the Convention *rights*.

---

[31] *Dudgeon* (1981) 4 EHRR 149 at 167 (para. 60).   [32] *Ibid.* at 164 (para. 51).

This presumption is still somewhat, though less and less, qualified by the Court's doctrine that national legislatures and governments have a 'margin of appreciation', within which their judgments, though doubted by the Court, will not be disturbed.[33] But that doctrine would have no hold on national courts empowered to enforce Convention provisions as bills of rights; for it rests on the ECtHR's peculiar status as organ of a treaty between states which retain full sovereignty.

The fate of the 'presumption of constitutionality' in American civil rights cases since 1937 suggests that our courts, too, might well come to allow little or no 'margin' for legislative or executive 'appreciation' in any case involving a 'preferred freedom' (in a modern bill of rights, presumably all rights named or enumerated therein). Instead, our courts would, I think, apply unqualified the doctrine which the ECtHR holds in a still qualified form and which is stated more frankly in America: the *presumption* (procedural matters aside) that laws qualifying or restricting an expressly or even an impliedly specified right are *un*constitutional.[34] In November 1977, before the ECtHR's interpretative doctrines had become quite so evident, Lord Scarman offered a reassurance to the Lords Select Committee:

if Parliament prescribed a limitation upon the right under consideration, then it would be enough for the judges and it would be presumed... that Parliament in enacting the limitation had had in mind requirements of a democratic society, the interests of public safety, the protection of public order, health and morals.[35]

---

[33] See e.g. *Handyside* (1976) ECHR Ser. A, vol. 24, 22 (para. 48); *Sunday Times v United Kingdom* (1979) 2 EHRR 245 at 275–6 (para. 59). The scope of the 'margin of appreciation' is diminishing under the impact of a conception (not yet fully admitted) that the Court can take into account 'progressive' changes in social and legal norms in Europe, and require backward countries to catch up or get into line: see Andrews, n. 1, 304 at 496–510; [and e.g. *Schalk and Kopf v Austria* application 30141/04, Judgment of the First Section, ECtHR, 24 June 2010, paras 28, 105, 109].

[34] See Frankfurter J's critical history of the emergent doctrine of preferred freedoms in *Kovacs v Cooper* 336 US 77 at 90–4 (1949). For the established doctrine, see *Roe v Wade* 410 US 113 at 155–6 (1973); Tribe, *American Constitutional Law*, 564 et seq. On the presumption of constitutionality applied by the Judicial Committee of the Privy Council in appeals from Commonwealth countries with bills of rights, see *A-G v Antigua Times* [1976] AC 16 at 32; *Hinds v R* [1977] AC 195 at 224. For the reversal of the presumption, by virtue of an onus of proof on parties relying on an 'exception' under the Canadian Charter of Rights and Freedoms [entrenched by the Constitution of Canada of 1982], see e.g. *Quebec Protestant School Board v A-G Quebec* (1982) 140 DLR (3d) 33 at 59 (SC, Que.), upheld in result, *A-G Quebec v Quebec Association of Protestant School Boards* [1984] 2 SCR 66 (SC, Can.).

[35] *Minutes of Evidence taken before the Select Committee on a Bill of Rights*, House of Lords paper no. 254 of 1976–7, 370 (Q. 807). Lord Scarman restricted his reassurance by the hypothesis that parliamentary legislative sovereignty had been undisturbed by the (extremely weak form of) incorporation discussed by the Committee. But it is hard to see why judges who knew that their judgments would cause no impediment to the legislative will should be *more* deferential to that will than judges charged with the heavy responsibility of overturning it for repugnance to the (more strongly incorporated) bill of rights.

I venture to think it improbable that that would long remain 'enough for the judges'.

The presumption of the unconstitutionality of laws delimiting preferred or specified rights is obviously supported by the theory we are considering, that rights are matters of principle, the province of the courts, and (save where the public need is sufficiently grave) prevail over policy and collective welfare, the province of the legislature. What, then, should we say of this theory?

It rests on an incomplete analysis and justification of rights, and trades on an unwarranted assumption that utilitarianism is a moral-political theory sufficiently coherent to yield results which need to be, and can be, trumped by considerations of individual rights.[36]

V

Two versions of utilitarianism figure in these jurisprudential debates. One I can call the special theory; Dworkin calls it 'neutral utilitarianism', and thinks that it 'has for some time been accepted in practical politics [and] ... supplied ... the working justification of most of the constraints on our liberty through the law that we accept as proper'.[37] This 'takes as the goal of politics the fulfilment of as many of people's goals for their own lives as possible',[38] and is 'neutral toward all people and preferences',[39] so that preferences are to be given full weight even when they 'combine to form a contemptible way of life'.[40]

Special or neutral utilitarianism is, I believe, both flatly unacceptable, and regarded as such in every civilized community.[41] As our practical

---

[36] Admittedly, in its most abstract statements, the theory treats the idea of rights as the following *formal* idea: of a consideration which provides a political justification for an individual's decision or action even when the 'general background' goals and justifications for political decisions and actions would (but for the trumping right) justify impeding or preventing that individual's decision or action—and the 'general background' goals and justifications need not be utilitarian. See Dworkin in Cohen, *Ronald Dworkin and Contemporary Jurisprudence*, 281; also *TRS* 169, 364–5, and *A Matter of Principle*, 370–1. But in practice, the theory treats utilitarianism, in one form or another, as the only background justification to be found in western political practice, and certainly as the only political theory which needs to be met by the theory of rights. The most obvious and (if developed) eligible alternative background theory, having been labelled platonist, is brushed aside: 'I doubt that it appeals to many people': *A Matter of Principle*, 415. See also *TRS* 272–3 ('I presume that we all accept [that] government must not constrain liberty on the ground that one citizen's conception of the good life ... is nobler or superior to another's.')

[37] *A Matter of Principle*, 370.   [38] *Ibid.*, 360; also *TRS* 364.
[39] Dworkin in Cohen (ed.), 282.   [40] *A Matter of Principle*, 360.
[41] Cf. Dworkin, *A Matter of Principle*, 360:

Suppose some version of utilitarianism provided that the preferences of some people were to count for less than those of others in the calculation how best to fulfill most preferences overall ... because the preferences in question combined to form a contemptible way of life. This would strike us as flatly unacceptable, and in any case much less appealing than standard forms of utilitarianism.

politics broadly accepts, certain preferences are not merely outweighed by the competing preferences of others; rather, if there were to be a counting, weighing, and aggregating—or, more pertinently, whenever opportunities and restraints are to be distributed—these preferences should not be included at all. A few examples: the preference for seeing other human beings or animals suffer, for copulating with one's own infant children, for getting one's way *by trickery*, for getting more than one's fair share (just as such, regardless of one's desire or need for the object being shared out), and for a lifetime of self-immolation in slavery, sexual bondage, or drug-induced fantasy and oblivion. You will supply other examples.[42]

The other prevalent version is so general, or vague, that one may doubt its utilitarian identity. It asserts that law and government are to advance 'the general interest', 'the general welfare', 'the public interest', and 'the interests of the community as a whole'; it further asserts that those terms are synonymous with 'the collective good', 'the collective welfare', 'greater benefit overall, in the aggregate', and 'aggregate collective good'. In the pursuit of any such goal, 'in each case distributional principles are subordinate to some conception of aggregate collective good'.[43]

Now claims of right are certainly claims to exclude, override, or be immune from, some competing interest or claim of one or many other persons. But we should not seek to explicate the 'trumping' or 'exclusionary' capacity of rights by a contrast with 'aggregate collective good'. Concerning all these notions of a collective good supposedly specifiable prior to the specification of distributional principles, we ought instead to say what Philippa Foot said concerning the corresponding notions in personal ethics:

...we have no reason to think that we must accept consequentialism in any form.... there is simply a blank where consequentialists see 'the best state of

In making this unplausible statement plausible to its author, how important are the words 'of some people' and 'combined'? Consider the following, from Cohen (ed.), 284:

> The good utilitarian, who says that the push-pin player is equally entitled to the satisfaction of that taste as the poet is entitled to the satisfaction of his, is not for that reason committed to the proposition that a life of push-pin is as good as a life of poetry. Only vulgar critics of utilitarianism would insist on that inference. The utilitarian says only that nothing in the theory of justice provides any reason why the political and economic arrangements and decisions of society should be any closer to those the poet would prefer than those the pushpin player would like. It is just a matter, from the standpoint of political justice, of how many people would prefer the one to the other and how strongly.

The critic of utilitarianism is driven to the 'vulgar' inferential imputation by the extreme implausibility of the alternative inference: that the utilitarian thinks a 'theory of justice' can do without any theory of human good. (Does not this sort of utilitarian trade on the idea that a 'preference', as distinct from a mere desire, has at least the worth of having been *chosen*? If so, does he have any *reason* for not counting other aspects of human good as relevant in determining the demands of justice?)

[42] Some relevant further examples are mentioned by Haksar, *Equality, Liberty, and Perfectionism*, 260–1.

[43] *TRS* 91.

affairs'...the concept of 'the best state of affairs' should disappear from moral theory.[44]

The notion of a determinable 'aggregate greater collective welfare' turns out to be no more coherent than the (quite different, but similarly illusory) notion of 'the biggest natural number'. The incoherence results from the incommensurability of the goods that make up individual welfare, and of the individual states of well-being (in the broadest sense of 'well-being') that make up the well-being of some 'collectivity'. There is a generic verification of this incommensurability whenever an unbiased and intelligent chooser, confronted with a state of affairs claimed to instantiate greater collective welfare than alternative states of affairs, *could choose* one or more of those alternative states of affairs. There is the proximate mark of incommensurability when alteration of the goods or bads in one or more of these various states of affairs leaves them all eligible; for that shows that the original multiple eligibility was not a mere tie between commensurable aggregate quantities of good.[45]

Thus the contrast between 'collective' good and 'individual' right cannot make good the contrast between policy and principle, legislative and judicial domains. The collectivity is of individuals, and the good (or well-being) of each individual and of their community involves, as an intrinsic aspect, that he or she is treated with fairness. Moreover, the good of each individual involves incommensurable aspects: there is a sense in which one's life-and-health is always better than one's death, a sense in which it is better to risk death on the Marylebone Road than abandon participation in normal affairs and responsibilities, and a sense in which one were better dead than be a betrayer of friends or a corrupter of children.[46] Reasonable choice, personal and social, is regulated not by the attempt to 'aggregate' goods, but by the attempt to foster or at least respect every basic human good according to criteria of fairness, respect (in every choice) for every basic good of every person, fidelity to commitments, creativity in pursuit of human good(s), and so on.

But are there not plain cases of preferring collective to individual good, or at least collective good to individual right? No, not in any strict sense. We loosely talk thus, of course, when, say, one man's house is blown up to save the suburb from burning. But what will burn is the houses of other individuals, each with a claim to be protected from fire. The plan is to protect these individuals by clearing combustibles from the fire's path. *This combustible is a man's house.* Can he complain of unfairness if we raze

---

[44] Foot, 'Utilitarianism and the Virtues' at 209; and 'Morality, Action and Outcome' at 36.
[45] See *FoE* 89–90; *NDMR* ch. ix, sec. 6.   [46] Cf. Matt. 18: 6; 26: 24.

it? Well, he retains all his rights—genuine rights, properly specified—unimpaired. Genuine, carefully specified rights are not mere fair-weather friends. So he can complain of unfairness, injustice, if our action is pointless because as much will be lost as will be saved, or if our motives are mixed with favouritism or hostility unrelated to the menace of the fire, or if we will not compensate him by contribution from all whose interests are preserved by our fire-fighting measures, or if we choose to prefer any amount of other people's *property* (after all, an instrumental good) to his children (whose good is personal, not instrumental) by blowing them up with the house. Beyond that his rights do not go (and, properly understood, never did). And we do all this practical moral-political reasoning the more clearly if we avoid the mistiness of 'collective' or 'aggregate' good.

But what about the fire brigade? Is not that the instrument of a collective goal? Yes, but only in the following sense. The protection of individuals from fires is one of the purposes we share, and whose sharing constitutes us a community. Protection from fires is thus an aspect of a good which you could call 'collective' but might do better to call 'common' or 'communal': shared. And the instruments for pursuing the various aspects of that good—instruments such as taxation systems, drainage, fire-fighting, police, courts, currency, and so forth—are irreducibly communal: public, not private, if not in ownership then in utility and dedication. But nowhere here do we find a collective welfare determinable apart from the individual rights which define, shape, and constitute the common good, the public interest. As our courts regularly and rightly say, the protection of individual rights is in the *public* interest.[47]

In the 1977 Maccabaean lecture, it was said that in Britain

> political debate centers on the...idea of the general welfare or collective good. When political debate talks of fairness, it is generally fairness to classes or groups within the society (like the working classes or the poor), which is a matter of the collective welfare of these groups.[48]

But is it not widely understood that the 'collective welfare' of the poor is simply the welfare of indigent individuals, and that any unfairness involved in their inadequate welfare is simply unfairness to each and all of the individuals within the (logical) class 'the poor'? In relation to the welfare of the poor, don't the words 'general' and 'collective' merely idle?

---

[47] See e.g. *Dumbell v Roberts* [1944] 1 All ER 326 at 329, per Scott LJ; *Mohammed-Holgate v Duke* [1984] AC 437, [1984] 1 All ER 1054 at 1059a, per Lord Diplock.

[48] *A Matter of Principle*, 31 = Proc Brit Acad, lxiv, at 286. See also *A Matter of Principle*, 65: '...a group interest in having the same opportunities as those of other races'.

May not the confusion they signify be in the beholder, rather than in the British political debate?

But more: the contrast between rights and collective welfare does mischief to rights themselves. While teaching that (all) rights are trumps, it also teaches that (all) rights must give way to so-called collective welfare. Each right's presumptive priority (it is said) can be rebutted, and is rebutted whenever the threat to this 'collective welfare' is sufficiently great. This grand picture, then, gives the utilitarian or consequentialist what he needs for his purpose of setting aside the truly inviolable rights.

To hold fast to these rights, one must hold fast to a distinction fundamental to western moral thought, perhaps increasingly though still only very hesitantly acknowledged in the explicit doctrine of our criminal law,[49] but ignored in the theory of rights which we are considering. The distinction, which I cannot here explore, is that between what one chooses (or: intends, whether as end or as means, and whether as act or omission) and what one merely accepts (rightly or wrongfully) as a side effect of one's choices. For if there are truly inviolable rights which, when precisely specified, do trump, and not merely presumptively, *all* competing considerations, that is because the correlative wrong (or breach of duty) is the *choosing* to destroy, damage, or impede some basic aspect of a human person—which is always wrong. The utilitarian,[50] denying any significant distinction between choosing death and accepting it as a side effect of what one chooses (say, as a means of alleviating pain), urgently wishes our law to permit choices to kill, for example handicapped babies. His projects of reform get aid and comfort, willy-nilly, from the claims much heard in contemporary jurisprudence: that (all) rights are trumps but (all) are outweighed by *some* 'collective goals', and that the paradigm case of a fairly weighty right is 'the right to free speech'—which, as everyone admits, is rightly qualified in scores of ways and whose elevation to the rank of a paradigm therefore teaches, subliminally, that rights need not be taken too seriously.[51]

---

[49] See *Hyam v DPP* [1975] AC 55, [1974] 2 All ER 41 at 52, per Lord Hailsham; contrast 63, per Lord Diplock, and *R v Lemon* [1979] AC 617, [1979] 1 All ER 898 at 905, per Lord Diplock.

[50] Not, of course, every utilitarian. It goes without saying that utilitarians (and other sorts of consequentialist or proportionalist) differ among themselves; for their 'method' *cannot* (in morally significant issues) amount to more than a rationalization of opinions formed on some basis other than the method (e.g. convention, sentiment, self-interest): *FoE* ch. IV.3. Moreover, since utilitarians characteristically want to get things done, they usually are loath to allow their calculations to take them too far from the consensus of their society and era.

[51] At one point, Dworkin entertains the category of 'absolute rights'; but he immediately renders it ridiculous by giving as his only hypothetical example 'a right to freedom of speech as absolute': *TRS* 92. His own teaching is that 'even the grand individual rights are not absolute, but will yield to especially powerful considerations of consequence': *ibid.*, 354.

VI

I return, once more, to the proposed constitutional division. Its proponents have never denied that legislation properly goes beyond 'policies' of pursuing 'collective goals', and gives principled effect to rights. Rights mentioned as proper objects of legislative concern include the 'right to a decent level of medical care',[52] the right to protection against the 'moral harm' of being convicted (however accidentally) when innocent,[53] the right of the young to social provision of resources to avoid the 'moral harm' of neglect of education,[54] and so on.

The utilitarian models which were meant to give sense to the presumptive priority (and the exceptional though not infrequent subordination) of rights have lately been departed from yet more widely. Concern for general welfare, it is said, includes concern for moral welfare.[55] Now moral welfare is the welfare of individuals. And the preservation of their own and their children's moral welfare is a task which individuals undertake as an essential exercise of their freedom. Suppose a court decides that the Convention's 'right of privacy' requires that use of pornography in private be permitted. Such a decision, as Dworkin says, would

> sharply limit the ability of individuals consciously and reflectively to influence the conditions of their own and their children's development. It would limit their ability to bring about the cultural structure they think best, a structure in which sexual experience generally has dignity and beauty...[56]

So interpreted, a right to privacy 'limits choice':

> those who wish to form sexual relationships based on culturally supported attitudes of respect and beauty, and to raise their children to that ideal, may find

---

[52] Dworkin in Cohen (ed.), 268, 270–1 [1983].

[53] *A Matter of Principle*, 80, 92–3 [1981]. NB:

> The injustice factor [moral harm] in a mistaken punishment will escape the net of any utilitarian calculation, however sophisticated, that measures harm by some psychological state along the pleasure-pain axis, or by the frustration of desires or preferences or as some function over the cardinal or ordinal rankings of particular people, even if the calculus includes the preferences that people have that neither they nor others be punished unjustly (*ibid.*, 81).

[54] *Ibid.*, 84. NB: this moral wrong, if it exists, is 'not captured in any ordinary utilitarian calculation'.

[55] *A Matter of Principle*, 29: 'the general welfare (Viscount Simonds called it the "moral welfare") of society'. Here 'of society' means just what 'public' means in 'conspiring to corrupt public morals': the moral welfare to be protected, preserved, or corrupted, is the moral welfare not merely of this individual or his household intimates, but of other individuals too; what matters is not that these other individuals be many, but that they be ascertained otherwise than by their private association with the individual in question: thus, any passer-by, any reader of an advertisement exposed to 'the public' in a 'public place', and so on.

[56] *A Matter of Principle*, 349 [1981]. See also *ibid.*, 350: recognition of a right of privacy of that sort 'gives most people less rather than more control over the design of their environment'.

their plans much harder to achieve if pornography has taken too firm a hold in popular culture, which it may do even without public display.[57]

Suppose, then, that a court decided disputed questions about 'privacy' without due regard to the fact that its decision to favour the 'right of privacy' would impose limitations on individual choice, self-determination, and parental capacity, in a matter which so affects human dignity, respect, and beauty of action. Would it not be doing an injustice or, if you prefer, violating *rights*?

Why, then, should anyone hold that a right such as privacy (embodied in the European Convention, and imaginatively inferred from the US Constitution by the Supreme Court) should trump a concern for 'morals'? That concern, we can now say, is no mere concern for continuance of the *mores* and *esprit de corps* of the tribe. It is a rational concern for human goods, not only beauty and respect in most significant relationships, but also the self-determination of those individuals who strive for an environment which enhances, not corrodes, such relationships, a milieu which they consider they have a right to create and preserve, in the interests of, at least, their children's rights.

VII

To the question, why *certain* rights (or certain exercises of certain rights) trump moral welfare (and, indeed, many other rights and interests), two types of answers are given, the one pragmatic, the other philosophical. The philosophical answer, offered by several contemporary jurisprudents,[58] is that to override these rights, in favour of worthwhile forms of life and in opposition to 'demeaning or bestial or otherwise unsuitable' forms of life, is to deny equality of concern and respect to those whose freedom of speech or 'privacy' (lifestyle) is overridden.

A first version of this claim was that legislative protection of morals manifests official or majority contempt for those whose preferred conduct is proscribed or impeded. That version was untenable because, on the contrary, such legislation may manifest precisely a sense of the equal worth and human dignity of those people, whose mistaken conception is impeded

---

[57] *Ibid.*, 415.
[58] See e.g. MacCormick, *Legal Right and Social Democracy*, 36 (enforcing morality treats others as 'not capable of morally proper choice'). Likewise Raz, 'Liberalism, Autonomy, and the Politics of Neutral Concern' at 113 ('...coercion...normally is an insult to the person's autonomy. He or she is being treated as a nonautonomous agent, an animal, a baby, or an imbecile'). These defenders of autonomy here seem simply to overlook the category of the autonomous individual who is capable of living rightly, but through temptation, bad example, and so forth, wrongly chooses to live otherwise (and who could be discouraged from doing so).

precisely on the ground that it misunderstands and betrays human worth and dignity (and thus their worth and dignity, along with that of others). So the new version relies instead on the idea of a hypothetical loss of, or incompatibility with, *self*-respect (one's own sense of one's equal worth):

> liberalism based on equality...insists that government...must impose no sacrifice or constraint on any citizen in virtue of an argument that a citizen could not accept without abandoning his sense of his equal worth....no self-respecting person who believes that a particular way to live is most valuable for him can accept that this way of life is base or degrading....So liberalism as based on equality justifies the traditional liberal principle that government should not enforce private morality...[59]

But this too fails. To forbid someone's preferred conduct does not require him to 'accept an argument'. And if he did accept the argument on which the law is based, he would be accepting that his former preferences were indeed unworthy of him (or, if he had always recognized that, but had retained his preferences nonetheless, it would amount to an acknowledgement that they had been unconscientious preferences). The phenomenon of conversion or, less dramatically, of regret and reform, shows that one must not identify the person (and his worth as a human being) with his current conception of human good. In sum: either the person whose preferred conduct is legally proscribed comes to accept the concept of human worth on which the law is based, or he does not. If he does, there is no injury to his self-respect; he realizes that he was in error, and may be glad of the assistance which compulsion lent to reform. (Does this sound unreal? Think of drug addicts.) And if he does not come to accept the law's view, the law leaves his self-respect unaffected; he will regard the law, rightly or wrongly, as pitiably (and damagingly) mistaken in its conception of what is good for him. He may profoundly resent the law. What he cannot accurately think is that the law does not treat him as an equal; for the justifying concern of this law, as an effort to uphold morality, is (may we not suppose?) for the good, the worth, and the dignity of everyone without exception.[60]

---

[59] *A Matter of Principle*, 205–6 [1983].

[60] Sometimes Dworkin distinguishes between the worth of people and of their preferences (e.g. *A Matter of Principle*, 360); but usually he thinks that (to use the old jargon) to condemn the sin is to manifest contempt for the sinner—a mistake encouraged by his ambiguous phrase 'people of bad character' (*ibid.*, 357). He thus overlooks another aspect of transparency: what is transparent for me, viz. the quality of *my* choices for the quality of *my* character, is not transparent when I am making judgments about other people, their choices, and their character. Since I do not know the deepest grounds of their choices, I can condemn those choices without condemning (the character of) those who made them.

VIII

The philosophical argument for priority of 'free speech' and 'privacy' failed because it sought to identify rights without proceeding from an understanding of human good (which feeds and is fed by an understanding of human nature). With the failure of that argument, there remains a pragmatic one: free speech and privacy are rights declared in the European Convention and other standard bills of rights, the fruits of historical experience. Specified and 'enshrined' in a public commitment, and protecting the individual against the state, they must extensively prevail over the competing considerations which have usually found a place in bills of rights only, if at all, in vague mention of 'morals' or 'public morals'.

The European Convention is indeed a product of historical experience. The draftsmen of 1950 had before their eyes the Nazi and Fascist lawlessness (often under cloak of legality), with its withdrawals of all human rights from unfavoured categories of person within the jurisdiction, on grounds such as race, language, religion, political opinion, association with a national minority, and so forth (Arts 1 and 14); its exterminations (Art. 2), tortures (Art. 3), forced labour (Art. 4), arbitrary and indefinite detentions (Art. 5), mock trials (Art. 6), retroactive criminal laws (Art. 7), arbitrary searches and seizures and disruption of families and family bonds (Art. 8),[61] repression of religious freedom (Art. 9), censorship, jamming, and persecution for transmitting opinion or information (Art. 10), destruction of unions and other intermediate or voluntary associations (Art. 11), and suppression of marriage and procreation by some categories of persons (Art. 12). Hence the selection of enumerated rights for protection.

The draftsmen were aware that there are many other ways in which human good can be affected by the conditions of life in community. These they referred to only compendiously, by such phrases as 'national security', 'public safety', 'prevention of disorder and crime', 'protection of health', and 'protection of morals'. Some of the named rights were not to be derogated from or qualified, even in the states of emergency which the Convention envisages, whether by reference to national security or anything else; these, being inviolable and (mostly) sufficiently specified, really do deserve the name *rights*; their unqualified identification is the European Convention's cardinal (though not unflawed)[62] virtue.‡ But the Convention stipulates,

---

[61] Graphically sketched by Judge Sir Gerald Fitzmaurice (dissenting) in *Marckx v Belgium* (1979) 2 EHRR 330 at 366 (para. 7).

[62] When the time comes, judges will, I expect, be found who will read 'deprived of his life', in Art. 2.1, as significantly different from 'deliberately killed' (or cognates such as 'intentionally hastening death'); and thus the Convention may provide no great obstacle to killing certain handicapped persons for whom 'termination of life is no deprivation', etc.

as I have said, that 'the exercise of' other named rights (privacy, Art. 8, and freedom of expression, Art. 10) can be subjected to interferences, restrictions, and penalties of a certain kind.

This uncraftsman-like language of 'interference' with exercises of the right carries an inappropriate implication: that when I am arrested in my cellar for making drugs, bombs, or freeze-proofed wines down there, the unwelcome irruption is not merely into my privacy but also into my exercise of my right. Would it not be more accurate to say that in such use of my cellar, I take myself outside the true ambit of my right? The limitations indicated by the Convention's references to public health, prevention of crime, and so on, are limitations which specify the limits of my right; they are in fact a part—or at least a compendious reference to an intrinsic part—of the right's own definition.§

More important than its conceptual inelegance is the Convention's fundamental remission of responsibility: a court must delimit various tersely named but undefined rights (or their exercise) by reference to what is 'necessary in a democratic society for the protection of' health or morals or reputation or national security or maintaining the authority and impartiality of the judiciary, and so forth.

'Necessary...for'—not merely appropriate, fitting, justifiable in view of ... Now American constitutional analysis can help clarify this matter. The necessity that must be shown is twofold: the law under challenge must be necessary for the public purpose it purports to protect (say public health, or morals), *and* that purpose must be a 'compelling state interest',[63] one whose importance outweighs, in a democratic society, the importance of the right (or: exercise of the right) which the challenged law restricts. As the ECtHR says, that law must be 'proportionate'. The significance of this opaque term emerges from the Court's use of it: the law must be proportionate not only to its own goal but also to the restriction it imposes on the right (a right treated in the Convention's conceptual structure, as we have just seen, as embracing the prohibited activity). The Court weighs the value of the relevant exercise of the right, against the value of the good secured by the challenged law.

What metric, what scales, are provided? The Convention refers us only to the concept of 'a democratic society'. How, you may ask, does the concept of democracy bear on the scope of the Convention's protection afforded to security, reputation, morals, judicial authority...? (Surely it is not a matter of the sort of things that came to mind when we heard the complaint that judicial review is undemocratic?) The ECtHR thinks it largely a matter of

---

[63] See e.g. *Roe v Wade* 410 US 113 (1973) at 316.

'tolerance and broadmindedness'.[64] Thus, superficiality and the short view are read into the Convention.

Is it the task of our judges to take another view? Is it *their* role to do what every legislature has, in any case, the responsibility to do? I mean: to hold in mind the good of autonomous and authentic choice, the evil of hypocrisy, bribery, blackmail, and police corruption, the costliness and scarcity of investigative and prosecutorial resources, the clumsiness of the legal process in analysing and resolving human character and relationships, the dignity of helping others to identify and choose consistently for the worthwhile amongst peddlers of decay, the importance of compulsion to education, the elusiveness of consensus in a pluralistic society, the fragility of allegiance in a society seeming to honour none but formal principles (such as the mysterious equality of immunity—for the safely born, and healthy—from interference)... Is it the proper role of judges to hold in view all these (and similar) goods and evils, opportunities, and perils, and to *choose commitments*, backed by legal compulsion, in relation to education, public or social means of communication, and recreation (newspapers, cinemas, videos, amusement arcades, bath-houses), research (human embryo banks, human embryo and fetal clearing-houses, human and humanoid genetic manipulations), family life (incest), institutional ideals, symbols, and structures (marriage, and its simulations in bigamy and homosexual unions)...?

A good citizen's sense of allegiance may be wounded, of course, when Parliament determines to permit, organize, and fund abortions of convenience, or to approve and fund the conditional proposal and dedicated systems for destroying millions of foreign citizens in nuclear city swaps and final retaliation. One may indeed wonder how far to be concerned about the constitutional order, let alone the morals, of a society which sponsors such wrongs of thought and deed. But there is, I suggest, a special humiliation when the judiciary is originating sponsor of wrongs. Why so? And if so, must there not be some deep difference in function and character between courts and legislature, a difference so much of my argument may have seemed to deny?

I have denied only one version of the constitutional division of responsibilities. I deny that courts are the uniquely appropriate forum for practical judgment about those rights and principles which comprise the

---

[64] *Handyside v United Kingdom* (1976) ECHR Ser. A, vol. 24, 23 (para. 49); *Dudgeon v United Kingdom* (1981) 4 EHRR 149 at 165 (para. 53). Tolerance is one thing; 'tolerance and broadmindedness' has a different ring. [These terms continue on their destructive judicial career as solvents of reasonable standards of justice, in (e.g.) *Hirst v United Kingdom (No. 2)* (2005) 42 EHRR 41 at para. 70. See first endnote below.]

bulk of manifestos like the European Convention and which extend their (defeasible, fair-weather) protection far beyond traditional common law protections against slavery, wrongful imprisonment, torture, and the like. The legislator, I have argued, has a high responsibility for the human goods which modern 'manifesto rights' and 'principles' pick out as basic goods to be shared in by all. His responsibility is to enact his laws (which can only rarely be *deduced* from principle) so as to give every relevant principle due practical acknowledgement in every legislative act.

The special responsibility and competence of courts I can here scarcely even sketch. Is it not to ensure that their decisions are consistent with (that is, 'fit') the derivative, *institutional* rights and principles created by the public commitments already made by the relatively determinate sources which can be the subject of legal *learning*: legislation, custom, and judicial precedent? What is 'necessary in a democratic society for the protection of, say, morals' is, it seems to me, an issue not to be mastered by legal learning or lawyerly skills. Perhaps, recalling my criticism of the ECtHR's protestations of moral neutrality, you will say that, on my view, courts that venture on these issues are damned if they do embrace moral neutrality and damned if they don't. And that is my point.

When a legislator considers human interests in terms of rights and principles, such as the right to privacy or the right of children and their progenitors and guardians to a decent milieu, his judgment may well be corrupted by false beliefs, passion, ineptitude, horse-trading, and all the other vices of political process. A community living without judicial review of legislation lives dangerously. How dangerously? That depends on the political community, its composition and its history. The political horizon of many American constitutional lawyers has been dominated by the simple judgment that the racial desegregation accomplished by judicial programmes, such as that of *Brown v Topeka Board of Education* 347 US 483 (1954), could not soon have been accomplished otherwise (say by Congressional legislation under the post-civil war amendments). But not every society has to unravel its own formerly entrenched injustices under the legal and political constraints of federalism. And the horizon of other constitutional lawyers is dominated by a gloomy spectacle: the analytical confusion and bad legal history, the doctrinal pieties and the moral evasions of an 'improvident and extravagant' exercise of 'raw judicial power',[65] to strike down the laws of fifty jurisdictions: *Roe v Wade* (1973).

[65] *Roe v Wade* 410 US 113 at 222, per White J (dissenting).

IX

Courts are a forum of principle. But when a judge has to determine, not what rights and principles have been established by the existing law as a whole, but whether existing laws measure up to the 'inspirational' terms of a novel constitutional instrument, may not his judgment, too, be deflected—say, by a narrow concern for precedent, the formulae of the text, the bounds of the pleadings and arguments addressed to it, and the parties' special circumstances, and by the political vices (more discreetly indulged), and mistaken political theories (such as utilitarianism, neutral liberalism, or social-cohesion conservatism), which enjoy a wider success amongst the sophisticated?

Here, perhaps, is the special insult added to the injury done when courts, in the name of rights, have overturned statutes and thereby sustained, abetted, or even imposed child labour, widespread pornography, and abortion.[66] It is not so much that the constitutional status of the bill of rights impedes prompt remedies for these injustices. Rather, it is the inauthenticity of the appearances which the courts in these cases kept up—the appearance of doing what courts characteristically do when doing justice according to law. Only out of court will the judge say what Mr Justice Kenny of the Irish Supreme Court said, reflecting approvingly on twenty years of 'active' interpretation of the Irish bill of rights: 'Judges have become legislators and have the advantage that they do not have to face an opposition.'[67]

Yet this was not mere usurpation. The constitutional text, by confusing education and inspiration with government, has required or at least invited judicial excursions beyond legal learning. The exigencies of federation virtually oblige the constitution-maker to impose extraordinary responsibilities on the courts who must supervise the distribution of powers between coordinate central and local legislatures. One must ask oneself whether some comparable exigency suggests that we should impose on our courts the task of confronting either legislation or common law with the uncharted 'necessities of a democratic society'.

---

[66] In the view of the British member of the European Commission on Human Rights, the Convention creates a right to abortion on demand at least until the unborn child is 'capable of independent life': *Bruggeman and Scheuten v Federal Republic of Germany* (1977) 3 EHRR 244 at 255–7 (Fawcett, dissenting). The Commission disagreed; the Court has not pronounced [but in *Vo v France* (2007) and *A, B & C v Ireland*, 2010 the Court held that one cannot determine whether the unborn are persons protected by the Convention (and states may thus allows abortion on demand or restrict it to cases where the mother's life is at stake)].

[67] Kenny, 'The Advantages of a Written Constitution incorporating a Bill of Rights' at 196. As Kelly, *The Irish Constitution*, 475 n. 29, points out, Kenny J's 'have become' refers to the epoch inaugurated by his own judgment in *Ryan v A-G* (1965) IR 294.

X

Have I been arguing against a bill of rights for Britain? Is there a grand balance sheet to be drawn up? No. Does either option, for or against a justiciable bill of rights, require us to choose to wrong someone? Not yet, or not certainly. I am suggesting just this. Forgoing a justiciable bill of rights means accepting some real risks of injustices. But adopting a bill of rights, in any form now practicable, means accepting a time-bound text which downgrades some human rights by its flawed craftsmanship and its failure to envisage more recent challenges to justice—flaws magnified by the ECtHR's interpretative methods. It also means accepting into our country's institutional play of practical reasoning and choice a new, or greatly expanded, element of make-believe, and new or ampler grounds for alienation from the rule of law.¶

NOTES

† *A different sort of lawyer* …(p. 20). For example: in May 2010, on the day of the United Kingdom general election, a leading human rights barrister, Lord Pannick QC, thought it persuasive to address voters as follows:

> In a close contest, when the result in many seats may depend on a small number of seats, the unlawful exclusion of 85,000 prisoners from the right to vote is a constitutional disgrace that undermines the legitimacy of the democratic process…. There could not be a clearer demonstration of why this country needs a proper Bill of Rights. (*The Times* [London], 6 May 2010, 21)

As Lord Pannick well knows, the statutory disqualification of convicted prisoners, enacted in 2000 by Parliament in line with the unanimous recommendation of an all-party committee, is 'unlawful' only in the sense that, in 2005, it was held by a majority of the Grand Chamber of the European Court of Human Rights to be contrary to the human rights protected by the European Convention on Human Rights, which like all treaties has no effect in English law save what Parliament ascribes to it.

Parliament had not acted to give effect to the ECtHR's judgment in *Hirst v United Kingdom (No. 2)* (2005) 42 EHRR 41, essentially because that judgment is wholly unpersuasive in its argumentation and its all too easygoing dismissal of the English courts' contrary holding about the same Convention provision. The ECtHR's *Hirst* decision became even less attractive in April 2010, when in *Frodl v Austria* (judgment of the First Section, ECtHR, 8 April 2010, para. 28) it was given a significant though unargued and unadmitted interpretative widening (to Lord Pannick's enthusiastic approval), so that now, in his words, 'disenfranchisement may lawfully be imposed only on a small number of prisoners' and then only one-by-one, by a judge.

The ECtHR in *Hirst* purports to accept as legitimate the 'aim(s)' of the statutory disenfranchisement. But it makes no attempt to formulate such aim(s) in its own words, and as the judgment proceeds it emerges that the only aim accepted by the Court is

> to protect [democratic society] against activities intended to destroy the rights or freedoms set forth in the Convention … [by] … restrictions on electoral rights … imposed on an individual who has, for example, seriously abused a public position or whose conduct threatened to undermine the rule of law or democratic foundations … (para. 71).

In reality, the statutory aims which the Court pretended to accept are far different, and wider: (1) to promote civic responsibility by giving expression to the link between the exercise of social rights (such as voting) and the acceptance of social duties such as respect for the lawful rights of other citizens—acceptance and respect plainly violated by the commission of offences serious enough to be met by imprisonment; and (2) to enhance the essential retributive rationale of punishment by accompanying the punitive deprivation of liberty of movement with pro rata punitive deprivation of the civil liberty of exercising the office of elector. (See *Hirst* paras 16, 24, 37, 50.) Since it is scarcely possible to carry out a proper assessment of the 'proportionality' of means without constantly keeping in mind the precise ends ('aims') for which those means were adopted, the ECtHR's failure to give more than passing and inarticulate lip service to Parliament's purposes makes its judgment of disproportionality quite unpersuasive, indeed arbitrary.

Moreover, the ECtHR's terse allusion, at a critical point (para. 58), to the Rule of Law makes clear enough that it inclines to the very questionable legal/political philosophy advanced by the narrow Supreme Court majority in the corresponding Canadian case, *Sauvé v Attorney General of Canada (No. 2)* [2002] 3 SCR 519, according to which (in the ECtHR's paraphrase, para. 36) 'the legitimacy of the law [sc. the entire legal system] and the obligation to obey the law [flow] directly from the right of every citizen to vote.'

‡ *Absolute rights the cardinal virtue of the European Convention on Human Rights* ... (at n. 62). Here the essay has been overtaken by judicial interpretations of Art. 3's prohibition of torture and inhuman or degrading treatment, misapplying it by extending the absoluteness (exceptionlessness and quasi-unbounded diffusiveness) of the prohibition beyond acts *of* or *intended to* facilitate torture, to encompass also all acts (however motivated or needed for public purposes such as the upholding of human rights) that happen to create, despite every precaution, a 'real risk' that someone else will engage in torture etc. See essay 9 n. 58 on *Chahal* and *Saadi*.

§ *The uncraftsmanlike language of 'interference'* ...(p. 40). See Webber, *The Negotiable Constitution: On the Limitation of Rights*, esp. ch. 2 ('The Received Approach'):

> Under the received approach, the analysis of a rights-claim proceeds in two stages, divorcing the question of the right from the question of its limitation. By reading the 'limitation' of a right as synonymous with the 'infringement' or 'overriding' of a right, the received approach characterizes a limitation clause as akin to ... 'savings clauses' or a 'defence', whereby the infringement of a right may be saved or defended in the name of the public interest.... The result is an expansive reading of all rights, the frequent infringement of rights by the State in pursuit of the public interest, and the appeal to the limitation clause (or not) to justify (or not) the infringement of constitutional rights (p. 56).

(See also Miller, 'Justification and Rights Limitation'.) Webber's critique of this very widely received approach can be detached from his endorsement of the questionable (though also rather widely accepted) thesis that 'a constitution ought to remain open, on an ongoing basis, for democratic renegotiating' (p. 55) by or between legislative and judicial organs which the constitution does not profess to endow with constituent authority.

¶ *Judicial review on human rights grounds as a new element of make-believe and cause of alienation from the rule of law* ...(p. 44). There have been a good many gravely flawed, uncraftsman-like instances of decision-making in the highest courts of the United Kingdom since the Human Rights Act 1998 incorporated the ECHR into the law of the United Kingdom (albeit not in the more or less entrenched form envisaged throughout this essay: see text after n. 4 above). One high-profile example is examined in 2007a (see preliminary n. to essay 9). More recent is *HJ (Iran) v Secretary of State for the Home Department* [2010] UKSC 31, concerning the application of the international Convention and Protocol relating to the Status of Refugees. Here Lord Rodger JSC, and the three other judges expressing agreement with him, ignored the body of doctrine most recently articulated in *Januzi v Secretary of State for the Home Department* [2006] UKHL 5, [2006] 2 AC 426, according to which it is reasonable to expect that, rather than travelling to a foreign country to claim refugee status, persons who could escape persecution by moving to another part of their own country should do so—indeed, should do so even if they would still 'not there enjoy the basic norms of civil, political and socio-economic human rights'—unless requiring of them such evasive measures would be unconscionably harsh, bearing in mind the standards of their own country, and of basic humanity, rather than the higher standards of the country in which they sought refuge (and in which the court is sitting). The remaining judge, Lord Hope DPSC, did attend, albeit briefly, to that body of doctrine, and (in a visibly confused way) to the argument from analogy based on it by the government. But he proceeded on the basis of a 'principle'—one for which only slender authority could be adduced, and which obviously does not cohere with the *Januzi* body of doctrine—viz. that a refugee's claims cannot be resisted on the basis that he should instead have taken evasive measures in his own country if in fact he would be *unwilling* to take those measures. The result is an unprincipled exception made in favour of those persons unwilling to practise either continence or concealment of their 'random [non-marital] sexual activity'. (And see endnote to essay 20.) Whether or not one agrees with the policy objectives and 'sexual identity' doctrines of the 'gay rights movement' and with opening the United Kingdom to all who face discrimination or penalty for *openly* living that 'lifestyle', it is clear that the Supreme Court judgments in this case do injury to the rule of law. More grave in its impact on the common good is another instance of the same kind of injury: the set of judgments, all manifestly unsatisfactory (see 2009i), given on the basis of an ECHR 'right to private life' in *R (Purdy) v Director of Public Prosecutions* [2009] UKHL 45 (assistance in suicide).

2

DUTIES TO ONESELF IN KANT*

I

My duty towards myself cannot be treated juridically; the law touches only our relations with other men; I have no legal obligations towards myself; and whatever I do to myself I do to a consenting party....[1]

So Kant's students understood him to say in his lectures on ethics in 1780–81. At about the same time, the *Critique of Pure Reason* proclaimed that legislation should be guided by the Idea of '*a* constitution allowing *the greatest possible human freedom* in accordance with laws by which *the freedom of each is made to be consistent with that of all others.*'[2] And there are sentences in his own later writings which might seem to confirm the apparent meaning and interrelation of those assertions. For example:

[The concept of Right] [*der Begriff des Rechts*]... applies only to the external and—what is more—practical relationship of one person to another in which their actions can in fact exert an influence on each other (directly or indirectly).[3]

...

If, therefore, my action or my condition in general can coexist with the freedom of everyone in accordance with a universal law, then anyone who hinders me in performing the action or in maintaining the condition does me an injustice....[4]

---

[*] 1987c ('Legal Enforcement of "Duties to Oneself": Kant v. Neo-Kantians').

[1] Kant, 'Duties to Oneself', in *Lectures on Ethics*, 117.

[2] *Kritik der reinen Vernunft* A316/B373. (Page references to Kant's *other* published writings, except where otherwise indicated, are to the pages of the appropriate volume of *Kants gesammelte Schriften* (the Prussian Academy edition); for the *Rechtslehre* and the rest of the *Metaphysik der Sitten* (1797) see vol. VI; for the *Grundlegung zur Metaphysik der Sitten* (1785) see vol. IV; for the *Kritik der praktishen Vernunft* (1788) and the *Kritik der Urteilskraft* (1790) see vol. V; for the other political writings published by Kant and cited below see vol. VIII.)

[3] *Rechtslehre* 230 (Ladd, *The Metaphysical Elements of Justice* reads *Recht* here as 'justice', which is not necessarily a sheer mistake; see text at n. 81 below).

[4] Ibid.; see also 237 on 'the innate equality belonging to every man which consists in his right to be independent of being bound by others to anything more than that to which he may also reciprocally bind them'.

Passages such as these may seem to ally Kant with those among our contemporaries who are willing or even keen to label Kantian their political theory that (a) the state (government, the law) should be neutral amongst competing conceptions of what is good or right for individuals (the *neutrality principle*), and/or (b) the state has no right to use coercion directly or indirectly to discourage conduct not harmful to persons other than those who consent to engage in it (the *harm principle*).

If Kant did consider that his ethical and legal theory required, or was consistent with, either the neutrality principle or the harm principle, that would be ground to doubt his theory. For our contemporaries' efforts to defend one or other, or both, of those two principles are notably unsuccessful. In sec. II of this essay, I examine the attempts of John Rawls and Ronald Dworkin; in sec. III, I examine an attempt by D.A.J. Richards, who more explicitly claims the patronage of Kant's general theory of freedom and autonomy.

As the critique of Richards' theses will suggest, however, Kant's critical writings adhere neither to the neutrality nor to the harm principle. Rather, as I argue in sec. IV, they repudiate those principles. (One who, like Kant, rejects the harm principle will reject the neutrality principle, though many who reject the neutrality principle uphold the harm principle.) Kant seems to me broadly correct in many of his practical conclusions,[5] but his defence of them is weakened, as I argue in sec. V, by well-known structural weaknesses in his ethical theory.

II

Rawls does not argue for the neutrality principle and the harm principle as such, but for a principle which, so far as its content can be specified at all,[6] seems almost identical in its force and practical implications: that 'everyone should have the greatest equal liberty consistent with a similar liberty for others'.[7]

[J]ustice as fairness requires us to show that modes of conduct interfere with the basic liberties of others or else violate some obligation or natural duty before they can be restricted.[8]

---

[5] But not all—not e.g. his condonation of infanticide of illegitimate children: *Rechtslehre* 336. Still, *pace* Richards, this essay is not concerned to discuss which of Kant's practical conclusions are sound, and which unsound.

[6] See the serious doubts raised about the intelligibility and specifiability of this 'principle' by Hart, 'Rawls on Liberty and Its Priority'.

[7] *TJ* 327–8; cf. Kant's sentence quoted n. 2 above and accompanying text.

[8] *TJ* 331. In Rawls's terminology, all obligations are obligations of fairness and all natural duties are duties owed to others. *Ibid.* at 112, 115. On the interpretation of this passage, see Hart, 'Rawls on Liberty and Its Priority' at 541–2.

What, then, are Rawls's arguments against the rival view, which he calls 'perfectionist'? This is the view that the state has the responsibility and right to foster the good, the well-being, flourishing, and excellence, of all its citizens and to discourage them, even coercively, from at least some of the actions and dispositions which would injure, degrade, or despoil them, even some actions and dispositions which as such are 'self-regarding'. Rawls expressly admits that:

> [T]he freedom and well-being of individuals, when measured by the excellence of their activities and works, is vastly different in value.... Comparisons of intrinsic value can obviously be made; and ... judgments of value have an important place in human affairs. They are not necessarily so vague that they must fail as a workable basis for assigning rights.[9]

Having conceded this, he offers two arguments against perfectionism. The first, and primary, is that perfectionist principles would not be chosen in the Original Position, in which principles to regulate social life in a well-ordered society are chosen by persons ignorant of what will be their own personal interests, beliefs, and highest ends. And perfectionist principles would not be chosen because:

> To acknowledge any such standard would be, in effect, to accept a principle that might lead to a lesser religious or other liberty.... They [persons in the Original Position] cannot *risk their freedom* by authorizing a standard of value to define what is to be maximized by a teleological principle of justice.[10]

For:

> They cannot *take chances with their liberty* by permitting the dominant religious or moral doctrine to persecute or to suppress others if it wishes.... [T]o gamble in this way would show that one did not take one's religious or moral convictions seriously....[11]

The supporting consideration advanced in the sentence last quoted suggests the fragility of the whole argument. For, in times when certain religious and moral convictions precisely were taken with great seriousness, rational people were indeed willing to admit the perfectionist principle and thereby 'gamble' that the *right* (from their own point of view) religious and moral beliefs would be enforced. When beliefs wrong from their point of view were enforced, they did not complain that that was unfair in principle—but only that it was unjust in fact, because the beliefs were erroneous—and they sought whatever means of resistance or reform promised an opportunity

---

[9] *TJ* 328.   [10] *TJ* 327–8 (emphasis added).   [11] *TJ* 207 (emphasis added).

to enforce correct ones. So: Rawls's argument must do without its final supporting flourish.

And without that flourish it fares badly. Its premise is simply that, for reasons of sheer prudent self-interest (quite independent of morality or fairness), perfectionism would not be chosen in the Original Position. Its conclusion is that perfectionism is not a just principle. The non sequitur is obvious enough. (But it centrally flaws Rawls's entire construction in *A Theory of Justice*.) The conditions of the Original Position do secure that the principles which would be chosen in it would be fair, in as much as those conditions systematically exclude the sources of interpersonal bias (favouritism) and thus guarantee impartiality.[12] But nothing in logic or in Rawls's argument, anywhere in the book, entitles him to conclude that a principle which would *not* be chosen in the Original Position cannot be a principle of justice in the real world.

Perfectionist principles were rejected by Rawls, not as unfair, but as inimical to the self-interest of anyone whose views or desires might conflict with some application of those principles—and to that self-interest *as conceived in ignorance of moral principles and other standards of excellence*. Rawls's argument is thus helpless against claims that applying 'perfectionist' principle(s) will be in the best interests, truly conceived, of everyone, even of those who have to be coercively prevented from damaging their own best interests.

Here, then, we come to Rawls's second argument, extractable from an uneasily shifting paragraph which begins by conceding that it is indeed not easy to argue against moderate perfectionism. 'Moderate perfectionism' relies not on a single conception of the good life, to secure which all other lives must be subordinated, but on claims about the excellent and the degrading which are balanced 'intuitionistically' against liberty and equality. Rawls's uneasy argument asserts first that 'criteria of excellence are imprecise as political principles', and that 'their application to public questions is bound to be unsettled and idiosyncratic'.[13] It then shifts abruptly to an assertion even more obviously questionable and contingent: that appeals to perfectionist criteria are made 'in an ad hoc manner', and made *because* other criteria of political choice, consistent with (in effect) the harm principle, are unavailable. But this assertion is in turn immediately qualified; it is not always but only 'often' or 'likely' true.[14] His conclusion

---

[12] But the Rawlsian construction does not escape bias as between conceptions of the good and thus also as between *conceptions of* the person. See Raz, *The Morality of Freedom*, 117–33; Nagel, 'Rawls on Justice' at 8–10.

[13] *TJ* 330.   [14] *TJ* 331.

is appropriately weak: '[I]t seems best to rely entirely on the [i.e. his] principles of justice which have a more definite structure.'[15]

But plainly it will 'seem best' only to those who are content with the peculiar 'modern conditions' of chaotic disagreement about good and evil; these are the conditions for which, alone, Rawls seeks to identify principles of justice.[16] Manifestly, the whole argument, even if accepted, is quite incapable of showing that it is always *unjust* to use state power in violation of the neutrality and harm principles.

Efforts, then, have been made to supply what Rawls so clearly failed to supply: an argument that the neutrality principle and/or the harm principle are principles required by justice. Ronald Dworkin's well-known effort was in fact, I think, first advanced as a fundamental reinterpretation of Rawls's basic construction:

> The original position...as a device for testing...competing arguments...supposes, reasonably, that political arrangements that do not display equal concern and respect are those that are established and administered by powerful men and women who, whether they recognize it or not, have more concern and respect for members of a particular class, or people with particular talents *or ideals*, than they have for others.[17]

As Dworkin later said, on his own behalf:

> Government must not only treat people with concern and respect, but with equal concern and respect.... It must not constrain liberty on the ground that one citizen's conception of the good life of one group is nobler or superior to another's.[18]

---

[15] *Ibid.*

[16] See Rawls, 'Kantian Constructivism in Moral Theory' at 518:

> [W]e are not trying to find a conception of justice suitable for all societies regardless of their particular social or historical circumstances. We want to settle a fundamental disagreement over the just form of basic institutions within a democratic society under modern conditions.

See likewise 539 '[J]ustice as fairness assumes that deep and pervasive differences of religious, philosophical, and ethical doctrine remain.' Likewise Rawls, 'Justice as Fairness; Political Not Metaphysical' at 225, 230–1. Note Rawls's conclusion in 'Kantian Constructivism' at 570:

> [F]or all that I have said it is still open to the rational intuitionist to reply that I have not shown that rational intuitionism is false or that it is not a possible basis for the necessary agreement in our judgments of justice. It has been my intention to describe constructivism by contrast and not to defend it, much less to argue that rational intuitionism is mistaken.

[17] *TRS* 181 (emphasis added). Dworkin continues:

> Men who have no idea of their own conception of the good cannot act to favor those who hold one ideal over those who hold another. The original position is well designed to enforce the abstract right to equal concern and respect, which must be understood to be the fundamental concept of Rawls' deep theory.

For Rawls's tempered denial of this, see 'Justice as Fairness' at 236 n. 19. Dworkin later ascribed a similar view to J.S. Mill: see *TRS* 263.

[18] *TRS* 272–3.

I shall not delay on this claim that legislative protection of morals manifests official or majority contempt for those whose preferred conduct is proscribed or impeded. I think Dworkin has tacitly conceded its untenability. Briefly: it fails because such legislation *may* manifest, not contempt, but rather a sense of the equal worth and human dignity of those people whose conduct is outlawed precisely on the ground that it expresses a serious misconception of, and actually degrades, human worth and dignity, and thus degrades their own personal worth and dignity, along with that of others who may be induced to share in or emulate their degradation.[19] To judge persons mistaken, and to act on that judgment, is not to be equated, in any field of human discourse or practice, with despising those persons or preferring oneself.

So Dworkin has now offered a revised version of his argument. The new version relies instead on the idea of a hypothetical loss of, or incompatibility with, self-respect (one's own sense of one's equal worth):

[L]iberalism based on equality...insists that government...must impose no sacrifice or constraint on any citizen in virtue of an argument that the citizen could not accept without abandoning his sense of his equal worth.... [N]o self-respecting person who believes that a particular way to live is most valuable for him can accept that this way of life is base or degrading.... So liberalism as based on equality justifies the traditional liberal principle that government should not enforce private morality....[20]

But this argument is as impotent as its forerunners. To forbid people's preferred conduct does not require them to 'accept an argument'. And if they did accept the argument on which the law is based, they would be accepting that their former preferences were indeed unworthy of them (or, if they had always recognized that, but had retained their preferences nonetheless, it would amount to an acknowledgement that they had been unconscientious). The phenomenon of conversion or, less dramatically, of regret and reform, shows that one must not identify persons (and their worth as human beings) with their current conception(s) of human good. In sum: either those whose preferred conduct is legally proscribed come to accept the concept of human worth on which the law is based, or they do not. If they do, there is no injury to their self-respect; they realize that they were in error, and may be glad of the assistance which compulsion lent to reform. (Does this sound unreal? Think of drug addicts.) And if they do not come to accept the law's view, the law leaves their self-respect unaffected; they will regard the law, rightly or wrongly, as pitiably (and damagingly)

---

[19] For another way of showing that the claim is untenable, see *NLNR* 221–3.
[20] Dworkin, *A Matter of Principle*, 205–6.

mistaken in its conception of what is good for them. They may profoundly resent the law. What they cannot accurately think is that the law does not treat them as an equal; for the justifying concern of this law, as an effort to uphold morality, is (we can here suppose) a concern for the good, the worth, and the dignity of everyone without exception.[21]

III

Before turning directly to Kant's own account of these matters, it will be helpful to observe the use to which certain words taken from that account are put by a current defender of the neutrality and harm principles, David Richards. Richards offers to derive principles of public and constitutional morality from a concept of human rights explicated 'in terms of an autonomy-based interpretation of treating persons as equals':[22]

Crucially, the idea of 'human rights' respects this capacity of persons for[23] rational autonomy—their capacity to be, in Kant's memorable phrase, free and rational sovereigns in the kingdom of ends [citation to *Grundlegung* 433–4]. Kant characterized this ultimate normative respect for[24] the revisable choice of ends as the dignity of autonomy [citation to *Grundlegung* 434–5], in contrast to the heteronomous, lower-order ends (pleasure, talent) among which the person may choose. Kant thus expressed the fundamental liberal imperative of moral *neutrality with regard to the many disparate visions of the good life*: the concern embodied in the idea of human rights is not with maximizing the agent's pursuit of any particular lower-order ends, but rather with respecting the higher-order *capacity* of the agent to exercise rational autonomy in choosing and revising his ends, *whatever they are*.[25]

With the neutrality principle which he announces in that passage, Richards links a principle tantamount to the harm principle:

Consistent with the autonomy-based interpretation of treating persons as equals, the principles underlying a just criminal law require forms of action

---

[21] Sometimes Dworkin distinguishes between the worth of people and the worth of their preferences. See e.g. *ibid.* 360. Usually, however, he thinks that (to use the old jargon) to condemn the sin is to manifest contempt for the sinner—a mistake encouraged by his ambiguous phrase 'people of bad character'. *Ibid.*, 357. He thus overlooks one of the important aspects of what I have called 'transparency'. See *FoE* 70–4, 140–2: what is transparent for me, viz. the quality of *my* choices for the quality of *my* character, is not transparent when I am making judgments about other people, their choices and their character. Since I do not know the deepest grounds of their choices, I can condemn those choices without condemning (the character of) those who made them.

[22] Richards, *Sex, Drugs, Death and the Law*, 8.

[23] But on the adjacent page, Richards describes the capacities (which he there lists) as 'capacities that *constitute* autonomy': 8 (emphasis added); see Richards, 'Rights and Autonomy' at 7.

[24] Why Richards supposes that *respect for* the revisable choice of ends can intelligibly be described as the *dignity* of something remains unelucidated by anything that Richards (or, of course, Kant) says.

[25] Richards, *Sex, Drugs, Death and the Law*, 9 (emphasis added). In the version of this paragraph in 'Rights and Autonomy' at 7 there is a citation, for the 'liberal imperative of moral neutrality', to Dworkin, 'Liberalism'.

and forbearance from action that express, on terms fair to all, basic respect for the *capacity* of persons responsibly to pursue their ends, *whatever they are*. Such principles impose this constraint: only those forms of action and forbearance that violate rights of the person to forms of respect defined by the underlying principles of obligation and duty may properly be criminalized.[26]

In his initial discussion of autonomy, Richards does refer to the relevance of 'principles of conduct and canons of ethics to which [those exercising autonomy] have given their rational assent', and of 'the capacity to use normative principles, including, *inter alia*, principles of rational choice, to decide which among several ends may be most effectively and coherently realized'.[27] But 'effectiveness' and 'coherence' already sound rather different from Kant, and the differences broaden and deepen as Richards discloses his own authorial understanding of the two not-unambiguous paragraphs which I have just quoted from him. For his working interpretation of Kant's conception of autonomy soon drops all reference to norms of choice:

In [Kant's] central statements of ethical theory, moral personality is described in terms of autonomous independence—the capacity to order and choose one's ends as a free and rational being.[28]

... [T]he autonomy-based concept of treating persons as equals rests on respect for the individual's ability to determine, evaluate, and revise the meaning of his or her own life.[29]

The focal weight... give[n] to the freedom and rationality of the individual as the creator of his own life *is* the ideal fundamental to the autonomy-based interpretation of treating persons as equals, the basis of the human rights perspective in politics and law.[30]

The 'fundamental right' which Richards derives from these considerations is the right of persons 'to determine the meaning of their own lives'.[31]

It is hard to find a more inexact rendering of Kant's conceptions of autonomy, rationality, dignity, and the kingdom of ends.

We might begin with the 'memorable phrase' which introduces Kant as sponsor of *Sex, Drugs, Death and the Law*: 'free and rational sovereigns in the kingdom of ends'. The phrase does not, of course, occur in Kant, either at the pages from which Richards claims to have memorized it, or anywhere else. For on the pages to which Richards refers us, Kant states not only that the kingdom of ends is 'certainly only an ideal', but also,

---

[26] Richards, *Sex, Drugs, Death and the Law*, 17 (emphasis added). [27] *Ibid.*, 8.
[28] *Ibid.*, 109. Identical statement, *ibid.*, 177. [29] *Ibid.*, 172.
[30] *Ibid.*, 274, where Richards ascribes this view to 'the Pico [Della Mirandola]-Sartre tradition', but refers back also to Kant as one of the greatest philosophers of human rights and an upholder (though with tensions and inconsistencies in practice) of 'the moral ideal of autonomy'.
[31] *Ibid.*

and more importantly, that even a rational legislator in a kingdom of ends would not be sovereign unless he were 'a completely independent being, without needs and with an unlimited power adequate to his will'[32]—a godlike, not a human being. As if already vexed by Richards' misreading, Kant wrote a few years later, in the *Critique of Practical Reason*:

> We are indeed legislative members of a moral realm which is possible through freedom and which is presented to us as an object of respect by practical reason; yet *we are* at the same time *subjects in it, not sovereigns*, and to mistake our inferior position as creatures and to deny, from self-conceit, respect to the holy law is, in spirit, a defection from it [the moral law] even if its letter be fulfilled.[33]

But already in the *Grundlegung*, on the two pages following those cited by Richards, Kant had made pellucidly clear how different from Richards' is his understanding of the 'dignity of autonomy'. What has 'intrinsic worth [*Werth*], i.e., dignity [*Würde*]' has only the worth 'determined for it by the [moral] law'.[34] 'Therefore morality, and humanity so far as it is capable of morality, is the only thing which has dignity.'[35] The capacities mentioned by Richards (some of which are here specifically mentioned by Kant)[36] have a 'market value [*Marktpreis*]' and/or an 'affective [or: fancy] price [*Affectionspreis*]' (another merely relative value), but morally upright actions (such as fidelity in promises and benevolence on principle) have intrinsic 'worth [*Würde*]'. Morally good dispositions can lay claim to dignity, just because they and only they afford to rational creatures participation in giving universal laws and thus *fit* such creatures to be members and legislators in a possible kingdom of ends. The maxims of rational choosers (that is, their rationales for their choices) have dignity only when those maxims could harmonize with a possible kingdom of ends, by treating not only other persons but also each of the choosers themselves (that is, their own rational nature) as no mere means but also an end. 'Autonomy is *therefore* the ground of the dignity [*Würde*] of human nature and of every rational nature.'[37]

---

[32] *Grundlegung* 433–4 (Abbott trans., *Groundwork of the Metaphysic of Morals*, 52).

[33] *Kritik der praktischen Vernunft*, 82–3 (emphasis added) (Beck trans. 85).

[34] *Grundlegung*, 435–6 (trans. Beck). Contrast Richards, *Sex, Drugs, Death and the Law*, 20: 'the only thing Kant claimed to be of unconditional worth, personal dignity' (citing *Grundlegung*, 434–5).

[35] *Ibid.*, 435.

[36] These capacities, just as such, Kant in fact regards as *talents*, which fit one to pursue 'any kind of ends' (cf. Richards' references to one's ends 'whatever they are'), and which at best are worthy only of a respect which is no more than analogous to the respect due to the worth of the moral law and choice in conformity with that law: *Kritik der praktischen Vernunft*, 41, 77–8. Cf. n. 88 below.

[37] *Grundlegung*, 436 (emphasis added). On Kant's attribution of dignity to (i) humanity, (ii) rational nature, (iii) morality, (iv) persons, (v) those who conform to duty, and (vi) dispositions to do one's duty for duty's sake, see Hill, 'Humanity as an End in Itself' at 91–2.

In short, one has autonomy just insofar as one does in fact make one's choices, not on the basis of one's interests, but out of respect for the demands of morality.[38] And:

[A]ll claims of self-esteem which precede conformity to the moral law are null and void. For the certainty of a disposition which agrees with this law is the first *condition of any worth [Werth] of the person...*, and any presumption [to worth] prior to this is false....[39]

It might, indeed, have been better to begin these summary comments on Richards where Kant begins his ethical teaching—with the concept of intrinsic human *worth (Würde)*. We can overhear him in his lectures of 1780–81:

The supreme created good is the most perfect world, that is, a world in which all rational beings are happy *and are worthy of happiness*. The ancients realized that mere happiness could not be the one highest good. For if all men were to obtain this happiness without distinction of just and unjust, the highest good would not be realized, because though happiness would indeed exist, worthiness of it would not.... Man can hope of being happy only in so far as he *makes himself worthy* to be happy, for this is the condition of happiness which reason itself proposes.[40]

Or we can look at the opening gambit in the Moral Catechism which Kant proposed in his most mature published reflections on ethics—the decisive first move by which teachers are to dislodge pupils from their exclusive concern with happiness. Supposing you had power to dispense happiness at no cost to yourself:

[W]ould you see to it that the drunkard is never short of wine and whatever else he needs to get drunk?...

No, I would not.

You see, then, that if you had all happiness in your hands and, along with it, the best will, you still would...first try to find out to what extent each [person] is *worthy [würdig]* of happiness.[41]

---

[38] See *Grundlegung*, 433, where 'autonomy' is first introduced. Consider also Kant's concept of the *state's* autonomy as its formation and maintenance of itself 'in accordance with the laws of freedom [*nach Freiheitsgesetzen*]': *Rechtslehre*, 318. Richards is aware that Kant's conception of autonomy has something (to say the least) to do with acting from moral duty; see 'Rights and Autonomy' at 15. But Richards persists (*ibid.*) in his reductive presentation; autonomy, he says, is a matter of the 'separateness of persons'.

[39] *Kritik der praktischen Vernunft*, 73 (trans. Beck, 76) (emphasis added); see also *ibid.* at 147 (Beck at 152).

[40] *Lectures on Ethics* at 6 (emphasis added); see also at 252 (in the concluding moments of the lectures); *Kritik der praktischen Vernunft*, 110: '[V]irtue (as the worthiness [*Würdigkeit*] to be happy) is the supreme condition of whatever appears to us to be desirable and thus of all our pursuit of happiness and, consequently,...is the supreme good' (trans. Beck 114), and 111–19 (trans. Beck 115–24).

[41] *Metaphysik der Sitten*, 480 (trans. Gregor, *The Doctrine of Virtue*, 154).

Kant admonishes teachers to exalt 'above everything else in actions' the 'dignity [*Würde*]' of *virtue*. For otherwise the concept of duty dissolves and 'man's consciousness of his own nobility then disappears and he is for sale and can be bought for a price [*Preis*] that the seductive inclinations offer him.'[42]

Richards is in another world. He thinks, for example, that Kantian autonomy involves 'sovereignty over the qualities of one's experience'.[43] Many young heroin users in the United States enjoy such sovereignty, he says, by choosing to allow their drug use a 'psychological centrality' which 'may, from the perspective of their own circumstances, not unreasonably organize their lives and ends',[44] because that use of heroin and the like

> generates its own social tasks and standards of successful achievement, its own forms of status and respect, and its own larger meaning centering on the perceived qualities that the drug brings to the users' personal experiences, such as relief of anxiety and, sometimes, euphoric peace.[45]

Let us here ignore everything Kant ever said about drunkards and the use of euphoric opiates (and about any other particular question of duty to oneself). It remains clear that Richards has nothing but equivocation, mere punning, upon which to ground his claim that Kant's conception of *autonomous freedom* inherently involves such choices as the choice to become 'psychologically devoted' to heroin—to sell oneself, as Kant would say, to the seductions of the inclinations (perhaps very seductive 'from the perspective of one's own circumstances'). And the point here is not simply that such a choice entrains (*pace* Richards) enslavement, but more importantly that such 'determining and revising the meaning of one's life' (*a fortiori* choosing to find that 'meaning' in 'personal experiences')[46] is utterly remote from Kant's autonomy; the rational identification of, and

---

[42] *Ibid.*, 483 (trans. Gregor, 156).   [43] *Sex, Drugs, Death and the Law*, 177.
[44] *Ibid.*, 176.   [45] *Ibid.*, 175.
[46] Cf. Richards, 'Rights and Autonomy' at 16: 'Kantian principles can be shown to justify a fundamental right to autonomy in deciding whom and how to love *in order to preserve underlying values of personal emotional integrity and self-expression* in intimate relations' (emphasis added). Equally distant from Kant is the concern with 'self-definition' (by choices of e.g. 'the form and nature of...intensely personal bonds'—involving e.g. homosexual sodomy) which is foundational to the principal dissent in *Bowers v Hardwick* 478 US 186 at 205 (1986) (Blackmun J, dissenting) [and to *Lawrence v Texas* 539 US 558 (2003) overruling *Bowers v Hardwick*:

> 'the most intimate and personal choices a person may make in a lifetime, choices central to personal dignity and autonomy.... the right to define one's own concept of existence, of meaning, of the universe, and of the mystery of human life. Beliefs about these matters ... define the attributes of personhood.' Persons in a homosexual relationship may seek autonomy for these purposes (Kennedy J, for the court, at 574, quoting *Planned Parenthood v Casey* 505 US 833 at 851 (1992)).]

respectful submission to, the moral law which, *precisely as universal*, imposes on each one of us duties to oneself.[47]

But what about Kant's conception of freedom? I shall have more to say about Kantian freedoms in the next section. But I should say something about the conception of freedom that is, for Kant, the conception relevant to, and on the same plane as, his ethical conception of autonomy. The main thing to be said is that this freedom—freedom in the strictest sense—is known only through our consciousness of the moral law.[48] And 'the human will by virtue of its freedom is directly determined by the moral law';[49] man 'is the subject of the moral law which is holy, because of the autonomy of his freedom'.[50] To be conscious of freedom indeed precisely is to be conscious of the moral law.[51] If the will is not determined by the moral law, it is not free, for it is determined either by that law or by inclinations[52]—but to be determined by inclinations is precisely to be subject to heteronomy, that is, to lack autonomy.[53] Thus 'the *autonomy* of the will is the sole principle'—not merely the presupposition—'of all moral laws and of the duties conforming to them'.[54]

But, of course, individuals are conscious of their own freedom not only through their awareness of being able to resist the seduction of the inclinations, but also through their experience of being able to reject the categorical imperatives of morality. In a strategic paragraph of his lectures on ethics, Kant holds before his hearers the double significance of freedom.

---

[47] Wolff, *The Autonomy of Reason*, 178, frankly concedes that in talking of autonomy, 'Kant turns out *not* to be saying what I [Wolff] want him to say.' For Wolff, autonomy means that rational agents are bound to substantive policies and principles because and only because they have freely chosen them; 'the substance or content of moral principles derives from collective commitments to freely chosen ends': *ibid.*, 181. But as Wolff rightly stresses (*ibid.*), this belief is 'incompatible' with the belief 'that there are objective, substantive, categorical moral principles which all rational agents, insofar as they are rational, acknowledge and obey'—and the latter is a belief which Kant certainly held (*ibid.*), and wished to explain by the notion of *disinterestedness* central to what he called autonomy: *ibid.*, 179. As Wolff observes, autonomy Wolff-style [or, similarly, Richards-style] has 'the most far-reaching consequences for politics as well as for ethics' (178)—e.g. anarchism, as he defends it in his *In Defense of Anarchism*—but autonomy of *this* sort is simply 'not at all what Kant had in mind': *The Autonomy of Reason*, 178. (Wolff finds it 'unsettling' that Kant thus uses the word 'autonomy': 179. But his explanation of Kant's meaning seems to set aside what is perhaps the key: that one's will is autonomous or self-legislative just insofar as nothing determines it save one's conception of the will's (i.e. practical reason's) own *worth*: see Jones, *Morality and Freedom in the Philosophy of Immanuel Kant*, 102–12.) However, in stressing that Kant's concept of giving law to oneself has nothing to do with Richards' concept of 'meaning giving', I do not wish to suggest that Kant's conception of self-legislation is any more coherent than his conception of the self: see e.g. Ward, *The Development of Kant's View of Ethics*, 166–74.

[48] *Kritik der praktischen Vernunft*, 29, 30, 31, 47, 70; *Rechtslehre*, 225, 226.

[49] *Kritik der praktischen Vernunft*, 38 (trans. Beck, 40).   [50] *Ibid.*, 87 (trans. Beck, 90).

[51] See *ibid.*, 46 (trans. Beck, 47); for 'a free will and a will under moral laws are identical': *Grundlegung*, 447 (trans Beck); *ibid.*, 450; cf. 'Duties to Oneself', in *Lectures on Ethics* at 29 ('The more he can be morally compelled, the freer a man is').

[52] See *Kritik der praktischen Vernunft*, 72 (trans. Beck, 75).   [53] See *Grundlegung*, 433.

[54] *Kritik der praktischen Vernunft*, 33 (trans. Beck, 33); also 39; also *Grundlegung*, 452–3.

III.2 DUTIES TO ONESELF IN KANT

First, freedom is 'the inner value of the world'. For: 'The inherent value of the world, the *summum bonum*, is freedom in accordance with a will which is not necessitated to action.'[55] 'But on the other hand', he goes on,

> freedom unrestrained by rules of its conditional employment is the most terrible of all things.... If the freedom of man were not kept within bounds by objective rules, the result would be the completest savage disorder. There could then be no certainty that man might not use his powers to destroy himself, his fellows, and the whole of nature.[56]

Sophisticates may smile at Kant's references here and elsewhere[57] to savage disorder, wild lawless freedom, and so forth. Anarchy, one may feel, belongs to the past, or to other peoples. But Kant is here[58] thinking on principle, not primarily predictively or prudentially,[59] let alone pictorially. His 'savage disorder' can be exemplified not only by the 1980s gay-bar/bathhouse, in which lust courts even homicide and self-destruction, but also by the coolly unprincipled national choice to treat North Atlantic democracy as exempt from the moral law against murder by preparations and readiness to carry out a vast holocaust of innocents (and even of 'the whole of nature') in the face of defeat.[60]

At all events, Kant's precise purpose in holding before his students the Janus faces of freedom was, by inducing in them a sense of freedom's grandeur and facility for degradation, to persuade them of the (moral) *necessity* of respecting humanity (rationality, the source of all worth) *in oneself*, as the precondition for respecting it in the person of others. In that very paragraph he proceeds to identify and condemn certain 'victimless'

---

[55] 'Duties to Oneself', in *Lectures on Ethics* at 122.
[56] *Ibid.*; see also 123, 125, 151.   [57] See e.g. *Rechtslehre*, 316.
[58] Of course, there is elsewhere a strain of inadequately grounded progressivism (taking hope for destiny) in Kant's view of the future course of history. See e.g. Kant, *Idea for a Universal History*, 21. [*NLNR* 373–4, 377, 411.]
[59] Kant carefully denies that in pointing to the abyss of lawless freedom he is advancing a prudential (or, as we would now say, a consequentialist) argument: 'Duties to Oneself', in *Lectures on Ethics* at 125.
[60] See *NDMR*. Richards, 'Kantian Ethics and the Harm Principle: A Reply to John Finnis' at 466 says the text sentence above is my 'picture of homosexuality'—a claim false to the text and to my discussion of choices to engage in homosexual acts in the 'esoteric' writings which, oddly enough, I freely cite (as in n. 85 below), where relevant, in my 'exoteric' works. The rest of Richards' agitated response to the text sentence fails to attend to the only fact I there asserted, viz. the fact witnessed to by, among others, Denis Altman (an Australian university teacher and well-known pro-homosexual writer), in his *AIDS and the New Puritanism*, 155 (1986) ('My own observations during the course of writing this book suggested that while quite major shifts in behavior have taken place, surprising numbers of people continue to use the baths in the same way as before the epidemic') (published in the United States as *AIDS in the Mind of America*). Richards, in n. 53 of his Reply, is as inaccurate as his other interpretations, when he asserts that, in the article there cited (1985e), I stated that homosexual acts are only 'usually' wrong; in fact I said that they are only usually *promiscuous*, but on a moral analysis are always objectively wrong, like all other essentially masturbatory sexual acts. For the reasoning, partly burlesqued and mostly ignored by Richards, see 1985e [and now also essays 20–22].

or 'self-regarding' moral evils which excite Richards' broadly approving concern: drug use, sodomy, and suicide. And the same paragraph states the principle of Kant's condemnation:

The supreme rule is that in all actions which affect himself a man should so conduct himself that every exercise of his power[s] is compatible with the fullest employment of them.... The conditions under which alone the fullest use of freedom is possible, and can be in harmony with itself, are the essential ends of humanity. It must conform with these. The principle of all duties is that the use of freedom must be in keeping with the essential ends of humanity.[61]

And '[o]ur duties towards ourselves constitute the supreme condition and the principle of all morality; for moral worth is the worth of the person as such....'[62] If one thought oneself justified in treating oneself as a mere means, what *reason* would one have not to consider oneself justified in treating other persons likewise?

IV

It is time to consider more directly whether Kant thought that his ethical and political or legal theory required or was consistent with the 'harm principle' which I identified and labelled in sec. I. For besides the freedom with which sec. III was concerned, there is, of course, another freedom: the political or natural-law liberty which Kant calls outer or external freedom. And:

Freedom (independence from the constraint of another's will), insofar as it is compatible with the freedom of everyone else in accordance with a universal law [*nach einem allgemeinen Gesetz*], is the one sole and original right that belongs to every human being by virtue of his humanity.[63]

Like the passages from Kant which I quoted at the beginning of sec. I, this may seem to confirm that Kant thought it wrong for the law of a state to

---

[61] 'Duties to Oneself', in *Lectures on Ethics* at 123–4. He expresses the same principle in the words used in his later moral writings: 'actions must be in keeping with humanity itself'. *Ibid.* at 125; and 121.

[62] *Ibid.* at 121. Having reached the end of this section, readers will note that of the forty-five passages from Kant which are cited in it against Richards' interpretation of Kant's conception of autonomy, only one involves Kant's 'casuistry', i.e. his views on sex, drugs, killing, the harm principle, etc. For the whole section is concerned with his fundamental 'philosophical vision', a vision in which it is simply false to say that moral reasonableness constrains only 'interpersonal conduct' (as Richards continues to claim in e.g. his Reply at 461 n. 22). Richards' main defence against my critique—viz. his assertion that my 'interpretive approach puts a fundamental weight on Kant's casuistry' (etc., etc.)—will be found surprising not only by readers of this section but also any who read sec. IV, in which I do say something about Kant's casuistry, in its place. Whether Richards, when he turns to my own works, actually adheres to the sensible principles of interpretation articulated in his Reply, readers will easily judge.

[63] *Rechtslehre*, 237.

hinder one's violation of one's moral duties to oneself. That Kant did indeed thus subscribe to the harm principle is maintained by good commentators, such as Mary Gregor:

> Law [*Recht*] has to do only with the relations of one person to another in so far as their actions, as physical events in time, can have an influx on one another. By this Kant excludes from the scope of Law all actions which affect only oneself, even though it is conceivable that some of these actions could be prevented by outer [e.g. state] legislation. Certain actions affecting only oneself are morally impossible, but the ground of their impossibility lies in man's obligation to moral integrity and virtue; and since virtue, as an interior attitude of will, lies beyond the scope of outer legislation, juridical laws ought not to prohibit actions of this sort. Though such violations of duty to oneself may involve external actions, juridical laws ought not to prohibit these actions except in so far as they might, at the same time, have injurious effects on other people.[64]

I challenge this interpretation. (I have no *a priori* interest in claiming Kant as a supporter of my own view that neither the harm principle nor, *a fortiori*, the neutrality principle are entitled to a place in a sound general political philosophy. For Kant's ethical theory, and therefore his political theory too, seem to me deeply inadequate. So it would be no embarrassment to me if my challenge foundered and this conventional interpretation were vindicated. Still, I think the interpretation erroneous, and shall say why.)

The most obvious difficulty which the interpretation faces is that Kant displays no discomfort with criminal laws forbidding conduct which seems 'self-regarding', that is, not harmful to others. In the supplementary explanations he appended to the second edition of the *Rechtslehre*, Kant discusses the proper measure of punishment required by his principle of talion. His discussion touches on 'crimes...called unnatural because they are committed against humanity itself': rape, pederasty, and bestiality.[65] The list suggests Kant's lack of interest in the harm principle; even if *Paederastie* be read (which it by no means need be) as restricted to perverted sexual acts with a child, and even if the child's consent is discounted and psychological and moral harm to the child is conceded, there remains Kant's reference to bestiality, conduct which in itself affects no other person. The appropriate punishment for bestiality, in Kant's view, is permanent expulsion from civil society, since 'the criminal guilty of bestiality is

---

[64] Gregor, *Laws of Freedom*, 35 (Gregor gives no citations at this point, but seems to be commenting largely on *Rechtslehre*, 229–30). See likewise e.g. Murphy, *Kant: The Philosophy of Right*, 94; Reiss, *Kant's Political Writings*, 22; Fletcher, 'Human Dignity as a Constitutional Value' at 175.

[65] *Rechtslehre*, 363 (trans. Ladd, 132–3). One aspect of the meaning of 'against humanity itself' is shown by the phrase at 362–3: 'the respect due the humanity in the person of the miscreant (that is, due the human species)' (Ladd, 131–2). Cf. n. 68 below.

unworthy of remaining in human society'.⁶⁶ All this the conventional interpretation would have to explain away as some sort of slip, or mere gross inconsistency (and hands might be waved in the direction of Kant's 'pietistic upbringing', and so forth).

Almost equally obvious, and perhaps more telling, is the account of juridical duties to oneself, an account which Kant gives eight or nine pages after the passages in the *Rechtslehre* which are principally relied upon by the conventional interpretation. In the earlier passages, as will be recalled from sec. I above, Kant had stated:

> [The concept of *Recht*] applies only to the external and—what is more—practical relationship of one person to another in which their actions can in fact exert an influence on each other (directly or indirectly).... *Recht* is therefore the aggregate of those conditions under which the will of one person can be conjoined with the will of another in accordance with a universal law of freedom.⁶⁷

I have been quoting from pages 230 and 237 of the *Rechtslehre*. On pages 239–40, however, Kant states bluntly that all duties are either juridical duties (*Rechtspflichten*) or duties of virtue (*Tugendpflichten*); that for juridical duties, but not for duties of virtue, external legislation is possible; and that perfect *juridical* duties are of two classes: duties to others, corresponding to 'the right of mankind [*Menschen*] in others', and *duties to oneself,* corresponding to 'the right of humanity [*Menschheit*] in our own person'.⁶⁸

Gregor has argued that Kant operates with two completely different conceptions of 'juridical duty', one treating duties as juridical (rather than ethical) according to the type of legislation and/or constraint (in particular, external penalty) accompanying the law creating them, and the other treating duties as juridical (rather than ethical) according as they

---

⁶⁶ *Ibid.*, 366. The next sentence in my text predicted the sort of response which, in the event, Richards has made.

⁶⁷ *Ibid.*, 230.

⁶⁸ *Ibid.*, 239–40. This distinction between the right *of Menschheit* in one's own person and the right of *Menschen* in the person of others is one of the reasons why I am unpersuaded by Fletcher's view that

> the Kantian ideal is clearly communitarian, for our focus is not on our own selves, but on the vindication of the dignity of all human kind.... [S]olidarity [for Kant] is more important than the fulfillment of the private self (Fletcher, 'Human Dignity as a Constitutional Value' at 176, 177).

As to the point made in my text, which is fundamental to my interpretation of Kant's views on legal enforcement of duties to (humanity in) oneself, I may record that in the 'close parsing' to which n. 14 of Richards' Reply appeals for support, Douglas P. Dryer felt obliged to declare that the table in *Rechtslehre* at 240 is false to Kant's 'mature view' (published virtually simultaneously) not just in one but in two respects. He also asserted that the correct translation of '*Rechtspflichten*' is one not hitherto adopted in any of the published English translations ('duties for which there are correlative rights'). I do not say he was mistaken, though I find the proposed translation surprising. Dryer's strong measures with Kant's text were of a piece with his willingness to junk Kant's still more mature statements about bestiality (and, probably, pederasty) in *Rechtslehre*, 363. [In the event, Professor Dryer's close parsing was not published by the Columbia Law Review.]

relate to actions themselves (rather than merely to the maxims of actions). She is thus enabled to maintain that while juridical duties in the first sense must relate to other men, juridical duties in the second sense can relate to uses of one's own person.[69] Thus she seeks to preserve her view that Kant restricted the proper field of state law to actions affecting others, and thus upheld something approximating the harm principle.

I think her attempt fails. All on the same two pages of the *Rechtslehre* to which I have referred, Kant lays it down explicitly that juridical duties may be enforced by external legislation and that juridical duties include duties to oneself (as distinct from duties to others). It is not credible that he has here passed from one sense of 'juridical' to another quite different sense, without seeking to relate the one to the other, and quite unconscious of the confusion such a transition would create.

Moreover, Kant in fact takes care, then and there, to explain why duties which are not juridical but merely ethical are not proper subjects of external legislation. And his explanation has nothing to do with the right to freedom (still less with Richards's 'autonomy' or Justice Brandeis's 'right to be let alone'[70]). It is simply that the subject-matter of ethical duties is an internal act of the mind—as he says elsewhere, 'intentions and not actions only'[71]—that no external legislation can bring about.[72] (He adds, however, that external legislation can command actions which would be *conducive to* that internal virtue and its end.[73]) Thus Kant incorporates Gregor's proposed 'different point of view' (her second sense of 'juridical duty')[74] *within* his explanation of juridical duty in her first sense, and then moves promptly and smoothly to his flat denial that juridical duties must be duties to others.

Here, then, we have Kant's explicit theoretical framework for affirming the propriety, in principle, of external (for example, state) laws proscribing and penalizing pederasty and bestiality (to go no further than Kant's own later examples).

But what are we to make of the passages which I quoted in sec. I and have amplified in the last paragraph but one?

---

[69] Gregor, *Laws of Freedom*, 115–16.
[70] *Olmstead v United States* 277 US 438, 478 (1928) (Brandeis J, dissenting); see also *Bowers v Hardwick* 478 US 186 at 199 (1986) (Blackmun J, dissenting). [Likewise Lord Hope DPSC's 'fundamental right to be what they are ...': *HJ (Iran) v Secretary of State for the Home Department* [2010] UKSC 31 at para. 11.]
[71] *Kritik der praktischen Vernunft*, 71 (Beck, 74).   [72] *Rechtslehre*, 239 (Ladd, 45).
[73] *Ibid.*; see, further, text at nn. 87–90 below.
[74] Which is indeed one sense in which Kant speaks of juridical (as opposed to ethical) duty: see the section title at *Metaphysik der Sitten*, 388: 'Ethics does not give laws for *Actions* (*Ius* does that) but only for the *Maxims* of actions' (trans. Gregor, 48).

Observe, first, that in the many passages of the *Rechtslehre* which speak of one's will, freedom, action, or condition *coexisting* with the will, etc., of others, Kant always adds a further *necessary condition*: that the coexistence, consistency, or compatibility of wills, etc., be 'in accordance with a universal law'.[75] Our contemporary neo-Kantians standardly omit this condition (as Kant himself had omitted it fifteen years earlier, in the *Critique of Pure Reason*, with a glancing and rhetorical reference to a constitution 'of the greatest human freedom'). Other interpreters, for example Fletcher, do not overlook it, but read it down as requiring merely that the choices be compatible 'as these choices are universalized across the legal system as a whole'.[76] I suggest, however, that the phrase 'in accordance with a universal law' was certainly meant to import Kant's own conception expounded in the three principal forms or formulations of the categorical imperative—(i) universalizability of form, (ii) respect of humanity as an end in itself, (iii) harmonization of individual maxims within a kingdom of ends—'fundamentally only so many formulas of the very same law'.[77]

Now, as Kant indicated in the *Grundlegung*, a genuine universal law contains the ground not only of duties to others but also of *duties to oneself*.[78] Hence, in insisting that, to be right, one's will must not only be compatible with others' wills but must be 'in accordance with a universal law', Kant was indicating why certain acts and choices, fully compatible with the wills of others, are nonetheless violations of perfect juridical duties to oneself—duties which, being juridical, can in principle be legally enforced. As he says a little further on in the *Rechtslehre*, recalling the *Grundlegung*'s second formulation of the categorical imperative, one has a *juridical* duty

[t]o assert[] one's own worth as a human being in relation to others, and this duty is expressed in the proposition: 'Do not make yourself into a mere means for others, but be at the same time an end for them.'[79]

(Here one can recall Kant's view that the essence of the 'carnal crimes against nature', and of sexual promiscuity in general, is that human beings do thereby make themselves mere objects of enjoyment for someone's sexual

---

[75] Notably *Rechtslehre*, 230–1 (trans. Ladd, 34–5). The syntax is ambiguous, and it may well be right to prefer Abbott's translation: 'Act externally so that the free use of thy elective will may not interfere with the freedom of any man so far as *it* agrees with universal law': Abbott, *Kant's Theory of Ethics*, 307n (emphasis added).
[76] Fletcher, 'Human Dignity as a Constitutional Value' at 175.
[77] *Grundlegung*, 436 (trans. Beck); also 421.   [78] *Ibid.*, 430n.
[79] *Rechtslehre*, 236 (Ladd, 42). Kant adds: 'This duty will be explained later as an obligation resulting from the right of humanity in our own person (*lex justi*).'

desire. Such conduct, even if it can coexist with the conduct of others, thus cannot do so 'in accordance with a universal law'.[80])

What, then, of the passage in which Kant states that the concept of *Recht* applies only to the external relationship of one person to another, insofar as the action of one person can directly or indirectly affect the other? I will say nothing here about the extent to which Kant's reference to indirect effects might erode the harm principle. Rather, I shall simply recall that Kant's whole treatment of the question 'What is *Recht*?' remains within the conventional framework of western thought, a framework which he here recalls by his use of the Latin, *quid sit iuris*, and his use of *justum* and *injustum* to translate *Recht* and *Unrecht*.[81] In that traditional framework, justice and right are conceptually tied to relationships of one person to (an)other(s).[82] Thomas Aquinas, for example, would have no difficulty in saying that an act of recreational use of heroin (or consensual homosexual intercourse) is not, or not necessarily, an act of injustice or a violation of anyone else's right. But he and the tradition would add that it does not follow that the *prohibition* of such acts is an act of injustice or a violation of right. Nor does such an act of prohibition fall outside Kant's conception of the sphere of *Recht*; it precisely satisfies the criterion of that conception: an act which applies to the 'external and...practical relationship of one person [here: the lawgiver or the sovereign] to another' in which the action of the former can exert an influence on the actions of the latter.[83]

In the last analysis, the conceptual framework articulated in Kant's paragraph on the concept of *Recht* does not seem in any way intended to settle disputed questions about the proper range of state law. At the very least, it offers no normative premises for a normative conclusion such as the harm principle.

There remains only the passage which I put at the head of this essay: 'My duty towards myself cannot be treated juridically; the law touches only our relations with other men....' It is a passage from the students' transcription of Kant's lectures of 1780–81, and as such it cannot stand against the clear statements, both general and particular, in the long-gestated *Rechtslehre*.[84]

---

[80] 'Duties to Oneself', in *Lectures on Ethics* at 124; 'Duties Towards the Body in Respect of Sexual Impulse', in *ibid.* at 163–6; 'Crimina Carnis', in *ibid.* at 170; *Rechtslehre*, 278.

[81] *Rechtslehre*, 229–30.

[82] See *NLNR* 161–3. As Kant says elsewhere: 'towards oneself one can never do an injustice [*unrecht*]'. *On the Common Saying: 'This May be True in Theory, But It Does Not Apply in Practice'*, in Reiss, *Kant's Political Writings*, 294–5.

[83] *Rechtslehre*, 230. Recall, too, that such prohibited or prohibitable actions, being in Kant's view incapable of being willed as universal law, violate the categorical imperative and are thus *illicit* and not the matter of 'moral right as a warrant or title of action [*Befugniss*] (*facultas moralis*)': 222; also 223–4.

[84] Similarly, in *Lectures on Ethics* at 48, Kant is seen distinguishing the ethical from the legal by a series of indicia, by no means all of which are maintained in the *Rechtslehre*.

Moreover, there is a sense in which the passage remains true, even if one rejects the harm principle and concedes the propriety of punishing bestiality. The duty to treat oneself as an end, as honourable, and not as a mere means to gratifying one's own or others' inclinations, is a duty which can only be truly and fully fulfilled by maintaining a certain intention/disposition (*Gesinnung*)—and there is a sense in which the state's law, as such, indeed cannot reach or 'treat' dispositions. All that the law can do directly is authorize one man (the executive sovereign, Kant would say) to interfere with the *actions* of another, for example, the pederast.

V

But why interfere with those actions? Kant's claim—a matter of ethics—that such actions are immoral ('violations of duties to oneself') is inadequately argued. And he fails to offer any significant argumentation for his evident view—a matter of political theory—that the state can rightly punish such violations of duties to oneself, even when they violate no duty to others (a view incompatible not only with the harm principle but also with the neutrality principle). I must say something about the roots of Kant's failure to supply the argumentation needed for this theorem of his political theory. But I shall here say little or nothing about the just-mentioned deficiency in his ethical theory,[85] though my discussion of the weaknesses of Kant's political theory will hint at how I think his ethical theory might be enriched in ways that would allow the immorality of (that is, the unreasonableness and self-mutilation inherent in) human actions of these types to be articulated and clarified.

The political-philosophical principle which Kant needs, and virtually lacks, is the principle that the point and justification of state law is the *common good*. As L.T. Hobhouse put it in his classic exposition of liberalism:

The common good includes the good of every member of the community, and the injury which a man inflicts upon himself is matter of common concern, even apart from any ulterior effect upon others. If we refrain from coercing a man for his own good, it is not because his good is indifferent to us, but because it cannot be furthered by coercion.[86]

---

[85] But see 1985e at 43–55. On the weaknesses of Kant's ethical theory, see *FoE* 122–4; on the extent of the parallelism with a better moral theory, see *NDMR* ch. 10; Grisez, *Christian Moral Principles*, 108–9; Boyle, 'Aquinas, Kant, and Donagan on Moral Principles'. In distinguishing ethical from political theory as I do in the text, I take for granted, with Kant and almost everybody, that 'the claims of ethics' can and should be distinguished from 'the [legally, coercively] enforceable claims of ethics'—as Richards' Reply, at nn. 25–37, manifestly fails to do.

[86] Hobhouse, *Liberalism*, 142–3. Thus Hobhouse rejects (142) Mill's distinction between self-regarding and other-regarding acts (and the principle Mill sought to found on it): 'first because there are no actions which may not directly or indirectly affect others, secondly because even if there

So far as I know, Kant's own publications scarcely discuss, in a political context, the question of fact which Hobhouse thus raises: can the good of a human person be advanced by coercion?[87] In an ethical context, Kant does advance a very weak argument against making the *perfection* of (an)other(s) one's responsibility. The *happiness* of others is among one's fundamental responsibilities, but not their perfection, for:

> it is contradictory to say that I make another person's *perfection* my end and consider myself obligated to promote this. For the perfection of another man, as a person, consists precisely in *his own* power to adopt his end in accordance with his own concept of duty; and it is self-contradictory to demand that I do (make it my duty to do) what only the other person himself can do.[88]

This will not do. We can agree that the necessary condition of human perfection is indeed authenticity: that one has adopted one's commitments in accordance with one's own conception of duty. But I deny that education, coercive deterrence, and coercive denial of opportunities can do nothing to assist persons to avoid choices which will degrade or in some other way harm them. And in several of his unpublished reflections, as we shall see, Kant admits that coercive measures can indeed be efficacious for this purpose.

It is important, at this point, to make a distinction. Coercing people to adopt or profess a religion is—if attempted for religious motives—self-stultifying in a way which could merit Kant's protean word '(self-)contradictory'. For the good of adherence to the propositions of religious faith intrinsically involves that the propositions be adhered to as *true*, that is, as disclosing a transcendent *reality* which is a *fit* object of adoration, petitionary prayer, and so forth. To the extent that the propositions are professed because their profession is convenient, both they and the professing of them obscure rather than disclose that reality.

But there is nothing analogously self-stultifying in coercing people to abstain from drug-taking or pederasty, whether by threatening them with criminal penalties, or by threatening those who would supply them with

---

were they would not cease to be matter of concern to others.' *Ibid*. But he goes on to argue, in rather Kantian fashion, that '[t]o try to form character by coercion is to destroy it in the making', or (weaker version) 'it is not possible to compel morality because morality is the act or character of a free agent' (143). He admits exceptions:

> [I]n the case of the drunkard—and I think the argument applies to all cases where overwhelming impulse is apt to master the will—it is a[n]...elementary duty to remove the sources of temptation, and to treat as anti-social in the highest degree every attempt to make profit out of human weakness, misery, and wrong-doing. (153)

[87] Unless one counts the statement noted in the text above at n. 73.

[88] *Metaphysik der Sitten*, 386 (trans. Gregor, 44–5). There is no need to dwell here on the fact that Kant's conception of perfection is here, in Rawlsian terminology, a 'thin theory'. See n. 36 above.

opportunities for indulgence in the vice, or merely by threatening those who would corrupt them while young. Nor has it been demonstrated that this need render the persons coerced unfit to integrate their characters around other personal commitments, freely chosen by them from the vast range of diverse but upright forms of life.[89]

Nor indeed has it been demonstrated that western tradition was mistaken in holding, with Aristotle and Aquinas, that people who are prone to vice, and resistant to verbal persuasion, not only can be restrained by coercive threats from depraved actions but also can often be led—by an acculturation which those philosophers called habituation—to make, willingly (that is, by their own authentic *free choice*), the very types of choices (to abstain from vice and to pursue worthwhile commitments) which, earlier, they made only 'under coercion' and unwillingly.[90]

And it is clear that Kant shared the factual judgment made by the tradition:

Man must be trained, so as to become domesticated and become virtuous later on. The coercion of government [*Regirungszwang*] and education make him supple, flexible and obedient to the laws; then reason will rule.[91]

But Kant could not bring this factual premise into conjunction with a normative premise about the common good.

For a workable conception of the common good requires that we reject several of the notorious Kantian dualisms. There is first the dualism of the phenomenal world (including human persons) subject to the reign of natural determinism and impulse *versus* the noumenal realm of 'selves' or 'subjects', of free will and moral law. The second dualism follows: of the

---

[89] As Joseph Raz says (using 'autonomy' not in the Kantian sense but in a normal modern sense rather like that which Richards had in mind):

only very rarely will the non-availability of morally repugnant options reduce a person's choice sufficiently to affect his autonomy.... The ideal of autonomy requires only the availability of morally acceptable options (*The Morality of Freedom*, 381; also 412, 417).

However, Raz contends, with notable abruptness, that *coercive* interference does violate autonomy because (i) it expresses an attitude of disrespect for the coerced individual, and (ii) its interference is 'global and indiscriminate': *ibid.*, 418. These grounds seem fragile; Raz's conception of the mechanisms of state coercion (and threats of coercion) is itself global and indiscriminate. (Contrast his more discriminating discussion in Raz, 'Liberalism, Autonomy, and the Politics of Neutral Concern' at 113.) But his strictures may well apply to some of Kant's views about the extent of punishment; permanent banishment e.g. seems too severe a penalty for homosexual intercourse [assuming a case where, by reason of its public character, some instance of that falls properly within the coercive jurisdiction of state government and law].

[90] See *NE* X.9: 1179b30–1180b28; *ST* I–II q.95 a.1 ('Is human law useful?').

[91] Kelly, *Idealism, Politics and History*, 145, translating Kant, *Gesammelte Schriften*, vol. XV, 522–3 no. 1184 (c. 1773–8); see also Kelly at 170, translating Kant, *Gesammelte Schriften*, vol. XIX, 202 no. 6906 (c. 1776 (?c. 1769)) ('Each man is by nature bad and becomes good only to the extent that he is subject to a power that obliges [*nöthigt*] him to be good. But he has the capacity to become progressively better without coercion [*Zwang*] if the dispositions for good within him are progressively developed.') See also Kant, *Idea for a Universal History* at 23 (sixth thesis: man needs a master ...).

human person's naturally determined impulse to *happiness*, understood by Kant as a self-love[92] dominated by experienced satisfaction with one's own condition (with the assurance that that satisfaction will last)[93] *versus* the rationally determined will to a *perfection* consisting essentially only in conformity for duty's sake to a moral law whose intelligibility is found not in the prospect of human fulfilment for its own sake but simply in the universalizability of principles directing choice. These dualisms block off Kant's view of all *intelligible* intrinsic human goods other than the good of practical reasonableness as such.

Kant rightly sees in practical reasonableness an intelligible worth (intrinsic goodness) which cannot be exhaustively reduced to any determinate state(s) of affairs which could be a technical objective. (Hence his justified rejection of all forms of consequentialism.) But just as the Critical philosophy inconsistently denies those forms of *understanding* of *reality* which Kant admits in the particular case of understanding the reality of the understanding and choosing subject (himself, oneself),[94] so too Kant inconsistently denies that we can understand aspects of human personal flourishing (other than practical reasonableness itself) as having an intelligible worth which cannot be exhaustively reduced to determinate states of affairs or definite objectives, but which—as inexhaustible prospects of human fulfilment—provide *reasons* for considering many possible determinate states of affairs to be choiceworthy opportunities.[95] These basic aspects of human flourishing—basic human goods—include not only practical reasonableness but also human life itself (and its transmission), knowledge (and aesthetic appreciation), excellence in performance (whether in 'work' or 'play'), and the interpersonal harmony (involving both respect and favour) which we call friendship or love in its various forms.[96]

Now in friendship—including concern for one's political community— the friends envisage a truly *common* good which transcends both self-love and mere altruism[97]—and which also transcends Kant's dualistic reduction

---

[92] See *Kritik der praktischen Vernunft*, 22, 70, 73 (Beck, 20, 73, 76).

[93] *Metaphysik der Sitten*, 387; see also *Kritik der Urteilskraft*, 434n (Meredith trans. 1973): 'enjoyment'.

[94] See the illuminating discussion in Grisez, *Beyond the New Theism*, 152–80, esp. 155–6 on *Critique of Pure Reason* A546–7/B574–5.

[95] See *NDMR* ch. 10.

[96] On basic human goods, see *NLNR* 81–99; on their intelligibility, see *FoE* 26–55. Not envisaging a multiplicity of basic aspects of human worth, Kant also did not steadily envisage the need for and possibility of requirements of practical reasonableness other than the requirement of consistency (universalizability) in choosing (which he eked out with a requirement of mastery over the animal inclinations). On the multiple requirements of right choosing, see *NLNR* 100–33; *FoE* 66–79; *NDMR* chs 10–11.

[97] On friendship and the idea of common good, see *NLNR* 141–4, 154–8, 210–18; on 'altruism,' see *ibid.*, 158.

of motives to the stark alternatives: self-love or sheer duty; desire for sensuous satisfactions or bare respect for one's rationality itself.

Given the more adequate concept of common good, there is no reason (and certainly nothing in Kant or our neo-Kantians which gives good grounds) to conclude that the justifying rationale of civil association and law is anything other than the good of all those who, by their cooperation, can reasonably hope to advance the common good of their community. Favouring the good of one's fellow citizens can rightly involve the use of coercive measures, primarily to dissuade them from morally evil forms of life, and secondarily to punish them, *not* for violating 'duties to themselves', but for wilfully failing to cooperate in the community's effort of reducing those evils and of maintaining forms of life more conducive to authentic human flourishing.[98†]

An essay on Kant and neo-Kantians is certainly not the place to offer a full, and fully nuanced, justification and critique of laws proscribing and/or withholding juridical recognition and lawful status from drug-use, sodomy, assistance in suicide, and so forth.[99] I add just one or two remarks.

Certainly there is room for much caution—not the *a priori* risk-aversion of Rawls, but the sober Kantian reminder that, if man is an animal who needs a master, the masters, too, are just such animals.[100] Masters are prone to do evil not merely out of self-love or malice, but out of misguided zeal. And very common forms of misguided zeal include (i) mistaking the common good for some determinate end-state to which present individual lives are treated as mere means, and (ii) forgetting that the common good is instantiated in the good of each and every individual, that no individual has *a priori* a claim to a fuller share in the common good than any other individual, and that the individual good includes some aspects of practical reasonableness which Kant's dualism of sense versus reason led him to slide over: the inner integrity by which senses and inclinations are not merely mastered by but in partnership with reasonableness, and the outer authenticity by which one's bodily and social behaviour does not merely simulate an imposed or opportunistically convenient pattern but actually manifests one's conscientious will.

---

[98] Thus the West German Basic Law (1949), whose Kantian inspiration is often mentioned by commentators, rightly provides in Art. II(1) that everyone has the right to the free flourishing of his personality provided that he does not violate the rights of others or the constitutional order 'or the moral law [*das Sittengesetz*]'. Thus the Basic Law is more Kantian than neo-Kantian.

[99] See *NLNR* 221–3, 229–30; Haksar, *Equality, Liberty, and Perfectionism*, 236–87; Raz, *The Morality of Freedom*, 390–5, 400–17. The latter two books state strong reasons for rejecting the neutrality principle, and thus go far towards undermining the harm principle.

[100] See *Idea for a Universal History* at 23.

NOTE

† *Common good and justified coercion* ... (text at n. 98). This sentence is unsatisfactory. It rightly rejects pure paternalism (punishment for violation of duties to oneself), but is obscure in all the other points it makes. The coercive measures which, as distinguished from punishment for engaging in morally evil forms of life, are spoken of as justified 'to dissuade [persons] from morally evil forms of life' refer to measures such as suppression of pornography (especially depicting or available to children), of propaganda for drug-taking, suicide, prostitution, and the like. The punitive measures which the later part of the sentence speaks of as justified 'for wilfully failing to cooperate in the community's effort of reducing those evils ... etc.' could again be justified only if directed against interpersonal activities offensive to justice, such as (i) inducing children into the use of heroin or of pornography, or of incest, paedophilia, bestiality, etc., or (ii) public propaganda for these and similar activities, or for suicide, prostitution, etc. And see Introduction at p. 10.

3

RAWLS'S *A THEORY OF JUSTICE**

1. (*Rawls*). A theory of justice interprets our sense of justice, that is, our strong and effective desires to act on the basic principles of justice. Such desires will not be strong and effective unless it is rational for us, given the system of wants, aims, and ends we happen to have, to want the state of affairs secured by general compliance with those principles. The theory of justice is also part of the theory of rational choice.

2. (*Rawls*). Whatever else one happens to want, the realization of one's nature in a complex way is both enjoyable and a necessary condition of self-respect, and thus is something it is rational for one to want. So, *if* acting on the principles of justice either (a) is the only or main way to express one's nature as a free and equal rational being, or (b) is the only or main way to win that esteem of one's fellows which is the other condition of one's self-respect, then it is rational for one to want so to act. But esteem can be thus gained from one's fellows only if they recognize much the same principles as one does oneself; and it is in any case rational to act on principles of justice only if one's fellows are similarly acting on them. So there is need of some standpoint or perspective in which (or by imagining which) rational, free, and equal men can attain unanimity, and indeed objectivity, about principles of justice. Any such standpoint shall be named an 'initial situation'.

3. Western moral theory typically selects as 'initial' the situation of the impartial but benevolent or sympathetic spectator equipped with all requisite information and powers of reasoning. Rawls allows that this viewpoint is suitably general and objective; but he objects that 'benevolence is at sea' since the 'rational self-love' and thus the 'claims' of the various persons it loves conflict. Now the relevant reply is that the benevolent spectator cares, not for the conflicting self-loves that the objects of his benevolence happen to have and the conflicting claims they

* 1973a.

happen to raise, but rather for the intrinsic value of the goods they could be educated to enjoy and of the various perfections and excellences they thus could variously realize. The view expressed in this reply Rawls calls 'perfectionism'. His own argument against perfectionism is that perfectionist principles would not be acceptable in that initial situation which he constructs, prefers, and names 'the original position' (OP).

4. (*Rawls*). The OP is constructed in order to eliminate bias and to allow the derivation of principles of justice from the weakest possible assumptions. Men's situations are to be compared by reference solely to things that *all* men prefer more of, things necessary to advance any man's aims whatever his aims are. Such things are 'primary goods': above all, self-respect, and then liberty, opportunity, and wealth. To be in the OP is to be a person concerned solely to guarantee that, in whatever society he may find himself after leaving the OP, he and his family will then have as much of those primary goods as he can now secure by agreeing to principles to regulate any well-ordered society (viz., any society in which people fully comply with the principles thus chosen).

More particularly, each party to any such agreement in the OP has no ethical motivations, no particular conceptions of intrinsic goods or excellences, and no concern for the interests of others, is not benevolent, egoistic, or envious, and must agree to principles (if any) while behind a veil of ignorance—he does not know in which society or at what stage of civilization he will have to live, or what will be his own status, natural assets, psychology, or conception of (intrinsic) value; but he does know general political and economic theory, and such general facts or assumptions about real societies outside the OP as, for example, that individuals have deeply opposed interests and take no interest in one another's interests. Then we can say: principles of justice are those that would be unanimously agreed to, by such persons thus situated in the OP, as principles for any (well-ordered) society in which any of the parties to the agreement might turn out to have to live.

5. The OP is constructed thus in order to generate principles of liberty and equality that fit moral beliefs which are 'settled' (amongst East Coast academics now, though not, I may say, amongst the authors of contemporary national and international declarations of human rights). Above all, each person is to have 'an equal right to the most extensive total system of equal basic liberties compatible with a similar system of liberty for all'—(but what is the 'extent' of a 'total system' of incommensurable liberties such as communication and privacy, free movement, and freedom from pollution, injury, or disturbance?)—and such liberty can be restricted *only* for the sake of liberty (at least, when a certain level of wealth and civilization has

been reached!). For each person in the OP would choose these principles of equal liberty and priority of liberty because he would think it imprudent (i) to gamble his liberty by acknowledging principles allowing others (save for the sake of 'public order') to restrict his freedom to pursue whatever his plan of life might turn out to be; or (ii) to run the risk that, having acknowledged principles favouring activities in proportion to their intrinsic value, he might turn out to have preferences and criteria of excellence that could accordingly be treated as trashy and insupportable.

Rawls's second main principle of justice is similarly grounded: the arrangement of social and economic inequalities is to be to the advantage (measured in terms only of 'primary goods') of the least advantaged class, and attached to offices and positions open to all—for (i)(a) no one can afford to risk turning out to be *abandoned* at the bottom of the social heap; (i)(b) the least advantaged might rebel against any principle other than this; and (ii) in the OP all ignore conceptions of worth and so, for example, would never agree that the principle of distribution might be shaped by criteria of merit or of deserving effort *even if* they could agree on these criteria.

6. I agree that the strange conditions of the OP do eliminate mere bias and so do guarantee that if a principle were agreed on in the OP it would be fair (at least as between the parties to the agreement). But, since 'if' is not equivalent to 'only if', it is a mere fallacy to *infer* from this (as much loose writing in the book invites the reader to infer) that if a principle would not be chosen in the OP it therefore would, in the real world, be unfair or not a proper principle of justice. If the book's arguments for particular principles and sentiments of justice do not rest altogether on that fallacy, they rest on this assumption: that to introduce into the real world (seen from the standpoint, say, of the impartial benevolent spectator) principles which discriminate between liberties, and adjust the distribution of goods, in order to secure certain forms of life preferred for their intrinsic excellence (moral or pre-moral) is necessarily to abandon objectivity for bias simply because judgments of excellence are inevitably biased. But that assumption Rawls makes no effort to justify. Indeed, he admits (as one should expect of a man so fruitfully concerned for quality of thought and excellence of style) that in our everyday life 'comparisons of intrinsic value can obviously be made' and that the 'freedom and well-being of individuals, when measured by the excellence of their activities and works, is vastly different in value'.

7. I left in suspense some links in Rawls's argument (para. 2 above) for the rationality of acting on just principles. *Is* adherence to Rawls's principles of justice the only or main way to get what it is rational to want in the way of (a) expressing one's nature and (b) securing from one's fellows the esteem necessary for one's self-respect? Yes, on Rawls's view, because (a) 'it is not

our aims' (such as truth, friendship, creativity,...) 'that primarily reveal our nature but rather the principles that we would acknowledge', out of a cautious, self-interested, prudential calculation, in a situation of profound ignorance and mistrust; and (b) self-respect is sufficiently secured by gaining, through one's conformity to those principles, the esteem of one's similarly conforming fellows, however trashy their motives, tastes, and values, however mediocre their aims and lifestyle. Some self-respect. Some nature.

8. What inspired the vast labours which (in ways I haven't been able even to indicate here) illuminate much in philosophy and economics, but which arrive by an essentially ramshackle argument at conclusions such as these? I do not know. But Rawls's last sentence redefines 'purity of heart' by ringing the changes on other moral symbols of our civilization: 'grace' and 'self-command' have already been given their new, reduced meanings, and to complete his purpose Rawls need only add, as he does, that the OP 'enables' us to see the world *'sub specie aeternitatis'*: for 'the perspective of eternity is not the point of view of a transcendent being'. To make the world *safe* for men without the divine measure: perhaps that is the inmost aspiration of the liberalism that Rawls has so integrally re-presented.

NOTE

On Rawls's second principle of justice, see also essay 7, sec. IV.

4

DISTRIBUTIVE JUSTICE AND THE BOTTOM LINE*

Stanley Kleinberg wants us to say that distribution of food by lot, in time of famine, is unjust but justified; that distribution of offices amongst equally qualified or unqualified persons by lot (or some other procedure which is regular and unbiased but is incapable of detecting intrinsic 'qualification' for office) is unjust but justified; and in general that justice can be overridden by utility, and hence that to establish that something is unjust is not at all to establish that it is unjustified.

Kleinberg's conception of justice is thus the characteristic modern conception, which emerges in the twentieth century as part of the vast movement of thought in which the language of the classical philosophy of human affairs was redefined, that is, gutted and refurbished. The change in respect of 'justice' is closely related to the change in the concept of '*jus*' or 'right' ('a right'), which I discuss in Chapter VIII ('Rights') of *Natural Law and Natural Rights*. It is characteristic, and a characteristic inconvenience (not to say mystification), of the modern usage of the word 'rights' that people have all sorts of rights to do things which, it is admitted, it would be wrong or unjustified for them to do, and all sorts of rights to treatment (or non-interference) which, it is admitted, it would be wrong to accord them. The obfuscation reaches its famous climax in talk of 'inalienable' rights which, however, in 'their exercise' (more plainly, in their reality or content!) are subject to all manner of other such rights and other considerations of public policy.

So the first thing to be said is that the classical writers would have been stupefied at our tolerance of imprecise and misleading ways of speaking about right and wrong in human conduct. The next thing to say is that, whatever the merits of the issue between the classics and the moderns, you

* Unpublished response to a commentary by Stanley Kleinberg, of the Department of Political Studies in the University of Stirling, on my paper 'A New Sketch of the Classical Theory of Justice'—a draft version of *NLNR* Chapter VII ('Justice')—at the 1979 conference of the Society of Public Teachers of Law.

will not begin to understand the classical conceptions of justice unless you accept that, on those conceptions, it is nonsense to speak of an unjust but justified action. That is why one of the most popular classical definitions of justice was 'the constant and perpetual willingness to give/render to each and every person his due/his right(s)/what he is owed/what is his [*jus suum* or simply *suum*]'—the phrase 'constant and perpetual' meaning unconditional: *not* subject to further calculations of utility or other assessments of the 'justified and the unjustified'. What is due to somebody correlates with what ought not to be done, or omitted to be done, to or for him, as judged when *all* the relevant considerations are in. Classical justice is on the bottom line, as American bureaucrats would say.

This does not in the least entail (*pace* Kleinberg) that the classics, by a conceptual move, 'demonstrated' (even within their own system) that we should not cast lots for officers or food rations. The classics would have asked Kleinberg why he imagines that it is unjust to cast lots, or to follow the fall of the dice when it is cast. And I do not see how he can plausibly reply. After all, if we need officers, and cannot distinguish between the candidates on their merits, what could be fairer than giving all an equal chance in a procedure free from all bias? It seems a paradigm case of just treatment.

The classics would have gone on to ask Kleinberg why he thinks the consent of all the candidates is required for the proceeding to be even 'fair *as a procedure*'. Again, of course, his perspective is characteristic of the modern era. But I for one must say that I regard all manner of laws as making just claims upon me, and imposing real obligations of justice on me, notwithstanding that (so far as I can recall) I have never consented in any form to any of them. Please don't say 'Oh, but you have voted in elections'. Have I ever voted for the winning party? And there has never been an election in which the law and procedure for election and parliamentary government was itself the subject on which a vote, even implicitly, could be cast. This is not to say that there are no good reasons for voting; still less is it to say that there are no good reasons for democratic systems of electing and dismissing legislators and rulers generally. Nor is it to say that consent is irrelevant. The consent of the governed is indeed not a necessary condition for the just imposition of obligations on them; but what is a necessary condition is that both the content of the obligations and the manner of imposing them should be such that the governed *ought* to consent to them. That does not mean: ought to vote for them. Rather, it means that a *reasonable* subject *would* consent *to be governed by* them once they have been created.

That was something of a digression. But it does put me in a position to say that in a situation in which officers are clearly required but cannot be selected on their merits, all potential officers ought to consent to some unbiased selection procedure, for example the lottery, and, whether or not they actually consented to such a procedure, ought to recognize the authority of those selected by it (at least until such time as the incompetence of those selected and the competence of possible substitutes for them has become manifest). Being favoured by the fall of the dice in such circumstances is to be 'relevantly different'.

This is not to deny that there are situations of what Kleinberg calls dilemma, that is, predicaments in which the standards of justice that suffice for ordinary situations, and which therefore have become the basis for people's legitimate expectations and reliances, prove inadequate—that is, inadequate *in justice*. These are not dilemmas between justice and utility. Outside limited technical contexts, utility is a literally senseless criterion, not merely 'practically unworkable'; I elaborate on this extensively in *NLNR*, and will not do so here. But even if it were not, it would remain true that utility, as Mill insists in the last chapter of *Utilitarianism*, both (a) incorporates a criterion of justice imported *ab extra* to save 'the greatest good of the greatest number' from being merely 'unmeaning', and (b) is itself a criterion of justice, that is, just conduct. In any event, assuming that unequal distribution of food in a famine is justified, the justification must be in terms of the common good; it must be on the basis that what the principle that each person's good is to be favoured requires, in *this* situation, is that *each* should be given the chance of being a survivor, given that some but not all can survive. Justice does not require that the survival of some must be secured whenever the alternative is the perishing of all. If the *only* means whereby some can survive is the murder or suicide of others, or even of one—which is always excluded by commutative justice—then the securing of such survival is not the preferable policy; the preferable policy is not to be defined as 'the perishing of all' but 'abstention from murder or suicide notwithstanding that the perishing of all is avoidable only by such murder or suicide'. But I assume, without deciding, that unequal distribution of rations is not inevitably murder or suicide, since it does not involve a direct choice to bring about death, but merely accepts the death of some as a *side* effect of a choice of means of securing the survival of some.

I don't expect that I have won many friends, or influenced many people, by my last few sentences. Nor do I contend that all the classics would have assented to my casuistry. But I do say that all the classics would take it that what Kleinberg (with the moderns) treats as a 'dilemma of justice against utility' is, rather, a competition—or rather, a question of demarcating—between normally applicable and exceptionally applicable norms of justice.

But there is a complication here, which, conveniently, relates to some things that Kleinberg says when he considers a supposition I made in arguing that function can be a criterion of distributive justice: the supposition that it might be right to require the general population to go short for the sake of equipping, feeding, and encouraging the fighting men (or Amazons). And he objects that failure to do this, in a situation in which doing it would be right, is not unjust *to the fighting men*. I agree. That is why the Roman definition of justice, which I quoted, about giving every man his due, is not wholly adequate; and if what I say [in the second paragraph of *NLNR* 162] comes too close to that, it needs revision. The *distributive* injustice of failing to institute the distribution necessary for the maintenance of the army and thus the defence of the community against the unjust enemy is an injustice, not to the fighting men as such, but to everyone in the community who is going to suffer from the enemy's victory. The scheme was, if you like, due/owed to these potential victims of a defeat. Of course, once the scheme has been adopted, then, relative to the scheme, there is a *commutative* injustice on the part of anyone who (as commonly happens in these situations) converts goods in transit to the front line to his own use and profit; and this injustice can, I think, be said to be specifically (though not exclusively) a denial to the soldiers of what is due *to them* as such.

I am afraid there are other complications that must be borne in mind if the classical conception of justice is to be used plausibly and coherently. One such complication is the distinction between objective injustice and subjectively culpable injustice. Stanley Kleinberg's ascetics who, as he says, 'wrongly' refuse to permit private ownership because they fail to see its benefits, are no doubt not acting unjustly in the subjective sense: they are still thinking, not of personal or partisan advantage, but of the common good. But their decision, being wrong, *is* unjust, objectively. To whom? To everyone who suffers (for example from the lack of medicines in underfinanced Soviet hospitals) from the wrong decision. But here there is a final complication, touched on in that parenthetical sentence of mine at *NLNR* 162, and elaborated extensively in my account, in other chapters, of the derivation of positive from natural law: apart from wrong decisions, there is a vast field of potential decisions whose rightness or wrongness cannot be established by reasoning, concerning matters on which there is a range of contrary views, all *reasonable*. This should make us hesitant to ascribe injustice, *tout court*, to people with whom we disagree on matters the assessment of which involves *commitment* to one or more of a range of *incommensurable* values. The decision to be a monk involves rejecting, for oneself, the life of the relatively powerful and wealthy spouse and father—but it does not involve regarding it as wrongful; and vice versa. And societies can reasonably commit themselves to forms and styles of life that, within limits, sacrifice material efficiency for other values. My assessment of the pros and cons of private ownership was, as Stanley Kleinberg has discerned, far from complete. Its aim was in large measure conceptual: to show how both the concept of the common good, and the quite different concept of common stock and matters intrinsically common, could be compatible with and even, conceptually speaking, require forms of private, that is, non-common management, exploitation, and ownership. I do, of course, grant that the fact that a system is 'more efficient in the provision of consumer durables' does not entail that the system is 'an overall benefit to non-owners'.[1] And I willingly concede that my draft is obscure and confusing about what I count as 'private ownership'. When Kleinberg says: 'Compared with a system of common ownership of means of production, private ownership is likely to be an obstacle in the pursuit of the good of many members of the community', I agree if by 'common ownership' he means cooperative owner/management on a scale small enough to allow participation by workers in management; if he means what I had in mind by what I sometimes call common and more often call public ownership, that is, management of 'nationalized' enterprises by public officials, I of course disagree (since we are both talking here of the good of individual autonomy, self-direction). I should have said all along that I count cooperative enterprises, on a small scale, as privately owned.

When it comes to the distribution by private owners of their surplus, I was a bit surprised to find my analysis described as the erecting of a state of nature alternative to Nozick's. I don't believe that I am talking about a state of nature alternative to anyone's. I certainly *want*, like all the classics, to regard any postulation of a state of nature, or any other genetic hypothesis, as pretty irrelevant to the analysis of justice (in any sense of analysis). I meant simply that here and now, owners have obligations of distributive justice. I don't think that owners can be left to decide for themselves how to carry out all their redistributive obligations. Kleinberg's

---

[1] *NLNR* 169:
... where individuals ... can help themselves by their own private efforts and initiatives without thereby injuring ... the common good.... It is unjust to require them to sacrifice their private initiative by demanding that they participate instead in a public enterprise; it remains unjust even if the material dividend they receive from the public enterprise is as great as or even somewhat greater than the material product of their own private efforts would have been.

Kleinberg made the reasonable counterpart observation, that the bare fact that a system of *private* ownership of the means of production yields greater material dividends ('more consumer durables') for non-owners does not *entail* that it is an overall benefit, or fully just, to non-owners. I agree. The radical inferiority and injustice of economic systems such as those of the Soviet Union and its satellites [,or of Albania in the 1980s or North Korea today,] is not a simple matter of measuring the availability or distribution of consumer durables on either side of the comparison of systems.

postulated situation in which people are starving because owners are more interested in fulfilling their obligations in other ways was precisely what I had in mind, or part of what I had in mind, in speaking, tersely, of inability (not 'failure', but inability) to coordinate their redistribution effectively,[2] that is, to coordinate them to the degree required by the common good.

A few scattered remarks about the later pages of Kleinberg's paper. Questions about the propriety of the distributor acquiring goods in the first place are not always questions of commutative justice; often enough the distributor will hold the 'goods' as a public officer, and although his entitlement to do so, and the bases of his subsequent distribution, will be determined by settled rules (and *thus* be a matter of the commutative justice of doing one's legal duty), those settled rules can be assessed for their justice, and that assessment will usually be substantially a matter of distributive justice.

I don't think of distributive justice as 'secondary' to commutative—I don't see any priority here, though I would accept Kleinberg's other formulation of my position, that it is a function of commutative justice to determine the framework within which it is permissible to raise questions of distributive justice. Some things are never to be done to people, and therefore they are not to be done to other people (commutative justice) and are not to be done in distributing goods to other people (distributive justice).

To raise a doubt about this, Kleinberg suggests that 'questions about what [bodily organs] may not properly be collected should not always be settled in advance of questions about distribution'. To test my 'presupposition that parts of individual persons should be excluded from the scope of distributive justice' he raises the hypothesis that someone has 'finger nails that contain a rare ingredient that could provide someone else's cancer cure', and says that the 'we might have some reason to doubt the assumption that the person with the valuable nails could not justly be required to clip them earlier than he might have wished and to yield the clippings'. What is significant is that Kleinberg has chosen a borderline case: for we treat parts of our finger nails as barely parts of ourselves.

But it turns out that he is on his way to considering the non-borderline case of 'a society of rational and virtuous utilitarians' who arrange their society on the basis that some members with many healthy organs are selected (evidently by lot) for killing, so that their organs could be

---

[2] *NLNR* 173:
Where owners will not perform these duties [of distributing their surplus], *or cannot effectively coordinate* their respective efforts to coordinate them, then public authority may rightly help them to perform them by devising and implementing schemes of distribution, e.g. by 'redistributive' taxation for purposes of 'social welfare', or by a measure of expropriation.

distributed with the intended and actual result that 'on the whole people lived longer and healthier lives'. Kleinberg argues, skilfully and rightly, that this kind of society is to be rejected because (in summary)

> we have a morality which does not just incorporate a concern with human needs but also a concern with how members of the community should relate to one another ... a conception of what is appropriate to a person.

I agree entirely, and only demur at his suggestion, in beginning his dialectic, that if you couldn't convince these 'tough-minded utilitarians', you would not have any reasons to give them.

5
LIMITED GOVERNMENT*

I

In any sound theory of natural law, the authority of government is explained and justified as an authority limited by positive law (especially but not only constitutional law), by the moral principles and norms of justice which apply to all human action (whether private or public), and by the common good of political communities—a common good which I shall argue is inherently instrumental and therefore limited. If 'limited government' is not a term widely used in natural law theories, that is doubtless because it is so ambiguous. For the proper limits on government and political authority are quite various in their sources, as I have just indicated. Being 'limited' is only to a limited extent a desirable characteristic of government anyway: bad and powerful people and groups want government limited so that they can bully and exploit the weak, or simply enjoy their wealth untroubled by care for others. So 'limited' cannot be a framework term like 'just'.

The first theorist of government to articulate as a specific concept the desideratum that governmental authority/power be legally 'limited' seems to have been Thomas Aquinas. (However, these questions of priority are not to be taken too seriously.[1]) On the first substantive page of his commentary on Aristotle's *Politics*, Aquinas gives an explanation of the distinction, which Aristotle at that point draws but does not explain, between *political* and *regal* types of government or regimen. In 'regal' forms of government, says Aquinas, the rulers have plenary authority,[2] while in 'political' forms,

---

* 1996a ('Is Natural Law Theory Compatible with Limited Government?'; an earlier version is 1994c. See the commentary in the ante-penultimate paragraph of sec. I of the Introduction, above.)

[1] It goes without saying that insofar as the concept of legal limitations on government is contained implicitly or virtually in Aristotle's conception of the rule of law, to that extent there is little original in Aquinas on this matter save the articulation of the term 'limited'.

[2] See also *ST* I–II q.105 a.1 ad 2.

their authority is 'limited [*coarctata*] in accordance with certain laws of the polity'.[3]

Why limit legally the authority of rulers? Well, Aquinas's uncompleted commentary ends before the passages where Aristotle discussed the desirability of a 'rule of laws and not of men'.[4] But in his commentary on Aristotle's *Ethics*, at the point in Book V where Aristotle briefly summarizes the merits of the rule of law,[5] Aquinas expands and perhaps deepens the summary a little: right government does not tolerate an unregulated rule by rulers ('rule of men'), but calls for rulers to be ruled by law, precisely because law is a dictate of *reason*, while what threatens to turn government into tyranny (rule in the interests of the rulers) is their human *passions*, inclining them to attribute to themselves more of the good things, and fewer of the bad things, than is their fair share. And the commentary on the *Politics* suggests another reason:

> Political [as opposed to despotic government] is the leadership of free and equal people; and so the roles of leader and led (ruler and ruled) are swapped about for the sake of equality, and many people get to be constituted ruler either in one position of responsibility or in a number of such positions.[6]

Such regular changeovers in political office—standardly correlated with elections[7]—obviously need to be regulated by the laws which constitute (define) these offices; those who at any one time hold office accordingly do so 'according to law' (*secundum statuta*).[8] The guiding thought is: 'free and equal'. Indeed, in his own free-standing theological works Aquinas will say that the best arrangement of governmental authority (*optima ordinatio principum*) will include this, that 'everyone (*omnes*) shares in government, both in the sense that everyone is eligible to be one of the rulers, and in the

---

[3] '...politicum autem regnum est quando ille qui praeest habet *potestatem coarctatam* secundum aliquas leges civitatis': Aquinas, *In Pol.* I.1 (Marietti ed., 1951, n. 13). In his *De Regno*, I, 6, Aquinas states that where one person is ruler, that person's power/authority should be 'limited' (*temperetur postestas*), lest it slide into tyranny (i.e. into government for private rather than common good). Aquinas's distinction between regal and political rule is enthusiastically taken up by Sir John Fortescue, *The Governance of England* (c. 1475), c. 1; likewise his *De Natura Legis Naturae* ('On the nature of natural law') (c. 1462), c. 16; similarly his *De Laudibus Legum Angliae* ('In praise of the laws of England') (c. 1469), cc. 2–4. Thence it finds its way into Coke and the mainstream of English constitutional thought. The first editor of Sir John Fortescue's *Governance* (Lord Fortescue of Credan, when Solicitor-General to the Prince of Wales, in 1714) titled the work, 'The Difference Between an Absolute and Limited Monarchy'. In c. 1 of the *Governance*, as elsewhere in his writings on this theme, Fortescue appeals to the authority of Aquinas, explicitly to the *De Regno*; there is, however, no evidence that he read Aquinas's commentary on the *Politics*: see Plummer (ed.), *The Governance of England*, 172–3.

[4] e.g. *Pol.* III.10: 1286a9, etc.   [5] *NE* V.6: 1134a35–b1.

[6] *In Pol.* I.5 (n. 90): 'politica est principatus *liberorum et aequalium*: unde commutantur personae principantes et subiectae propter aequalitatem, et constituuntur etiam plures principatus vel in uno vel in diversis officiis.'

[7] *Ibid.*, n. 152.   [8] *Ibid.*

sense that those who do rule are elected by everyone'.[9] And those who go beyond constitutional limits by enacting *ultra vires* laws are thereby acting unjustly;[10] their action is merely another way of getting more than their fair share (in this case, of authority, if of nothing else).

The account of the rationale and content of the *Rechtsstaat* or Rule of Law, and thus of the point and scope of the legal limits on government, has subsequently become ampler and more detailed. Suffice it to note that, like these early teachings of Aristotle and Aquinas, later accounts enriched by historical experience and the reflections of public lawyers properly pertain to natural law theory, in ways which I hope to make clearer in what follows.

II

Deeper and more demanding than any constitutional or other legal limits on governments are the moral principles and norms which natural law theory considers to be principles and norms of reason,[11] and which are limits, side-constraints, recognized in the conscientious deliberations of every decent person. The public responsibilities and authority of rulers do not exempt them from these limits:[12] no intentional killing of the innocent, no rape, no lies, no non-penal enslavement, and so forth.

---

[9] *ST* I–II q.105 a.1c. On sharing in government as the essence of citizenship, see *In Pol.* III.1 (n. 354).

[10] This is one form of unjust law (and so more a matter of violence than of law properly understood): *ST* I–II q.96 a.4c.

[11] See Plato, *Republic* IV, 444d; IX, 585–6 on acting according to reason and thus according to nature. More explicitly, *ST* I–II q.71 a.2c:

> The good of the human being is being in accord with reason, and human evil is being outside the order of reasonableness...So human virtue...is in accordance with human nature *just* in *so* far as it is in accordance with reason, and vice is contrary to human nature just in so far as it is contrary to the order of reasonableness.

[12] 'When it is a matter of the moral norms prohibiting intrinsic evil, there are no privileges or exceptions for anyone. It makes no difference whether one is the master of the world or the 'poorest of the poor' on the face of the earth. Before the demands of morality we are all absolutely equal.' (John Paul II, Encyclical *Veritatis Splendor* 'Regarding Certain Fundamental Questions of the Church's Moral Teaching' (6 August 1993), s. 96.)

'Intrinsic evil' has earlier in the document been explained as follows:

> acts which, in the Church's moral tradition, have been termed 'intrinsically evil' (*intrinsece malum*)...are such always and per se, in other words, on account of their object, and quite apart from the ulterior intentions of the one acting and the circumstances (s. 80).

The 'object' of an act had been explained as 'the proximate end of a deliberate decision which determines the act of willing on the part of the acting person': s. 78. An earlier, less precise statement;

> [t]he same law of nature that governs the life and conduct of individuals must also regulate the relations of political communities with one another...Political leaders...are still bound by the natural law...and have no authority to depart from its slightest precepts. (John XXIII, Encyclical *Pacem in Terris* (1963), part III, paras 80–1. See *NDMR* 205.)

86   PART ONE: HUMAN RIGHTS AND COMMON GOOD

The reassertion of the truths that there are indeed such limits on government, and that they can well be articulated in the relatively modern language of truly inviolable rights, is one of the principal teachings in the new encyclical *Veritatis Splendor*.[13] The justification of the traditional claim (reaffirmed in *Veritatis Splendor*) that these are truths which both pertain to revelation and are accessible to reason unaided by revelation would be matter for another treatise, or series of treatises.[14] Here I want merely to underline the importance for political theory of these unconditional, exceptionless limitations on government.

It may be appropriate to highlight the centrality of this point by recalling Strauss's explicit rejection of such limitations, in a passage surely central to his thought and perhaps to some of his influence. The passage occurs, fittingly enough, in the precisely central pages (pp. 160–2) of Strauss's (323-page) book, *Natural Right and History*, in the core of his discussion of the central (the Aristotelian) type among the 'three types of classic natural right teachings'.[15] The climax of this striking passage is the blunt assertion—*propria voce*—that, even (and precisely) for 'a decent society', in war '[t]here are *no limits* which can be defined in advance, there are no *assignable limits* to what might become just reprisals'.[16] Of course, many liberal politicians have acted upon such notions, for example in maintaining the strategic deterrent set up in the years when Strauss was (by unmistakably deliberate implication) articulating its supposed moral underpinnings (1949–53). Those politicians will not have thanked Strauss for going on to observe that these are teachings which cannot coherently be restricted to external affairs, and that the kind of 'suspension of rules of natural right' which he considers justified applies also to governmental dealings with 'subversive elements within society'.[17]

---

[13] The treatment of inviolable human rights, based on the moral norms exceptionlessly prohibiting intrinsically evil kinds of act, centres on ss. 95–101 of *Veritatis Splendor*.

[14] I have done something towards that project in the last four chapters of *NDMR* and in my little, more recent book *Moral Absolutes*.

[15] Strauss, *Natural Right and History*, 146. Indeed, these and the other pages in question are from the book's *central* chapter, too, when we count the Introduction and the two demarcated halves of chs V and VI respectively.

[16] *Ibid.*, 159–60 (emphasis added).

[17] But war casts its shadow on peace. The most just society cannot survive without 'intelligence', i.e. espionage. Espionage is impossible without a suspension of certain rules of natural right. Considerations which apply to foreign enemies may well apply to subversive elements within society. Let us leave these sad exigencies covered with the veil with which they are justly covered. (*Ibid.*, 160.)

In these and neighbouring pages Strauss is making the pleas which other philosophers and theologians have more carefully argued for: moral judgment has its truth only in and for 'particular situations'; in situations of 'conflict' (159) one should decide by reference to a particular 'common good' which relativizes the principles of justice and suspends certain 'rules of natural right'; 'there is not a single [moral] rule, however basic, which is not subject to exception' (160); and what matters in

A natural law theory which rejects Strauss's defence of a right of governments *in extremis* to kill the innocent, and denies that it is better that one (innocent) man die (by such killing) than that the people perish, must undertake a radical critique of the assumptions about value, deliberation, and choice which underlie every such consequentialism, utilitarianism, proportionalism, or situationism (labels to gesture towards a family of arguments many of which are hinted at or rapidly deployed in these remarkable pages of Strauss).[18] Such a critique must be open and public (as it is in the work of, say, Germain Grisez and others who have followed him in rethinking and developing the classic theory of natural law).[19] For a natural law theory of government certainly involves that, while governments rightly can have secrets and deliberate in deep secrecy, the moral principles by virtue of which they have authority to affect their subjects' deliberations, and which morally limit the exercise of their governmental powers, must all be publicly justifiable. Natural law theory explores, expounds, and explains the deep structure of morality, but morality is a matter of what reasons require, and reasons are inherently intelligible, shared, common.

III

The government of political communities is rationally limited not only by constitutional law and by the moral norms which limit every decent person's deliberation and choice, but also by the inherent limits of its general justifying aim, purpose, or rationale. As Strauss observed in the passage I have recalled, that rationale is the common good of the political community. And that common good, as he did not observe, is (I shall argue) not basic, intrinsic, or constitutive, but rather, instrumental. How should it be explained?

---

situations is not what one does but that one does it (unlike a Machiavellian *tout court*) with an *attitude* e.g., of 'reluctance' (162).

[18] A plea in mitigation for Strauss could fairly note that, when he wrote, the defenders of the 'Thomistic doctrine of natural right' which he was repudiating (see 163) in the passages above had scarcely undertaken that radical critique. Note also that although Strauss was professing to be finding 'a safe middle road between...Averroes and Thomas' (159), his own views, starkly expressed on pp. 160–2, correspond most closely to 'the view characteristic of the *falasifa* (i.e., of the Islamic Aristotelians' as well as of the Jewish Aristotelians' (158), namely, the view that what are presented in the Thomistic account of natural right (and indeed in a reading of Aristotle which Strauss fails to explore) as 'universally valid general rules' are in truth only generally valid—so that, as presented, without qualifications and exceptions, they are 'untrue...not natural right but conventional right' (158). For the alternative reading of Aristotle, see *MA* 31–41, 36.

[19] See e.g. Grisez, 'Against Consequentialism'; *NDMR* 238–72; George, 'Does the "Incommensurability Thesis" Imperil Common Sense Moral Judgments?'.

Every community is constituted by the communication and cooperation among its members. To say that a community has a common good is simply to say that that communication and cooperation has a point which the members more or less concur in understanding, valuing, and pursuing. How does a critical political theory go about identifying, explaining, and showing to be fully reasonable, the various types of intelligible point or common good, and thus the various fully reasonable types of human community? It can do so only by going back to first principles. And the first principles of all deliberation, choice, and action are the basic *reasons for action*. What gives reason for action is always some intelligible benefit which could be attained or instantiated by successful action, such as: (1) *knowledge* (including aesthetic appreciation) or reality; (2) *skilful performance*, in work and play, for its own sake; (3) *bodily life* and the component aspects of its fullness: health, vigour, and safety; (4) *friendship* or harmony and association between persons in its various forms and strengths; (5) the sexual association of a man and a woman which, though it essentially involves both friendship between the partners and the procreation and education of children by them, seems to have a point and shared benefit which is irreducible either to friendship or to life-in-its-transmission and therefore (as comparative anthropology confirms and Aristotle and the 'third founder' of Stoicism, Musonius Rufus, came particularly close to articulating)[20] should be acknowledged to be a distinct basic human good, call it *marriage*, the *conjunctio* of man and woman which Aquinas speaks of when identifying the basic goods in his list of first practical principles; (6) the harmony between one's feelings and one's judgments (inner integrity), and between one's judgments and one's behaviour (authenticity), which we can call *practical reasonableness*; and (7) *harmony* with the widest reaches and *ultimate source* of all reality, including meaning and value. The propositions which pick out such basic human goods precisely as giving (underived, non-instrumental) reasons for action to instantiate those benefits, and for avoiding what threatens to destroy, damage, or impede their instantiation, are propositions called by Aquinas the first principles of natural law or, synonymously for him (if I dare to say so here), of natural right[21]—natural, not because they are principles deduced from some prior theoretical account of human nature, but rather because precisely by one's originally practical understanding of these aspects of human flourishing and fulfilment one comes both to realize (make actual in practice) and

---

[20] Everyone knows and few even profess to deny Aristotle's teaching that people are by nature social and indeed political animals. Many fewer seem aware of his teaching (*NE* VIII.12: 1162a15–29) that people are by nature *even more primarily conjugal*.

[21] *ST* I–II q.94 aa.2c, 3c.

reflectively and theoretically to understand the nature of the sort of being (the human person, *homo*) who is fulfilled in these ways.[22]

With all this in mind, let me go back to the question of the basic types of *common* good and human community. There are three types of common good each of which provides the constitutive point of a distinctive type of community and directly instantiates a *basic* human good: (i) the affectionate mutual help and shared enjoyment of the friendship and *communio* of 'real friends'; (ii) the sharing of husband and wife in married life, united as complementary, bodily persons whose activities make them apt for parenthood—the *communio* of spouses and, if their marriage is fruitful, their children; (iii) the *communio* of religious believers cooperating in the devotion and service called for by what they believe to be the accessible truths about the ultimate source of meaning, value, and other realities, and about the ways in which human beings can be in harmony with that ultimate source. Other human communities have a common good which is instrumental rather than basic, though association and cooperation even when for an instrumental good (such as a business enterprise) have more than a merely instrumental character in as much as they instantiate the basic good of friendship in one or other of its central or non-central forms.

Thus the political community—properly understood as one of the forms of collaboration needed for the sake of the goods identified in the first principles of natural law—is a community cooperating in the service of a common good which is instrumental, not itself basic. True, it is a good which is 'great and godlike'[23] in its ambitious range:

to secure the whole ensemble of material and other conditions, including forms of collaboration, that tend to favour, facilitate, and foster the realization by each individual [in that community] of his or her personal development.[24]

---

[22] On the fundamental but often overlooked Aristotelian and Thomistic methodological axiom, that natures are understood by understanding capacities, and capacities by understanding their actuations, and acts by understanding their objects (and on the basic human goods as the objects of acts of will), see *FoE* 21–2. A further methodological note may be in place. Although the worth of all these types of intrinsic benefit, of basic human goods, is obvious, a reflective account of them can and should be discursive and critical, assembling reminders of the experience, practices, and institutions which evidence the intelligibility and point of these forms of good, and defending the account against doubts and objections. For the inherent self-evidence of some propositions does not preclude a rational defence of them; one argues for such a proposition dialectically, i.e. by relating it to other knowledge, and showing that denying it has rationally unacceptable consequences. Once again one can observe that when Strauss wrote, this work of argumentation and critical dialectic had been only patchily begun; but since then it has been essayed quite vigorously. See 1987f and its bibliography at 148–51; George, 'Recent Criticism of Natural Law Theory'.

[23] *NE* I.1: 1094b9.

[24] *NLNR* 147. As I indicate, *ibid.* 160, this account of the common good of the political community is close to that worked out by French commentators on Aquinas in the early mid-twentieth century. A similar account was adopted by the Second Vatican Council: e.g. 'the sum of those conditions of social life which allow social groups and their individual members relatively thorough and

(which will in each case include, constitutively, the flourishing of the family, friendship, and other communities to which that person belongs). True too, its proper range includes the regulation of friendships, marriage, families, and religious associations, as well as all the many organizations and associations which, like the state itself, have only an instrumental (for example, an economic) common good. But such regulation of these associations should never (in the case of the associations with a non-instrumental common good) or only exceptionally (in the case of instrumental associations) be intended to take over the formation, direction, or management of these personal initiatives and interpersonal associations. Rather, its purpose must be to carry out a function which the Jesuit social theorists of the early twentieth century taught us to call subsidiarity (that is, helping, from the Latin *subsidium,* help): the function[25] of assisting individuals and groups to coordinate their activities for the objectives and commitments they have chosen, and to do so in ways consistent with the other aspects of the common good of the political community, uniquely complex and far-reaching in its rationale and peculiarly demanding in its requirements of cooperation.[26]

The fundamentally instrumental character of the political common good is indicated by both parts of the Second Vatican Council's teaching about religious liberty, a teaching considered by the Council to be a matter of natural law (that is, of 'reason itself'[27]). The *first* part of the teaching is that everyone has the right not to be coerced in matters of religious belief and practice. For, to know the truth about the ultimate matters compendiously called by the Council 'religious', and to adhere to and put into practice the truth one has come to know, is so significant a good and so basic a responsibility, and the attainment of that 'good of the human spirit'[28] is so inherently and non-substitutably a matter of

---

ready access to their own fulfillment' (*Gaudium et Spes* [1965] para. 26; similarly, *Dignitatis Humanae* [1965], para. 6).

[25] See *NLNR* 146–7, 159.

[26] Of course, the common good of the political community has important elements which are scarcely shared with any other community within the polity: e.g. the restoration of justice by punishment of those who have offended against just laws; the coercive repelling and restraint of those whose conduct (including negligent omissions) unfairly threatens the interests of others, particularly those interests identified as moral ('human') or legal rights, and corresponding compulsory measures to secure restitution, compensation, or reparation for violations of rights; the specifying and upholding of a system of holding or property rights which respects the various interests, immediate and vested or remote and contingent, which everyone has in each holding. But the fact that these and various other elements of the political common good are peculiar to the political community and the proper responsibility of its leaders, the government, in no way entails that these elements are basic human goods or that the political common good is other than in itself instrumental.

[27] Declaration, *Dignitatis Humanae*, para. 2. In paras 9–15, the Declaration treats the matter as one of divine revelation.

[28] It is one of the *animi humani bona* mentioned in *ibid.*, para. 1.

personal assent and *conscientious* decision that, if a government intervenes coercively in people's search for true religious beliefs, or in people's expression of the beliefs they suppose true, it will harm those people and violate their dignity even when its intervention is based on the correct premise that their search has been negligently conducted and/or has led them into false beliefs. Religious acts, according to the Council, 'transcend' the sphere which is proper to government; government is to care for the temporal common good, and this includes [the subsidiary function of] acknowledging and fostering the religious life of its citizens; but governments have no responsibility or right to direct religious acts, and *'exceed their proper limits'* if they presume to do so.[29]

The *second* part of the Council's teaching concerns the proper restrictions on religious freedom, namely those restrictions which are

required for [i] the effective *protection of the rights* of all citizens and of their peaceful coexistence, [ii] a sufficient care for the authentic public peace of an ordered common life in true justice, and [iii] a proper upholding of *public morality*. All these factors constitute a fundamental part of the common good, and come under the notion of *ordre public*.[30]

Here too the political common good is presented as instrumental, serving the protection of human and legal rights, *public* peace and *public* morality—this last involving the preservation of a social environment conducive to virtue. Government is precisely not presented here as dedicated to the coercive promotion of virtue and the repression of vice, as such, even though virtue (and vice) are of supreme and constitutive importance for the well-being (or otherwise) of individual persons and the worth (or otherwise) of their associations.

Is the Council's natural law theory right? Or should we rather adhere to the less complex view suggested by a quick reading of Aquinas's *On Government*, that government should command whatever leads people towards their ultimate (heavenly) end, forbid whatever deflects them from it, and coercively deter people from evil-doing and induce them to morally decent conduct?[31] Perhaps the most persuasive short statement of that teaching is still Aristotle's famous attack on theories which, like the sophist

---

[29] 'Potestas igitur civilis, cuius finis proprius est bonum commune temporale curare, religiosam quidem civium vitam agnoscere eique favere debet, sed *limites suos excedere* dicenda est, si actus religiosos dirigere vel impedire praesumat': *ibid.*, para. 3.

[30] *Ibid.*, para. 7. I use the French 'ordre public' to translate the Latin *ordinis publici*, for reasons explained in *NLNR* 215.

[31] *De Regno* c. 14 (...*ab iniquitate coerceat et ad opera virtuosa inducat*). [But in context, this and related passages in *De Regno* may be consistent with e.g. *ST* II–II q.104 a.5c which teaches that human government has no authority over people's minds and the interior motions of their wills. See *Aquinas* ch. VII esp. 228–31.]

Lycophron's, treat the state as a mere mutual insurance arrangement.[32] But in two crucial respects, at least, Aristotle (and with him much of the tradition) has taken things too easily.

First, if the object, point or common good of the political community were indeed a self-sufficient life, and if self-sufficiency (*autarcheia*) were indeed what Aristotle defines it to be—a life lacking in nothing, of complete fulfilment[33]—then we would have to say that the political community has a point it cannot hope to achieve, a common good utterly beyond its reach. For subsequent philosophical reflection has confirmed what one might suspect from Aristotle's own manifest oscillation between different conceptions of *eudaimonia* (and thus of *autarcheia*), that integral human fulfilment is nothing less than the fulfilment of all human persons in all communities (in principle) and cannot be achieved in any community short of the heavenly kingdom, a community envisaged not by unaided reason (natural law theory) but only by virtue of divine revelation and attainable only by supernatural divine gift. To be sure, integral human fulfilment can and should be a conception central to a natural law theory of morality and thus of politics. For nothing less than integral human fulfilment, the fulfilment of all persons in all the basic human goods, answers to reason's full knowledge of, and the will's full interest in, the human good in which one can participate by action. And so the first principle of a sound morality must be as follows: in voluntarily acting for human goods and avoiding what is opposed to them, one ought to choose and will those and only those possibilities the willing of which are compatible with integral human fulfilment. To say that immorality is constituted by cutting back on or fettering reason by passions is equivalent to saying that the sway of feelings over reason constitutes immorality by deflecting one to objectives not in line with integral human fulfilment. This ideal community is thus the good will's most fundamental orientating ideal. But it is not, as early

---

[32] '...the *polis* was formed not for the sake of life only but rather for the good life...and...its purpose is not [merely] for the sake of trade and business relations...any *polis* which is truly so called, and is not one merely in name, must have virtue/excellence as an object of its care [*peri aretēs epimeles einai:* be solicitous about virtue]. Otherwise a *polis* sinks into a mere alliance, differing only in space from other forms of alliance where the members live at a distance from each other. Otherwise, too, the law becomes a mere social contract [*synthēkē:* covenant] or (in the phrase of the sophist Lycophron) "a guarantor of justice as between one man and another"—instead of being, as it should be, such as will make [*"poiein"*] citizens good and just...' The *polis* is 'not merely a sharing of a common locality for the purpose of preventing mutual injury and exchanging goods. These are necessary preconditions of the existence of a *polis*...but a *polis* is a *communio* [*koinōnia*] of clans [and neighbourhoods] in living well, with the object of a full and self-sufficient [*autarkous*] life...it must therefore be for the sake of truly good (*kalōn*) actions, not of merely living together...' Aristotle, *Pol.* III.5: 1280a32, a35, 1280b7–13, b30–31, b34, 1281a1–4.

[33] *NE* I.7: 1097b16–17. This, incidentally, differs widely from what Macedo, *Liberal Virtues*, 215–17, means by 'an autarchic person'.

natural law theories such as Aristotle's prematurely proposed, the political community.

Secondly: when Aristotle speaks of 'making' people good, he constantly[34] uses the word *poiēsis* which he has so often contrasted with *praxis* and reserved for techniques ('arts') of manipulating matter.[35] But helping citizens to choose and act in line with integral human fulfilment must involve something which goes beyond any art or technique. For only individual acting persons can by their own choices make themselves good or evil. Not that their life should or can be individualistic; their deliberating and choosing will be shaped, and helped or hindered, by the language of their culture, by their family, their friends, their associates and enemies, the customs of their communities, the laws of their polity, and by the impress of human influences of many kinds from beyond their homeland. Their choices will involve them in relationships just or unjust, generous or illiberal, vengeful or charitable, with other persons in all these communities. And as members of all these communities they have some responsibility to encourage their fellow members in morally good conduct and discourage them from morally bad conduct.

To be sure, the political community is a cooperation which undertakes the unique tasks of giving coercive protection to all individuals and lawful associations within its domain, and of securing an economic and cultural environment in which all these persons and groups can pursue their own proper good. To be sure, this common good of the political community makes it far more than a mere arrangement for 'preventing mutual injury and exchanging goods'. But it is one thing to maintain, as reason requires, that the political community's rationale requires that its public managing structure, the state, should deliberately and publicly identify, encourage, facilitate, and support the truly worthwhile (including moral virtue), should deliberately and publicly identify, discourage, and hinder the harmful and evil, and should by its criminal prohibitions and sanctions (as well as its other laws and policies) assist people with parental responsibilities to educate children and young people in virtue and to discourage their vices. It is another thing to maintain that that rationale requires or authorizes the state to direct people to virtue and deter them from vice by making even secret and truly consensual adult acts of vice a punishable offence against the state's laws. So a third way in which Aristotle takes things too easily is his slide from upholding government's responsibility to assist or substitute for the direct parental discipline of youth, to claiming

---

[34] Apart from the passage just cited, see *NE* I.10: 1099b32; II.1: 1103b4; X.9: 1180b24.
[35] e.g. *NE* VI.5: 1140a2; *Pol.* I.2: 1254a5.

that this responsibility continues, and in the same direct coercive form, 'to cover the whole of a lifetime, since most people obey necessity rather than argument, and punishments rather than the sense of what is truly worthwhile'.[36] There was a sound and important distinction of principle which the Supreme Court of the United States overlooked in moving from *Griswold v Connecticut* 381 US 479 (1965) (*use* of contraceptives by spouses) to *Eisenstadt v Baird* 405 US 438 (1970) (*public distribution* of contraceptives to *unmarried* people).[37] The truth and relevance of that distinction would be overlooked again if laws criminalizing private acts of sodomy between adults were to be struck down by the Court on any ground which would also constitutionally require the law to tolerate the advertising or marketing of homosexual services, the maintenance of places of resort for homosexual activity, or the promotion of homosexualist 'lifestyles' via education and public media of communication, or to recognize homosexual 'marriages' or permit the adoption of children by homosexually active people, and so forth.

IV

It is, I think, a mistake of method to frame one's political theory in terms of its 'liberal' or 'non-liberal' (or '[anti-]conservative' or '[non-]socialist' or '[anti-]capitalist') character. Fruitful inquiry in political theory asks and debates whether specified principles, norms, institutions, laws, and practices are 'sound', 'true', 'good', 'reasonable', 'decent', 'just', 'fair', 'compatible with proper freedom', and the like—not whether they are liberal or incompatible with 'liberalism'.[38] Still, many who style their own thought 'liberal' offer to identify limits on government which go beyond those I have outlined above. So we can usefully ask whether these suggest a conception of limited government which natural law theory would be wrong to reject or overlook.

---

[36] *NE* X.9: 1180a1–6.

[37] The law struck down in *Griswold* was the law forbidding use of contraceptives even by married persons; Griswold's conviction as an accessory to such use fell with the fall of the substantive law against the principals in such use. Very different, in principle, would have been a law directly forbidding Griswold's activities as a public promoter of contraceptive information and supplies. If US constitutional law fails to recognize such distinctions, it shows its want of sound principle.

[38] Inquiries framed in the latter way enmesh the would-be theorist in the shifting contingencies of political movements or programmes which, taken in their sequence since the term 'liberal' emerged in political use in the 1830s, having virtually nothing significant in common and, as movements, no principle for identifying a central case or focal sense. The only sensible way to deal with philosophical claims framed in terms of liberalism, liberal political institutions, etc., is to treat them as rhetorical code for 'sound', 'true', 'warranted', 'just', or the like; one translates accordingly and carries on with the consideration of the arguments or claims on their merits.

One proposal is that government not constrain liberty on the ground that one conception of what is good or right for individuals is superior to another. This proposal has been put forward by the later Rawls as appropriate for nearly-just, modern constitutional democracies such as he takes the United States to be. But this same, latter-day Rawls abstains from claiming that his theory is true, valid, or sound; it is advanced instead as suitable to ensure stability and social unity from one generation to the next, by bringing about or maintaining an 'overlapping consensus' on certain constitutional principles (notably this one).[39] To claim validity or truth for his theory, or the principles it promotes, would be (Rawls claims) to violate the conditions of pluralism and (as other 'liberals' put it) 'neutrality' and to move from the proper domain of political theory and practice into the domain of private ideals and conceptions of the good—from public reasons for action to private reasons. Ronald Dworkin, on the other hand, has proposed that the requirement of government neutrality between conceptions of good and bad ways of life is an implication of a *true* political principle, that everyone is entitled to equal concern and respect.

Rawls's refusal to offer any further justification for these principles has attracted devastating criticism from Joseph Raz,[40] and others.[41] The essential point, in my opinion, is that any position like Rawls's postulates or presupposes an untenable distinction between public and private reasons for action, since like Rawls it will admit that in one's private deliberations, unlike public deliberations, one may and doubtless should be motivated by a conception of good and bad lives, a conception which one considers true. The untenability of this distinction is evident. For every political actor/agent is a human person or at least, in the case of the social acts of groups (states, corporations, teams...), has no existence apart from the personal acts of the people who are the group's leaders and/or other members. Each person's reasons for choosing to perform some political act must be, or at least be based upon, reasons which for that person are ultimate/basic (in need of no further, rationally motivating and thus justifying reason); and these reasons must all be consistent with the acting person's other reasons or principles of action. For one's public acts are at the same time one's private acts: they are part of one's one and only real life. One's engagement in a 'political' act must not be merely logically consistent with one's conception of a good and decent life; it must actually be rationally motivated by that conception (which after all can be nothing other than

---

[39] See the expository discussion of Rawls in Raz, 'Facing Diversity: The Case of Epistemic Diversity' at 12.
[40] *Ibid.* (the article also effectively criticizes the analogous proposals made by Thomas Nagel).
[41] Macedo, *Liberal Virtues*, 53, 55, 60–4.

one's conception of what are good reasons for one's acting). So one's 'public' reasons for acting must also be one's 'private' reasons (though it does not follow that all one's reasons for action need be 'made public'). Moreover, political actions often have the gravest consequences both for the actor and for others; so, the public reasons are not good (adequate) reasons unless they justify the act, so to speak, all the way down, that is, justify the actor in doing it. To postulate that political acts are all to be done for reasons publicly undiscussable ('private ideals') is to propose that the political order should refuse to offer its participants any good (adequate) reason for participating in it or for accepting the burdens of citizenship.

As for Dworkin's attempts to derive a constraint of neutrality from the 'principle of equal concern and respect', refutations of them are perhaps well enough known to need no repeating here.[42] A careful, fair, and decisive summation and development of these critiques can be found in Robert George's book, *Making Men Moral: Civil Liberties and Public Morality*.[43]

That enables me to turn, instead, to a proposal more recent and more cautious than either Rawls's or Dworkin's. Stephen Macedo rejects the claim that liberal justice is neutral among human goods or ways of life.[44] But government should do nothing disrespectful of its subjects, and respect for persons requires, he argues, that they be subjected to no constraint not

---

[42] To constrain people's actions on the ground that the conception of the good which (if they are done in good faith) those actions put into effect is a bad conception, may manifest not contempt but rather a sense of the equal worth and human dignity of those people; the outlawing of their conduct may be based simply on the judgment that they have seriously misconceived and are engaged in degrading human worth and dignity, including their own personal worth and dignity along with that of others who may be induced to share in or emulate their degradation. In no field of human discourse or practice should one equate judging persons mistaken (and acting on that judgment) with despising those persons or preferring those who share one's judgement. See *NLNR* 221–3. After 1980 Dworkin revised his argument. Equality of concern and respect is violated whenever sacrifices or constraints are imposed on citizens in virtue of an argument they could not accept without abandoning their sense of their equal worth—for 'no self-respecting person who believes that a particular way to live is most valuable for him can accept that this way of life is base or degrading': Dworkin, *A Matter of Principle*, 206. But this argument is as impotent as its forerunners. To forbid people's preferred conduct does not require them to 'accept an argument'. And if they did accept the argument on which the law is based, they would be accepting that their former preferences were indeed unworthy of them (or, if they had always recognized that, but had retained their preferences nonetheless, it would amount to an acknowledgement that they had been unconscientious). People can come to regret their previous views and conduct; so one must not identify persons (and their worth as human beings) with their current conception(s) of human good. In sum: either those whose preferred conduct is legally proscribed come to accept the concept of human worth on which the law is based, or they do not. If they do, there is no injury to their self-respect; they realize that they were in error, and may be glad of the assistance which compulsion lent to reform. (Think of drug addicts.) And if they do not come to accept the law's view, the law leaves their self-respect unaffected; they will regard the law, rightly or wrongly, as pitiably (and damagingly) mistaken in its conception of what is good for them. They may profoundly resent the law. What they cannot accurately think is that a law motivated by concern for the good, the worth, and the dignity of everyone without exception, does not treat them as an equal. See essay 2, sec. II at nn. 17–21.

[43] George, *Making Men Moral: Civil Liberties and Public Morality*, 83–109.

[44] *Liberal Virtues*, 265.

publicly justifiable. 'People may rightly be coerced by the state only for certain limited reasons',[45] namely, public reasons—'reasons that all ought to be able to accept'.[46]

Thus stated, this is a limit which a natural law theorist will gladly accept. Natural law theory is nothing other than the account of all the reasons-for-action which people ought to be able to accept, precisely because these are good, valid, and sound as reasons. But Macedo, here following Rawls, proposes to interpret the limit differently:

> ...*public* moral justification...does not aim to identify what are simply the best reasons, where best is a function of only the quality of the reasons as reasons leaving aside the constraints of wide accessibility.[47]

Now this is not a crude appeal to majority rule. It is intended as a substantive principle, limiting government action even where a majority support the action. For such a support is sometimes based not on reasons but on respect for tradition or mere uncritical *mores*. In such a case, despite the fact that a law or other governmental action has majority support and is, in truth, supported by the best reasons, the limit which Macedo proposes would be transgressed—and those subjected to the law would be treated without due respect—if the reasons supporting the action, though sound and true, involve 'very difficult forms of reasoning'.[48] The rational justification for the government's action must be 'accessible to people as we know them'.[49] But (he goes on) in a natural law theory such as Aquinas's or the new classical theory of Grisez, Boyle, Finnis, George, and others, there is a gap between first principles and specific moral norms such as we find in the Decalogue, a logical space which must be filled by inferences *some* of which 'require a wisdom or reasonableness "not found in everyone or even in most people"'.[50] So, Macedo concludes, relevant parts of the natural law (even if true), or at least the inferences (even if sound) on which they depend, may be 'beyond the capacities of "most people"' and therefore not proper grounds for law.[51]

But in fact these natural law theorists do not admit that the actual norms of the Decalogue, or even the inferences on which they rationally depend, are beyond the *capacities* of most people, or that they are inaccessible, or that they *cannot* be appreciated by most people. Macedo, throughout his

---

[45] *Ibid.*, 263   [46] *Ibid.*, 195; cf. 41: 'that all reasonable people should be able to accept'.
[47] *Ibid.*, 50.
[48] *Ibid.*, 46; also 48 ('excessively subtle and complex forms of reasoning'), 63–4 ('too complex to be widely understood, or otherwise incapable of being widely appreciated by reasonable people').
[49] *Ibid.*, 43.
[50] *Ibid.*, 212; the internal quotation is from my 1985e at 52, which in turn is citing and summarizing *ST* I–II q.100 aa. 1c, 3c, 11c.
[51] *Liberal Virtues*, 212.

work, ignores the distinction between native and formed capacity, between faculty and competence, that is, the fact that I both *do* and *do not* have the capacity to speak Icelandic. And in each of the passages which Macedo implicitly relies upon, Aquinas says that the precepts of the Decalogue can be known from first principles with only a little reflection[52] and even ordinary folk can make the inference to them and see their point,[53] though it *can happen that* some people get confused about them;[54] *other* moral norms, inferable from the precepts of the Decalogue, are ones which *are known* (*cognoscuntur*)[55] by the wise rather than by others, who unlike the wise *do not* (not 'could not') diligently consider the relevant circumstances.[56] So, even on the face of the texts, there is no admission that the moral principles of the Decalogue are outside the domain of 'public justification' and public 'accessibility'.[57]

V

Macedo brings his proposed limit to bear on two main issues. *The first* is an embarrassing and difficult one to discuss, and that embarrassment turns out to be relevant to the political-theoretical issue in more ways than one. For laws and public policies should indeed be based on reasons, not merely emotions, prejudices, and biases, and a sub-rational prejudice does not become a moral judgment merely by being labelled so. So if the promotion of certain types of conduct through, for example, educational facilities or legally supported domestic arrangements is deliberately discouraged by law (which will often have the side effect of disadvantaging those who are ready and willing to engage in that sort of conduct), and if the decision to discourage that type of conduct is premised on the judgment that such conduct is morally deleterious and is thus a matter of legitimate concern in designing educational and socially supported domestic arrangements, then the law will be justified only if that adverse normative judgment is reasonable and not merely an expression of loathing. But Macedo's first

---

[52] *ST* I–II q.110, a.3c: 'modica consideratione'.
[53] a.11c: 'quorum rationem statim quilibet, etiam popularis, potest de facili videre'.
[54] a.11c: 'circa huiusmodi contingit judicium humanum perverti'.
[55] a.3c. [56] a.1c: 'quas considerare diligenter non est cuiuslibet sed sapientum'.
[57] Admittedly, large numbers of people can get confused even about one or another norm of the Decalogue, as (Aquinas remarks) the Germans encountered by Julius Caesar were morally confused about robbery. *ST* I–II q.94 a.4c. The conventions of a culture, reinforced by self-interest and a habit of following some passion, can obscure many people's understanding of a moral norm, deflecting rational inference by alluring images and by sophistical objections and rationalizations engendered by intelligence in the service of feeling. Moreover, what is principle and what is conclusion, and how they are related, can be outside the habits of reflection and powers of articulation of many who nonetheless, given time and skilful dialectic, could be brought to a reflective and articulate grasp of them.

issue is (as he frames it) homosexual conduct, and the discussion of that issue, indeed even private reflection upon it, is dogged by an embarrassment which renders most people more than usually inarticulate, and thus makes it more than usually difficult to differentiate between a reasonable though unarticulated judgment and a mere unthinking hostility.

So we are in a difficulty. On the one hand there is commonsense wisdom, articulated in the second half of the first century AD by Musonius Rufus: 'One begins to lose one's hesitation to do disgraceful things when one loses one's hesitation to speak of them.'[58] On the other hand, a judgment like the judgment of the Court in *Bowers v Hardwick*,[59] by its silence about why and in what respects homosexual conduct is bad, raises the suspicion that the laws on that matter (and even laws discouraging homosexual conduct in ways more in keeping with the state's subsidiary function) are grounded in sub-rational motivations.

Yet the fact is that many great philosophers—Socrates, Plato, and Aristotle—and other outstanding thinkers of classical antiquity rejected homosexual conduct.[60] Even those people inclined to it by their nature[61] viewed it as something degrading to the humanity of those who engage in it.[62] What is most striking about that rejection is not merely that it was the judgment of profoundly reflective thinkers untouched by the revealed teachings of the Old and New Covenants. It is that the judgment was reached very deliberately and carefully and, in the case at least of Socrates, Plato, and Aristotle reached in the midst of a distinctively homoerotic culture, and that its essential content was this: homosexual *conduct* (and indeed all extra-marital sexual gratification) is radically incapable of participating in, actualizing, the common good of friendship. Friends who engage in such conduct are following a natural impulse and doubtless often wish their genital conduct to be a good 'way to participate in the goods of intimate friendship'. But in supposing that it can in truth be that, they are deceiving themselves.

[58] See Musonius Rufus, Fragment 26, in Lutz, 'Musonius Rufus "The Roman Socrates"' at 131.
[59] 478 US 186 (1986).
[60] See 1994b at 1055–63. In those pages will be found sufficient reason for treating with the greatest caution everything said in Nussbaum, 'Platonic Love and Colorado Law'. Note in particular that the passages quoted by her from letters written to her by Sir Kenneth Dover and Anthony Price leave entirely intact the judgments of Dover and Price quoted and cited in my article, loc. cit. Indeed, passages quoted by her from these letters implicitly contradict statements made on oath by Professor Nussbaum herself, in October 1993, in the circumstances described in my article. See also George, '"Shameless Acts" Revisited: Some Questions for Martha Nussbaum'.
[61] A case expressly envisaged by Aristotle, *NE* VII.6: 1148b30.
[62] Vlastos, *Platonic Studies*, 25, citing Plato, *Phaedrus*, 251A1 and *Laws*, 636–7. Not all Vlastos's interpretations can be accepted, but this one is sound. See also Plato, *Republic*, 403a–c; *Laws*, 836–7, 840–1. For Musonius Rufus, see discourse XII in Lutz, 'Musonius Rufus "The Roman Socrates"', 84–9 (Greek/English), or Festugière, *Deux Prédicateurs de l'Antiquité: Télès et Musonius*, 94–5. For Plutarch, see his *Erotikos* (*Dialogue on Love*), 751c–d, 766e–771d.

In his book, Macedo had put the opposing case like this:

[n]on-promiscuous homosexual relationships...also participate in real human goods (friendship, play, knowledge). And for those whose attractions nature has directed toward members of the same sex, homosexual love may be the best way to participate in the goods of intimate friendship.[63]

So we must look more deeply into the foundations of the Socratic-Platonic judgment.

Here we can recall the reflections on marital communion in Musonius Rufus[64] and, a little later in the same generation, Plutarch.[65] And one could add Plato's identification of the work of Eros in the *Symposium* as paradigmatically that intercourse of man and woman which is a begetting and a divine thing.[66] These reflections become the more accessible to us if we set aside the long-dominant theological tradition whose dominance was inaugurated by Augustine's *De Bono Conjugali*. In this influential little treatise, Augustine taught that the marital good is an instrument good, in the service of the procreation and education of children so that the intrinsic, non-instrumental good of friendship will be promoted and realized by the propagation of the human race, and the intrinsic good of inner integration will be promoted and realized by the 'remedying' of the disordered desires of concupiscence.[67] Now, when considering sterile marriage, Augustine had identified a further good of marriage, the natural *societas* (companionship) of the two sexes.[68] Had he truly integrated this into his synthesis, he would have recognized that in sterile and fertile marriages alike, the communion, companionship, *societas*, and *amicitia* of the spouses—their being married—is the very good of marriage, and is an intrinsic, basic human good, not merely instrumental to any other good. And this communion of married life, this integral amalgamation of the lives of the two persons (as Plutarch[69] put it before John Paul II[70]) has as its intrinsic elements, as essential parts of one and the same good, the *bona* and *fines* to which the theological tradition for a long time subordinated that communion. It took a long and gradual process of development of doctrine, through the *Roman Catechism* issued after the Council of Trent, the teachings of Pius XI and Pius XII, and eventually those of Vatican II—a

---

[63] *Liberal Virtues*, 211.   [64] Discourses, XIIIA, XIIIB, and XIV (Lutz ed.).
[65] Plutarch, *Life of Solon*, 20, 4; *Erōtikos*, 768–70.
[66] *Symposium*, 206c; see also the comments by Allen, *The Dialogues of Plato*, vol. II, *The Symposium*, 18. And see Plato, *Laws*, 838–9, esp. 839b on familiarity and love between spouses in a chastely exclusive marriage.
[67] *De Bono Conjugali*, 9.9.   [68] Ibid., 3.3.
[69] *Erōtikos*, 769f.; *Conjugalia Praecepta*, 142f.
[70] Address to Young Married Couples at Taranto, October 1989, quoted in *LCL* 571 at n. 46: '...a great project: *fusing* your persons to the point of becoming "one flesh"'.

process brilliantly illuminated in the new, second volume of Germain Grisez's masterly treatise on moral theology[71]—to bring the tradition to the position that procreation and children are neither the end (whether primary or secondary) to which marriage is instrumental (as Augustine taught), nor instrumental to the good of the spouses (as much secular and 'liberal Christian' thought supposes), but rather: parenthood and children and family are the intrinsic fulfilment of a communion which, because it is not merely instrumental, can exist and fulfil the spouses even if procreation happens to be impossible for them.

Now if marriage is a basic human good, there fall into place not only the elements of the classic philosophical judgments on non-marital sexual conduct but also the similar judgments reached about such conduct by decent people who cannot articulate explanatory premises for those judgments, which they reach rather by an insight into what is and what is not *consistent with* realities whose goodness they experience and understand at least sufficiently to will and choose. At the heart of the Platonic-Aristotelian and later ancient philosophical rejections of all homosexual conduct, and thus of the modern 'gay' ideology, are three fundamental theses: (i) the commitment of a man and woman to each other in the sexual union of marriage is intrinsically good and reasonable, and is incompatible with sexual relations outside marriage; (ii) homosexual acts are radically and peculiarly non-marital, and for that reason intrinsically unreasonable and unnatural; (iii) furthermore, according to Plato, if not Aristotle, homosexual acts have a special similarity to solitary masturbation, and both types of radically non-marital act are manifestly unworthy of the human being and immoral. These are the theses whose public accessibility and justifiability I wish to defend. Their defence will include an answer to the question I left hanging: why cannot non-marital friendship be promoted and expressed by sexual acts? Why is the attempt to express affection by orgasmic non-marital sex the pursuit of an illusion?

Plato's mature concern in the *Laws* for familiarity, affection, and love between spouses in a chastely exclusive marriage, Aristotle's representation of marriage as an intrinsically desirable friendship between quasi-equals, and as a state of life even more natural to human beings than political life,[72] and Musonius Rufus's conception of the inseparable double goods of marriage all find expression in Plutarch's celebration of marriage—as a union not of mere instinct but of reasonable love, and not merely for procreation but for mutual help, goodwill, and cooperation for their own

---

[71] *LCL* 556–659.
[72] *NE* VIII.12: 1162a16–30; see also the probably pseudo-Aristotle, *Oeconomica* I. 3–4: 1343b12–1344a22; III.

sake.[73] Plutarch's severe critiques of homosexual conduct (and of the disparagement of women implicit in male homosexual ideology)[74] develop Plato's critique of homosexual and all other extra-marital sexual conduct. Like Musonius Rufus, Plutarch does so by bringing much closer to explicit articulation the following thought. Genital intercourse between spouses enables them to actualize and experience (and in that sense express) their marriage itself, a single reality with two blessings (children and mutual affection).[75] Non-marital intercourse, especially but not only homosexual, has no such point and therefore is unacceptable.

Underlying these rejections of extra-marital sex, and the judgment that such conduct is radically incapable of participating in, actualizing, the common good of friendship, is a thought which may be articulated as follows. The union of the reproductive organs of husband and wife really unites them biologically (and their biological reality is part of, not merely an instrument of, their *personal* reality). Reproduction is one function and so, in respect of that function, the spouses are indeed one reality, and their sexual union therefore can *actualize* and allow them to *experience* their *real common good—their marriage* with the two goods, parenthood and friendship, which are the parts of its wholeness as an intelligible common good even if, independently of what the spouses will, their capacity for biological parenthood will not be fulfilled in consequence of that act of genital union. But the common good of friends who are not and cannot be married (for example, man and man, man and boy, woman and woman) has nothing to do with their having children by each other, and their reproductive organs cannot make them a biological (and therefore personal) unit.[76] So their genital acts together cannot do what they may hope and imagine. Because

---

[73] Plutarch reads this conception back to the dawn of Athenian civilization and, doubtless anachronistically, ascribes it to the great original Athenian law-giver, Solon: marriage should be 'a union of life between man and woman for the delights of love and the getting of children': Plutarch, *Life of Solon*, 20, 4. See also Plutarch, *Erōtikos*, 769:

In the case of lawful wives, physical union is the beginning of friendship, a sharing, as it were, in great mysteries. Pleasure is short [or unimportant *mikron*], but the respect and kindness and mutual affection and loyalty that daily spring from it convicts neither the Delphians of raving when they call Aphrodite 'Harmony' nor Homer when he designates such a union 'friendship'. It also proves that Solon was a very experienced legislator of marriage laws. He prescribed that a man should consort with his wife not less than three times a month—not for the pleasure surely, but as cities renew their mutual agreements from time to time, just so he must have wished this to be a renewal of marriage and with such an act of tenderness to wipe out the complaints that accumulate from everyday living.

[74] See *Erōtikos*, 768D–70A.
[75] Plutarch speaks of the union of husband and wife as an 'integral amalgamation' [*di' holōn krasis*]: *Erōtikos*, 769F; *Conjugalia Praecepta*, 142F.
[76] Macedo, 'The New Natural Lawyers' writes:

[i]n effect, gays can have sex in a way that is open to procreation, and to new life. They can be, and many are, prepared to engage in the kind of loving relations that would result in procreation—were conditions different. Like sterile married couples, many would like nothing better.

their choice to activate their reproductive organs cannot be an actualizing and experiencing of the marital good—as marital intercourse can, even between spouses who happen to be sterile—it can do no more than provide each partner with an individual gratification. For want of a *common good* that could be actualized and experienced *by this bodily union*, that conduct involves the partners in treating their bodies as instruments to be used in the service of their consciously experiencing selves; their choice thus disintegrates each of them precisely as acting persons.[77]

Reality is known in judgment, not in emotion, and in reality, whatever the generous hopes and dreams with which some same-sex partners may surround their genital sexual acts, those acts cannot express or do more than is expressed or done if two strangers engage in such activity to give each other pleasure, or a prostitute gives pleasure to a client in return for money, or, say, a man masturbates to give himself a fantasy of more human relationships after a gruelling day on the assembly line. This is, I believe, the substance of Plato's judgment[78]—in the *Gorgias*, a dialogue so important for political philosophy—that there is no important distinction in essential moral worthlessness between solitary masturbation, being sodomized as a prostitute, and being sodomized for the pleasure of it.[79]

In short, sexual acts are not unitive in their significance unless they are marital (actualizing the all-level unity of marriage) and (since the common good of marriage has two aspects) they are not marital unless they have not only the generosity of acts of friendship but also the procreative significance, not necessarily of being intended to generate or capable in the circumstances of generating but at least of being, as human conduct, acts of the reproductive kind—actualizations, so far as the spouses then and there can, of the reproductive function in which they are biologically and thus personally one.

The ancient philosophers do not much discuss the case of sterile marriages, or the fact (well known to them) that for long periods of time (for example, throughout pregnancy) the sexual acts of a married couple

---

Here fantasy has taken leave of reality. Anal or oral intercourse, whether between spouses or males, is no more a biological union 'open to procreation' than is intercourse with a goat by a shepherd who fantasizes about breeding a faun; each 'would' yield the desired mutant 'were conditions different'. Biological union between humans is the inseminatory union of male genital organ with female genital organ; in most circumstances it does not result in generation, but it is the behaviour that unites biologically because it is the behaviour which, as behaviour, is suitable for generation.

[77] For the whole argument, see *LCL* 634–9, 648–54, 662–4.
[78] *Gorgias*, 494–5, esp. 494e1–5, 495b3.
[79] Price, *Love and Friendship in Plato and Aristotle*, 223–35, esp. 233, 235, concludes (despite Price's own regret) from a study of Plato's teachings on marital and non-marital sex that Plato had just about found his way to the understanding which Price finds articulated most notably, for modern times, by Paul VI in 1968 and after him by John Paul II.

are naturally incapable of resulting in reproduction. They appear to take for granted what the subsequent Christian tradition certainly did, that such sterility does not render the conjugal sexual acts of the spouses non-marital. (Plutarch indicates that intercourse with a sterile spouse is a desirable mark of marital esteem and affection.[80]) For, a husband and wife who unite their reproductive organs in an act of sexual intercourse which, so far as they then can make it, is of a kind suitable for generation, do function as a biological (and thus personal) unit and thus can be actualizing and experiencing the two-in-one-flesh common good and reality of marriage, even when some biological condition happens to prevent that unity resulting in generation of a child. Their conduct thus differs radically from the acts of a husband and wife whose intercourse is masturbatory, for example sodomitic or by fellatio or coitus interruptus.[81] In law such acts do not consummate a marriage, because in reality (whatever the couple's illusions of intimacy and self-giving in such acts) they do not actualize the one-flesh, two-part marital good.

Does this account seek to 'make moral judgments based on natural facts'? Yes and no. No, in the sense that it does not seek to infer normative conclusions or theses from non-normative (natural-fact) premises. Nor does it appeal to any norm of the form 'Respect natural facts or natural functions'. But yes, it does apply the relevant practical reasons (especially that marriage and inner integrity are basic human goods) and moral principles (especially that one may never intend to destroy, damage, impede, or violate any basic human good, or prefer an illusory instantiation of a basic human good to a real instantiation of that or some other human good) to the realities of our constitution, intentions, and circumstances.

'Homosexual orientation', in one of the two main senses of that highly equivocal term, is the deliberate willingness to promote and engage in homosexual acts—the state of mind and will whose self-interpretation came to be expressed in the deplorable but helpfully revealing name 'gay'. This willingness treats human sexual capacities in a way which is deeply

---

[80] Plutarch, *Life of Solon*, 20, 3. The post-Christian moral philosophy of Kant identified the wrongfulness of masturbation and homosexual (and bestial) conduct as consisting in the instrumentalization of one's body, and thus ('since a person is an absolute unity') the 'wrong to humanity in our own person'. But Kant, though he emphasizes the equality of husband and wife (impossible in concubinage or more casual prostitution), did not integrate this insight with an understanding of marriage as a single two-part good involving, inseparably, friendship as well as procreation. Hence he was puzzled by the question why marital intercourse is right when the woman is pregnant or beyond the menopause. See Kant, *The Metaphysics of Morals*, 277–9, 220–2 (trans. Gregor, 96–8, 220–2). (The deep source of his puzzlement is his refusal to allow intelligible goods any structural role in his ethics, a refusal which sets him against a classical moral philosophy such as Aristotle's, and indeed against any adequate theory of natural law, and in turn is connected with his dualistic separation of body from mind and body, a separation which conflicts with his own insight, just quoted, that the person is a real unity.)

[81] Or deliberately contracepted, which I omit from the list in the text only because it would no doubt not now be accepted by secular civil law as preventing consummation—a failure of understanding. See also n. 37 above.

hostile to the self-understanding of those members of the community who are willing to commit themselves to real marriage in the understanding that its sexual joys are not mere instruments or accompaniments to, or mere compensations for, the accomplishment of marriage's responsibilities, but rather are the *actualizing and experiencing* of the intelligent commitment to share in those responsibilities. The 'gay' ideology treats sexual capacities, organs, and acts as instruments to be put to whatever suits the purposes of the individual 'self' who has them, and so is radically inconsistent with the constitutive self-interpretative judgment of married people and their family, that adultery is per se (and not merely because it may involve deception), and in an important way, inconsistent with conjugal love. So a political community which judges that the stability and educative generosity of family life is one of the basic goods which political association itself exists to serve can rightly judge that it has a compelling interest in denying that 'gay lifestyles' are a valid, humanly acceptable choice and form of life, and in doing whatever it properly can, as a community with uniquely wide but still subsidiary functions, to discourage such conduct. This should not, I have argued, be done by way of a law of the type upheld in *Bowers v Hardwick*, but rather by other legal arrangements supervising not the truly private conduct of adults but the *public realm or environment*. For that is (1) the environment or public realm in which young people (of whatever sexual inclination) are educated, (2) the context in which and by which everyone with responsibility for the well-being of young people is helped or hindered in assisting them to avoid bad forms of life, and (3) the milieu in which and by which all citizens are encouraged and helped, or discouraged and undermined, in their own resistance to being lured by temptation into falling away from their own aspirations to be people of integrated good character, autonomous, and self-controlled persons, rather than slaves to the passions.[82]

VI

I have cut a long story rather short, partly because of the embarrassment which even tough Callicles felt in taking up such matters,[83] and partly because the second issue raised by Macedo is in itself more important.

---

[82] Macedo, loc. cit.:
All we can say is that conditions would have to be more radically different in the case of gay and lesbian couples than sterile married couples for new life to result from sex...but what is the moral force of that? The new natural law theory does not make moral judgements based on natural facts.

Macedo's phrase 'based on' equivocates between the first premises of normative arguments (which must be normative) and the other premise(s) (which can and normally should be factual and where appropriate can refer to natural facts such as that the human mouth is not a reproductive organ).

[83] See *Gorgias*, 494e5.

Macedo argues that governments should limit their protection of the unborn by a 'principled moderation' which demands that those with the best case should 'give something' to those who have put up a 'case that is very strong'. For, he says,

> [t]here are...many reasonable arguments on both sides of the abortion debate...and it is easy to see how reasonable people can come down on either side...[A]bortion...seems to come down to a fairly close call between two well-reasoned sets of arguments.[84]

But Macedo's proposal unreasonably assumes a dialectical symmetry which in reality does not hold. For if the better case is that what the abortions in dispute deliberately seek to kill are living human persons, then, however 'well reasoned' the contrary arguments may be, it will be a grave wrong to the unborn that the right to deliberately kill them is the 'something' to be 'given' away to show our 'respect' for people who had denied the reality of the unborn's existence, nature, and rights. But if the better case were some contrary (what?), then the loss of 'autonomy' or 'liberty' given away to honour the pro-life reasoners would involve no deliberate assault on mothers but merely an extension of those restrictions on intentionally destructive individual action which are the very first duty of government and the very basis of the common good. So there is no symmetry, and in this matter the responsibility of governments is to reach the right answer.

Indeed, a government which attends strictly to the arguments and is not distracted by the numbers and respectability of those who propose them, will find that (apart from the question whether killing is intended in cases where the pregnancy itself threatens the mother's life) the issue is not even a close call. Pro-choice arguments on abortion, however well reasoned, nicely fit Macedo's description: arguments whose key premises are manifestations of prejudice (in this case, rationalizing the self-preference of men and women). They yield conclusions which, as he says about 'racism' and anti-Semitism, we should not wish to compromise with but should, as a community, approach 'with resoluteness rather than moderation'. For there are fundamental matters in which a sound theory of government is indeed incompatible with limitations based on an appeal to 'principled moderation' rather than to truth.

---

[84] *Liberal Virtues*, 72.

6

VIRTUE AND THE CONSTITUTION*

The five questions put to our panel provide a suitable framework for my reflections.

1. Does the Constitution require or presuppose, or thwart or even forbid, a formative project of government inculcating in citizens the civic virtue necessary to promote and sustain a good society?
2. To what extent can the institutions of civil society support or even supplant government in inculcating civic virtue?
3. What is the content of the civic virtue that should be inculcated in circumstances of moral disagreement, and how does it relate to traditional moral virtue?
4. Does it include respect for and appreciation of diversity?
5. Should a formative project include cultivating attitudes that are critical of practices that deny liberty and equality?

I. CIVIC VIRTUES ARE MORAL VIRTUES

Since it is sensible to think about ends before considering the means to them, it may be best to start with the central question, the third: What is civic virtue? How does it 'relate to traditional moral virtue'? How is its content affected by circumstances of diversity?

As Plato and Cicero make clear, civic virtue is a more 'traditional' category than moral virtue. Just insofar as civic virtue is one's practical horizon, the traditions of one's *civitas*, one's polity, bound one's critical autonomy and one's appropriation of practical reasonableness. If the traditions of one's polity about what a decent person does are decent

---

* 2001b ('Virtue and the Constitution of the United States'). The panel of five on 'The Constitution of Civic Virtue for a Good Society' in the symposium on 'The Constitution and the Good Society', at Fordham University Law School in New York City in September 2000, included Stephen Macedo (see n. 1 below).

traditions, one will be encouraged in virtue. If not, not. If one has the misfortune to belong to a certain kind of traditional southern Italian community, and cannot break with the pagan traditions alive under surface forms of Catholicism, one will make one's own the ethos of vendetta and an honour which is steeped in murder and deceit. If one has the misfortune to belong to the leisured male upper classes of the brilliant commercial republic of fifth-century Athens, and lives in its traditions, one will be a contented slave-owner, wise in the ways of seducing and masturbating on boys, with no thought of one's wife's true equality: that is how good citizens are, and affirm each other in being. And so forth.

When one breaks tradition's hold, by the asking and pressing of questions which we formalize as 'philosophy', or by hearing and living by a new and true gospel, one gets clear that there is only one genuine kind of virtue. In our language, it is moral virtue, of which civic virtue is one aspect. For virtue is nothing other than the whole set of dispositions which fit one as an individual and responsible acting person to make authentically reasonable choices—morally good and right choices—in every context where one can choose and act. So civic virtue, coherently considered, is simply the moral virtues insofar as they bear on one's participation in community which extends beyond family to the forms of civic and political association: schools, cities, shops and marketplaces, highway travelling, churches, charitable, sporting, and other voluntary associations, firms, professional dealings and associations, and state governmental activities such as jury trials, elections, military service, public administration, judging, legislating, and so forth.

Relative to the distorted subordination of neighbourliness to family in the vendetta, true civic virtue is morality's demand that justice be administered and wrongs righted by an impartial civic/political institution, the judge, and not by passionate *parti pris*. Relative to the private indulgence of classical Greek homosexual culture, and its Roman analogues, true civic virtue was located in morality's demand that one look with more egalitarian respect to one's wife, free one's slaves, and treat one's neighbours' sons as persons, still children, but to be fulfilled as spouses in loving marriage not as unequal and passive partners in one's own sensual indulgence, and so forth. All these reformations of 'private' vices would tend, as Augustus to some extent perceived when enacting his *Leges Iuliae* against adultery and easy-going divorce, to benefit the city and the wider republic and empire—and not *simply* demographically.

Here are a few instances of key elements in civic virtue: the *impartial and zealous dutifulness* of, say, the doctor or fireman who treats and rescues all who need that help, even those who are abusers of themselves or others or are in loathsome condition or feeble-minded or unconscious; the *probity* of the lawyer who fearlessly upholds the traditions of the Bar and ethics of the profession against the pressures of unfair judges, importunate clients, unscrupulous opponents, and the constant temptation to make success in the present proceedings the overriding criterion of choice; the *honesty* of the scholar who refuses to join the teams of scholars who regularly pollute the marketplace of ideas by manufacturing false histories in order to promote legal and other social causes they value; the *fidelity* of those who honour their contracts, marital or commercial, carry out their responsibilities as public or private trustees, and pay their debts, especially to needy creditors, rather than treat bankruptcy as wiping their own moral slate clean. And so on.

How is all this affected by circumstances of diversity? Obviously, many of the aspects of virtue which I have mentioned involve overcoming hostility to the unfamiliar or the despised, and reaching to the person in need. Getting and maintaining these virtues may be specially difficult when there are long-standing traditions of presuming that everyone of a certain category has certain vices or weaknesses. So one model of civic virtue is the courage and clear-headedness of the Northern Irish Catholic who, precisely in order to be a good citizen of the *res publica*, joins the Royal Ulster Constabulary and uses her talents to participate in the daily work of thwarting and rectifying the injustice of criminals and of a ruthless armed force engaged in obviously unjust war against that *res publica*, the polity. The dangers and harms she is willing to undergo include not only murderous reprisals but blinkered hostility from those who will not consider the common good of the present community as it really is but prefer to remain in the horizons of old struggles and the loyalties and patterns of exclusion and reaction they fostered.

II. CIVIC VIRTUE INCLUDES RESPECT FOR AND APPRECIATION OF PERSONS, HOWEVER DIVERSE

Our fourth question asks whether civic virtue includes respect for and appreciation of diversity. The answer is clear enough. Diversity is a blessing for any community just to the extent that many diverse gifts make for more resourceful and adequate mutual help, and richer authentic human fulfilment for all. Diversity is a tragedy, a cross, for any community just to the extent that diversity of opinions and dispositions about fundamental questions about right and wrong, virtue and vice, blocks that community's pursuit of and participation in decent ways of living and interacting, and its ability to reform and overcome unworthy ways of living together: slavery, wealth-accumulation without sharing with those in need, baby-farming, cultivation of demeaning stereotypes (Prods and Micks), the socially facilitated and approved choice to destroy a baby rather than accept motherhood or fatherhood; and so forth. John Stuart Mill's neo-Humboldtian affection for diversity is little more than an aesthetic preference worthy of little admiration unless it extends to what is really at stake: not 'diversity' but *persons* in and notwithstanding their diversity.†

What civic virtue calls for is respect for people of every kind, and appreciation of their humanity and of whatever good use they have been able—if they have—to make of their gifts and talents, however diverse those good uses and talents. In season and out, the 'more traditional forms of Roman Catholicism'[1] hold before us models such as the Missionaries of Charity, works of charity, reconciliation, peace-making, and a humility which does not kneel before wrong opinions and dispositions, or teach anyone to be indifferent to their wrongness, but 'respects and appreciates' wrongdoers (all of us in some measure). This is a model of civic virtue, as the non-Christian government and good citizens of Calcutta most readily acknowledge. There are many other models for combining respect for people in their diversity with refusal to accommodate their injustice. For injustice comes in very diverse and appealing forms. So, since the polity's jurisdiction is to secure justice,[2] a culture of civic virtue needs to teach in deed as well as word that diversity merits no respect or appreciation where it is a manifestation of personal or group injustice. And to add, in word and deed, that the ending of respect and appreciation need not and often should not be the beginning of violent, particularly private, action against the injustice.

'Does civic virtue include respect for and appreciation of diversity?' If 'diversity' here is code for, especially, willingness to engage in and promote homosexual conduct, as it is in various environments familiar to us, the answer, I suggest, is: No, indeed not. To respect such a willingness, or anybody's willingness to engage in any other form of non-marital sex acts, is to endorse an important falsehood about what is good for human persons, and is to make a contribution towards the collapse of marriage as a civic institution and personal reality,[3] and so to do one's bit to harm,

---

[1] [Stephen Macedo's contribution to the panel discussion is 'Constitution, Civic Virtue, and Civil Society: Social Capital as Substantive Morality', and says at 1578: 'Some religions (like the more traditional forms of Roman Catholicism) seem to undermine at least some important civic virtues, especially the civic virtues of generalized cooperativeness …'.]

[2] See *Aquinas* ch. VII.

[3] See essay 22; *Aquinas* 143–54. The core of the argument is a reflection, found already in Aquinas, on the pre-conditions for spouses to *actualize, experience, and express* their marriage in their

unjustly, all the people who will suffer as children and therefore also as adults by being raised in more or less non-marital environments.[4] A civic virtue of some importance at this time is having the resolution to think this matter through, analyse and assess the self-indulgent and unjust claims to equality of treatment, tell the truth about this matter in uncomfortable contexts, and act on it in legitimate contexts such as national, state, and local elections, or school government—while maintaining proper civility and respect for all persons involved.

III. PROJECTS FOR INCULCATING CIVIC VIRTUES SHOULD CRITIQUE PRACTICES DENYING JUST LIBERTY AND AUTHENTIC EQUALITY

The fifth question seems to insinuate that fostering 'liberty and equality' should have a kind of priority in projects of encouraging civic virtue. In their obvious political meaning, these are great goods rightly emphasized in the aftermath of empire and slavery, and so in the Constitution of the United States and its Fourteenth Amendment. But though, for the same reason, they head up the Gettysburg address, the political thought of the address comes to rest in the proposition that government by the people is both of and for the people. Government of people entails restriction of their liberties, even if it is intended to preserve the liberties of others; and government for people implies that it is for the benefit of all aspects of people's needs and well-being, not simply their freedom and equality of status.

So liberty and equality have their place in the project, but the priority must go to encouraging people to distinguish between just liberty and the

---

acts of marital intercourse. Confused questions and interjections at the conference make it advisable to add that it is as intrinsic to the idea of marriage that it be between a man and woman as it is that it be between only two persons. It is absurd for 'gay rights' advocates to claim that a commitment between two persons of the same sex can instantiate *marriage*—and this absurdity is made manifest as soon as one asks supporters of gay ideology why they keep talking about *couples*: the ideology offers no *reason* whatever for such a restriction, any more than it offers reason for fidelity and exclusiveness within 'marriage'.

[4] It does not follow that engaging in such acts, with full adult consent and in total privacy, should be criminalized, and I have long held that it should not be: see 1994b; essay 21, sec. I and n. 20. Nor do I raise the question of homosexual conduct out of any hostility to people disposed to engage in such conduct, or any special hostility to that kind of conduct. My concern in this area is with all kinds of disposition and conduct opposed to marriage (e.g. fornication, adultery, the dissemination of pornography, etc.). I had researched and published in the area for decades before the accidents of the Colorado Amendment 2 litigation in 1993 occasioned my first research and publication on homosexual conduct and 'orientation'. Still, there is a case for giving attention to the 'gay' ideology: it is a particularly shameless assault on the idea of marriage, even—and to some extent especially— when it claims for same-sex couples, triples, quadruples, etc., a 'right to marry'. And true marriage is really important for justice to children, i.e. to everyone in their early years.

unjust liberty of the snake oil merchant, the child abuser, the monopolist, the lying advocate, and so forth; and between equality in fundamentals, such as was unjustly denied in slavery and is today denied in the right of the strong to abort the weak, and equality wrongly claimed for people whose actions and dispositions are rightly regarded as unjust or causes of injustice. The US Supreme Court has rightly denied that there is a constitutional liberty-right to be killed (by euthanasia or assistance in suicide), and an important premise in the argument was that this liberty of a few would (i) endanger the liberty of many to live free from the terror of being killed because their life has been judged by someone to be not worth living, and (ii) equally endanger the equality of those too poor to escape being treated in institutions, public or private, which have great economic incentives to secure their early death.[5] But there are many ways of harming the welfare, especially of children, which should not be forced into the straitjacket of violations of the children's liberty or equality, rather than what they are: ways of harming their formation in generosity, self-control, fair-mindedness, the chastity which supports and informs good marriage, and so forth.

Looking at questions 4 and 5 together, one seems to detect an insinuation: there should be more endorsement of the anti-life and anti-marital practices that Christian culture always opposed, and less tolerance of those persons and organizations (such as the Catholic Church) that are critical of those practices. If that is indeed the suggestion, my reply is twofold: (1) broadly speaking, it has the truth exactly backward, but (2) one can say little useful for or against the suggestion without doing what self-styled liberal theorists, with honourable exceptions such as Macedo, are usually reluctant to do—consider the merits of the practices and critiques in question.

IV. THE CONSTITUTION OF THE UNITED STATES PERMITS GOVERNMENTAL ENCOURAGEMENT TO VIRTUE

With emphasis, the Constitution proclaims that the powers of the United States are only a fraction of the proper powers and responsibilities of government, and that all such governmental powers not delegated to the United States or prohibited by it to the states are retained by ('reserved

---

[5] See *Washington v Glucksberg* 521 US 702 (1997) at 719, 730–2, 737, 747, 782–7, 789–90; *Vacco v Quill* 521 US 793 (1997) at 808–9, esp. the references to the Report of the New York State Task Force on Life and the Law, *When Death is Sought: Assisted Suicide and Euthanasia in the Medical Context*; and essay 16.

to') each of the states. Those retained powers include that general residual power to legislate for the common good, which bears an unfortunate historical label 'police power', where police has nothing to do with 'police' in the modern sense of law-enforcement agent, and everything to do with the well-being of the polity.[6] It is the inherent authority of a government to impose restrictions on private conduct and holdings, for the sake of the public goods of justice, order, peace, security, and welfare. That general power includes the power to legislate for and in other ways make provision for the preservation of public morality, which certainly includes the protection of children from moral corruption of every kind that bears on their fitness for living. 'Public morality' is a category in some danger of withering away; unlike 'rights' and 'liberties' it does not confer on any individual or private group a standing to sue. But it is greatly important for the common good, the well-being of persons.

So the Constitution does not 'require or presuppose, or thwart or even forbid' a governmental project of encouraging civic virtue. The organizers' four candidate verbs manage to miss the mark. The right verbs are 'permits' and in the long term 'depends upon'. Some Supreme Court decisions purporting to apply the Fourteenth Amendment against the states, on the basis that what the state or states deem a vice harmful to others is in the Court's view not harmful, have certainly had the effect of thwarting sound projects of encouraging civic virtue. But there has not been, and is no constitutional basis for, a general prohibition on state laws advancing or supporting such projects.

V. PRIMARY RESPONSIBILITY FOR INCULCATING CIVIC VIRTUE RESTS WITH FAMILIES, SCHOOLS, AND OTHER INSTITUTIONS OF CIVIC SOCIETY. GOVERNMENTS' ROLE IS SUBSIDIARY

Question 2, which I have left until last, seems significantly skewed: 'To what extent can the institutions of civil society support or even supplant government in inculcating civic virtue?' That is, it seems to presuppose the top-down statism characteristic of much thought and practice commonly but complacently called 'liberal', such as the assumption that schooling of children should be 'public' in the sense that it is owned, managed, conducted, and administered from top to bottom by a governmental agency; and the accompanying presumption that 'private' schooling is an anomalous and

---

[6] [See Legarre, 'The Historical Background of the Police Power'.]

civically unfortunate side effect of the constitutional guarantees of religious and associational freedom.

The people of the Soviet Union had to learn the hard way—and at huge and continuing cost to their civic virtue at every level—that the principle of subsidiarity articulated by the Popes in the face of socialism is a true principle of justice, and that putting services like schooling into the hands of state monopolists made irresponsible by making their product free at the point of supply not only has devastating bad side effects but is a serious injustice to the parents and children who could otherwise have been helped, where necessary, to organize their own institutions for schooling children in truth, honesty, generosity, courage, respect for others as individuals, and concern for wider circles including, but in a subsidiary way, the state, its government, and its political, legal, and international life. Personal life, the real life of individuals, became in radically socialist countries intensely *privatized*: that is, at every level civic virtue as a personal disposition became stunted to the point of withering away, as I could observe when visiting an underground 'university' in late-Communist Bratislava, and a Russian-speaking child of mine could often observe in late-Soviet Leningrad and contemporary Moscow.

Less dramatically, and *mutatis mutandis*, similar phenomena can be observed in America. Even when differences in education, income, race, age, family structure, region, and hours per week worked by parents were all controlled for, the American families whose children attended public schools were found in 1996 to be *more privatized* than the families whose children attended Catholic or other private schools or were home schooled—that is to say, they were *less* likely to be involved in civic activities on each and all of the nine dimensions of involvement used by 1996 Household Education Survey conducted by the US Department of Education's National Center for Education Statistics.[7]

That is anecdotal evidence, though more to the point than the anecdotal evidence Steve Macedo kindly retailed to us from southern Italy.[8] The answer to the question is supplied by a sound analysis of the foundations of politics:[9] governments do have a primary role in cultivating *some* elements of civic virtue—those that pertain to the performance of political roles

---

[7] Smith and Sikkink, 'Is Private Schooling Privatizing?'.

[8] [Macedo, 'Constitution, Civic Virtue, and Civil Society'.] One of the more striking and sustained manifestations of civic virtue in my lifetime was the rescue of many Australian trade unions from the grip of Communists by Catholic activists led by the southern Italian 'traditional Catholic' intellectual and activist Bob Santamaria, at a time (c. 1949–52) when the secular and largely Protestant national government was concentrating futilely on top-down state measures such as dissolving the Communist Party.

[9] See e.g. *NLNR* 146 and 159 (definition of subsidiarity), 169, 233.

and responsibilities, such as fair competition in elections for public offices, doing one's duty if called for service on a jury, refusing bribes, as a citizen, to vote for certain candidates or, as a legislator, for certain bills, etc. As to the many other important elements of civic virtue, however, government can and must support but should not supplant the ongoing educative project of the civic institutions (families, schools, churches, etc.) which rightly have primary responsibility for inculcating these elements.

NOTE

† *Mill and von Humboldt* ... (p. 110). Mill quotes, as *On Liberty*'s epigraph or motto:

> 'The grand, leading principle, towards which every argument unfolded in these pages directly converges, is the absolute and essential importance of human development in its richest diversity' (Wilhelm von Humboldt, *The Sphere and Duties of Government* [([c. 1792] 1854), ch. VI para. 148]).

Mill also adopts von Humboldt's conception of human flourishing or perfection. Mill says (*On Liberty*, ch. 1 para. 11):

> It is proper to state that I forgo any advantage which could be derived to my argument from the idea of abstract right, as a thing independent of utility. I regard utility as the ultimate appeal on all ethical questions; but it must be utility in the largest sense, grounded on the permanent interests of a man as a progressive being.

Humboldt, *The Sphere and Duties of Government* ch. II (para. 84) says:

> The true end of Man, or that which is prescribed by the eternal and immutable dictates of reason, and not suggested by vague and transient desires, is the highest and most harmonious development of his *powers* to a complete and consistent whole. Freedom is the grand and indispensable condition which the possibility of such a development presupposes; but there is besides another essential,—intimately connected with freedom, it is true,—a variety of situations.

On the rational superiority of Mill's (and thus also Humboldt's) approach compared with, say, Hart's, and on a fundamental element of myth in Mill's, see essay IV.11 (2009b), sec. IV, and essay I.18, sec. III.

7

MIGRATION RIGHTS*

Because the basic goods intrinsic to human flourishing are multiple, and because each human being belongs to a number of communities (each of whose common good is an aspect of the intrinsic good of each of its members), our responsibilities are complex. Similarly complex is the theory which accurately identifies these goods, communities, and responsibilities—natural law theory. The complexity of this theory is enhanced by the complexity of rational choice and action, in which ends, means, and unintended but foreseen side effects each fall within the chooser's responsibility, but in very different ways.

Both Ann Dummett's and Paul Weithman's essays seem to me to oversimplify the theory. Since my role is only to suggest some comments, I shall take no position on the question of what is just and what unjust in the international movement of people and funds. Nor shall I attempt to state the extent of my agreement with either of the essays. It should not be assumed that the policies I favour involve less far-reaching reforms than theirs. I shall merely indicate some points at which I think the logic of their arguments fails.

I

Ann Dummett thinks that the Home Secretary, Mr Edward Shortt, KC, was rejecting a natural law concept of justice when he said that steps to secure national safety are just even when they result necessarily in 'the infliction of hardship upon an alien'. I think her assessment is hasty. Mr Shortt's statement is ambiguous, and although nothing in his speech itself resolves the ambiguity, neither his words nor the traditions of British public discourse they take for granted commit him to the view that the

---

* 1992b ('A Commentary on Dummett and Weithman', responding to Dummett, 'The transnational migration of people seen from within a natural law tradition' and Weithman, 'Natural law, solidarity and international justice').

interest of a single political unit is a complete moral guide, or that aliens have no human rights valid against a nation-state.[1]

Suppose a heckler had asked whether Mr Shortt was asserting that aliens could be held hostage, tortured, or killed in order to secure national safety. Nothing in the statement of this Liberal politician (and judge) would have been negated by the reply he would certainly have given: that such an assertion was far from his meaning and unacceptable both to him and to the nation. The heckler's intervention would thus have brought to the surface the ambiguity between hardship imposed *as a means* and hardship *resulting as an unintended though foreseen side effect*. The word 'infliction' fosters this ambiguity—though probably unintentionally. If Shortt was not careful about the morally essential distinction, nor is Ann Dummett. And her own phrase 'promote the good of citizens *at the expense of others*' trades on the same ambiguity, even more misleadingly.

Consider a statement essential to Aquinas's account of the justice of self-defence:

One is not morally required to abstain—in order to avoid killing someone else—from an act of self-defence proportionate to the occasion; for one has a stronger obligation to preserve one's own life than the life of another.[2]

Aquinas is saying, if you like, that one may justly 'inflict' harm on another in self-defence, and that one may defend oneself at the expense of another. But more precisely, he is saying that one private individual may never *choose to* inflict death or any other harm *as a means* to his safety or any other good—may never *intend* death or any other harm to anyone;[3] one may only choose to stop the attack by those measures which are available to one, are no more than sufficient for stopping the attack, and impose no unfair side effects on the assailant or anyone else. One may not defend oneself by choosing to kill or harm hostages, even if doing so is the only 'means of self-defence' likely to suffice. In that sense, one may not act 'at the expense of others', that is, to impose on them a harm as a means to one's own gain or even one's security. (This negative norm of justice does not itself derive from the principle of fairness with which I shall later be concerned.)

---

[1] Anyone minded to infer that I am naïve about the morals of British statesmen and their public should first read *NDMR* 8–10, 38–44. But issues of honesty and hypocrisy are irrelevant to the point being made by Dummett. [Shortt was Secretary of State in 1919.]

[2] *ST* II–II q.64 a.7c: 'Nec est necessarium ad salutem ut homo actum moderatae tutelae praetermittat ad evitandum occisionem alterius, quia plus tenetur homo vitae suae providere quam vitae alienae'.

[3] *Ibid.*: 'illicitum est quod homo intendat occidere hominem ut seipsum defendat [it is impermissible to intend to kill someone in order to defend oneself]'.

Now consider a case which is like private self-defence as conceived by Aquinas, in that it involves a kind of preference for one's own security (or the interests of those for whom one has a special responsibility) over the interests of others, but which differs in that it involved no application of harmful force, no 'infliction of harm'. Suppose one comes home one evening to find squatters occupying one's house; one's children have nowhere to sleep and study; so one has the squatters put out into the street. Is one promoting the good of one's children at the expense of other human beings, in defiance of human rights and natural law? No. One acts to preserve and retain the space and facilities one had justly held in possession for one's children. If there is foreseeable loss to the squatters, that is a side effect, not a means. Perhaps there is no loss, since they are rich people who squat for fun. Perhaps there is loss, since they have nowhere else to go. In either case, their losing, precisely as such, is not a means to one's gain; and where there is loss it results from a lack (their lack of *anywhere else* to go) of which one is not oneself, as such, the cause. Does this exhaust one's responsibilities? By no means. If it is an icy night and the squatters are sick or thinly clad, one has some responsibilities… And if a political party credibly proposes fair means of alleviating homelessness, one has a responsibility to count that a serious reason for favouring that party.

II

Ann Dummett's next major proposition about natural law or the natural law tradition is: since, by natural law, one's rights arise from one's being human (not from one's being a citizen), any legal or political arrangement in which citizens have rights which aliens do not have must contradict natural law and be unjust. This argument seems to me invalid and mistaken.

Some of my children's rights are predicated on no fact other than that they are human: notably, their right not to be intentionally killed or harmed in their health and bodily integrity, their right not to be lied to, their right to be considered in any sharing of the world's resources, their right not to be punished without fair trial. Some of their most important rights, however, are predicated on the combination of their being human with some further, so to speak more contingent fact(s), such as that they are mine, or that I have paid such-and-such a school to educate them: hence their right to be fed and clothed and educated *by me*, and their right to be cared for during school hours *by that school* and *its* responsible employees and agents (not to mention their right to attend gatherings for alumni of the school). Other important rights which they have are predicated on the fact that they have made the commitments they have, by which they undertook responsibilities and enjoy rights which fairly correspond to those responsibilities—for example as spouses, or as owners of property, or as members of a college. Some other rights and duties of theirs—such as their right to vote—have an intelligible correspondence to responsibilities such as their contingent liability as citizens to do military or other national service, responsibilities which they have without having voluntarily undertaken them, but which are predicated on facts which include the undertakings which others have made and maintain and the responsibilities which others respect and fulfil for the sake of benefiting members of the community as members of which my children have precisely these obligations or liabilities and corresponding rights.

Underlying the notion that such-and-such a right corresponds to such-and-such an obligation is a modality of the principle of fairness, a principle of natural law most pithily captured in the Golden Rule. This principle is fundamental to most of our specific affirmative obligations and to the correlative rights which we have (correlative to others' obligations to us). The modality in play in the last sentence of the preceding paragraph is: fairness requires that one who takes the benefits of a fair system of cooperation and mutual restraints and service should take the corresponding burdens; and that one who has assumed the burdens is entitled to the benefits. The application of this modality of fairness is, of course, conditional on the conformity of the system with all other moral norms, including fairness in its other modalities.

If Japan adopts a law like one under discussion there in mid-1990, permitting Malaysians to enter Japan for the purposes of employment on condition that no such immigrant may stay for more than two years, or be visited by any members of his or her family, must we condemn this as unjust? Suppose that such workers are paid wages ample for feeding, housing, and educating their families in Malaysia but less than the wages paid to Japanese who are doing comparable work but who need wages well above the Malaysian level to pay for the housing and education in Japan which these Malaysians will never have to provide for. Must we say that this is unjust? I can think of no plausible norm of justice which compels us to. And: to say this, is not to accept the fairness and justice of every system which allows in alien migrant workers to work for long periods in conditions and for emoluments inferior to those available to citizens.

III

Ann Dummett proposes a norm of justice which would condemn the Japanese-Malaysian proposal. The norm she proposes is: everyone has a right to enter any territory he or she chooses, with a view to living and working peacefully under the laws applicable to citizens, provided only that the exercise of this right does not coincide with its exercise by so many other people that the fundamental human rights of other human individuals are threatened—such fundamental human rights *not* including the right that the moral, demographic, economic, political, or other cultural character or well-being of a national or lesser community be preserved.

Her primary argument for this norm is that it is logically or rationally entailed by the norm—whose justice is widely admitted—according to which everyone has the right to emigrate. (It is not clear to me that the exercise of this right is, in justice, as free from conditions as western polities have asserted and Ann Dummett assumes.) But there simply is no such entailment. It is quite clear who has the duty correlative to the right to emigrate.[†] It is quite unclear that (as Ann Dummett seems to suggest) every other community everywhere has an equivalent duty to admit unlimited numbers of foreigners whatever the foreseeable consequences for the economic, political, and cultural life of its citizens (short of 'violation' of their 'recognized individual' fundamental rights defined as narrowly as she proposes).

It seems to me that the fundamental norms of justice which underlie the institution of property (*dominium*) are applicable, *mutatis mutandis*, to the institution of territorial dominion by politically organized communities. The first of these fundamental norms is that the world with its resources is radically common to all, for the benefit of each and every member of the human race. The second is that a system of dominion—entailing restrictions on the availability of defined parcels of land and resources—tends to result in important benefits to all and can be fair, provided that its immediate negative implications for those who remain in serious deprivation by reason of their exclusion from lands and/or resources are alleviated. Ann Dummett criticizes 'Western countries' for 'deliberately blurring' the distinction between 'the special claims of the persecuted or starving and the lesser claims of an ordinary migrant' (or would-be migrant). But the principal weakness of her own radical proposal is that it blurs—to the point of eliminating—that very distinction, one which seems to me inherent in the norms of justice I have mentioned (all too briefly) in this paragraph.

IV

Natural law theory is a reflective account of what practical reasonableness, oriented by an integral openness to and respect for the intrinsic human goods, requires of human choosers in the various sorts of conditions in which they have to make and carry out their choices. It has no particular interest in states of affairs of a type no one is likely to encounter, such as the state of affairs in which 'individuals and institutions... comply perfectly with the principles of justice'.[4] Moreover, justice and injustice are not properties of any state of affairs, except insofar as it may be considered precisely *qua* exemplifying the fulfilment or neglect of responsibilities of justice by ascertainable people.

Justice, in short, is essentially a property of choices and dispositions which bear on choice. Choices and dispositions are just insofar as they satisfy all that morality requires of a choice, or other disposition of will, which impacts on other people. (I say 'people' deliberately; *pace* Weithman, one's moral responsibilities to respect and promote the subhuman realm of nature are not, I think, helpfully assimilated to responsibilities of justice in response to claims, for example, of bodies of water, etc.) That is the fundamental reason why a sensible theory of justice has little or nothing to do with imagining states of affairs in which resources would be distributed according to a pattern which the theory identifies as just, under conditions which more or less guarantee that no one's choices or actions could move us from the world in which we live to that state of affairs.

Rawls's second principle of justice, as articulated in the formula quoted by Weithman,[5] seems to me to be either a commendation of injustice, or no principle of justice/injustice at all. Who can properly define their role as 'arranging social and economic inequalities'? Anyone who undertook such a role would be undertaking to act unjustly. To say that, is not of course to say that anyone should undertake to *eliminate* all social and economic inequalities; that too would be a work of injustice. It is to say that justice has to do with fair choices, and that fairness—whose rational criteria are complex and in their application partly relative to non-rational factors such as feelings ('Do as you would *be willing* to be done by')—accepts inequalities

---

[4] Nor do I agree that the social teaching of the Popes since Vatican II has been directed towards that 'ideal' state of affairs, whose unattainability in this world is guaranteed by important Christian teachings about original sin, the transcendence of the Kingdom, and the portents which will precede the Kingdom's definitive installation. Certainly the essay of Donal Dorr which Weithman cites ['Solidarity and Integral Human Development'] hugely exaggerates the methodological difference between Vatican II and Paul VI, and simply overlooks the continuity between the pre-Vatican II concept of the common good and Paul VI's concept of integral development. But since I think it unsafe to assume that Catholic social teaching is directed solely by principles knowable independently of revelation, or that recent documents of the US Catholic Conference adequately represent Catholic social teaching, I here make no arguments about or by reference to Catholic teaching, beyond saying that nothing in it seems to me inconsistent with what I say in this essay.

[5] ['Rawls's second principle of justice reads: "Social and economic inequalities are to be arranged so that they are both (a) to the greatest benefit of the least advantaged and (b) attached to offices and positions open to all under conditions of fair equality of opportunity"', Weithman, citing Rawls, *A Theory of Justice*, 83.] [Cf. essay 3, para. 5.]

only as a side effect of choices concerned with other matters and not as an objective to be attained by some 'arrangement' of means to ends.

But where one's action is such that some whom one could otherwise have helped are left worse-off than if one had helped them, it can be unfair to accept such a side effect; one can have a responsibility, in accordance with the principle of fairness, to make an alternative choice which avoids that side effect and helps those people. So the justice of the 'Difference Principle' can be tested by asking: Can it ever be fair for anyone, in the exercise of responsibilities in and for a community (family, voluntary association, nation, church, and so on), to make a choice in such a way that the least advantaged people in the world are not benefited by that choice? Weithman's answer appears to be: No, such a choice could never be fair.§

That answer seems to me very implausible, and the argument advanced in defence of it seems quite inadequate. The strong form of the argument is clearly guilty of the fallacy I have noted in sec. I above, of confusing means with side effects. This is the 'Kantian' argument that: 'to *permit* lesser prospects for some to be justified by greater benefits for others would be to permit the treatment of some *as a means for* the well-being of others'. Not so. If a couple spend £100 on educating their children, thereby permitting every other child (anywhere) who could have benefited from that £100 to have lesser prospects than if they had spent it on that child, they are not thereby treating (or permitting the treatment of) any other child (let alone every other child) *as a means for* the well-being of their own children.

The weaker version of Weithman's argument for the Difference Principle is not clearly fallacious, but I see no clear reason to accept it. It asserts that accepting the principle would 'foster the goods of community' better than any other principle of justice. To me it seems highly probable that if anyone arrogated to themselves the role of 'arranging inequalities' so that those inequalities were 'to the greatest benefit of the least advantaged' anywhere in the world, there would result a far-reaching disruption of community as soon as people found all their particular commitments, undertakings, roles, and communities being deflected and overridden for the sake of a single supreme objective—the bettering of the (currently?) least advantaged. But, more to the point, there would very probably be well-founded complaints, raised by many people who are poor but not of the class of 'the least advantaged' (however one may specify that vague category), that the arrangements designed to benefit the least advantaged more than any alternative arrangements were arrangements which imposed on them, the poor-but-not-poorest, burdens quite disproportionate to the burdens (if any) imposed on the really well off. Such complaints are often justly made about the politics of our own real-world societies, in which welfare policies fashioned by the rich and powerful in the interest of the poorest are financed by exactions which bear unfairly heavily on the not quite so poor, or the lower middle class. Rawls's one-dimensional Difference Principle ignores this and many other sources and forms of unfairness in distributions of benefits and burdens in communities.

The poverty of the worst off is an evil which very many people, in very many different ways, have a responsibility to do something to alleviate. The responsibility of any particular person or institution to be of service to the worst off is a responsibility which, under the general principle of fairness (and consistently with all other moral requirements), is specified in moral norms (norms of natural law) corresponding to that person or institution's resources and other responsibilities. For people *in extremis*, all the world with its resources is again common: no claim to property or dominion is, precisely as such, morally valid against them. It does not follow that particular owners, trustees, or possessors have the obligation to make the service of such people the dominant end to which every use of their resources must be a means, regardless of their own opportunities of putting those resources to other good uses and of the extent to which others in their position are cooperating with, free-riding on, or defecting from cooperative efforts to provide the services which the worst off need. Still less have they the obligation to harness all their resources to the service of world 'community' or 'solidarity',[6] conceived of as a dominant end, a future end-state of affairs to be achieved by efficient arrangements of means.

NOTES

† *The right to emigrate* ... (p. 120). Although this involves a Hohfeldian liberty (no duty not to emigrate), what is more important about it, especially in international declarations of it, is the claim-right to be allowed to emigrate (not to be prevented from emigrating, and not to be expropriated on occasion of emigrating). Hence there is indeed a correlative duty—primarily of the government of the state from which someone is seeking to emigrate.

§ *A worldwide, cosmopolitan, globalized Difference Principle?*...(p. 122). A few years after this essay, John Rawls rejected the thesis of former students of his such as Thomas Pogge[7] and Paul Weithman, who proposed that his second principle of justice (the Difference Principle, quoted in n. 5 above) applies to the worldwide human community considered as if it were a single political community. In

---

[6] Weithman seems to treat 'community' as synonymous with the 'solidarity' which is thematic in John Paul II's encyclical *Sollicitudo Rei Socialis* (30 December 1987). But the word is not used by the encyclical to refer to an end-state which might be achieved by skilful 'selection' of principles efficient for promoting a certain future state of affairs. Instead, it is used to pick out a specific moral attitude or virtue by which individuals fulfil themselves by including the *common* good in their own *proper* (individual) good. The word thus corresponds closely to the virtue of 'general (or legal) justice' as that term was understood by Aquinas, but not as the term was used in later scholastic writing: see *NLNR* 184–6.

[7] Pogge, *Realizing Rawls*, Part Three ('Globalizing the Rawlsian Conception of Justice').

his *The Law of Peoples* Rawls argues that his principles of justice are to be regarded as applying to the community whose members are politically independent peoples. For a people's political independence is one of a number of *values* that would be sacrificed by attempting to apply the Difference Principle directly to the worldwide community of persons. See essay II.7 at nn. 7–21. Rawls's arguments about justice are generally unsound (see sec. IV above; essay 2, sec. II; and essay 3), but his judgment in this matter converges with that expressed tersely in the penultimate paragraph of this essay. It is one thing to predicate justice of decisions intended to promote end-state patterns of human relationships postulated to be attainable under conditions of universal full compliance with justice. It is quite another thing to predicate injustice of decisions which take reasonable account of their likely side effects, in the real world, on the pre-conditions for the flourishing, with just (Golden Rule-compliant) dispositions, of individuals, families, civil associations, economic undertakings, and politically organized communities. Rawls's rejection of the Pogge-Weithman thesis tacitly (and belatedly) but plainly, and reasonably, acknowledges this difference.

8
BOUNDARIES*

I. INTRODUCTION

When I taught law in the University of Malawi between 1976 and 1978, I lived in houses owned by the university in succession to the government, houses formerly occupied by colonial civil servants. From my first house in Zomba, I looked over the roof of the adjacent Parliament House, across the trees hiding the university down on the plain, and on towards the mountains of Mozambique, an even more newly independent country. At night we could see, out on the plain beyond the university, the arc lights around the prison camp where several hundred prisoners were detained on Presidential orders, including the most recent holders of the offices of Registrar of the University and Principal of the university college of which the Law Faculty was part. The President's powers of detention without trial were copied from powers used sometimes by the British government of the Nyasaland Protectorate. That protectorate, or colonial administration of the territory, had been inaugurated partially and informally in 1884, formally but partially in 1889, and formally and entirely in 1891, and terminated formally in 1964 (in substance in February 1963).

The Nyasaland protectorate was inaugurated against the long-standing wishes of the Foreign and Colonial Offices of the British Government, under pressure of public opinion keen to prevent the humanitarian disaster of an immense and long-standing slave trade conducted by Arabs with the willing assistance of the tribe that dominated the southern and southeastern shores of Lake Nyasa and preyed on peaceable but loosely organized Nyanja peoples just as the Angoni, pushed back from southern Africa by the Zulu, annually pillaged and slaughtered the Maravi on the western and northern shores of the lake. Had I been looking out over the plain from

---

* 2003a ('Natural Law and the Re-Making of Boundaries', a response to Tuck, 'The Making and Unmaking of Boundaries from a Natural Law Perspective').

the same spot a longish lifetime earlier, I could have seen the long slave columns beginning their death march 750 miles north-east as the crow flies to Zanzibar, to the slave market on the site of the cathedral there. To humanitarian and missionary British public opinion, Cecil Rhodes and a few others added some commercial suggestions, as inducements for the parsimonious British Government. The first acts of *imperium* and jurisdiction by the new Commissioner, Harry Johnston, on his arrival in 1891 were the forcible suppression of the slave trade and the cancelling of a large number of land purchases made by enterprising Europeans from native chiefs. His stated objects in respect of land were

firstly, to protect the rights of the natives, to see that their villages and plantations are not disturbed, and that sufficient space is left for their expansion; secondly, to discourage land speculation; and thirdly, to secure the rights of the Crown in such a way that the Crown shall profit by the development of this country.

His broader purposes were stated by him to his Whitehall superiors in 1893: 'we do not come here necessarily to subjugate; we come to protect and instruct'. The government school for Zomba children whose families speak English at home bears his name to this day.

In 1936, the Native Trust Land Order in Council confirmed and protected the position about settlement reached after forty years: Native Trust Land, administered and controlled by the Government for the use and common benefit, direct or indirect, of the natives of the Protectorate, comprised over 87 per cent of the land in the Protectorate; 7.65 per cent was held as forest reserves, townships, and leasehold crown land; and 5.1 per cent was alienated in freehold to European settlers—an amount much larger than the few hundred farmers and planters could cultivate. Settlement had never been a substantial motive or justification advanced for the establishing of the Protectorate.

There were a number of important injustices in the Protectorate's administration and laws—the head tax, for example, designed to force the population into some kind of commercial life, the failure to institute any government plan for and encouragement of education (left entirely to the missionaries), the unprotected status of squatters on uncultivated freehold land, the inadequate albeit real measures to protect public health, and so forth.

But it would, in my view, be unreasonable to judge that the decisions to declare the Protectorate, to enforce its administration of justice, and to maintain it for three-score years and ten, against German attack in 1914 and the one significant act of internal subversion (the Chilembwe uprising in 1915) were unjust or unjustified decisions. They were decisions made with generally good motives and just intentions, and were in all the circumstances fair and reasonable. It would have been, it seems to me, unjust and unreasonable for persons with the opportunities open to the British authorities in 1884 to have decided to leave the peoples of the territory under the sway of local rulers quite indifferent to the rule of law and incapable of defending their people against ruthless aggression, pillage, ethnic cleansing, and slavery at the hands of other Africans, or to a languid and capricious rule by Portuguese who had for centuries done little or nothing about those very evils, or to the generally brutal rule of the German East Africa colonial authorities.

The boundaries of Nyasaland were negotiated in the late 1880s between the British, Portuguese, and German governments, far from the scene. They make little intrinsic sense, cutting through a number of tribal areas. But it was clearly appropriate that some such boundaries should have been drawn in order to determine where a particular magistrate's jurisdiction—responsibility for maintaining peace and justice—ended or, perhaps, began. As one drives north along the highlands on the western shore of Lake Nyasa, one finds that the road itself, nothing more, marks the boundary between Malawi and Mozambique. To get, say, breakfast one must drive off a few hundred yards into Mozambique; the locals move back and forth between countries without apparent care or concern. But if a dispute arises between neighbours, or a man murders his wife or his neighbour or the shopkeeper, who is to exercise the kind of jurisdiction that only states can exercise with the prospect of due and impartial process of law? A Malawian or a Mozambiquan judge, with the help of whose police? When one gets to the outer reaches, the marches, a boundary provides a hardly dispensable service to fairness and to peace.

It would be summary but reasonable to say that British state rule in Nyasaland did not invade any state, did not transgress any state boundaries, respected existing property or quasi-property rights, and supplanted the jurisdiction only of rulers of manifest unfairness (if not always of bad faith), unwillingness to respect the boundaries of others, and incapacity to defend let alone appropriately promote the common good of their peoples. The era has now passed. But its contours remain relevant to any reflection on the justice of boundaries.

II

The principles of public reason that since Plato have been called natural law, natural justice, or natural right suggest and justify a territorial division and assumption of political/state jurisdiction for reasons closely analogous to those that suggest and justify the appropriation of land and other natural and artificial resources to private owners, individual or corporate. Those reasons can be summarized in headline form: services to common good (ultimately to the common good of all persons); responsibility for such service, and consequent authority to legislate, adjudicate, and administer (jurisdiction, *imperium* and, *mutatis mutandis*, *dominium*); and reciprocity.

One or two applications and illustrations. The domination of a nomadic tribe over the territory it happens to control at the present stage of its wandering, in the present balance of power with neighbouring nomadic or non-nomadic tribes, does not constitute it as a state, a political community organized for justice and peace, and does not establish for it *boundaries* to be respected by persons interested in bringing peace and justice to the area. This thought is relevant to a consideration of the justice of instituting colonial government in, say, Australia or, as I suggested, in parts of Africa.[1] Or again, a ruler's or ruling group's forcible domination of a people for the gratification of the ruling person's or group's own interests and advantage is tyrannical rule that has no title to respect by persons who intend and are equipped to protect and promote the common good of that same people. This thought, too, is relevant to reflections on Australia and some parts of Africa.

Richard Tuck says that Aquinas, like other Dominicans, 'disagreed profoundly with any theory of world authority, preferring instead a vision of a world of independent and equal political communities'. I doubt this. To me its seems a cardinal feature of Aquinas's treatment of political matters that he abstracts entirely from all questions about the conditions under which it is proper for political communities to be brought into being or dissolved or otherwise replaced.[2] His theory, it seems to me, is of a political community,

---

[1] There has been a tendency to suppose that if nineteenth-century judges were using a false factual premise in treating the colonization of Australia as occupation of a *res nullius*, it follows that that colonization lacked moral or legal title. *Non sequitur*, as the sixteenth-century discussions mentioned at nn. 9–12 below make clear.

[2] See *Aquinas* 219–21:

Aquinas's most important treatment of political matters is perhaps his treatise on law (*ST* I–II qq. 90–108), a discussion shaped by a methodological decision and a theoretical thesis. The thesis is that law exists, focally or centrally, only in complete communities (*perfectae communitates*). The methodological decision is to set aside all questions about which sorts of multifamily community are 'complete', and to consider a type, usually named *civitas*, whose completeness is simply posited. It is not a decision to regard the *civitas* as internally static or as free from external enemies. Revolutions and wars, flourishing, corruption, and decay are firmly on the agenda. But not the question which people are or are entitled to be a *civitas*.

The methodological decision... has important consequences. He is well aware that in his own world, though there are some city-*states* (*civitates*), there are also many cities (*civitates*) which make no pretension to being complete communities but exist (perhaps established rather like castles to adorn a kingdom) as parts of a realm; and *civitates*, kingdoms, and realms may be politically organized in sets, perhaps as 'provinces' (of which he often speaks) or empires (about which he discreetly remains almost wholly silent). He is well aware of the idea, and the reality, of

whether it be as small as Sparta or Florence or as large as France or indeed the world. His silence about the Holy Roman Empire seems to me just that: silence—like his silence about the Crusades: a kind of abstracting from radically contingent circumstances, enterprises, and institutions, in favour of keeping the focus upon the essential principles of good government:

... if the good for one human being is the same good [i.e. *human good*] as the good for a whole *civitas*, still it is evidently a much greater and more perfect thing to procure and preserve the state of affairs which is the good of a whole *civitas* than the state of affairs which is the good of a single human being. For: it belongs to the love which should exist between human persons that one should seek and preserve the good of even one single human being; but how much better and more godlike that this should be shown for a whole people and *for a plurality of civitates*. Or: it is lovable that this be shown for one single *civitas*, but *much more godlike that it be shown for the whole people embracing many civitates*. ('More godlike' because more in the likeness of God who is the universal cause of all goods.) This good, *the good common to one or many civitates*, is what the theory, i.e. the 'art' which is called 'civil', has as its point [intendit]. And so it is this theory, above all—as the most primary [principalissima] of all practical theories—that considers the ultimate end of human life.[3]

Of course, there is no reason to think that Aquinas considered world government a desirable possibility in any concretely foreseeable circumstances. How could anyone in the world he knew claim with justice to be able to promote, and therefore be potentially responsible for, the political common good, the justice and peace, of people in India?[4]

> peoples (*gentes*; *populi*) and nations (*nationes*) and regions (*regiones*). As we have seen [see passage quoted at n. 3 below], Aquinas is willing to raise his eyes to relationships of friendship between states, and to the widest horizons of human community, and he envisages treaties and other binding sources of law or right even between warring states. His methodological decision allows him to abstract from all this.
> It also allows him to abstract from a number of deep and puzzling questions: how—and indeed by what right—any particular *civitas* comes into being (and passes away); how far the *civitas* should coincide with unities of origin or culture; and whether and what intermediate constitutional forms there are, such as federations or international organisations. Liberated from such questions, Aquinas will consider the *civitas* rather as if it were, and were to be, the only political community in the world and its people the only people. All issues of *extension*—of origins, membership, and boundaries, of amalgamations and dissolutions—are thereby set aside. The issues will all be, so to speak, intensional: the proper functions and modes and limits of government, authoritative direction, and obligatory compliance in a community whose 'completeness' is presupposed.

[3] *In Eth*. I. 2 nn. 11–12 [29–30].
[4] See *Aquinas* 126 n. 112:

> Who then is my neighbour, my *proximus*? If 'people in Ethiopia or India', as Aquinas says (*Virt*. q. 2 a. 8c), can be benefited by my prayer, they are my neighbours, though he mentions them to his thirteenth-century audience as people so *remote* that we cannot and therefore morally need not seek to benefit, i.e. to love, them in any other way. As he explains in his discussion of the neighbour-as-oneself principle in *ST* II–II q. 44 a. 7c, 'neighbour' is synonymous here with 'brother' (as in 'fraternity') or 'friend' or any other term which points to the relevant affinity

Tuck (at 154) goes further: 'the Thomist answer [to the question whether the world was exhaustively divided among independent and jurisdictionally equal states] has always been that it was'. Tuck contrasts this with the rejected thesis that there was a Christian *dominium mundi*.[5] But the alternative theses do not exhaust the possibilities. A third possibility was that some parts of the world are administered as states and others are not, yet. (And a fourth possibility would question the jurisdictional equality of states.) It seems to me that Thomism was quite open to that third possibility. Certainly Aquinas seems quite relaxed when he himself writes about the responsibilities of rulers to found *civitates* or *regna* by choosing a good, temperate, fertile, beautiful (but not too beautiful) location for the realm and then, within that realm, selecting a site suitable for the building of a city—and all this in some place where no realm or city was already established.[6]

True, Vitoria—taking up the mantle of St Thomas in the 1530s—thinks that 'after Noah the world was divided into various countries and kingdoms'.[7] But he says this to refute the thesis that the whole world is or has been under the one emperor, not to refute the thesis that some parts of the world are as yet not part of the territory of any political community. True, too, Vitoria denies that the Spaniards acquired the 'Indies' by discovery 'just as if they had discovered a hitherto uninhabited desert'. But he is concerned here to refute the thesis that the Indies were 'unoccupied' or 'deserted' or otherwise outside 'true public and private dominion'.[8] He is not concerned to deny that there are or may be regions which *are* outside such dominion, such as that 'hitherto uninhabited desert'. So he is not claiming that the world is exhaustively divided among states.

Moreover, at the end of his discussion of the seven or eight *just* titles the Spanish *might* have had for assuming the administration of the Indies as their territorial possessions, Vitoria states that 'there are many things which they [the native peoples and rulers of the Indies] regard as uninhabited, or which are common to all who wish to appropriate them'.[9] This harks back

(*affinitas*), which consists in sharing a common human nature (*secundum naturalem Dei imaginem*). 'We ought to treat every human being as, so to speak, neighbour and brother (*omnem hominem habere quasi proximum et fratrem*)': II–II q. 78 a. 1 ad 2.

[5] Note that the would-be Thomist who 'completed' Aquinas's treatise *De Regno* [*De Regimine Principum*], and whose work was long accepted as Aquinas's by good Thomists (e.g. Francisco de Vitoria), considered that the whole world was subject to the Roman emperor at the time of, and as regent for, Christ—seeing nothing inappropriate in that. See *Reg.* 3 c. 13; cf. Vitoria, *De Indis* I q.2 a.1 in *Vitoria Political Writings*, 255–6, arguing that that this does not mean quite what it seems to say, and is inconsistent with other works of Aquinas.

[6] Aquinas, *De Regno* II cc. 2, 5–8 (ed. Phelan and Eschmann, 1949, 56–7, 68, 71, 74–5, 78).
[7] Vitoria, *De Indis*, I q.2 a.1 (255).   [8] *Ibid.*, I q.2 a.3 (264–5).
[9] *Ibid.*, I q.3 conclusion: *multa enim sunt quae ipsi pro desertis habent, vel sunt communia omnibus volentibus occupare.* (My translation departs in more than one respect from Pagden/Lawrance's 'they

to the first of these just titles, to which he gives the headline: 'natural partnership [*societas*] and interaction [*communicatio*]'. The thrust of the argument is that even though the native peoples and their rulers have governmental jurisdiction and genuine ownership of their territories and of any privately or publicly owned lands within them, they nonetheless are bound by natural justice and the quasi-positive law common to all peoples (the *ius gentium*) to allow well-intentioned travellers into their territories as tourists, missionaries, and traders, and as miners, pearl-fishers, and collectors of other kinds of *communia* or *res nullius*. Unowned natural resources are to be available to peaceful and well-intentioned foreigners on essentially the same terms as they are available to citizens. The division of resources for the purposes of private appropriation is in almost all human circumstances a requirement of justice, and results in ownership, *dominium*, which is just but also is far from absolute. *Dominium* is subject to override for the prevention of criminal or harmful activities, and to outright expropriation for the satisfaction of debts (including taxes), the relief of others' urgent necessities, eminent domain for road-building, fire-prevention, and so forth. Just so, the state's or political community's jurisdiction over its boundaries is far from absolute, and the boundaries themselves are quite permeable.[10] For a state to close its borders to well-intentioned strangers, exclude them from its territories or from the fair exploitation of its natural resources or from its markets, and enforce these exclusions by force, would be unjust aggression entitling those whose rights are so violated to undertake a defensive war of conquest—a war intended, that is to say, for the purposes of establishing on a stable footing a substantially just regime of government and property.[11]

This line of thought about just titles for taking territorial possession of lands that are *not* empty *res nullius* appears in Tuck's essay, but rather late—in his discussion of Grotius, nearly a century after Vitoria. (Tuck at 157 remarks parenthetically, however, that 'the Spaniards and other Europeans had pleaded [these titles] against native peoples'.) It is important to notice that it is a line of thought that Vitoria advances substantially as a matter of *ius gentium* rather than as a sheer implication of the principles of natural law or justice. One may think that Vitoria does not work hard enough to show that the customs of all or most peoples treat such offences of exclusion as grounds for a war not simply of satisfaction but of conquest. And one can certainly think that the international law that has supplanted

---

have many possessions which they regard as uninhabited, which are open to anyone who wishes to occupy' (291) and from Gwladys Williams's 'there are many commodities which the natives treat as ownerless or as common to all who like to take them'.)

[10] *Ibid.*, I q.3 a.1 (278–81).   [11] *Ibid.* (281–4).

the old, relatively informal *ius gentium* has set its face not only against such *casus belli* but also against the notion that boundaries are properly required to be as permeable to non-citizens as Vitoria contends or assumes.

It is not, perhaps, so clear that the modern *ius gentium* entirely excludes another title that Vitoria advances for the just suppression or overriding of boundaries: defence of the innocent against tyranny or other unjust attacks on human life.[12] We hear talk of justified resort to force to prevent a humanitarian disaster—or at least, if we cannot prevent it, or have perhaps unintentionally provoked it, to put an end to such radical injustice—and establish a more or less international protectorate for ensuring, so far as fairly possible, that injustice of that kind does not quickly resume.

The informing principle is no more and no less precise than the Golden Rule, the requirement of reciprocity, a genuine willingness to consider what one would wish for, or be content to see done to, one's closest friends if they were the ones whose possessions (with their boundaries) were in question.

---

[12] *Ibid.*, I q.3 a.5 (287–8).

9
NATIONALITY AND ALIENAGE*

I. CONSTITUTIONAL PRINCIPLES: BASIC ASPECTS OF OUR COMMON GOOD

Our courts call some principles of our law 'constitutional'.[1] Some rights, too, were picked out as constitutional, well before the courts were charged with enforcing rights as 'human'.[2] Constitutional principles and rights prevail over ordinary norms of statutory interpretation; the presumption that statutes do not overturn these rights and principles qualifies the ordinary subordination of common law to parliamentary authority. They correspond to aspects of our common good which are of special concern to the judiciary. Many of them concern the responsibility of the courts themselves to be available to all, not least to protect everyone within their jurisdiction from legally unwarranted detention.

'The power to admit, exclude and expel aliens was among the earliest and most widely recognized powers of the sovereign state',[3] and the power

---

* 2007a ('Nationality, Alienage and Constitutional Principle'). Secs V and VI of the published original are here omitted for reasons of space. They argue that the widely acclaimed decision of the House of Lords in *A v Secretary of State for the Home Department* [2004] UKHL 56, [2005] 2 AC 68 was not only inattentive to the constitutional principle articulated in this essay but also radically erroneous because entirely neglectful of both (a) the court's duty under the Human Rights Act 1998, s. 3(1) to interpret legislation 'so far as it is possible to do so... in a way which is compatible with the [European] Convention [on Human Rights] rights' imported into English law by that Act and (b) the obvious possibility and good sense of reading the relevant statutory provision of the Anti-Terrorism, Crime and Security Act 2001 as authorizing detention of alien suspected international terrorists *just so long as good faith efforts* were demonstrably being made to deport them.

[1] e.g. *A v Secretary of State for the Home Department (No. 2)* [2005] UKHL 71, [2006] 2 AC 221 at paras 12, 51; *R (Gillan) v Commissioner of Police for the Metropolis* [2006] UKHL 12, [2006] 2 AC 307 at para. 1.

[2] *Bray v Ford* [1896] AC 44 at 49; *Scott v Scott* [1913] AC 417 at 477 (Lord Shaw of Dunfermline); Church of England Assembly (Powers) Act 1919, s. 3(3); *Wheeler v Leicester City Council* [1985] AC 1054 at 1065 (CA, Browne-Wilkinson LJ, dissenting).

[3] *R (European Roma Rights Centre) v Immigration Officer at Prague Airport* [2004] UKHL 55, [2005] 2 AC 1 at para. 11 (Lord Bingham of Cornhill).

remains 'undoubted'.[4] But unless it is understood to be a constitutional principle, or the instrument of constitutional principle, the power will crumble, eroded by newly enforceable constitutional principles of equality before the law, and by rights as ancient as liberty (immunity from coercion or imprisonment) or as newly fecund as 'respect for [one's] private life'. For *principle*, adequately conceived, is not merely a matter of general normative propositions; more fundamentally, it retains its connotative link to *principium*, a starting point and source. And the source of normativity, in legal or moral schemes of right, is value, purpose, point—in short, common good. So the power of exclusion needs to be understood with its underlying principle, which in turn needs to be understood as one of those elements of the common good which the law of our constitution articulates and promotes.

The fundamentally equal protection which our law has long accorded aliens (foreigners)[5] within the realm is grounded on a venerable constitutional maxim of reciprocity: presence within the realm entitles foreigners to the protection of subjects and with it the obligations of subjects. Taken with the abolition of banishment as an option for dealing with risks posed by our own nationals, and the contemporaneous re-articulation of the liability of foreigners to be expelled when their presence is responsibly determined to be adverse to our public good, it yields a principle of constitutional weight:

Risks to the public good that must be accepted when posed by the potential conduct of a national (citizen) need not be accepted when posed by a foreigner, and may be obviated by the foreigner's exclusion or expulsion.

Though a foreigner's legally cognizable misconduct, actual or reasonably apprehended, does not automatically nullify the onerous obligations of protection which our law and government accept as arising from his presence, the consequent damage or risk to the common good entitles the public authorities to prevent or terminate that presence by lawful process. A foreigner's recalcitrant failure to assimilate his conduct, in matters of weight, to the particular conceptions of common and public good that are embodied in our constitution and law can lawfully and appropriately be met by refusing him entry, or requiring his departure. These applications of the deep principle of reciprocity cohere with, support, and are supported by the mutual trust, the give and take, and tolerance of shared risks that

---

[4] Counsel for seven of the nine appellant applicant detainees in *A v Secretary of State for the Home Department* [2004] UKHL 56, [2005] 2 AC 68 at 78.

[5] This essay uses these two words interchangeably and synonymously, to mean non-national/non-citizen.

are a precondition for democracy, social welfare, the defence of the realm, and the constitutional rule of law. The Lords in *A v Home Secretary* (2004)[6] were led away from these constitutional principles by argumentation which seems partly erroneous and partly *per incuriam*.[7]

II. ALIENS AS CONDITIONAL SUBJECTS

The maxim of reciprocity was articulated by Coke, with the Lord Chancellor and almost all England's judges, in *Calvin's Case* (1608): *protectio trahit subjectionem, et subjectio protectionem*: protection entails subjection, and the status of subject entails entitlement to protection by Crown, law, and courts.[8] So the presence within the realm of a friendly (non-enemy) alien, by drawing with it the protection of those institutions, entails the alien's duty of allegiance during his stay.[9] Commenting on Littleton, Coke would ground the legal status of foreigners present within the realm upon their right to sue in personal actions, a right he was the first to assert firmly.[10] Magna Carta, regularly treated by Coke as declaring common law rights, had distinguished enemy from non-enemy foreigners (s. 41). So the supposed incapacity of aliens to pursue personal actions at law was limited, he concluded, to enemy aliens: subjects of a state at war with the Crown.

Thus, in the seventeenth-century doctrinal and political settlement which shapes the constitutions of English-speaking countries around the world, foreigners within the realm (speaking always of non-enemy aliens)[11] enjoy the subject's common law right to freedom from every act of a government servant or agent which if done by a private person would be a tort. Because the Crown can neither do nor authorize wrong, any such act of an official against an alien must be tortious unless demonstrably warranted by common law or statute.[12] And this inference will underlie both the doubt of eighteenth-century lawyers about the existence of a prerogative of expelling aliens, and the Crown's long abstention from

---

[6] *A v Secretary of State for the Home Department* [2004] UKHL 56, [2005] 2 AC 68.
[7] In this the case resembles other notable cases where skilful advocacy led the House of Lords unanimously astray: e.g. *Haughton v Smith* [1975] AC 476, and again *Anderton v Ryan* [1985] AC 560. *A v Home Secretary* is not quite unanimous, but Lord Walker of Gestingthorpe's dissent scarcely challenges the six majority judgments at their questionable roots.
[8] *Calvin's Case* (1608) 7 Co Rep 1a, 5a; *Joyce v DPP* [1946] AC 347 at 366.
[9] *Calvin's Case* at 5b–6a.
[10] Coke, *Commentary on Littleton* (1628), 129b; Hale, *Historia Placitorum Coronae* (1678) I, 542 ratifies the doctrine; Holdsworth, *Hist.* ix, 95.
[11] But 'even alien enemies, if they were resident in this country with the express or even with the tacit permission of the Crown, must be treated as alien friends': Holdsworth, *Hist.* x, 396; ix, 101. Holdsworth's 'must' takes for granted that Parliament can dispose otherwise.
[12] Holdsworth, *Hist.* ix, 98.

purported exercise of it. If expulsion were by royal proclamation, defiance of it must go without penalty since the Crown cannot make criminal what hitherto was not criminal.[13] But if it were by arrest, detention, and forcible movement towards the boundaries of the realm, would it not be mere assault, trespass, and false imprisonment, axiomatically incapable of non-statutory authorization, and liable to the alien's personal action for damages against the officers and their agents? Dicey dramatized the constitutional position evocatively, in 1885: if 'foreign anarchists come to England and are thought by the police on strong grounds of suspicion to be engaged in a plot, say for blowing up the Houses of Parliament', but the responsible minister is not in a position to put them on trial, there are 'no means of arresting them, or of expelling them from the country'. No rule of common or statutory law authorized interference with their liberty, Dicey implied, and their application for habeas corpus must succeed.[14]

But when Dicey last passed this passage for the press in 1908, the law had begun to leave him behind. In authorizing detention pending deportation, the Aliens Act 1905 did not deal with Dicey's unconvicted foreign terrorists.[15] But soon after its enactment, the Judicial Committee of the Privy Council articulated constitutional foundations for doing so:

One of the rights possessed by the supreme power in every State is the right to refuse to permit an alien to enter that State, to annex what conditions it pleases to the permission to enter it, and to expel or deport from the State, at pleasure, even a friendly alien, especially if it considers his presence in the State opposed to its peace, order, and good government, or to its social or material interests: *Vattel, Law of Nations* book 1 s. 231; book 2, s. 125.[16]

By carefully not specifying 'the supreme power of the State', the Privy Council skirted the unresolved question whether *our* executive has any inherent power of excluding foreigners, or is altogether dependent upon parliamentary authority for doing so.

Johnstone v Pedlar (1921) riveted into our constitution the fundamental and extensive equality, within the realm, of friendly aliens and British nationals. But each Law Lord pointed, without deciding, to a prerogative or inherent power of the Crown to 'revoke its licence expressed or implied to

---

[13] *Case of Proclamations* (1611) 12 Co Rep 74 at 75, 76.
[14] Dicey, *Introduction to the Study of the Law of the Constitution* (1st edn, 1885), 239–40; (7th edn, 1908), 226–7.
[15] On the occasion and limited purpose of the Aliens Act 1905, see Beatson, 'Aliens, Friendly Aliens and Friendly Enemy Aliens' at 80.
[16] *A-G for Canada v Cain* [1906] AC 542, 546, quoted in the single judgment in *R (Saadi) v Secretary of State for the Home Department* [2002] UKHL 41, [2002] 1 WLR 3131 at para. 31, and described there as 'this principle'; quoted by Lord Bingham in *R (European Roma Rights) v Prague Immigration Officer* [2004] UKHL 55, [2005] 2 AC 1 at para. 12.

an alien to reside'.[17] The Crown having made no such purported revocation, its officer's seizure of the alien Pedlar's money was simply tortious, and actionable at his suit, despite all the trappings of a Secretary of State's ratification and the treasonable savour of the alien's activities. The issues, decided and undecided, rest today where the Privy Council left them in 1906 and 1921: there is constitutional authority, whether by prerogative or not,[18] to exclude an alien in the interests of the community's well-being. Since 1919, at latest, Parliament as the state's supreme authority has vigorously asserted, and ever more carefully regulated, our state's (nation's, political community's) capacity lawfully and rightfully to exclude.[19]

III. THE DEVELOPED CONSTITUTIONAL DIFFERENTIATION AND ITS PRINCIPLE

The legislation made by or under parliamentary authority during the first twenty years of the twentieth century defines principal effects of the constitutional distinction between nationals and aliens. Aliens have no liberty to enter the realm without leave of an immigration officer, may be admitted subject to 'such conditions as the Secretary of State may think fit',[20] and may be deported either (i) if a court sentencing them for an offence punishable only with imprisonment so recommends and the Secretary of State concurs or (ii) 'if the Secretary of State deems it to be conducive to the public good'.[21] Where a deportation order has been made, or a certificate has been given by a court with a view to the Secretary of State making such an order, a foreigner may be detained pending removal.[22] This basic pattern of duties and (Hohfeldian) liabilities is confirmed in the next great settling of status, the Immigration Act 1971, which begins with 'General Principles':

1. All those who are in this Act expressed to have the right of abode in the United Kingdom shall be free to live in, and to come and go into and

---

[17] [1921] 2 AC 263 at 283, per Lord Atkinson; see also 273 (Viscount Finlay), 276 (Viscount Cave), 293–4 (Lord Sumner, concessively), 297 (Lord Phillimore). Holdsworth, *Hist.* x, 393–400, assembles the seventeenth-century practices and judicial dicta, and the eighteenth and nineteenth-century opinions of lawyers, firmly asserting a prerogative of both exclusion and expulsion.

[18] Prerogative powers are preserved, if not asserted, in successive statutory saving clauses, e.g. Immigration Act 1971, s. 33(5).

[19] See Aliens Restriction Act 1919, authorizing the Aliens Order 1920, S.R. & O. 1920/448 and 2262. The Order as amended remained in force until 1953, its provisions being eventually transformed into the Immigration Act 1971 and the associated Immigration Rules.

[20] Aliens Order 1920, art. 1(4).   [21] *Ibid.*, art. 12(6)(c).

[22] *Ibid.*, art. 12(4). Powers of detention pending actual removal from the realm were created by the Aliens Act 1905, e.g. s. 7(3) (detention in custody awaiting a ship's departure or pending the Secretary of State's determination after certification by a court of conviction for a deportable offence).

from, the United Kingdom without let or hindrance except such as may be required under and in accordance with this Act to enable their right to be established or as may be otherwise lawfully imposed on any person.
2. Those not having that right may live, work and settle in the United Kingdom by permission and subject to such regulation and control of their entry into, stay in and departure from the United Kingdom as is imposed by this Act....

The right of abode, under the Act, is defined in the next section as belonging to United Kingdom citizens (since 1981 called British citizens) and a now vestigial sub-class of Commonwealth citizens. The third section's 'general provisions for regulation and control' provide first for exclusion—grant or refusal of leave to enter, and the conditions which may be attached to such leave, all regulated by Rules made under parliamentary scrutiny—and then for expulsion by deportation of any who overstay their leave of entry or fail to observe any of its conditions, or who obtain leave to enter by deception, or are recommended by a court for deportation on their conviction for an imprisonable offence,[23] or whose deportation the Secretary of State 'deems to be *conducive to the public good*'. More drastically, the British Nationality Act 1981, s. 40,[24] empowers the Secretary of State to make an order depriving of that status a British citizen who, he is satisfied, has done 'anything seriously prejudicial to the vital interests of the United Kingdom or a British overseas territory', unless such deprivation would result in statelessness.

The constitutional scheme's main features embody two legal constitutional principles, each resting on a moral-constitutional principle. (1) Subject to the limitations on employment or occupation that may have been imposed as conditions of their entry, and to liabilities which, for all foreigners, are entailed by the Crown's authority to expel them, non-enemy aliens present within the realm have all the rights and obligations that nationals have.[25] This rests on the justificatory (moral-constitutional) principle that resident aliens, having the duties of subjects, should reciprocally enjoy the rights of subjects. (2) The citizen, on the other hand,

---

[23] For the principles on which the courts exercise this function, see *R v Nazari* [1980] 1 WLR 1366; [1980] 3 All ER 880, CA. A court's refusal to make such a recommendation creates no presumption that the Secretary of State should not order deportation, although the court's recommendation does create some presumption in favour of such an order: *M v Secretary of State for the Home Department* [2003] EWCA Civ 146, [2003] 1 WLR 1980.

[24] As substituted by Nationality, Immigration and Asylum Act 2002, s. 4. On the wider (in certain respects) effect of s. 40 as enacted in 1981, see *Secretary of State for the Home Department v Hicks* [2006] EWCA Civ 400, [2006] INLR 203.

[25] *R v Secretary of State for the Home Department, ex p. Khawaja* [1984] 1 AC 74 at 111–12, per Lord Scarman. The alien's rights are subject to another exception: those rights that, as Aristotle said, define the central case and focal sense of citizenship, viz., rights of participation in governing (electorally, legislatively, executively, or judicially): *Pol.* III.1, 2 and 7; *NLNR* 253–4, 259.

can never be excluded from the realm: this was the trajectory and principle[26] albeit not the letter[27] of our law long before the United Kingdom signed up to a strict articulation of that proposition in Art. 3 of Protocol No. 4 (1963) to the European Convention on Human Rights ('ECHR').[28]

What principle underlies the executive's authority—now highly regulated both legislatively and judicially[29]—to exclude foreigners? Connoted by 'not conducive to the public good' (which doubtless means 'in some way deleterious to, or putting at risk, the public good'), the principle is this: the political community, while it cannot shift to other communities the risks presented by one of its own nationals,[30] need not unconditionally accept the *risk presented by aliens*. That is, the presence in the community of an alien who, individually considered,[31] can fairly be said to present some genuine *risk*, even relatively slight, to the rights of others, or to national security, public safety, the prevention of crime, the protection of health or morals or maintenance of *l'ordre public*, or to anything else of 'public interest in a democratic society', *need not be accepted*. Instead such risk can properly be sought to be prevented by exclusion, or terminated by expulsion, on the grounds that such presence within the community, even if it has not been already forfeited by commission of an imprisonable offence, is nonetheless 'not conducive to the public good'.

This principle is fully compatible with our moral and legal obligations to accept refugees or other immigrants, and to accept some costs and burdens in doing so. Vattel said that 'the first general law to be found in the very end of the society of nations is that each nation should contribute as far as it can to the happiness and advancement of other nations,'[32] and that 'no nation may, without good reason, refuse even a perpetual residence to one who has

---

[26] See e.g. Co. Litt. 133a; Blackstone, *Commentaries* I, 133 [137]; Holdsworth, *Hist.* x, 393.

[27] Provisions enacted in 1829 for the banishment or transportation for life of e.g. Jesuits were not repealed until the Roman Catholic Relief Act 1926, but had long been in desuetude. On expatriation, banishment and related concepts, see *Trop v Dulles* 356 US 86 (1958) at 102.

[28] Lest it confer a right of abode on certain classes of people belonging to present or former dependent territories, the United Kingdom has not yet ratified the Fourth Protocol, which subject to the usual kinds of authorized restrictions provides that 'No one shall be expelled, by means either of an individual or of a collective measure, from the territory of the State of which he is a national' and 'No one shall be deprived of the right to enter the territory of the state of which he is a national'.

[29] Immigration Act 1971, s. 15(1), conferring rights of appeal against any deportation order except (by s. 15(3)) any order made purportedly 'in the interests of national security or of the relations between the United Kingdom and any other country or for other reasons of a political nature'; that exception was disapproved by the European Court of Human Rights ('ECtHR') in *Chahal v United Kingdom* (1996) 23 EHRR 413, resulting in the rights of appeal to a Special Immigration Appeals Commission ('SIAC') established by the Special Immigration Appeals Commission Act 1997. See *Secretary of State for the Home Department v Rehman* [2001] UKHL 47, [2003] 1 AC 153.

[30] Dual nationality would be accommodated by a more precise statement of the principle.

[31] ECHR Protocol No. 6, Art. 4: 'Collective expulsion of aliens is prohibited.' Exclusion (denial of permission to enter) of wide classes (collectivities) of foreigners on grounds of their numbers or their collective characteristics is a different matter.

[32] Vattel, *Le Droit des Gens* (1758), Introduction sec. 13.

been driven from his country',[33] or to a body of fugitives or exiles unless its own territory 'could scarcely supply the needs of its own citizens'.[34] We might accept all this and more—even an extensive immigration programme, adopted as a duty of justice[35]—and yet justly demand of the foreigners that, at peril of being expelled (even if only to make way for others), they abstain from conduct (act or omission) that damages or puts at risk the public good. Indeed, we might hold that the more extensive the nation's willingness to accept newcomers, the less willing it need be to accept dangers created by the presence, especially the actual or reasonably foreseeable conduct, of particular foreigners (or, indeed—while eschewing collective expulsion—particular kinds of foreigners).

IV. DETENTION PENDING (WITH A PURPOSE OF) REMOVAL

The principle that *risks to the public good which must be accepted when arising from the presence of a national need not be accepted from the presence of an alien and may be obviated by the alien's exclusion or expulsion* has long been recognized as having an immediate practical consequence. Foreigners who are to be lawfully removed from the country may be detained pending their removal. Indeed, where reasonable grounds appear for investigating and deciding whether to remove particular foreigners, they may be detained pending the decision and its execution. Provision for such detention was made in the Aliens Act 1905 and more fully in all later enactments governing expulsion. The ECHR provides in Art. 5(1)(f) that the right to liberty and security of person is not infringed by '(f) the lawful...detention of a person...against whom action is being taken with a view to deportation...'.

The key concept in Art. 5(1)(f) is of ongoing purposive activity: the detention must at all times be part of action being taken 'with a view to' the non-citizen's removal from the territory. Likewise, in the governing provision of the Immigration Act 1971, Sch. 3, para. 2(3):

Where a deportation order is in force against any person, he may be detained under the authority of the Secretary of State pending his removal or departure from the United Kingdom...

---

[33] *Ibid.*, book I sec. 231.   [34] *Ibid.*

[35] The original commonality of all the earth's resources, as available in justice for all and each of earth's human inhabitants, is abrogated neither by the instituting of private property (see n. 62 below) nor by the appropriation of territories to states; and just as property rights are subject to a kind of moral trust or 'social mortgage' (a requirement of justice not merely of charity) for the benefit of the poor in their necessity (see *Aquinas* 188–96; *NLNR* 169–73), so the right of states to exclude aliens from their territory is subject in principle to an analogous qualification or burden. See sec. V below, and essays 7 and 8.

Here an ongoing purpose of removal is connoted not only by the word 'pending' but by the provision on which Sch. 3 depends, s. 5(5).[36]

As judicially interpreted, these provisions for detention 'pending' and 'with a view to' deportation, like similar provisions in other countries, fall far short of providing that an alien against whom a deportation order has been made may be detained for as long as ministers wish and regardless of their purposes and methods. The *locus classicus* is a dictum, largely if not wholly obiter, of Woolf J in *ex parte Hardial Singh* (1984). The case concerned very dilatory arrangements for a deportation, but there was little or no suggestion that deportation might even temporarily be 'impossible', in the sense of prevented by obstacles immovable for the foreseeable future. However, Woolf J's statement concerns itself mainly with that hypothesis, although it does not neglect to give primacy to *purpose of removal*:

Although the power which is given to the Secretary of State in paragraph 2 to detain individuals is not subject to any express limitation of time, I am quite satisfied that it is subject to limitations. First of all, it can only authorise detention if the individual is being detained...pending his removal. *It cannot be used for any other purpose.* Secondly, as the power is given in order to enable the machinery of deportation to be carried out, I regard the power of detention as being impliedly limited to a period which is *reasonably necessary for that purpose.* The period which is reasonable will depend upon the circumstances of the particular case. What is more, if there is a situation where it is apparent to the Secretary of State that he is not going to be able to operate the machinery provided in the Act for removing persons who are intended to be deported within a reasonable period, it seems to me that it would be wrong for the Secretary of State to seek to exercise his power of detention.[37]

Woolf J here assumes that inability to deport 'within a reasonable period' is somehow incompatible with maintaining and acting on a purpose of deporting, and/or with that being reasonable. As will become apparent, such an assumption is questionable and has been challenged both legislatively and judicially.

Woolf J's dicta were treated as a sound guide in interpreting Hong Kong's more elaborate statutory provisions in *Tan Te Lam v Superintendent of Tai A Chau Detention Centre* (1996).[38] The Judicial Committee of the Privy Council ruled that 'if it becomes clear that removal is not going to be possible within a reasonable time, further detention is not authorized'. But dicta and ruling alike were treated as implications of a governing

---

[36] Immigration Act 1971, s. 5(5): 'The provisions of Schedule 3...shall have effect with respect to...the detention...of persons *in connection with deportation*' (emphasis added).

[37] *R v Governor of Durham Prison, ex p. Hardial Singh* [1984] 1 WLR 704 at 706 (emphases added). The suggestion that detention might be improper *ab initio* goes wider than the treatment of Art. 5(1)(f) in *Chahal v United Kingdom*, 23 EHHR 413; see nn. 55–8 below.

[38] [1997] AC 97.

principle: 'in conferring such a power to interfere with individual liberty the legislature intended that such power could only be exercised reasonably'.[39] The Judicial Committee expressed agreement with the trial judge's findings that, although the period during which the applicant Vietnamese boat people had been in detention pending deportation (in one case over five years in all)[40] was 'truly shocking' and 'at first blush, an affront to the standards of...civilized society', it was *nonetheless reasonable* and lawful, given circumstances such as the policies and practices of the Vietnamese authorities, the refusal of some detainees to apply for repatriation, and in another case the detainee's apparent withdrawal of his application.[41]

Detention for removal was subjected to a 'reasonable length of time' limitation, by constitutionally motivated statutory interpretation, in the US Supreme Court's decision in *Zadvydas v Davis* ten weeks before 9/11 (the New York and Washington atrocities of 11 September 2001).[42] The statute provided for a ninety-day removal period, after which certain categories of foreigners (criminals, security risks, persons certified likely to abscond or a risk to the community, etc.)[43] 'may be detained beyond the removal period and, if released, shall be subject to...supervision'. By majority the Court held that this post-'removal period' detention could[44] continue only 'for such time as is reasonably necessary to secure the alien's removal', and presumptively only for a further ninety days, after which even criminal or risky aliens would be entitled to release if they 'provide good reason to believe that there is no significant likelihood of removal in the reasonably foreseeable future'.[45] Reasonableness is to be measured 'primarily in terms of the statute's basic purpose, namely assuring the alien's presence at the moment of removal'.[46] The consequent risks to the public could be obviated:

the alien's release may and should be conditioned on any of the various forms of supervised release that are appropriate in the circumstances, and the alien may no doubt be returned to custody upon a violation of those conditions.[47]

---

[39] *Ibid.* at 111.
[40] By the time of the determination of the appeal, 40 months 'pending removal'.
[41] [1997] AC at 109, 114–15 (no need to decide, since applicants successful on another ground).
[42] 533 US 678, 150 L Ed 2d 653 (2001).
[43] But in the case of terrorist aliens ordered to be removed but whom 'no country is willing to receive', Congress had authorized the Attorney-General 'notwithstanding any law, [to] retain the alien in custody' on six-monthly administrative review, a provision noted without adverse comment by the Court (533 US at 697).
[44] The Court (at 696) seems to accept that, notwithstanding the resident alien's constitutionally significant liberty interest, Congress could have authorized (if sufficiently explicit about its intent) the indefinite detention of a deportee for whom there was no reasonable prospect of finding any receiving country within a reasonable period.
[45] 533 US at 701.   [46] 533 US at 699.   [47] 533 US at 700.

The Court seems to imply that such conditions of supervision, perhaps stringent, might equally be 'indefinite and potentially permanent', so long as the certified flight risk or danger to the community persists and is reaffirmed from time to time with procedural due process, and provided always that the government's purpose remains to deport this person as soon as possible.

Into the notably more severe[48] Australian statutory scheme—mandatory removal of all unlawful non-citizens 'as soon as reasonably practicable' and *mandatory* detention 'until...removed'—the High Court read restrictions pertaining to the purpose of the detention as ancillary to the purpose of removal. Although *Al Kateb v Godwin*[49] (6 August 2004) declines to read into the statute a temporal limitation of the *Hardial* or *Zadvydas* type (terminating detention when there is 'no real likelihood or prospect of removal in the reasonably foreseeable future'), it implicitly accepts[50] the Solicitor-General's submission that 'detention cannot continue indefinitely without bona fide efforts being made to remove the detainee, and the court has power to order that reasonable efforts be made' and to 'review...whether reasonable efforts are being made to effect removal'.[51] The majority Justices[52] vigorously reject the claim that extended or even indefinite delay is incompatible with maintaining the indispensable *purpose* of deporting the detainee. As Hayne J (Heydon J agreeing) puts it:

the most that could ever be said in a particular case where it is not now, and has not been, reasonably practicable to effect removal, is that there is *now* no country which will receive a particular non-citizen whom Australia seeks to remove, and it cannot *now* be predicted when that will happen.... That is not to say that it will *never* happen.

---

[48] Note, however, that ECHR Art. 5(1)(f), on its face, authorizes detention without limit of time 'to prevent [a person's] effecting an unauthorized entry into the country'.

[49] [2004] HCA 37, (2004) 219 CLR 562, decided simultaneously with *Minister for Immigration & Multicultural & Indigenous Affairs v Al Khafaji* [2004] HCA 38, (2004) 219 CLR 664, with the same majority (McHugh, Hayne, Callinan, and Heydon JJ) and minority.

[50] See [224–5] (Hayne J, Heydon J agreeing), [294] (Callinan J, who at [290–1], however, goes further and holds that the purpose of removing the detainee is to be presumed unless 'formally and unequivocally abandoned'—perhaps too narrow a version of the implied limitation by purpose).

[51] 219 CLR at 567 per Bennett S-G., who prefaced this with: 'Removal will never be impossible because it is always possible that there will be a change of regime or a change of mind in the subject country or that some other country will take an altruistic view.'

[52] Gleeson CJ, dissenting, also accepted that 'it cannot be said that it will never be reasonably practicable to remove [the detainee]'. But he considered that where removal is not 'currently practicable, and is not likely to become practicable in the foreseeable future', the detention's primary purpose of removal is 'in suspense' (para. 18), and that in respect of such cases the statute should be presumed not to have intended to authorize indefinite detention regardless of 'the circumstances of individual cases, including, in particular, danger to the community and likelihood of absconding' (para. 22).

Even a finding of '"no real likelihood or prospect of removal in the reasonably foreseeable future"...does not mean that continued detention is not for the purpose of subsequent removal' or that the purpose of detention for removal is spent.[53] What matters is that the executive keep trying to carry out their duty to remove, by taking what reasonable steps they can to accomplish what may at present seem not reasonably practicable.

Had *Al Kateb* been cited in *A v Home Secretary* (argued in October 2004), neither counsel nor Law Lords could have been as carefree as they were in treating the appellant detainees as persons who '*cannot*' be deported, a simplification which reaches its extreme in Baroness Hale of Richmond's summary: 'These foreigners are only being detained because they cannot be deported. They are just like a British national who cannot be deported'![54] The Australian majority judges, like the dissenters in *Zadvydas*, demonstrate that what is 'temporarily impossible', or 'not possible for the indefinite future', may tomorrow become possible because of some change of regime abroad, or a breakthrough in negotiations with some other state; and that therefore it would be quite wrong to treat either of these phrases (or other similar phrases) as equivalent to '[simply] impossible [in practice]'. Removal in such a situation (assuming always that the executive had not begun to treat removal as impossible, and ceased trying to work around the obstacles) would better be said to be 'prevented (temporarily or indefinitely)'. And that was the language of the statutory provision condemned, with no attention to the spectrum of situations it signified, in *A v Home Secretary*.

That condemnation took the form of a declaration of incompatibility with ECHR Arts 5 and 14, made effective in the United Kingdom by the Human Rights Act 1998 ('HRA'). So the requirements stated in *Hardial* are now reinforced by Art. 5(1)(f), permitting detention while 'action is being taken with a view to deportation'. In *Chahal v United Kingdom* (1996), the ECtHR had held that, if action is being taken with due diligence[55] with a view to deportation, Art. 5(1)(f) does *not* require that the detention be considered necessary, 'for example to prevent his committing an offence or

---

[53] 219 CLR at paras 229, 231. To the same effect is Callinan J at paras 290, 291 and in *Al Khafaji*, 219 CLR at para. 45:

> The reference of [the trial judge] to reasonable practicability and reasonable foreseeability was directed to the situation 'at present'. The Migration Act imposes no such temporal qualification. It is to purpose [that] attention must be paid, and the purpose of deportation has not been abandoned. As I have observed in *Al-Kateb*, in the nature of human and international affairs, long periods may be involved just as circumstances may change very quickly.

[54] *A v Home Secretary* [2004] UKHL 56, [2005] 2 AC 68, para. 235; see also paras 222 and 228; the simplification is explicit in paras 9 and 13 (Bingham), 84 (Nicholls), 126 (Hope), 162 and 188 (Rodger), and 210 (Walker).

[55] 23 EHHR 413 at para. 113.

fleeing'.[56] It held, moreover, that the proceedings for Chahal's deportation had been conducted with such diligence that four (indeed, over six) years' detention of the alien deportee was compatible with Art. 5(1)(f). And this despite the fact that, so the Court also held, the purpose of deporting him to his national territory, India, was at all relevant times incompatible with the requirements of Art. 3, prohibiting torture and ill-treatment. It was not unreasonable for the Secretary of State to have taken over thirteen months to deliberate about the alien's claim that his deportation to India would contravene Art. 3. Thus the question whether an alien 'cannot be deported' (because there is a 'real risk' of torture or ill-treatment) is not open and shut, but 'involves considerations of an extremely serious and weighty nature' and decisions that should not 'be taken hastily, without due regard to all the relevant issues and evidence'.[57]

Since 1998, of course, deportation 'contrary to' Art. 3 as read or misread by *Chahal*[58] is now 'impossible', if not strictly as a matter of law (though

---

[56] At para. 112.

[57] At para. 117. Lord Bingham's statement in *A v Secretary of State for Home Department* at para. 9 of what *Chahal* decided about Art. 5(1)(f) is mistaken or at best elliptical:

[the ECtHR] reasserted (para 113) that 'any deprivation of liberty under article 5(1)(f) will be justified only for as long as deportation proceedings are in progress'. In a case like Mr Chahal's, where deportation proceedings are precluded by article 3, article 5(1)(f) would not sanction detention because the non-nationals would not be 'a person against whom action is being taken with a view to deportation'.

In fact, however, the court held that, although Chahal's deportation was precluded by Art. 3, his detention for four or six years *was sanctioned* by Art. 5(1)(f) while the authorities took action to ascertain whether or not his deportation could be carried out compatibly with the United Kingdom's obligations. No doubt those authorities did not have the clear view of Art. 3 imposed in that case by the court. But even if they had had such a view, they might reasonably have taken steps, with all deliberate speed (on the part of the United Kingdom authorities) but perhaps lengthy in duration (not least if lengthened by the dilatoriness of foreign governments), to ascertain the risks and seek ways of obviating them by agreement with India or some other state.

[58] If *Chahal*'s rulings on Art. 5 are unhelpfully terse, its pronouncements on Art. 3, both in the majority and the principal dissenting judgments, are notably ill-reasoned. The absoluteness of a state's obligation not to engage in torture and other practices contrary to Art. 3 in no way entails that the person with such an absolute right has thereby the right not to be subjected to any form of treatment (e.g. deportation) that might have the foreseeable but unintended and unwelcome side effect of his being tortured or ill-treated by some other persons. All who seriously reflect upon normative absolutes recognize that they would entail intolerable paradoxes and deliberative incoherence unless their exceptionless prohibitions define the excluded conduct by reference to the *proximate intentions* (or *object*) of the person(s) they bind: see *MA* 68–74, 81–3. It is one thing for a state to deliver persons to another state *so as* to enable the latter to torture them, and quite another matter to remove/deliver them to another state with all practically possible precaution against their being tortured thereafter and with the sole object of removing the real threat their presence poses to the lives of people in the removing state. *Chahal*'s Art. 3 ruling treats the intentions of the removing state as completely irrelevant and declares that the deportee's activities, '*however undesirable or dangerous*, cannot be a material consideration' ([80], emphasis added). Taking into account Art. 3's extension beyond torture to 'degrading treatment', and the breadth of that concept in recent ECtHR jurisprudence, *Chahal*'s ruling on Art. 3 is juridically unsound by over-breadth, and shocking to conscience by its indifference to the human rights threatened *by* the would-be deportee. [The same is regrettably true of the ECtHR Grand Chamber's unanimous ratification of this central ruling in *Chahal* in *Saadi v Italy* [2008] ECHR 179, 49 EHRR 30; on all the main

that is how the courts unhesitatingly treat it), at least as a matter of treaty obligation. But even as it articulated this rule, *Chahal* made it clear that the rule's application to particular cases may involve contingencies which preclude, as unacceptably simplistic, any notion that deportation is from the outset impossible. Rather, the existence of a 'real risk' that the deportee would be tortured or ill-treated will in various cases not be so indisputable as to render deportation (and thus detention with a view to removal) impossible from the outset or at any definable moment thereafter. So this is yet another way in which the 'possibility' or 'impossibility' of removal, and of having a purpose of removing, is often relative, provisional, qualified and arguable.

V. THE CONSTITUTIONAL PRINCIPLE'S RATIONALE

What, then, is the rationale or, in the more rigid language of ECHR jurisprudence, 'legitimating aim', of the principle of nationality-differentiated risk-acceptability? What basic aspect of the common good does it represent, promote or protect?

The principle informs two undoubted rules, not merely one: foreigners can be deported; nationals cannot. Associated with the latter is the rule that nationals cannot be deprived of their citizenship if doing so would leave them without a nationality. The rules signal a fundamental understanding and disposition: the human community is politically and juridically organized into states, groups that are national political communities ('nations'). Whoever and wherever one may be, one is both entitled and bound to regard oneself as belonging to one of them: statelessness is an anomaly, a disability, and presumptively an injustice, to be systematically minimized.[59]

What constitutes such a political community? Aristotle famously tried out the hypothesis that a *polis* (state) is a set of people given identity-establishing *form* by a constitution (*politeia*), with the entailment that the identity of the *polis* (state) changes when its constitution changes, say from

points the submissions of the United Kingdom, intervening, were sound but rejected by the Court with the mantra that Art. 3 is absolute (sc. in all its extensions and applications however extended or indirect).]

[59] Measures for rectifying the anomaly are instituted by the Convention relating to the Status of Stateless Persons 1954 (ratified by the United Kingdom in 1959 and in force since 1960), which provides for the state of their lawful residence to treat them so far as possible as other aliens, and looks (Art. 32) towards eventual 'assimilation and naturalization', subject (Art. 2) to the stateless person's duties 'to the country in which he finds himself', in particular to 'conform to its laws and regulations as well as to measures taken for the maintenance of public order'.

a tyranny to a democracy. But this will not do, as Aristotle tacitly concedes by concluding his discussion with the question whether agreements entered into and debts incurred by the state under the previous constitution can rightly be repudiated (or regarded as nullities) by the new state—a question which he promises but fails to try to answer.[60] Working out the implications of Kelsen's and Hart's accounts of legal systems, Joseph Raz and I, quite independently, concluded that a legal system's subsisting unity through time cannot be explained without foundational reference to the group whose legal system it is.[61]

To be sure, groups with a complex and far-reaching membership and purpose such as a worldwide and ecclesial religion may reasonably organize and count themselves as having a legal system, parallel to and in principle compatible with the legal systems of the states in which their adherents are citizens. And those states are appropriately many and particular, not universal. For just as experience shows compellingly that the resources on which human life and well-being depend are best husbanded, developed, and made available by a system of appropriation of particular resources to particular owners,[62] so experience compellingly shows—and the *international* order by its structures and regulating principles confirms— that human persons need to live in polities or states, political communities which hold as their own a defined territory subject to a national legal system defining, inter alia, a national constitution.

About this need we can and should be still more specific. Addressing an ethnically and culturally diverse audience in Germany, Raz showed why political societies need a common bond. They authoritatively require individuals to make sacrifices for the benefit of other members: witness redistributive taxation and all the other institutions of the welfare state. But 'the willingness to share is not purchased easily. Without it political society soon disintegrates, or has to rely on extensive force and coercion.' And this willingness to share itself cannot be maintained without a common culture, grounding the needed 'ability of people to feel for others', which 'depends on their ability to understand and empathise with other people's experiences, aspirations and anxieties'. Thus the political unity presupposed by any welfare state

depends on people's free and willing identification with the political society they belong to: on the fact that they feel German, that their sense of their own identity

---

[60] *Pol.* III.3: 1276a7–b15; *Aquinas* 28, 53.
[61] *CLS* 101–5, 188, 210; and essay IV.21 (1971a).
[62] See *NLNR* 170–1 (and see n. 35 above on the defeasibility of all such appropriations).

as German is totally instinctive and unproblematic. And it depends on the fact that they are proud to be German.[63]

States, occupying valuable territory as they do, can be confronted, moreover, with challenges more urgent and far-reaching, more existential, than maintaining the welfare state. These challenges too will call upon their members' sense of identification with their fellow members—upon the 'solidarity among citizens that', as David Miller argues, 'democratic politics requires'.[64] Much recent political theory shows how equal laws, public probity, impartial government, social justice, and democratic deliberation towards the undertaking of collective commitments and obligations and international action all depend upon—and in turn foster—a generalized trust sufficient to outweigh *competing* bonds of kin, caste, religion, or ethnicity, a level of trust and common sympathies attainable only within bounded political communities, nation-states.[65] The distinction between nationals and aliens is an indispensable framework for articulating, expressing, ratifying, and demanding such willingness to share, such awareness of being part owner of a shared inheritance and future,[66] such integration in and assimilation to *this* nation-state rather than some other.

But that willingness, as joint and common inheritors, to share a common fate, promote a common life, and accept and contribute towards common burdens and benefits, should not be conceived as suppressing the liberties of individuals, families, and other associations to occupy their own space and enjoy, as of right, their own freedom of initiative, self-direction, and self-determination. Such freedoms entail, as a side effect, the unintended but real creating of risks to others and to the common life. (This reciprocity underpins the reciprocity of protection and subjection that *Calvin's Case* articulated in the language of allegiance, language which should not obscure either the duties of governors or the truth that everyone's root political and legal-moral obligations are not so fundamentally to our rulers or institutions of governance as to our fellow subjects.[67]) The

[63] Raz, 'Multiculturalism' at 202–3. Since policies of assimilation or integration may be intended precisely to preserve the benefits, for all, of national solidarity which are so cogently described by Raz, his further thesis that such policies insult the members of immigrant cultures is mistaken.

[64] Miller, *Citizenship & National Identity*, 62.

[65] See Canovan, *Nationhood & Political Theory*, 44 and passim. To witness an unabashedly national pride—patriotism—being rooted in history and used as a ground of judicial reasoning and decision, see e.g. *A v Secretary of State for the Home Department (No. 2)* [2005] UKHL 71, [2006] 2 AC 221, at [82], [99], [152], [171]; or again *A v Secretary of State for the Home Department* [2004] UKHL 56, [2005] 2 AC 68 at [86], [96] (Lord Hoffmann).

[66] See Canovan, 54–75; also Raz, *Ethics in the Public Domain*, 172–3, on a common culture as needed for the civic solidarity which in turn is 'essential to the existence of a well-ordered political society' (172). [On this, and the issues in nn. 63–65, see essay II.7.]

[67] *NLNR* 359.

benefits of those politically (legally) respected and defended freedoms, and the burdens of the attendant risks, are part of what we share as members of this political community. And this is the rationale of the principle that we should be willing to accept from fellow members a level of adverse risk that we need not accept from non-members.

Here our constitutional law intervenes to remind us that while they are among us, non-members are to be treated as members so far as is compatible with maintaining the core of the distinction between members and non-members—between members by right and members by revocable permission. So our justifiable lesser willingness to accept risks from non-members warrants, not a set of special duties, liabilities, or disabilities of foreigners within the realm, but only their individual liability to be removed from the nation's territory and, with a view to and pending that removal, to be kept apart from the community by humane detention or control.[68]

The problem of the indefinitely 'irremovable' foreigner, as in *Zadvydas v Davis*, in *Al Kateb v Godwin*, and in *A v Home Secretary*, is a boundary problem of the intersection of these two building blocks of our constitutional scheme. The argumentation in the American and Australian judgments, majority and minority alike, reveals the problem's contours perceptively;[69] *A v Home Secretary* does not.

Beyond that boundary problem there lies, of course, the deeper challenge to constitutional order and theory posed by *nationals* who regard their nationality as a form of alienage because, doubtless like some if not all the detainees in *A v Home Secretary*, they believe their true Nation lies altogether beyond—but is ordained to have dominion over—the bounds and territories, and the constitutional principles and rights,[70] that frame and structure our nation's common good.

---

[68] The liability of *enemy aliens*—a category not considered in this essay, and hitherto conceived of as nationals of a state at war with ours—to statutorily authorized detention in time of war might be understood as a form which that liability to removal reasonably takes when circumstances prevent (or make unreasonable) actual removal.

[69] So too does the Canadian Supreme Court's decision in *Charkaoui v Canada* [2007] SC 9, which accepts that there need be no breach of human or constitutional rights in open-ended detention for the purposes of deportation provided that regular review keeps all factors in view, not least the burden on the detainee compared with any remaining danger he presents to national security or the safety of any person: see paras 110, 126–7.

[70] See the Cairo Declaration on Human Rights in Islam, unanimously approved by 45 states at the Nineteenth Islamic Conference of Foreign Ministers, 5 August 1990, English trans. UN Doc. A/CONF.157/PC/62/Add.18 (UN GAOR, World Conference on Human Rights., 4th Sess., Agenda Item 5) (1993), especially preamble and Arts 10, 19, 22–5; and see generally essay II.7; essay V.1 (2009c) sec. VII; essay V.4 sec. VII (2006a at 122–7); and essay 2009e, sec. 4.

Part Two
Justice and Punishment

10

HART'S PHILOSOPHY OF PUNISHMENT*

Beneath the rich contemporary reference of these essays there moves the ground-swell of time in western civilisation. Our guides through 'doctrines' and 'theories' are the never stressed but ever present sea-marks which give Hart's collection its settled rhythm: the 'now' contrasted with the 'then', the 'older' with the 'newer', the 'traditional' with the 'modern', the 'antiquated' and 'outmoded' with the 'nowadays...' Still, this rhythm is not to be misunderstood. The classical or the traditional or the merely antiquated and outmoded usually turn out to be the doctrines and theories of eighteenth-century enlightenment. And the 'latest opinions' are interpreted, more often than not, as invitations to a 'descent into Erewhon' or the Brave New World, and as such are politely declined. The omnipresent 'we', the 'modern men', of the book are stood between the fallacies of a past that was proud of its modernity and the menaces of a future that is proud of its modernity, too. So strong a sense of recurrent error and illusion commonly promotes a general scepticism; but if there is a moral to the book it is that the scepticisms of enlightenment are to be resisted as fallacious or menacing. The word 'scepticism' is used and repeated in almost every essay. Of course, Professor Hart is too urbane either to give the word itself any pejorative force or to express the moral we have suggested. Indeed, he might not thank us for suggesting it. But at the end of the day the reader will find that Hart has consistently been neutral against scepticism. One's only doubt can be whether this Irish sort of neutrality is quite enough to restore order to the intellectual chaos of the age. Hart would be the first to agree with Sir Henry Maine, the first holder of his own chair of Jurisprudence: 'All theories on the subject of punishment have more or less broken down, and we are at sea as to first principles.'

---

* 1968a ('Old and New in Hart's Philosophy of Punishment': a review of Hart, *Punishment and Responsibility*).

I

The nine essays were originally published between 1957 and 1967, and it might be possible to trace certain lines of development of doctrine. But, as Hart hints by arranging them out of chronological order, the exercise would not be too profitable. The main themes are few, simple, and consistent. The general justifying aim of punishment is its beneficial social consequences, but any morally tolerable account of the institution of punishment will have to recognize that justice 'forbids the use of one human being for the benefit of others except in return for his voluntary action against them' (p. 22). Thus there is a principle of retribution governing, not the aim, but the distribution of punishment. This principle is not explicable on purely utilitarian lines, and Bentham's attempt to provide a utilitarian explication, on the ground that punishment of involuntary breaches of law must be inefficacious as a deterrent, 'is in fact a spectacular non sequitur' (p. 19; Hart's argument is repeated in a strikingly rich diversity of formulations on pp. 40–3, 77, 179, and 230). Since the retributive principle of distribution of punishment is the rationale of legal excuses, the relevance of excusing conditions must be defended against determinist sceptics (ch. II). Since, on the other hand, the retributive principle is neither the justification of punishment nor a 'natural' measure of its severity, the question of the death penalty is to be resolved in the light of the (qualified) utilitarian demand that any penalty, being prima facie evil as a pain, must be justified by positive evidence that it is required in order to minimize crime (ch. III). Again, the concept of voluntariness underlying the retributive rationale of distribution and excuses must be distinguished from the eighteenth-century theory (adopted by many English legal writers) that criminal responsibility is predicated on the occurrence of desire for muscular contractions, followed by the contractions, followed by foreseen consequences. In truth, Hart says, a movement is not relevantly involuntary unless it occurred 'though the agent had not reason for moving his body in that way', and omissions are not relevantly involuntary unless the agent either was unable to do any conscious action or was unable to make the particular movements required by law (ch. IV). Indeed, the whole notion of *mens* ought to be extended beyond the rationalistic elements of desire and foresight, so as to include the capacities and powers of normal persons to think about and control their conduct. So scepticism about the justifiability of imposing criminal liability for negligence is unwarranted (ch. VI). Similarly, the rationalistic and utilitarian scepticism about the possibility of deterring negligent conduct is unwarranted, since threats may not only guide one's deliberations but may also goad one to think (ch. V).

Thus far, the argument has amounted to a sustained reconstruction of classical and traditional notions of action, responsibility, and liability against enthusiastic doubts deriving from eighteenth-century enlightenment (This is not how Hart presents the issue: in his presentation 'tradition' usually denotes the conceptions that have come down to us from the enlightenment. Plato is the only classical thinker to appear, and then only in the guise of a reformer who condemned all backward looking in the treatment and cure of criminals). But the argument then turns against the modern scepticisms about 'the whole institution of punishment so far as it contains elements which differentiate it from a system of purely forward-looking social hygiene' (p. 193). This progressivist scepticism in large part stems from 'the ideology of science' (p. 179), in the name of which we are invited to abandon the idea that a man could, or could be known to have been able to, have done something which he in fact did not do. The invitation is to be refused; fairness and the value of individual liberty are sufficient to vindicate the principle of responsibility. Human nature in human society being as it actually is, human movements are interpreted as manifestations of intentions and choices, and the absence of intention or choice, or of capacity or opportunity to intend or choose, does and should modify our assessments of responsibility and liability (ch. VII). To say this does not imply the retributive theory of punishment so repugnant to progressives,

for though we must seek a moral licence for punishing a man in his voluntary conduct in breaking the law, the punishment we are then licensed to use may still be directed solely to preventing future crimes on his part or on others' and not to 'retribution' (ch. VIII, p. 208).

II

So Hart's essays, though free from party and polemical spirit, provide a resourceful defence of some main lines of the traditional (that is, Greek and Judaeo-Christian) moral conceptions of punishment and responsibility, as against progressivisms old and new. Their philosophical underpinnings will therefore attract some scrutiny.

Hart does not waste much time on expositions of philosophical method. Considerations of method do, however, rise to the surface in his attack on John Austin's theory of action. This theory, as we noted, 'splits an ordinary action into three constituents: a desire for muscular contractions followed by the contractions, followed by foreseen consequences' (p. 101). This account, says Hart, 'is really nothing more than an out-dated fiction'. Why? Because 'such a division is quite at variance with the ordinary man's experience and the way in which his own actions appear to him'. For only on some special occasions (for example, when a gymnastic instructor orders one to raise one's arm and contract the muscles of the upper arm) would it be appropriate to say that one desired to and did contract one's muscles. 'I draw attention to this not as a matter of language, but because language here does usefully mark a vital, factual distinction which the theory we are criticizing ignores' (p. 102).

Before commenting on this, let us take one other passage which displays Hart's philosophical method, this time employed in the attack on contemporaries such as Lady Wootton.

> Human society is a society of persons; and persons do not view themselves or each other merely as so many bodies moving in ways which are sometimes harmful and have to be prevented or altered. Instead persons interpret each other's movements as manifestations of intention and choices... If one person hits another, the person struck does not think of the other as just a cause of pain to him... If the blow was light but deliberate, it has a significance for the person struck quite different from an accidental much heavier blow... the judgment that the blow was deliberate will elicit fear, indignation, anger, resentment... [and] the same judgment will enter into deliberations about my future voluntary conduct towards you... This is how human nature in human society actually is and as yet we have no power to alter it (pp. 182–3).

Reflection on the foregoing sets of remarks will forestall many facile opinions about 'linguistic' philosophy or jurisprudence. Not only is Hart not examining language for its own sake—he also is examining 'factual distinctions' which language may 'usefully mark' 'here', but which in other contexts language, one supposes, might misleadingly mark or fail to mark. Hart is adverting directly to features of human nature: (1) 'the ordinary man's experience'; (2) the way in which his own and other people's actions 'appear to him' or are 'interpreted' or 'judged' by him; (3) the responses ('not voluntary' p. 183) which these judgments 'will elicit', and (4) the range of judgments, based on 'deliberations', as to the 'significance' of the actions for 'future voluntary conduct' towards the actor. Using the word 'experience' perhaps (but perhaps not) more broadly than in the preceding sentence, we can say that Hart is engaging us with a full-scale (though unstressed) philosophy of experience, and is appealing directly to our own personal experience for verification. As against the Procrustean doctrinaires who have troubled philosophy and jurisprudence, attention to language has had the salutary effect of promoting attention to language-users and to the full range of experience grounding their uses of language.

In this enterprise, Hart is assisted (and assists his readers) by attention to the wealth of reflection embodied in the law. For lawyers are working close to vivid and commonplace occurrences and actions, and must work with a shared and generally intelligible stock of deliberate assessments of those occurrences and actions. Thus both 'experience' and 'doctrine' are subject to continual refinement and control. Aberration is of course possible. But at almost every point Hart sees fit to steer 'theory' back towards the doctrine accepted in at least the practice, if not always the explanations, of the courts. Hart might agree with Aquinas's suggestion that common-lawyers, as a whole, should get the benefit of Aristotle's maxim: 'we ought to attend to the undemonstrated sayings and opinions of experienced and older people and of people of practical wisdom not less than to demonstrations; for because experience has given them an eye they see aright' in human affairs (*NE* 1143b11 [; *ST* I–II q. 95 a. 2 ad 4]).

But does Hart go far enough in his pursuit of human experience and nature? I think not. Since the sense of doctrinal ebb and flow in the time of western civilization is so strong throughout the book, it may be as well to tackle the question tangentially, by looking into Hart's references to the classical origins of the civilization. These references are to Plato—fittingly, since the range of experiences of the western soul is adumbrated so fully and influentially in Plato. Hart suggests, as we noted before, that Plato

> thought it superstitious to look back and go into questions of responsibility or the previous history of a crime except when it might throw light on what was needed to cure the criminal (pp. 51–2; 163).

The principal citation is to *Protagoras* 324. Readers will feel some misgivings when they observe that the opinion there expressed is that of Protagoras the sophist, the incompleteness and inadequate basis of whose views on the teachability of virtue Socrates points up throughout the dialogue. The other reference is to *Laws* 861, 865; but these are the very passages in which Plato is struggling to establish the previously unelaborated doctrine that involuntary harms are not wrongs. And the 'cure' which the Athenian Stranger posits as the end of human punishment is by no means the 'cure' proposed by the modern reformer; for some criminals the cure is above all death: *Laws* 855, 957. Moreover, the preambles to human laws are to state the 'true doctrine' that beyond the grave the criminal will pay the natural penalty of being done by as he did: *Laws* 870, 872, 905. The great eschatological myths of the *Republic*, the *Gorgias* and the *Phaedo* do indeed stress punishment's cathartic and deterrent ends. But overshadowing everything is simply their drama of the restoration of order by rewarding the just, who will have suffered in this life, and punishing the wicked, who may in a sense have prospered. While Christianity brought this retributive function into prominence, by eliminating the myth of the cycles and metempsychosis, it was able confidently to adopt the Platonic maxims that punishment is never to be inflicted for harm's sake (*Laws* 854) and that what is once done can never be undone (*Laws* 934). For Christianity retained the fundamental Platonic experiences which Protagoras did not mention: the experience of the disorder effected by crime, in the soul of the criminal and as between the criminal and society (or cosmos or God); and the sense that this disorder can be, not in itself eliminated, but absorbed into an overarching order of justice in the fullness of time (for Plato the time of the cycles, for Christianity the judgment beyond time). All this is radically distinct from, though not incompatible with, the reformer's interest in the disorder revealed by crime in the soul of the criminal.

These conceptions of transcendental retribution are mentioned here because they bring to light features shared by the ordinary man's more mundane sense of order, disorder, and the restoration of order in the soul and in society, all viewed in the perspective of time. For the past, present, and future of the criminal and his fellows are seen as a whole, and this whole is experienced as disorderly (quite apart from deterrence and reform) if, for no good reason, no adjustments in the criminal's position are made in response to the crime. Everyone concerned with justice admits that fair shares are to be assessed in view of the whole (set of values and disvalues) available and the whole (set of people) to whom it is available. Retributive justice simply sees the whole in the further dimension of time, as does anyone who assesses fairness or justice or rightness in terms such as merit, reward, desert, praise, blame, thanks, remorse, or who shares the all but universal sense of the disorder of the prosperity of the unrighteous.

Hart, on the other hand, wants to deny that retribution can be a justifying aim of punishment. It is not that he lacks or ignores the experience of order, disorder, and the restoration of order. On the contrary, he has in *The Concept of Law* given us an elegant account of the order of justice ('an artificial equality' created by a 'structure of reciprocal rights and obligations'), of the disorder effected, not by all harm, but by harm 'wantonly', intentionally, or negligently inflicted, and of the restoration of order by, for example, paying back to the victim something equivalent to the 'profit' which was gained ('not literally') at the victim's 'expense' by the wrongdoer's own 'indulging his wish' to injure (pp. 160–1). Indeed, this notion of paying 'the price of some satisfaction obtained from breach of law' recurs in *Punishment and Responsibility* (pp. 47, 23, 130). Hart uses the notion in defending his theory that justice in distribution of punishment demands that punishment be retributive in the sense that only voluntary wrongdoers should be punished. What he never explains is why it should not be an aim of punishment to restore the order of justice, by getting the criminal to pay a price for the ill-gotten satisfactions he obtained in indulging his wish to injure and in preferring his will to the will of society—satisfactions which his law-abiding fellows have denied themselves. (Moreover, Hart does not explain why there should be only one aim of punishment, not several: there is something suspiciously rigid about his differentiation between Definition, General Justifying Aim (singular), and Distribution.) Alternatively, one may ask why retribution, understood as the restoration of an order of fairness between citizens, should not be included within Hart's utilitarian General Justifying Aim. For that aim is 'beneficial consequences to society'; but is it not an integral component of the good of society that there should be maintained a continually adjusted order of fairness between citizens, so that ill-gotten 'satisfactions' (retaining here a terminology perhaps open to criticism) are not enjoyed with impunity and so that enjoyment of the benefits of social living is conditioned on, and proportioned to, willingness to play the social game? (We can agree with Hart [p. 161] that 'there is no natural relationship to be discerned between wickedness and punishment of a certain degree or kind'. But this is not a modern insight. Aristotle and Aquinas insisted that, though it is a principle of natural law that crimes should be punished, there is no natural measure of punishment; the degree and kind of punishment is in fact a traditional stock-example of what is left to pure positive law: *NE* 1134b22; *ST* I–II, q.95, a.2c.)

If the use of the term 'experience' in the foregoing remarks should appear philosophically troublesome, attention will at least have been drawn to parallel problems in Hart's technical apparatus. We have observed that in describing human action and practical responses to human action, Hart employs such terms as 'experience', 'interpretation', 'significance'; and in speaking of justice he regularly talks of its 'principles'. But in speaking of retribution (as an aim of punishment) he regularly uses the term 'theory' (sometimes enclosing it in inverted commas, as a sign perhaps of uneasiness). What is the relation between experience, interpretation, principle, and theory? (Not to mention the much relied-upon 'convictions which most of us share'—another case of heeding 'the undemonstrated sayings...' perhaps?) Hart says that 'the absolutist [sc. retributionist] must simply expose for inspection and acceptance his claim' about the true moral basis of punishment (p. 75). But that is a fate no moralist can escape in the presentation of his 'claims'. It can be doubted, however, whether a mature ethical epistemology will retain the curiously external notions of 'exposing claims' for 'inspection and acceptance'.

I think it is at least clear that for Hart, retribution as an aim of punishment is 'mere' theory; his essays convey little of any experience of which 'retribution' in this strong sense could be an appropriate symbolization.

His statement of 'retributive theory', even in the pages devoted to it in the last essay, is always notably flat, brief, and unhelpful: usually he mentions no more than 'the return of suffering for moral evil voluntarily done' (p. 231) or the theory that 'wicked conduct injuring others itself calls for punishment' (p. 234; cf. pp. 8, 52, 81, 165). The repeated terms 'evil' and 'wickedness' contrive to make the 'theory' sound distant and archaic. The lack of variation in his statements of the theory contrasts sharply with the fecundity of formulation we noticed in his argument against Bentham. It is easy to see what Hart has made his own and what remains external to him, a mere item in the baggage of western culture, to be treated in unusually gentlemanly fashion but, in the last resort, without sympathy.

Finally, one must point to relics of unreconstructed utilitarianism left over from (may we not say?) an earlier time. Notable among these is the definition of punishment in terms of pain and pleasure (p. 4); this definition prejudices all the subsequent remarks on justification against the possibility of retribution as a justifying aim, since retributive accounts of punishment will prefer to define it in terms of subjection of wayward will, or perhaps denial of benefits of social living. Another relic is the unexamined distinction between 'act' and 'result' or 'outcome' in the discussion of the 'Catholic doctrine of double effect' (pp. 122–4). These leftovers are the more visible in the light of Hart's remarkable, if incompletely successful, rethinking of so much of the (may we not say?) classical theory of punishment and responsibility.

11

THE RESTORATION OF RETRIBUTION*

In 'Three Mistakes About Retributivism', Jeffrie G. Murphy argues that the retributivist claim that crime deserves punishment may be taken, not as the assertion of an intuited, primitive, and unanalysed proposition, but as one particular application of, or theorem within, a general theory of political obligation. Thus, if political obligation is based on the justice of reciprocity or fair play in the sharing of the burdens and benefits of social life, then crime may be analysed as gaining (or putting oneself in a position to gain: Murphy is not specific about this) an unfair advantage over those who, even when they do not desire to do so, voluntarily obey the law; and punishment can be analysed as the attempt 'to maintain the proper balance between benefit and obedience by insuring that there is no profit in criminal wrongdoing' (p. 166); and the general principle of fairness between citizens then justifies punishment for crime.

This argument is clearly superior to appeals to unanalysed 'desert'. It can be further strengthened if certain obscurities are cleared up, and if it is removed from a strictly Kantian setting.

As I have already hinted parenthetically, Murphy's exposition is obscure about *how* the criminal profits from his crime. Murphy says: 'If a man does profit from his own wrongdoing, from his disobedience, this is *unfair* or *unjust*, not merely to his victim, but to all those who have been obedient' (p. 167). This formulation provokes the question: *When* does the criminal unfairly profit? Is it at the moment when he commits the crime (in which case it might be more exact to speak of punishment, not so much as *maintaining* a proper balance between benefit and obedience, but rather as *restoring* a balance upset)? Or is it when he is allowed to avoid paying back what Murphy calls (p. 168) 'the costs in life and labour of certain kinds of crime'? Murphy might seem to favour the latter view, since he speaks of calculating first these costs of crime and

---

* 1972a.

then 'the costs of punishments', 'so that retribution could be understood as *preventing* criminal profit' (p. 168, emphasis added)—as if the unfair profit arose from a wrongful failure to make restitution (not, of course, restitution to the victim, which is quite another matter, but rather 'to all those who have been obedient'). The latter view is more or less the view that retributivism is a theory of moral accounting, connected, as William Kneale has argued, 'with an attempt to assimilate all moral obligations to the obligations undertaken by borrowers'.[1] And such an attempt is none too plausible.

These obscurities about the nature and occasion of the criminal's profiting can be cleared up if we go further than Murphy, and say that:

(1) what the criminal gains in the act of committing crime (whatever the size and nature of the loot, if any, and indeed quite apart from the success or failure of his overall purpose) is the advantage of indulging a (wrongful) self-preference, of permitting himself an excessive freedom in choosing—this advantage (of exercising a wider freedom and of acting according to one's tastes: I vary the formulations to avoid any suggestion of an esoteric 'doctrine') being something that his law-abiding fellow citizens have denied themselves insofar as they have chosen to conform their will (habits and choices) to the law even when they would 'prefer' not to;

(2) this advantage is gained at the time of the crime, because and insofar as the crime is (as may indeed not be the case of all or many of the performances that lead to a *legally* correct finding of 'criminal' guilt) a free and 'responsible' exercise of self-will; the wrongfulness of gaining this advantage is the specifically relevant moral turpitude adverted to in the retributivist's talk of criminal 'guilt'; and the advantage is one that cannot be lost, unless and until

(3) the criminal has the disadvantage of having his wayward will restricted in its freedom by being subjected to the representative 'will of society' (the 'will' which he disregarded in disregarding the law) through the process of punishment; a punishment is thus to be defined not, formally speaking, in terms of the infliction of pain (nor as incarceration), but rather in terms of the subjection of will (normally, but not necessarily, effected through the denial of benefits and advantages of social living: compulsory employment on some useful work which the criminal would not of himself have chosen to do would satisfy the definition).

---

[1] Kneale, 'The Responsibility of Criminals'.

Such an account of the relation between crime and retributive punishment is both younger and older than Kant's. Main elements of the account are implicit in H.L.A. Hart's account of restorative justice in *The Concept of Law* (1961), which may be rendered as an account (i) of an order of justice (that is, an 'artificial equality' created by a 'structure of reciprocal rights and obligations'); (ii) of the disorder brought about, not by all harm, but by harm 'wantonly, intentionally or negligently' inflicted; and (iii) of the restoration of order by, for example, paying back to the victim something equivalent to the 'profit' which was gained ('not literally') at the victim's 'expense', by the wrongdoer's 'indulging his wish' to injure or by his 'not sacrificing his ease to the duty of taking adequate precautions'.[2] Indeed, this notion of paying 'the price of some satisfaction obtained by breach of law' recurs in Hart's essays, *Punishment and Responsibility* (1968).[3] But Hart omits to recognize, in *The Concept of Law*, that it is not just the victim and the wrongdoer who should be put back on a footing of equality: the 'satisfaction' which the wrongdoer gains is an advantage not only as against the victim but also as against all those who might have been wrongdoers but restrained themselves. This Hart partially recognizes on p. 131 of *Punishment and Responsibility*, when he notes that, in connection with the punishment of unsuccessful attempts to commit crime,

it is pointed out that in some cases the successful completion of a crime may be a source of gratification, and in the case of theft of actual gain, and in such cases to punish the successful criminal more severely may be one way of depriving him of these illicit satisfactions which the unsuccessful have never had.

Again we must note what Hart fails to observe: that it is not merely the unsuccessful criminals, but also all the law-abiding, who have never had 'these illicit satisfactions'. What is most odd, however, is that Hart should describe as 'an interesting addition to the theories of punishment' the principle that 'the wicked should not be allowed to profit by their crimes'— surely that has always been at the root of people's sense of the rightness of punishment as a *response* to crime, and Murphy is right to restore it to its lost prominence in the philosophical debate.

So much for a very recent (and partial and hesitant) account of retribution. Much earlier, in *Summa Theologiae* I–II q.87 a.6, Aquinas raised the question whether liability to punishment should persist after the criminal's activity is finished, on the assumption that the criminal does not wish to engage in crime again. An objector is put up to suggest that, as Aristotle said, all

---

[2] *CL* 160–1 (*CL*² 165). [3] *Punishment and Responsibility*, 47 (and cf. 23, 130).

punishments are medicinal, and such a criminal is in no need of a cure. Aquinas replies (I compress his remarks slightly):

> Criminal activity makes a man worthy of punishment [*reum poenae*] in so far as he violates the order of justice [*ordinem justitiae*]. He does not return to that order except by way of some sort of punitive recompense [*per quandam recompensationem poenae*] which brings [him] back [into] the equality of justice [*aequalitatem justitiae*]; anyone who has indulged his will more than he ought [*plus voluntati suae indulsit quam debuit*], by transgressing the law, should either of his own accord or without his consent undergo something opposed to what he wills—so that the equality of justice may thus be restored [*reintegretur*].

And this restoration of the order of fairness lends point and justification to the punishment even of the 'reformed' criminal under discussion.

On this view, as amplified by those clarifications of Murphy's views which I have offered above, we can say (what Hart is so concerned to deny in *Punishment and Responsibility*) that the restoration of a fair distribution of advantages and disadvantages as between citizens is *an aim* of punishment. Of course, the crime and the harm it causes can never be *undone*. But that fair distribution (or balance or order) whose disruption is entailed by the now past crime can be subsumed under a new order by an adjustment of the criminal's position relative to his fellows—an adjustment in the precisely relevant respect, that is, by deprivations in respect of his wrongfully (but necessarily profitably) indulged disposition towards self-preference—so that, taking a period of time rather than one or another moment in the life of a society, a long-term order of fairness is maintained (by renovation). Naturally, it would be better if the order of fairness were never disrupted; but often it is, and at the end of a period one should be able to look back over the *whole* period and say that, because of the adjustments that were made in response to criminal disruption of that order, no one has (overall and taking the period as a whole) been disadvantaged unfairly by attempting to live in strict accordance with that basic order of fairness. Punishment is forward-looking or future-regarding (though not in the 'utilitarian' sense), in that it is imposed, *during* the period in question, in contemplation of that future backward-looking scrutiny from the vantage point of the end of the period.

Finally, for Kant retribution is both an unconditional, categorical imperative and a *lex talionis*, demanding like for like. And Murphy says (without guarding against the ambiguity of 'regardless') that 'retributive theories of punishment maintain that criminal guilt merits or deserves punishment, regardless of considerations of social utility' (p. 166). But in the classical and more standard view, represented by Aquinas for example, while it is clear that crime should ordinarily be punished, the questions of time, place, circumstance, and degree are a matter of pure positive law, and cannot be determined by abstract moral reasoning. (See, for example, *Summa Theologiae* I–II q.95 a.2.) And this position seems more reasonable than Kant's. For although fairness is a component of the overall social good, it is only a component, and it would be silly to sacrifice important social goods simply to secure a scrupulously restored order of fairness. Indeed, if it is unfair to law-abiding citizens not to punish criminals, it is more unfair to them to punish criminals when it is clear that the punishment will lead to more crime, more unfairness by criminals, and more danger and disadvantage to law-abiding citizens. Thus, while the retributive restoration of the order of fairness is the most specific and essential aim of punishment, it is not necessarily the most important aim in the practical sense of determining the forms and degrees of punishments.

In short, where Hart is content to say that it is *unfair to punish the innocent*, and where Kant is keen to insist that it is *wrong not to punish the guilty*, we should say that it is more reasonable morally (and more representative of western common sense) to argue that it is *unfair not to aim at punishing the guilty* (or, that it is unfair *ceteris paribus* not to punish the guilty)—but also that fairness is not the sole ground of political obligation and so need not be pursued regardless of consequences. And this account of the aim of punishment (as distinct from other social institutions and practices, such as the incarceration of enemy aliens and of lunatics) explains why it is unfair to *punish* the innocent, the insane, the infant, and those 'suffering from diminished [capacity-] responsibility',[†] even when it may be right to treat such people to coercive restrictions on other grounds and with other aims. For it is a principal weakness of any theory, such as Hart's, which denies that retribution is a justifiable aim of punishment (while asserting that the distribution of punishments is to be limited by a retributive principle), that such a theory cannot explain why the retributive principle of distribution is so important in punishment while it is of no importance in other coercive social institutions, given that (as that theory is keen to assert, and as I am here concerned to deny) punishment shares with these other social institutions the same exclusively 'utilitarian' aim(s).

NOTE

[†] *Diminished responsibility*... (text and n. 4). Homicide Act 1957, s. 2 provides:

> 2. *Persons suffering from diminished responsibility*
>   (1) Where a person kills or is a party to the killing of another, he shall not be convicted of murder if he was suffering from such abnormality of mind (whether arising from a

[4] Cf. Homicide Act 1957 (UK), s. 2 (sidenote/heading).[†]

condition of arrested or retarded development of mind or any inherent causes or induced by disease or injury) as substantially impaired his mental responsibility for his acts and omissions in doing or being a party to the killing.

(2) On a charge of murder, it shall be for the defence to prove that the person charged is by virtue of this section not liable to be convicted of murder.

(3) A person who but for this section would be liable, whether as principal or as accessory, to be convicted of murder shall be liable instead to be convicted of manslaughter.

Subsection (1) is amended by Coroners and Justice Act 2009, so that, under the same heading about 'Persons suffering from diminished responsibility', it reads:

(1) A person ('D') who kills or is a party to the killing of another is not to be convicted of murder if D was suffering from an abnormality of mental functioning which—

    (a) arose from a recognised medical condition,

    (b) substantially impaired D's ability to do one or more of the things mentioned in subsection (1A), and

    (c) provides an explanation for D's acts and omissions in doing or being a party to the killing.

(1A) Those things are—

    (a) to understand the nature of D's conduct;

    (b) to form a rational judgment;

    (c) to exercise self-control.

(1B) For the purposes of subsection (1)(c), an abnormality of mental functioning provides an explanation for D's conduct if it causes, or is a significant contributory factor in causing, D to carry out that conduct.

Where this defence applies, D remains criminally liable to conviction for manslaughter, and the sentencing guidelines employed by the English courts assume that in some cases D retained such substantial responsibility for his acts that he may be punitively imprisoned (rather than detained merely because a danger to the public, or for psychiatric treatment): *Chambers* (1983) 5 Cr App R (S) 190. My reference in the text to diminished responsibility ignores this category of cases.

12

RETRIBUTION: PUNISHMENT'S FORMATIVE AIM[*]

I

The account of punishment offered by Friedrich Nietzsche in a central section of his *On the Genealogy of Morals* (1887) helps explain why this proudly malicious[1] and profoundly confused thinker still is to be regarded as a participant in philosophy's conversation. There are, he says, two aspects of the problem of punishment to be distinguished:

> on the one hand, that aspect of punishment which is relatively *enduring*—the custom, the act, the 'drama', a certain strict sequence of procedures—and, on the other hand, that aspect which is *fluid*—the meaning, the aim, the expectation which is attached to the execution of such procedures.[2]

Thus, things are not 'as our naive genealogists of morality and law have previously assumed, thinking as they all do that the procedure was *invented* specifically for the purpose of punishment...'.[3] Rather, it is to be assumed that 'the procedure itself will be something older, earlier than its use as a means of punishment...'.[4] Thus,

> in a very late stage of cultural development (as, for example, in contemporary Europe) the concept 'punishment' in fact no longer possesses a *single* meaning, but a whole synthesis of 'meanings'. The whole history of punishment up to this point, the history of its exploitation to the most diverse ends, finally crystallises in a sort of unity which is difficult to unravel, difficult to analyse, and—a point which must be emphasised—completely *beyond definition*. (Nowadays it is impossible to say *why* people are punished: all concepts in which a whole process is summarised in signs escape definition; only that which is without history can be defined.)[5]

Nietzsche here puts his finger on a genuine problem for social theory, the problem of defining social-historical concepts—or, more precisely, of

---

[*] 1999b.
[1] 'self-assured intellectual malice which belongs to great health': Nietzsche, *On the Genealogy of Morals*, II.24 at 76.
[2] *Ibid.* II.13 at 60.   [3] *Ibid.*   [4] *Ibid.*   [5] *Ibid.*

giving any theoretical and general account of them beyond a listing of the various historically given terms ('signs'). (In the first two pages of *NLNR* I give my own statement of the problem, and the rest of the chapter is my response—visibly to jurists such as Bentham, Kelsen, Hart, and Raz, invisibly to this passage from Nietzsche, on which I lectured in the early 1970s.[6]) Nietzsche's discussion proceeds to offer a list, 'far from exhaustive', of eleven 'meanings' or 'intentions' of punishment: a way of rendering harmless and preventing further damage; compensation for the victim; the isolation and containment of something which disturbs equilibrium; a means of instilling fear of those who determine and carry it out; 'a form of forfeit [compensation] due in return for the advantages which the criminal previously [up to that point] enjoyed (as, for example, when he is made useful as slave-labour in the mines)'; elimination of a degenerate element or branch; festivity, the violation and humiliation of an enemy; a means of producing a memory, whether for the person on whom the punishment is imposed (so-called rehabilitation) or for those who witness it; a form of remuneration in return for protection from excesses of revenge; a compromise with the spirit of revenge; a declaration of war against an enemy deemed dangerous and traitorous.[7]

This is a pretty good inventory. But Nietzsche is after bigger fish, the genealogy of morality itself, and in particular of conscience and one's 'sense' or consciousness of guilt. Punishment itself, he says, does not normally induce a sense of guilt or bad conscience—indeed it typically, and historically, hinders or hindered the development of a sense of guilt,[8] and in its origins it had nothing to do with desert or responsibility. Rather, it originated in notions of equivalence modelled on barter and sale. The criminal was debtor and the damaged creditor received compensation in the form of 'the pleasure of being able to vent his power without a second thought on someone who is powerless ... the pleasure of violation [rape; doing violence]'.[9] But as the community grows stronger it ceases to regard crimes quite so seriously and begins to shield the offender from popular indignation and the fury of the person whom the offender has injured.[10] And so we arrive at Nietzsche's 'hypothesis' about the origins of conscience, in the first instance of 'bad conscience' or guilt (part II.16), but fundamentally of conscience itself (part II.22). In this hypothesis we see the forerunner of the Freudian,[11] the socio-biological, and countless other

---

[6] [On the intentions of that chapter, see also 2008d, sec. I; *ibid.*, sec. II revisits this discussion of Nietzsche.]

[7] *On the Genealogy of Morals*, II.13 at 61.   [8] *Ibid.*, II.14 at 62.   [9] *Ibid.*, II.5 at 46.

[10] *Ibid.*, II.10.

[11] See Jones, *The Life and Work of Sigmund Freud*, 596, summarizing Freud's thesis in *Civilization and Its Discontents* (1930).

III.12 RETRIBUTION: PUNISHMENT'S FORMATIVE AIM

reductive attempts to explain conscience as the sublimation or product of repression, death wishes, instincts, and so on.

I take conscience to be the deep sickness to which man was obliged to succumb under the pressure of that most fundamental of all changes—when he found himself definitively locked in the spell of society and peace.... Every instinct which does not vent itself externally *turns inwards*—this is what I call the *internalization* of man: it is at this point that what is later called the 'soul' first develops in man.... Those fearful bulwarks by means of which the state organization protected itself against the old instincts of freedom—punishment belongs above all to these bulwarks—caused all the instincts of the wild, free, nomadic man to turn backwards *against man himself.* Hostility, cruelty, pleasure in persecution, in assault, in change, in destruction,—all that turning against the man who possesses such instincts: *such* is the origin of 'bad conscience'. The man who is forced into an oppressively narrow and regular morality, who for want of external enemies and resistance impatiently tears, persecutes, gnaws, disturbs, mistreats himself, this animal which is to be 'tamed', which rubs himself raw against the bars of the cage, this deprived man consumed with homesickness for the desert, who had no choice but to transform himself into an adventure, a place of torture, an uncertain and dangerous wilderness—this fool, this yearning and desperate prisoner became the inventor of 'bad conscience'.[12]

In short: bad conscience, that is to say, one's conscience passing adverse judgment on one's own past conduct, is 'the will to mistreat the self',[13] the 'will to self-torture, that downtrodden cruelty of the internalized animal man who has been chased back into himself, of the man locked up in the "state"'—locked up originally at the hands of 'some horde or other of blond predatory animals [blond beasts], a race of conquerors and masters'[14] (Nietzsche's admiration for whom is unconcealed)—'in order to be tamed, the man who invented bad conscience in order to inflict pain on himself after the *more natural* outlet for this desire to inflict pain was obstructed...'[15] etc. Thus, says Nietzsche at the end of this exposition of his 'hypothesis', he has taken care 'once and for all, of the origin of the "holy God"', by which he means both conscience (which Kant had called our holy Lord) and God, another sublimation and projection of the tormented 'sad, insane beast, man'.[16]

Within a few pages, Nietzsche has turned to the third and last part of his *On the Genealogy of Morals*. In it he drives his reflections and his rhetoric to their self-stultifying conclusion or impasse. The will to be truthful, to seek

---

[12] *On the Genealogy of Morals*, II.16 at 64–5.
[13] *Ibid.*, II.18 at 68.
[14] *Ibid.*, II.17 at 66.
[15] *Ibid.*, II.22 at 72.
[16] *Ibid.*, II.22 at 73.

and hold to the truth, is itself a product of that sickness, conscience. The truth that conscience is a sickness and that God, the only ground of truth's value, is non-existent therefore puts in question, renders problematic, the will to truth, the value of truth, and of being truthful: 'the value of truth must for once, by way of experiment, be *called into question...*'.[17] Nietzsche's phrase 'by way of experiment' reveals the ultimately frivolous, dilettantish character of his thought, or the depth of the impasse to which his arbitrary assertions and denials have driven him. But he does not deny, indeed he here, at this juncture, admits that the 'core'[18] of conscience is, in fact, the will to truth, to truthfulness.[19]

It will be good to get away from the stale air of Nietzsche's writing room. This part of the book—a book whose seductiveness you can see infecting a good deal in the academy today (quite evident, for example, in Judge Posner's Holmes Lectures at Harvard Law School in 1997)[20]—is headed by a quotation from an earlier work by Nietzsche:

Unconcerned [carefree], contemptuous [mocking], violent—this is how wisdom would have *us* be [or: thus wisdom wants *us*]: she is a woman, she only ever loves a warrior.[21]

Here the word 'warrior' helps Nietzsche give gloss and lustre to his admiration for rape (and to his truculence about self-contradiction, the truculence which motivates the quotation). To get out of Nietzsche's study consider a real rape by real soldiers. A good account of such an act of violence by soldiers upon a woman, in November 1966 on Hill 192 (as the military designated it) in central South Vietnam, was written up by Daniel Lang in 1969.[22] The account is told from the viewpoint of one of the five soldiers in a patrol whose leader, Sergeant Meserve, decided in advance to capture a young village woman, Phan Thi Mao, use her, with her hands tied, for sexual intercourse, and then kill her and conceal her body. All save one of

---

[17] *Ibid.*, III.24 at 128. Also at 126:

these hard, severe, abstemious, heroic spirits ... these pale atheists, anti-Christians, immoralists, nihilists ... these men in whom the intellectual conscience is alone embodied and dwells today.... These men are far from *free* spirits: *for they still believe in the truth!*...

And here Nietzsche associates himself with the *secretum* of the highest grades of 'that invincible order of the Assassins, that order of free spirits *par excellence*', the *secretum* that 'nothing is true, everything is permitted'. He calls this a 'proposition' (true? false?) with 'labyrinthine *consequences*' (*ibid.*), and it seems to be this that he has in mind when he says, III.27 at 135: 'from now on morality will be *destroyed* through the coming to consciousness of the will to truth', viz. its becoming 'conscious of itself as a *problem*'; and 'this is the great drama in a hundred acts which is reserved for Europe over the next two thousand years, the most fearful, most questionable and perhaps also most hopeful of all dramas...'.

[18] *Ibid.*, III.27 at 134. [19] *Ibid.* at 134–5.
[20] Posner, 'The Problematics of Moral and Legal Theory'.
[21] Nietzsche, 'What is the Meaning of Ascetic Ideals?,' in *On the Genealogy of Morals* at 77.
[22] Lang, *Casualties of War*.

the men participated in the rape or the murder or both. This man, Private Eriksson, realized then and there that 'unless he took it upon himself to speak out, the fact of Mao's death would remain a secret'.[23] He did report the crime to his superiors back at base, who eventually and reluctantly did prosecute the other four for rape and murder. But the obstacles, the delays, and the warnings of the risks of revenge which Eriksson was running in pressing the charges were such that he could rely upon nothing other than interest in the truth being known and acknowledged, and thus upon the conscience of his superiors in the army and its justice system. At the trials, witnesses and defendants alike indicated their incredulity that useful fighting men should be being put on trial, though no one denied in principle that crimes such as rape and murder should be punished.

In Luke's Gospel, 23: 39–41, we read:

> One of the criminals who were hanging [on their crosses] kept deriding him and saying 'Aren't you the Messiah? Save yourself and us!' But the other rebuked him, saying, 'Don't you fear God, since you are under the same sentence of condemnation. And we indeed have been condemned justly, for we are getting our due for our actions, but this man has done nothing wrong.'

Is Nietzsche right in holding that this acknowledgement of guilt and the accompanying recognition of punishment's justice are a mere sickness somehow transmitted from earlier generations of self-lacerating slaves and fools?

We should regard Nietzsche's genealogy of conscience and morality as factually, historically, far from grounded in evidence. But even if it were far better grounded in evidence than it is, we should also have to bear in mind, and adopt, Nietzsche's own recognition—acknowledged by him regardless of its subversion of his own project—that

> there is a world of difference between the reason for something coming into existence in the first place and the ultimate use to which it is put, its actual application and integration into a system of goals.[24]

Our reactive inclinations, like our desires and aversions generally, can well be constitutionally ordered and directed by our understanding, by our capacity to understand and reason about opportunities and benefits, and the corresponding defaults and losses, common to us all. Our reactive instincts, even when they are interior to our intellectual capacities, our will, can be and, for truth's sake, should be integrated into this constitutional order in the soul, which is the source of all constitutional, decent order between persons, all society.

[23] *Ibid.*, 54.   [24] *On the Genealogy of Morals*, II.12 at 57.

What is it, then, that with whatever admixture of emotion and confusion was nevertheless truly understood by the penitent malefactor and by Private Eriksson witnessing his fellow soldiers' crimes on Hill 192?

II

The intrinsic worth of what truly benefits me has the same worth in the lives of any other persons who do or could share in that kind of benefit. This truth and our primary understanding of it are the primary source of all human community, more decisive than any emotion of sympathy or subrational instinct of solidarity. These emotions and instincts fittingly support and enliven one's intelligent grasp of the truth that every human good is a common good, but they also must contend with competing emotions or inclinations of self-indulgence and pride, dear to Nietzsche's heart. It is our practical knowledge, our understanding of intelligible opportunities and benefits precisely when we are thinking about what to choose and do, that can be and so, for the sake of truth and friendship, should be decisive. We have in mind the commanding status of this judgment in our deliberations, and in our reflections on our past choices and actions or omissions, when we speak of conscience: *judgment* about what is truly worthwhile and ought to be pursued, or done, or avoided.

Nietzsche claimed that generations of infliction of ferocious punishments were needed to create in human persons the *memory* required to take seriously one's own promise or to acknowledge one's 'guilt' or responsibility.[25] But what Nietzsche thus freely asserts, quite without evidence, should be freely denied. It is not lack of memory that stands or stood in the way of acknowledging the obligatoriness of one's promises or of one's duties of restitution or recompense. At most it was some kind of submerging of memories, a kind of overriding of stable willingness, of fidelity, of responsibility, and of regret, by countervailing desires to attend to one's own interests and pursue one's inclinations from now forward into the future, or perhaps by countervailing conventions encouraging indifference to the interests of persons outside a group. Part of the profound unity of our complex nature as individual human persons is one's capacity to recognize oneself as a being who lasts, from one end of this sentence to the other, from the beginning of deliberation through choice to execution of choice and enjoyment of the benefit one first envisaged (or regret at failing in one's purpose). And equally one can effortlessly recall and recognize as one's own one's parents, the undertakings others have

[25] *Ibid.*, II.1–3.

made and on which one has relied or thought of relying, the harms one has done to others, the relationships one has formed, or maintained, or violated, the work one has done and now seeks payment for.

So Private Eriksson and the repentant malefactor (the 'good thief') were, first and foremost, being truthful about the past and about how one person is related to another or others by virtue of what was done in time past. In stressing this, I do not concede that retribution is 'purely backward-looking', as is so often said. The retributive shaping point of punishment, like other purposes to which punishment can be adapted, is forward-looking. The 'medicinal' or 'healing' point of punishment, of which Aquinas often speaks, is envisaged by him as *including* its purpose of retribution. There is a notable difference here between St Thomas's terminology and the language of the *Catechism of the Catholic Church*. The catechism uses the term 'medicinal' to refer exclusively to punishment's possible value as reformative: 'Finally punishment has a medicinal value; as far as possible it should contribute to the correction of the offender.'[26] But when he speaks of punishment's medicinal function, Aquinas has in mind not only reform and deterrence and restraint and coercive inducement to decent conduct, but also the function which the *Catechism* calls primary: the redressing of the disorder caused by the offence. Why is this medicinal, curative healing? Because it is the healing of a disorder—precisely an unjust inequality—introduced into a whole community by the wrongdoer's criminal choice and action.

To understand this, it is necessary to set aside the assumption made all too casually by Nietzsche, but also by Bentham, Hart, and countless other theorists—the assumption that the essence of punishment is the infliction of *pain*.[27] Putting punishment on the level of the sensory, sentient, and emotional is an efficient way of blocking all understanding of its real point and operation, which is on the level of the will, that is to say of one's responsiveness to the *intelligible* goods one *understands*.

The essence of punishments, as Aquinas clearly and often explains, is that they subject offenders to something *contrary to their wills*—something *contra voluntatem*.[28] This, not pain, is of the essence. Why? Because the essence of offences is that in their wrongful acts offenders 'yielded to

---

[26] *CCC*, para. 2266.
[27] See Hart, *Punishment and Responsibility*, 4: 'I shall define the standard or central case of "punishment" in terms of five elements: (i) it must involve pain or other consequences normally considered unpleasant...'. Here it is worth recalling that the French word for pain is *douleur* not *peine* (the French word for punishment), just as the Latin for pain is *dolor* not *poena* (punishment).
[28] *Sent.* II d.42 q.1 a.2c; *ST* I–II q.46 a.6 ad 2: 'est de ratione poenae quod sit contraria voluntati'; likewise I q.48 a.5c; I–II q.87 a.2c and a.6c; *ScG* III, c.140 n.5 [3149]. Still, punishment can be undergone and accepted voluntarily and freely {libenter}, on one's own account or on behalf of one's friend: *Sent.* IV d.21 q.1 a.1 sol.4c. See *Aquinas* 212.

their will more than they ought',[29] 'followed their own will excessively',[30] 'ascribed too much to their own preferences'[31]—the measure of excess being the relevant law or moral norm for preserving and promoting the common good.[32] Hence the proposition foundational for Aquinas's entire account of punishment: the order of just equality in relation to the offender is restored—offenders are brought back into that equality—precisely by the 'subtraction' effected in a corresponding, proportionate[33] suppression[34] *of the will which took for itself too much* (too much freedom or autonomy, we may say).[35] In this way punishment 'sets in order' the guilt[36] whose essence was wrongful willing; and this (re)ordering {ordinativa} point of punishment can either be accounted remedial {medicinalis},[37] or contrasted (for the *Catechism of the Catholic Church* is adopting *one* of Aquinas's ways of speaking) with the remedial (deterrent, reformative).[38]

Nietzsche saw the origins of punishment in the debtor-creditor relationship. Perhaps; the evidence is scant. But we should be concerned

---

[29] *ST* I–II q.87 a.6c {plus voluntati suae indulsit quam debuit}; III q.86 a.4c (same); *De Rationibus Fidei ad Cantorem Antiochum* c. 7 [998] (same).

[30] *ST* II–II q.108 a.4c {peccando nimis secutus est suam voluntatem}.

[31] *Compendium Theologiae ad fratrem Reginaldum*, I c. 121 {plus suae voluntati tribuens quam oportet}. At the time of his *Sent.*, Aquinas seems not to have understood the will's offence in terms of excess, and so did not squarely identify punishment as subtraction in the field of willing: see e.g. *Sent.* IV d.15 q.1 a.4c; but *Sent.* II d.42 q.1 a.2c and ad 5 gets very close to the clarity of the late works.

[32] So the criminal's criminal offence is not, as such, against the victim so much as against 'common justice', like the case discussed in *ST* II–II q.66 a.5 ad 3: I lend you something and, when its return is overdue, I take it back by force or stealth instead of persuasion or due process of law; this conduct 'does not harm {gravet} [you] but is an offense against common justice, inasmuch as [I am] usurping to [myself] the judgment on the matter and setting aside the due process of law {iuris ordine praetermisso}.'

[33] *Sent.* II d.42 q.1 a.2 ad 5:

to the extent {tantum} that one has obeyed one's own will by transgressing the law..., to that extent {quantum} one should compensate in the opposite direction {in contrarium}, so that thus the equality of justice may be respected.

[34] *ST* I–II q.87 a.1c: the essence of punishment, whether by one's own conscience in remorse, or by some external governing authority, is this suppression {depressio} by or on behalf of the order against which the wrongdoer was in insurrection. Note that, by contrast, the principal purpose of restitution (which is always to the victim) is 'not that someone who has an excess {plus quam debet} should cease to have it, but that the person who has a deficiency {minus} should have it made good': II–II q.62 a.6 ad 1.

[35] *ST* II–II q.108 a.4c: 'the equality of justice is restored {reparatur} by punishment inasmuch as they undergo something contrary to their will'; *Compendium Theologiae* I c. 121 [237]: 'there is a restoring {reductio} to the order of justice by punishment, through which something is subtracted from the will'; *ST* I–II q.87 a.6c; likewise III q.86 a.4c: 'through punishment's recompense {recompensationem} the equality of justice is restored {reintegretur}'; *De Rationibus Fidei ad Cantorem Antiochum* c. 7 [998]: 'to restore them to the order of justice, something that they want needs to be taken away from {subtrahitur} their will—which punishment does by taking away goods they want to have or imposing bads they are unwilling to undergo'. See also *In Eth.* V.6 n. 6 [952], dealing simultaneously but to some extent distinctly with criminal punishment and civil compensation. Relevant goods which punishment takes away, and corresponding bads which it imposes, are life, bodily security, liberty, wealth, homeland, and honours {gloria}: *ST* II–II q.108 a.3c.

[36] *ScG* III, c.146 n.1 [3193].   [37] As in e.g. *Sent.* II d.36 q.1 a.3 ad 3.

[38] As in e.g. *ST* II–II q.108 a.4c.

not with origins but with practical, moral intelligibilities. The debts from which just punishment liberates the offender[39] are not debts to the victims who might be plaintiffs in a civil proceeding or might understandably but wrongly desire revenge. Rather, we may say, those debts are the advantage—the inequality—which, in the willing of an offence, is wrongly gained *relative to all the offender's fellows* in the community against whose law, and so whose common good, the offence offends:[40] the advantage of freedom from external constraints in choosing and acting.[41]

Though the distinction between laws we call *civil* and laws we call *criminal* is no more clearly marked by Aquinas than by Aristotle or by Roman law, Aquinas does identify the basis for that distinction: the difference between one's duty to compensate and one's liability to punishment. Equally clearly he identifies the fundamental similarity of purpose: each of these branches of law concerns the restoration of an upset equality, the elimination of an unjustified inequality between persons; the restoration which justice requires can in either branch be called a recompense {recompensatio}. But the one branch looks to the losses incurred by specific persons, the other to a kind of advantage gained over all the other members of a community. For compensation {reparatio; restitutio; satisfactio} is essentially a matter of restoring to specific losers—to those who now have less than they ought[42]—what they have been deprived of.[43] But punishment {poena; retributio[44]} is essentially a matter of removing from wrongdoers a kind of advantage they gained, precisely in preferring their own will to the requirements authoritatively specified for that community's common good.[45] So in litigation of the kind we call civil, the court has the duty to give plaintiffs their rights {ius suum}, everything to which they are

---

[39] *Compendium Theologiae*, I c. 226 [470].

[40] So one merits reward or deserves punishment (which can only be rightly imposed by persons responsible for a community, administering its law) precisely as someone who is (or, like a visitor, is reasonably taken to be) a part of a community: *ST* I–II q.21 a.3 ad 2, a.4c and ad 3; q.92 a.2 ad 3. There is, in the focal sense, no punishment (or reward) of subhuman animals: see *Compendium Theologiae*, I c. 143 [285].

[41] So punishment cures and removes this inequality: *Sent.* IV d.15 q.1 a.1 sol.3c; *ScG* III, c.140 n.5 [3149]; and n. 35 above.

[42] *Sent.* IV d.38 q.2 a.4 sol.1 ad 1; *ST* II–II q.67 a.4c.

[43] *ST* II–II q.62 a.5c. Sometimes Aquinas distinguishes compensation {satisfactio} for wrongful acts from return {restitutio} of something which has been, or would otherwise be, wrongfully detained: *Sent.* IV d.15 q.1 a.5 sol.1c. But often *restitutio* is a synonym for *reparatio* as the general category of civil compensation. The loss for which it would be unjust not to make restitution need not have resulted from the defendant's fault {iniustitia}: *ST* II–II q.62 a.3c.

[44] Caution: *retributio*, unlike the modern usage of the English word 'retribution', extends (like 'retribution' in older English) to reward of merit as well as punishment for guilt (see e.g. *ST* I–II q.21 a.3c); like many other key terms in Aquinas it takes its meaning-in-use from its context.

[45] See e.g. *ST* I–II q.87 a.6c and ad 3.

entitled as compensation for their injurious losses.[46] But in proceedings of the kind we call criminal, the court can be authorized to impose, relax, remit, or withhold penalties with a view to wider considerations of public good {publicae utilitati}.[47]

In short, retribution is one element in the general function of government: to uphold the proportionate equality of a just distribution of advantages and disadvantages, benefits and burdens, among the members of (and sojourners within) a political community. The precise benefit or advantage whose fair distribution it is the primary and shaping purpose of punishment to uphold is the advantage of freedom, in one's choosing and acting, from external constraints including the constraints appropriately imposed by laws made for the common good. Hart came close to identifying punishment's formative point and its place in the wider responsibility of the state's government and law to secure equality in justice. For he saw that morality—and he should have added, law—puts the strong and the cunning on a level with the weak and simple (something that disgusted Nietzsche).

Their cases are made morally alike. Hence the strong man who disregards morality and takes advantage of his strength to injure another is conceived as upsetting this equilibrium, or order of equality, established by morals; justice then requires that this moral status quo should as far as possible be restored by the wrongdoer.[48]

Here he is speaking of civil law, especially of tort, and its function and effect of compensating the victim of wrongdoing. He shows how the wrongdoer's advantage-taking applies even in cases of mere negligence:

One who has physically injured another either intentionally or through negligence is thought of as having taken something from his victim; and though he has not literally done this, the figure is not too far-fetched: for he has profited

---

[46] *ST* II–II q.67 a.4c: note that the plaintiff is here called *accusator* and the defendant a guilty person (*reus*) who is to be penalized {puniatur} by the award of damages; moreover, *ibid.* ad 3 states that victims of wrongdoing can be harmed by unwarranted remission of punishment, inasmuch as part of the compensation {recompensatio} to which they are entitled is a kind of restitution of a dignity interest {restitutio honoris} through the punishment of the injurer(s). Note also: the civil court's order to pay compensatory damages or to return goods does no more than reaffirm a moral obligation which the defendant ought already to have discharged; but in respect of any (civil or criminal) *penalties*, defendants are morally entitled to await the court's order: II–II q.62 a.3c. But where there was an offence, the ruptured relationship between the parties (wrongdoer and victim) is not fully restored by restitution of what the victim lost; there must be some further making amends, some specific *humilitas*, by the wrongdoer: *Sent.* IV d.15 q.1 a.5 sol.1 ad 1.

[47] *Sent.* IV d.38 q.2 a.4 sol.1 ad 1; *ST* II–II q.67 a.4c. Being an aspect of the overall 'care of the community', punishment can be imposed only by the authority of the supreme ruler(s): *ST* I–II q.21 a.4c.

[48] *CL*² 165.

at his victim's expense, even if it is only by indulging his wish to injure or not sacrificing his ease to the duty of taking adequate precautions.[49]

Reflecting, I believe, on this passage, Hart's student Herbert Morris was able to envisage punishment as retributive in aim by having the restoration of equality as its point: equality between the wrongdoer and the law-abiding.[50] His argument was taken up by Jeffrie Murphy,[51] and it remained only to identify the precise advantage gained by the offender relative to the law-abiding. When that advantage was identified as being what Aquinas had pointed to—indulgence of will—the point of punishment, its general justifying aim, became once again clear.[52] Hart never envisaged this line of thought clearly enough to reject it; it was blocked from his view by his assumption that punishment is by definition the infliction of pain—for how can adding pain to wrong restore anything or balance any account?[53]

What is done cannot be undone. But the purpose of retributive punishment is forward-looking, and not in vain. It is to secure that over the span of time which extends from before the crime until after the punishment, no one should have been disadvantaged—in respect of this particular but real kind of advantage—by choosing to remain within the law's confines. Punishment does not negate the crime, but it does negate, cancel out, the advantage the offender gained in the crime—the advantage not necessarily of loot or psychological satisfaction, but of having pursued one's own purposes even when the law required that one refrain from doing so. That there is point, value, merit, fittingness, in thus restoring equality between offenders and law-abiding, and cancelling the wrongdoer's unfair profit (advantage over them), is a truth which Eriksson and the good malefactor acknowledged. It stands undefeated by the assaults of Nietzsche and the neglect and misunderstanding of many.

Retributive punishment, the only genuine and justified form of punishment (whatever other purposes may rightly be pursued on the

---

[49] Ibid.
[50] Morris, 'Persons and Punishment'.   [51] Murphy, 'Three Mistakes about Retributivism'.
[52] See essay 11; *NLNR* 261–6.
[53] Hart, *Punishment and Responsibility*, 12 (also 18) tries to show that retributive principles of distribution, which he accepts (especially that only offenders should be punished, and only in proportion to their offence), 'cannot be explained as merely a consequence of the principle [which he does not accept] that the General Justifying aim is Retribution...'. The argument is that if a law demanded immoral acts, so that disobedience to it was not immoral but morally required, punishment of persons who had *not* disobeyed it 'would be a further *special* iniquity'. But this is not convincing. Suppose that Y disobeys the 'hideously immoral' law and X does not. Y has as much moral right as X to be immune from punishment, and X cannot rightly complain that he, X, should have been given the opportunity of obeying the law before being punished. At most, X could complain that there was no just reason for selecting him for punishment rather than Z or anyone else in the whole population. But this is no longer a complaint about violation of *retributive* principles of distribution; it is the same complaint as X could make if he were selected for death in a programme having nothing to do with offences, e.g. a programme of reducing population pressures by culling one person in ten.

occasion and, in a sense, by means of it), is thus remote indeed from revenge. Punishment cannot be imposed by the victim as such. Indeed, it cannot rightly be imposed on behalf of the victim as such, but only on behalf of the community of citizens willing to abide by the law. Any practice of giving victims some role in criminal proceedings other than as witnesses, amongst other witnesses, to the fact of the offence must be highly questionable.

III

Nietzsche spoke of the doctrine of hell as the very climax of man's insane self-laceration, 'a kind of madness of the will in psychic cruelty which simply knows no equal'.[54] But he understood neither the doctrine nor the seriousness of wrongdoing—indeed, his envious admiration for lawless and immoral deeds of outrageous cruelty is scarcely concealed. He misconceived the notion of hell, in its sober essentials, because he conceived of punishment as infliction of pain, and failed to understand that hell is only by an extended analogy a matter of punishment. And the core of the analogy is not the choosing to inflict a penalty, a choosing (sentencing) which is central to human punishing. The analogy consists only in these two elements: subjection of the offender's will, and restoration of an equality between persons[55] which was disturbed by the offender's wrongdoing. And even the subjection of will is essentially a matter of incompatibility between the offender's self-chosen stance (a stance now rendered unchangeable by that person's death)[56] and the appropriate order within and between the creatures of the universe and their creator. The pains of loss are a bad side effect of this chosen stance, not the point of some selection of sentence.

In human punishments, on the other hand, penalties must be chosen by the judge from a range. There is no 'natural' measure of punishment, that is to say, no rationally determinable and uniquely appropriate penalty to fit the crime. Punishment is the tradition's stock example of the need for *determinatio*, a process of choosing freely from a range of reasonable options none of which is simply rationally superior to the others. So there

---

[54] *On the Genealogy of Morals*, II.2 at 73.
[55] Cf. John Paul II, *Crossing the Threshold of Hope*, 186:

[T]here is something in man's moral conscience itself that rebels against any loss of this conviction [that there is eternal damnation]: Is not God who is Love also Justice? Can He tolerate these terrible crimes, can they go unpunished? Isn't final punishment in some way necessary to reestablish moral equilibrium in the complex history of humanity?

[56] Cf. *CCC* para 1033:

To die in mortal sin without repenting and accepting God's merciful love means remaining separated from him forever by our own free choice. This state of definitive self-exclusion from communion with God and the blessed is called 'hell'.

is no 'natural', that is, rational, requirement that murder, even the most atrocious, be punished capitally.

NOTE

The fact that the offence against the law-abiding community can be articulated as taking too much freedom does not entail that restrictions of freedom by fine or imprisonment are the only proper criminal penalties. Other measures that are presumptively against the will (the self-interested will) of the offender can be entirely reasonable, such as compulsory labour for the good of the community and/or the victims; corporal punishment without damage to health has been excluded by a recently emerged *jus publicum Europaeum* or *jus gentium* which can be respected as a matter of positive law (whose adoption has its roots in justified revulsion against many abuses and excesses, culminating in Nazi atrocities, and in unjustified confusion between pleasure/pain and substantive human goods), not natural right. It is quite arbitrary (substantially unreasoned, and unreasonable) for the European Court of Human Rights to hold, as it did in *Hirst v United Kingdom (No. 2)* (2005) 42 EHRR 41, that human rights are violated by including among retributive measures in response to serious crime an automatic deprivation of the right to vote during imprisonment: see first endnote to essay 1 above.

Part Three
War and Justice

13

WAR AND PEACE IN THE NATURAL LAW TRADITION*

I. PEACE AND WAR

Law, and a legalistic morality and politics, can define peace and war by their mutual opposition. Any two communities are either at peace or at war with one another. If they are at war, each is seeking a relationship to the other ('victory over', 'prevailing over') which that other seeks precisely to frustrate or overcome. If they are at peace, each pursues its own concerns in a state of indifference to, non-interference in, or collaboration with the concerns of the other.

But sound moral and political deliberation and reflection is not legalistic. Despite some tendencies towards legalism, the Catholic tradition of natural law theory very early articulated and has steadily maintained a richer and more subtle conception of peace and war. From the outset, the philosophers in the tradition have accepted that social theory (a theory of practice) should have a distinct method, appropriate to its uniquely complex subject-matter. It should not seek to articulate univocal terms and concepts which, like the concepts a lawyer needs, extend in the same sense to every instance within a clearly bounded field. Rather, it should identify the central cases of the opportunities and realities with which it is concerned, and the focal meanings of the terms which pick out those opportunities and realities. What is central, primary, and focal, and what peripheral, secondary, and diluted, is a function of (that is, is settled by reference to) what is humanly important, which in turn is a function of what are the good reasons for choice and action. So there are central and secondary forms of community, of friendship, of constitution, of the rule of law, of citizenship—and of peace. The secondary forms are really instances. But a reflection which focuses on them will overlook much that is important both for conscientious deliberation (practice) and for a fully explanatory reflection (theory).

---

* 1996b ('The Ethics of War and Peace in the Catholic Natural Law Tradition'; the essay follows a template specified by the organizers of a symposium in which the ethics of war and peace were studied in relation to various 'traditions').

So: to describe or explain peace as the absence of war is to miss the important reasons why, as the tradition affirms, peace is the point of war. That affirmation is not to be taken in the diluted and ironical sense of the Tacitean *ubi solitudinem faciunt, pacem appellant*.[1] The tradition knows well enough that wars are sometimes, in fact, waged to annihilate, out of hatred or sheer delight in inflicting misery, destruction, and death, and that even such wars can be said to be 'for the sake of peace', that is, for the inner peace of satiation of desire and the outward peace of an unchallenged mastery over one's domain.[2] But even the inner peace attainable by such means is partial, unstable, and unsatisfying, and the peace of an unfair and cruel mastery is deeply disordered and deficient. More adequately understood, peace is the 'tranquillity of order', and 'order is the arrangement of things equal and unequal in a pattern which assigns to each its proper position'.[3]

But a definition of peace in terms of things resting tranquilly in their proper places still fails to articulate the peace which could be the point of war. It remains too passive. The account needs to be supplemented by, indeed recentered on, what Augustine had treated as primary in the two immediately preceding sentences: *concordia* and *societas*, concord and community. For concord is agreement and harmony in willing, that is, in deliberating, choosing, and acting, and community is fellowship and harmony in shared purposes and common or coordinated activities. Peace is not best captured with metaphors of rest. It is the fulfilment which is realized most fully in the active neighbourliness of willing cooperation in purposes which are both good in themselves and harmonious with the good purposes and enterprises of others.

Peace, then, is diminished and undermined generically by every attitude, act, or omission damaging to a society's fair common good—specifically, by dispositions and choices which more or less directly damage a society's concord. Such dispositions and choices include a proud and selfish individualism, estranged from one's society's (or societies') concerns and common good;[4] contentiousness, obstinacy, or quarrelsomeness;[5] feuding with one's fellow citizens[6] and sedition against proper authority;[7] and, most radically, war.

---

[1] Tacitus, *Agricola*, 30, imagining a speech by a British chieftain: 'They (the Romans) make a wilderness and call it peace.'

[2] Cf. Augustine, *De civitate Dei*, 19.12.

[3] *De civitate Dei*, 19.13: 'Pax omnium rerum tranquillitas ordinis. Ordo est parium dispariumque rerum sua cuique loca tribuens dispositio.'

[4] *ST* II–II q.37 aa.1 and 2 (*discordia in corde*).

[5] II–II q.38 aa.1 and 2 (*contentio in ore*).   [6] II–II q.41 aa.1 and 2 (*rixa*).

[7] II–II q. 42 aa.1 and 2 (*seditio*).

To choose war is precisely to choose a relationship or interaction in which *we* seek by lethal physical force to block and shatter at least some of *their* undertakings and to seize or destroy at least some of the resources and means by which they could prosecute such undertakings or resist our use of force.[8] (Do not equate 'lethal' with 'intended to kill': see under 'Attitudes toward War and Non-Violence' below.) In the paradigm case of war, the *we* and the *they* are both political communities, acting as such—what the tradition called 'complete or self-sufficient (*perfectae*) communities'. But there are only 'material', not 'formal' (essential, morally decisive), differences between that paradigm case ('war' strictly so called) and other cases:[9] the war of a political community against pirates; the revolt of part of a political community against their rulers, or the campaign of the rulers against some part of their community, or some other form of civil war; the armed struggle of a group or individual against gangsters, bandits, or pirates; the duel of one person against another. In each case, the relationship and interactions between *us* and *them* which we bring into being in choosing to go to war replace, for the war's duration, the neighbourliness and cooperation which might otherwise have subsisted between us and them. But the tradition teaches that a choice of means which involves such a negation of peace (of concord, neighbourliness, and collaboration) cannot be justified unless one's purpose (end) in choosing such means includes the restoration, and if possible the enhancement, of peace (concord, neighbourliness, and collaboration) as constitutive of the *common* good of the imperfect community constituted by any two interacting human societies.[10]

This requirement of a pacific intention is, for the tradition, an inescapable implication of morality; it is entailed by the truly justifying point of any and every human choice and action. For peace, in its rich central sense and reality, is materially synonymous with the ideal condition of integral human fulfilment—the flourishing of all human persons and communities.[11] And openness to that ideal, and the consistency of all one's choices with such openness, is the first condition of moral reasonableness.[12]

---

[8] The tradition is scarcely concerned with formulating a definition of war more satisfying than Cicero's *decertare per vim*, 'contending by force' (*De officiis*, 1.11.34).

[9] On the many forms of war in a general sense, see Francisco Suarez, *De bello*, prol., in Suarez, *Selections from Three Works*, 800.

[10] 'We wage war to gain peace. Be peaceful therefore even while you are at war, so that in overcoming those whom you are fighting you may bring them to the benefits of peace.' Augustine, *Epist. 189 ad Bonifacium* 6, cited in *ST* II–II q.40 a.1 ad 3. See also *ST* II–II q.29 a.2 ad 2.

[11] 'Perfect peace consists in the perfect enjoyment of the supreme good, ... the rational creature's last end': *ST* II–II q.29 a.2 ad 4.

[12] See e.g. 1987f at 125–31.

186   PART THREE: WAR AND JUSTICE

In the classic sources of the tradition, that primary moral principle is articulated not as I have just stated it, but as the principle that one is to love one's neighbour as oneself, a principle proposed as fundamental not only to the Gospel law but also to the natural law, to practical reasonableness itself.[13] Accordingly, the tradition's classic treatments of war are found in the treatises on *caritas*, precisely on love of neighbour.[14] Justice removes obstacles to peace, and is intrinsic to it, but the direct source of peace is love of neighbour.[15] And war is to be for peace.[16]

For true peace, not a false or seeming peace. War might often be averted by surrender. But the peace thus won would often be a false peace, corrupted and diluted by injustices, slavery, and fear. Preserving, regaining, or attaining true peace can require war (though war will never of itself suffice to achieve that peace[17]).

II. MOTIVE OR INTENTION

An act, a deed, is essentially what the person who chooses to do it intends it to be. Intention looks always to the point, the end, rather than to means precisely as such; intention corresponds to the question, 'Why are you doing this?' But any complex activity is a nested order of ends which are also means to further ends: I get up *to* walk to the cupboard *to* get herbs *to* make a potion *to* drink *to* purge myself *to* get slim *to* restore my health *to* prepare for battle *to*...[18] So, though intention is of ends, it is also of all the actions which are means.

English lawyers try to mark the distinction between one's more immediate intentions and one's further intentions by reserving the word 'motive' for the latter. The spirit in which one acts, the emotions which support one's choice and exertions, can be called one's motives, too, but become the moralist's direct concern only if and insofar as they make a difference to *what* is intended and chosen. If the proposal one shapes in deliberation and adopts by choice is partly moulded by one's emotional

---

[13] See *ST* I–II q.100 a.3 ad 1.
[14] In *ST* II–II q.41 (*de bello*), and embedded in qq.34–43 (vices opposed to *caritas*); see prol. to q.43; Suarez, *De bello*, disp. 13 in tract. 3 (*De caritate*) in his *De triplice virtute theologica* (1621).
[15] *ST* II–II q.29 a.3 ad 3.
[16] See n. 10 above; also Plato, *Laws*, 1.628d–e; 7.803c–d; *NE* X.7: 1177b5.
[17] Leo XIII, *Nostis errorem* (11 February 1889), *Acta Leonis XIII*, vol. 9 (Rome, 1890), 48:

Foundations should be sought for peace that are both firmer and more in keeping with nature. For while it is allowable consistently with nature to defend one's right by force and arms, *nature does not allow that force be an efficient cause of right*. For peace consists in the tranquillity of order, and so the concord of rulers, like that of private persons, is grounded above all in justice and charity. (My trans.; emphasis added.)

[18] The example, aside from the military purpose, is from Aristotle and Aquinas: Aquinas, *In II Phys.* lect. 8 (no. 214); *In VII Meta.* lect. 6 (no. 1382); *In XI Meta.* lect. 8 (nos 2269, 2284).

motivations (more precisely, by one's intelligence in the service of those emotions), then those motivations are to be counted among one's intentions (and motives), help make one's act what it is, and fall directly under moral scrutiny.

A war is just if and only if it is right to choose to engage in it. A choice is right if and only if it satisfies all the requirements of practical reasonableness, that is, *all* relevant moral requirements. If one's purpose (motive, further intention) is good but one's chosen means is vicious, the whole choice and action is wrong. Conversely, if one's means is upright (say, giving alms to the poor) but one's motive—one's reason for choosing it—is corrupt (say, deceiving voters about one's character and purposes), the whole choice and action is wrong. The scholastics had an untranslatable maxim to make this simple point: *bonum ex integra causa, malum ex quocumque defectu*, an act will be morally good (right) if what goes into it is entirely good, but will be morally bad (wrong) if it is defective in *any* morally relevant respect (bad end, or bad means, or inappropriate circumstances). Treatises on just war are discussions of the conditions which must *all* be satisfied if the war is to be just.

The preceding three paragraphs enable us to see that, in the tradition, no clear or clearly relevant distinction can be drawn between 'grounds for' war and 'motive or intention' in going to war. The proper questions are always: What are good reasons for going to war? What reasons must not be allowed to shape the proposal(s) about which I deliberate, or motivate my adoption of a proposal?

In the first major treatise on war by a philosophical theologian (as opposed to a canonist), Alexander of Hales (c. 1240) identifies six preconditions for a just war. The person declaring war must have (1) the right *affectus* (state of mind) and (2) authority to do so; the persons engaging in war must (3) not be clerics, and must have (4) the right *intentio*; the persons warred upon must (5) deserve it (the war must have *meritum*); and there must be (6) *causa*, in that the war must be waged for the support of the good, the coercion of the bad, and peace for all.[19] Here the word *causa* is less generic than in the maxim *bonum ex integra causa*, but less specific than in Aquinas's discussion of just war, about thirty years later. Aquinas (c. 1270) cuts the preconditions down to three: authority, *causa iusta*, and *intentio recta*. Aquinas's *causa* is essentially what Alexander of Hales had called *meritum*. There is a just *causa*, says Aquinas, when those whom one attacks deserve (*mereantur*) the attack on account of their culpability;

---

[19] Alexander of Hales, *Summa Theologica*, 3.466, carefully analysed in Jonathan Barnes, 'The Just War'.

just wars are wars for righting wrongs, in particular a nation's wrong in neglecting to punish crimes committed by its people or to restore what has been unjustly taken away.[20]

Thus it is clear that, in Aquinas, the term *causa* is not equivalent to 'a justifying ground'. Rather, it points to something more like the English lawyer's 'cause of action', a wrong cognizable by the law as giving basis for a complaint, a wrong meriting legal redress. As Francisco Suarez notes, 350 years later, a discussion of such *iustae causae* for war is primarily a discussion of the justifying grounds for war *other than* self-defence:[21] to act in self-defence really needs no *causa*. (Throughout I shall follow Article 51 of the UN Charter in using the term 'self-defence' to include all cases of justifiable defence, *légitime défense*.) So there is an important difference between a present-day inquiry into the justifying grounds for war and a mediaeval inquiry into *iusta causa*. Aquinas had more reason to distinguish (as he firmly does[22]) between *causa* (in his sense) and *intentio* than we now have to distinguish between 'ground' and 'motive or intention'.

Is there nonetheless some room, in considering the rightness of initiating or participating in a war or act of war, for an inquiry into the spirit or sentiment in which a people, an official, or a citizen acts? Perhaps there is. We might draw a distinction between 'grounds' and 'spirit' by recalling that war is paradigmatically a social and *public* act. Now, just as an individual's act or deed is essentially what the person who chooses to do it intends it to be, so the acts of a society are essentially what they are defined to be in the public policy which members of the society are invited or required to participate in carrying out. That defining policy, which organizes the *actions* of individual participants in a war (thus constituting their acts a social act),[23] and does so by more or less explicit reference to war aims and strategy, can often be distinguished both from any accompanying propaganda and from the emotions and dispositions of the leaders who shaped and adopted it. Thus individual citizens can, in principle, assess the public policy, the announced reasons for going to war, the announced war aims, and the adopted strategy (so far as they know it) and assess the justice of the war (taking into account the facts about the enemy's deeds, operations, and plans so far as they can discover them). Such an assessment can set aside the moral deficiencies of the society's leaders, except insofar as those deficiencies—manifest bellicosity, vengefulness, chauvinism, and

---

[20] *ST* II–II q.40 a.1c, quoting (in a slightly garbled form) Augustine, *Quaestiones in Heptateuchum*, 6.10; and see Barnes, 'The Just War', 778.

[21] Suarez, *De bello*, 4.1 (Williams, trans., 816).

[22] 'Even when a legitimate authority declares war, and there is *causa iusta*, it can be the case that the war is made immoral/illicit by wrongful *intentio*': *ST* II–II q.40 a.1c.

[23] See *NDMR* 120–3, 131, 288, 343–4; essay II.5 (1989a).

the like—should be taken into account in judging the truth of the leaders' claims about facts and about the absence of suitable alternatives to war.

Notice that this does not carry us very far. Individual citizens have (in varying measure) some duty to consider the justice of the war, even if there is a weighty presumption in favour of accepting the public policy; in carrying out that duty, they must not allow themselves to be swayed by exciting but evil motivations: 'the craving to hurt people, the cruel thirst for revenge, a bellicose and unappeasable spirit, ferocity in hitting back, lust for mastery, and anything else of this sort'.[24] The same goes for the leaders: the shaping and adoption of their choice to go to war, of their war aims, and of their strategy will be wrongful if *affected* by any such seductive emotions.

Yet that malign influence might (and perhaps not infrequently does) remain undetectable by those who are called upon to participate in the war. To these citizens, the grounds for war, and the war aims and strategy which provide the grounds for particular operations, may reasonably seem morally acceptable. Indeed, those grounds may sometimes *be* morally acceptable even when the leaders of the society would in fact not have acted on them but for their own immoralities of disposition ('spirit') and motivation ('intention').

III. GROUNDS FOR WAR

It is primarily by harnessing reason to devise rationalizations that emotions create temptations to injustice (and to other immoralities). Rationalizations are plausible grounds which make proposals for choice and action attractive to reason and will but which, in truth (as indeed the deliberating or reflecting agent could discern), fail to satisfy all the requirements of practical reasonableness. As we have seen, the first such requirement is openness to integral human fulfilment, articulated in the tradition as love of neighbour as oneself. (The tradition—even, tentatively, in its purely philosophical articulations[25]—adds, 'Out of love of God, source of the very being and life of self and neighbor alike.') All other moral principles are specifications, more and less general, of this primary moral principle. One of the most immediate specifications is the Golden Rule of fairness, in each of its forms, positive and negative: do to/for others as you would have them do to/for you; do not do to others what you would not be willing to have

---

[24] 'Nocendi cupiditas, ulciscendi crudelitas, impacatus et implacabilis animus, feritas rebellandi, libido dominandi, et si qua similia, haec sunt quae in bellis iure culpantur.' Augustine, *Contra Faustum*, 22.74; *ST* II–II q.40 a.1c.

[25] See e.g. Plato, *Laws*, 4.715e–716d; cf. *Republic*, 6.500c.

them do to you. This in turn is specified in the presumptive obligations to keep promises, to respect the domain and goods of others, to compensate for wrongful harm, and so forth. And these obligations in turn rule out a good many alleged grounds for war.

Sifting the types of reason put forward to justify or explain a decision to fight, the tradition became clear that only two could justify such a decision: self-defence, and the rectification (punitive or compensatory/restitutionary) of a wrong done.

Aquinas runs the two grounds together in a single, foundational proposition:

> Just as rulers rightly use the sword in lawful *defence* against those who disturb the peace within the realm, when they *punish* criminals ... so too they rightly use the sword of war to *protect* their polity from external enemies.[26]

Later scholastics, such as Vitoria (c. 1535) and Suarez (c. 1610), while not repudiating Aquinas's resort to arguments which assimilate defence to punishment, do distinguish between defensive and offensive wars: war is self-defensive if waged to avert an injustice still about to take place; it is offensive if the injustice has already occured and what is sought is redress.[27] And while they consider self-defence a ground so obviously just that it scarcely needs argument,[28] they consider offensive wars to be justified basically by the justice of retribution (*vindicatio*).[29] An offensive war is like the action of the police in tracking down and forcing the surrender of criminals within the jurisdiction, action assimilated (in this line of thought) with the action of the judge and the jailer or executioner.

As so often, Suarez's care brings nearer to the surface of the discussion an issue which seems to me to present the tradition with a notable difficulty. Private persons may forcibly defend themselves,[30] but 'a punishment inflicted by one's own private authority is intrinsically evil', that is, it is wrong in all circumstances, even when one cannot get retributive or compensatory

---

[26] *ST* II–II q.40 a.1c:

Sicut licite defendunt eam [rempublicam] materiali gladio contra interiores quidem perturbatores, dum malefactores puniunt, secundum illud Apostoli, 'Non sine causa gladium portat: minister enim Dei est, vindex in iram ei qui male agit', ita etiam gladio bellico ad eos pertinet rempublicam tueri ab exterioribus hostibus.

[27] Suarez, *De bello*, 1.6 (Williams, trans., 804); cf. Vitoria, *De iure belli* (1539), sec. 13, in Vitoria, *Political Writings*, 303.

[28] Vitoria, *De iure belli*, sec. 1 (*Political Writings*, 297); Suarez, *De bello*, 1.4, 6 (Williams, trans., 803, 804).

[29] Vitoria, *De iure belli*, secs 1, 44 (*Political Writings*, 297, 319; but note that the editors often mistranslate *vindicatio* and its cognates as 'revenge'; even 'vengeance' is, in modern English, misleading as a translation of *vindicatio*); Suarez, *De bello*, 1.5 (Williams, trans., 803–4).

[30] Thus Vitoria, *De iure belli*, sec. 3 (*Political Writings*, 299): 'Any person, even a private citizen, may declare and wage defensive war.'

justice from a judge.[31] (For punishment is essentially the restoration of a fair balance between the offender and the law-abiding, a balance which the commission of an offence disturbs by enacting the offender's willingness to take the advantage of doing as one pleases when the law requires a common restraint; and persons who are not responsible for upholding the balance of fairness in distribution of advantages and disadvantages in a community *cannot* by 'punitively' repressing wrongdoers accomplish that restoration of fairness which their act, by purporting to be punishment, pretends to accomplish.) It is because private punishment is always immoral that the tradition, following Cicero,[32] insisted on public authority as one of the essential preconditions for just war (meaning just offensive war). But in a world without any world government, are not states and their rulers in precisely the position of private persons? How can they punish if they are not world rulers, or even international rulers, and so lack the type of responsibility that grounds acts of punishment—responsibility for maintaining and restoring a balance of justice between wrongdoers and the law-abiding, or between wrongdoers and their victims? This difficulty is often raised in a slightly different form: how can a state or government rightly act as both judge and party? That is a fair question, which Suarez identifies and tries to answer,[33] but I think the form in which I have framed the difficulty is the more fundamental.

The issue is complicated, above all by the flexible extension of 'defence' and 'punishment' and their convergence or even overlap in a range of situations. Note first that a war, or a military operation, is not taken out of the class of *defensive* acts by the mere fact that it is initiated to forestall a reasonably anticipated and imminent unjust attack.[34] More importantly, defence is of rights and does not become inapplicable on the first success of a violation of them. If it is self-defence to resist forcibly the entry of squatters into my family house, is it not self-defence to eject them forcibly when I discover them on returning home in the evening? Defensive measures seem to extend to self-help reclamation of what one has just lost.[35] And why should the mere temporal immediacy, or delay, of one's measures make an essential difference? Again, Vitoria, without seeking to justify the Spanish appropriation or colonization of the Americas on this ground, upheld the

---

[31] Suarez, *De bello*, 2.2 (Williams, trans., 807) and 4.7 (820); cf. Vitoria, *De iure belli*, sec. 5 (*Political Writings*, 300). Behind them, Augustine, *De civitate Dei*, 1.17, 21. Contrast the non-Catholic tradition following Grotius, *De iure belli ac pacis* (1625), 2.20.8.2, in Grotius, *The Law of War and Peace*, 472, and thence Locke, *Two Treatises of Civil Government* (1689–90), 2.2.7.

[32] Cicero, *De officiis*, 1.11.36–7.   [33] Suarez, *De bello*, 4.6, 7 (Williams trans., 819).

[34] This is denied by some, e.g. Ottaviani, *Compendium iuris publici ecclesiastici*, 88.

[35] Vitoria, *De iure belli*, sec. 3 (*Political Writings*, 299); contrast, however, sec. 5 (300) and Vitoria *De bello*, in Scott, *Francisco de Vitoria and His Law of Nations*, cxvi: 'It is impermissible for a private person to avenge himself *or to reclaim his own property* save through the judge.'

right of the Spanish to make war on the Amerindians *in defence of* the many likely innocent Amerindian victims of Amerindian cannibalism, human sacrifice, and euthanasia of the senile.[36] 'For the defence of our neighbours is the rightful concern of each of us, even for private persons and even if it involves shedding blood.[37]

Moreover, much of what the tradition says about the *punitive* function of war between polities relates not to the punishment's primary, retributive rationale but to punishment's function as a deterrent, general or special. 'Without the fear of punishment to deter them from wrongdoing (*iniuria*), the enemy would simply grow more bold about invading a second time.'[38] May not the same thought play a legitimate part in one's deliberation as a private person deciding whether or not to expel squatters from some part of one's domain? Note how Vitoria not only moves back and forth between defence and punishment, but also treats each as an aspect of the other:

> The license and authority to wage war may be conferred by necessity. If, for example, a city attacks another city in the same kingdom, ... and the king fails, through negligence or timidity, to avenge [impose retribution for] the damage done (*vindicare iniurias illatas*), then the injured ... city ... may not only defend itself but may also carry the war into its attacker's territory and teach its enemy a lesson (*animadvertere in hostes*), even killing the wrongdoers. Otherwise the injured party would have no adequate self-defence; enemies would not abstain from harming others, if their victims were content only to defend themselves. By the same argument, even a private individual may attack his enemy if there is no other way open to him of defending himself from harm.[39]

Thus the conceptual boundaries between defence and punishment are somewhat blurred. Still, the distinction remains, and with it the question: Why is punishment morally allowable in the state and its government, but not in the individual whose rights are not and perhaps cannot be vindicated by the state? Suarez gives the technical answer:

> Just as the sovereign prince may punish his own subjects when they offend others, so he may exact retribution [*se vindicare*] on another prince or *state which by reason of some offense becomes subject to him*; and this retribution cannot be sought at the hands of another judge, because the prince of whom we are speaking has no superior in temporal affairs.[40]

---

[36] Vitoria, 'Lecture on the Evangelization of Unbelievers' (1534–35), para. 3, in *Political Writings*, 347; 'On Dietary Laws, or Self-Restraint' (1538), *ibid.*, 225–6; *De Indis* (1539), para. 15, *ibid.*, 288–9.
[37] Vitoria, 'Lecture on the Evangelization of Unbelievers', *ibid.*, 347.
[38] Vitoria, *De iure belli*, sec. 1 (*Political Writings*, 298); see also sec. 5 (300).
[39] Vitoria, *De iure belli*, sec. 9 (*Political Writings*, 302).
[40] Suarez, *De bello*, 2.1 (Williams trans., 806, emphasis added).

But the proposition I have italicized smuggles the conclusion into the premises. If this wronged state or government has no rightful human superior in secular matters, the same will be true of the offending state or government, and the proposition[41] that the offence puts the offending state (morally speaking) into a state of subjection is question-begging or a fiction.

A number of recent writers have surmised that the issue was obscured from the tradition's classical writers by the notion that all Christendom was one realm, so that the wars of a state or government within that quasi-universal realm could the more readily be supposed to be analogous to the use of police power to bring to justice wrongdoers within a realm.[42] But this hypothesis, though not altogether groundless, is scarcely satisfying; the emperor's sovereignty over Christendom was manifestly a fiction, and the existence of states outside the empire was all too well known. Moreover, the traditional position that punitive war is justified survived after the replacement of Christendom by states which everyone accepted were wholly independent sovereignties.

Without, I think, the benefit of much clear discussion among the tradition's representatives, recent witnesses to the tradition—notably Pius XII, John XXIII, and the Second Vatican Council—have spoken as if the only justifying ground for war were defence.[43] Several moralists who uphold the main lines of the Catholic natural law tradition argue

---

[41] e.g. Suarez, *De bello*, 2.3 (Williams trans., 807).

[42] Barnes, 'The Just War,' 776–7 and 775 n. 23; Regan, *Thou Shalt Not Kill*, 77–9; *NDMR* 315 n. 3; Grisez, *Living a Christian Life*, ch. 11.E.3.b.

[43] Pius XII, Christmas Message (24 December 1944), *AAS* 37 (1945), 18, teaches that there is a duty to ban 'wars of aggression as legitimate solutions of international disputes and as a means toward realizing national aspirations'. Pius XII, Christmas Message (24 December 1948), *AAS* 41 (1949), 12–13, teaches:

> Every war of aggression against those goods which the Divine plan for peace obliges men unconditionally to respect and guarantee and accordingly to protect and defend, is a sin, a crime, and an outrage against the majesty of God, the Creator and Ordainer of the world.

John XXIII, *Pacem in terris*, *AAS* 55 (1963), 291, teaches: 'In this age which boasts of its atomic power, it no longer makes sense to maintain that war is a fit instrument with which to repair the violation of justice.' Noting Pope John's point, Vatican II explains how 'the horror and perversity of war are immensely magnified by the multiplication of scientific weapons', and draws the conclusion: 'All these considerations compel us to undertake an evaluation of war with an entirely new attitude', *Gaudium et spes* (1965), para. 80 with n. 2 (n. 258 in the Abbott ed.). In para. 79, the Council states:

> As long as the danger of war remains and there is no competent and sufficiently powerful authority at the international level, governments cannot be denied the right *to legitimate defence* once every means of peaceful settlement has been exhausted. Therefore, government authorities and others who share public responsibility have the duty to protect the welfare of the people entrusted to their care and to conduct such grave matters soberly. But it is one thing to undertake military action for *the just defence of the people*, and something else again to seek the subjugation of other nations. (Emphasis added.)

None of these statements unambiguously repudiates the tradition's constant teaching that punitive and, in that sense, offensive war can be justified.

that this is a legitimate development of the tradition, that it renders the tradition more consistent with its own principles.[44] In as much as they rely on a supposed change in the nature of warfare by virtue of technological developments, their argument is unpersuasive. Many present-day wars are fought in traditional ways at more or less traditional levels of limited destructiveness. Moreover, although a world government can now be envisaged as in some sense a practical possibility (again by virtue of technological development), and although leaders and people ought to do what (if anything) they responsibly can to bring such a world government into being,[45] these considerations do not justify the conclusion that, in the meantime, states must behave precisely as if they already had a common superior, effectively responsible for maintaining the worldwide common good, on whom exclusively they must treat the police power (of bringing wrongdoers to justice) as having been devolved. If self-defence (*légitime défense*) is to be held to be the only just ground for war, it must be on the ground that the tradition (1) rightly judged that private individuals as such have no right to punish those who have wronged them, but (2) erred in supposing that independent states purporting to punish states which have wronged them are in an essentially different moral position from private persons purporting to punish people who have wronged them. Vitoria and Suarez uneasily ascribed the supposed moral difference between the positions of private persons and independent states to 'the consent of the world' and the customary positive law (*jus gentium*), not to natural law.[46] The same consent and custom grounded slavery.[47] As the customary institution of slavery came to be discerned by the tradition itself as contrary rather than supplementary to natural law, so the tradition has

---

[44] Grisez, *Living a Christian Life*, ch. 11.E.3.b; Augustine Regan, 'The Worth of Human Life', *Studia Moralia* 6 (1968), 241–3; Ottaviani, *Compendium iuris*, 88.

[45] John XXIII, *Pacem in terris*, paras 43–6, in *AAS* 55 (1963), 291–4. [Benedict XVI, Encyclical *Caritas in veritate* (29 June 2009), para. 67 recalls this statement and says that, for the sake of various desirable ends mentioned in para. 67, there is 'an urgent need for a true world authority'; but para. 67 also states a set of reasonable pre-conditions such that readers can judge that, for the foreseeable future, it would be irresponsible to incur any costs or risks to meet the need.]

[46] Vitoria, *De iure belli*, sec. 19 (*Political Writings*, 305) and sec. 46 (320); but cf. sec. 5 (300), seeking to derive the punitive authority of states from their self-sufficiency; Suarez, *De legibus* (1612), 2.19.8 (Williams, trans., 348):

> The law of war—in so far as that law rests upon the power possessed by a given state ...for the punishment, avenging (*vindicandam*), or reparation of an injury inflicted upon it by another state—would seem to pertain properly to the *ius gentium*. For it was not indispensable by virtue of natural reason alone that the power in question should exist within an injured state, since men could have established some other mode of inflicting punishment, or entrusted that power to some prince and quasi-arbitrator with coercive power. Nevertheless, since the mode in question, which is at present in practice, is easier and more in conformity with nature, it has been adopted by custom (*usu*) and is just to the extent that it may not rightfully be resisted. In the same class I place slavery.

[47] Suarez, *De legibus*, 2.19.8 (Williams trans., 348).

come (or is coming) to discern the true moral character of the custom ascribing to states the authority to levy punitive war.

IV. OTHER DISTINGUISHING CRITERIA

Having a good ground is not the only prerequisite for justly going to war (and fighting it). *Bonum ex integra causa, malum ex quocumque defectu*; there are other conditions which must all be satisfied if one's warring is to be justifiable. All of these further conditions are, I think, implications of the Golden Rule (principle) of fairness, rather than of the principle that one must never choose to harm the innocent. The most important of these implications is that it is unfair not only to the enemy but also to one's own people (1) to initiate or continue a war which has no reasonable hope of success, or (2) to initiate a war which could be avoided by alternatives short of war, such as negotiation and non-violent action.

The condition that the foreseeable side effects of going to war be not excessive ('disproportionate') was usually stated by the tradition in connection with the justification-conditions of punitive wars. A government's initiation of a war for the sake of retributively restoring an order disturbed by a wrong done to its own country could not be justified if the war were likely to expose that country unfairly to loss and risk of loss (for example, great risk of substantial loss, or significant risk of great loss). Indeed, it seems to be only such wars that the tradition explicitly declares to be subject to this condition.[48] But there can be little doubt that even the decision to put up a defence must be subject to the same sort of precondition. Modern restatements of the tradition which make defence the only just ground for war do treat *probability of success* and *proportionality* (of anticipated damage and costs to expected good results) as preconditions.[49]

That is not to say that a military unit faced with overwhelming odds must, in fairness, surrender. Everyone knows that one unit's willingness to fight to the last man can sometimes inflict such losses that the enemy's overall operation and strategy is weakened or delayed and so can be defeated—its victory over the unit destroyed was Pyrrhic. And everyone knows that an isolated unit, in the dust of conflict, can rarely discern with confidence how its resistance would affect the overall outcome of the war. Military discipline is therefore not unfair in imposing a strong presumption

---

[48] See e.g. Suarez, *De bello*, 3.8 (Williams trans., 821).
[49] Pius XII, Address to Military Doctors (19 October 1953) *AAS* 45 (1953), 748–9; United States National Conference of Catholic Bishops, *The Challenge of Peace*, Pastoral Letter of 3 May 1983 (Washington, DC: US Catholic Conference, 1983), paras 98–9.

in favour of fighting on. But, when standing alone against the enemy, those in command of the whole nation or its armed forces as a whole must very seriously ask whether it is consistent with the Golden Rule to undertake a hopeless resistance which will impose immense losses on the combatants of both sides, on non-combatants of both nations (especially the nation attacked), and perhaps on the citizens of neutral states lying, say, in the path of the fallout.

The same sort of fairness-based considerations underlie the requirement that war be considered a *last resort* after the exhaustion of peaceful alternatives.[50] The losses accepted in a negotiated settlement, however unpalatable, must be compared with the losses that would be borne by all those likely to be destroyed or injured by the alternative option, war.

How are such comparisons and judgments of (dis)proportion to be made? Not by the simply aggregative methods taken for granted by utilitarian, consequentialist, or proportionalist ethics, which blandly but absurdly ignore the incommensurability of the goods and bads at stake in human options.[51] It is a matter, rather, of adhering to the *rational* requirement of impartiality by an intuitive awareness of one's own *feelings* as one imaginatively puts oneself in the place of those who will suffer from the effects of the alternative options (not forgetting the different status of the various classes of potential sufferers, some of whom would have willed and initiated the war and thus accepted the risk). As the US Catholic bishops indicate, to identify proportionality one must 'tak[e] into account' both the expected advantages and the expected harms, but with the purpose (not of measuring incommensurables but rather) of 'assess[ing] the justice of accepting the harms', an assessment in which 'it is of utmost importance... to think about the poor and the helpless, for they are usually the ones who have the least to gain and the most to lose when war's violence touches their lives' (not forgetting, however, their fate in an unjust peace).[52] As we shall see when we consider unfairness ('disproportion') in the conduct of military operations, the deliberations and conduct of a party to the conflict will provide a referent against which to assess the requirements of impartiality as they bear on other conduct of that same party.

V. THE CONDUCT OF WAR

All the moral requirements which bear on the decision to go to war apply also to the willingness to carry on fighting and to the conduct of the war

---

[50] *The Challenge of Peace*, para. 96 (exhaustion of peaceful alternatives).
[51] See *NDMR* ch. 9. [52] *The Challenge of Peace*, para. 105.

in particular military operations. Indeed, they apply also to the adoption of a deterrent strategy in the hope that war will thereby be averted.[53] The distinction between *ius ad bellum* and *ius in bello* is scarcely part of the Catholic natural law tradition. Nor is it a helpful distinction. True, it teaches that the rightness of a decision to fight does not entail the rightness of everything done in fighting; but that is more fundamentally taught by the more general principle, applicable to all decisions and actions, *bonum ex integra causa, malum ex quocumque defectu: every* choice must satisfy all moral requirements.

So it must be clear at the outset that, in the Catholic natural law tradition, there can be no question of different moral constraints pulling one another. Each of the constraints is a necessary condition of justifiability, and compliance with one or some of them is never a sufficient condition. The combatants, like the leaders who opted for war, must have upright intentions: their motivations must be free from unfair bias and cruelty, they must intend to fight on some just ground, they must not be willing to impose unfair devastation. And, just as their leaders in deliberating about whether to go to war must not intend the death of innocents (non-combatants), either as an end (malice and revenge) or as a means (of breaking the enemy's will to fight, for example, or of bringing neutrals into the war), so, too, those who plan and carry out military operations are subject to precisely the same constraint, the same exceptionless requirement of respect for (innocent) human life. So too, indeed, are those who participate in the public polity and act of maintaining a strategy of deterrence involving threats which they hope will never (but could and, as far as the policy is concerned, would) be carried out.[54]

Curiously, Aquinas's little treatise *de bello* makes no reference to the exceptionless moral norm that innocents must not be deliberately killed. But there is no doubt that he held that norm to be applicable to war. For the norm itself is one which, a little later in the same part of the *Summa Theologiae*, he clearly affirms and defends as exceptionless.[55] And, as we shall see in the next section, he explicitly affirms (with the whole tradition) that such norms remain requirements of reason and thus of morality whatever the circumstances. As if to make the point economically, his treatment *de bello* affirms the exceptionless applicability to war of another moral norm which many people violate in war, indeed violate perhaps even more freely and with even fewer qualms of conscience: the moral norm excluding all lying (as distinct from subterfuges which do not involve

---

[53] *NDMR* esp. ch. 4.
[54] See *NDMR* ch. 5, on the impossibility of bluff in a complex society. [Also essay II.4 at 86–91.]
[55] *ST* II–II q.64 a.6.

affirming as true what one knows to be untrue).[56] And the whole tradition after him peacefully accepts the absolute immunity of non-combatants from deliberate attack, that is, attack intended to harm them either as an end or as a means to some other end.[57]

Combatants are all those whose behaviour is part of a society's use of force; if we are engaged in just defence, enemy combatants are those whose behaviour contributes to their society's wrongful use of force. Anyone whose behaviour during warfare could not be used to verify the proposition, 'That society is at war with us', is clearly a non-combatant. But some of those people whose wartime behaviour could be used to verify that proposition (little old ladies knitting khaki socks, for example) nevertheless contribute so little, and so merely symbolically, to the acts of war whose violation of just order is ground for war that they are reasonably considered non-combatants. The principle of discrimination—that one must not make non-combatants the object of attack as one makes combatants—requires one to respect the distinction between combatants and non-combatants, but does not presuppose that drawing the distinction is easy. There are in fact many borderline cases: farmers, workers in public utilities, members of fire brigades, and the like, who engage in certain performances specified by war and essential to it, yet very little different from their peacetime occupations and essential to the survival and well-being of all who are certainly non-combatants. Some theorists in the tradition have called them combatants, others in the tradition have called them non-combatants. But, on any view, the population of a political community includes many people who are certainly non-combatants; their behaviour would in no way help to verify that the society is engaged in operations of war against another society. They include in particular those who cannot take care of themselves, together with those whose full-time occupation is caring for the helpless. The behaviour of people of these sorts contributes nothing to a society's war effort, but actually diverts resources which might otherwise be used in that effort.

Non-combatants, then, are innocent; that is, they are not *nocentes*, not engaged in the operations which most of the tradition assimilated to capital crimes and which the newer conception proposed by, say, Grisez treats as activities warranting forcible resistance in self-defence. Non-combatants may not be directly harmed or killed; 'directly' here means 'as a means or

---

[56] *ST* II–II q.40 a.3; see also q.110 a.3. Likewise Suarez, *De bello*, 7.23 (Williams, trans., 852).
[57] Vitoria, *De iure belli*, secs 34–7 (*Political Writings*, 3, 14–17); Suarez, *De bello*, 7.6, 15 (Williams, trans., 840, 845); *The Challenge of Peace* (n. 49 above), paras 104–5.

as an end'.[58] (Does it follow that combatants may be directly killed? See the last section below.) But, without intending any harm to non-combatants, one may choose to plan and carry out military operations which one knows will in fact cause non-combatants injury or death; and such a non-homicidal choice can be justified provided that the choice is otherwise fair and well motivated (*malum ex quocumque defectu*). The proviso just mentioned is often expressed as 'provided that the death-dealing or other harmful effects on non-combatants are not disproportionate'. Here 'proportionate' can have a rational meaning which it could not have if it referred simply to sheer magnitude; its rational meaning is *unfair*, imposed by a biased and partial, not an impartial, measure and judgment. The standard is the Golden Rule, and I have sketched in the preceding section the ways in which it gains content. The basic measure is: what people do, or are unwilling to do, to themselves and their friends. For example: in 1944, Allied air forces followed a policy of precision bombing when attacking German targets in France, and a policy of blind or other imprecise bombing when attacking German military targets in Germany.[59] Thus they showed themselves willing to impose on German non-combatants a level of incidental harm and death which they were not willing to impose on French civilians. This was unfair; the collateral damage to German civilians was, therefore, disproportionate.

Are there prudential as well as moral constraints on the conduct of war once it has begun? Here I take 'prudential' in its modern meaning: in my/our own interests. Doubtless sane leaders will regulate their decisions with an eye to the consequences for themselves and their community. But the tradition is quite clear that there is no coherent and non-arbitrary prudence apart from a morally regulated, indeed morally directive, prudence which respects *all* the requirements of reasonableness, including fairness and respect for the humanity of *all* persons in every community. So, in the final analysis, it is futile and misleading to investigate a prudence distinct from morality. Machiavellianism, for all its impressive rules of practice and its attractions to the emotions of self-preference and the aesthetics of technique, is a mere rationalization which cannot withstand rational critique. For it cannot justify its horizon, its presupposed demarcation

---

[58] Thus 'direct' killing of the innocent is explained as killing either as an end or as a means by Pius XII (12 November 1944, in *Discoursi e radiomessaggi* 6: 191–2); by Paul VI (*Humanae vitae* [1968], n. 14); and by the CDF (*De abortu procurato*, 18 November 1974, para. 7; *Donum vitae*, 22 February 1987, n. 20). For similar explanations of 'direct' in terms of 'as an end or as a means', see Pius XII, *AAS* 43 (1951), 838 (killing) and 843–4 (sterilization), and *AAS* 49 (1957), 146 (euthanasia).

[59] *NDMR* 39–40, 264–5, 271–2. The attacks to which I am here referring are, of course, not the regular British obliteration or 'area' bombing raids of 1942–45, directed at cities and their inhabitants as such, but attacks on railway yards or on the submarines congregated at Kiel, etc.

of a range of persons or communities whose well-being it will then take as the measure of prudentially 'right' action. The so-called paradoxes of nuclear deterrence are merely one exemplary sign of the unreasonableness of every prudence which falls short of the requirements of morality's first principle.

VI. MORALITY IN EXTREMITY

The remarks in the preceding paragraph indicate the tradition's fundamental response to the question of morality in extremity. For 'extremity' denotes the grave and imminent danger that *we* will be overwhelmed or destroyed (unless we take certain measures). The tradition does not suggest that the requirements of morally decent deliberation take no account of such a danger. On the contrary, all the requirements of the Golden Rule are liable to be profoundly affected by the presence and degree of such risks.

The so-called rules of war include many norms which are valid and binding because they have been *adopted* (posited) by custom or agreement or enactment by some body empowered by custom or agreement to make such enactments. This is true not only of modern international conventions, but also of much in the tradition's moral treatises on war, where such norms are described as *de iure gentium* (as distinct from *de iure naturali*).[60] Now, the moral force of positive law, including the *ius gentium* in as much as it is positive law, rests on the Golden Rule (taken together with the rational requirement that one be concerned for the well-being of others and thus of the communities to which one belongs). Having taken the benefits of others' compliance with the rules, I cannot fairly renege on one of those rules when it requires compliance from me. But the principle articulated in the preceding sentence, though reasonable and usually decisive, is not absolute. That is to say, it does not apply exceptionlessly. For if the situation now is such that, had it obtained when compliance with some rule by others was in issue, I would not have wanted and expected (demanded) those others to comply, it can be fair for me to withhold my compliance; I can fairly do as I truly would have been willing for others *to* do in a like case.

So, in principle, those rules of war which depend on custom, agreement, or enactment are liable to be set aside in extremity. On the other hand, the tradition holds that where a rule, though positive (*de iure gentium*, not *de iure naturali*), has been adopted precisely *for* and *with a view to* regulating conduct in situations of extremity, it cannot rightly be set aside. Thus,

---

[60] e.g. Vitoria, *De iure belli*, sec. 19 (*Political Writings*, 305); Suarez, *De bello*, 7.7 (Williams trans., 820–41) and, very clearly and fundamentally, *De legibus*, 2.19.8 (quoted above, n. 46).

since the rules of fair trial for a capital crime are designed precisely for the extremity in which persons on trial for such crimes find themselves, those who are convicted on perjured testimony must patiently endure death,[61] and judges who know the truth but after every effort can find no legal way of proving it (or of excluding the false evidence) must follow the rules of evidence and sentence to death someone whom they know to be innocent.[62] So there may well be rules of war which, though positive, are not subject to dispensation in emergency, since they were adopted precisely for that type of extremity.

Moreover, not all 'rules of war' are merely positive. Some are true implications of the basic requirements of practical reasonableness, which are morality's (natural law's) foundational principles. And some of those basic requirements entail exceptionless moral norms. What Kant identified as the requirement that one treat human persons always as ends in themselves and never as mere means is a bundling together of the requirement that one never meet injury with injury (even when one could do so fairly), which excludes all acts of mere revenge, and the requirement that one not do evil (such as intentionally to destroy, damage, or impede a basic human good) for the sake of good—each requirement being, in turn, an implication of the first moral principle of openness to integral human fulfilment (love of neighbour as oneself). One of the exceptionless moral norms entailed by the requirement that evil not be done for the sake of good is the norm which excludes intending to kill, and intentionally killing, any (innocent) human being.

But, at least in situations of extremity, would it not be the lesser evil to kill a few innocents (say hostage children) to prevent the extermination of thousands and the utter ruin of a decent community? The whole tradition, while very attentive to the need to prevent bad consequences and to the bearing of likely bad consequences on duties of fairness, denies the claim that reason can identify such a killing of the innocent as the lesser evil.[63] It accepts the Socratic, Platonic, and Catholic maxim that it is better (a lesser evil) to suffer wrong than to do wrong,[64] and rejects as an understandable but ultimately unreasonable temptation the thought[65] that it is better for one innocent man to be framed and put to death than for the whole people to perish. It accepts that self-defence is a situation of necessity,[66] but

---

[61] Suarez, *De bello*, 9.5 (Williams trans., 859).
[62] *ST* II–II q.64 a.6 ad 3; q.67 a.2. [But see the endnote to essay IV.17.]
[63] On the killing of innocent hostages, see Vitoria, *De iure belli*, sec. 43 (*Political Writings*, 319).
[64] Plato, *Gorgias*, 508e–9d; Vatican II, *Gaudium et spes*, para. 27; see *FoE* 112–20; *MA* 47–51.
[65] Articulated for the tradition in John 1: 50; 18: 14.
[66] Vitoria, *De iure belli*, secs 1 (*Political Writings*, 298), 19 (305); Suarez, *De bello*, 1.4 (Williams trans., 803); 4.10 (823).

rejects as unreasonable and morally false[67] the Roman and Cromwellian maxim that necessity knows no law. Or rather, the maxim is given its proper, subordinate role: necessity (that is, great danger) can entitle one to make an exception to rules adopted for human convenience, or concerning human goods which are not basic; thus rules about fasting and Sabbath observance, or about rights of property, can be overridden 'by necessity', as fairness suggests and permits.[68] But the basic goods of the human person must be respected unconditionally.

One can find in the tradition occasional statements which clearly face up to the gravity of the matter:

> In such a situation, the law of God, which is also the rule of reason, makes exceptionally high demands.... The principles the Church proclaims are not for some ideal or theoretical world or for humanity in the abstract. They speak directly to the consciences of men and women in this world. They are principles that can on occasion demand heroic self-sacrifice of individuals and nations. For there are situations, for example in war, in which self-defence could not be effective without the commission of acts which must never be done, whatever the consequences. Innocent hostages, for example, must never be killed.[69]

But such statements are less frequent than one would think needful to prepare people to live up to the taxing responsibilities of suffering wrong rather than doing it in situations where everything is or seems to be at stake.

To be sure, the tradition's adherence to exceptionless moral norms is reinforced by faith in God's providence, redemption, and promise of eternal salvation. But it is not logically dependent upon that faith. Nor is it, ultimately, a legalism, in which exceptionless rules might be promoted for fear that allowing exceptions would have bad consequences (for example, by abusive extensions of the permission). It understands itself, rather, as an unconditional adherence to the truth about what reason requires. An understanding and defence of the tradition thus depends upon a critique of

---

[67] See *MA* 51–5; *NDMR* ch. 9.

[68] Grotius, though not Catholic, states the tradition accurately enough: '"Necessity", says Seneca, "... the great resource of human weakness, breaks every law", meaning, of course, every human law, or law constituted after the fashion of human law': *De iure belli ac pacis*, 2.2.6.4 (Kelsey trans., 193–4). In 1.4.7.1 (148–9), he exemplifies the latter category by pointing to the divine law of Sabbath rest, subject to a tacit exception in cases of extreme necessity. See also 3.1.2.1 (599). In Aquinas, the maxim *necessitas non subditur legi*, necessity is not subject to the law, is used just to make the point that, in an emergency so sudden that there is no time to consult authorized interpreters, it is permissible for the subjects to give to the law an interpretation that they think would have been approved by the law-maker (assumed to be a morally upright law-maker). 'Keep the city gates shut' e.g. can be regarded as subject to an interpretative exception 'except to admit your own army in flight from the battlefield', *ST* I–II q.96 a.6c and ad 1.

[69] Archbishops of Great Britain, 'Abortion and the Right to Live', 24 January 1980, para. 24.

claims that reason does not warrant these (or any) exceptionless specific norms.[70]

VII. RESISTANCE TO POLITICAL AUTHORITY

The tradition is not content with so cloudy, euphemistic, and characteristically modern a term as 'resistance'. The Resistance was trying to overthrow German rule in France, and in conscientious deliberations such a venture deserves to be known for what it is, and distinguished from disobedience, 'civil' or otherwise.

The tradition's reflections on the forcible overthrow of governments proceed in the same dialectic of private right and public authority, of defence and punishment, as its reflections on war between nations. For such overthrow is truly a war-like venture. There are two main sorts of unjust government which might rightly be overthrown: (1) governments which seized power unjustly and by force and have not been legitimized by effluxion of time and absence of alternatives, and (2) governments which came to power lawfully but govern with manifest gross injustice (looting, murdering, framing, etc.).[71] If a government of either type pursues certain private citizens in an attempt to kill or mutilate them, they can rightly use force in the exercise of their rights of self-defence, and doing so is not necessarily made unacceptable by the fact that it will have the side effect of killing even the supreme ruler.[72] But no private citizen, as such, can rightly undertake to kill any or all of the rulers, as punishment (or revenge) for their wrongdoing, however wicked, any more than private citizens can rightly kill a well-known murderer on the score that they are administering capital punishment (or vengeance).[73]

Still, might not such a citizen claim to be defending the community against the future crimes of the government? In the case where the government had come to power justly or acquired a moral entitlement to govern, the answer given by the tradition was: yes, if the wrongs such a citizen seeks to prevent are violent, but not otherwise; for in any other case, the attempt amounts to levying offensive war, which is never within private authority, any more than a private citizen can rightly resort to personal violence to incapacitate a forger. In the case where the government came to power illegitimately and remains illegitimate, the tradition is willing to

---

[70] Such a critique is available in e.g. *MA*.
[71] Suarez, *De iuramento fidelitatis regis Angliae* (1613), 4.1 (Williams trans., 705).
[72] *Ibid.*, 4.5 (709). As always, the side effects of the ruler's death or overthrow remain to be assessed for the fairness or unfairness of incurring them.
[73] *Ibid.*, 4.4 (708).

treat the government's acts of ruling, however peaceful in themselves, as amounting to a continuing act of violent injustice against the community (banditry). Accordingly, unless the community by some communal act makes it clear that it wishes no such deliverance, any private individual has the tacit and assumed public authority and constructive consent needed to seek an illegitimate government's violent overthrow, not as an act of punishment but as defence of self, country, and every innocent member of the community.[74] Such an act must, of course, satisfy all the other relevant requirements of proper motivation, exhaustion of alternatives, prospect of success, and fairness in accepting the foreseeable bad side effects.[75]

The risk that any attempt to overthrow a government by force will have very bad side effects is often great. The tradition, for the most part, inculcates caution and emphasizes the general desirability of preferring non-violent or 'passive' forms of resistance, always within the context of a wider teaching that government and positive law create moral obligations which, though by no means absolute or indefeasible or invariably strong, are significant and prevail over the contrary inclinations and desires of subjects in all cases save where the exercise of governmental power in question is certainly unjust. The tradition also recognizes other cases of justifiable disobedience, short of revolutionary violence intended to overthrow—that is, acts of war against—an unjust regime.

First, there is the important class of cases where administrative or legal requirements demand the performance of immoral acts (to surrender Jews to the Nazi authorities, for example). Violation of such requirements is both permissible and obligatory.

Secondly, government (or indeed private) property may be specifically dedicated to wicked activities: concentration camps, slave ships, abortoria, human-embryo experimentation equipment, nuclear weaponry deployed for deterrence by a strategy involving city-swapping and final countervalue retaliation, etc. In circumstances where destroying the property and impeding the evil activities would be likely to save some persons from serious injustice, those actions would be justified.

Thirdly, there is civil disobedience strictly so called. This involves essentially (1) overt violation of a law (2) to express one's protest against that law, or against something public closely connected with some application of that law, together with (3) ready submission to the law's

---

[74] *Ibid.*, 4.11–13 (714). Aquinas, in his youthful *Sent.* II d.44 q.2 a.2c, treats the killing of Julius Caesar as justifiable on this basis.

[75] Suarez, *De iuramento fidelitatis*, 4.7–9. 'The Church's Magisterium admits [recourse to armed struggle] as a last resort to put an end to an obvious and prolonged tyranny which is gravely damaging the fundamental rights of individuals and the common good': CDF, Instruction on Christian Freedom and Liberation, *Libertatis conscientiae*, 22 March 1986, para. 79.

sanctions (a submission not morally required in the other classes of justifiable disobedience). The violation must not involve doing anything otherwise immoral, and its manner and circumstances must make it clear to observers not only that it *symbolizes* opposition to some important and clearly identified matter of law or policy, but also that this opposition seeks justice, not advantage. Since civil disobedience must not involve doing anything otherwise immoral, its justification does not cover use of force against any person. Nor does it cover the destruction of property which is at all closely connected with the well-being of individual persons who would be damaged by its destruction, removal, or temporary or permanent inaccessibility. Above all, it shuns the maxim 'Evil may be done that [greater] good may come of it'; indeed, that is the maxim which underpins most (though not all) attempted justifications of the laws or policies or proposals which are the objects of the civilly disobedient protest. So-called civil disobedience will be corrupted and corrupting if the campaigners subscribe to that maxim and so are willing to do real harm, not in self-defence but to advance their cause. The 'harms' one does in justifiable civil disobedience must be actions which, in their full context (as set out in the definition just given), are of a type accepted by one's upright fellow citizens as essentially no more than vivid expressions of authentic moral-political concerns, and thus as not truly harms. The essential analogy here is with the blows given and received on the football field, or the touchings and jostlings in a rush-hour crowd; in their full context these are not harms, even though in other contexts they would constitute assaults.[76]

The most fundamental point and justification of civil disobedience is to *show* that the wickedness of the laws or policies in question takes them outside the ordinary web of politics and law, and undermines the very legitimacy of the state or government itself—a legitimacy founded on justice, not on calculations of advantage in which the lives of innocents might be directly sacrificed in the interests of others.

VIII. ATTITUDES TOWARD WAR AND NON-VIOLENCE

The tradition emerged and flourished in coexistence with a body of customary laws (*ius gentium*) which it in part reformed but in part accepted with a complacency which now seems disconcerting. But at no time was the tradition an apologia for war. Rather, its thrust has been, and ever more clearly is, to teach that wars are *certainly unjustified* unless a number

[76] See further *NDMR* 354–7.

of conditions are satisfied. It involves no belief that many wars are just, or that the conduct of any war is in fact free from wicked injustice. Even in teaching (as it used to do but now scarcely does) that offensive war could be justified to punish guilty rulers and their agents, the tradition required that war be the last resort, initiated only after communications, negotiations, and where practicable a ceding of rights for the sake of peace.

The tradition is still developing, on the basis of its own fundamentals. Those fundamentals entail, I think, that war can be justified only as defence. In the absence of a world government, no state or political community or ruler can rightly claim the authority to punish; the custom on which that authority was formerly rested[77] should now be regarded as immoral and ineffective. To purport to exercise such authority, in these circumstances, is to do no more than to reproduce the practice of feuding, writ large. And if there were a worldwide government, its rulers' justifiable powers against communities would be police powers: to take steps to bring offending individuals to justice, and to defend themselves and overcome resistance in the course of taking those steps, but not to administer punishment to whole communities, or to punish individuals otherwise than by impartial judicial trial and public sentence.

As it reaches this point in its development, one can discern that the tradition's fundamentals implicitly entail the rejection of a belief which is explicit not only in the tradition but also in both classic pacifism and 'political realism'—the belief that war must involve *intending to kill*. The act-analysis involved in Aquinas's discussion of private self-defence entails, as Aquinas makes clear, that defensive acts foreseen to be likely or even certain to kill can nonetheless be done without any intent to kill. One's choice in choosing such an act of defence need only be to stop the attack, accepting as a side effect the attacker's death, unavoidably caused by the only available effective defensive measure. Such choices do not violate the exceptionless moral norm excluding every choice to destroy a basic human good. They will be justifiable choices only if they also involve no violation of any other requirement, especially the requirement of fairness: a deadly deed cannot be fairly chosen to fend off a harmless blow; those who are themselves acting unjustly cannot fairly resort to deadly force to resist someone reasonably trying to apprehend them.

And the structure of the action of political societies can be the same as that of individuals' acts of self-defence. Deadly deeds can be chosen, not with the precise object of killing those (other societies and their members) who are using force to back their challenge to just order, but

---

[77] Vitoria, *De iure belli*, sec. 19 (*Political Writings*, 305); see the quotation from Suarez above, n. 46.

simply to thwart that challenge. If the social act is limited to the use of only that force necessary to accomplish its appropriate purpose, the side effect of the death of those challenging the society's just order can rightly be accepted.[78] The distinction between innocents (combatants) and non-innocents (non-combatants) remains: lethal force may rightly be used against persons whose behaviour is part of the enemy society's wrongful use of force (against combatants), but not against others. The innocent (non-combatants, those not participating in the use of force against just order) cannot rightly be made the objects of lethal force.

The tradition, even as substantially developed and refined by the exclusion of punitive justifications for war and of intent to kill in war, wholly excludes pacifism—that is, the claim that lethal force can never be rightly used. Pacifism is not to be found in the New Testament[79] (in which the Catholic understanding of natural law already emerges), read as an integrated whole. What does there emerge is the vocation of some individuals and groups to non-violence (unconditional abstention from such use of force) in witness to the truths that peace, like all true goods, is a gift from above—of divine grace working in a privileged way by healing mercy and reconciliation—and that war, though its point is peace, can never be the efficient cause of peace.

---

[78] See further *NDMR* 309–19.
[79] See Grotius, *De iure belli ac pacis*, 1.2.6–8 (Kelsey trans., 61–81).

Part Four

Autonomy, Euthanasia, and Justice

14

EUTHANASIA AND JUSTICE[*]

I. 'EUTHANASIA'

Devised for service in a rhetoric of persuasion, the term 'euthanasia' has no generally accepted and philosophically warranted core of meaning.

The Dutch medical profession and civil authorities define euthanasia as: killing at the request of the person killed. But I shall call that *voluntary euthanasia*, and distinguish it from non-voluntary euthanasia (where the person killed is not capable of either making or refusing to make such a request) and involuntary euthanasia (where the person killed is capable of making such a request but has not done so).[1] It is certain that deliberate killing of patients by Dutch medical personnel, with the more or less explicit permission of civil authority, extends well beyond cases where death has been requested by the person killed; the Dutch practice of euthanasia includes non-voluntary and perhaps some involuntary euthanasia. Rightly (as we shall see) the Dutch commonly reject as morally irrelevant the distinction sometimes drawn between 'active' and 'passive' euthanasia, that is, between killing by use of techniques or instrumentalities for hastening death, and killing by omitting to supply sustenance and/or treatment which, but for the decision and intent to terminate life, would have been supplied.

In Nazi discourse, euthanasia was any killing carried out by medical means or medically qualified personnel, whether intended for the termination of suffering and/or of the burden or indignity of a life not worth living

---

[*] 1995b, comprising the three stages of a debate with John Harris. Here the sections are numbered consecutively from beginning to end. Harris and I each wrote our first essay independently and without sight of the other's; our second essays were each a reply to the other's first (again written without sight of the other's reply); and the third round was conducted like the second. So: my first essay is secs I–IV, my second is secs V–VIII, and my third is (after a short preface) secs IX–XII.
[1] These definitions of 'voluntary', 'non-voluntary', and 'involuntary' euthanasia correspond to those employed by the House of Lords Select Committee on Medical Ethics (Walton Committee) (see House of Lords Paper 21-1 of 1993–94, para. 23), and seem more serviceable than the different definitions offered in Harris, *The Value of Life*, 82–3.

(*Lebensunwertes Leben*), or for some more evidently public benefit such as eugenics (racial purity and hygiene), *Lebensraum* (living space for Germans), and/or minimizing the waste of resources on 'useless mouths'.

In pluralist democracies today, there is understandable reluctance to be associated with Nazi ideas and practices. Racist eugenics are condemned, though one comes across discreet allusions to the burden and futility of sustaining the severely mentally handicapped. Much more popular is the conception that some sorts of life are not worth living; life in such a state demeans the patient's dignity, and maintaining it (otherwise than at the patient's express request) insults that dignity; proper respect for the patient and the patient's best interests requires that that life be brought to an end.

Since this essay is to present a philosophical case against euthanasia, my working definition of euthanasia should satisfy two requirements. It should ensure that the type of proposal to be argued against is identified under its most attractive or tempting true description. And it should also identify the full range or set of proposals which, for the purposes of applying the relevant moral principles and norms, fall within the same morally significant type and are the subject-matter of a single moral conclusion.

So I define the *central case* of *euthanasia* as the adopting and carrying out of a proposal that, as part of the medical care being given someone, his or her life be terminated on the ground that it would be better for him or her (or at least no harm) if that were done. But this definition should be taken with two related and interrelated points. The moral norms which, I shall argue, rule out the central case will rule out *every* proposal to terminate people's lives on the ground that doing so would be beneficial by alleviating human suffering or burdens, whether the proposal arises within or outside the context of medical care. And, conversely, if the central case of euthanasia is not morally ruled out, neither are proposals to terminate people's lives outside the context of medical care and/or on the ground that doing so would benefit *other people* at least by alleviating their proportionately greater burdens.

To make this last point is not to insinuate some crude 'slippery slope' argument from the anticipated bad consequences of allowing euthanasia of the paradigm sort. It is merely to indicate at the outset, proleptically, that neither the true moral principles at stake in the discussion, nor any plausible (though untrue) principles which if true would justify euthanasia of the paradigmatic type, give warrant for thinking that the conclusion of the moral argument might depend upon the medical (or non-medical) character or context of lethal conduct, or upon the identity of the person(s) for whose benefit a proposal precisely to terminate life might be adopted as a means. It is, in other words, to indicate that hereabouts one will find 'slippery slope' arguments of a valid[2] and sophisticated type, adverting not so much to predictions and attempted evaluative assessments of future consequences and states of affairs, but rather to the implications of consistency in judgment.

One of those valid arguments from consistency will conclude that there is no morally relevant distinction between employing deliberate omissions (or forbearances or abstentions) *in order to* terminate life ('passive euthanasia') and employing 'a deliberate intervention' for the same purpose ('active euthanasia'). So my definition even of the narrow central case of euthanasia is wider than the definition offered by those who, like the Walton Committee,[3] wish (for good reason) to oppose euthanasia but (for no detectable reason of principle) are unwilling to challenge the line between 'positive actions intended to terminate life' and 'omissions intended to terminate life'—the line drawn, for example, in *Airedale NHS Trust v Bland*[4] by Law Lords who admitted its legal misshapenness and moral irrelevance.[5]

II. HOW INTENTION COUNTS

The Select Committee on Medical Ethics (Walton Committee), which was set up by the House of Lords in the wake of the *Bland* case and reported in early 1994, unanimously rejected any proposal to 'cross the line which prohibits any *intentional* killing, a line which we think it essential to preserve'.[6] The Committee described the 'prohibition of intentional killing' as 'the cornerstone of law and of social relationships'.[7] They then showed their understanding of the nature and importance of *intention* by rejecting outright the view[8] that the rightness or wrongness of administering analgesics or sedatives, in the knowledge that the dose will both relieve pain and shorten life, depends not upon the intention with which the

---

[2] See Douglas Walton, *Slippery Slope Arguments* (1992).
[3] Report of the Select Committee on Medical Ethics (Chairman Lord Walton), 31 January 1994 (House of Lords Paper 21-1 of 1993–4), paras 20–1.
[4] [1993] AC 789.   [5] See essay II.19 (1993c).
[6] House of Lords Paper 21-1 of 1993–94, para. 260. Here as elsewhere emphases are by me unless otherwise indicated.
[7] *Ibid.*, para. 237.
[8] Expressed to the Committee by the British Humanist Association, thus:

The doctrine of double effect seems to us a sophistry which is morally particularly damaging. When there are two outcomes of a given action, one good and one bad, the action is justified only if the good outweighs the bad in moral significance; and the moral weights of the two outcomes depend on the outcomes and the overall context, and are quite independent of the doctor's self-described intentions. (*Ibid.*, para. 76.)

medication is administered and only upon the comparative value of the respective outcomes. The Committee's view was this:

[W]e are satisfied that the professional judgment of the health-care team can be exercised to enable increasing doses of medication (whether of analgesics or sedatives) to be given *in order to* provide relief, even if this shortens life. In some cases patients may in consequence die sooner than they would otherwise have done but this is not in our view a reason for withholding treatment that would give relief, *as long as* the doctor acts in accordance with responsible medical practice *with the objective of* relieving pain or distress, and *with no intention to kill*... [T]he doctor's intention, and evaluation of the pain and distress suffered by the patient, are of crucial significance in judging double effect. If this *intention* is the relief of pain or severe distress, and the treatment given is appropriate to that *end*, then the possible double effect should be no obstacle to such treatment being given. Some may suggest that intention is not readily ascertainable. But juries are asked every day to assess intention in all sorts of cases.[9]

In this passage, the Committee rightly deploy some of the various synonyms which common speech deploys as alternative ways of expressing what is signified by their key general term 'intentional': 'with the intention to', 'in order to', 'with the objective of' and 'to that end'.[10]

I mention the Walton Committee's conclusions not as an appeal to authority, but as convenient evidence of a fact confirmed in many recent philosophical studies. Intention is a tough, sophisticated, and serviceable concept, well worthy of its central role in moral deliberation, analysis, and judgment, because it picks out the central realities of deliberation and choice: the linking of means and ends in a plan or *proposal*-for-action *adopted* by *choice* in preference to alternative proposals (including: to do nothing). What one intends is what one chooses, whether as end or as means. Included in one's intention is everything which is part of one's plan (proposal), whether as purpose or as way of effecting one's purpose(s). The parts of the plan are often picked out by phrases such as 'trying to', 'in order to', 'with the objective of', 'so as to', or, often enough, plain 'to'.

In recent years, the English courts have firmly set their face against a view widely and for many years propounded by legal academics, but most clearly put by Henry Sidgwick:

for purposes of exact moral or jural discussion, it is best to include under the term 'intention' all the consequences of an act that are foreseen as certain or probable.[11]

---

[9] *Ibid.*, paras 242, 243.
[10] Thus the Committee make it clear that they use 'intentional' as equivalent to 'intended' or 'with intent to', and not in the weaker sense (equivalent to 'not unintentionally', i.e. not accidentally or mistakenly or unexpectedly) found in some common idiom and some philosophical treatments of these issues.
[11] *The Methods of Ethics*, 202.

It was settled by the Law Lords in *R v Moloney* (1985) and *R v Hancock* (1986) that it is a fatal misdirection to instruct a jury on Sidgwick's lines. Foresight of consequences is evidentially relevant to the question what the accused intended, but a jury can rightly hold that what one foresees as probable or even certain to result from one's action is nevertheless no part of what one intends.[12] (And 'jural discussion' about the law of murder is intended by the judges to track sound 'moral discussion'.) The 'oblique intention' of Bentham, Sidgwick, Holmes, and Glanville Williams is not intention at all; it is a state of foresight and acceptance that one will cause such-and-such as a side effect. These thinkers claim one *should* have the same moral responsibility for foreseen (or foreseeable?) side effects as one has for what one intentionally brings about. But that claim depends not on a clear and realistic analysis of action but on a (highly contestable) theory about the content of true moral norms. In a sound theory of human action, the utilitarian construct 'oblique intention' is a mere deeming, a fiction, but the *intention* known to common sense, law, and exact philosophy alike is action's central reality. It is what one forms in choosing to act on *this* proposal/plan rather than that or those. In carrying out one's intention, one *does* precisely what one intends. The primary and proper description of one's act, and thus its primary identity as a human act, morally assessable by reference to relevant moral norms, is settled by what one intends, what one means to do.

So, in common sense and law alike, there is a straightforward, non-artificial, substantive distinction between choosing to kill someone with drugs (administered over, say, three days in order not to arouse suspicion) in order to relieve them of their pain and suffering, and choosing to relieve someone of their pain by giving drugs, in a dosage determined by the drugs' capacity for pain-relief, foreseeing that the drugs in that dosage will cause death in, say, three days. The former choice is legally and morally murder (in mitigating circumstances); the latter is not. The latter *may* still be morally and legally culpable, not by virtue of the moral and legal norm which excludes intentionally terminating life, but by virtue of other legal and moral norms, those which apply to the causing and accepting of side effects unfairly or in some other way unreasonably. So if the pain were in any case likely to abate, and the patient was not in any case dying, the imposition of death even as an unintended consequence (side effect) of pain relief would normally be grossly unfair and unreasonable, and in law a case of manslaughter though not murder.

---

[12] See essay II.10 at 174–5, 182–3 (1991b at 33–5, 45–6); Goff 'The Mental Element in the Crime of Murder' at 42–3.

The distinctions between what is intended as means or end and what is accepted as a side effect do not depend upon whether the side effect is desired or undesired, welcomed or accepted with reluctance. Provided that one in no way adjusts one's plan so as to make them more likely, side effects may be welcomed as a 'bonus' without being intended. It can be reasonable for someone to welcome death precisely insofar as it involves an end to misery or is envisaged as the gate of heaven. Of course, such a desire for death can be or become a temptation to form an intention to terminate or secure the termination of one's life, even if only a conditional ('If things get worse, I'll...') or hypothetical intention ('If I had the nerve to do it, I'd...'). But a desire for death need not result in the forming of such an understandable but always fundamentally different (and immoral) intention.

So the moral argument which condemns euthanasia as a kind of intentional killing does not condemn the use of drugs which cause death as a side effect, and does not condemn the longing that some people have for death. Nor does it condemn the decision of those who decline to undergo some life-saving or life-sustaining form of treatment because they choose to avoid the burdens (for example pain, disfigurement, or expense) imposed by such treatment, and accept the earlier onset of their death as a side effect of that choice. Such decisions may be more or less immoral because lacking in fortitude and/or perseverance in reasonable commitment or because unfair to dependants or colleagues, and so forth. But provided that they in no way involve the choice (intention) to terminate life by omission, they are not suicidal, and a similar decision made on someone's behalf is not euthanasiast.

Turn the coin over. Intentionally terminating life by omission—starving someone to death, or withholding their insulin, etc., etc.—is just as much murder as doing so by 'deliberate intervention' ('commission', 'active euthanasia'). Without squarely confronting the issue, at least a majority of the Law Lords in *Bland* slid, via a confused analysis of 'duty of care', into a position tantamount to denying this implication of the significance of intention. And the Walton Committee unfortunately so arranged their definitions and discussions that they managed to avoid even confronting the need to identify euthanasia by deliberate omission for what it is, and to distinguish it from the refusal or withholding of burdensome or futile treatment.

III. WHY INTENTION COUNTS

The distinction between what one intends (and does) and what one accepts as foreseen side effect(s) is significant because free choice matters. There is a free choice (in the sense that matters morally) only when one is rationally motivated towards incompatible alternative possible purposes (X and Y, or X and not-X) which one considers desirable by reason of the intelligible goods (instrumental and basic) which they offer—and when nothing but one's choosing itself settles which alternative is chosen. In choosing one adopts a proposal to bring about certain states of affairs—one's instrumental and basic purposes—which are precisely those identified under the description which made them seem rationally appealing and choosable. And what one thus adopts is, so to speak, synthesized with one's will, that is, with oneself as an acting person. Rationally motivated choice, being for reasons, is never of a sheer particular. So one *becomes* a doer of the *sort* of thing that one saw reason to do and chose and set oneself to do and accomplish—in short, one becomes the sort of person who has *such* an intention. Nothing but contrary free choice(s) can reverse this self-constitution.

Forming an intention, in choosing freely, is not a matter of having an internal feeling or impression; it is a matter of *setting oneself* to do something. (Here and hereabouts 'do' and 'act' include deliberate omissions such as starving one's children to death.) No form of voluntariness other than intention—for example the voluntariness involved in knowingly causing the side effects one could have avoided causing by not choosing what one chose—can have the self-constituting significance of really forming an intention.

The distinction between the intended and the side effect is *morally* significant. One who chooses (intends) to destroy, damage, or impede some instantiation of a basic human good chooses and acts contrary to the practical reason constituted by that basic human good. It can never be reasonable—and hence it can never be morally acceptable—to choose contrary to a reason, unless one has reason to do so which is rationally preferable to the reason not to do so. But where the reason *not* to act is a *basic* human good—in an instantiation that one would be choosing to destroy, damage, or impede by so acting—there cannot be a rationally preferable reason to choose so to act. (For the basic goods are aspects of the human persons who can participate in them, and their instantiations in particular persons cannot, as reasons for action, be rationally commensurated with one another. Indeed, if they could be, the reason which measured lower on the scale would, by that very fact, cease to be a *reason* and the higher ranked reason, having *all* the value of the lower *and some additional value*, would be rationally unopposed; so the situation would cease to be one of morally significant choice, choice between rationally appealing alternatives. But, to repeat, because of many factors including the self-constitutive significance of free choices, reasons for action (goods and bads) involved in alternative proposals for action are not commensurable *prior* to *moral* judgment and choice. Immoral proposals, though not fully reasonable, can and often do have rational appeal and morally significant choice between right and wrong remains eminently possible.) So, one who *intends* to destroy, damage, or impede some instantiation of a basic human good necessarily acts contrary not merely to a reason but to reason, that is, immorally.

Such, in very abstract terms, is the rationale of the more concrete and traditional moral wisdom: there are means which cannot be justified by any end; do not do evil that good may come; it is better to suffer wrong than to do it—not to mention the restatement made by Kant in opposition to early utilitarianism: treat humanity in oneself and others always as an end and never as a mere means.

The exceptionless moral norms which give specificity to these principles are—and, if morality is to give coherent direction to conscientious deliberation, must be—negative norms about what is chosen and intended, not about what is caused and accepted as a side effect. But while one can always refrain from choosing to harm an instance of a basic human good (that is, from resorting to unjustifiable means, doing evil, doing wrong, treating someone's humanity as a mere means), one *cannot* avoid *causing harm* to some instances of human goods. For every choice and action has some more or less immediate or remote negative impact on—in some way facilitates the damaging or impeding of—some instantiation(s) of basic human good(s). And since such harm is inevitable, it cannot be excluded by reason's norms of action. For moral norms exclude irrationality over which we have some control; they do not exclude accepting the inevitable limits we face as rational agents. Accepting—knowingly causing—harm to basic human goods as side effects will be contrary to reason only if doing so is contrary to a reason of another sort, viz., a reason which bears not on choosing/intending precisely as such but rather on acceptance, awareness, and causation. As I indicated in relation to choices to administer pain-relieving drugs, or to refuse or withhold life-saving treatment, there certainly are reasons of this other sort—particularly reasons of impartiality and fairness (the Golden Rule), and reasons arising from role-responsibilities and prior commitments. Still, one can be certain that harmful side effects are *not* such as to give reason to reject an option, if the feasible alternative option(s) involve *intending* to destroy or damage some instantiation of a basic human good such as someone's life.

IV. WHY IT IS ALWAYS WRONG TO CHOOSE TO TERMINATE THE LIFE OF THE VERY YOUNG, THE VERY ILL AND/OR THE VERY OLD

The Walton Committee, having expressed its judgment that the prohibition of intentional killing is the cornerstone of social relationships, immediately adds: 'It protects each one of us impartially, embodying the belief that *all are equal*.'[13] All who/what? The answer is evident enough: people, including the vulnerable and disadvantaged.[14]

In virtue of what (if anything) are people, with all their manifold differences, equal and so entitled to be valued and treated as—not merely *as if*!—equals? To answer that question is also to answer the question of whether and why human life is a basic good which one may never rightly choose to destroy in any of its instantiations (living human beings).

What do all human beings have in common? Their humanity. This is not a mere abstraction or nominal category; nor is it Kant's thin, rationalistic reduction of one's humanity (*Menschlichkeit*) to that aspect of one's nature which one does not share with other terrestrial creatures: one's reason and rational will. Rather, one's humanity is one's capacity to live the life, not of a carrot or a cat, but a human being. And one's having this radical capacity is, again, no mere abstraction; it is, indeed, one's very life, one's being a living human being. Carrots and cats, too, are alive. But human life is not partly carrot-life and partly cat-life. It is human through and through, a capacity—more or less actualized in various states of existence such as waking, sleeping, infancy, traumatic unconsciousness, decrepitude, etc.—for human metabolism, human awareness, feelings, imagination, memory, responsiveness and sexuality, and human wondering, relating, and communicating, deliberating, choosing, and acting. To lose one's life is to lose all these capacities, these specific forms and manifestations of one's humanness; it is to lose one's very reality as a human being.

That reality is through and through the reality of a person, a being with the radical capacity to deliberate and choose. Free choice, as I have already said, is wonderful in its freedom from inner and outer determination and its world-shaping and self-determining creativity for participating in intelligible goods. Personal life accordingly has the dignity which the tradition sought to capture with the phrase 'image of God'—a phrase which serious philosophers such as Socrates, Plato, and Aristotle would not have dismissed as a mere theological flourish foreign

---

[13] House of Lords Paper 21-1 of 1993–94, para. 237. [14] See *ibid.*, para. 239.

to philosophy's reflection on the ultimate principles of everything.[15] That dignity is most fully manifested in the dispositions and activities of people and communities who think wisely, and choose and act with the integrity and justice of full reasonableness. But, once again, thinking (and thinking straight) and choosing (with the freedom of full reasonableness unfettered by deflecting emotions) are *vital* activities, life-functions, actualizations of that *one* radical, dynamic capacity which is actuated in all one's activities, metabolic, sensitive, imaginative, intellectual, and volitional.

Every living human being has this radical capacity for participating in the manner of a person—intelligently and freely—in human goods. That is, every living being which results from human conception and has the epigenetic primordia (which every hydatidiform mole and, even more obviously, every human sperm and every ovum lacks) of a human body normal enough to be the bodily basis of some intellectual act is truly a human being, a human person. But, to repeat again, the human being's life is not a vegetable life supplemented by an animal life supplemented by an intellectual life; it is the one life of a unitary being. So a being that once has human (and thus personal) life will remain a human person while that life (the dynamic principle for that being's integrated organic functioning) remains—that is, until death. Where one's brain has not yet developed, or has been so damaged as to impair or even destroy one's capacity for intellectual acts, one is an immature or damaged human person.

The alternative is some sort of dualism according to which a human person inhabits and uses a living, organically human body while that body is in a certain state of development and health, but at other times (earlier and in many cases also later) is absent from it because the body, though living, cannot yet or can no longer support personal existence. But dualism—every such attempt to distance human bodily life from person or selfhood—has been subjected to devastating philosophical criticism. For a dualistic account of personal existence undertakes to be a theory of something but ends up unable to pick out any unified something of which to be the theory. More specifically, it sets out to be a theory of one's personal identity as a unitary and subsisting self—a self always organically living but only discontinuously conscious, and now and then inquiring and judging, deliberating and choosing, communicating, etc.—but every dualistic theory renders inexplicable the unity in complexity which one experiences in every act one consciously does. We experience this (complex) unity more intimately and thoroughly than any other unity in the world; indeed, it is for us the very paradigm of substantial unity and identity. As I write this,

---

[15] See e.g. Aristotle, *Metaphysics*, XII.7–8: 1072a18–639.

I am one and the same subject of my fingers hitting the keys, the sensations I feel in them, the thinking I am articulating, my commitment to write this essay, my use of the computer to express myself. Dualistic accounts, then, fail to explain *me*; they tell me about two things, other and other, one a non-bodily person and the other a non-personal body, neither of which I can recognize as myself, and neither of which can be recognized as me by the people with whom I communicate my perceptions, feelings, thoughts, desires, and intentions by speaking, smiling, etc. Careful philosophical reflection on human existence rejects the casual, opportunistic dualism of the many bio-ethicists who want to justify the non-voluntary killing of small, weak, or otherwise impaired people but, for some ill-explained reason, are reluctant to accept that such killing puts to death persons. It also exposes the arbitrariness with which these bio-ethicists attempt to draw a line between living human beings deemed to be persons and living human beings deemed to be not yet or no longer or never persons.

In short, human bodily life is the life of a person and has the dignity of the person. Every human being is equal precisely in having that human life which is also humanity and personhood, and thus that dignity and intrinsic value. Human bodily life is not mere habitation, platform, or instrument for the human person or spirit. It is therefore not a merely instrumental good, but is an intrinsic and basic human good. Human life is indeed the concrete reality of the human person. In sustaining human bodily life, in however impaired a condition, one is sustaining the person whose life it is. In refusing to choose to violate it, one respects the person in the most fundamental and indispensable way.

In the life of the person in an irreversible coma or irreversibly persistent vegetative state, the good of human life is really but very inadequately instantiated. Respect for persons and the goods intrinsic to their well-being requires that one make no choice to violate that good by terminating their life. On the other hand, fair-minded persons may well be unwilling to impose on themselves or their families or communities the burden of expense involved in medical treatment and non-domestic care for the purpose of sustaining them in such a deprived and unhealthy state. To preserve human solidarity with such people, and to respect rather than violate the one good in which they still participate—bodily life bereft of participation in other human goods such as knowledge and friendship—the care to be provided to them need not, I think, be more than is provided (save in times of most desperate emergency) to anyone and everyone for whom one has any respect and responsibility: the food, water, and cleaning that one can provide at home. To do less than that (save in desperate emergency when one must attend to more urgent responsibilities) would scarcely be intelligible save as manifesting a choice—perhaps even a choice once made by the patient and set down in some advance directive—to proceed on the basis that such patients and/or anyone who is responsible for caring for them would be better off if they were dead. But such a choice involves the intent to terminate life and thus violates a basic and intrinsic good of human persons, and denies such people's still subsisting equality of value and worth, and their equal right to life.

Is this to say that the autonomy of the patient or prospective patient counts for nothing? By no means. Where one does not know that the requests are suicidal in intent, one can rightly, as a healthcare professional or as someone responsible for the care of people, give full effect to requests to withhold specified treatments or indeed any and all treatments, even when one considers the requests misguided and regrettable. For one is entitled and indeed ought to honour these people's autonomy, and can reasonably accept their death as a side effect of doing so.

But suicide and requests which one understands to be requests for assistance in suicide are a very different matter. It is mere self-deception to regard the choice to kill oneself as a 'self-regarding' decision with no impact on the well-being of people to whom one has duties in justice. The point is not merely that 'the death of a person affects the lives of others, often in ways and to an extent which cannot be foreseen'.[16] More importantly, it is this. If one is really exercising autonomy in choosing to kill oneself, or in inviting or demanding that others assist one to do so or themselves take steps to terminate one's life, one will be proceeding on one or both of two philosophically and morally erroneous judgments: (i) that human life in certain conditions or circumstances retains no intrinsic value and dignity; and/or (ii) that the world would be a better place if one's life were intentionally terminated. And each of these erroneous judgments has very grave implications for people who are in poor shape and/or whose existence creates serious burdens for others.

For: if one claims a right to suicide, assistance in suicide, and/or euthanasia, one is making a claim which is not and rationally cannot be limited by reference to one's own particular identity and circumstances. Nor can it plausibly be restricted to cases where the person to be killed has autonomously chosen to act on one or both of the two (erroneous) judgments. For the first judgment claims that death—and thus being killed—is no harm (indeed may be a benefit). So it renders unintelligible any principled moral exclusion of non-voluntary and even of involuntary euthanasia. And the second judgment, too, cannot be plausibly defended

---

[16] Walton Committee, House of Lords Paper 21-1 of 1993–94, para. 237.

by reasons such that its range of application would be limited to suicide, assisted suicide, and voluntary euthanasia; its sense and its grounds alike extend to include non-voluntary euthanasia.

The moral errors underlying claims to a right to assistance in suicide or to voluntary euthanasia are errors which do the most vulnerable members of our communities the great injustice of denying, in action, the true judgments on which depend both the acknowledgement of their dignity and their right to life (and so too all their other rights).

* * *

The notable differences between John Harris's essay and his earlier writings suggest the fragility of the grounds he offers for abandoning our deeply meditated traditions and embracing euthanasia. The ground he marks out is indeed shifting.

V. 'INDIVIDUAL'

Harris's definition of euthanasia, and much of his discussion, employs the term 'individual'. The theme of our exchange, of course, is not abortion. But it would be wrong to overlook his essay's striking assertion that 'the individual can be said to have come into existence when the egg is first differentiated or the sperm that will fertilise that egg is first formed'. Contrast this with chapter 1 of *The Value of Life* (often cited in the essay), where Harris maintained that 'fertilisation does not result in an individual even of any kind' and that 'the emergence of the individual occurs gradually', *after* conception.[17]

In 1985, Harris had two arguments for denying that a human individual begins at conception: that the 'fertilized egg' (that is, the early embryo) will divide into two elements (the embryo proper, as distinct from the placenta and related tissues), and that some early embryos split to form twins. Both those arguments are quite inadequate bases for denying what the definite article in the otherwise tendentious phrase '*the* fertilized egg' bears witness to: that from conception there is at all stages an individual organic entity. The specification of embryonic tissues into embryoblast and trophoblast, and the development of the latter into the placenta and related tissues, is neither more nor less than the development of an organ *of the embryo*, an organ which it will discard at birth. The division of an embryo into twins or triplets is simply a change from one individual into two; whether

[17] Harris, *The Value of Life*, 11.

or not the original individual was predetermined to become two, we find at all stages of this remarkable biological process nothing other than an individual or two or more individual human beings.

Before conception, on the other hand, it is not possible to say with confidence that 'the egg' will be fertilized. Still less is it possible to say which of many millions of sperm will fertilize it, if it is fertilized. Only the most unreconstructed Laplacean determinist could deny that the identity of the fertilizing sperm—that is, the question which one among the many millions of sperm which are formed at about the same time will in fact fertilize an egg—is a matter partly of chance and other non-determined factors (such as the free choice of the parents to have intercourse at such-and-such a precise time and in such-and-such a precise way). The first time at which the egg and sperm referred to by Harris become even in principle identifiable is the time of conception. Only by making an extravagant extrapolation backwards in time from that point can Harris suggest that the individual which emerges in the union of that egg and sperm already constituted an individual—indeed, already constituted *that* individual—from the earlier time when the fertilizing sperm was first formed. Harris's willingness to affirm that there is an individual from that earlier time is dependent upon his projecting forward the futures of two individuals (only hypothetically identifiable at that moment).

This willingness to project or extrapolate *individuals* backwards and forwards, in a manner quite foreign to a biologist's understanding of what is and is not an organism, not only stands in uneasy contrast to Harris's 1985 discussion. It also contrasts dramatically (and, I think, inexplicably) with his *un*willingness to project backwards or forwards those *capacities* which characterize the being of *persons*. His arbitrarily constrained conception of *having a capacity* is the basis of his artificial and fragile concept of being a person. It is thus the basis of his claims that a person does not exist until such-and-such a (very vaguely described) stage in the life of an individual human being, and that a person has ceased to exist before, perhaps long before, the death of the (so to speak) corresponding human individual.

VI. 'PERSON'

Like Harris, the tradition has an understanding of persons which 'allows for the possibility of there being non-human persons on other worlds'. That understanding is not anthropocentric; it respects and promotes the human, and recognizes inviolable human rights, not because humanity is *our* species and we just do favour our own, but because to be human is to have some share in the dignity of persons. Unlike Harris, however, the common tradition holds that where a product of human conception has the epigenetic primordia of a human body normal enough to be the organic basis of some intellectual act[18] it is not only a human being or individual but is indeed a person. And such a bodily individual is a bodily person not only from the outset but also, until death, irrevocably, whether or not he or she happens ever to engage in an intellectual act or is prevented temporarily or permanently from doing so by sleep, disease, injury, immaturity, or senility. Though there may be bodily persons who are not human, there are no human individuals who are not persons.

Like Harris, the tradition considers that self-consciousness and intelligence are 'criteria for personhood' in one sense of that very elusive phrase. To be a person is to belong to a kind of being which is characterized by rational (self-conscious, intelligent) nature.[19] To have a particular nature is to be so constituted, dynamically integrated, as to have certain *capacities* (for example for self-awareness and reasoning). But if being a person ('personhood') were not as radical and fundamental to one's dynamic constitution as being a human being is, but were rather an acquired trait—something as extrinsic and therefore potentially transient as, say, the magnetism of a piece of iron—then one's being a person would not have the significant depth, the dignity, which even Harris acknowledges.

What is distinctive about Harris's position, both in his essay and his book, is his attempt to link *being a person* with *being capable of valuing one's own existence.* Once again, the tradition accepts this link or criterion, provided that 'capable of' is understood as signifying having a nature of the kind whose flourishing involves such valuing, whether or not an individual or such a nature happens to be in a position to exercise those capacities. But if 'capable of' is understood as Harris does, then people's personhood will come and go.[20] If, furthermore, the term 'valuing' is taken to signify a self-conscious intellectual act (such as mice and dogs, though wanting things,

---

[18] Thus a hydatidiform mole, though an organic individual with human origins and a human genetic structure, is not a human person.

[19] See e.g. Wiggins, 'Locke, Butler and the Stream of Consciousness: and Men as a Natural Kind' and the works cited in his n. 33. Wiggins integrates Locke's conception of personhood into his own more adequate account.

[20] Sometimes the capacity is understood by Harris in such a narrow and stringent way that it becomes equivalent to exercising the capacity. Thus he says (*The Value of Life*, 18):

> To value its own life, a being would have to be aware of itself as an independent centre of consciousness, existing over time with a future that it was capable of envisaging and wishing to experience. Only if it could envisage the future could a being want life to go on, and so value its continued existence... On this concept of the person, the moral difference between persons and non-persons lies in the value that people *give to their lives.* The reasons it is wrong to kill a person is [sic] that to do so robs that individual of something they value and of the very thing that makes possible valuing anything at all. (Emphasis added.)

presumably cannot perform),[21] then personhood will be so much the more transient and the class of human persons so much the more restricted.

And since the presence or absence of this more than merely animal 'valuing' is so elusive, indeterminate, and non-determinable, the class of persons, of *people with equal rights*, becomes, even in principle, a matter of sheer decision, of selecting some point along a spectrum. Then the 'we' in Harris's 'What we have in common is our *capacity* to value our own lives and those of others'[22] takes on the somewhat sinister connotation of a self-defined discrimination between 'us' and 'you' or 'them' (the immature, the mentally defective, the senile...).

Harris preserves a discreet silence about Ronald Dworkin's recognition that a person who becomes demented remains a person.[23] But whether or not he in fact agrees with that judgment, the fact is that Harris's criterion of personhood allows him no rational basis for a judgment on the matter. All depends on how strongly and narrowly one understands 'able to value his own life', given that

to value its own life, a being would have to be aware of itself as an independent centre of consciousness with a future that it was capable of envisaging and wishing to experience.[24]

And why not pick out other features which characterize human nature in its flourishing—say, linguistic articulacy,[25] sense of humour, and/or friendship more deep, transparent, and supple than friendship between man and dog? Why not then call one or other or some set of these the capacity which, while it is enjoyed, makes us people and 'entitles an individual to be considered a person'?[26]

It is the fragility of Harris's method that impresses, its character as a process of *selecting grounds* on which to *adopt* a conception of personhood. It is a conception narrower and wider[27] than *humanity*, and it is selected, constructed, or interpreted, from a range of conceptions or interpretations, for its apparent congruence with current views about 'the peculiar *status that we give* to creatures possessing such features'.[28]

---

[21] 'For valuing is a conscious process and to value something is both to know what we value and to be conscious of our attitude towards it': *ibid.*, 15. But apes and perhaps some other creatures satisfy Harris's own understanding of his criteria for being a valuer: *ibid.*, 19–21.
[22] *Ibid.*, 16.   [23] Dworkin, *Life's Dominion*, 237.   [24] Harris, *The Value of Life*, 18.
[25] If there are, as there may well be, as many accounts of what it is that makes life valuable as there are valuable lives these accounts in a sense cancel each other out. What matters is not the *content* of each account but rather *that the individual in question has the capacity to give such an account.* (*Ibid.*, 16 (emphasis added to last 13 words).)
[26] *Ibid.*, 14. Some individual human beings, then, are not 'entitled' to be 'considered' persons.
[27] 'I think that she [Washoe, a chimpanzee] clearly can [speak] and is therefore equally clearly a person': *ibid.*, 20.
[28] *Ibid.*, 15 (emphasis added).

As the discussion in section I above suggested, Harris fails to understand organic identity, and the *substantial* change—change of organic identity—which occurs at conception and death.[29] His notion of *capacity* is as narrow and shifting as it is because, misconceiving organic identity, he misconceives what he calls 'the potentiality argument' and mistakenly thinks he has refuted 'it'. He misconceives the relevant point as a claim that 'since the fertilised egg is potentially a human being we must invest [!] it with all the same rights and protections that are possessed by actual human beings'.[30] But the relevant argument instead claims that the embryo is actually a human being because it already possesses, albeit in undeveloped or immature form, all the capacities or potential that any other human being has. Harris's counter-arguments fail. They are worth considering here, not because our theme is abortion, but because failure to grasp what is involved in organic integration, unity, and identity makes it impossible to give a true account of the changes which an organism undergoes in illness, decay, injury, and the process of dying.

Harris's first argument about 'potentiality' is that

the bare fact that something will become X... is not a good reason for treating it now as if it were in fact X. We will all inevitably die, but that is an inadequate reason for treating us now as if we were dead.[31]

This argument fails to grasp the difference between an active capacity and a vulnerability or susceptibility. An organic capacity for developing eyesight is not 'the bare fact that something will become' sighted; it is an existing reality, a thoroughly unitary ensemble of dynamically interrelated primordia of, bases and structures for, development.

Harris's second counter-argument equally disregards the real distinction between what pertains to one organism and what does not. 'The unfertilised egg and the sperm [which sperm?] are equally potentially new human beings'.[32] But this claim flies in the face of the biological understanding of reality to which it appeals. Even if 'the sperm' could be identified in advance of fertilization (as even in principle it cannot), there is no sense whatever in which the unfertilized ovum and that sperm constitute one organism, a dynamic unity, identity, whole. The zygote is precisely that: a new human being. It will remain one and the same (unless it twins) until its death, whether days or decades later. The same organizing principle which integrates a human individual and directs his or her development continues to do so until death. So this individual remains the same organic individual even if gravely impaired by immaturity, senility, or illness.

[29] And, it seems, in the relatively rare case of twinning.
[30] *Ibid.*, 11.   [31] *Ibid.*   [32] *Ibid.*; see also 12.

Someone may say that to speak of organisms is one thing but to speak of persons quite another. And it is true that just as physics as such knows nothing of chemical compounding, and chemistry as such knows nothing of the living cell, so biology as such knows nothing of persons. But a philosophical anthropology attentive to all the relevant data, including biological and zoological realities, can make a well-grounded affirmation of the personal nature of the human organism. An organism of human genetic constitution normal enough to provide, or develop sufficiently to provide, at least the organic basis of some intellectual act is a personal entity, even when too impaired to perform such an act. To deny this is either to ignore the personal characteristics of normal adult human existence (characteristics most perfectly represented by the bodily-intellectual reality of language), or else to embrace a kind of dualism according to which a person temporarily *inhabits*[33] an organism. That kind of dualism is unsustainable for reasons some of which I sketched in my first essay.[34]

VII. 'CRITICAL INTERESTS'

We now reach the most interesting aspect of Harris's essay—interesting not least for its divergence from the position advanced in his book *The Value of Life*. It is the theory, which he adopts or perhaps adapts from Dworkin, of *critical interests*. The link between this new theme and the matters just discussed can be seen in Harris's remarkable thesis: a human being who—or rather, which, or that—has ceased to be a person may nonetheless retain critical interests. One can have a critical interest, he says, even when one can no longer want or value anything; Tony Bland, when 'no longer a person', 'could and did still have critical interests'.[35] This whole thesis dramatizes the artificiality of Harris's conception of personhood. The idea of critical interests also, as I shall argue, undermines his case for voluntary euthanasia and his 'liberal' objections to the 'tyranny' or 'paternalism' allegedly involved in proscribing it.

Harris makes some acute observations on Ronald Dworkin's case for euthanasia. But, so it seems, he now accepts the idea which Dworkin names *critical interests*.

---

[33] See e.g. Dworkin, 'The Right to Death' at 17.
[34] [*Scil.* sec. IV at 220–21.] See also Braine, *The Human Person: Animal and Spirit*. (This is a book which itself is in more ways than one a triumph of the human as described in its sub-title.)
[35] 'An important feature of critical, as opposed to experiential, interests is that they survive the permanent loss of the capacity to know whether or not these interests are being fulfilled': Harris, 'Euthanasia and the Value of Life'. Why this should be so Harris never, I think, even vaguely indicates.

Dworkin distinguishes between experiential and critical interests. One's experiential interests, he says, are one's interests merely because one likes the experiences involved in satisfying them; and 'the value of these experiences...depends precisely on the fact that we do find them pleasurable or exciting *as experiences*'.[36] But critical interests are 'interests that it does make [one's] life genuinely better to satisfy, interests [one] would be mistaken, and genuinely worse off, if one did not recognise'.[37] So these are not just interests which one happens to have and happens to want satisfied. Rather they are 'critical' precisely because they are interests which one judges one '*should* want' (Dworkin's italics).[38]

[W]e not only have, in common with all sensate creatures, experiential interests in the quality of our future experiences but also critical interests in the character and value of our lives as a whole. These critical interests are connected...to our convictions about the intrinsic value...of our own lives. A person worries about his critical interests because he believes it important what kind of a life he has led, important for its own sake and not merely for the experiential pleasure that leading a valuable life (or believing it valuable) might or might not have given him...he is the kind of creature, and has the moral standing, such that it is intrinsically, objectively important how his life goes.[39]

Harris notes, indeed headlines, that 'critical interests are objective'. He notes how this objectivity entails that one can misunderstand what is important about life and mislocate one's critical interests, and how this possibility provides the basis for a 'defence of paternalistic interference with an individual's desires "in her own critical interests"'. He seems unhappy with this implication of the notion of critical interests, yet rejects neither the soundness of the implication nor the notion of critical interests itself. Indeed his essay concludes by accepting and deploying the notion, if not the implication, with some enthusiasm. He seems not to see what havoc it plays with his fundamental conclusion that forbidding voluntary euthanasia is 'a form of tyranny which like all acts of tyranny is an ultimate denial of respect for persons'.

Harris's allegation about the tyrannical character of laws found in all civilized states cannot be sustained. The argument of sec. IV is here reinforced by the conception of critical interests. For if it is the case, as I argued, that those who choose to ask to be killed are (in Harris's paraphrase of Dworkin) 'tragically misinterpreting' their own life and its

---

[36] Dworkin, *Life's Dominion*, 201.   [37] *Ibid.*, 201.
[38] *Ibid.*, 202. Dworkin illustrates his point: 'Having a close relationship with my children is not important just because I happen to want the experience; on the contrary, I believe a life without wanting it would be a much worse one.'
[39] *Ibid.*, 235–6.

meaning—not to mention the meaning and value of the life of any bodily person and thus any human being—it must also be the case that action to prevent persons from acting on such a misinterpretation need involve no 'ultimate denial of respect for persons' but rather can manifest the most profound respect for persons, including even the persons so prevented.

I suspect that Harris hopes to escape this implication of the idea of critical interests by 'reinterpreting' the idea. On Dworkin's understanding of it, what is objectively important is how one's life goes, and one can rightly speak of the 'intrinsic, cosmic importance of human life itself'.[40]

Harris hopes, I think, to replace this understanding of *critical interests* with a more subjective understanding of it: what is 'of intrinsic, cosmic importance' (as Harris puts it) is the individual's *opinions about* what it means for his or her own life to go well. But this subjectivizing of Dworkin's conception cannot be carried through without abandoning the very notion of critical interests. Dworkin could of course accept, and may well in fact accept, that amongst the items of cosmic importance are the strong and genuine preferences and self-referential opinions of persons—right or wrong. But there is no plausibility whatever in the notion—which seems to be what Harris is hinting at—that the *only* items of cosmic importance are the preferences or self-referential opinions themselves, regardless of their rightness. If nothing else about human existence and its forms and conditions be of objective importance, there are no grounds for thinking that the sheer fact of having an opinion or preference *is* of such importance and does call for such respect.

As Dworkin says, in a passage quoted by Harris with qualified approval, opinions about the importance of human life concern values which 'no one can treat...as trivial enough to accept other people's orders about what they mean'.[41] Swept along by his prejudicial rhetoric about 'orders' and his imminent declamation about 'devastating, odious tyranny', Dworkin fails to see that his thesis in this passage cuts both ways. Since the 'values' are indeed as important as he says, one can hardly treat them as trivial enough to stand idly by when someone within one's care makes a mistake about them which threatens to have irreversible consequences, directly for that person and indirectly for others. Harris in turn fails to see that if the values themselves lack 'cosmic importance', so too must people's opinions about them. For if a human person's very being, self, and flourishing or ruin are of no cosmic importance, it is mere baseless conceit to attribute that kind of importance (as Harris does) to people's self-assessments or self-disposition.

[40] *Ibid.*, 217.   [41] *Ibid.*

VIII. NON-VOLUNTARY AND INVOLUNTARY EUTHANASIA

Harris says 'the real problem of euthanasia is the tragedy of the premature and unwanted deaths of the thousands of people in every society who die for want of medical or other resources'. By thus deliberately treating *intention to kill* as irrelevant, Harris wilfully obfuscates the debate about euthanasia. According to him, 'whenever life-saving resources are "spent" on things other than saving lives',[42] those who decide to spend these resources on something other than saving life have (or treat themselves as having) 'moral reasons for killing' the person whom they could have saved, and are indeed killing that person.[43] Since money can almost always buy life-saving resources, almost everyone who spends money on anything other than such resources is deciding to kill, and killing. This debauching of our language by Harris is most readily explicable as intended to soften up his readers to support wide programmes of deliberate, intentional killing.

The definitions of voluntary and non-voluntary euthanasia offered in his first essay are significantly different from those offered in his book, *The Value of Life*. But all are syntactically misleading. The phrase common to all of them, 'decision that a particular individual's life will come to an end', would be taken in good faith by most readers as meaning the same as 'decision *to* bring an individual's life to an end', that is, a decision executing a choice or *intention to* terminate life (whether by 'act' or omission). But Harris intends the phrase to include decisions by Parliament not to increase the health budget by the sums that would be required to save every life that could be saved—that is, all decisions to spend money on something other than life-saving. On this basis, he can freely and quite misleadingly denounce 'the government's euthanasia programme'.[44] His definition's allusion to 'a *particular* person's life' is thus a red herring, and it is hard to think of any appropriate reason for his including it.

Harris is fully entitled, of course, to argue that more should be spent on life-saving, and that failure to do so is very culpable. He is fully entitled to argue (though he will be mistaken in doing so) that the distinction between what is intended and what is merely accepted as a side effect has no moral significance. But it is, I suggest, profoundly misleading of him simply to ignore the distinction, without fair notice, and to hijack the term 'murder'—which centrally connotes *intention to kill*, both in law and common morality—by claiming, as he in substance does, that any governmental or

---

[42] Harris, *The Value of Life*, 160.   [43] Ibid., 65–6.   [44] Ibid., 84–5.

private limiting of life-saving is 'involuntary euthanasia or murder'. This sleight of hand even does duty to relieve him of his obligation to *argue* that such limiting is unjustified.

Meanwhile, everyone should notice what the moral principles, the conception of value and the conception of responsibility employed by Harris entail. On his view of things, there is no barrier of principle which excludes either non-voluntary euthanasia (whether on his definition or Walton's and mine) or involuntary euthanasia (again, on his or my definition). Even his 'liberal' conception of respect for people's 'autonomy' is subject to a tacit qualification that autonomy, being one value among many, can be outweighed.[45] Since the weights and measures for this 'balancing' of values are not supplied by reason, our right not to be deliberately killed could scarcely—if Harris were correct—be a right, so radically subject would it be, even in principle, to the sentiments of those who subscribe to arguments like his. Shifting, unsteady ground.

* * *

John Harris's second essay depends upon some striking misunderstandings of the positions central to my first essay, 'A philosophical case against euthanasia'. These misunderstandings or misstatements are of more than local or personal interest. They are characteristic of euthanasiast attempts to rationalize the sentiments which are the movement's real guide.

Harris's second essay is notable also for its open reliance upon the thought that there are persons who simply 'should die'. To the notion that there are people who lack the status of 'persons', the thought that some innocent people who concededly do have that status nevertheless *should* die, and so should be killed, adds something equally sinister.

I am writing, of course, without having seen Harris's third essay. But at the end of the debate readers will, I think, wish to ask: Has Harris offered any clear and settled reason for doubting that all living human beings are people (persons), however disabled? Or for doubting that intention matters to the content of our fundamental rights, and duties of respect? Or that allowing sentiment to preside in these matters will propel us down a slippery slope into fearful oppression of the aged and infirm?

IX. RESPONSIBILITY FOR SIDE EFFECTS

Although he even quotes one of the passages in which I speak about our serious moral and legal responsibility for side effects of our choices, Harris

---

[45] See *ibid.*, 66.

insinuates that on my 'theory of action' one can 'ignore' all side effects, such as the hangovers or liver disease one incurs through over-drinking. 'For Finnis, an agent...is...only responsible for the world he intends.' Battling against this straw man, Harris contends that 'our moral responsibility [covers] what we knowingly and voluntarily bring about'. On other occasions, however, he tacitly acknowledges that my theory indeed affirms moral (and legal) responsibility for side effects. But his acknowledgements are misshapen.

For he claims that, on my view, we are '*less* responsible for things we...do not *positively desire*, or which are not our *primary objective*', we do not 'have *the same* responsibility', or '*full* moral responsibility' for side effects. I have italicized the misstatements. Intention, on my account, is not a matter of desire, still less of positively desiring; rather, it is a matter of choosing ends and means, often against the tug of contrary desires. Intention extends not only to primary objectives, but also to secondary objectives and chosen means (however reluctantly they may be chosen). The difference between our responsibility for what we intend and our responsibility for what we cause is not that the latter cannot be 'full', or is necessarily 'less' than (and in that quantitative sense not the 'same' as) the former. It is rather, as the very passage Harris quoted makes clear, a real and often very grave moral responsibility, but one governed, measured, and identifiable by moral norms *different* from those applicable to our intending and choosing of ends and means.

Harris's misunderstanding is not merely of my text and my theory of action and account of morality. It is a thoroughgoing misunderstanding of the whole common tradition recently manifested in passages of the Walton Report noted in my first essay. Where Walton, the law, the common tradition and I all distinguish between giving drugs *to kill* and giving the same drugs *to suppress pain*, Harris 'fail[s] to see any moral distinction at all'. (His changing my hypothetical euthanasiast doctor's motives for taking three days to do the job is quite beside the point.) Each of these two administrations of drugs, says Harris, is '*to* bring about the death'. This claim is false, for the very reasons which Harris acknowledges when he admits, against Sidgwick, that the average drunkard does not drink *to* get a hangover or to get liver disease.

Nor does the point depend upon whether the side effects are altogether unwanted (as hangovers and liver disease usually are) or unwanted in one respect but welcome in another. Suppose a commander orders the bombing of a factory, regretting as a human person the civilian deaths (unwanted side effect) from inevitable misses but also welcoming as a combatant the impact ('bonus' side effect) of these civilian deaths on enemy morale. He can truthfully say that (unlike many immorally ruthless commanders) he is not bombing *to* undermine civilian morale at all, but only *to* destroy the factory. This claim will be true if he has in no way calibrated or adjusted his plans so as to achieve civilian deaths—not even as a secondary objective—and if he stops the bombing as soon as the factory is destroyed.

Harris thinks this sort of distinction is of interest only to people who, like me (he says), are 'more interested in moral character—in the state of a person's soul—than what happens in the world'. This contrast is misconceived. The moral principles and norms which rely on the distinction between the intended and the unintended (side effect) are vastly important for 'what happens in the world'. The effects, 'in the world', of abandoning those principles, so as to treat ends (consequences) as potentially justifying any and every type of means, are and will be enormous. To the extent that we accept Harris's (or Machiavelli's or Bentham's) invitation to set aside moral norms which pivot on intention, and to make moral judgments by looking only to ends or expected or actual results, we become persons and societies of a different sort, we change character in a way that must (*if and to the extent that we are self-consistent*) involve extensive changes in the ways we act and thus in 'the worlds we create'.

Recognition of the absolute human (personal) rights and exceptionless duties of respect, so central to the morality Harris rejects, has had incalculably beneficial effects on these worlds, that is, on the real people who would otherwise be the victims of acts intended to suppress their life. The beneficial effects on character, on the souls of those who unconditionally respect personal dignity, have been and are side effects (albeit inbuilt and welcome), not the primary motivation of that respect. It is, as Elizabeth Anscombe has observed, 'quite characteristic of very bad degenerations of thought on such questions that they sound edifying'.[46] She was speaking precisely of the thesis which Harris articulates thus in his second essay:

the agent chooses...the world which results from her actions (or conscious omissions)...we are responsible for the whole package of consequences which we know will result from the choices we make.

This sounds edifying. So too does Harris's later claim that those who choose a regime of treatment which results in earlier death are choosing to kill because there is an alternative which (at whatever cost) will delay the patient's death. But such claims are manifestations of a thought which is manifested also by one of Harris's claims on which I commented in my second essay, the claim that when Parliament chooses to spend funds on education which might have been spent on life-saving surgery it is choosing

[46] Anscombe, 'Modern Moral Philosophy' at 35.

and running a programme of euthanasia. The same thought entails also the conclusion that when one chooses to take one's children for a walk, thus passing up the opportunity to take a plane to Calcutta to save street children, one is responsible for the deaths of—indeed, is choosing to kill (by omission)—those far-away street children.

Taken with the refusal to acknowledge that there are moral norms which relate precisely to what one intends as distinct from what one foresees and causes as a side effect, this thought yields the conclusion that intentional killing—indeed as much intentional killing as seems likely to promote overall human welfare—is not merely justified but actually required. The degeneration involved in reaching such a conclusion is not only of personal and social character, with grave consequences for everybody (the world). It is, in Anscombe's words, a degeneration *of thought*, a refusal or failure to attend steadily and openly to reality, to real distinctions between trying to get and accepting, and to real and insuperable limitations on our knowledge and capacities and thus on our responsibility.

X. PEOPLE 'WHO SHOULD DIE'

Harris misunderstands that common tradition of moral thought, and thus too my first essay, when he offers to explain why, as I said, it could well be grossly wrong to administer pain-killing drugs for the purpose exclusively of relieving pain (and in no way intending to kill) but knowing that the dosage is liable to kill someone who might otherwise recover from their illness. He thinks that what makes such a knowingly though not intentionally lethal administration immoral is that, independently of any moral assessment of the choice to administer drugs, the person in question 'should not die'. Correspondingly, there are people who (he says) 'should die', and to whom drugs can therefore rightly be administered precisely with the intent to kill them.

Harris's willingness thus to categorize *people as people who should live* and *people who should die* is a vivid illustration of the change of character, heart—and thus of conduct and world—which is introduced by the shift from the common tradition to his consequentialist ethic. In the common tradition, the question whether a lethal but not intentionally lethal act or omission[47] is culpable is answered not by making such a categorization.

---

[47] As Lord Mustill rightly noted in *Bland*, and as I noted at the end of sec. I, there is no morally relevant distinction between a positive act intended to achieve an effect and an omission intended to achieve the same effect. The unargued assumption by some of the Law Lords in *Bland*, that the withdrawal of life-sustaining measures was being chosen by the plaintiffs in that case with the intention (aim, purpose) of terminating Bland's life, may well have been a justified assumption on the record of the proceedings in that litigation. But it in no way amounts to a ruling, nor does it in any way entail,

Rather it is answered by considering the interrelationships of the various competing responsibilities of the person whose acts or omissions are under consideration (who could also be the person whose life is at stake).

It can be perfectly reasonable to *feel* that death would be a welcome relief for someone suffering from hopeless debility or illness, or from intense and intractable pain, and to *wish for* that relief from suffering which death promises to bring. It cannot be reasonable to form the *judgment* that all things considered this person would be better off dead, or the world would be better off if this person were dead, or this person is someone who *should die*. Nor can it be reasonable to rely upon that judgment to 'outweigh' the reason which every basic and intrinsic good of a person gives one not to choose to destroy that basic good (see sec. III of Chapter 2). Making and relying thus upon such a judgment irrationally ignores the incommensurability of the personal goods and bads, and the incalculable perils and opportunities, involved in the life and death of anyone. It unreasonably treats the dignity of the person (whose life is his or her very existence as a person) as if it were a factor which like money or other instrumental goods can be weighed in a balance and found wanting.

The morality of choices which involve no intent to kill or harm but foreseeably will result in death is to be assessed by reference to moral standards of which the most important and pervasive is the standard of fairness, the Golden Rule. This is a *rational* standard, identifying and critiquing the unreasonableness of discriminating between persons (other than for reasons, for example, of commitment or vocation). But in determining what counts as discrimination, the Golden Rule relies primarily upon the measure of *feelings*. Do to others as you *would be* (that is, feel willing to be) done by. Do not do to others what you would not feel willing to do to those for whom you feel affection. And so on. (To play this proper and necessary role in giving content to a rational standard (fairness), such feelings must be coherent with the other requirements of practical reason—acknowledgement of the worth and pursuitworthiness of all the basic personal goods, fidelity to reasonable commitments, and so forth; but within the forms and limits established by those rational considerations, *feelings* (which themselves are not rational) *about the consequences of one's options* can be one's measure and guide in deliberation.) By such a discernment of feelings one can measure the extent of one's responsibility to undergo burdensome treatments to preserve or restore one's own health; or of one's responsibility to impose on one's family or

---

nor does judicial or other common sense suggest, that all withdrawals of 'treatment from people who will die without it' must be intended to end their life.

heirs or society the costs of expensive treatment (whether of oneself or of others) which promises rather little improvement.

In this way (here only sketched) one can justifiably make decisions and choices which one knows will or may well have the death of oneself or another person as their side effect. And one can reasonably reach such decisions without ever making a judgment of the form: this person is a *person who should die*. Such judgments are not only irrational, hubristic, and in their practical implications deeply sinister. They also are not necessary to the identification and justified rejection of treatment which is burdensome or futile, and thus excessive, inhumane, or unfair.

Each of Harris's attempts to explain how causing death as a side effect can be unfair and unreasonable is, in fact, absurd. First he suggests that it is unfair 'because these "side-effects" are someone's death'. But this ignores the many cases where such a consequence is the inevitable outcome of a 'triage' situation, or where death could be averted only by heroic efforts and expenditures far out of line with people's normal willingness to accept *lethal* risks avertable only at great expense. Then he suggests that it 'is unfair if she does not want to die'. But this ignores those cases where a person's wish could be satisfied only by imposing on others burdens which she would not accept if she were in their shoes. Finally he proposes that the fairness or unfairness of causing death depends on the judgment whether or not 'the person should die'—a judgment for which no criteria are offered except the implicit appeal to an imagined assessment of how killings of innocent persons would, overall, sufficiently (!) diminish 'the level of suffering in the world' or perhaps sufficiently enhance some other 'very weighty cause'.[48] But this, as I have argued, absurdly exaggerates the power of human reasoning to commensurate the consequences of choices, and overlooks the dignity of the persons whose intrinsic goods make rational claims to our untradeable respect.

For good measure, this paragraph in Harris's second essay (Chapter 3) ends by openly asserting that the morality of causing death (whether intentionally or by side effect) cannot be determined without 'first determining whether or not this death is morally permissible in these circumstances howsoever caused'. That is a hopelessly vicious circle. It also involves a category mistake about permissibility, which is predicable only of actions and their consequences precisely as such, and not of events or occurrences considered prior to any consideration of a human action.

In this same essay, Harris more than once suggests that 'the persons whose deaths are permitted must autonomously choose to die'. This

[48] See Harris, *The Value of Life*, 81.

purported restriction of permissible euthanasia to voluntary euthanasia must be taken cautiously and with a large pinch of salt. Cautiously, because as he says in the essay's chilling final words, 'non-persons, even if human, are... a different matter'. And with a large pinch of salt, because in his book *The Value of Life* Harris unambiguously affirms that the persons who may rightly (indeed should) be killed include not only those who autonomously choose to die but also 'those who are living in circumstances to which death is preferable or who face a future in which this will be true, but who are unable to express a preference for death',[49] and also those other innocents whose death, although not desired by them, is expected to 'promote [ ] other values' of sufficient weight.[50] Are Harris's present essays really recanting his book's promotion of both non-voluntary euthanasia and the deliberate and intentional killing of innocent and unwilling persons? It would be rash to think so.

XI. RADICAL CAPACITY, CAPACITY, AND DUALISM

The discussion of capacity, personhood, and dualism in Harris's second essay is another tissue of muddles.

Ignoring, even while quoting, my distinction between 'capacity' and 'radical capacity', Harris claims that I 'want [ ] to hold that when human beings lack these capacities, they are still persons'. But 'these capacities' refers back to his own immediately preceding sentence, in which he says that I 'need [ ] persons to have this *radical* capacity to deliberate and choose'. Thus his exposition severely mangles my claim, which was this. Every living human being has the *radical capacity* to deliberate and choose, even when a given individual human person's capacity to do so—ability to exercise the radical capacity—has been destroyed. And why is this is so? Because, as I said,

> thinking... and choosing... are *vital* activities, life-functions, actualizations of that *one* radical, dynamic capacity which is actuated in all one's activities, metabolic, sensitive, imaginative, intellectual, and volitional.

---

[49] *Ibid.*, 78. See also 83:

> Non-voluntary euthanasia... will be wrong unless it seems certain that the individual concerned would prefer to die rather than go on living under the circumstances which confront her *and* it is impossible to find out whether the individual concerned shares this view. (Harris's emphasis.)

On Harris's peculiar use of 'wrong', which will allow other cases of fully justifiable non-voluntary (and involuntary) euthanasia, see n. 50 below.

[50] *Ibid.*, 81. Harris sometimes uses the word 'wrong' in a confined, technical, and highly idiosyncratic way, according to which an action can be 'wrong' but fully justifiable and precisely the caring thing to do. Thus at 83 he sums up his position: 'So that involuntary euthanasia [killing an individual against that individual's express wishes: 82] will always be wrong, although it may be *justifiable* for any of the reasons considered earlier' (Harris's emphasis)!

The alternative, as I showed, is some kind of dualism which overlooks the *unity* of the bodily and mental in the life of the human being. I recalled the experience we have of this unity—say, the experience (as one composes on a word processor) of being the single subject of one's fingers hitting the keys, the sensations in those fingers, the thinking one is articulating, and so forth. Harris quotes this passage, and then declares that:

all the things Finnis mentions as examples of experiencing unity in complexity are dimensions of what it is to have intelligence and autonomy. They are, as he rightly demonstrates, manifestations of that intelligence and autonomy which has no separate existence.

Harris is quite mistaken. I 'rightly demonstrate' no such thing. For some of the things I mention are not 'manifestations' or 'dimensions' of 'what it is to have intelligence and autonomy'. Sensing one's fingers hitting keys, for example, is rather a 'dimension' or 'manifestation' of what it is to be a living body, intelligent or not. Of course, in the human subject bodily life in all its manifestations is a dimension of the *one human life* by which a person composing onto a word processor *also* exercises and experiences intelligence and autonomy, and by which a sleeping person breathes, metabolizes air and food, dreams, and responds to stimuli.

Having thus yet again mutilated my argument, Harris provides a fairly clear affirmation of his dualism. A living human being in persistent vegetative state is 'a living human body' but no longer the body of a person. But this affirmation entails that one and the same living human body at one time was the body of a person and at another time was not. The person comes (at some ill-defined stage in fetal or infant development) and goes (at some ill-defined stage in illness or decay), while the bodily life of the being that can move and perhaps also sense its fingers subsists throughout, until death. This division between person and body is the very dualism to which my arguments were directed, and they remain unanswered.

I called such dualism casual and opportunistic because the grounds for it, for example in Harris's *The Value of Life*, seem to me just that. In his case, they are little more than a definition of 'person' resting uncritically on the authority of an under-interpreted and rationally most vulnerable proposal by Locke.[51]

The living principle (dynamic and constitutive inner source) which actively animates, organizes, and informs every aspect of one's existence from one's conception to one's death establishes, constitutes, one's radical capacity to metabolize, feel, move, notice, understand, respond, want,

---

[51] *Ibid.*, 15. On the incoherences in Locke's account of persons and the arbitrariness in contemporary quasi-Lockean definitions such as Harris's, see Teichman, 'The Definition of a Person'.

choose, and carry out choices all in a human way. That radical capacity remains even when the breakdown of one or more of one's organs deprives one of the capacity (ability) to exercise that radical capacity in one or more of its dimensions. A Tony Bland in deep and irreversible persistent vegetative state is in a profoundly disabled state. He has lost the capacity (ability) to think and feel—but not the humanity, the *human* life, which until his death goes on shaping, informing, and organizing his existence *towards* the feeling and thinking which are natural to human life (that is, which human life is radically capable of and orientated towards).

The 24-year-old patient 'S', who died in southern England in January 1994 after the judicially authorized discontinuance of nutrition and hydration and all other life-sustaining measures, was judged by his nurses and at least one of the neurologists attending him to be suffering pain from time to time, making non-verbal noises and moving about in his bed.[52] He was less disabled than Bland, occupying a somewhat different place on the great spectrum of human beings in different states of flourishing and impairment of capacity. That is the spectrum which Harris divides somewhere into two: those states of human life which qualify one as a person and those which qualify one as now a mere living human body without rights or intrinsic value. His division, as I argued in sec. VI, is a matter of sheer decision, so indeterminate and indeed shifting are his criteria.

XII. AUTONOMY, VALUE, AND UNFAIR GROUNDS OF CHOICE

At the end of my first essay I argued that if one is really exercising autonomy (not merely yielding to impulse or compulsion) in choosing to kill oneself or to be deliberately killed, one will be proceeding on one or both of two philosophically and morally erroneous judgments: (i) that human life in certain conditions or circumstances retains no intrinsic value or dignity; and/or (ii) that the world would be a better place if one's life were intentionally terminated; and that these erroneous judgments, being inherently universal, have grave implications for the weak and disabled.

Despite Harris's free and not too carefully posited assertions that I was mistaken, my argument stands. But it could be made more precise. The first of the two types of erroneous judgment which I identified could be stated more exactly: (i) that one's human life in certain conditions or circumstances retains no intrinsic value or dignity, or on balance no net

---

[52] *Frenchay NHS Trust v S* [1994] 1 WLR 601, [1994] 2 All ER 403 at 407, 410.

value, so that one's life is not worth living and one would be better-off dead.

Against this, Harris asserts that 'one can rationally hold' that even people whose life has no net value have a right not to be killed against their will or without the exercise of their autonomous choice. Harris's use of the indefinite passive phrases 'one can sensibly hold' and 'one can rationally hold' is significant. Whatever others might rationally hold, no one with a theory of value and morality such as Harris's can rationally, that is, consistently and for reasons, hold that there are human rights (or entitlements and corresponding disentitlements) not grounded in assessments of the overall balance of values and disvalues in the situation. As I indicated at the end of sec. X above, Harris's book contends that many people (persons) can rightly be killed without having made a choice to be killed, and that at least some persons can be killed against their will. Autonomy, in his scheme of things, is a value and can be outweighed by other values, by 'very weighty causes'.[53]

In the common tradition which I have been defending and Harris wishes to replace, autonomy is indeed a great good. But its exercise should be consistent with the rights of others and with all the other requirements of humane and decent behaviour. No man is an island. That is why it is important to try to understand the premises on which autonomous choices are made, and to reflect on the implications of those premises. Exercises of autonomy which proceed from premises which are both false and, in their implications, injurious to other members of society, can rightly be overridden by law.

---

[53] See Harris, *The Value of Life*, 81.

15

ECONOMICS, JUSTICE, AND THE VALUE OF LIFE*

I

Among the most serious efforts to settle ethical questions by economic reasoning is the Economic Analysis of Law. Richard Posner, a cultured and sophisticated professor of law at Chicago, led a movement which has undertaken a wide-ranging description and evaluation of legal arrangements in terms of their economic efficiency (maximization of social wealth, particularly by minimization of wasted 'transaction costs'). At the movement's zenith, Posner himself proposed that the ethics of wealth maximization is superior to other aggregative theories of morality, notably utilitarianism, and provides 'a comprehensive and unitary criterion of rights and duties'.[1] Some of its results—such as that 'people who are very poor...count only if they are part of the utility function of someone who has wealth'—do (he conceded) 'grate on modern sensibilities'; but none of its positions or implications, he urged, are 'violently inconsistent with our common moral intuitions'.[2] Ten years later, and now a high-ranking federal judge, Posner withdrew his claim that Economic Analysis of Law affords an appropriate 'comprehensive criterion' of moral judgment, and conceded that it is open to criticisms which cannot be answered. One may doubt the philosophical depth of his formulation of the deepest criticism: that wealth maximization's potential for approving slavery is 'contrary to the unshakable moral intuitions of Americans'.[3] But the reluctant admissions of these ambitious and perceptive theorists are relevant to a reflection on the issues discussed in this book.

Disciplined economic thought is helpful. It brings to light the complexity of the impact which one's choices have, beyond their purpose or intention.

---

* 1992c.
[1] Posner, 'Utilitarianism, Economics, and Legal Theory' at 140.   [2] *Ibid.*, 128, 131.
[3] Posner, *The Problems of Jurisprudence*, 377.

And it constantly reminds us that to spend on one thing is to use up what might have been spent (time and labour, money, other resources) on other purposes. But it cannot capture the idea of justice or the sense of our purpose to be just and to do justice. For economic thought, as such, cannot comprehend and explain either of the two basic forms of justice's requirements: that one abstain from those types of choice and action which are incompatible with decent, proper, acceptable treatment of another human being; and that one abstain from causing and accepting (let alone intending) unfair consequences, even 'mere' side effects of one's chosen action and of its intended effects.

The problem with any and every kind of economic reasoning taken as a comprehensive criterion of rational choice is that it seeks the maximization of value, measuring better and worse, greater good and lesser evil, by aggregating units of a single measure of value—what people are willing and able to pay in dollars or dollar equivalents.[4] But if reason could accomplish such an aggregation—that is, if the action involving overall aggregate net greatest good were identifiable—*choice*, morally significant and rationally guided election between open alternatives, would be neither necessary nor, strictly speaking, possible. For the alternative courses of action, involving aggregate lesser good, would have *no* rational attraction. In reality, of course, morally significant choices are everywhere open and pressing, precisely because the goods involved, especially the goods fundamental to human persons, cannot be weighed and measured in the way that economics, like every aggregative method proposed for directing choice (for example utilitarianism), requires. Such choices involve incommensurables.[5]

By no means all measurements and comparisons relevant to human action are impossible or outside the range of reason. For example, the precise goal of some particular procedure or intervention or administration of drugs provides a rational measure of efficacy and, in that sense, of benefit; some at least of the costs involved in seeking that goal can similarly be rationally assessed by reference to specific measures such as money, or pain imposed compared with pain relieved.

But any full assessment of options in the treatment of elderly long-term-care patients will escape the bounds of measurability. For the irreversible debility and dependence of the patient raises a question, not so much about the physiological benefit or futility of specific treatments, but rather about whether the specific benefit obtainable from any treatment, even the most ordinary and inexpensive, is a benefit which, *all things considered*, is worth

---

[4] See Posner, 'Utilitarianism, Economics, and Legal Theory' at 119–20.
[5] *NDMR* 243–72; 1990f (Boyle, Grisez, and Finnis, 'Incoherence and Consequentialism (or Proportionalism)—A Rejoinder').

seeking and having. Perhaps this patient's continued existence, even with the comfort and sustenance afforded by a meal or a drink, is of no benefit to anyone? What we should think in response to that question is the theme of the next section. My present point concerns the practical context in which the question is a live issue, the context of choice between alternative options.

For: many people have come to think that one should guide one's moral judgment by first identifying one option as promising greater overall net good or less overall net bad than alternative options. But such a calculus of greater pre-moral good and lesser pre-moral bad is impossible (not merely impracticable: impossible) wherever there is a morally significant choice. And the present context well illustrates one of the main sources of this pre-moral incommensurability of options. A first option is to continue to give or accept sustenance. A second option is to withhold or withdraw it, in the belief that the patient's continuing life in itself involves and imposes costs outweighing any benefits obtainable from it and its sustenance; the proposal is to terminate life in order to cut these costs by discontinuing sustenance—in other words, to kill the patient by deliberate omission, omission chosen as a means to an end. A third option is to withhold or withdraw sustenance, on the subtly different ground that giving sustenance is wasteful because the patient's continuing life yields no net benefit; one's purpose again is to minimize costs, and one's proposal is not precisely to kill (as a means of reducing overall costs) but to *abandon* the patient to death (judging that the means of sustaining the patient would better be kept for or devoted to some other purpose). My point, then, is this: the benefits and costs involved in alternative options such as these are real and striking, but elude an economic calculus or any other process of aggregating pre-moral goods. Each is an option with enormous implications and ramifications for everyone's life and existence. Whichever proposal is adopted or recommended, the choice (or recommendation) is one which will impact on the character of the chooser (or recommender) and of every potential chooser, on the character of healthcare professionals, on the relationship of trust between healthcare professionals and their clients, on the attitude of everyone to his or her own body and bodily life, on the whole substance of solidarity between the strong and the weak at all stages of life...And all these effects quite elude measurement, yet are very real and are really involved, as benefits and harms, in the only relevant object of weighing and comparing: the alternative *options* (of treating/sustaining, of killing, and of abandoning the patient) to be considered in deliberation and accepted or rejected in free choice.

II

To have a just understanding of, and disposition towards, the value of a human being's bodily life it is not enough to be aware of the fallacies of every economism which would apply a technique (legitimate in resolving technical problems) to non-technical decisions. One of the sternest and most effective critics of Economic Analysis of Law has been Ronald Dworkin, long-time Professor of Jurisprudence at Oxford and later also at New York University. And Dworkin, whose interpretation of liberalism expresses attitudes and policies widely accepted and often applied, has recently taken to affirming what he calls 'the intrinsic value of human life'.

But by this phrase, Dworkin means no more than: 'once a human life has begun it is terribly important that it goes well'.[6] The implication is that there are human lives which are not going, or are likely not to go, 'well enough' to be worth living. Thus the phrase hitherto taken as foundational for the 'pro-life' case against abortion is purloined to convey a meaning from which 'it sometimes follows that abortion is morally recommended or required'.[7]

Correspondingly, Dworkin vehemently rejects the view that the life of the comatose has any value: the life of the permanently vegetative is 'not valuable to anyone'.[8] It is not in their interests to live on, indeed it is plausible or right to think that continuing to live on is, for them, a net disadvantage, and that they are better off dead.[9] Polishing the similar rhetoric of Justice Stevens of the US Supreme Court, more cautiously shared by the other three dissenting Justices in *Cruzan v Director Missouri Department of Health* 497 US 261 (1990), Dworkin holds: 'There is no way in which continued life can be good for such people.' Indeed, 'it is at least a reasonable view that a permanently comatose person is, for all that matters, dead already'; the 'bodies they used to inhabit' are only 'technically alive'. And: to care for them is to show 'pointless and degrading solicitude'.[10]

This is not the place to attempt any full unravelling of the ways one's intrinsic dignity is related to and yet not determined by indignities which one may undergo or by the undignified aspects of one's dependence in illness, disintegration, dying...Certainly, a comatose person can be subjected to indignities, for example by being treated as a sex object, or by being dumped into the garbage, or by being systematically called a vegetable. But the rhetoric which Dworkin takes over from (dissenting) judgments of Supreme Court Justices is sinister in its systematic confusion

---

[6] Dworkin, 'The Right to Death' at 17.   [7] *Ibid.*   [8] *Ibid.* at 15.   [9] *Ibid.* at 16.
[10] *Ibid.*

of the emotionally repugnant aspects of long-term coma (the mess of excrement and so forth) with lack of human dignity. These distinguished lawyers, offering to speak for the interests of the comatose, shroud these people with epithets calculated to de-humanize them (preparatory, it is to be feared, to justifying the deliberate termination of their lives). So it is said that for such people 'the burden of maintaining the corporeal existence degrades the very humanity it was meant to serve'; their life is one of degradation; someone on life support has a 'degraded existence' (Brennan J in *Cruzan*). In short, all such remarks confuse the emotional sense of 'dignity', 'dignified/undignified', and 'indignity' with the rational and essential sense of 'human dignity'. For in the latter sense it is indeed true to say that one who helps the comatose, or other severely mentally disabled people, is affirming and serving their dignity and expressing solidarity with them as, while gravely disabled, still human persons.

But is such care pointless? Does it at best affirm a value which is absent, and at worst impose on the object of care still further disvalue? Do the unconscious (or other severely mentally disabled persons) who can no longer do good things or have good experiences benefit at all from their continued existence? Does caring for them benefit either them or others? Does it maintain human solidarity with them, or is it just sentimental folly?

If, as Dworkin and Stevens explicitly and Brennan and others implicitly contend, one's life without cognitive-affective function, one's mere physical existence, is of no value, constitutes no benefit, then that bodily life must be merely an instrumental good, something which persons have and use for their specifically human or personal purposes but which remains really distinct from what human persons *are*. One who has only this has ceased to be *as* a person, has *no personal interests* at stake, 'is for all that matters dead already'.

But this is an issue to be decided by reason, not feeling and rhetorically stirred imagination. When one considers living in a coma, one is overwhelmed by the distance between this condition and the integral good of a flourishing human person. Nobody wants to be in that condition; no decent person wants anyone to be in it. The good of human life is *very inadequately* instantiated in such a life, so deprived and so unhealthy. But this does not show that human life considered in abstraction from all other human goods such as play, friendship, awareness of truth and beauty, is of no intrinsic goodness. *No* human good, considered *apart from* all the others, in a mode of existence (if it were possible) deprived of all the others, is appealing. But this does not show that basic human goods, such as those I have just mentioned, are instrumental, or other than intrinsically good. No more does the unappealing nature of comatose life show it to be valueless. For it is the very actuality of one's living body, and one's living body is one's person.

To deny that one's living body is one's person is to accept some sort of dualistic theory of human persons, according to which human beings are inherently disembodied realities who only *have* their bodies, only inhabit them and use them. (This is clearly the basis on which Stevens J proceeds in *Cruzan's* case: unconscious, therefore not a person, *therefore* not really living.)

No form of dualism is rationally defensible. For every dualism sets out to be a theory of one's personal identity as a unitary and subsisting self—a self always organically living but only discontinuously conscious, and now and then inquiring and judging, deliberating and choosing, and employing techniques and instruments to achieve purposes. But every form of dualism renders inexplicable the unity in complexity which one experiences in every act one consciously does. We experience this (complex) unity more intimately and thoroughly than any other unity in the world; indeed, it is for us the very paradigm of substantial unity and identity. As I write this, I am the unitary subject of my fingers hitting the keys, the sensations I feel in them, the thinking I am articulating, my commitment to write this essay, my use of the computer to express myself. So the one reality that I am involves at once consciousness and bodily behaviour; and dualism sets out to explain *me*.

But every dualism ends by denying that there is any *one* something of which to be the theory. It does not explain *me*; it tells me about two things, one a nonbodily person and the other a nonpersonal body, neither of which I can recognise as myself.[11]

So, one's living body is intrinsic to one's personal reality. One does not merely possess, inhabit, or use one's body, as one possesses and uses an instrument or inhabits a dwelling. Thus, human life, which is nothing other than the very actuality of one's body, is a good intrinsic to one. It is not merely an instrumental good of the person, or extrinsic to the person. Intrinsic to the original unity of the person, it shares in the dignity of the person.

Like other basic, intrinsic human goods, human bodily life can be instantiated more or less perfectly. When instantiated most perfectly, it includes vital functions such as speech, deliberation, and free choice; then it is most obviously proper to the person. But even an impoverished

---

[11] Grisez, 'Should Nutrition and Hydration be Provided to Permanently Comatose, and Other Mentally Disabled Persons?' at 37; see also *NDMR* 304–9; essay II.5, sec. I (1989a at 267–8).

instantiation of the good of life remains specifically human and proper to the person whose life it is. Human life is inherently good, and does not cease to be good when one can no longer enjoy a degree of cognitive-affective function or attain other values. Human bodily life, even the life of one in a coma, has value. To choose to kill even such a person is to choose to harm that person. It is therefore inconsistent with a rational love of that person, and (however much motivated by feelings of affection and compassed about with thoughts and words of respect) is inconsistent with respect for and justice to the person. Whatever the feelings of solidarity which may accompany and suggest such a choice, it is a choice incompatible with a reasonable solidarity with the person so killed.

Such a choice differs radically from two other sorts of choice or attitude with which euthanasiasts usually confuse it. (i) Whereas the choice to confer relief from suffering or embarrassment ('indignity') or expense *by* killing (by action or omission) is a choice to impose harm *to the whole person as a means* (of benefiting the person), the choice to remove a diseased organ or limb in order to save the patient is not a choice *of harm to the person* at all.[12] What is and is not harming is to be judged by reference to the whole person whose organically integral bodily well-being is the reason for choosing to remove the diseased part, not by reference to the part whose disease threatens that organic integration nor by reference to any part which is damaged as an unavoidable side effect of the treatment. Therapeutic surgery is not a case of choosing to do harm (or any other sort of evil) for the sake of good. (ii) The choice not to undergo further medical treatment, because of its expense, riskiness, painfulness, or other burdens, can be a reasonable choice even in cases where it is known that the consequence of the choice will be an early death. Here death is not sought as a means (still less as an end), but is simply accepted as a side effect.

Such an acceptance need not be based on any attempt (which would be doomed to failure) to evaluate continued life as valueless, or as objectively less valuable than relief from expense, risk, pain, or other burdens. It may be based simply on aversion to the burdens or costs of the treatment. These are burdens or costs which rational deliberation can take into account; they provide reasons for forgoing the treatment. But in situations of morally significant choice, as I have already stressed, reasons constituted by costs and burdens cannot be measured by aggregating them for comparison with ('weighing' against) net benefits. Deliberating will come down, instead, to a matter of one's personal response to the competing reasons. One's

---

[12] *Pace* McCormick, *Notes on Moral Theology 1965 through 1980*, 647; on McCormick's analysis of amputation, Daniel Maguire builds the ethical theory of 'proportionate reason' that he employs to defend and advocate euthanasia: Maguire, *Death by Choice*, 71, 126.

deliberation should set aside *merely* emotional motivations such as feelings of anxiety. But it will not exclude one's affective response to the relevant reasons.

The feelings involved in such an affective response are not themselves required or shaped by reason. Nor, in someone of upright character, will they be contrary to reason. But every choice of (intention to do) harm to the person will be contrary to reason because contrary to a reason (for example 'the basic human good of life and health is to be pursued and respected') that cannot be rationally outweighed. So, whatever one's feelings, it cannot be right to intend death or any other harm to oneself or another. It can be reasonable to act on one's aversion to the costs and benefits, provided one is not making a choice contrary to any of the rational requirements which we call moral standards. These standards include not only the norm excluding intent to kill or harm, and the norm requiring fairness to others (for example one's children or others dependent upon one's continued life and activity), but also highly specific standards that one has made relevant to oneself by one's commitments, vocation, and particular undertakings.[13]

III

Talk of maintaining solidarity with and fidelity to the very dependent can sound vague and high falutin', not to say abstract and fishy. But the papers of the healthcare professionals in this collection[14]—particularly those of Graham Mulley, Marion Hildick-Smith, and Robert Stout—convey something of solidarity's practical substance and realism. The considerations and measures they advance are relatively simple and straightforward (though they certainly call for imagination and sympathy). But these considerations and measures are the working out of an attitude which classical philosophy and theology called *general justice*: an all-round decency of individuals both in their individual capacities and as making decisions on behalf of a community (whether at the level of hospital, local authority, or central government).

As for fairness—that rational standard whose particular content is, however, dependent upon feelings and other contingencies—its requirements cut both ways. Politically demanding and effective groups of the elderly can propose and secure the placing of unjustifiable burdens on younger

---

[13] This paragraph does no more than sketch some essentials; for a much fuller and more nuanced discussion, involving similar principles and judgments, see Grisez, 'Should Nutrition and Hydration be Provided to Permanently Comatose, and Other Mentally Disabled Persons?'; [also *LCL*, 8.F.3–4; Grisez, *Difficult Moral Questions*, QQ. 44–7.]

[14] Gormally (ed.), *The Dependent Elderly.*

persons with immediate responsibility for children; levels of pensions, and arrangements about house ownership, for example, can in some modern western democracies impose unfair burdens in the interests of the elderly. But that should not distract us from the very real concerns ventilated in the papers of Michael Banner, Joseph Boyle, and Luke Gormally. And John Keown's survey of the emergence and wildfire spread of euthanasia in the Netherlands provides us with a striking example of the downward spiral in which an irrational attitude to human bodily life (treating an intrinsic and basic good as if it were extrinsic and instrumental) reinforces and is reinforced by an irrational belief in the possibility of rationally aggregating the costs and benefits involved in the alternative options: (a) killing out of compassion, and (b) care which excludes both the choice to kill (by act or omission) and the choice to continue treatment which is futile or imposes burdens one has no responsibility in fairness or fortitude to bear.

Some questions of allocation or rationing of resources are easy to make, as Robert Stout suggests. Others will always remain difficult questions, about which reasonable people will reasonably disagree with each other, making different and incompatible choices within the range of not unreasonable options. But some problems of allocation or rationing will remain questions which we can and should answer prior to all reasonably disputable issues of allocation, and which we can and should answer in a definite direction, thereby establishing boundaries for all subsequent allocative choices. Luke Gormally indicates one of these boundaries:

...what is *minimally* required in the provision of health care for the debilitated elderly is a quality of care which so far as possible reduces the temptation to doctors, nurses and others to think that they would do better to kill some of their patients rather than provide them with manifestly inadequate care, i.e. care of a kind which leads to rapid deterioration or which fails to palliate. The inadequate care of patients creates the temptation to dispose of patients who are obviously held in low esteem. By contrast, adequate care signifies that the patients are valued.[15]

This, of course, identifies what is 'minimally required' in a well-resourced society; there can be social conditions where no treatment actually available prevents rapid deterioration or succeeds in palliating distress, and where what care and sustenance is available is fairly reserved for the young. But even in such conditions, which are far from the conditions of our society, justice excludes all choices to kill, and reason undercuts every claim that the life of the dependent elderly is a null or negative value which one may reasonably choose to terminate.

---

[15] Gormally, 'The Aged: Non-Persons, Dignity and Justice' at 187.

16

EUTHANASIA AND THE LAW*

I

Arguments for legalizing euthanasia rely on claims about autonomy rights, or claims about political pluralism, or on both sorts of claim. My response will make three main points.

First, those demanding this legalisation have shirked their elementary obligation to describe the alleged right, identify who has it, and delineate its boundaries as a right supposed to trump other goods, interests, and the well-being or rights of others.

Secondly, they have neglected, or at best hugely underestimated, the casualties who would be, and in some places already are being, created by the success of their campaign. That is to say, they are neglecting basic responsibilities of fairness and justice.

Thirdly, they proceed on an inadmissible conception of the nature and value of human life and dignity—on a theory which should be rejected for the same sorts of reasons of equality and dignity that lead us to reject *as a matter of principle*[1] the alleged right (often recognized in former societies) to free yourself from perhaps crushing burdens by selling yourself into slavery.

We are all going to be involved in this debate, this struggle for power, this great collective deliberation, for the rest of our lifetimes. We will need to keep our critical faculties all the way through. There will be majority

---

* 1998b (a lecture given on 22 November 1996 along with, and in response to, Ronald Dworkin's lecture on the same themes, 'Euthanasia, Morality and Law'; the occasion fell between the decision of the Ninth Circuit in *Compassion in Dying* in March 1996 and the decision of the Supreme Court in *Glucksberg* in June 1997, decisions which respectively correspond substantially with Dworkin's views and mine).

[1] In his lecture, Dworkin described this sort of rejection in principle as 'extraordinary', 'blunt', 'blanket', and 'crude'—in the case of euthanasia. He did not take the opportunity, afforded then by my remarks, to say whether these epithets apply also to our law's rejection of slavery, torture, coerced confessions, etc.

decisions by courts, legislatures, electorates, sometimes by wide margins labelled 'consensus'. But to resolve these great issues of moral truth and judgment we each have standards by which we, anyone, can critically assess and *judge* legislatures, Fuhrers, courts. The 'right-thinking' people who call the tune in law schools, media, and courts may well be like the right-thinking people who decided for individual autonomy against social justice in *Lochner v New York*[2] or for quality of life against radical human dignity in *Buck v Bell*[3] ('three generations of imbeciles are enough', said Justice Holmes to justify sterilizing a mentally retarded girl). And, on the other hand, perhaps the laws against homicide, so often re-enacted and confirmed over the centuries, impose as Ronald Dworkin thinks a 'serious, unjustified, unnecessary...',[4] crippling, humiliating...,[5] devastating, odious form of tyranny',[6] when applied to prevent physicians killing terminally ill patients. That's a thought we should certainly consider on its merits.

But if we are to keep our critical freedom we cannot accept that 'History has decided', or is deciding this issue; or has settled other issues so that as a matter of principle and integrity this issue must now be decided in a certain way.[7] Conscience judges, not by the play of judicial or any other majoritarian

---

[2] 198 US 45 (1905).   [3] 274 US 200, 207 (1927).   [4] Dworkin, *Freedom's Law*, 146.
[5] Dworkin, 'When Can a Doctor Kill?'.   [6] Dworkin, *Life's Dominion*, 217.
[7] In his own lecture, Dworkin advanced precisely such a claim, making central to his address the contention that in *Cruzan v Missouri Department of Health* 497 US 261 (1990), the American people had resolved, or at least supposed (with definitive effect), that patients and their doctors may lawfully, as a matter of constitutional right, *aim at death*. This claim was doubly erroneous. If *Cruzan* had indeed made such a decision, or supposition, it would now be open to the court and to the people to judge it a false step, an abandonment of the historic and morally sound foundations of the law of murder, a mistaken decision ripe for reform by overruling. But, secondly, it is historically and juridically crystal clear that *Cruzan* neither decided, nor supposed, nor even entertained the possibility that people and their doctors have a constitutional right to aim at death. The dissenting Justices accurately state the core of the majority opinion in the following terms:

> the Court, while tentatively accepting that there is some degree of constitutionally protected liberty interest *in avoiding unwanted medical treatment*, including life-sustaining medical treatment such as artificial nutrition and hydration, affirms the decision of the Missouri Supreme Court. (*Ibid.* at 302 (Justice Brennan, dissenting, joined by Justices Marshall and Blackmun) (emphasis added).)

They add:

> Justice O'Connor's [concurring] opinion *is less parsimonious*. She openly affirms that 'the Court has often deemed state *incursions into the body repugnant* to the interests protected by the Due Process Clause', that there is a liberty interest in avoiding unwanted medical treatment, and that it encompasses the right to be free of 'artificially delivered food and water'. (*Ibid.* at 304 (Justice Brennan, dissenting) (emphasis added).)

Thus the interest presupposed by the court was simply the interest in *refusing unwanted interventions on one's body*. The fact that some patients or doctors may foreseeably abuse or exploit the protected liberty interest by making it the instrument of an *aim* (intent, purpose, etc.) to bring about death in no way makes such motives a part of the constitutionally protected interest. The easily foreseeable fact that defendants will exploit their constitutionally protected *liberty to testify*, by aiming to deceive the jury, does not make such an aim a part of the constitutionally protected liberty right—as if that great liberty could be accurately understood as *'the right to lie'* and as if counsel, after hearing a

or elite power, opinion, will, but by looking for reasons good *as reasons*. So I shall be considering the issues as they arise for every contemporary community (including the United States), and not as matters of American constitutional law as such.

II

The opinion of Judge Reinhardt for eight judges of the Ninth Circuit in *Compassion in Dying v Washington*[8] uses the term 'euthanasia' in an almost uniquely eccentric way, as the *unrequested* putting to death of persons suffering from incurable and distressing disease.[9] Almost all other English-speakers call that *non-voluntary euthanasia*, and so shall I. I shall assume Ronald Dworkin's agreement, since he defines euthanasia simply as 'deliberately killing a person out of kindness'[10]—not very serviceable as a legal definition, but compatible with common usage and not with the Ninth Circuit's.

The official Dutch definition of 'euthanasia' is precisely opposite to the Ninth Circuit's, but equally eccentric: termination of life 'by someone other than the person concerned *upon the request of the latter*'.[11] Almost everyone in the English-speaking world calls that *'voluntary euthanasia'*, and so shall I.

We must have the odd Dutch definition firmly in mind when we read that 2 per cent of all deaths in the Netherlands in 1990 resulted from 'euthanasia'.[12] If we do, we will remember to read more deeply into the figures. Then we will find that a further nearly 1 per cent of all Dutch deaths—over 1,000 further deaths—followed immediately the administering of a drug 'with the explicit purpose of hastening the end of life without *an explicit request of the patient*'.[13] These 1,000 cases are not called euthanasia, in the eccentric Dutch sense; they are the *only* euthanasia in Holland, in the eccentric Ninth Circuit sense. In the more usual idiom which I am adopting they are of course cases of non-voluntary euthanasia.

---

client's unambiguous confession of guilt, would nevertheless have the constitutional right to put that client on the stand precisely in order to lie.

[8] 79 F3d 790 (9th Cir.), reversed by *Washington v Glucksberg* 521 US 702 (1997).

[9] *Compassion in Dying v Washington* 79 F3d at 832 n. 120.

[10] *Life's Dominion*, 3. Mysteriously, when he comes to the part of the book dealing with euthanasia, he offers a new and highly eccentric definition which greatly eases his task as an advocate: 'euthanasia in its various forms— suicide, assisting suicide, or withholding medical treatment or life support—may be [etc.]....': *ibid.*, 213.

[11] Keown, 'Euthanasia in the Netherlands: Sliding Down the Slippery Slope?', in Keown, *Euthanasia Examined* at 261, 270 (emphasis added).

[12] See *ibid.* at 268.   [13] *Ibid.*, 269.

In his new book, *Freedom's Law*, Ronald Dworkin says:

Some critics worry about the practice in Holland, where doctors have given lethal injections to unconscious or incompetent terminal patients who had not explicitly asked to die.[14]

Indeed 'doctors have'. But in fact about 40 per cent of those 1,000 people officially known to have been killed without their request were neither unconscious nor incompetent.[15] We might use the label 'involuntary euthanasia' for this subclass of non-voluntary euthanasia: killed while competent to request but not requesting death. We still lack an accepted label for physicians' terminating people's life against their request: perhaps 'contra-voluntary euthanasia'.

The definitions I have suggested so far leave one important matter unclear. I introduce it, again, by reference to Dutch experience, though it is of universal significance. Euthanasia and assisting suicide were exempted from criminal sanctions by a decision of the Dutch Supreme Court in 1984.[16] Three months earlier, the Royal Dutch Medical Association had set out criteria for permissible euthanasia, later adopted in national medical 'Guidelines for Euthanasia'.[17] In the Medical Association's report no distinction was drawn between 'active' and 'passive'. 'All activities *or non-activities* with the purpose to terminate a patient's life are defined as euthanasia'.[18]

This inclusion of 'non-activities', omissions, 'passive' conduct, is entirely reasonable. Euthanasia, on any view, is an exception or proposed exception to the law of homicide, more specifically the law of murder. And you can unquestionably commit murder by omission. Parents murder children sometimes with a pillow but sometimes by starvation, omitting to feed them. To inherit the fortune, I omit to give the diabetic child his insulin. To be free to marry his secretary, Dr D omits to switch his wife's life-support system back on after its daily service break. The core concept in the law of murder, everywhere, is *intention to cause death*. Causation—starvation, dehydration, insulin shock—plus intention: murder by omission. Of course, the accused must have had control over the deceased—care or an

---

[14] Dworkin, *Freedom's Law*, 144.

[15] *See* Loes Pijnenborg et al., 'Life-Terminating Acts Without Explicit Request' at 1197; New York State Task Force on Life and the Law, *When Death Is Sought: Assisted Suicide and Euthanasia in the Medical Context*, 134 n. 31 (1994) [hereinafter *When Death is Sought*]. Pijnenborg's study relates to a different series; the corresponding figures supplied by the official Committee state that 25 per cent of those killed without their request were stated by their doctors to be totally (14 per cent) or partly (11 per cent) competent to request. *See* Keown, *Euthanasia Examined* at 292 n. 104.

[16] See *ibid.* at 261; Keown, 'The Law and Practice of Euthanasia in The Netherlands' at 51–7.

[17] Promulgated jointly by the Royal Dutch Medical Association and the National Association of Nurses. *See* Keown, *Euthanasia Examined* at 264.

[18] See *ibid.* at 271, 290 (emphasis altered).

acknowledged, fulfillable duty of care—otherwise there's no intention but at most a wish.

In short, to make euthanasia lawful, the desired exception to the law of murder needs to cover cases of omission with intent to terminate life. The Dutch Guidelines take care to cover such cases.

But the official Dutch commentary on the 1990 *statistics* selects for presentation only the cases of euthanasia by *action*. One has to look to the underlying official figures to see all the many cases where treatment was withdrawn or withheld with the primary or secondary *purpose* of shortening life, as well as many cases in which pain medication was administered precisely *with the intent to* shorten life.[19]

When we sum up these official Dutch statistics for the fifth year of their euthanasia regime, we find that in 26,350 cases, death was accelerated by medical intervention intended wholly or partly to terminate life. That is *over 20 per cent of all Dutch deaths*. In the United States that would be over 400,000 deaths.[20] Of these, well over half—59 per cent (15,528)—were without any explicit request. In the United States that would be over 235,000 unrequested medically accelerated deaths per annum.[21]

---

[19] See *ibid.* at 268–73. The additional officially admitted 1,000 terminations without request included only those done by administering a drug with intent to terminate life. The missing cases—which are euthanasia under the Guidelines but carried out by *omission*—are grouped under two headings: 'Withdrawal or withholding of treatment partly with the purpose of shortening life' (9,042 cases), and 'Withdrawal or withholding of treatment with the explicit purpose [i.e. solely or primarily for the purpose] of terminating life' (5,508 cases [4,000 + 1,508])—a further 14,550 cases in all—about 9 per cent of all deaths in Holland. See *ibid.* at 270, Table I. (Of these additional deaths, the majority (60 per cent) were non-voluntary euthanasia.) Of course, treatment is often withdrawn without any purpose of terminating life, but knowing that death will result as a more or less inevitable side effect. The figures I have just given, where termination of life was a *purpose*, represent only a minority (about 47 per cent) of all the cases where treatment was withdrawn and death followed. Another set of cases not noticed in the soothing official commentary is those where pain- or symptom-relief was administered with the explicit [i.e. primary] purpose of shortening life (a further 1,350 cases), or partly with that purpose (another 6,750)—cases mostly of lethal, though not instantly lethal injections. *Ibid.*, Table I. Of these 8,100 cases, 68 per cent (5,508 cases [5,058 + 450]) are to be added to the 1,000 cases Dworkin presumably had in mind when he said that 'doctors have given lethal injections to unconscious or incompetent terminal patients who had not explicitly asked to die'. [For some updating of the statistics for Holland, without amelioration of the overall trend away from civilized practice and respect for the lives of the vulnerable, see Keown, *Euthanasia, Ethics and Public Policy*, 115–35.]

[20] Even if one excludes all the cases where terminating life was not the doctor's *primary* intention, it remains true that nearly 1 death in 12 is accelerated precisely and explicitly with the intent to terminate life—in the United States that would be over 160,000 deaths each year, over 80,000 of them being without explicit request. In sum, using my definition of euthanasia, the only definition which really fits with the surrounding law of murder, there would be at a minimum about 160,000 and more realistically over 400,000 cases in the United States of *euthanasia*—deaths caused by decisions and courses of conduct intended to bring it about. Less than half of these would be *voluntary* and the rest, the majority, would be *non-voluntary*. And more than a third of these cases of non-voluntary euthanasia would doubtless be the killing of patients who were at that time competent to make an explicit request but did not do so.

[21] Of course, these extrapolations to the United States are debatable. Holland suffered the horrors of Nazi invasion and purges, has a more effective and universally available healthcare system, and

Before leaving words and definitions, I should say something more about intention. The entire opinion of Judge Reinhardt for the Ninth Circuit in *Compassion in Dying* relies upon a law school definition of intention as including not only what you intend but also whatever you foresee as the certain or even likely[22] outcome of your conduct. So Judge Reinhardt derides the American Medical Association's insistence upon the distinction between giving painkillers with intent to kill and giving them with intent to suppress pain.[23] He declares that doctors who respect a patient's decision to forgo life-sustaining treatment *intend* to hasten their patient's death.[24] And that the laws authorizing people to refuse treatment are simply laws for authorizing suicide. In a delirium of rhetoric, he even suggests that laws for preventing suicide have 'an aim' of prolonging a dying person's suffering. And so on and on—this is the key to the whole opinion.

The word 'intention' can indeed be given a special extended meaning, including foreseen likely effects, which does not do much harm in the law of torts, but has had to be carefully expelled from the law of murder by a long course of decisions and enactments.[25] The extended meaning was always a legal fiction. Intention is a reality, not merely a word. That's why it is synonymous, in its non-fictitious sense, with many other words and phrases: 'with the aim of', 'with a purpose of', 'trying to', 'in order to', 'with a view to', or plain 'to' (as in 'He came to Loyola to give a lecture' or 'She gave the morphine to kill the patient to let the children claim under the expiring insurance policy'). You intend your end (aim, purpose, sought-after outcome) and your chosen means. Consequences which you foresee, even as certainties, are not intended unless they are one of your ends or your means. I foresee jetlag flying the Atlantic, the hangover after the party, the fading of drapes in bright sunlight, the annoyance of people who hear my stuttering, the death of my own troops in the assault I have ordered. I intend none of those consequences, however inevitable.

No less erroneously and arbitrarily than the Ninth Circuit, the Second Circuit in *Quill v Vacco*[26] wholly misrepresents both the intention of the

---

is relatively free from racial and underclass poverty. On the other hand, it has doubtless been affected more deeply than the United States by atheism and unbelief, and so by cynicism and despair.

[22] See *Compassion in Dying v Washington* 79 F3d 790 (9th Cir.) at 823, n. 95.

[23] See *ibid.* at 823–4 and n. 94. The distinction is firmly and ably defended by (i) Judge Kleinfeld, dissenting in *Compassion in Dying* 79 F3d at 858; and (ii) the Walton Committee: Report of the House of Lords Select Committee on Medical Ethics, HL Paper 21-1 of 1993–94 (31 January 1994), paras 242–4, reproduced in Keown, *Euthanasia Examined* at 103–4. [And see now the firm and clear statements of the Supreme Court in *Vacco v Quill* 521 US 793 (1997), especially the quotations from *United States v Bailey* 444 US 394, 403–6 (1980) and from Judge Kleinfeld's judgment.]

[24] See *Compassion in Dying* 79 F3d at 822.

[25] See *Sandstrom v Montana* 442 US 510, 513 (1979); and essay II.10 (1991b).

[26] 80 F3d 716 (1996).

legislative guarantees of the right to refuse medical treatment, and the type of intentions for the sake of which such legislation was enacted: not the intention of hastening or determining the time of my death but the intention to be free from unwanted burdens and interventions on my body, even if my death is a foreseeable consequence. The legislature of course foresaw that one consequence of its enactment would be that some people would use—abuse—this right by exercising it *with intent to* hasten death. But as a legislative declaration makes clear,[27] that was not part of the legislature's intent—no more than we intend the guilty to escape when we grant due process of law, or intend lawyers to conspire to lie when we grant an attorney-client privilege.

So much for words. If we are to tell what is being said, we need not only definitions but also propositions. We must not try to make do—or do anything—with non-propositional catchphrases such as 'sanctity of life', 'death with dignity', or 'right to die'.

Take the last, 'the right to die'. Where is the proposition specifying *who* has the right, to *what* acts, by *which* persons? Is it the right of terminally ill patients? (And what is terminal illness?) Or only of those who are suffering? (And what sort and degree of sufferings?) Or of all who are suffering whether or not their illness is terminal? Is it a right only to be assisted in killing oneself, as created in the suspended Oregon law of 1995? Or also that others be permitted (or perhaps under a duty) to kill me? (When I cannot do so myself? Or also when I choose?)[28]

In the United States the debate is currently fixated on assisting in suicide. But this is only a whistle stop.[29] The Ninth Circuit's opinion, behind its

---

[27] See Health Care Agents and Proxies Act, *NY Pub Health Law* §2989(3) (McKinney, 1993); *Quill* 80 F3d at 734 n. 7.

[28] The Dutch Supreme Court's 1984 decision exempted from criminal sanction not only euthanasia but also assisting in suicide, the subject of a different provision of the Dutch Penal Code. But assisted suicide is a minority pursuit in Holland. Against the 26,000 cases of euthanasia, only about 400 cases of assisted suicide are reported.

[29] Sometimes this way station is passed through within the confines of a single statute. Thus in the Northern Territory of Australia, the world's first and (for a brief period) only operative legislative enactment in the field, the Rights of the Terminally Ill Act 1995, is presented to the public as about assistance in killing *oneself*, and has a central provision which seems to mean precisely that:

> 4. A patient who, in the course of a terminal illness, is experiencing pain, suffering and/or distress to an extent unacceptable to the patient, may request the patient's medical practitioner to assist the patient to terminate the patient's life.

Rights of the Terminally Ill Act 1995 (N. Terr. Aust.), s. 4. But the Act's definition of 'assist' gives, at the very end of the list, 'and the administration of a substance to the patient': *ibid.*, s. 2. So this was a euthanasia law under colour of a law about assisting suicide. Coming into effect in July 1996, it was nullified by the federal legislature in March 1997: Euthanasia Laws Act 1997 (Cth. of Aust.), the operative provision of which nullifies any territorial enactments

> which permit or have the effect of permitting (whether subject to conditions or not) the form of intentional killing of another called euthanasia (which includes mercy killing) or the assisting of a person to terminate his or her life.

protective refusal to identify even in principle what class of people has the constitutional right it declares, made it quite clear that the court sees no relevant distinctions short of the distinction between 'voluntary and involuntary' (non-voluntary) termination of life.[30] And even that distinction is immediately revealed to be fuzzy: the footnote warns that the judges 'do not intimate any view' of non-voluntary or involuntary euthanasia, and that if 'a duly appointed surrogate decision maker' decides to terminate the life of a non-competent patient, that counts as 'voluntary' euthanasia.[31]

III

People say everyone has a right to autonomy—that as an American, one has 'the right to define one's own concept of existence, of meaning, of the universe, and of the mystery of human life'—the words in *Planned Parenthood v Casey*[32] relied upon by the Ninth Circuit in *Compassion in Dying*[33] and quoted approvingly in Ronald Dworkin's new book.[34] But healthy Americans who demand assistance in suicide, or actual euthanasia at the hands of medical personnel, will find themselves being told by our reformers that, well, after all the right belongs *not* to those with an autonomy interest in defining their own concept of existence and so forth, but to people whose lives are no longer worth living—and, that means whose lives are no longer worth living in the opinion of a court, or medical practitioners, in the context of legislative criteria adopted by courts or legislatures from time to time. Even when you fall seriously ill, or become clinically depressed, you will find (if the reformers are to be believed) that your right to autonomy does not give you the right to be assisted in suicide unless you are ill *enough* or suffering *enough*, or depressed severely and incurably *enough*—in each case 'enough' in the view of somebody else, *other people*. And this of course is no surprise. For what you are proposing is not a private act, but precisely an act in which you seek assistance from someone else, or which you are asking someone else to carry out, sharing your intent to destroy your personal life. It is no more a private act than a duel or an agreement to sell myself into slavery.

> It preserves the power of territorial legislatures to make laws 'with respect to:
> (a) the withdrawal or withholding of medical or surgical measures for prolonging the life of a patient but not so as to permit the intentional killing of the patient; and
> (b) medical treatment in the provision of palliative care to a dying patient, but not so as to permit the intentional killing of the patient; and
> (c) the appointment of an agent by a patient who is authorised to make decisions about the withdrawal or withholding of treatment; and
> (d) the repealing of legal sanctions against attempted suicide'.

[30] *Compassion in Dying v Washington* 79 F3d 790, 832 (9th Cir.). [31] *Ibid.* at 832 n. 120.
[32] 505 US 833, 851 (1992). [33] 79 F3d at 813. [34] See Dworkin, *Freedom's Law*, 144.

So the bottom-line issue becomes clearer. When should we allow some people to sit in judgment on the life of another human person, to judge that person's life worthless, and so to authorize themselves or others to carry out that person's request for death? And then, if such judgments about the worthlessness of a person's life are decisive, why not also when the judgment about insufficient or negative quality of life is the same but the request for help to terminate life cannot be made? Or has not been made?

Notice: the issue is *not* whether physicians can reasonably make the more limited assessment necessary to judge further treatment futile, or excessively burdensome, or not rewarding enough to be worth the costs in suffering, money, labour, or use of other resources. Those are difficult, inherently uncertain judgments. But they are in any case made, routinely, in countless ways in countless cases. They remain focused upon the treatment and the burdens and benefits, and fall short of the global assessment of a person's whole existence needed to warrant a decision focused precisely on terminating that existence—to undertake a course of conduct with the intent to kill (or assist in the killing of) that person, to destroy or assist in the deliberate destruction of his or her very being so far as is humanly possible.

IV

We should not try to estimate the impact of changing the law by looking at its new permission while holding steady and unchanged everything else in the picture. Ronald Dworkin has given the British public good advice: when considering the impact of introducing a justiciable Bill of Rights, do not for a moment assume that it will be interpreted and enforced by lawyers and judges with today's attitudes. A whole *new breed* of lawyers and law teachers and judges will rapidly come into existence to give effect to the new régime.[35]

So do not think of the euthanasia law being administered by today's medical practitioners and nurses and hospital administrators, whose codes of ethics exclude killing as a treatment and management option. If the law of murder were changed in the way proposed, and especially if it were

---

[35] *See* Dworkin, *A Matter of Principle*, 31. H.L.A. Hart, a passionate liberal reformer, never ceased to support the legislation of 1967 which legalized so-called therapeutic abortion in Britain. But in the 1970s he noted that its effects had been *greatly underestimated* by those who brought about the change. What had been envisaged by many as simply a permission, recognizing an area of liberty in place of prohibition, had proved to be the introduction of a vast structure of new relationships, institutions, funding, professional obligations, and so forth, involving changes in the ethics, practices, and dispositions of doctors, midwives, social workers, psychiatrists, and people at large. See Hart, 'Abortion Law Reform: The English Experience' at 408–9; and essay IV.11 at 278 n. 79 (2009b at 183).

changed by decision of the US Supreme Court declaring what is every American's right as part of the very meaning of liberty, the ethics of all those professions and classes would—and would be bound to—change. The change would be very rapid, hastened along by the not too gentle spur of the law of torts.

Don't be distracted here by conscience clauses. The question is not about the right of the few orthodox Catholics and Jews and other mavericks to opt out. It is about the bulk of ordinary decent professionals,[36] equipped with new 'treatment options' which would greatly simplify the management of difficult cases, by the elimination of the human being causing the trouble.

Our doctors have always had the power to kill us. And to disguise their deed. This time last year I watched my father die of cancer. The doctor who gave him morphine towards the end had the power to decide to terminate his life under the guise of deciding what would quell his pain. In many, many situations, nothing prevents the doctor deciding to kill save an ethic which simply excludes that option—the ethic derided by the Ninth Circuit for insisting upon the very same difference as the law of murder: between intending to kill and accepting death as a side effect (possibly welcome but still unintended) of something done with no such intent. Now change the law and the professional ethic. Killing with intent becomes a routine management option. Oh yes, there are restrictions, guidelines, paperwork. Well meant. Not utterly irrelevant. But as nothing compared with our doctors' change in heart, professional formation, and conscience.

So our doctors would enter our sickrooms as men and women trained to be willing to kill on the occasions of their choosing, guided we trust by new professional and legal standards which shift to and fro searching for the bright *line* lost with the majoritarian judicial or legislative overthrow of the line between intending to kill and intending to heal, treat, alleviate, palliate...

A new zone of silence. Can I safely speak to my physician about the full extent of my sufferings, about my fears, about my occasional or regular wish to be free from my burdens? Will my words be heard as a plea to be killed? As a tacit permission? And why does my physician need my permission, my request? The Dutch guidelines, insisted upon in court pronouncements, and described in the Dutch press and literature with robotic, mantra-like regularity as 'strict' and 'precise', demand that euthanasia be preceded by

---

[36] Like e.g. all who massively opposed the introduction of Great Britain's Abortion Act 1967 as a violation of the profession's age-old ethics, whose Medical Defence Union told them in 1968 that changing the criminal law entailed changing their civil law duties of care in tort, and who within a few years became massively opposed to any reform that might slightly reduce the treatment options that had become available to them. See Keown, *Abortion, Doctors and the Law*, 84–109.

an explicit request. But within five years *most* Dutch medical killings are without any explicit request whatever. And though reporting is required by the guidelines, and non-reporting is a criminal offence, 87 per cent are not reported. In a famously law-abiding country.

Another zone of fearful silence. Outside the door are the relatives. What will they be telling the doctor about my condition and my wishes? What is it prudent to tell them about my suffering, my depression, my wishes? Are they interpreting my state of mind just as I would wish? Are their interests in line with mine? Many people will find that their nearest and dearest are less and less near, and less and less dear.[37]

Dutch doctors give the official (anonymous) inquiries two main reasons why they almost always violate the Guidelines and the criminal law by falsifying the death certificate and reporting that death was from 'natural causes'. One is to avoid the fuss of legal investigation. The other, almost equally strong, is the desire to protect relatives from official inquiry.[38]

Ronald Dworkin's new book responds to such concerns. Even now, he says, 'doctors sometimes deliberately give dying patients large enough doses of pain-killing drugs to kill them'.[39] He ignores the question of their intent in doing so, and says that this is a 'covert decision much more open to abuse than a scheme of voluntary euthanasia would be'.[40] He neglects to note that, whatever the 'scheme of voluntary euthanasia would be', the power and opportunity of doctors to administer lethal doses of painkillers would remain absolutely unfettered. But that same power and opportunity will be in the hands of a 'new breed of doctors' (like Dworkin's projected 'new breed' of lawyers and judges for Britain), doctors directed to regard *intentional killing* as a therapeutic option, something good doctors quite often do. And now the 'covert decision' to use lethal doses of painkillers will be a readily available end-run around the law's paperwork requirements for legal voluntary euthanasia—an end-run for those doctors who don't wish to use the alternative end-run employed by Dutch doctors in seven out of eight cases of plain euthanasia—ignore the paperwork. Either way: avoid fuss. Don't involve the relatives in tiresome legal process.[41]

---

[37] See Scruton, 'Not Mighty But Mundane', a sympathetic review of Keizer, *Dancing with Mister D*, by a sensitive and philosophically inclined ex-Catholic Dutch euthanasiast doctor who recounts his experiences in killing his patients, the astonishing ease with which one gets and uses this licence to kill, the rapid informality of the actual killing (a speed and informality necessary to maintain the sense that this is a *medical* event), and the frequently blasé attitude of the relatives. In Scruton's final words: '[A]s atheism, cynicism and the practice of euthanasia spread, your nearest and dearest will be less and less near, and less and less dear'.

[38] See Keown, *Euthanasia Examined* at 281.   [39] Dworkin, *Freedom's Law* at 145.

[40] Ibid.

[41] Most of the non-reporting Dutch doctors gave two reasons for violating their clear legal duty to report: avoid the fuss of legal investigation; protect the relatives from judicial inquiry. See Keown, *Euthanasia Examined* at 281.

In his evidence before the Walton Committee (the British Parliamentary Committee on euthanasia in 1993), Dworkin was asked again and again about these problems. His answers can be fairly summarized in one quotation. This sort of bad consequence of legalization

> is not an argument for caution, because it would be wrong to harm a lot of people [by keeping the present law against euthanasia] just because we feel that in some instance a decision might be made on the wrong basis. Those in charge of these decisions, and the doctors would be to the frontline, would simply have to be very careful to observe the kinds of conditions that the model Uniform Statute on Living Wills... directs doctors to attend to.[42]

But of course, doctors would simply *not* 'have to', and the Committee unanimously rejected his reassurances.

His response in his new book is equally unconvincing: 'states plainly have the power to guard against requests influenced by guilt, depression, poor care, or economic worries'.[43] Nearly everyone who has thought seriously about this has concluded that the power is practically empty.

Be that as it may, it is very important to see what's going on here. *Suppose* for a moment that there is a right (moral or constitutional) to choose when to die, that is, to choose precisely to hasten one's death. Even more evidently there is a right to choose *not* to be killed. The question is which legal framework will *take those rights most seriously*. That is a largely empirical question. It is a question which Dworkin accepts, but has wholly failed to answer plausibly. Here, at the nub of the debate, we are not dealing with a legal theorist's vision of what our constitution requires as a matter of integrity, or with a Herculean grasp of the principles of an entire legal system and its history. We are all dealing with a question on which ordinary folk have as good a grasp as anyone: in the new world of medical law and ethics, what conceivable legislative pronouncements, elegant preambles, government pamphlets, elaboration of hospital paperwork, physician reporting, official inquiries, and all that, could remove or even appreciably diminish the patient's subjection to the pressure of the thought that my being killed is what my relatives expect of me and is in any case the decent thing to do, even though I utterly fear it and perhaps perceive it as the uttermost and ultimate indignity, an odious, devastating subjection to the needs and will of others? And likewise with the other sources of tyranny, the new power, opportunity, and ethic of doctors, and the real and novel power of the relatives.

---

[42] House of Lords Select Committee on Medical Ethics, HL Paper 91-vii of 1992–93 (29 June 1993), 162, para. 452.

[43] *Freedom's Law*, 144.

At this point in his new book Dworkin terminates his brief response to such concerns. These 'slippery-slope arguments', he declares, 'are very weak ones; they seem only disguises for the deeper convictions that actually move most opponents of all euthanasia'.[44] To represent these convictions of *most people who oppose euthanasia* he takes care to select a Catholic priest who links euthanasia with contraception! But it is my colleague Ronald Dworkin's own assessment of those effects and implications that is truly 'very weak'. The Walton Committee of thirteen members included only one Catholic, and a spread of liberal and secular opinion—medical, legal, philosophical—representative of worldly, secular British society. They heard him, read his book, took a mountain of other evidence, visited Holland for discussions with the Dutch medical and legal authorities. They unanimously recommended against changing the law defining murder or assisted suicide. They judged unanimously that 'any change' in the prohibition of *intentional killing* is to be rejected because it 'would have such serious and widespread repercussions'.[45]

[W]e do not think it possible to set secure limits on voluntary euthanasia.... [I]t would not be possible to frame adequate safeguards against non-voluntary euthanasia if voluntary euthanasia were to be legalized.[46]

And so on, to the conclusion that 'any decriminalisation of voluntary euthanasia would give rise to more, and more grave, problems than those it sought to address'.[47]

The insinuation that most of those who state such deeply informed judgments are disguising their real convictions is even more vividly refuted by the 1994 report of the New York State Task Force on Life and the Law.[48] If you want a single, up-to-date, and American work as a basis for your reflections on the whole question, this is the one. The twenty-four members of the Task Force, set up in 1984 by Governor Mario Cuomo, were perhaps even more representative, secular, liberal, than the Walton Committee. Some of them think suicide and euthanasia morally acceptable in conscience.[49] After considering a mass of evidence (including Ronald Dworkin's work, to which they carefully reply),[50] with

[44] *Ibid.*, 145.
[45] Report of the House of Lords Select Committee on Medical Ethics, HL Paper 21-1 of 1993–94 [hereafter *Walton Report*], para. 237. Excerpts reproduced in *Euthanasia Examined* at 102.
[46] *Walton Report* para. 238; *Euthanasia Examined* at 103.   [47] *Ibid.*
[48] *When Death is Sought.*   [49] *Ibid.*, xii–xiii, 119–20.
[50] *Ibid.*, 74 n. 112:

Advocates of legalized assisted suicide or euthanasia often fail to engage in [the] crucial balancing process. For example, Ronald Dworkin suggests that, because '[t]here are dangers both in legalizing and refusing to legalize' euthanasia, society has an obligation to carve out a middle ground. See R. Dworkin, *Life's Dominion* 198 (New York: Knopf, 1993) ('[O]nce we understand that legalizing *no* euthanasia is itself harmful to many people...we realize that doing our best

the aid of consultants at least one of whom is strongly pro-euthanasia, they 'unanimously concluded that legalizing assisted suicide and euthanasia would pose profound risks to many patients', especially

those who are poor, elderly, members of a minority group, or without access to good medical care.... The clinical safeguards that have been proposed to prevent abuse and errors would not be realized in many cases.[51]

These and their other reasons for unanimously recommending that there be no change in the law forbidding euthanasia and assistance in suicide are carefully argued with full documentation over about 200 pages.

The Task Force took at face value the Dutch figures for 'euthanasia' in 1990 as given in the soothing and misleading official commentary, overlooking the overwhelmingly greater numbers revealed in the Tables behind that commentary.[52] But even the massaged Dutch figures, extrapolated to the United States (36,000 cases of voluntary euthanasia and 16,000 non-voluntary per annum), were judged by the members of the Task Force to be an 'unacceptable' risk, a risk of abuse which, they added,

is neither speculative nor distant, but an inevitable byproduct of the transition from policy to practice in the diverse circumstances in which the practices would be employed.[53]

The bottom line: the secular, highly experienced, and sophisticated members of the Walton Committee and the New York Task Force judge that if euthanasia were legalized at all, the right *not* to be killed would be catastrophically nullified for very many more people than the few whose supposed right to die is compromised by present law. The Ninth and Second Circuits' countervailing judgment, by comparison, seems sophistical, naïve, and careless.

As the fraud lawyers say, *Follow the money*. Who can doubt that if assisted suicide is introduced by judicial fiat, it will be followed if not accompanied

to draw and maintain a defensible line...is better than abandoning those people altogether'.). Dworkin's argument loses much of its force once it is recognized that the number of people genuinely harmed by laws prohibiting euthanasia or assisted suicide is extremely small, and that legalizing euthanasia or assisted suicide for the sake of these few—whatever safeguards are written into the law—would endanger the lives of a far larger group of individuals, who might avail themselves of these options as a result of depression, coercion, or untreated pain.

Dworkin's argument loses the rest of its force when one notices that he has entirely neglected to offer any account of a 'defensible line' that might be drawn and maintained. He suggests that if he were to offer a 'detailed legal scheme' it would include rules for deciding 'when doctors may hasten the death [soft words!]...of unconscious patients who cannot make' the choice to die. *Life's Dominion*, 216. For the rest he contents himself with attacking the 'tyranny' of the existing law—'the jackboots of the criminal law': *ibid.*, 15.

[51] *When Death is Sought*, xiii; see also 120.   [52] See at nn. 19–21 above.
[53] *When Death is Sought*, 134.

by voluntary euthanasia, and that the *subsequent*, inexorable course of litigation (whose outcome seems to be forecast in the Ninth Circuit's footnote)[54] to establish that these autonomy rights must be exercisable for and on behalf of the incompetent would be litigation substantially funded by healthcare financial interests? Who can doubt that meanwhile, in the words of the New York Task Force:

> Limits on hospital reimbursement based on length of stay and diagnostic group, falling hospital revenues, and the social need to allocate health dollars may all influence physicians' decisions at the bedside... Under any new system of health care delivery, as at present, it will be far less costly to give a lethal injection than to care for a patient throughout the dying process.[55]

No one's pain, delirium, or other physical distress is untreatable.[56] In a tiny proportion of cases the treatment might have to extend to keeping the patient unconscious.[57] But the care-providers may well have an objection to that: the cost of care.

V

And we should be *looking out for the will to power*. Any permission of euthanasia, voluntary or involuntary, will obviously be a huge accession of power to physicians and healthcare personnel. Dutch doctors not only regularly and with effective impunity kill non-consenting patients. With equal freedom they refuse thousands of requests for euthanasia. Patients are radically dependent and, in the Task Force's words, 'generally do what their doctors recommend'.[58] As they also say:

> Physicians who determine that a patient is a suitable candidate for assisted suicide or euthanasia may be far less inclined to present treatment alternatives, especially if the treatment requires intensive efforts by health care professionals.[59]

And much more in the same vein, persuasively spelt out and documented by the Task Force.

The Task Force speaks on the basis of wide, hands-on medical and other relevant practical experience. From my quite different position let me just suggest another possible relevance of the will to power. Ronald

---

[54] *Compassion in Dying v Washington* 79 F3d 790, 832 n. 120.
[55] *When Death is Sought*, 123.
[56] My Oxford colleague, Dr Robert Twycross, who has treated thousands of patients dying of cancer over the past twenty years, gives reasons for thinking that the proportion of such cases where mastery of pain is difficult for skilful practitioners is of the order of 1 per cent, and the proportion where nothing less than complete sedation will suffice is much less than 1 per cent. See Twycross, 'Where There Is Hope, There Is Life: A View From the Hospice' at 147–9, 165–6.
[57] Ibid.   [58] *When Death is Sought*, 122.   [59] Ibid., 124.

Dworkin's theory of the right to euthanasia—a theory in which there is indeed something to admire, especially his account of 'critical interests' and his rejection of scepticism[60]—is a theory driven by a conception that it is reasonable (and, he insinuates, right) to regard one's life as a narrative of which one is the author, so that when one ceases to be in *command* of the plot, one's remaining life—denounced as mere biological life—is valueless if not indeed 'indecent' and contemptible. And here he quotes with evident approval passages in which Nietzsche fiercely attacks those who do not choose to die 'when it is no longer possible to live proudly'.[61] Whatever Dworkin's own views, there is much to reflect upon hereabouts—not least Nietzsche's passionate contempt for the weak, and for compassion with them. Nietzsche's conception of morality as a kind of aesthetics—the aesthetics of a self-created life, indeed a self-narrated life, and in that way a life of noble, authorial power—deeply and pervasively misunderstands morality and thus the very foundations of human rights. A theme I cannot pursue here.

VI

The Ninth Circuit ransacks the language to describe the 'unrelieved misery or torture' from which its decision will rescue people. The judgment's last words are 'painful, protracted, and agonizing deaths'.[62] But as Dr Peter Admiraal, leading Dutch exponent and practitioner of euthanasia, said in the mid-1980s, pain is never a legitimate reason for euthanasia because methods exist to relieve it,[63] indeed in most cases it can be adequately controlled without adverse effect on the patient's normal functioning.[64] An expert committee of the World Health Organization concluded in 1990:

> now that a practicable alternative to death in pain exists, there should be concentrated efforts to implement programs of palliative care, rather than yielding to pressure for legal euthanasia.[65]

Though Dworkin toys with talk of 'terrible pain'[66] and 'prolonged agony',[67] his primary argument for wanting legalization of euthanasia lies elsewhere, so far as I can see—in the view that it is reasonable to have a quasi-Nietzschean, aesthetic hatred of dependence and loathing for the spectacle

---

[60] *Life's Dominion*, 201–7.   [61] *Ibid.*, 212.
[62] *Compassion in Dying v Washington* 79 F3d 790, 814, 839.
[63] See Twycross, 'Where There is Hope, There is Life' at 141.
[64] See Admiraal, 'Justifiable Euthanasia' at 362.
[65] World Health Organization, *Cancer Pain Relief* (1986). [For the background see Meldrum, 'The Ladder and the Clock'.]
[66] *Life's Dominion*, 209.   [67] Dworkin, 'Sex, Death, and the Courts' at 47.

of, say, Sunny von Bulow, wholly unconscious for years but visited daily by her hairdresser. 'Really obscene' he told the Walton Committee.[68]

It is indeed hard for people like judges, professors, classical scholars, and so forth—used to mastery, achievement, and control—to accept the prospect of becoming or being subject to great deprivation and more or less complete dependence. They—we—are understandably but misguidedly tempted to view such a state as spoiling their 'narrative'. The view is radically mistaken: the narrative of which they can (where they rightly can) be proud is a narrative which ends when their actual ability to carry out choices ends. Beyond that point, as (in one's earliest years) before it, there is life which is real, human, and personal, but without a story of which to be proud or ashamed. An utterly common human condition. Aesthetic objections to being reduced to this equality of dependence and powerlessness are, I suggest, no adequate basis for imposing on the many the grave injustices—the terror of being put to death and the reality of coerced and unrequested extinction—inherent in any working regime of euthanasia.

VII

What I have said about pain is one explanation why I have said so little about the realities of suffering which tempt people to commit suicide or seek assistance in doing so or demand that doctors be legally authorized to kill them. Another reason is this. For every harrowing case you can depict or report which would fall within any legalization of euthanasia seriously defended in public debate today, there can be found dozens of cases quite comparably harrowing which fall on the other side of any such line. Read the euthanasiast, confused, but (it seems) honest Dr Lonny Shavelson's *A Chosen Death*.[69] Of the half-dozen harrowing cases he describes, only one or two would fall within any plausible euthanasia campaigner's script (and one of those, an AIDS patient who kept moving his 'line in the sand', dies naturally). Read accounts of the experience of long-time physicians in hospices for the dying.[70]

The hard cases, the real sufferings of real people, are not to be shuffled away in our deliberations about euthanasia. We need to ponder them, not least to ask ourselves what we should be doing about pain and depression and other relievable sources of misery. But we also should look for the line,

---

[68] House of Lords Select Committee on Medical Ethics, HL Paper 91-vii of 1992–93 (29 June 1993) at 162. See also *Life's Dominion*, 210.
[69] Shavelson, *A Chosen Death: The Dying Confront Assisted Suicide.*
[70] See e.g. Twycross, 'Where There is Hope, There is Life' at 141–68.

any line seriously proposed, and ask the line-drawers what sense they can make of distinguishing between the cases on each side of it—in matters so important as autonomy, oppression, and existence itself.

In his latest publication on euthanasia, Dworkin describes the right he contends for as 'the basic right of citizens to decide for themselves whether to die *at once* or after prolonged agony'.[71] But 'once' what? Decide to die *when*? The great majority of people who request euthanasia in hospices change their minds and come to value their last months or weeks of illness, severe though this often is. Few of those who are *dying* of AIDS request euthanasia; most of the many suicides of AIDS patients are by rather healthy people fairly soon after being told of their prognosis.[72] Those who hang on very often find that their hope is eventually transferred from living on to dying well—albeit in extremities of disfigurement and debility—dying affirmed and not abandoned by their relatives or friends. These many, many people, having left behind the falsely exclusive and dominating ethic or aesthetic of control, mastery, and achievement, have found a deeper, more humble but more human understanding of the worth of simply being, with what remains of what one was given.

VIII

Last but by no means least, we should wish to remain uncorrupted by the terrible euthanasiast confusion between *being in an undignified situation or condition* and *lacking human dignity*. Mindful of the Nazi horror, most American and English euthanasiasts have not yet turned their talent for rhetorically demeaning the dying or the comatose—'vegetables', and so forth—to doing the same for the mentally handicapped. What reason of principle have they for this abstention?

The deepest mistakes in Ronald Dworkin's approach to euthanasia are encapsulated in the favour which *Life's Dominion* suggests he has for the view that nurses who care for the permanently comatose, and who believe that they are doing it for a comatose person, are in fact caring only for a 'vegetating body with...the ultimate insult: the conviction that they do it for *him*'.[73] He does not explain how it could be reasonable to think that a body supposed to be merely vegetative and no longer personal could be insulted by respectful and loving care. And he does not defend the incoherent person-body dualism[74] involved in declaring the nurses erroneous in their belief that they are acting for a person, albeit one in

---

[71] Dworkin, 'Sex, Death, and the Courts' at 47 (emphasis added).
[72] See Twycross, 'Where There is Hope, There is Life' at 152–4.   [73] *Life's Dominion*, 212.
[74] See e.g. *NDMR* 304–9; essay 14, sec. IV at 220–1.

the extremities of illness and disability. Like the nurses, and the whole tradition of respecting radical human equality, I think we should judge, and act on the basis, that: persons keep their radical dignity until death— all the way through.

As the Walton Committee, immediately after setting out Dworkin's thesis, expressed the essential point: the 'prohibition of intentional killing...is the cornerstone of law and social relationships, it protects each one of us impartially, embodying the belief that all are equal'.[75] The Committee had seen through the arguments from autonomy and pluralism; unless doctors are to be permitted to kill anyone and everyone who makes a 'stable and competent' request for death, they are going to have to proceed on a classification of lives as 'worth living' or 'not worth living'. Benign as its present authors and promoters doubtless generally are, such a classification would create in our society a new structure of radical inequality, with implications of the most sinister kind.[76]

---

[75] *Walton Report*, paras 236–7; *Euthanasia Examined* at 102:

236. [W]e gave much thought too to Professor Dworkin's opinion that, for those without religious belief, the individual is best able to decide what manner of death is fitting to the life which has been lived.

237. Ultimately, however, we do not believe that these arguments are sufficient reason to weaken society's prohibition of intentional killing.

No other person is distinguished by name in the Committee's long report.

[76] These implications are readily discerned by members of disfavoured and vulnerable groups. Three reports to the legislative committee responsible for Aboriginal affairs in the legislature of the Northern Territory of Australia, dated 28 June, 9 July, and 23 July 1996, were made by Mr Chips Mackinolty, the consultant commissioned by the Northern Territory Government to explain to Aboriginal communities throughout the Northern Territory of Australia the meaning, limits, and benefits of the Territory's euthanasia statute (see n. 29 above). Despite his support for the principles of the statute, Mr Mackinolty's experience of the fear and opposition of the Aboriginal communities—opposition which grew rather than diminished as they heard his explanations—led him to advise the Northern Territory legislature to repeal the statute. First:

The level of fear of and hostility to the legislation is far more widespread than originally envisaged....While it was expected that Aboriginal people out bush would be opposed and would be highly unlikely to avail themselves of the Act, opposition to its existence must be viewed as near universal....One central Australian community, after hearing out some of the education program, became extremely angry at the legislation's existence. ('[I]t might be all right for that man in Darwin to kill his mother, but we don't do that here!'), and asked us to leave—It has been expressed to us by a number of individuals that euthanasia is seen by some as a further method of genocide of Aboriginal people....Conversely, there has been genuine interest from health workers and community leaders in finding out exactly what is in the legislation (albeit with a sense of trying to work out what these crazy whitefellas are up to now!)....As expected there has been considerable interest in Palliative Care, which has been seen by all as 'the Aboriginal way'.

Report by Chips Mackinolty to the Northern Territory of Australia Legislative Committee for Aboriginal Affairs (28 June 1996). A fortnight later, the legislation having come into effect:

Going on from the previous report, I would reiterate in the strongest possible terms the comments made previously with regard to Aboriginal attitudes to the legislation and the damage it is causing Territory Health Services' reputation and standing out bush.

Report by Chips Mackinolty to the Northern Territory of Australia Legislative Committee for Aboriginal Affairs (9 July 1996). Finally, after another fortnight:

Dworkin now argues that there must be no 'official orthodoxy' about what makes human life of value. He says that 'no one can treat [the values in question] as trivial enough to accept other people's orders about what they mean'.[77] He says that

> [w]hatever view we take...we want the right to decide for ourselves, and so we should therefore be ready to insist that any honorable constitution, any genuine constitution of principle, will guarantee that right for everyone.[78]

But the guarantee he proposes is worthless. While exposing almost everyone to violations of a true right (not to be deliberately killed), it would secure for few the supposed 'right to decide for themselves' but for many more would transfer to doctors the discretion to grant or withhold autonomy itself. And in exercising their discretion, the doctors, like those petitioning them for their lethal attentions, would be proceeding on a radically false valuation of the value and dignity of human life. We should not treat 'the values in question' as 'trivial enough' to allow doctors, judges, and other powerful people to impose this false valuation by whittling down and circumventing the law of murder.

Do we hear this talk of 'official orthodoxy' when it comes to matters like slavery or paedophilia? A just society cannot be maintained, and people cannot be treated with the equal concern and respect to which they are all entitled, unless we hold fast to the truth—or, if you will, the axiom—that none of us is entitled to act on the opinion that the life of another is not worth living. To trash this truth—or axiom—as a mere, unconstitutional 'official orthodoxy' is to discard the very foundations of just and *equal respect* for persons in their liberty, their pursuit of happiness, and their life.

> I would love to report some sort of epiphany on the road to the ROTI [euthanasia] legislation, but it just hasn't happened. If anything I feel a bit more gloomy about the whole business and its impact on the Health Department.... The greatest fear and reluctance about the legislation would appear to be coming from Aboriginal Health Workers themselves... [F]eelings about the legislation are far more widespread than originally envisaged, that is, they are not limited to those communities who have strong 'Church' followings....

Report by Chips Mackinolty to the Northern Territory of Australia Legislative Committee for Aboriginal Affairs (23 July 1996).

[77] *Life's Dominion*, 217.   [78] *Ibid.*, 239.

Part Five
Autonomy, IVF, Abortion, and Justice

17

C.S. LEWIS AND TEST-TUBE BABIES*

Lewis's own discussion of test-tube babies is in the third and last of the Riddell Memorial lectures he gave and published these forty years ago, in 1943. That lecture's title he used for the series and the book: *The Abolition of Man*.[1] The title is not the best thing about the book or the lecture; it comes from a strand of thought which I don't think Lewis really made good, the thought that 'when Man by eugenics, by pre-natal conditioning, and by an education and propaganda based on perfect applied psychology, has obtained full control over himself', then both the Conditioners and the conditioned will have ceased to be men:[2]

It is not that they [the Conditioners] are bad men. They are not men at all. Stepping outside the *Tao* [the natural law, the order of true human goods within the universal order], they have stepped into the void. Nor are their subjects necessarily unhappy men. They are not men at all: they are artefacts. Man's final conquest has proved to be the abolition of Man.[3]

As I say, I don't think that Lewis really thought that. The true core of his thought on creation and abolition is more adequately conveyed in his letter to the Anglican nun, Sister Penelope on 20 February 1943, just the time of the lectures:

'Creation' as applied to human authorship...seems to me an entirely misleading term. We...re-arrange elements He has provided. There is not a *vestige* of real creativity *de novo* in us. Try to imagine a new primary colour,

---

* Unpublished, 1984, for the C.S. Lewis Society, Oxford.
[1] Lewis, *The Abolition of Man*. [John Lucas's fiftieth anniversary Riddell Lecture, 'The Restoration of Man', gives a nuanced and illuminating account of the central argument (from self-referential inconsistency) of the first two lectures, against ethical scepticism, relativism, and subjectivism, but does not attend at all to the theme that I consider central to the third lecture, and take up in this essay. The target of Lewis's critique in the first lectures is a book for schools and schoolteachers, on reading and writing, published in 1939 and quickly popular; it argued that all values are subjective, and evaluative propositions mere statements (or expressions) of feelings; one of its two authors, M.A. Ketley, taught me at St Peter's School Collegiate in Adelaide in the 1950s. Lewis's first academic post was as tutor ('Lecturer') in Philosophy at his (and my) Oxford college, University College.]
[2] Lewis, *The Abolition of Man*, 37.   [3] Ibid., 39–40.

[in his second Riddell lecture, 'The Way', at a crucial point, Lewis had said this: 'the human mind has no more power of inventing a new value than of imagining a new primary colour...'[4]]

a third sex, a fourth dimension, or even a monster which does not consist of bits of existing animals stuck together. Nothing happens, and that surely is why our works (as you said) never mean to others quite what we intended; because we are re-combining elements made by Him and already containing *His* meanings. Because of those divine meanings in our materials it is impossible that we should ever know the whole meaning of our own works, and the meaning we never intended may be the best and truest one. Writing a book is much less like creation than it is like planting a garden or begetting a child; in all three cases we are only entering as *one* cause into a causal stream which works, so to speak, in its own way. I would not wish it otherwise.[5]

No: the real theme of the lecture was not the abolition of man but the enslavement of man—the enslavement of the Conditioners, who repudiate the *Tao*, by their own necessarily irrational impulses; and the enslavement of all the rest by the Conditioners. This theme is developed masterfully, in passages that have continued to speak to many, confronted now by real man-making:

...all long-term exercises of power, especially in breeding, must mean the power of earlier generations over later ones.... In order to understand fully what Man's power over Nature, and therefore the power of some men over other men, really means, we must picture the race extended in time from the date of its emergence to that of its extinction. Each generation exercises power over its successors.... If any one age really attains, by eugenics and scientific education, the power to make its descendants what it pleases, all men who live after it are the patients of that power. They are weaker, not stronger: for though we have put wonderful machines in their hands we have pre-ordained how they are to use them.... There is therefore no question of a power vested in the race as a whole steadily growing as long as the race survives. The last men, far from being the heirs of power, will be of all men most subject to the dead hand of the great planners and conditioners and will themselves exercise least power upon the future. The real picture is that of one dominant age—let us suppose the hundredth century A.D.—which resists all previous ages most successfully and dominates all subsequent ages most irresistibly, and thus is the real master of the human species. But even within this master generation (itself an infinitesimal minority of the species) the power will be exercised by a minority smaller still. Man's conquest of Nature, if the dreams of some scientific planners are realised, means the rule of a few hundreds of men over billions upon billions of men.[6]

[4] *Ibid.*, 30.
[5] Hooper, *C.S. Lewis. Collected Letters*, vol. II, 555 (on Sister Penelope CSMV see *ibid.*, 1055–9).
[6] *The Abolition of Man*, 35–6.

Later in the lecture, admittedly, this is linked to the theme of the abolition of man, that is the abolition of human practical understanding (intelligent grasp of true human goods) and the abolition of free choice (an abolition which Lewis had no good reason to suppose even in 'the hundredth century A.D.'). For we find him saying:

> ...without the judgment 'Benevolence is good'—that is, without reentering the *Tao*—they [the Conditioners] can have no ground for promoting or stabilizing these impulses rather than any others. By the logic of their position they must just take their impulses as they come, from chance. And Chance here means Nature. It is from heredity, digestion, the weather, and the association of ideas, that the motives of the Conditioners will spring.... Nature, untrammelled by values, rules the Conditioners and, through them, all humanity. Man's conquest of Nature turns out, in the moment of its consummation, to be Nature's conquest of Man.[7]

But there is some equivocation in this line of argument, which speaks as if nature and human nature would really become just as the Conditioners' false philosophy (mis)conceives them to be. To see what I mean, take a slightly less complex instance of the argument. Lewis says, about the Conditioners who 'devote themselves to the task of deciding what "Humanity" shall henceforth mean':[8]

> 'Good' and 'bad', applied to [the Conditioners], are words without content: for it is from them that the content of these words is henceforward to be derived.[9]

Doubtless that is what the Conditioners would think about good and bad, and about 'good' and 'bad'. But in truth and reality, human goods and human evil, human intelligence and human free choice would remain as the Creator made and makes them. Admittedly, the Conditioners whom Lewis imagines, enslavers of so many, would themselves be slaves not only to their own impulses but also to an illusion of *creative* mastery, an illusion which Lewis's lectures, according to their real drift, tear aside. Yet that illusion would be providing for them an intelligible motivation, confused and uncritical no doubt, but something distinct from a mere impulse or other sub-rational, 'natural' (animal) motive. Critical thought, and reflective deliberation about how to exercise their freedom of choice *well*, would remain for them as close as...—well, as one thought is to the next.

In the real world discussed by Lewis in his letter to Sister Penelope, we can choose, and constitute ourselves (not create ourselves!) by our free choices. We can and should make moral judgments, which are assessments of those choices, not only for their motives and for their expected consequences but

---

[7] *Ibid.*, 39–40. [8] *Ibid.*, 39. [9] *Ibid.*

also for the essential human character of the act of choice itself. Choices are not mere isolated events, but take up a stance towards human goods, and mould the chooser's character, which not only tends to find expression in socially significant acts and attitudes, but will also last into eternity, unless repudiated by another free choice to repent and change…

So I want to say a little about the human character of the acts of choice involved, not in conditioning the whole human species for the whole future, but in making a single test-tube baby. I want to suggest that there is a moral flaw in all test-tube baby-making, even when it is not accompanied (as in fact it virtually always is) by the willingness to kill, and even when it fully respects (as often and increasingly it will not) the goods and bounds of marriage (bounds which are goods for any child as source of its stable identity).

The core of my argument is this: the IVF child comes into existence, not as *a gift supervening on an act expressive of marital unity*, and so not in the manner of a new partner in the common life so vividly expressed by that act, but rather in the manner of a product of a making (and indeed, typically, as the end-product of a process managed and carried out by persons other than his parents).

In procreation by sexual intercourse, *one and the same act of choice*, made by each spouse, governs *both* the experienced and expressive sexual union *and* the procreation of the child. There is one intentional act, and its intention remains governing even when procreation depends on supplementing the act of intercourse by some technical means.

But in IVF, there are irreducibly separate acts of choice, all indispensable, and all the independent acts of different people: the acts of those involved in *producing and collecting sperm* (a process which might involve an act of intercourse but in practice does not); the act(s) of the mother and those involved in *collecting an ovum or ova*; the act(s) of those who *mix sperm and ovum*, and again of those who *transfer the product* of that mixing or uniting; and the choice of the mother to *permit that transfer*. Perhaps none of these choices is the one on which procreation should be said to be radically dependent; or if one has this primary originating significance it is the mixing of the gametes. Each of the sets of actions I have listed is inherently necessary to the outcome; each involves free choices which may be withheld; and *none has the character of a person-to-person act of mutual involvement*.

To choose to have a child by IVF is to choose to have a child as the product of a making. But the relationship of product to maker is a relationship of radical inequality, of profound subordination. Thus the choice to have or to create a child by IVF is a choice in which the child does not have the status which the child of sexual union has, a status which is a great good for any child: the status of radical equality with parents, as partner like them in the familial community.

Of course, the childless parents of the IVF *want* a *child*, and the child once conceived is not *in fact*, in relation to the human race, a mere object or product; and IVF teams devoted to work with the infertile do so to help meet the parents' need. But just as conceiving a child by extra-marital intercourse violates proper marital and parental relationships even when done 'for the sake of the marriage' and 'to give us a child', so too, a moral analysis of IVF cannot stop at the level of motives and expected consequences.

The nuclear family is a community. Though founded and sustained by the voluntary choice and commitment of the spouses, it is not a mere 'voluntary association'. It involves its members in responsibilities which go beyond anything they envisaged and as such consented to on becoming a member. The marriage partners' commitment is 'for better, for worse, for richer, for poorer'; it thus involves a radical *submission* by the couple to the contingencies, however unforeseen, of so unreserved a mutual commitment. The gift and responsibility of children is one of the most important of those contingencies, for parents cannot rightly *determine* the character of their children or reject children whom they dislike.

Let me return to Lewis. In *That Hideous Strength* (1945), the modern fairy tale for grown-ups which, he says in its Preface, 'has behind it a serious "point" which I have tried to make in my *Abolition of Man*',[10] Merlin the Stranger asks Ransom: 'Why is the womb barren on one side? Where are the cold marriages?'. Ransom replies that

Half of her [the Moon's, Sulva's] orb is turned towards us and shares our curse. Her other half looks to Deep Heaven...On this side the womb is barren and the marriages cold. There dwell an accursed people, full of pride and lust. There when a young man takes a maiden to marriage they do not lie together, but each lies with a cunningly fashioned image of the other, made to move and to warm by devilish arts, for real flesh will not please them, they are so dainty (*delicati*) in their dreams of lust. Their real children they fabricate by vile arts in a secret place.[11]

'"You have answered well", said the stranger.'

One of the themes of the novel is the erotic significance—indeed the 'erotic necessity'[12] of humility; and not simply the humility of one partner before the other, setting aside concern for equality with that other, but more particularly the humility of both towards what is greater than

[10] Lewis, *That Hideous Strength*, 7.   [11] *Ibid.*, 337.   [12] *Ibid.*, 179.

them both. 'Those who are enjoying *something*, or suffering something together, are companions. Those who enjoy or suffer one another are not'...'Courtship knows nothing of [equality]; nor does fruition'.[13] The Director (Ransom) is talking to Jane, whose *willed* barrenness, defeating the purpose of God, is later denounced by Merlin, and who at the end, like her husband, 'descends the ladder of humility' to a bed that is no longer 'barren' but rather 'rich'. And the third step of this ladder, the step that takes her to the half-way point is: 'she thought of children, and of pain and death...'.[14]

The act of sexual intercourse profoundly embodies, expresses, and enacts this submission to membership in a partnership. In this respect there is a profound difference between procreation by IVF and procreation by intercourse, even an act of intercourse which the spouses hope and expect will result in procreation. Such an act, even if engaged in at a time calculated by them most likely to be fertile, will properly be an act inherently expressive of the marital partnership and thus quite different from any human acts of making, producing, or acquiring a possession. Freely chosen by the spouses, it has nonetheless a physical and emotional structure making it inherently apt to be experienced by each partner as a giving of self and receiving of the other, a giving which may be complemented by the gift of a child. That gift of a child will have come, then, not from any act of mastery, even jointly agreed mastery, over extraneous materials, even natural biological materials. Rather, *the child will have come from an act of mutual involvement between persons* (involvement at all levels, physical, emotional, intelligent, and moral).

In thus giving and submitting themselves each to the other, these partners in marriage are opening themselves up (and submitting themselves) both to the profound source of life from which the child (they hope) may come, and to service of the child and of each other in the unforeseeable contingencies of their new role as parents, a role which will subsist until death parts the family.

That, very briefly, is why the child of such a union, although weak and dependent, enters the community of the family not as an object of production but as a kind of *partner* in the familial enterprise; and as such this child has a fundamental *parity or equality with the parents.*

The essential conditions of the IVF child's origin, on the other hand, tend to assign this child, in its inception, the same status as other objects of acquisition. The technical skills and decisions of the child's makers will have produced, they hope, a good product, a desirable acquisition.

---

[13] *Ibid.* (emphasis added).   [14] *Ibid.*, 476.

The great evils of destructive experimentation, observation, and selection, are also *signs*, I think, of the moral flaw with which I'm now concerned: of decisions in which human children are envisaged as products. For products typically are subject to quality control, utilization, and discard.[15] Another (lesser) sign of the same flaw is the fact that those who work in the IVF field frequently express anxiety about the *ownership* of the human gametes with which they work *and of the human embryos* which they have produced.

If the parents are to be good parents, they will strive to assign the child his or her true status as a member of the human race and of their own family. But in so doing, *they will be labouring against the real structure of the decisive choices and against the deep symbolism of all that was done to bring that child into being*. They will have to resist all pressures to create 'extra' embryos for the sake of enhancing the chances of achieving pregnancy, all pressures to select out 'unfit' or 'inferior' or 'wrong sex' or other 'unwanted' embryos, and all pressures to mould the normal child's genetic constitution to some special pattern which they or their society favour. But in the very act of resisting such pressures, which is morally admirable, they will find that in choosing IVF they have chosen to put themselves in a position which is not truly familial, in a position of *dominance which is not truly parental*. (Unlike parents such as we are imagining, many other IVF parents, and most IVF teams working today, do follow through the 'logic' of radical domination.) This position of radical dominance is also inherent in the fact that, after the IVF child's conception, the parents (or at least the mother) must make a distinct and positive act of choice: to authorize the transfer of this embryo to her womb.

I should say a word about the death-dealing aspects of IVF, from the point of view, so to speak, of the human being so produced and subjected to domination and, often enough (far more often than not), to destruction. Since the culmination of the process of fertilization, each one of us has maintained not only the same genetic code or, more precisely, genetic constitution (practically unique to himself or herself) but also an organic integration which will remain until death. So it is not *only* the identity and singularity of genetic constitution of each stage (and indeed in each cell) which justifies this fundamental proposition: the human person's bodily life begins at conception and lasts until the death of that individual.

---

[15] I am not saying that this attitude to children is peculiar to IVF, or even that it is seen at its worst in IVF practice. On the contrary, the widespread practice of amniocentesis with a view to the destruction of supposedly defective unborn children is a more gross manifestation of the attitude in which children appear as objects of acquisition, to be assessed as desirable or undesirable and accepted or discarded accordingly.

Something of what I am saying is conveyed by Dr R.G. Edwards, the pioneer of IVF, in his account of 'the beginning of life':

> the embryo is passing through a critical period of life of great exploration: it becomes magnificently organised, switching on its own biochemistry, increasing in size, and preparing itself quickly for implantation in the womb.[16]

Dr Edwards's assessment seems inescapable, that the conceptus, even in the 'pre-implantation stage', is 'a microscopic *human being*—one in its very earliest stages of development.'[17]

Respect for human persons demands respect for each human being at all stages of his or her bodily life. This in turn demands more than merely a certain mental attitude (for example, 'I reverence this human being whose life I hereby destroy') such as might accompany even the grossest acts of exploitation. Rather, an adequate respect for the human person rules out certain sorts of *decisions* and *acts*. In particular it rules out deliberate and direct killing or injuring of innocent human beings (for example, human beings not contributing to any unjust attack on another). It also rules out deliberate neglect and wastage of human lives which are under one's direct responsibility and control.

Certain aspects of much current IVF practice are, therefore, fundamentally unacceptable and ought to be prohibited by any civilized community. There are many such practices and procedures which are widely accepted amongst reputable medical practitioners and scientists in the IVF field in this country and elsewhere in Europe, the United States and Australia:

- many forms of observation of a human embryo which damage or destroy that human embryo, or endanger it by delaying the time of its transfer and implantation, and are observations not made for the benefit of that embryo itself;
- freezing or other storage done without genuine and definite prospect of subsequent transfer, unimpaired, to a mother;
- selection among living and developing human embryos, with a view to transferring and implementing only the fittest or most desirable.

All these practices and procedures involve one human being sitting in judgment on the very life of another and treating that other as a mere means to an end (perhaps a very worthy end); or one human being acting with a disregard for that other's well-being which amounts to treating

---

[16] Edwards and Steptoe, *A Matter of Life*, 101. [17] *Ibid.* (emphasis added).

that other as a mere means. To permit such sitting in judgment, or such disregard, in an area of decision so radically removed from any question of self-defence, is to undermine the basic dignity of human beings. It is thus corrupting, as well as in itself unjust.

To rule out these practices would also rule out the maintenance of embryos in 'banks' as resources for tissue—or organ—transplants or for drug-testing. But there are other practices which should be excluded from the human community on the basis of a different but closely related principle: that humanity itself is to be respected. Consider the practice of *fertilizing human with non-human gametes, or non-human with human.* By such production of 'chimaeras', however short-lived, humanity is submerged ambiguously in a lower order of being, with affront to the dignity of the human in each such chimaera. Doubt is cast on the boundaries of the human and thus on the basic equality of each member of the human race.

I have been concealing the fact that Lewis never spoke of 'test-tube babies'. In the *Abolition of Man* what he speaks of, I mean the word he uses, is 'contraception'.[18] What he was exploring there, and especially in *That Hideous Strength*, is what happens when procreation is *taken out* of marital intercourse; procreation becomes *reproduction*, a form of production entailing the radical maker-product, master-slave relationship of total domination (for howsoever benevolent motives, perhaps); and marital intercourse becomes a kind of mutual masturbation in which even actual mutual involvement will be set aside if the *experiences* will thereby be enhanced: 'each lies with a cunningly fashioned image of the other...'. Later Lewis was to become, like so many Christians, reticent and uncertain[19] and accepting of contraception. In the choosing of his motto for the title page of his book, Lewis saw more clearly on this than, perhaps, he saw later.

The Master said, He who sets to work on a different strand destroys the whole fabric.—Confucius, *Analects* II.16

---

[18] *The Abolition of Man*, 40 (second page of the final lecture).
[19] See his letter to Mrs E.L. Baxter, 19 August 1947: Hooper ed., 798.

18

THE RIGHTS AND WRONGS OF ABORTION*

Fortunately, none of the arguments for and against abortion *need* be expressed in terms of 'rights'. As we shall see, Judith Thomson virtually admits as much in her article.[1] But since she has chosen to conduct her case by playing off a 'right to life' against a 'right to decide what happens in and to one's body', I shall begin by showing how this way of arguing about the rights and wrongs of abortion needlessly complicates and confuses the issue. It is convenient and appropriate to speak of 'rights' for purposes and in contexts which I shall try to identify; it is most inconvenient and inappropriate when one is debating the moral permissibility of types of action—types such as 'abortions performed without the desire to kill', which is the type of action Thomson wishes to defend as morally permissible under most circumstances. So in sec. I of this essay I shall show how her specification and moral characterization of this type of action are logically independent of her discussion of 'rights'. Then in sec. II I shall outline some principles of moral characterization and of moral permissibility, principles capable of explaining some of the moral condemnations which Thomson expresses but which remain all too vulnerable and obscure in her paper. In sec. III I shall show how the elaboration of those principles warrants those condemnations of abortion which Thomson thinks mistaken as well as many of those attributions of human rights which she so much takes for granted. In sec. IV I briefly state the reason (misstated by Thomson and also by Wertheimer)[2] why the fetus from conception has human rights, that is, should be given the same consideration as other human beings.

---

[*] 1973b
[1] 'A Defence of Abortion'. Otherwise unidentified page references in the text are to this article.
[2] Wertheimer, 'Understanding the Abortion Argument'.

I

Thomson's reflections on rights develop in three stages. (A) She indicates a knot of problems about what rights are rights to; she dwells particularly on the problem 'what it comes to, to have a right to life' (p. 55). (B) She indicates, rather less clearly, a knot of problems about the source of rights; in particular she suggests that, over a wide range (left unspecified by her) of types of right, a person has a right only to what he has 'title' to by reason of some gift, concession, grant, or undertaking to him by another person. (C) She cuts both these knots by admitting (but all too quietly) that her whole argument about abortion concerns simply what is 'morally required' or 'morally permissible'; that what is in question is really the scope and source of the mother's responsibility (and only derivatively, by entailment, the scope and source of the unborn child's rights). I shall now examine these three stages a little more closely, and then (D) indicate why I think it useful to have done so.

(A) How do we specify the content of a right? What is a right a right to? Thomson mentions at least nine different rights which a person might rightly or wrongly be said to have.[3] Of these nine, seven have the same logical structure;[4] viz., in each instance, the alleged right is a right with respect to P's action (performance, omission) as an action which may affect Q. In some of these seven instances,[5] the right with respect to P's action is P's right (which Hohfeld[6] called a privilege and Hohfeldians call a liberty). In the other instances,[7] the right with respect to P's action is Q's right (which Hohfeldians call a 'claim-right'). But in all these seven instances

---

[3] Rights which Thomson is willing to allow that a person has:
R1. a right to life (p. 51);
R2. a right to decide what happens in and to one's body (p. 50) (to be equated, apparently, with a just prior claim to one's own body, p. 54);
R3. a right to defend oneself (i.e. to self-defence, p. 53);
R4. a right to refuse to lay hands on other people (even when it would be just and fair to do so, p. 54)—more precisely, a right not to lay hands on other people....
Rights which she thinks it would be coherent but mistaken to claim that a person has or in any event always has:
R5. a right to demand that someone else give one assistance (p. 63)—more precisely, a right to be given assistance by...;
R6. a right to be given whatever one needs for continued life (p. 55);
R7. a right to the use of (or to be given, or to be allowed to continue, the use of) someone else's body (or house) (p. 56);
R8. a right not to be killed by anybody (p. 56);
R9. a right to slit another's throat (an instance, apparently, of a 'right to be guaranteed his death') (p. 66).

[4] Namely, R3 to R9 in the list of n. 3 above.
[5] Namely, R3, R4, and, in one of their senses, R7 and R9.
[6] Hohfeld, *Fundamental Legal Conceptions as Applied in Judicial Reasoning*.
[7] Namely, R5, R6, R8, and, in another of their senses, R7 and R9.

there is what I shall call a 'Hohfeldian right': to assert a Hohfeldian right is to assert a three-term relation between two persons and the action of one of those persons insofar as that action concerns the other person.

The other two rights mentioned by Thomson have a different logical structure.[8] In both these instances, the alleged right is a right with respect to a thing (one's 'own body', or the state of affairs referred to as one's 'life'). Here the relation is two-term: between one person and some thing or state of affairs. Rights in this sense cannot be completely analysed in terms of some unique combination of Hohfeldian rights.[9] P's right to a thing (land, body, life) can and normally should be secured by granting or attributing Hohfeldian rights to him or to others; but just which combination of such Hohfeldian rights will properly or best secure his single right to the thing in question will vary according to time, place, person, and circumstance. And since moral judgments centrally concern *actions*, it is this specification of Hohfeldian rights that we need for moral purposes, rather than invocations of rights to things.

Since Thomson concentrates on the problematic character of the 'right to life', I shall illustrate what I have just said by reference to the 'right to one's own body', which she should (but seems, in practice, not to) regard as equally problematic. Now her two explicit versions of this right are: one's 'just, prior claim to his own body', and one's 'right to decide what happens in and to one's body'. But both versions need much specification[10] before they can warrant moral judgments about particular sorts of action. For example, the 'right to decide' may be *either* (i) a right (Hohfeldian liberty) to do things to or with one's own body (for example to remove those kidney stones, or that baby, from it—but what else? anything? do I have the moral liberty to decide not to raise my hand to the telephone to save Kitty Genovese from her murderers? cf. pp. 62–3); *or* (ii) a right (Hohfeldian claim-right) that other people shall not (at least without one's permission) do things to or with one's own body (for example draw sustenance from,

---

[8] Namely, R1 and R2.

[9] This proposition is elaborated in a juridical context by Honoré, 'Rights of Exclusion and Immunities against Divesting'.

[10] Insufficient specification causes needless problems, besides those mentioned in the text. E.g.: against 'so using the term "right" that from the fact that A ought to do a thing for B, it follows that B has a right against A that A do it for him', Thomson objects that any such use of the term 'right' is 'going to make the question of whether or not a man has a right to a thing turn on how easy it is to provide him with it' (pp. 60–1); and she adds that it's 'rather a shocking idea that anybody's rights should fade away and disappear as it gets harder and harder to accord them to him' (p. 61). So she says she has no 'right' to the touch of Henry Fonda's cool hand, *because*, although he ought to cross the room to touch her brow (and thus save her life), he is not morally obliged to cross America to do so. But this objection rests merely on inadequate specification of the right as against Henry Fonda. For if we say that she has a right that Henry Fonda should cross-the-room-to-touch-her-fevered-brow, and that she has no right that he should cross-America-to-touch-her-fevered-brow, then we can (if we like!) continue to deduce rights from duties.

or inhabit, it—but what else? anything?); *or* (iii) some combination of these forms of right with each other or with other forms of right such as (a) the right (Hohfeldian power) to change another person's right (liberty) to use one's body by making a grant of or permitting such use (*any* such use?), or (b) the right (Hohfeldian immunity) not to have one's right (claim-right) to be free from others' use of one's body diminished or affected by purported grants or permissions by third parties. And as soon as we thus identify these possible sorts of right, available to give concrete moral content to the 'right to one's body', it becomes obvious that the actions which the right entitles, disentitles, or requires one to perform (or entitles, disentitles, or requires others to perform) *vary* according to the identity and circumstances of the two parties to each available and relevant Hohfeldian right. And this, though she didn't recognize it, is the reason why Thomson found the 'right to life' problematic, too.

(B) I suspect it was her concentration on non-Hohfeldian rights ('title' to things like chocolates or bodies) that led Thomson to make the curious suggestion which appears and reappears, though with a very uncertain role, in her paper. I mean, her suggestion that we should speak of 'rights' only in respect of what a man has 'title' to (usually, if not necessarily, by reason of gift, concession, or grant to him).

This suggestion,[11] quite apart from the dubious centrality it accords to ownership and property in the spectrum of rights, causes needless confusion in the presentation of Thomson's defence of abortion. For if the term 'right' were to be kept on the 'tight rein' which she suggests (p. 60), then (a) the Popes and others whose appeal to 'the right to life' she is questioning would deprive her paper of its starting point and indeed its pivot by simply rephrasing their appeal so as to eliminate all reference to rights (for, as I show in the next section, they are not alleging that the impropriety of abortion follows from any grant, gift, or concession of 'rights' to the unborn child); and (b) Thomson would likewise have to

---

[11] It is perhaps worth pointing out that, even if we restrict our attention to the rights involved in gifts, concessions, grants, contracts, trusts, and the like, Thomson's proposed reining-in of the term 'right' will be rather inconvenient. Does only the donee have the 'rights'? Suppose that uncle U gives a box of chocolates to nephew N1, with instructions to share it with nephew N2, and asks father F to see that this sharing is done. Then we want to be able to say that U has a right that N1 and N2 shall each get their share, that N1 shall give N2 that share, that F shall see to it that this is done, and so on; and that N1 has the right to his share, the right not to be interfered with by F or N2 or anyone else in eating his share, and so on; and that N2 has a similar set of rights; and that F has the right to take steps to enforce a fair distribution, the right not to be interfered with in taking those steps, and so on. Since disputes may arise about any one of these relations between the various persons and their actions and the chocolates thereby affected, it is convenient to have the term 'right' on a loose rein, to let it ride round the circle of relations, picking up the action in dispute and fitting the competing claims about 'the right thing to do' into intelligible and typical three-term relationships. Yet some of the rights involved in the gift of the chocolates, e.g. U's rights, are not acquired by any grant to the right-holder.

rephrase claims she herself makes, such as that innocent persons certainly have a right to life, that mothers have the right to abort themselves to save their lives, that P has a right not to be tortured to death by Q even if R is threatening to kill Q unless Q does so, and so on. But if such rephrasing is possible (as indeed it is), then it is obvious that suggestions about the proper or best way to use the term 'a right' are irrelevant to the substantive moral defence or critique of abortion.

But this terminological suggestion is linked closely with Thomson's substantive thesis that we do not have any 'special [sc. Good Samaritan or Splendid Samaritan] responsibility' for the life or well-being of others 'unless we have assumed it, explicitly or implicitly' (p. 65). It is this (or some such) thesis about *responsibility* on which Thomson's whole argument, in the end, rests.

(C) Thomson's explicit recognition that her defence of abortion *need* not have turned on the assertion or denial of rights comes rather late in her paper, when she says that there is 'no need to insist on' her suggested reined-in use of the term 'right':

If anyone does wish to deduce 'he has a right' from 'you ought,' then all the same he must surely grant that there are cases in which it is not morally required of you that you allow that violinist to use your kidneys....[12] And so also for mother and unborn child. Except in such cases as the unborn person has a right to demand it...nobody is morally *required* to make large sacrifices...in order to keep another person alive (pp. 61–2).

In short, the dispute is about what is 'morally required' (that is, about what one 'must' and, for that matter, 'may' or 'can' [not] do: see p. 52); that is to say, about the rights and wrongs of abortion. True, on page 61 there is still that 'right to demand large sacrifices' cluttering up the margins of the picture. But when we come to the last pages of her paper (pp. 64–5) even that has been set aside, and the real question is identified as not whether the child has a 'right to demand large sacrifices' of its mother, but whether the mother has a 'special responsibility' to or for the child (since, if she has, then she may be morally required to make large sacrifices for it and *therefore* we will be able to assert, by a convenient locution, the child's 'right to [demand] those sacrifices').

---

[12] The sentence continues: 'and in which he does not have a right to use them, and in which you do not do him an injustice if you refuse'. But these are merely remnants of the 'rhetoric' in which she has cast her argument. Notice, incidentally, that her suggestion that 'justice' and 'injustice' should be restricted to respect for and violation of rights in her reined-in sense is of no importance since she grants that actions not in her sense unjust may be self-centred, callous, and indecent, and that these vices are 'no less grave' (p. 61).

(D) So in the end most of the argument about rights was a red herring. I have bothered to track down this false trail, not merely to identify some very common sorts and sources of equivocation (more will come to light in the next two sections), but also to show how Thomson's decision to conduct her defence in terms of 'rights' makes it peculiarly easy to miss a most important weak point in her defence. This weak point is the connection or relation between one's 'special responsibilities' and one's ordinary (not special) responsibilities; and one is enabled to miss it easily if one thinks (a) that the whole problem is essentially one of rights, (b) that rights typically or even essentially depend on grant, concession, assumption, etc., (c) that special responsibilities likewise depend on grants, concessions, assumptions, etc., and (d) that therefore the whole moral problem here concerns one's *special* responsibilities. Such a train of thought is indeed an enthymeme, if not a downright fallacy; but that is not surprising, since I am commenting here not on an argument offered by Thomson but on a likely effect of her 'rhetoric'.

What Thomson, then, fails to attend to adequately is the claim (one of the claims implicit, I think, in the papal and conservative rhetoric of rights) that the mother's duty not to abort herself is *not* an incident of any special responsibility which she assumed or undertook for the child, but is a straightforward incident of an ordinary duty everyone owes to his neighbour. Thomson indeed acknowledges that such ordinary non-assumed duties exist and are as morally weighty as duties of justice in her reined-in sense of 'justice'; but I cannot discern the principles on which she bases, and (confidently) delimits the range of, these duties.[13]

She speaks, for instance, about 'the drastic limits to the right of self-defence': 'If someone threatens you with death unless you torture someone else to death, I think you have not the right, even to save your life, to do so' (p. 53). Yet she also says: 'If anything in the world is true, it is that you do not...do what is impermissible, if you reach around to your back and unplug yourself from that violinist to save your life' (p. 52). So why, in the first case, has one the strict responsibility not to bring about the death demanded? Surely she is not suggesting that the pain ('torture') makes

---

[13] Perhaps this is the point at which to note how dubious is Thomson's assertion that 'in no state in this country is any man compelled by law to be even a Minimally Decent Samaritan to any person', and her insinuation that this is a manifestation of discrimination against women. This sounds so odd coming from a country in which a young man, not a young woman, is compelled by law to 'give up long stretches of his life' to defending his country at considerable 'risk of death for himself'. True, he is not doing this for 'a person who has no special right to demand it'; indeed, what makes active military service tough is that one is not risking one's life to save *anybody* in particular from any *particular* risk. And are we to say that young men have *assumed* a 'special responsibility' for defending other people? Wouldn't that be a gross fiction which only a lame moral theory could tempt us to indulge in? But it is just this sort of social contractarianism that Thomson is tempting us with.

the difference, or that it *is* morally permissible to kill *painlessly* another person on the orders of a third party who threatens you with death for non-compliance? And, since she thinks that

> nobody is morally *required* to make large sacrifices, of health, of all other interests and concerns, of all other duties and commitments, for nine years, or even for nine months, in order to keep another person alive (p. 62)

will she go on to say that it is permissible, when a third party threatens you with such 'large sacrifices' (though well short of your life), to *kill* (painlessly) another person, or two or ten other persons?

If Thomson balks at such suggestions, I think it must be because she does in the end rely on some version of the distinction, forced underground in her paper, between 'direct killing' and 'not keeping another person alive'.

The more one reflects on Thomson's argument, the more it seems to turn and trade on some version of this distinction. Of course she starts by rejecting the view that it is always wrong to directly kill, because that view would (she thinks) condemn one to a lifetime plugged into the violinist. But she proceeds, as we have noted, to reject at least one form of killing to save one's life, on grounds that seem to have nothing to do with consequences and everything to do with the formal context and thus structure of one's action (the sort of formal considerations that usually are wrapped up, as we shall see, in the word 'direct'). And indeed the whole movement of her argument in defence of abortion is to assimilate abortion to the range of Samaritan problems, on the basis that having an abortion is, or can be, justified as *merely* a way of *not rendering special assistance*. Again, the argument turns, not on a calculus of consequences, but on the formal characteristics of one's choice itself.

Well, why should this apparently *formal* aspect of one's choice determine one's precise responsibilities in a certain situation whatever the other circumstances and expected consequences or upshots? When we know *why*, on both sides of the debate about abortion, we draw and rely on these distinctions, then we will be better placed to consider (i) whether or not unplugging from the violinist is, after all, direct killing in the sense alleged to be relevant by Popes and others, and (ii) whether or not abortion is, after all, just like unplugging the captive philosopher from the moribund musician.

II

Like Thomson's moral language (setting off the 'permissible' against the 'impermissible'), the traditional rule about killing doubtless gets its peremptory sharpness primarily (historically speaking) from the injunction, respected as divine and revealed: 'Do not kill the innocent and just.'[14] But the handful of peremptory negative moral principles correspond to the handful of really basic aspects of human flourishing, which in turn correspond to the handful of really basic and controlling human needs and human inclinations. To be fully reasonable, one must remain *open* to every basic aspect of human flourishing, to every basic form of human good. For is not each irreducibly basic, and none merely means to end? Are not the basic goods incommensurable? Of course it is reasonable to concentrate on realizing those forms of good, in or for those particular communities and persons (first of all oneself), which one's situation, talents, and opportunities most fit one for. But concentration, specialization, particularization is one thing; it is quite another thing, rationally and thus morally speaking, to make a choice which cannot but be characterized as a choice *against* life (to kill), *against* communicable knowledge of truth (to lie, where truth is at stake in communication), *against* procreation, *against* friendship and the justice that is bound up with friendship. Hence the strict negative precepts.[15]

The general sense of 'responsibility', 'duty', 'obligation', 'permissibility' is not my concern here, but rather the *content* of our responsibilities, duties, obligations, of the demands which human good makes on each of us. The general demand is that we remain adequately open to, attentive to, respectful of, and willing to pursue human good insofar as it can be realized and respected in our choices and dispositions. Now most moral failings are not by way of violation of strict negative precepts—that is, are not straightforward choices against basic values. Rather, they are forms of negligence, of *insufficient* regard for these basic goods, or for the derivative structures reasonably created to support the basic goods. And when someone is accused of violating directly a basic good, he will usually plead that he was acting out of a proper care and concern for the realization of that or another basic value in the *consequences* of his chosen act though not in the act itself. For example, an experimenter accused of killing children in order to conduct medical tests will point out that these deaths are necessary to these tests, and these tests to medical discoveries, and the discoveries to the saving of many more lives—so that, in view of the foreseeable consequences of his deed, he displays (he will argue) a fully adequate (indeed, the only adequate) and reasonable regard for the value of human life.

---

[14] Exodus 23: 7; cf. Exodus 20: 13, Deuteronomy 5: 17, Genesis 9: 6, Jeremiah 7: 6 and 22: 3.
[15] These remarks are filled out somewhat in essay 1970b. See also Grisez, *Abortion: The Myths, the Realities and the Arguments*, ch. 6. My argument owes much to this and other works by Grisez.

But to appeal to consequences in this fashion is to set aside one criterion of practical reasonableness and hence of morality—namely, that one remain open to each basic value, and attentive to some basic value, in each of one's chosen acts—in favour of quite another criterion—namely, that one choose so to act as to bring about consequences involving a greater balance of good over bad than could be expected to be brought about by doing any alternative action open to one. Hare has observed that '*for practical purposes* there is no important difference' between most of the currently advocated theories in ethics; they all are 'utilitarian', a term he uses to embrace Brandt's ideal observer theory, Richards's (Rawls's?) rational contractor theory, specific rule-utilitarianism, universalistic act-utilitarianism and his own universal prescriptivism.[16] All justify and require, he argues, the adoption of 'the principles whose general inculcation will have, all in all, the best consequences'.[17] I offer no critique of this utilitarianism here; Thomson's paper is not, on its face, consequentialist. Suffice it to inquire how Hare and his fellow consequentialists know the future that to most of us is hidden. How do they know what unit of computation to select from among the incommensurable and irreducible basic aspects of human flourishing; what principle of distribution of goods to commend to an individual considering his own interests, those of his friends, his family, his enemies, his *patria*, and those of all men present and future? How do they know how to define the 'situation' whose universal specification will appear in the principle whose adoption (singly? in conjunction with other principles?) 'will' have best consequences;[18] whether and how to weigh future and uncertain consequences against present and certain consequences? And how do they know that net good consequences would in fact be maximized (even if *per impossibile* they were calculable) by general adoption of consequentialist principles of action along with consequentialist 'principles' to justify non-observance of consequentialist 'principles' in 'hard cases'?[19] One cannot understand the western moral tradition, with its peremptory negative (forbearance-requiring) principles (the positive principles being relevant in all, but peremptory in few, particular situations), unless one sees why that tradition rejected consequentialism as mere self-delusion—for Hare and his fellow consequentialists can provide no satisfactory answer to any of the foregoing lines of inquiry, and have no coherent rational account to give of any level of moral thought above that of the man who thinks

---

[16] Hare, 'Rules of War and Moral Reasoning' at 168.   [17] *Ibid.* at 174.
[18] Cf. Castañeda, 'On the Problem of Formulating a Coherent Act-Utilitarianism'; Zellner, 'Utilitarianism and Derived Obligation'.
[19] See Hodgson, *Consequences of Utilitarianism*.

how good it would be to act 'for the best'.[20] Expected total consequences of one's action do not provide a sufficient ground for making a choice that cannot but be regarded as *itself* a choice directly against a basic value (even that basic value which it is hoped will be realized in the *consequences*)—for expected total consequences cannot be given an evaluation sufficiently reasonable and definitive to be the decisive measure of our response to the call of human values, while a choice directly against a basic good provides, one might say, its own definitive evaluation of itself.

I do not expect these isolated and fragmentary remarks to be in themselves persuasive. I do not deny that the traditional western willingness, (in theory) to discount expected consequences wherever the action itself could not but be characterized as against a basic value, is or was supported by the belief that Providence would inevitably provide that 'all manner of things shall be well' (that is, that the whole course of history would turn out to have been a fine thing, indisputably evil deeds and their consequences turning out to have been 'all to the good' like indisputably saintly deeds and their consequences). Indeed, the consequentialist moralist, who nourishes his moral imagination on scenarios in which by killing an innocent or two he saves scores, thousands, millions, or even the race itself, rather obviously is a post-Christian phenomenon—such an assumption of the role of Providence would have seemed absurd to the pre-Christian philosophers[21] known to Cicero and Augustine. I am content to suggest the theoretical and moral context in which the casuistry of 'direct' and 'indirect' develops, within the wider context of *types* of action to be considered 'impermissible' (I leave the term incompletely accounted for) because *inescapably* (that is, whatever the hoped-for consequences) choices *against* a basic value of human living and doing. In short, one's responsibility for the realization of human good, one's fostering of or respect for human flourishing in future states of affairs at some greater or lesser remove from one's present action, does not override one's responsibility to respect each basic form of human good which comes directly in question in one's present action itself.

But how does one choose 'directly against' a basic form of good? When is it the case, for example, that one's choice, one's intentional act, 'cannot but be' characterized as 'inescapably' anti-life? Is abortion always (or ever) such a case? A way to tackle these questions can be illustrated by reference

[20] 20: Cf. Hare, 'Rules of War and Moral Reasoning' at 174:

The defect in most deontological theories...is that they have no coherent rational account to give of any level of moral thought above that of the man who knows some good simple moral principles and sticks to them.... [The] simple principles of the deontologist...are what we should be trying to inculcate into ourselves and our children if we want to stand the best chance...of doing what is for the best.

[21] Not to mention the Jewish moralists: see Daube, *Collaboration with Tyranny in Rabbinic Law*.

to three hard cases whose traditional 'solutions' contributed decisively to the traditional judgment about abortion. The relevance of these 'hard cases' and 'solutions' to the discussion with Thomson should be apparent in each case, but will become even more apparent in the next section.

(i) *Suicide*. Considered as a fully deliberate choice (which it doubtless only rather rarely is), suicide is a paradigm case of an action that is always wrong because it cannot but be characterized as a choice directly against a fundamental value, life. The characterization is significant, for what makes the killing of oneself attractive is usually, no doubt, the prospect of peace, relief, even a kind of freedom or personal integration, and sometimes is an admirable concern for others; but no amount of concentration on the allure of these positive values can disguise from a clear-headed practical reasoner that it is *by* and *in* killing himself that he intends or hopes to realize those goods. And the characterization is given sharpness and definition by the contrast with heroic self-sacrifices in battle or with willing martyrdom.[22] Where Durkheim treated martyrdom as a case of suicide,[23] anybody concerned with the intentional structure of actions (rather than with a simplistic analysis of movements with foreseen upshots) will grant that the martyr is not directly choosing death, either as end or as means. For, however certainly death may be expected to ensue from the martyr's choice not to accede to the tyrant's threats, still it will ensue through, and as the point of, *someone else's* deliberate act (the tyrant's or the executioner's), and thus the martyr's chosen act of defiance need not be interpreted as itself a choice against the good of life.

The case of suicide has a further significance. The judgments, the characterizations, and the distinctions made in respect of someone's choices involving his *own* death will be used in respect of choices involving the death of *others*. In other words, *rights* (such as the 'right to life') are not the fundamental rationale for the judgment that the killing of other (innocent) persons is impermissible. What is impermissible is an intention set against the value of human life where that value is directly at stake in any action by virtue of the intentional and causal structure of that action; and such an impermissible intention may concern my life or yours—and no one speaks of his 'right to life' as against himself, as something that would explain why *his* act of self-killing would be wrongful.

Indeed, I think the real justification for speaking of 'rights' is to make the point that, when it comes to characterizing intentional actions in terms

---

[22] Note that I am not asserting (or denying) that self-sacrificial heroism and martyrdom are moral duties; I am explaining why they need not be regarded as moral faults.

[23] *Le Suicide: étude de sociologie*, 5. Cf. also Daube's remarks on Donne in 'The Linguistics of Suicide' at 418–21.

of their openness to basic human values, those human values are, and are to be, realized in the lives and well-being of others as well as in the life and well-being of the actor. That is, the point of speaking of 'rights' is to stake out the relevant claims to equality and non-discrimination (claims that are not to absolute equality, since *my* life and my well-being have some reasonable priority in the direction of *my* practical effort, if only because I am better placed to secure them). But the claims are to equality of *treatment*; so, rather than speak emptily of, say, a 'right to life', it would be better to speak of, say, inter alia, a 'right not to be killed intentionally'—where the meaning and significance of 'intentional killing' can be illuminated by consideration of the right and wrong of killing oneself (that is, of a situation where no 'rights' are in question and one is alone with the bare problem of the right relation between one's acts and the basic values that can be realized or spurned in human actions).

Finally, the case of suicide and its traditional solution remind us forcefully that traditional western ethics simply does not accept that a person has 'a right to decide what shall happen in and to his body' a right which Thomson thinks, astonishingly (since she is talking of Pius XI and Pius XII), 'everybody seems to be ready to grant' (p. 50). Indeed, one might go so far as to say that traditional western ethics holds that, because and to the extent that one does not have the 'right' to decide what shall happen in and to one's body, one *therefore* and to that extent does not have the right to decide what shall, by way of one's own acts, happen in and to anyone else's body.[24] As I have already hinted, and shall elaborate later, this would be something of an oversimplification, since one's responsibility for one's own life, health, etc. is reasonably regarded as prior to one's concern for the life, health, etc. of others. But the oversimplification is worth risking in order to make the point that the traditional condemnation of abortion (as something one makes happen in and to a baby's body) *starts* by rejecting what Thomson thinks everyone will admit.

(ii) *D's killing an innocent V in order to escape death at the hands of P, who has ordered D to kill V.* This case has been traditionally treated on the same footing as cases such as D's killing V in order to save Q (or Q1, Q2…Qn) from death (perhaps at the hands of P) or from disease (where

---

[24] As one example of this general point, consider the practice of duelling to satisfy private honour or privately avenge wrongs: strongly upheld by aristocratic, military, and some other elements of secular culture down to the early twentieth century, it was condemned by Christian teachers with ever increasing severity. (The Council of Trent e.g. condemned it in 1563 as a mortal sin which must be expunged from the Christian world, excommunicated and penalized rulers who permitted it, duelists and their seconds or sponsors, denied Christian burial to any who perished in a duel, and so forth). It involves the exercise of a (morally falsely) supposed right to put one's own body and life at risk, by one's own choice (not as a means of self-defence, but—in the central case—in order to be in a position to destroy the body and life of another, as a means of vindicating one's honour.

D is a medical researcher); for all such cases cannot but be characterized as choices to act directly against human life. Of course, in each case, the reason for making the choice is to save life; but such saving of life will be effected, if at all, through the choices of other actors (for example P's choice not to kill D where D has killed V; or P's choice not to kill Q) or through quite distinct sequences of events (for example Q's being given life-saving drugs discovered by D).

Hence the traditional ethics affirms that 'there are drastic limits to the right of self-defence' in much the same terms as Thomson. 'If someone threatens you with death when you torture someone else to death...you have not the right, even to save your own life, to do so' (p. 53). And it was this very problem that occasioned the first ecclesiastical pronouncement on abortion in the modern era, denying that 'it is licit to procure abortion before animation of the foetus in order to prevent a girl, caught pregnant, being killed or dishonoured'.[25] The choice to abort here cannot but be characterized as a choice against life, since its intended good life- or reputation-saving effects are merely expected consequences, occurring if at all through the further acts of other persons, and thus are not what is being *done* in and by the act of abortion itself. But I do not know how one could arrive at any view of this second sort of hard case by juggling, as Thomson seems to be willing to, with a 'right to life', a 'right to determine what happens in and to your own body', a 'right of self-defence', and a 'right to refuse to lay hands on other people'—all rights shared equally by D, V, P, and Q, Q1, Q2...!

(iii) *Killing the mother to save the child*. This was the only aspect of abortion that Thomas Aquinas touched on, but he discussed it thrice.[26] For if it is accepted that eternal death is worse than mere bodily death, shouldn't one choose the lesser evil? So if the unborn child is likely to die unbaptized, shouldn't one open up the mother, rip out the child and save-it-from-eternal-death-by-baptizing-it? (If you find Aquinas's problem unreal, amend it—consider instead the cases where the child's life seems so much more valuable, whether to itself or to others, than the life of its sick or old or low-born mother.) No, says Aquinas. He evidently considers (for reasons I consider in sec. III) that the project involves a direct choice against life and is straightforwardly wrong, notwithstanding the good consequences.

So the traditional condemnation of therapeutic abortion flows not from a prejudice against women or in favour of children but from a straightforward

---

[25] Decree of the Holy Office, 2 March 1679, error no. 34; see *DS* 2134; Grisez, *Abortion*, 174; John T. Noonan, Jr., 'An Almost Absolute Value in History', 34.
[26] See *ST* III, q.68, a.11; *Sent.* IV d.6 q.1. a.1 qa.1 ad 4; and [without explicit reference to abortion] d.23 q.2 a.2 qa.1 ad 1 and 2; Grisez, *Abortion*, 154; Noonan, op. cit., 24.

application of the solution in the one case to the other case, on the basis that mother and child are *equally* persons in whom the value of human life is to be realized (or the 'right to life' respected) and not directly attacked.[27]

III

But now at last let us look at this 'traditional condemnation of abortion' a little more closely than Thomson does. It is not a condemnation of the administration of medications to a pregnant mother whose life is threatened by, say, a high fever (whether brought on by pregnancy or not), in an effort to reduce the fever, even if it is known that such medications have the side effect of inducing miscarriage. It is not a condemnation of the removal of the malignantly cancerous womb of a pregnant women, even if it is known that the fetus within is not of viable age and so will die. It is quite doubtful whether it is a condemnation of an operation to put back in its place the displaced womb of a pregnant woman whose life is threatened by the displacement, even though the operation necessitates the draining off of the amniotic fluids necessary to the survival of the fetus.[28]

But why are these operations not condemned? As Foot has remarked, the distinction drawn between these and other death-dealing operations 'has evoked particularly bitter reactions on the part of non-Catholics. If you are permitted to bring about the death of the child, what does it matter how it is done?'[29] Still, she goes some way to answering her own question; she is not content to let the matter rest where Hart had left it, when he said:

Perhaps the most perplexing feature of these cases is that the overriding aim in all of them is the same good result, namely...to save the mother's life. The differences between the cases are differences of causal structure leading to the applicability of different verbal distinctions. There seems to be no relevant moral difference between them on any theory of morality...[to attribute moral relevance to distinctions drawn in this way] in cases where the ultimate purpose is the same can only be explained as the result of a legalistic conception of morality as if it were conceived in the form of a law in rigid form prohibiting all intentional killing as distinct from knowingly causing death.[30]

---

[27] Pius XII's remark, quoted by Thomson, that 'the baby in the maternal breast has the right to life immediately from God' has its principal point, not *(pace* Thomson, 51) in the assertion of a premise from which one could deduce the wrongfulness of direct killing, but in the assertion that *if* anybody—e.g. the mother—has the right not to be directly killed, *then* the baby has the same right, since as Pius XII goes on immediately 'the baby, still not born, is a man in the same degree and for the same reason as the mother'.

[28] The three cases mentioned in this paragraph are discussed in a standard and conservative Roman Catholic textbook: Zalba, *Theologiae Moralis Compendium*, I, 885.

[29] Foot, 'The Problem of Abortion and the Doctrine of Double Effect'.

[30] Hart, 'Intention and Punishment' in his *Punishment and Responsibility*, 124–5.

Foot recognizes that attention to 'overriding aim' and 'ultimate purpose' is not enough if we are to keep clear of moral horrors such as saving life by killing innocent hostages, etc. As a general though not exclusive and not (it seems) at-all-costs principle, she proposes that one has a duty to refrain from doing injury to innocent people and that this duty is stricter than one's duty to aid others; this enables her to see that 'we might find' the traditional conclusion correct, that we must not crush the unborn child's skull in order to save the mother (in a case where the child could be saved if one let the mother die): 'for in general we do not think that we can kill one innocent person to rescue another'.[31] But what is it to 'do injury to' innocent people? She does not think it an injury to blow a man to pieces, or kill and eat him, in order to save others trapped with him in a cave, *if he is certain to die soon anyway*.[32] So I suppose that, after all, she *would* be willing (however reluctantly) to justify the killing by D of hostages, V, V1, V2, whenever the blackmailer P threatened to kill *them too*, along with Q, Q1, Q2, unless D killed them himself.† One wonders whether this is not an unwarranted though plausible concession to consequentialism.

In any event, Foot was aware, not only that the 'doctrine of the double effect' 'should be taken seriously in spite of the fact that it sounds rather odd...',[33] but also of what Thomson has not recorded in her brief footnote (p. 50 n. 3) on the technical meaning given to the term 'direct' by moralists using the 'doctrine' to analyse the relation between choices and basic values, namely that the 'doctrine' requires more than that a certain bad effect or aspect (say, someone's being killed) of one's deed be not intended either as end or as means. If one is to establish that one's death-dealing deed need not be characterized as directly or intentionally against the good of human life, the 'doctrine' requires further that the good effect or aspect, which *is* intended, should be proportionate (say, saving someone's life), that is, sufficiently good and important relative to the bad effect or aspect: otherwise (we may add, in our own words) one's choice, although not intentionally to kill, will reasonably be counted as a choice inadequately open to the value of life.[34] And this consideration alone might well suffice to rule out abortions performed in order simply to remove the unwanted fetus from the body of women who conceived as a result of forcible rape, even if

---

[31] Foot, 'The Problem of Abortion and the Doctrine of Double Effect', 15.   [32] *Ibid.*, 14.
[33] *Ibid.*, 8.
[34] *Ibid.*, 7. This is the fourth of the four usual conditions for the application of the 'Doctrine of Double Effect'; see e.g. Grisez, *Abortion*, 329. Anscombe, 'War and Murder' at 57 [*Collected Philosophical Papers*, 58], formulates the 'principle of double effect', in relation to the situation where 'someone innocent will die unless I do a wicked thing', thus: 'you are no murderer if a man's death was neither your aim nor your chosen means, *and if you had to act in the way that led to it or else do something absolutely forbidden*' (emphasis added). [In 1973b at 135 my phrase 'although not intentionally to kill' read 'although not directly and intentionally to kill', which made the sentence incoherent.]

one were to explicate the phrase 'intended directly as end or as means' in such a way that the abortion did not amount to a directly intended killing (for example because the mother desired only the removal, not the death of the fetus, and would have been willing to have the fetus reared in an artificial womb had one been available).[35]

Well, how *should* one explicate these central requirements of the 'doctrine' of double effect? When *should* one say that the expected bad effect or aspect of an action is not intended either as end or as means and hence does not determine the moral character of the act as a choice not to respect one of the basic human values? Since it is in any case impossible to undertake a full discussion of this question here, let me narrow the issue down to the more difficult and controverted problem of 'means'. Clearly enough, D intends the death of V *as a means* when he kills him in order to conform to the orders of the blackmailer P (with the object of thereby saving the lives of Q et al.), since the good effect of D's act will follow only by virtue of *another* human act (here P's). But Grisez (no consequentialist!) argues that the bad effects or aspects of some *natural* process or chain of causation need not be regarded as intended as means to the good effects or aspects of that process even if the good effects or aspects *depend* on them in the causal sense (and provided that those good effects could not have been attained in some other way by that agent in those circumstances).[36] So he would, I think, say that Thomson could rightly unplug herself from the violinist (at least where the hook-up endangered her life) even if 'unplugging' could only be effected by chopping the violinist in pieces. He treats the life-saving abortion operation in the same way, holding that there is no direct choice against life involved in chopping up the fetus if what is intended as end is to save the life of the mother and what is intended as means is no more than the removal of the fetus and the consequential relief to the mother's body.[37] As a suasive, he points again to the fact that *if* an artificial womb or restorative operation were available for the aborted fetus, a right-thinking mother and doctor in such a case would wish to make these available to the fetus; this shows, he says, that a right-thinking mother and doctor, even where such facilities are *not* in fact available, need not be regarded as intending the death of the fetus they kill.[38] For my part, I think Grisez's reliance on such counter-factual hypotheses to specify the

[35] Grisez argues thus, *Abortion*, 343; also in 'Toward a Consistent Natural-Law Ethics of Killing'.
[36] Ibid., 333 and 89–90 respectively.   [37] Ibid., 341 and 94 respectively.
[38] Ibid., 341 and 95 respectively. I agree with Grisez that the fact that, if an artificial womb were available, many women would *not* transfer their aborted offspring to it shows that those women are directly and wrongfully intending the *death* of their offspring. I suspect Judith Thomson would agree; cf. 66.

morally relevant meaning or intention of human acts is excessive, for it removes morally relevant 'intention' too far from commonsense intention, tends to unravel the traditional and commonsense moral judgments on suicide (someone would say: 'It's not death I'm choosing, only a long space of peace and quiet, after which I'd willingly be revived, if that were possible'!), and likewise disturbs our judgments on murder and in particular on the difference between administering (death-hastening) drugs to relieve pain and administering drugs to relieve-pain-by-killing.

In any event, the version of traditional non-consequentialist ethics which has gained explicit ecclesiastical approval in the Roman church these last ninety years treats the matter differently; it treats a bad or unwanted aspect or effect of act A1 as an *intended* aspect of A1, not only when the good effect (unlike the bad) follows only by virtue of another human act A2, but also *sometimes* when both the good effect and the bad effect are parts of one natural causal process requiring no further human act to achieve its effect. *Sometimes*, but not always; so when?

A variety of factors are appealed to explicitly or relied on implicitly in making a judgment that the bad effect is to count as intended-as-a-means;‡ Bennett would call the set of factors a 'jumble';[39] but they are even more various than he has noted. It will be convenient to set them out while at the same time observing their bearing on the two cases centrally in dispute, the craniotomy to save a mother's life and that notable scenario in which 'you reach around to your back and unplug yourself from that violinist to save your life'.

(1) Would the chosen action have been chosen if the victim had not been present? If it would, this is ground for saying that the bad aspects of the action, viz. its death-dealing effects on the victim (child or violinist), are not being intended or chosen either as end or means, but are genuinely incidental side effects that do not necessarily determine the character of one's action as (not) respectful of human life. This was the principal reason the ecclesiastical moralists had for regarding as permissible the operation to remove the cancerous womb of the pregnant woman.[40] And the 'bitter' reaction which Foot cites and endorses—'If you are permitted to bring about the death of the child, what does it matter how it is done?'—seems, here, to miss the point. For what is in question, here, is not a mere matter of technique, of different ways of doing something. Rather it is a matter of the very reason one has for acting in the way one does, and such reasons can

---

[39] Bennett, 'Whatever the Consequences' at 92 n. 1.
[40] See the debate between A. Gemelli and P. Vermeersch, summarized in Ephemerides Theologicae Lovaniensis 11 (1934): 525–61; see also Noonan, *The Morality of Abortion*, 49; Zalba, *Theologiae Moralis Compendium* I, 885.

be constitutive of the act as an intentional performance. One has no reason even to want to be rid of the fetus within the womb, let alone to want to kill it; and so one's act, though certain, causally, to kill, is not, intentionally, a choice against life.

But of course, *this* factor does not serve to distinguish a craniotomy from unplugging that violinist; in both situations, the oppressive presence of the victim is what makes one minded to do the act in question.

(2) Is the person making the choice the one whose life is threatened by the presence of the victim? Thomson rightly sees that this is a relevant question, and Thomas Aquinas makes it the pivot of his discussion of self-defensive killing (the discussion from which the 'doctrine' of double effect, as a theoretically elaborated way of analysing intention, can be said to have arisen). He says:

> Although it is not permissible to intend to kill someone else in order to defend oneself (since it is not right to do the act 'killing a human being,' except [in some cases of unjust aggression] by public authority and for the general welfare), still it is not morally necessary to omit to do what is strictly appropriate to securing one's own life simply in order to avoid killing another, for to make provision for one's own life is more strictly one's moral concern than to make provision for the life of another persons.[41]

As Thomson has suggested, a bystander, confronted with a situation in which one innocent person's presence is endangering the life of another innocent person, is in a different position; to choose to intervene, in order to kill one person to save the other, involves a choice to make himself a master of life and death, a judge of who lives and who dies; and (we may say) this context of his choice prevents him from saying, reasonably, what the man defending himself can say:

> I am not choosing to kill; I am just doing what—as a single act and not simply by virtue of remote consequences or of someone's else's subsequent act—is strictly needful to protect my own life, by forcefully removing what is threatening it.

Now the traditional condemnation of abortion[42] concerns the bystander's situation: a bystander cannot but be choosing to kill if (a) he rips open the mother, in a way foreseeably fatal to her, in order to save the child from the threatening enveloping presence of the mother (say, because the

---

[41] *ST* II–II q.64 a.7:
Nec est necessarium ad salutem ut homo actum moderatae tutelae praetermittat ad evitandum occisionem alterius: quia plus tenetur homo vitae suae providere quam vitae alienae. Sed quia occidere hominem non licet nisi publica auctoritate propter bonum commune, ut ex supra dictis patet [a.3], illicitum est quod homo intendat occidere hominem ut seipsum defendat.

[42] *Ibid.*, aa.2 and 3.

placenta has come adrift and the viable child is trapped and doomed unless it can be rescued, or because the mother's blood is poisoning the child, in a situation in which the bystander would prefer to save the child, either because he wants to save it from eternal damnation, or because the child is of royal blood and the mother low born, or because the mother is in any case sick, or old, or useless, or 'has had her turn', while the child has a whole rich life before it); or if (b) he cuts up or drowns the child in order to save the mother from the child's threatening presence. 'Things being as they are, there isn't much a woman can safely do to abort herself', as Thomson says (p. 52)—at least, not without the help of bystanders, who by helping (directly) would be making the same choice as if they did it themselves. But the unplugging of the violinist is done by the very person defending herself. Thomson admits (p. 52) that this gives quite a different flavour to the situation, but she thinks that the difference is not decisive, since bystanders have a decisive reason to intervene in favour of the *mother* threatened by her child's presence. And she finds this reason in the fact that the mother *owns* her body, just as the person plugged in to the violinist owns his own kidneys and is entitled to their unencumbered use (p. 53). Well, this too has always been accounted a factor in these problems, as we can see by turning to the following question.

(3) Does the chosen action involve not merely a denial of aid and succour to someone but an actual intervention that amounts to an assault on the body of that person? Bennett wanted to deny all relevance to any such question,[43] but Foot[44] and Thomson have rightly seen that in the ticklish matter of respecting human life in the persons of others, and of characterizing choices with a view to assessing their respect for life, it *can* matter that one is directly injuring and not merely failing to maintain a life-preserving level of assistance to another. Sometimes, as here, it is the causal structure of one's activity that involves one willy-nilly in a choice for or against a basic value. The connection between one's activity and the destruction of life may be so close and direct that intentions and considerations which would give a different dominant character to mere non-preservation of life are incapable of affecting the dominant character of a straightforward taking of life. This surely is the reason why Thomson goes about and about to represent a choice to have an abortion as a choice *not* to provide assistance or facilities, *not* to be a Good or at any rate a Splendid Samaritan; and why, too, she carefully describes the violinist affair so as to minimize the degree of intervention against the violinist's

---

[43] Bennett, 'Whatever the Consequences'.
[44] Foot, 'The Problem of Abortion and the Doctrine of Double Effect' at 11–13.

body, and to maximize the analogy with simply refusing an invitation to volunteer one's kidneys for his welfare (like Henry Fonda's declining to cross America to save Judith Thomson's life).

If anything in the world is true, it is that you do not commit murder, you do not do what is impermissible, if you reach around to your back and unplug yourself from that violinist to save your life (p. 52).

Quite so. It might nevertheless be useful to test one's moral reactions a little further: suppose, not simply that 'unplugging' required a *bystander's* intervention, but also that (for medical reasons, poison in the bloodstream, shock, etc.) unplugging could not safely be performed unless and until the violinist had first been dead for six hours and had moreover been killed outright, say by drowning or decapitation (though not necessarily while conscious). Could one then be *so* confident, as a bystander, that it was right to kill the violinist in order to save the philosopher? But I put forward this revised version principally to illustrate *another* reason for thinking that, within the traditional casuistry, the violinist-unplugging in Thomson's version is *not* the 'direct killing' which she claims it is, and which she *must* claim it is if she is to make out her case for rejecting the traditional principle about direct killing.

Let us now look back to the traditional rule about abortion. If the mother needs medical treatment to save her life, she gets it, subject to one proviso, even if the treatment is certain to kill the unborn child—for after all, her body is *her* body, as 'women have said again and again' (and they have been heard by the traditional casuists!). And the proviso? That the medical treatment not be *via* a straightforward assault on or intervention against the child's body. For after all *the child's body is the child's body, not the woman's*. The traditional casuists have admitted the claims made on behalf of one 'body' up to the very limit where those claims become *mere (understandable) bias, mere (understandable) self-interested* refusal to listen to the *very same* claim ('This body is *my* body') when it is made by or on behalf of another person.[45] Of course, a traditional casuist would display an utter want of feeling if he didn't most profoundly sympathize with women in the desperate circumstances under discussion. But it is vexing to find a philosophical Judith Thomson, in a cool hour, unable to see when an argument cuts both ways, and unaware that the casuists have seen the point before her and have, unlike her, allowed the argument to cut both ways impartially. The child, like his mother, has a 'just prior claim to his own body', and abortion involves laying hands on, manipulating, that

---

[45] Not, of course, that they have used Thomson's curious talk of 'owning' one's own body with its distracting and legalistic connotations and its dualistic reduction of subjects of justice to objects.

body. And here we have perhaps the decisive reason why abortion cannot be assimilated to the range of Samaritan problems and why Thomson's location of it within that range is a mere (ingenious) novelty.

(4) But is the action against someone who had a duty not to be doing what he is doing, or not to be present where he is present? There seems no doubt that the 'innocence' of the victim whose life is taken makes a difference to the characterizing of an action as open to and respectful of the good of human life, and as an intentional killing. Just how and why it makes a difference is difficult to unravel; I shall not attempt an unravelling here. We all, for whatever reason, recognize the difference and Thomson has expressly allowed its relevance (p. 52).

But her way of speaking of 'rights' has a final unfortunate effect at this point. We can grant, and have granted, that the unborn child has no Hohfeldian *claim-right* to be allowed to stay within the mother's body under all circumstances; the mother is not under a strict duty to allow it to stay under all circumstances. In *that* sense, the child 'has no right to be there'. But Thomson discusses also the case of the burglar in the house; and he, too, has 'no right to be there', even when she opens the window! But beware of the equivocation! The burglar not merely has no claim-right to be allowed to enter or stay; he also has a strict duty *not* to enter or stay, that is, he has no Hohfeldian *liberty*—and it is *this* that is uppermost in our minds when we think that he 'has no right to be there': it is actually unjust for him to be there. Similarly with Jones who takes Smith's coat, leaving Smith freezing (p. 53). And similarly with the violinist. He and his agents had a strict duty not to make the hook-up to Judith Thomson or her gentle reader. Of course, the violinist himself may have been unconscious and so not himself at fault; but the whole affair is a gross injustice to the person whose kidneys are made free with, and the injustice to that person is not measured simply by the degree of moral fault of one of the parties to the injustice. Our whole view of the violinist's situation is coloured by this burglarious and persisting wrongfulness of his presence plugged into his victim.

But can any of this reasonably be said or thought of the unborn child? True, the child had no *claim-right* to be allowed to come into being within the mother. But it was not in breach of any *duty* in coming into being nor in remaining present within the mother; Thomson gives no arguments at all in favour of the view that the child is in breach of duty in being present (though her counter examples show that she is often tacitly assuming this). (Indeed, if we are going to use the wretched analogy of owning houses, I fail to see why the unborn child should not with justice say of the body around it: 'That is my house. No one *granted* me property rights in it, but equally no one *granted* my mother any property rights in it.' The fact is that both persons *share* in the use of this body, both by the same sort of title, viz., that this is the way they happened to come into being. But it would be better to drop this ill-fitting talk of 'ownership' and 'property rights' altogether.) So though the unborn child 'had no right to be there' (in the sense that it never had a claim-right to be allowed to *begin* to be there), in another straightforward and more important sense it *did* 'have a right to be there' (in the sense that it was not in breach of duty in being or continuing to be there). All this is, I think, clear and clearly different from the violinist's case. Perhaps forcible rape is a special case; but even then it seems fanciful to say that the child is or could be in any way at fault, as the violinist is at fault or would be but for the adventitious circumstance that he was unconscious at the time.

Still, I don't want to be dogmatic about the justice or injustice, innocence or fault, involved in a rape conception. (I have already remarked that the impermissibility of abortion in any such case, where the mother's life is not in danger, does not depend necessarily on showing that the act is a choice directly to kill.) It is enough that I have shown how in three admittedly important respects the violinist case differs from the therapeutic abortion performed to save the life of the mother. As presented by Thomson, the violinist's case involves (i) no bystander, (ii) no intervention against or assault upon the body of the violinist, and (iii) an indisputable injustice to the agent in question. Each of these three factors is absent from the abortion cases in dispute. Each has been treated as relevant by the traditional casuists whose condemnations Thomson was seeking to contest when she plugged us into the violinist.

When all is said and done, however, I haven't rigorously answered my own question. When should one say that the expected bad effect or aspect of an act is not intended even as a means and hence does not determine the moral character of the act as a choice not to respect one of the basic human values? I have done no more than list some factors. I have not discussed how one decides which combinations of these factors suffice to answer the question one way rather than the other. I have not discussed the man on the plank, or the man off the plank; or the woman who leaves her baby behind as she flees from the lion, or the other woman who feeds *her* baby to the lion in order to make good her own escape; or the 'innocent' child who threatens to shoot a man dead, or the man who shoots that child to save himself;[46] or the starving explorer who kills himself to provide food for his fellows, or the other explorer who wanders away from the party

---

[46] This case is (too casually) used in Brody, 'Thomson on Abortion'.

so as not to hold them up or diminish their rations. The cases are many, various, instructive. Too generalized or rule-governed an application of the notion of 'double effect' would offend against the Aristotelean, common law, Wittgensteinian wisdom that here 'we do not know how to draw the boundaries of the concept'—of intention, of respect for the good of life, and of action as distinct from consequences—'except for a special purpose'.[47] But I think that those whom Aristotle bluntly calls wise can come to clear judgments on most of the abortion problems, judgments that will not coincide with Thomson's.

IV

I have been assuming that the unborn child is, from conception, a person and hence is not to be discriminated against on account of age, appearance, or other such factors insofar as such factors are reasonably considered irrelevant where respect for basic human values is in question. Thomson argues against this assumption, but not, as I think, well. She thinks (like Wertheimer,[48] *mutatis mutandis*) that the argument in favour of treating a newly conceived child as a person is merely a 'slippery slope' argument (p. 47), rather like (I suppose) saying that one should call all men bearded because there is no line one can confidently draw between beard and clean shavenness. More precisely, she thinks that a newly conceived child is like an acorn, which after all is not an oak! It is discouraging to see her relying so heavily and uncritically on this hoary muddle. An acorn can remain for years in a stable state, simply but completely an acorn. Plant it and from it will sprout an oak sapling, a new, dynamic biological system that has nothing much in common with an acorn save that it came from an acorn and is capable of generating new acorns. Suppose an acorn is formed in September 1971, picked up on 1 February 1972, and stored under good conditions for three years, then planted in January 1975; it sprouts on 1 March 1975 and fifty years later is a fully mature oak tree. Now suppose I ask: When did that oak begin to grow? Will anyone say September 1971 or February 1972? Will anyone look for the date on which it was first noticed in the garden? Surely not. If we know it sprouted from the acorn on 1 March 1975, that is enough (though a biologist could be a trifle more exact about 'sprouting'); that is when *the oak* began. *A fortiori* with the conception of a child, which is no *mere* germination of a seed. Two sex cells, each with only twenty-three chromosomes, unite and more or

---

[47] Cf. Wittgenstein, *Philosophical Investigations*, sec. 69.
[48] 'Understanding the Abortion Argument'.

less immediately fuse to become a new cell with forty-six chromosomes providing a unique genetic constitution (not the father's, not the mother's, and not a mere juxtaposition of the parents') which thenceforth throughout its life, however long, will substantially determine the new individual's make-up.[49] This new cell is the first stage in a dynamic integrated system that has nothing much in common with the individual male and female sex cells, save that it sprang from a pair of them and will in time produce new sex cells. To say that *this* is when a person's life began is not to work backwards from maturity, sophistically asking at each point 'How can one draw the line *here*?' Rather it is to point to a perfectly clear-cut beginning to which each one of us can look back and in looking back see how, in a vividly intelligible sense, 'in my beginning is my end'. Judith Thomson thinks she began to 'acquire human characteristics' 'by the tenth week' (when fingers, toes, etc. became visible). I cannot think why she overlooks the most radically and distinctively human characteristic of all—the fact that she was conceived of human parents. And then there is Henry Fonda. From the time of his conception, though not before, one could say, looking at his unique personal genetic constitution, not only that 'by the tenth week' Henry Fonda would have fingers, but also that in his fortieth year he would have a cool hand. That is why there seems no rhyme or reason in waiting 'ten weeks' until his fingers and so on actually become visible before declaring that he *now* has the human rights which Judith Thomson rightly but incompletely recognizes.

NOTES

† *'Direct' in the 'doctrine' of 'double effect'*...(p. 296 after n.32). Here my argumentation jumbles together two distinct issues: what is intended as a means, and what can fairly be imposed as a side effect. To be 'not an injury', death or harm must have been caused neither as a means (or end) nor unfairly ('disproportionately'). The question whether hostages are going to die anyway is relevant to the second issue but not to the first.

‡ *A variety of factors are appealed to explicitly or relied on implicitly in making a judgment that the bad effect is to count as intended-as-a-means*...(at n. 39). As noted in essay II.13 at n. 11, my understanding of intention and action was underdeveloped at the time of the present essay: I had not grasped the significance of the proposal adopted by choice and consisting of the whole sequence of ends (almost all also means) and means (almost all also ends), all of which are intended under the description that, in the deliberation which shapes the proposal, makes them choiceworthy. (For the developed account, see essays II. 8 (1987b), II.9 (1991a), II.10 (1991b), and II.13 (2001a).) The discussion in sec. III of the present essay is set up as a consideration of the differences between unplugging Thomson's violinist and performing a craniotomy. My discussion at no point affirms that the craniotomy is always impermissible; in criticizing Grisez's use of counter-factual hypotheses as a suasive for his conclusion that craniotomy need not be direct (i.e. intended) killing, I neither denied nor affirmed his conclusion. But I went on to consider what could be said by or on behalf of the moral tradition approved by the Roman ecclesiastical authorities since 1884 ('these last ninety years', looking back from 1973) to differentiate craniotomy (assumed to be wrongful) from unplugging (granted to be permissible).

[49] See Grisez, *Abortion*, ch. 1 and 273–87, with literature there cited.

(Actually, the Roman ecclesiastical authorities deliberately abstained from pronouncing craniotomy to be wrongful: for citations and discussion see sec. III of essay II.13 (2001a).) If craniotomy done by a doctor to relieve the mother of the imminent threat to her life from the unborn baby's presence in her birth canal is accepted, as in essay II.13, to be permissible, there remains a vast range of abortions (starting with the craniotomies conventionally called partial birth abortions, done to prevent the baby being born alive) to which some or all of the enumerated differences from unplugging remain relevant. Some of these impermissible abortions differ from unplugging because they are done not to relieve the mother from pregnancy but from post-natal childcare and/or the grief of surrendering the child for adoption. Some differ from unplugging because, though done to relieve the mother from the burdens of pregnancy, they unfairly discriminate against the unborn child in the ways enumerated in sec. III as (2), (3), and/or (4).

19

JUSTICE FOR MOTHER AND CHILD*

If the unborn are human persons, the principles of justice and non-maleficence (rightly understood) prohibit every abortion; that is, every procedure or technical process carried out with the intention of killing an unborn child or terminating its development. In [the essay (II.16) with which this essay was originally conjoined] I argue that the only reasonable judgment is that the unborn are indeed human persons. Now I explore the ways in which the principles of justice and non-maleficence bear on various actions and procedures which harm or may well harm the unborn. The right understanding of those principles is sketched in [another essay originally written for the same volume on medical ethics, essay 1993d]. That essay has a theological setting, but the considerations which I set out in the present essay in no way depend on faith; they are philosophical and natural-scientific considerations valid and, in my view, properly decisive for everyone, quite independently of any religious premise.

I

Every attempt to harm an innocent human person violates the principles of non-maleficence and justice, and is always wrong. Every procedure adopted with the intention of killing an unborn child, or of terminating its development, is an attempt to harm, even if it is adopted only as a means to some beneficent end (purpose) and even if it is carried out with very great reluctance and regret. Such procedures are often called 'direct abortion'. But here 'direct' does not refer to physical or temporal immediacy, but to the reasons for the procedure: whatever is chosen as an end or (however

---

* 1993a ('Abortion and Health-care Ethics') (second part). The large edited volume on medical ethics for which both the essay of which this was a part and a co-authored companion essay (1993d) were written was editorially framed around the 'four principles of medical ethics' proposed by Beauchamp and Childress, *Principles of Biomedical Ethics*: beneficence, non-maleficence, autonomy, and justice. Essay 1993d makes a number of criticisms of these principles and of their use to guide reflection and deliberation in medical ethics and bioethics. The present essay makes some

reluctantly) as a means is 'directly' willed.[1] What is only an unintended side effect is 'indirectly' willed. Using this terminology, one can rightly say that 'direct abortion' is always wrong, while 'indirect abortion' is not always wrong. But it would be clearer to reserve the word 'abortion' (or 'induced abortion' or 'therapeutic abortion') for procedures adopted with the intent to kill or terminate the development of the fetus, and to call by their own proper names any therapeutic procedures which have amongst their foreseen but unintended results the termination of pregnancy and death of the fetus.

The ethics governing therapeutic procedures which impact fatally on the unborn can be summarized as follows:

(1) The direct killing of the innocent—that is, killing either as an end or as a chosen means to some other end—is always gravely wrong. This moral norm excludes even the choice to kill one innocent person as a means of saving another or others, or even as a means of preventing the murder of another or others.

(2) Every living human individual is equal to every other human person in respect of the right to life. Since universal propositions are true equally of every instance which falls under them, *equality in right to life* is entailed by the truth of two universal propositions: (a) every living human individual must be regarded and treated as a person, and (b) every innocent human person has the right never to be directly killed.

(3) The unborn can never be considered as aggressors, still less as unjust aggressors. For the concept of aggression involves action. But it is only the very existence and the vegetative functioning of the unborn (and not its animal activities, its movements, its sensitive reactions to pain, etc., real as these are) that can give rise to problems for the life or health of the mother. So the concept of aggression extends only by metaphor to the unborn. Moreover, the unborn child, being in its natural place through no initiative and no breach of duty of its own, cannot be reasonably regarded as intruder, predator, or aggressor; its relation to its mother is just that: mother and child.[2]

---

reference to them just to the extent that they seem rightly applicable. The essay refers to Catholic moral teaching because it was commissioned for that purpose; but part of that teaching is that it is philosophically sound, and indeed *philosophically based* and therefore fully accessible (in epistemically propitious circumstances) to anyone whether or not they accept those parts of Catholic belief which rely on revelation and thus, though philosophically sound, are not philosophically based.

[1] Pius XII, Address of 12 November 1944, *Discorsi & Radiomessaggi* 6: 191–2; CDF, *De abortu procurato, Declaration on Abortion* (18 November 1974), para. 7; *MA* 40, 67–77.

[2] Essay 18, sec. III.

(4) Provided that bringing about death or injury is not chosen as an end in itself (say, as fun or revenge) or *as a means* to some further end (even the purpose of preserving life), an action which is necessary to preserve the life of one person can be permissible even if it is certain also to bring about the death or injury of another or others.

(5) Not every indirect killing is permissible; sometimes, though indirect, it is unjust, for example because there is a non-deadly alternative to the deadly procedure which could be used for preserving life.

A just law and a decent medical ethic forbidding the killing of the unborn cannot admit an exception formulated as: 'to save the life of the mother'. Many of the laws in Christian nations used to include exactly that exception (and no others), but there are two decisive reasons why a fully just law and medical ethic cannot include a provision formulated in that sort of way. First, that sort of formulation implies that, in this case at least, killing may rightly be chosen *as a means* to an end. Second, by referring only to the mother, any such formulation implies that her life should *always* be preferred, which is unfair.

However, a just law and a decent medical ethic cannot delimit permissible killing by limiting its prohibition to 'direct killing' (or 'direct abortion'). For this would leave unprohibited the cases where indirect killing is unjust (for example because it could have been delayed until the time when the unborn child would survive the operation; or because it was done to relieve the mother of a condition which did not threaten her life).

Where the life of the mother or of the unborn child is at stake, the requirements both of a decent medical ethic and of just law can be expressed in the following proposition:

If the life of either the mother or the child can be saved only by some medical procedure which will adversely affect the other, then it is permissible to undertake such a procedure with the intention of saving life, provided that the procedure is the most effective available to increase the overall probability that one or the other (or both) will survive, i.e. to increase the *average probability* of their survival.

This proposition does not say or imply that killing as a means can be permissible. It does not give an unfair priority to either the mother or the child. It excludes any indirect killing which would be unfair.

Nevertheless, it may seem at first glance that the proposition would admit direct abortion in certain cases. For people often assume, and many Catholic theologians argue, that any procedure is direct abortion if in the process of cause and effect it *at once* or *first* brings about the damage to the unborn child.

But even amongst Catholic theologians who reject every kind of compromise with secular consequentialism and proportionalism, there are some who propose an alternative understanding of direct killing, using the framework of Thomas Aquinas's analysis of acts with two effects and of Pope Pius XII's interpretation of 'direct killing' as an action which aims at the destruction of an innocent human life either as an end or as a means.[3] The directness which is in choosing a means is to be understood, according to these theologians, not by reference to immediacy or priority in the process of cause and effect, as such, but by reference to the intelligible content of a choice to do something inherently suited to bring about intended benefit.

The proposition I have set out above requires that any procedure which adversely affects the life of either the mother or the unborn child be intended *and inherently suited* to preserving life (both lives) so far as possible. It thus falls within an acceptable understanding of Catholic teaching on 'direct' abortion. At the same time it demands that any such procedure satisfy the requirements of justice (fairness) which are conditions for the moral permissibility of 'indirect abortion' (as it can be called, though other names are better, as I have said above). The most obvious and likely application of the proposition is in cases where four conditions are satisfied: some pathology threatens the lives of both the pregnant woman and her child; it is not safe to wait, or waiting will very probably result in the death of both; there is no way to save the child; and an operation that can save the mother's life will result in the child's death. Of these cases the example most likely to be met in modern health care is that of ectopic pregnancy (assuming that the embryo cannot be successfully transplanted from the tube to the uterus).[4]

Abortion to 'save the life of the mother' because she is threatening to commit suicide (or because her relatives are threatening to kill her) obviously falls outside the proposition and is a case of direct, impermissible killing. It is neither the only means of saving her life (guarding or restraining her or her relatives is another means), nor is it a means suited of its nature to saving life; of itself, indeed, the abortion in such a case does nothing but kill.

---

[3] Zalba, 'Nihil prohibet unius actus esse duos effectus' at 567–8.; Grisez and Boyle, *Life and Death with Liberty and Justice*, 404–7. [See also essay II.13 (2001a) for a full discussion of the issues relating to intention and causation.]

[4] [On the principles, and the analysis of choice and action, employed in this essay and defended in essays II.9–11 and II.13, it can be right to treat ectopic pregnancy not only by salpingectomy (removing the fallopian tube containing the embryo) but also, where medically indicated, by salpingostomy (removing the embryo through an incision, leaving the tube in place). And in the rare but not unknown cases where the mother is so ill that attempting to carry the child through to viability will kill her before viability, removal of the unborn child, though certain to result in termination of his or her development (and in death), can rightly be undertaken to relieve the mother of the child's dependence on her system, the dependence which is threatening her life.]

II

A woman who is the victim of rape is entitled to defend herself against the continuing effects of such an attack and to seek immediate medical assistance with a view to preventing conception.[5] (Such efforts to prevent conception are not necessarily acts of contraception, for they seek to prevent conception not *as* the coming to being of a new human life but rather *as* the invasion of her ovum as a final incident in the invasion of her body by her assailant's bodily substances.) But the possible presence of an unborn child changes the moral situation notably. Even if a procedure for terminating pregnancy were undertaken without any intention, even partly, to terminate the development and life of the unborn child, but *solely* to relieve the mother of the continued bodily effects of the rape, that procedure would be unjust to the unborn child, who is wholly innocent of the father's wrongdoing. For people are generally willing to accept, and expect their close friends and relatives to accept, grave burdens short of loss of life or moral integrity in order to avert certain death. So imposing certain or even probable death on the unborn child in these circumstances is an unfair discrimination against the child.

However, if a procedure such as the administration of the 'post-coital pill' is undertaken for the purpose only of *preventing* conception after rape but involves some *risk* of causing abortion *as a side effect* (because it is not known at what stage of her cycle the woman is), there can be no universal judgment that the adoption of such a procedure is unjust to the unborn. For there are many legitimate activities which foreseeably cause some risk of serious or even fatal harm, a risk which in many cases is rightly accepted by upright and informed people as a possible side effect of their choices to engage in those activities.[6]

III. PRENATAL SCREENING AND GENETIC COUNSELLING

Examinations and tests done with the intention of, if need be, treating the unborn or preparing for a safe pregnancy and delivery are desirable and right when undertaken on the same criteria as other medical procedures. Examinations and tests done to allay anxiety or curiosity are justifiable

---

[5] Catholic Archbishops of Great Britain, *Abortion and the Right to Live* (London: Catholic Truth Society, 1980), para. 21.

[6] Catholic Bishops' Joint Committee on Bio-ethical Issues, (i) 'The morning-after pill: some practical and moral questions about post-coital "contraception"', *Briefing* 16 (1986), 33–9; (ii) 'The morning-after pill–a reply', *Briefing* 16 (1986), 254–5.

only if they involve no significant risk to the child. But anyone who does or accepts a test or examination with the thought of perhaps suggesting or arranging or carrying out an abortion if the results show something undesirable, is already willing, conditionally, abortion, and so is already making himself or herself into a violator of the principles of non-maleficence and justice.

Healthcare personnel who respect those principles have a responsibility not only to refrain from recommending or conducting tests or examinations with a view to seeing whether or not abortion is 'medically indicated', but also the responsibility of telling a woman within their care which of the various tests she may be offered by others are done only or mainly for that immoral (but widely accepted) purpose and which are done to safeguard the health of the unborn child.[7]

IV. PARTICIPATION

Anyone who commands, directs, advises, encourages, prescribes, approves, or actively defends doing something immoral is a cooperator in it if it is done, and even if it is not in the event done has already willed it to be done and thus already participates in its immorality. So a doctor who does not perform abortions but refers pregnant women to consultant obstetricians with a view to abortion wills the immorality of abortion.

On the other hand, some people whose activity contributes to the carrying out of an immoral act need not will the accomplishment of the immoral act; their cooperation in the evil is not a participation in the immorality as such. Their cooperation is often called 'material', to distinguish it from the so-called 'formal' (intended) cooperation of those who (for whatever reason and with whatever enthusiasm or reluctance) will the successful doing of the immoral act. Formal cooperation in immoral acts is always wrong; material cooperation is not always wrong, but will be wrong if it is unfair or a needless giving of a bad example. So a nurse in a general hospital who is unwilling to participate in abortions but is required by the terms of her employment to prepare patients for surgical operations (cleaning, shaving, etc.) may prepare patients for abortion without ever willing the killing or harming of the unborn child; she does only whatever she does towards any morally good operation; so her cooperation can be morally permissible *if* in all circumstances it is not unfair and a needless occasion of scandal (morally corrupting example to others). The surgeon, on the other hand, must will the harm to the unborn, since that is the point

---

[7] Sutton, *Prenatal Diagnosis: Confronting the Ethical Issues*.

of the immoral abortion and he or she must will the operation's success; so he or she is a participant, indeed a primary participant, in immorality, even if he or she too is doing so only in order to retain employment or gain medical qualifications.[8] Hospital managers who want every patient to give written and full consent to operations must want women who come to the hospital for abortions to consent precisely to abortion; so these managers willy-nilly encourage the women's immoral willing of abortion; indeed, the managers' immoral commitment of will may well be greater than that of women whose consent is given in a state of emotional upheaval and distress.

All healthcare personnel have a moral right (and duty) of non-participation in wrongdoing. This right is not in essence one of 'conscientious objection', since it is founded not on the sheer fact of having made a good-faith judgment of conscience—which might be mistaken—but on the basic human duty and corresponding right not to participate in what really is a moral evil. But where the state recognizes a legal right of 'conscientious objection' to participation in abortion, healthcare personnel have the moral right and duty to avail themselves of that legal right wherever they would otherwise incur any kind of legal obligation or institutional responsibility to cooperate 'formally' (that is, intentionally) in abortion. They should take the appropriate steps in good time (but even if they have culpably failed to take those steps, should still refuse all formal cooperation in any of the immoral activities now so widespread in the practice of health care).

V. EMBRYO EXPERIMENTATION

What has been said above about abortion applies, of course, to embryos living in vitro—understanding by 'embryo' any human individual from the beginning of fertilization. Any form of experimentation on or observation of an embryo which is likely to damage that embryo (or any other embryo which it might engender by twinning), or to endanger it by delaying the time of its transfer and implantation, is maleficent or unjust or both, unless the procedures are intended to benefit that individual itself. Any form of freezing or other storage done without genuine and definite prospect of a subsequent transfer, unimpaired, to the proper mother is unjust unless done as a measure to save the embryo in an unexpected emergency. Any procedure whereby embryos are brought into being with a view to selecting among them the fittest or most desirable for transfer and implantation

---

[8] Grisez, *Christian Moral Principles*, 300–3.

involves a radically unjust and maleficent intention, however good its further motivations.[9]

VI. BENEVOLENCE AND AUTONOMY

The open acceptance of abortion into reputable medical practice during the past quarter of a century—an ethical and civilizational collapse of historic magnitude and far-reaching effects—creates a profound challenge for all who remain willing to adhere to the proper meaning of non-maleficence and justice. They need a proper sense of their own autonomy, as upright moral subjects who preserve and respect the truth amid a social fabric of untruths and rationalizations. They also need to retain and live out a full respect for the principle of beneficence. By refusing their participation in abortion they show beneficence to the unborn (even though these will almost certainly be killed by others); and to the mothers of the unborn (however little they appreciate it at the time); and to all whose lives are endangered by the spread of an ethos of 'ethical killing' in the name of compassion or autonomy. They retain a full responsibility for the compassionate care of pregnant women and for women whose pregnancy was terminated by abortion, no less than of women threatened by or suffering in or after miscarriage or stillbirth. They should be aware of the very real special needs and vulnerabilities of those who have had an induced abortion, even though those needs and sequelae are widely denied by those who promote abortion and produce rationalizations for doing and undergoing it.

---

[9] Fisher, *IVF: The Critical Issues*; 1983e; CDF, *Donum Vitae. Instruction on Respect for Human Life in its Origin and the Dignity of Procreation* (1987); [essays 17 and II.17 (2000b)].

Part Six
Marriage, Justice, and the Common Good

20

MARRIAGE: A BASIC AND EXIGENT GOOD[*]

I

Marrying is an act, the chosen act of the two spouses who thereby commit themselves to living as husband and wife. Marriage as a state or way of life—being married—is the couple's living out of that constitutive act of commitment in countless further acts, and in each spouse's disposition or readiness both to do such acts of carrying out their commitment, and to abstain from choices inconsistent with it, until they are parted by death. Marriage as an institution is the network of legal and other social norms which—in view of the good of that way of life—hold out stable ways of marrying and being married, support such acts and dispositions by benefiting fidelity to marital commitment, and discourage conduct impeding the making and living out of marital commitment.

That stipulates, for this essay, the focal meaning of 'marriage'. The paragraph's purpose, however, was neither linguistic stipulation nor lexicography. It was to begin to articulate, summarily, a set of strongly evaluative judgments about a field of human opportunity and practice. Those judgments pick out the central case of an institution, way of life, and kind of act which is found also in many more or less non-central cases both in our society and era and in other societies and other times. They display that central case both as a social reality available for description[1] and as a very choiceworthy kind of opportunity. To articulate such judgments is to contribute to discourse by offering a set of propositions for critical consideration and discussion. The discussion can go well only if those who participate in it are aware that, in the last analysis, it is preparatory to the making of judgments and choices which, being more than discursive, change lives.[2]

---

[*] 2008c.
[1] On the evaluative conditions for such description advanced in a general descriptive theory of human affairs, see essay IV.10 (2007b).
[2] See *FoE* 1–6.

What is its point? This is the first question about any act, or kind of act. The answer I give to the question about marriage's point will extend through this whole essay. It begins with two summary thoughts: that marriage's point is twofold, procreation and friendship;[3] and that marriage is one of those kinds of human good which are so basic and constitutive in human fulfilment that each can be said to be an intrinsic good.

Moral thinking, in its central critical-practical form, begins with an understanding of the desirability and worth of such basic human goods as life and health, knowledge, friendship, marriage, and so forth, and terminates in judgments about what kinds of act it is not unreasonable to choose. The understanding of basic forms of human opportunity parallels the findings of empirical sociology about the basic aspects of human social existence, but does not depend upon or, typically, begin from such findings.[4] The eventual moral judgments are exercises of the judging person's conscience, framed in the first person singular—about what I ought to be respecting and realizing in what I chose and do—not exercises in praising or blaming the conduct or worthiness of other persons or societies. Yet, since they aspire to be rational and, indeed, reasonable,[5] they cannot fail to be exercises of public reason in its most fundamental sense. That is, they aspire to be judgments such as anyone else could and should make, and free from the dispositional and other sources of error which render judgment 'subjective'. They aspire to be correct, objective judgments, judgments in which, under ideal epistemic conditions, everyone would concur.[6]

Moreover, basic human goods are not intelligible in an essentially individualistic way. They are understood as aspects of human well-being that are good not only for me but for anyone 'like me'—a qualifier than turns out to include any human person. They are good as realized in the life of a stranger in the same way, in principle, as in my life. Moreover, my own participation in these goods is radically dependent upon the various other persons by whose actions and forbearances I came into being and have begun and continued, more or less, to flourish and be able, for my own part, to contribute to *their* or others' well-being.

---

[3] Some find 'friendship' too cool a term in this context, and some think it fails to refer to the biological union involved in a marriage. But alternatives such as 'love' and 'communion' have distracting connotations for many, friendships can be passionate, and it is marriage's orientation to procreation that makes it possible for biologically unitive marital intercourse, even when engaged in with no prospect, intent, or hope of procreation, to have the multiple significance which (see secs II and III below) it has.

[4] See essay IV.1 (2003b) at nn. 2–12.

[5] On this distinction between 'rational' and 'reasonable' see *FoE* 29–30, 52–3.

[6] On such consensus under ideal conditions as a mark, *not* a criterion, of truth, and on objectivity in general, see *FoE* 62–6.

Marriage is a distinct fundamental human good[7] because it enables the parties to it, the wife and husband, to flourish as individuals and as a couple, both by the most far-reaching form of togetherness possible for human beings and by the most radical and creative enabling of another person to flourish, namely, the bringing of that person *into existence* as conceptus, embryo, child, and eventually adult fully able to participate in human flourishing on his or her own responsibility. The understanding that this two-sided good is a profoundly desirable and profoundly demanding opportunity entails that marriage is utterly misunderstood when conceived as no more than an official status, imposed by law and accompanied by government entitlements and mandates. Its intelligible and inherent connection with human flourishing (and thus with human nature) makes it far more than a function of legal arrangements and definitions. The intelligibility and worth of its contours are bases for rejecting some legal arrangements and definitions and mandating others.

At the centre of the range of activities that go to make up the marital sharing of life and lives is the kind of sexual act fittingly called marital. The commitment of marriage has at its centre the agreement to engage together, with full mutuality, in such acts.[8]

II

What in the mating of other animals is sheerly instinctual behaviour is in marital intercourse a mating which actualizes, expresses, and enables the spouses to experience, at all levels of their being, their marriage itself in each of its essential dimensions: friendship and openness to procreation. In *their* marital union of their shared lives as a whole these spouses actualize, to the full extent they can, the intelligible good of marriage, and in the sexual union of their marital acts they epitomize their marriage in the three ways just mentioned: actualizing, expressing, and experiencing it. Their

---

[7] The discussion of basic human goods in *NLNR* failed to reach any clear or stable position on the place of transmission of life, procreation, and marital friendship. Aquinas (when correctly translated) had it right (in this respect): see *Aquinas* 83; he was right for the kinds of reasons outlined, in relation to the identification of basic human goods in general, in *NLNR* 81–6.

[8] More precisely, the consent and commitment is to be open to the other's wish (whether expressed or unexpressed) for such intercourse, provided there is not, in the circumstances of the relevant time and place, some sufficient reason not to engage in intercourse. Such reasons may legitimately vary widely; at the far end of the spectrum is an example found in Christian tradition, as accepted and articulated by Aquinas: on the one hand, Mary and Joseph, the parents of Jesus of Nazareth, had each, earlier and independently, resolved upon virginity, believing that God had for her/him a special vocation, but adhering to this resolve was not inconsistent with them marrying, because each of them had qualified it with a further, conditional act of will of the form: 'but if God ever so wills it, I consent to sexual intercourse with my spouse': *Sent.* IV d.30 q.2 a.1 qa.1c; qa.2 ad 3; d.28 q.1 a.4c.

commitment is an act of reasonable will (free choice) which illuminates, integrates, extends, and deepens all that is instinctual and passionate in their motivation to make the commitment.

That motivation, as with all morally good acts, must not be understood on the Humeian and Kantian models, in which sub-rational motivations set the ends, goals, purposes, and reason comes in only to devise means and/or to eliminate the irrationality of contradiction. No, the commitment of marriage has the motivating intelligibilities, the sufficiently attractive and desirable *reasons* already mentioned: as enabling us two to help each other as friends, lovers, who can hand on our life in the procreation of new persons, *our* children whom we can help become self-determining in their own right (*sui iuris*) and who will contribute to the survival of our people. The enterprise to which we commit ourselves can scarcely be other than arduous, and the ardour and joy possible in the marital act reinforce—and are confirmed by—both the judgment that the commitment does make sense, and the ongoing willingness to be faithful to it.

III

Moral thought or commentary on sex and marriage today often leans heavily on a historicist claim, or assumption, that the moral standards of the central tradition widely rejected today were shaped or influenced by non-moral beliefs and attitudes now obviously unacceptable. Almost all of us grew up believing that mediaeval people thought the world is flat. More fool us. Mediaeval people, even school children, knew like us that it's a sphere.[9] Almost everyone believes that mediaeval people, or at least the institutions of mediaeval culture, thought marital sex (i) right only when done for the sake of procreating and (ii) morally tainted if chosen for the sake of pleasure, and (iii) a matter, for the woman, of passivity with no entitlement to and scant expectation of orgasmic pleasure. Wrong again, as unequivocal texts of Aquinas[10] plainly show, and the pre-reformation liturgies of marriage[11] (not to mention Boccaccio and Chaucer) confirm.

---

[9] See (referring also to the Enlightenment fabrication of this myth about mediaeval times) *Aquinas* 4, 16.

[10] On this, and on the massive, fundamental misreadings and misrepresentation of Aquinas in Noonan, *Contraception*, see essay 22 at nn. 18–80; also *Aquinas* 143–54. Noonan's misrepresentations have their baleful influence everywhere; they wreck e.g. the treatment of sex in marriage in the early modern era in Sommerville, *Sex and Subjection*, 118–40, though she rightly rejects outright (2, 130, 139, etc.) the myth that companionate marriage emerged from Protestantism (or Puritanism).

[11] The liturgy known as the Sarum Rite, widely used in England and predating the Protestant Reformation by 450 years or more, begins its marriage rituals with the declaration that they are to join two bodies (*ad conjugendum duo corpora*), so that these in a way become one flesh, two souls (*ut amodo sint una caro et duae animae*); the central identical statement which each makes in order to give his or her commitment (*det fidem*) to the other, exclusively and permanently, is supplemented

The first of those three modern myths is the most important here. Aquinas's uncontradicted teaching was that it is entirely acceptable for wife or husband to invite and engage in marital intercourse simply as a matter of pleasurably expressing and experiencing *fides*, without thought of procreation. This *fides* is what I have been calling the commitment of each spouse to the other that is their marriage. If we translate it 'faithfulness' we must enrich that word, for the *fides* spoken of in the teachings about marriage handed on by Aquinas is not simply abstention from infidelity. It is more a positive motive for all the acts involved in living out a marriage, and most intensely a sufficient motive for proposing intercourse. In making clear that the prospect of the mutual pleasures of marital intercourse, expressive of the spouses' loving or friendly commitment, is an utterly reasonable motive for intercourse, Aquinas affirms that this is true even though both parties know very well that their pleasure may well transport them beyond all reasoning.[12]

So too, when he says that intercourse 'for the sake of pleasure' is morally flawed, Aquinas repeatedly makes his meaning clear. Here 'for the sake of pleasure' is just shorthand for the real thesis: intercourse 'for the sake of pleasure *alone*' is flawed. And an act of marital intercourse is not for the sake of 'pleasure alone' if it expresses and embodies personal commitment to one's spouse and the marital relationship with him or her. It is for 'pleasure alone' (*intendens* solam *delectationem*) in the flawed sense only if either (i) one or both would be willing to have sex with some other attractive person then and there, or (ii) one spouse (or both), though resolved to have sex only 'within marriage,' is so indifferent to the identity or personality of the other that the spirit of his or her engagement in their sexual activities is just as if he were doing it with a call-girl or she with a gigolo. Aquinas, like Augustine and the central tradition, is not concerned to downplay pleasure, the wife's any more than the husband's, but only to teach against depersonalized sex which in its interior motivation is already half-way non-marital and, in the worse of the two kinds of case, case (i), is inwardly devoid of, and opposed to, one of marriage's foundations: devotion to the unique person of one's spouse.[13]

The two relatively subtle sorts of sexual immorality just mentioned are discussed by Aquinas more than any other sort. This fact points us to a sound

by the wife's undertaking to 'be bonere and buxom [affable and willing] in bed and at board' and the husband's declaration 'with my body I thee worship'. See Palmer, *Origines Liturgicae*, II, 209–13; Freeborn, *From Old English to Standard English*, 6.

[12] On this and the other aspects of Aquinas's theses on sex and marriage, see *Aquinas* 143–54; on pleasure in intercourse, see also *ibid.*, 76 nn. 64–5; also, in some respects fuller, essay 22, secs I–III.

[13] For all matters in this paragraph, see essay 22, sec. II and see nn. 2, 51, 115, 127 in that essay on female pleasure in marital intercourse.

account of specifically sexual immoralities, one continuous with, perhaps implicit in, the central tradition he exemplifies.[14] In each of the two cases discussed by Aquinas, the de-maritalizing and de-personalizing of sexual choice and activity is identified as a kind of conditional willingness—in the one case, present conditional willingness to have sex with such an other *if* such an other were available; in the other, present willingness to act with the same attitudes as one *would* have with a prostitute or other adulterous 'lover'. Behaviour which is marital, because with one's spouse, is in such cases not truly marital *action* because it is not the carrying out of a choice shaped by marital commitment, and so does not *really* actualize, express, or enable the couple to experience their marriage. Moreover, still more significantly, a willingness to approve (and where possible to engage in) such sexual activity entails denying that doing this together *is* actualizing, expressing, and experiencing marriage. Doing this together becomes, instead, just an instance of the kind of thing done by people in countless non-marital ways; trying to *clothe* it with additional significance is at best an imposing, and at worst an illusory imagining, rather than a finding or a participating in true significance. Marital intercourse, so important to the full intelligibility of marital commitment (and thus to marriage as an institution, and to the children who could be benefited by marital devotion), only actualizes, expresses, and enables the spouses to experience in it their marriage on condition that they reject—and where need be repent of—any willingness, however attitudinal or conditional, to engage in any non-marital sex act.[15] That thesis is the core of the traditional language of 'purity' and 'chaste marital intercourse', and of the commonsense thought that one should 'keep oneself' for marriage and trust or hope that one's spouse has done likewise—or has really repented of not having done so.

The account, or argument, is completed by its universalizing. If the married couple cannot reasonably hope to participate, really, in authentically marital intercourse without resolving upon an exceptionless reservation of their sex acts to the marital before and during marriage, so too none of us can coherently judge marriage a form of life that enables such participation, unless we too judge that sex acts are to be reserved to the marital kind. That judgment implies the wrongness of the subtly ('psychologically') non-marital kinds of sex act enumerated above; and also of the many less subtly, more manifestly non-marital kinds. Sex acts cannot be marital in kind unless they actualize, express, and enable the spouses

---

[14] For this account, see *Aquinas* 152; much more fully, essay 22, sec. IV.

[15] I use 'sex act' to signify an act or sequence of performances engaged in with the intention or willingness that it secure orgasmic sexual satisfaction for one or more person doing or participating in the act. The term is morally entirely neutral. See further essay 22 at n. 2.

to experience not only their commitment to their marriage but also their marriage's dual point. Whatever the person or persons engaging in it imagine or suppose, a sex act cannot do that unless it actualizes, expresses, and enables the experiencing of a marriage's freely chosen commitment to equality between the spouses, exclusivity, permanence, and openness to procreation.

So all morally bad kinds of sex act are bad because their choosing sets the wills of the choosers, willy-nilly, against[16] the good of marriage. Because we are directed to that good by a first principle of practical reason, such choosing against the marital good is unreasonable. In any understanding of morality that is not childish or merely conventional, it is in such unreasonableness that the immorality of bad consensual sex acts consists.

IV

The moral, that is rational, norms just given a summary articulation—reservation of all sex acts to the truly marital—are widely rejected, scorned, and reviled as arbitrarily oppressive, rooted in denigration of sexuality, gender stereotyping, refusal to admit polymorphic 'sexual identity', and so forth.[17] The extent to which essentially these norms were judged true by the most profound and critical philosophers of many ages is widely unrecognized or even, by a kind of forgery, denied.[18]

---

[16] One who reasonably chooses a worthwhile form of life which entails responsibilities incompatible with the commitment and responsibilities of marriage does not thereby choose *against* the good of marriage, unless he or she engages in sex acts (in which case the choice to engage in them is against that good for the reason already stated: briefly, judging it reasonable to engage in sex acts non-maritally entails judging that the sex acts of a married couple do not *really* actualize, express, and enable them to experience their marriage). [And see essay 21 in the paragraph to which n. 25 of that essay is cued; and essay 22 at nn. 75–7 and at nn. 110–14.]

[17] Thus Taylor, 'Sex and Christianity: How Has the Moral Landscape Changed?' lists the main features of the 'sexual revolution':

(1) the rehabilitation, continued from the 1920s, of sensuality as a good in itself; (2) the continued affirmation of the equality of the sexes, and in particular the expression of a new ideal in which men and women come together as partners freed of their gender roles; (3) a widespread sense of Dionysian, even 'transgressive' sex as liberating; and (4) a new conception of one's sexuality as an essential part of one's identity, which not only gave an additional meaning to sexual liberation, but also became the basis for gay liberation and the emancipation of a whole host of previously condemned forms of sexual life.

He ends:

...we have to recognize that the moral landscape has changed. People who have been through the upheaval have to find forms that allow for long-term loving relations between equal partners who will in many cases also want to become parents and bring up their children in love and security. But these can't be simply identical to the codes of the past, insofar as they were connected with the denigration of sexuality, horror at the Dionysian, fixed gender roles, or a refusal to discuss identity issues. It is a tragedy that the codes that churches want to urge on people still (at least seem to) suffer from one or more—and sometimes all—of these defects.

[18] Showing how far the sex ethics of Socrates, Plato, and Aristotle, not to mention philosophically minded transmitters of their tradition such as Musonius Rufus and Plutarch, corresponds to

The moral requirement that sex acts be marital is no denigration of sexuality, but instead a pointing out of the conditions under which its intense pleasures are human, that is, attentive to the relevant intelligible goods as they can be actualized in the lives of others (as oneself).[19] The conflict between adultery's 'Dionysian' pleasures and respect for one's spouse and children is only an example, exemplary and easily grasped, of the kinds of inhumanity to which the 'pleasure principle' gives a meretricious glamour. The conflict between taking contracepted sex acts to be truly marital and the maintenance of marriage as a coherent social institution and individual opportunity is less easily grasped, no doubt. But the conflict has been becoming steadily more palpable, not only in the unravelling of ecclesial communities which explicitly proposed that they could admit contraception while retaining the rest of their sexual ethic, but also in the secular realities of western societies. In these societies, marriage is in process of being replaced by scarcely committed cohabitation or by decades of sexually active living alone. Taxes and other social mechanisms of redistribution of wealth have been altered to minimize or remove the benefits of marital status. Arrangements for housing and employment likewise. The concept of a family wage, around which a major progressive industrial politics was constructed in the early twentieth century, has been banished with hostility and contempt. Large minorities or even majorities of children are being raised by their mothers without their fathers or any committed stepfather. And above all: these are societies confronted by the inexorable, ever more evident reality that any people whose women give birth, on average, to only two or fewer children will become extinct, and on the way down and out will forfeit to other peoples much of what it has and is. Yet they remain unwilling, both officially and in the preponderant decisions of private citizens, to begin making any of the revisions of judgment and preference, or taking any of the measures, needed to avert their fate. At the core of such measures would have to be a re-maritalizing of their understanding of sexual capacities and relationships.

The foregoing neither attempts nor insinuates a rule-utilitarian or any other kind of consequentialist weighing of overall consequences.

that expounded in this essay, and how far Martha Nussbaum was willing to go in misrepresenting Plato: 1994b and 1994d; on her reply, see essay 22 at n. 109; essay 5, n. 60; George, '"Shameless Acts" Revisited: Some Questions for Martha Nussbaum'.

[19] In the sense recalled by Hermia to her beloved Lysander in the woods in *A Midsummer Night's Dream* 2.2:

But, gentle friend, for love and courtesy Lie further off; in human modesty, Such separation as may well be said Becomes a virtuous bachelor and a maid, So far be distant; and, good night, sweet friend: Thy love ne'er alter till thy sweet life end!

See likewise *The Tempest* 4.1.14–31, 51–6, 84–97, 106–17. For all his bawdy, there is nothing in Shakespeare to set against these repeated expressions of the rightness—the necessity, if great goods are to be preserved and attained—of reserving sex for marriage.

Rather it explores further the conditions on which marriage is a genuine opportunity rather than a snare or a delusion. Why undertake the burdens and unquantifiable risks involved in its defining commitments if not, in part, out of care for the future of one's people (and one's forebears' families) and, in part and more immediately, out of an uncomplacent wonder at the reality of a new person's coming to be, utter dependence, intrinsic worth but relative fragility in health, character, and attainments. There can be no reasonable ethics of sex and marriage, and no reasonable politics of education, employment, and family support, without this clear-eyed, unsentimental wonder.

Marriage, with the exclusiveness and moral permanence that define its central case, makes sense because the children to whose procreation, nurture, and education its structure is thoroughly adapted are each an icon of the non-fungibility of persons. The contracting of the spouses, and their fulfilment of their promises, is itself an icon not only of their families' and their people's past and future hopes and achievements, but of free and self-directing citizenship. And their commitment and fidelity weave the cradle of new, eventually independent and responsible citizens. (*Liberi* [children] on the way to being *liberi* [fully self-determining free persons].) These are goods sufficiently important, exigent, and unsubstitutable to falsify the thought that the moral restraints which guard them are cruel or arbitrarily oppressive, difficult though the living out of those restraints certainly is for many (in some respects for almost everyone willing to follow a well-formed conscience in making choices about sex).

V

We all live our lives in four distinct and irreducible kinds of order: the natural (including physical, chemical, biochemical, biological, and psychosomatic systems/orders), the logical (involving all aspects of our reasoning), the technical domain of systems (including language) for mastering matter to achieve specific goals, and the domain of self-determining, morally significant choices.[20] Marriage, too, involves all four kinds of order. But since it is at bottom an act, and the carrying out of that constitutive act in countless other acts, its primary reality is moral, presupposing and engaging the natural, and supported by the cultural. To say that polygamy is not truly marriage, but only a version so watered down and defective as to be rather an imitation, is not to make a linguistic or other culture-relative claim. Rather it is to make a moral assertion, which

---

[20] See e.g. essay II.2 (2005c).

must be validated by moral arguments. (These arguments will point, for example, to the inequality of—in polygamy's standard form, polygyny—the multiple 'wives' both with each other and with the 'husband'; and to the fractured relations of siblings and half-siblings.)

Similarly with 'gay marriage'. What the phrase means is clear enough. To judge such marriages no marriage is like judging invalid arguments no argument, quack medicines no medicine; the point is not linguistic but in those two analogies is logical and technical respectively, and in the case in issue is both cultural and moral. In our culture, the normative definition, both cultural and legal (until only the other day), has been the same as the moral judgment unfolded in previous sections of this essay: lifelong and exclusive sexual commitment to a single spouse, in an institution oriented towards, and socially supported precisely for the sake of, the children whom this sexual union may well generate, is truly choiceworthy, and exigently important to—irreplaceably beneficial for—the whole community. Since the sexual acts of same-sex partners (couples, threesomes, foursomes...) have no tendency at all to generate children, there is no reason why whatever commitment such partners wish to make to one another (as couples, threesomes, foursomes... for life or for five years...) should be thought of as marriage. Their relationship is physically, biologically, psychosomatically different from the spectrum of really marital relations.

For in marital relations the marital act culminates in the very kind of activity—ecstatic genital giving and genital accepting of semen—that sometimes results in generation. Thus, even when it does not have that result, it is an act of the kind[21] that links the spouses triply to the dual good of marriage, by enabling[22] them to actualize, experience, and express the marital commitment. That commitment is to be open to procreation, even though marital acts are incapable of resulting in procreation on the great majority of days, and throughout any pregnancy, and then throughout the period that begins, usually quite gradually, with the coming of menopause. In short, marital acts retain that triple link to both elements of the dual good of marriage even when those who choose and engage in the acts believe themselves sterile because of the time of the month, pregnancy, or aging, or because of a medical condition which yet leaves them potent to engage in such acts.[23] Whatever imaginings or longings accompany them,

---

[21] Namely, what the tradition—as expressed in e.g. Aquinas—calls acts of the generative kind. These are acts which, as Aquinas carefully notes, can be engaged in even by couples who know that they are sterile: see *Aquinas* 150 n. 84; for much fuller citation and quotation, see essay 22 at n. 127.

[22] Necessary, not sufficient: the triple link to marital commitment fails if the parties to the act are engaging in it 'solely for pleasure' in the precise, depersonalizing sense explained above.

[23] See further essay 22 at n. 127; 132. On the arguments of Stephen Macedo and Andrew Koppelman attempting to assimilate same-sex sex acts to the marital intercourse of spouses who

neither solitary sex acts nor the sex acts of same-sex partners can be more than fictionally marital.[24]

Notoriously, moreover, ethical positions which present themselves as 'gay' include no norm requiring or making sense of exclusiveness of sexual partnership, and much evidence suggests that the great majority of same-sex male couples or wider groupings have 'open' relationships.[25] In all such cases the imitation of authentic marriage is even more threadbare, more parodic. Indeed, the drive for same-sex marriage seems in large measure an element in a strategy of parrying and finally de-legitimizing cultural-moral critiques of same-sex sex acts, critiques which in their proper form are critiques of *all* non-marital sex acts, heterosexual and homosexual alike. This de-legitimizing strategy finds a willing aide in the ideologists of equality of entitlement to esteem. The ideology, which of course subjects its equality axiom to arbitrary exceptions, draws support from all whose scepticism about all human value prevents them from assessing reasonably whether the ways of life esteemed are all equally or even sufficiently compatible with common good. Such scepticism is kept from plunging into utter nihilism only by this devotion to equality, which functions for the devotees like a rotting bough over the stream just above the misted lip of the falls.

The successes of the gay movement's strategy are further signs of our culture's—not least its educated elites'—faltering grasp of the human goods at stake and the conditions under which these goods can be actualized well. If most modern marriages involve no commitment to exclude either consensual divorce (with a view to remarriage or extra-marital sex) or contraception, and so are watered-down instances of marriage—though

believe themselves sterile (and have done nothing to render themselves or their act sterile), see essay 21, sec. V.

[24] Macedo, 'Homosexuality and the Conservative Mind' at 280, says:

The focus on procreation [in the sex ethics represented by the present article] appears opportunistic: selected so as to allow sterile heterosexuals into the tent while keeping homosexuals out.

But (1) there has been no selection of focus, however motivated; marriage is the form of life that corresponds to the need for a new generation of human persons to sustain all human goods, and to the need for children for the nurture of committed friends who take seriously their responsibility for bringing new persons in to the world; and the marital act does embody this commitment to the marital form of life by its uniting of the reproductive organs and all other levels of the spouses' being. And (2) in this ethics, the non-marital sex acts of heterosexuals, solitary or with another or others, are 'outside the tent', too.

[25] For evidence and argument, see essay 22 at nn. 130-4; that evidence warrants the conclusion there formulated:

Only a small proportion of homosexual men who live as 'gays' seriously attempt anything even resembling marriage as a permanent commitment. Only a tiny proportion seriously attempt marital fidelity, the commitment to exclusiveness; the proportion who find that the attempt seems to make sense, in view of the other aspects of their 'gay identity,' is even tinier. Thus, even at the level of behavior—i.e. even leaving aside its inherent sterility—gay 'marriage,' precisely because it excludes or makes no sense of a *commitment* utterly central to *marriage*, is a sham.

authentic enough as instances of the cultural form now held out as marriage to those contemplating it—the question arises whether there remains rational ground for resisting the extension of the present legal-cultural form of marriage to same-sex couples.

Should not that question be answered in much the same way as another current question? Should one help defend one's country (*patria*) against colonization and takeover, demographic if not violent, if many of its native people and institutions have themselves, with cultural approval, become coarsely decadent, selectively homicidal, and legally intolerant of certain true beliefs held, until recently, by virtually everyone, while the colonizers do not share these vices? Much depends, surely, on the character of the colonizers. Suppose that their culture, while embodying a range of virtues and condemning a number of our own culture's vicious traits, has its own traits which, albeit in different ways, are lascivious, dishonest, homicidal, inequitable, and oppressive, and that it further lacks those institutions of freedom which keep open the way to legal, political, moral, and cultural *conversion*—and that, worse still, it forbids, with even capital penalties, all conversion *from* its errors. Then the rational love we all should have for that country which, for all its faults and falsehoods, helped enable us to participate in all the true goods we do, and is, at least presumptively, for us the non-fungible embodiment of many lasting forms of common good,[26] should be sufficient ground for willingly defending it by cultural, political, and other morally acceptable means of repelling the takeover and the preparatory colonization.

So too, then, the great flaws in the modern cultural form of marriage do indeed impair, but do not eliminate, its fundamental intelligibility and worth as oriented towards exclusivity and permanence for the sake both of children and of a corresponding and unique kind of friendship—of man with woman, in a complementarity which makes up for what each sex or gender lacks as a type-instantiation of human flourishing and nature. To try to graft into this root legal-cultural form a kind of sexual relationship which has no structural orientation or inherent intelligible ground for either exclusivity and permanence, no deep complementarity, no connection between its sexual interactions and any children the partners may acquire, and no inherent commitment to the arduous parenting of children, is to do what one can to make the root institution and practice unintelligible, and to demote it, culturally, from a worthy ideal to one more or less arbitrary fancy amongst others. It is also to install sexual immorality officially at the heart of this primary social institution. In even the short term, this

---

[26] Essay II.6 (2008b).

subjecting of the legal-cultural definition of marriage to the revolutionary and shattering transformation of excising 'of one *man* with one *woman*' strips the law, the culture, and its institution of marriage of any coherent response to claims that equality of esteem demands excision of the exclusive 'one with one' and extension of marriage first to polygamy/polygyny and then in short order to a polyamory which excises also all even aspirational commitment to permanence. An elementary respect for children, one of justice's demands, and for one's own people as a lasting community linking past, present, and future, justifies and indeed mandates the defence even of modern marriage against such evacuations of its meaning and intelligibility as an ideal and a summons to thoroughgoing commitment for a non-illusory common good.

VI

And then there are the travails, failures, miseries of many who have made the commitment of true marriage in its central form, but whose hopes of it have been betrayed by the fault of one or both of them, or by some other kind of rupture or dissolution of their friendship which makes it reasonable for one or both of them to separate from the other and end their living together as spouses (*divortium a mensa et thoro*)—and wholly understandable if they (and their friends) wish also that each could start afresh in a new marital commitment to a new spouse.

But to start afresh by 'remarriage' during the life of one to whom one had freely made the commitment of marriage would entail that, in that commitment, the undertaking to be married to this person 'for better for worse, for richer for poorer, *'til death us do part*' was illusory. For, on the hypothesis that marriage can be terminated by the radical divorce (*divortium a vinculo*) which would leave the parties free to remarry (just as if one of them had died), the undertaking of *permanent* exclusivity would be subject to an unspoken but foreknown and therefore implied negation ('though not if...'). On this hypothesis, the parties entering on this uniquely far-reaching friendship would have to regard themselves as incapable of making a commitment not conditioned by some implied negation of its permanent exclusivity. But there is no good reason to treat everyone as lacking the capacity to make so far-reaching a commitment.

The issue here is philosophically interesting, and important for understanding why any political theory offering a 'social contract' as the foundation of political obligation must fail. The bond (*vinculum*) of marriage is in each case unquestionably dependent upon the choice, the will of the parties to it to enter upon the commitment, by their exchange of promises, that is, their contract or covenant of marriage here and now (*de praesenti*). But such acts of will could not have the moral effect of making it true that the parties are morally obligated, that is, bound to each other in the way and to the extent they undertake, unless it is morally true, prior to and independently of their promising, that such promises can rightly be made and have the enduring morally binding effect they profess and intend (at the time of their making) to have. And that moral proposition—which has acts of will as its subject-matter but not as the ground for its truth—is indeed true, for two kinds of reason. (1) Persons do not have the moral incapacity presupposed by the theory of necessarily dissoluble marriage. And, more fundamentally, (2) the idea of an interpersonal relationship created by choice precisely *as*—under the description of—a relationship not dissoluble by choice or circumstance is an idea that can and should be affirmed, in view of the great dual good it makes realizable, the good of (i) bringing offspring into existence as the embodiment of (ii) the friendship of two friends committed to accepting each child as a (i) gift supervening on and extending that (ii) friendship and to responding to that gift by (i) shouldering the lifelong responsibility of carrying out, through countless choices to act *maternally* and *paternally*, their originating choice to enact (ii) their friendship by uniting biologically, joyfully, lovingly—maritally—at all levels of their being, in marital acts. Thus the rationality of willing a permanent and exclusive marital union emerges by unfolding the implications of the dual good outlined in previous sections of this essay: children's needs and interests entitle them, doubtless not absolutely but really and exigently, to very firm parental intention and commitment to maintaining a framework of common life in mutual cooperation, father with mother, and each with children who are and entitled to be treated as *theirs*, in a relationship thoroughly dissimilar in kind to the relation of producers to their products or owners to their property, and ever more similar in kind to that of friend to friend.

It is much the same with political obligation, and indeed with the authority of posited law. No contract of the members of a society with each other and/or with a putative leader could have the effect of making performance of the contract obligatory, unless there were sound reasons, independent of any agreement, for grouping into political communities and acknowledging as authoritative certain prescriptions of persons acknowledged to be rulers. No such law-making prescriptions could have a moral obligation-imposing effect tracking, presumptively, the obligatory force they purport to have, unless it were a standing requirement of practical reason (of integral human fulfilment) that government and law be acknowledged as authoritative for the sake of fundamental aspects of common good (especially justice and its maintenance again injustice) not otherwise securable. Positive law, in short, adds much content to the principles and standards of practical reasonableness traditionally called natural law. Yet, for its relevance in practical reason and the judgments of conscience, it depends upon natural law with its master principle of 'love of neighbour as oneself' and its more specific principles identifying kinds of act compatible with intelligent love of human persons and their fulfilment, and kinds incompatible with it.

Natural law's invitation to, and underwriting of, the commitment to truly marital union points to and provides a moral reality, our marriage. That reality not only has the intelligible dual point articulated above, but also answers to and is an objective correlate of those central elements in erotic attraction, love, and affection which make lovers—especially but not only in the act of love—yearn for and profess an undying union, exclusive and permanent. The natural law principles leave a good many questions about the boundaries (for example as to consanguinity) and implications of unions of this type, all to be settled by *determinatio* by the relevant authorities, ecclesiastical or political, along with many other questions about the spouses' status, property, rights *inter se* and in relation to their children, in marital breakdown, and so forth. There can even, I think, be ground for the law of the state to diverge from the morally true contours of marriage, just as the Mosaic law of marriage and divorce diverged (it has been said with some authority[27]) because of the people's 'hardness of heart'. The wider the divergence, the greater the risk that real marriage's intelligibility, and thus its desirability, will be obscured. Since marriages, not unlike positive legal systems, are *factual* realities whose coming to be and lasting depends upon people's grasp of marriage's truth ('reality', 'worth') as an *ideal*, that risk is one to be accepted only with reluctance, caution, and willingness to go 'back' as well as 'forward'.

There are other relevant matters within the law's proper jurisdiction, which is to protect and promote *public* good, that is, justice and the public morality that protects justice (especially justice to children and other vulnerable people). The effective, not merely nominal, prohibition of distributing pornography has always been regarded, and rightly so, as a necessary public witness to the truth about marriage's worth and importance, and as an empirically (though of course incompletely) efficacious restraint on the impurities which, if unresisted, darken natural reason's understanding of the link between purity and the proper significance and value of marital acts.

[27] Mark 10: 5.

VII

An institution so lived in as marriage is attracts in full measure the resentment, satirical denunciation, ribaldry, scorn and sophisticated ennui of those many whom—or whose associates—it has disappointed or wounded in their idealism, their self-interest, or both. As was said already, in more particular contexts, in sec. V above, marriage's moral claims cannot be justly assessed if its defective instantiations are compared with alternative ideals considered as ideals. Much the same goes for long-lived-in institutions such as political society, government, and the rule of law, each constantly the occasion and even cause of dreadful abuses and failures, yet each plainly a worthwhile ideal to be reconstructed, again and again, in preference to the anarchic or tyrannical alternatives.

So one makes no progress by imagining alternative worlds in which everything is the same as our world save that law and government give no endorsement to marriage and, subject to a few prohibitions, leave couples, threesomes... fivesomes... to make their own arrangements for sex acts and for the generation and upbringing of children—and then to simply postulate that in such a world children will generally be loved and cared for. Nor does one make progress—clarify issues and get closer to sound judgment—by overlooking the fundamental disparities between mothers and fathers, the former bound to their children by physical and psychological ties vastly closer and more durable than the latter's, which need last no longer than a single act of insemination. The well-nigh complete unravelling of marriage and family, and destruction of fatherhood, experienced in some ethnic groups during the past thirty years, and its broad and intricate consequences, summon everyone to reflection on the real nature of alternatives to marriage. On the real inhumanity, for example, of a mother's bonding, not so much with transient and irresponsible sexual partners as with the offices, officials, and funds of a government bureaucracy.

NOTE

The sheer scale of the normative revolutions in our societies since the 1950s can be assessed by reading the judgments of each of the five Justices in *HJ (Iran) v Secretary of State for the Home Department* [2010] UKSC 31. Set aside their proper concern with grossly persecutory acts (public hanging, castration by lynch mobs, and the like) and their argumentation about persecution and the Refugee Convention (on which see last endnote to essay 1). Set aside also their particular concern with homosexual inclinations and activities. What is central, pervasive, and unchallenged in these judgments is this. Everyone has a sexual 'identity' defined, not just as hetero- or homo- but by any 'along a broad spectrum' of the types of sex acts and relationships he or she is inclined to, and by the strength of his or her inclinations. Though this identity or 'orientation' may change from time to time, it is 'so fundamental to identity or human dignity that it ought not to be required to be changed', and open manifestation of it in search for, and activities with, numerous sexual partners ought positively to be allowed and facilitated, both by law and by social attitudes and opinion. Contrast this with the moral teachings and social traditions and laws all substantially overthrown by the normative revolutions. Central to them is and was a contrary proposition, with its corollary. Human dignity itself requires that one's inclinations be disciplined and reformed so as to be in line with marriage and marital paternity or maternity. And, for the sake of marriage as an institution essential to the survival of the group and its culture and freedom, and for the sake of justice to children whose true well-being depends on a marital upbringing, those whose inclinations unfit them for marriage, or who opt not to marry, or who cannot find anyone willing to marry them, or whose spouse becomes sexually disabled, can reasonably be publicly called upon to live in a way that at least openly does not defy these propositions.

21

LAW, MORALITY, AND 'SEXUAL ORIENTATION'*

I

During the past thirty years there has emerged a standard form of legal regulation of sexual conduct. This 'standard modern position' has two limbs. On the one hand, the state is not authorized to, and does not, make it a punishable offence for adult consenting persons to engage, in private, in immoral sexual acts (for example, homosexual acts). On the other hand, states do have the authority to discourage, say, homosexual conduct and 'orientation' (that is, overtly manifested active willingness to engage in homosexual conduct). And typically, though not universally, they do so. That is to say, they maintain various criminal and administrative laws and policies which have as part of their purpose the discouraging of such conduct. Many of these laws, regulations, and policies discriminate (that is, distinguish) between heterosexual and homosexual conduct adversely to the latter.

The concern of the standard modern position itself is not with inclinations but entirely with certain *decisions* to *express* or *manifest* deliberate promotion of, or readiness to engage in, homosexual *activity/ conduct*, including promotion of forms of life (for example purportedly marital cohabitation) which both encourage such activity and present it as a valid or acceptable alternative to the committed heterosexual union which the state recognizes as marriage. Subject only to the written or unwritten constitutional requirement of freedom of discussion of ideas, the state laws and state policies which I have outlined are intended to discourage decisions which are thus deliberately oriented towards homosexual conduct and are manifested in public ways.

The standard modern position considers that the state's proper responsibility for upholding true worth (morality) is a responsibility *subsidiary* (auxiliary) to the *primary* responsibility of parents and

---
* 1997c. See the first endnote.

non-political voluntary associations. This conception of the proper role of government has been taken to exclude the state from assuming a directly parental disciplinary role in relation to consenting *adults*. That role was one which political theory and practice formerly ascribed to the state on the assumption that the role followed by logical necessity from the truth that the state should encourage true worth and discourage immorality. That assumption is now judged to be mistaken (a judgment for which I have argued in various places).†

So the modern theory and practice draws a distinction not drawn in the former legal arrangements, a distinction between (a) supervising the truly private conduct of adults and (b) supervising the *public realm or environment*. The importance of the latter includes the following considerations: (i) this is the environment or public realm in which young people (of whatever sexual inclination) are educated; (ii) it is the context in which and by which everyone with responsibility for the well-being of young people is helped or hindered in assisting them to avoid bad forms of life; (iii) it is the milieu in which and by which all citizens are encouraged and helped, or discouraged and undermined, in their own resistance to being lured by temptation into falling away from their own aspirations to be people of integrated good character, and to be autonomous, self-controlled rather than slaves to impulse and sensual gratification.

Type (a) supervision of truly private adult consensual conduct is now considered to be outside the state's normally proper role (with exceptions such as sadomasochistic bodily damage, and apparent but not real exceptions such as assisting in suicide). But type (b) supervision of the moral-cultural-educational environment is maintained as a very important part of the state's justification for claiming legitimately the loyalty of its decent citizens.

The standard modern position is part of a politico-legal order which systematically outlaws many forms of discrimination. Thus the European Convention on Human Rights (the model for many national bills of rights adopted over the past thirty-five years) provides that the protection of the rights it sets out is to be enjoyed without discrimination on any ground such as 'sex, race, colour, language, religion, political or other opinion, national or social origin, association with a national minority, property, birth or other status'.

But the standard modern position deliberately rejects proposals to include in such lists the item 'sexual orientation'. For the phrase 'sexual orientation' is radically equivocal. Particularly as used by promoters of 'gay rights', it ambiguously assimilates two things which the standard modern position carefully distinguishes: (I) a psychological or psychosomatic disposition inwardly orienting one *towards* homosexual activity; (II) the deliberate *decision* so to orient one's public *behaviour* as to express or *manifest* one's active interest in and endorsement of homosexual *conduct* and/or forms of life which presumptively involve such conduct.

Indeed, laws or proposed laws outlawing 'discrimination based on sexual orientation' are always interpreted by 'gay rights' movements as going far beyond discrimination based merely on (i) A's belief that B is sexually attracted to persons of the same sex. Such movements interpret the phrase as extending full legal protection to (ii) *public* activities intended specifically to promote, procure, and facilitate homosexual *conduct*.

So, while the standard position accepts that discrimination on the basis of type I dispositions is unjust, it judges that there are compelling reasons both to deny that such injustice would be appropriately remedied by laws against 'discrimination based on sexual orientation', and to hold that such a 'remedy' would work significant discrimination and injustice against (and would indeed damage) families, associations, and institutions which have organized themselves to live out and transmit ideals of family life that include a high conception of the worth of truly conjugal sexual intercourse.

II

The standard modern position involves a number of explicit or implicit judgments about the proper role of law and the compelling interests of political communities, and about the evil of homosexual conduct. Can these be defended by reflective, critical, publicly intelligible, and rational arguments? I believe they can. The judgment that it is morally wrong need not be a manifestation either of mere hostility to a hated minority, or of purely religious, theological, and sectarian belief.

I have been using and shall continue to use the terms 'homosexual activity', 'homosexual acts', and 'homosexual conduct' synonymously, to refer to bodily acts, on the body of a person of the same sex, which are engaged in with a view to securing orgasmic sexual satisfaction for one or more of the parties.

Let me begin by noticing a too little noticed fact. All three of the greatest Greek philosophers, Socrates, Plato, and Aristotle, regarded homosexual *conduct* as intrinsically shameful, immoral, and indeed depraved or depraving. That is to say, all three rejected the linchpin of modern 'gay' ideology and lifestyle.

Socrates is portrayed by Plato (and by Xenophon) as having strong homosexual (as well as heterosexual) inclinations or interest, and as promoting an ideal of homosexual romance between men and youths, but at the same time as utterly rejecting homosexual conduct. This is made clear in Sir Kenneth Dover's famous book;[1] in Dover's summarizing words: 'Xenophon's Socrates lacks the sensibility and urbanity of the Platonic Socrates, but there is no doubt that both of them condemn homosexual copulation.'[2] It is also made clear by Gregory Vlastos in his last book, precisely on Socrates: in Socratic *eros* involving relationships of affection between men and boys or youths, intimacy is limited to mind- and eye-contact and 'terminal gratification' is forbidden[3] (and *a fortiori* in relationships between adult males, since virtually all Athenians regarded sex acts between adult males as intrinsically shameful).[4] Vlastos thus makes it clear that Socrates forbids precisely what I have been calling homosexual conduct.

What, then, about Plato? Well, the same Plato who in his *Symposium* wrote a famous celebration of *romantic and spiritual* man-boy erotic relationships, made very clear that all forms of sexual *conduct* outside heterosexual marriage are shameful, wrongful, and harmful. This is particularly evident from his treatment of the matter in his last work, the *Laws*, but is also sufficiently clear in the *Republic* and the *Phaedrus*, and even in the *Symposium* itself. This is affirmed unequivocally both by Dover and by Vlastos, neither of whom favours these views of Plato. According to Vlastos, for example, Plato

saw anal intercourse as 'contrary to nature,' [footnote: *Ph*[*ae*]*dr*[*us*] 251A1, *L*[*aws*] 636–7] a degradation not only of man's humanity, but even of his animality...[5]

It is for Plato, Vlastos adds, a type of act far more serious than any mere going 'contrary to the rules'.[6]

---

[1] *Greek Homosexuality* 154–9. See also the letter from Sir Kenneth Dover to John Finnis, dated 23 January 1994, in 1994b at 1057, 1059.

[2] *Ibid.*, 159.   [3] *Socrates, Ironist and Moral Philosopher*, 38–9.

[4] Hindley and Cohen, 'Debate: Law, Society and Homosexuality in Classical Athens' at 179–80, 188 n. 14.

[5] In the footnote, Vlastos complains that by *para physin*, 'contrary to nature', Plato here and in 836B–C meant something 'far stronger' than the phrase 'against the rules', which Dover had used in a 1966 article on *erōs* and *nomos*. Sometime before the revised edition, Vlastos and Dover corresponded about this complaint, and Vlastos records a letter from Dover:

What [Plato] did believe was that the act was 'unnatural', in the sense 'against the rules'; it was a morally ignorant exploitation of pleasure beyond what was 'granted' (*kata physin apodedosthai*, [*Laws*] 636C4), the product of an *akrateia* ([636]C6 which can be aggravated by habituation and bad example. His comparison of homosexuality with incest ([*Laws* 837E8–838E1]) is particularly revealing.

And Vlastos immediately remarks that Dover's allusion to Plato's comparison of homosexuality with incest shows that Dover acknowledges the great force with which Plato is condemning what Vlastos called 'anal intercourse' and Dover, loosely, 'the act' and 'homosexuality'.

[6] Anthony Price's valuable book, *Love and Friendship in Plato and Aristotle* at 89 firmly rejects Vlastos's theory that Socrates and Plato, though forbidding homosexual acts, accepted that lovers could nevertheless rightly engage in the sort of petting spoken of in *Phaedrus* 255e.

As for Aristotle, there is widespread scholarly agreement that he rejected homosexual conduct. In fact, such conduct is frequently represented by Aristotle (in some cases directly and in other cases by a lecturer's hint) as intrinsically perverse, shameful, and harmful both to the individuals involved and to society itself.[7]

Although the ideology of homosexual love (with its accompanying devaluation of women) continued to have philosophical defenders down to the end of classical Greek civilization, there equally continued to be influential philosophical writers, wholly untouched by Judaeo-Christian tradition, who taught that homosexual conduct is not only intrinsically shameful but also inconsistent with a proper recognition of the equality of women with men in intrinsic worth. (The ancients did not fail to note that Socrates' homoerotic orientation, for all its admirable chastity—abstention from homosexual conduct—went along with a neglect to treat his wife as an equal.) A good example of such late classical writing is Plutarch's *Erōtikos* (Dialogue on Love) 751C–D, 766E–771D, written probably some time in the early second century, but certainly free from Judaeo-Christian influence. Plutarch's vast literary-historical and philosophical corpus of writings is an effort to recapture and recapitulate the highest achievements of classical civilization, and had a very substantial influence on western thought down to recent times. I shall say more about Plutarch's thought on these matters below.

Another example is the Stoic, Musonius Rufus (who taught at Rome c. 80 AD and again was not influenced by Jewish or Christian thought). He rejects all homosexual conduct as shameful. Sexual conduct is decent and acceptable only within marriage. The point of marriage includes not only procreation and raising of children but also, integrally and essentially, a complete community of life and mutual care and affection between husband and wife.

At the heart of the Platonic-Aristotelian and later ancient philosophical rejections of all homosexual conduct, and thus of the modern 'gay' ideology, are three fundamental theses. (1) The commitment of a man and woman to each other in the sexual union of marriage is intrinsically good and reasonable, and is incompatible with sexual relations outside marriage. (2) Homosexual acts are radically and peculiarly non-marital, and for that reason intrinsically unreasonable and unnatural. (3) Furthermore, according to Plato, if not Aristotle, homosexual acts have a special similarity

---

[7] See *NE* VII.5: 1148b29; *Pol.* II.1: 1262a33–9, together with the hints in II.6: 1269b28 and II.7: 1272a25. See e.g. Price, *Love and Friendship in Plato and Aristotle* 225, citing Plato, *Republic* 403b4–6 and Aristotle, *Pol.* 1262a32–7.

to solitary masturbation,[8] and both types of radically non-marital act are manifestly unworthy of the human being and immoral.

III

I want now to offer an interpretation of these three theses which articulates them more clearly than was ever attempted by Plato or, so far as we can tell, by Aristotle. It is, I think, an interpretation faithful to what they do say, but takes up suggestions in Plutarch and in the eighteenth-century Enlightenment philosophy of Immanuel Kant (who likewise rejected all homosexual conduct), though even these writers' indications, too, remain relatively terse. My account also articulates thoughts which have historically been implicit in the judgments of many non-philosophical people, and which have been held to justify the laws adopted in many nations and states both before and after the period when Christian beliefs as such were politically and socially dominant. And it is an application of the theory of morality and natural law developed over the past thirty years by Germain Grisez and others. A fuller exposition can be found in the chapter on marriage, sexual acts, and family life, in the new second volume of Grisez's great work on moral theology.[9]

Plato's mature concern, in the *Laws*, for familiarity, affection, and love between spouses in a chastely exclusive marriage, Aristotle's representation of marriage as an intrinsically desirable friendship between quasi-equals, and as a state of life even more natural to human beings than political life,[10] and Musonius Rufus's conception of the inseparable double goods of marriage all find expression in Plutarch's celebration of marriage—as a union not of mere instinct but of reasonable love, and not merely for procreation but for mutual help, goodwill, and cooperation for their own sake.[11] Plutarch's severe critiques of homosexual conduct (and of the

---

[8] See Plato, *Gorgias*, 494–5, esp. 494e1–5, 495b3.

[9] Grisez, *Living a Christian Life*, esp. 555–74, 633–80.

[10] *NE* VIII.12: 1162a16–30; see also the probably pseudo-Aristotle, *Oeconomica* I, 3–4: 1343b12–1344a22; III.

[11] Plutarch reads this conception back to the dawn of Athenian civilization and, doubtless anachronistically, ascribes it to the great original Athenian law-giver, Solon: marriage should be 'a union of life between man and woman "for the delights of love and the getting of children"': Plutarch, *Life of Solon*, 20, 4. See also Plutarch, *Erōtikos*, 769:

In the case of lawful wives, physical union is the beginning of friendship, a sharing, as it were, in great mysteries. Pleasure is short [or unimportant: *mikron*], but the respect and kindness and mutual affection and loyalty that daily spring from it convicts neither the Delphians of raving when they call Aphrodite 'Harmony' nor Homer when he designates such a union 'friendship'. It also proves that Solon was a very experienced legislator of marriage laws. He prescribed that a man should consort with his wife not less than three times a month—not for the pleasure surely, but as cities renew their mutual agreements from time to time, just so he must have wished this

disparagement of women implicit in homosexual ideology),[12] develop Plato's critique of homosexual and all other extra-marital sexual conduct. Like Musonius Rufus, Plutarch does so by bringing much closer to explicit articulation the following thought. Genital intercourse between spouses enables them to actualize and experience (and in that sense express) their marriage itself, as a single reality with two blessings (children and mutual affection).[13] Non-marital intercourse, especially *but not only* homosexual, has no such point and therefore is unacceptable.

Why cannot non-marital friendship be promoted and expressed by sexual acts? Why is the attempt to express affection by orgasmic non-marital sex the pursuit of an illusion? Why did Plato and Socrates, Xenophon, Aristotle, Musonius Rufus, and Plutarch, right at the heart of their reflections on the homoerotic culture around them, make the very deliberate and careful judgment that homosexual *conduct* (and indeed all extra-marital sexual gratification) is radically incapable of participating in, actualizing, the common good of friendship?

Implicit in the philosophical and commonsense rejection of extra-marital sex is the answer to these questions. The union of the reproductive organs of husband and wife really unites them biologically (and their biological reality is part of, not merely an instrument of, their *personal* reality); reproduction is *one* function and so, in respect of that function, the spouses are indeed one reality. So their union in a sexual act of the reproductive kind (whether or not actually reproductive or even capable of resulting in generation in this instance) can *actualize* and allow them to *experience* their *real common good*. That common good is precisely *their marriage* with the two goods, parenthood and friendship, which are the parts of its wholeness as an intelligible common good even if, independently of what the spouses will, their capacity for biological parenthood will not be fulfilled by that act of genital union. But the common good of friends who are not and cannot be married (for example, man and man, man and boy, woman and woman) has nothing to do with their having children by each other, and their reproductive organs cannot make them a biological (and therefore personal) unit.[14] So their sexual acts together cannot do what

    to be a renewal of marriage and with such an act of tenderness to wipe out the complaints that accumulate from everyday living.

[12] See *Erōtikos*, 768D–770A.

[13] The core of this argument can be clarified by comparing it with St Augustine's treatment of marriage in his *De Bono Coniugali*. There the good of marital communion is presented primarily as an instrumental good, in the service of the procreation and education of children: see 1994b at 1064–5; and essay 5 at nn. 68–71.

[14] Macedo, 'The New Natural Lawyers', writes:

    In effect, gays can have sex in a way that is open to procreation, and to new life. They can be, and many are, prepared to engage in the kind of loving relations that would result in procreation—were conditions different. Like sterile married couples, many would like nothing better.

they may hope and imagine. Because their activation of one or even each of their reproductive organs cannot be an actualizing and experiencing of the *marital* good—as marital intercourse (intercourse between spouses in a marital way) can, even between spouses who *happen* to be sterile—it can *do* no more than provide each partner with an individual gratification. For want of a *common good* that could be actualized and experienced *by and in this bodily union*, that conduct involves the partners in treating their bodies as instruments to be used in the service of their consciously experiencing selves; their choice to engage in such conduct thus dis-integrates each of them precisely as acting persons.[15]

Reality is known in judgment, not in emotion. In reality, whatever the generous hopes and dreams and thoughts of *giving* with which some same-sex partners may surround their 'sexual' acts, those acts cannot express or do more than is expressed or done if two strangers engage in such activity to give each other pleasure, or a prostitute pleasures a client to give him pleasure in return for money, or, say, a man masturbates to give himself pleasure and a fantasy of more human relationships after a gruelling day on the assembly line. This is, I believe, the substance of Plato's judgment—at that moment in the *Gorgias* 494–5 which is also decisive for the moral and political philosophical critique of hedonism[16]—that there is no important distinction in essential moral worthlessness between solitary masturbation, being sodomized as a prostitute, and being sodomized for the pleasure of it. Sexual acts cannot *in reality* be self-giving unless they are acts by which a man and a woman actualize and experience sexually the real giving of themselves to each other—in biological, affective, and volitional union in mutual commitment, both open-ended and exclusive—which like Plato and Aristotle and most peoples we call *marriage*.

In short, sexual acts are not unitive in their significance unless they are marital (actualizing the all-level unity of marriage) and (since the common good of marriage has two aspects) they are not marital unless they have not only the generosity of acts of friendship but also the procreative significance, not necessarily of being intended to generate or capable in the circumstances of generating but at least of being, as human conduct,

---

Here fantasy has taken leave of reality. Anal or oral intercourse, whether between spouses or between males, is no more a biological union 'open to procreation' than is intercourse with a goat by a shepherd who fantasizes about breeding a faun; each 'would' yield the desired progeny 'were conditions different'.

Biological union between humans is the *inseminatory* union of male genital organ with female genital organ; in most circumstances it does not result in generation, but it is the behaviour that unites biologically because it is the behaviour which, as behaviour, is suitable for generation. (See also n. 28 below [and for comment on the unsatisfactory formulating of the first part of the preceding sentence, see essay 22 n. 125.])

[15] For the whole argument, see *LCL* 634–9, 648–54, 662–4.
[16] *Gorgias*, 494–5, esp. 494e1–5, 495b3.

acts of the reproductive kind—actualizations, so far as the spouses then and there can, of the reproductive function in which they are biologically and thus personally one.

The ancient philosophers do not much discuss the case of sterile marriages, or the fact (well known to them) that for long periods of time (for example throughout pregnancy) the sexual acts of a married couple are naturally incapable of resulting in reproduction. They appear to take for granted what the subsequent Christian tradition certainly did, that such sterility does not render the conjugal sexual acts of the spouses non-marital. (Plutarch indicates that intercourse with a sterile spouse is a desirable mark of marital esteem and affection.)[17] For: a husband and wife who unite their reproductive organs in an act of sexual intercourse which, so far as they then can make it, is of a kind suitable for generation, do function as a biological (and thus personal) unit and thus can be actualizing and experiencing the two-in-one-flesh common good and reality of marriage, even when some biological condition happens to prevent that unity resulting in generation of a child. Their conduct thus differs radically from the acts of a husband and wife whose intercourse is masturbatory, for example sodomitic or by fellatio or coitus interruptus.[18] In law such acts do not consummate a marriage, because in reality (whatever the couple's illusions of intimacy and self-giving in such acts) they do not actualize the one-flesh, two-part marital good.

Does this account seek to 'make moral judgments based on natural facts'?[19] Yes and no. No, in the sense that it does not seek to infer

---

[17] Plutarch, *Life of Solon*, 20, 3. The post-Christian moral philosophy of Kant identified the wrongfulness of masturbation and homosexual (and bestial) conduct as consisting in the instrumentalization of one's body, and thus ('since a person is an absolute unity') the 'wrong to humanity in our own person'. But Kant, though he emphasizes the equality of husband and wife (impossible in concubinage or more casual prostitution), did not integrate this insight with an understanding of marriage as a single two-part good involving, inseparably, friendship as well as procreation. Hence he was puzzled by the question why marital intercourse is right when the woman is pregnant or beyond the menopause. See Kant, *The Metaphysics of Morals*, 277–9, 220–2 (1991, trans. Gregor, 96–8, 220–2).

(The deep source of his puzzlement is his refusal to allow intelligible goods any structural role in his ethics, a refusal which sets him against a classical moral philosophy such as Aristotle's, and indeed against any adequate theory of natural law, and in turn is connected with his dualistic separation of body from mind and body, a separation which conflicts with his own insight, just quoted, that the person is a real unity. [See essay 2, sec. V at nn. 92–7.])

[18] Or deliberately contracepted, which I omit from the list in the text only because it would no doubt not now be accepted by secular civil law as preventing consummation—a failure of understanding.

[19] Macedo, loc. cit.,

All we can say is that conditions would have to be more radically different in the case of gay and lesbian couples than sterile married couples for new life to result from sex...but what is the moral force of that? The new natural law theory does not make moral judgments based on natural facts.

Macedo's phrase 'based on' equivocates between the first premises of normative arguments (which must be normative) and the other premise(s) (which can and normally should be factual

normative conclusions or theses from only non-normative (natural-fact) premises. Nor does it appeal to any norm of the form 'Respect natural facts or natural functions'. But yes, it is to the realities of our constitution, intentions, and circumstances that the argument applies the relevant practical reasons (especially that marriage and inner integrity are basic human goods) and moral principles (especially that one may never *intend* to destroy, damage, impede, or violate any basic human good, or prefer an illusory instantiation of a basic human good to a real instantiation of that or some other human good).

IV

Societies such as classical Athens and contemporary England (and virtually every other) draw a distinction between behaviour found merely (perhaps extremely) offensive (such as eating excrement), and behaviour to be repudiated as destructive of human character and relationships. Copulation of humans with animals is repudiated because it treats human sexual activity and satisfaction as something appropriately sought in a manner as divorced from the expressing of an intelligible common good as is the instinctive coupling of beasts—and so treats human bodily life, in one of its most intense activities, as a life appropriately lived *as* merely animal. The deliberate genital coupling of persons of the same sex is repudiated for a very similar reason. It is not simply that it is sterile and disposes the participants to an abdication of responsibility for the future of humankind. Nor is it simply that it cannot *really* actualize the mutual devotion which some homosexual persons hope to manifest and experience by it, and that it harms the personalities of its participants by its disintegrative manipulation of different parts of their one personal reality. It is also that it treats human sexual capacities in a way which is deeply hostile to the self-understanding of those members of the community who are willing to commit themselves to real marriage in the understanding that its sexual joys are not mere instruments or accompaniments to, or mere compensations for, the accomplishment of marriage's responsibilities, but rather enable the spouses to *actualize and experience* their intelligent commitment to share in those responsibilities, in that genuine self-giving.

Now, as I noted in sec. I, 'homosexual orientation', in one of the two main senses of that highly equivocal term, is precisely the deliberate willingness

---

and where appropriate can refer to natural facts such as that the human mouth is not a reproductive organ).

to promote and engage in homosexual acts—the state of mind, will, and character whose self-interpretation came to be expressed in the deplorable but helpfully revealing name 'gay'. So this willingness, and the whole 'gay' ideology, treats human sexual capacities in a way which is deeply hostile to the self-understanding of those members of the community who are willing to commit themselves to real marriage.

Homosexual orientation in this sense is, in fact, a standing denial of the intrinsic aptness of sexual intercourse to actualize and in that sense give expression to the exclusiveness and open-ended commitment of marriage as something good in itself. All who accept that homosexual acts can be a humanly appropriate use of sexual capacities must, if consistent, regard sexual capacities, organs, and acts as instruments for gratifying the individual 'self' who has them. Such an acceptance is commonly (and in my opinion rightly) judged to be an active threat to the stability of existing and future marriages; it makes nonsense, for example, of the view that adultery is inconsistent with conjugal love, in an important way and *intrinsically*—not merely because it may involve deception. A political community which judges that the stability and protective and educative generosity of family life are of fundamental importance to the whole community's present and future can rightly judge that it has compelling reasons for judging that homosexual conduct—a 'gay lifestyle'—is never a valid, humanly acceptable choice and form of life, in denying that same-sex partners are capable of marrying, and in doing whatever it *properly* can, as a community with uniquely wide but still subsidiary functions (see sec. I above), to discourage such conduct.[20]

---

[20] The criminal law upheld in *Bowers v Hardwick* 478 US 186 (1986) seems to me unsound in principle. But there was a sound and important distinction of principle which the US Supreme Court overlooked in moving from *Griswold v Connecticut* 381 US 479 (1965) (*private use* of contraceptives by *spouses*) to *Eisenstadt v Baird* 405 US 438 (1970) (*public distribution* of contraceptives to *unmarried* people). (The law struck down in *Griswold* was the law forbidding use of contraceptives even by married persons; Griswold's conviction as an accessory to such use fell with the fall of the substantive law against the principals in such use. Very different, in principle, would have been a law directly forbidding Griswold's activities as a public promoter of contraceptive information and supplies.) The truth and relevance of that distinction, and its high importance for the common good, would be overlooked again if laws criminalizing private acts of sodomy between adults were to be struck down by the court on any ground which would also constitutionally require the law to tolerate the advertising or marketing of homosexual services, the maintenance of places of resort for homosexual activity, or the promotion of homosexualist 'lifestyles' via education and public media of communication, or to recognize homosexual 'marriages' or permit the adoption of children by homosexually active people, and so forth. [In the event, *Lawrence v Texas* 539 US 558 (2003), which overrules *Bowers v Hardwick* and strikes down laws of the kind it upheld, does so not on the sound ground that purely private conduct between consenting adults is outside the proper jurisdiction of state government and laws but on the ground that law must not 'demean' or impose a 'stigma' on homosexual conduct—a premise obviously capable of being employed to require the forms of toleration mentioned in the preceding sentence.]

V

The preceding sections of this essay—an essay which bears the marks of its origin in 1993 as an affidavit of evidence in the 'Colorado Amendment 2 case', *Evans v Romer*‡ —were published (in a rather longer version) in 1994 and have attracted various responses including the essay by Andrew Koppelman [published alongside 1997c]. Koppelman takes it for granted that the kind of argument developed in my essay, the argument of 'the new natural lawyers', is radically different from (and, he claims, less coherent than) 'Aquinas' insistence on natural teleology'. He is right in thinking that Grisez, George, Bradley and I reject as fallacious (and never argue on the basis of) any proposition like 'natural functions or tendencies are moral standards and ought to guide deliberation and choice'. But, though this fallacy is certainly to be found from time to time in the tradition, Koppelman is mistaken in thinking that Aquinas's sex ethics depends upon it.

The question of sex ethics which seems to have interested Aquinas far more than any other is: When must sex acts *between spouses*, even acts of intercourse of the generative kind, be regarded as seriously wrongful? His answer is, in effect: When such acts are de-personalized, and de-maritalized. That is to say, if I choose this act of intercourse with my spouse, not for the sake of pleasurably actualizing and expressing our marital commitment, but *'solely* for pleasure', or *solely* for the sake of my health, or *solely* as a relief from temptations to masturbation or extra-marital sex, and *would be just as (or more!) willing* to be having intercourse with someone else—so that I am seeing in my spouse, in this act of intercourse, no more than I would see in a good-time girl or a gigolo or another acquaintance or someone else's spouse—then my sex act with my spouse is *non-marital* and is in principle seriously wrong.[21] It is contrary to reason, and therefore[22] contrary to nature. It is contrary to reason because it is contrary to—dis-integrated from—an intrinsic good to which we are directed by one of the first principles of practical reason (and therefore of natural law), a good which may therefore be called primary, fundamental, or basic: the good of marriage itself.[23]

---

[21] See *Sent* IV q.26 q.1 a.4c (= *ST Supp.* q.41 a.4c); d.31 q.2 a.2 (= *Supp.* q.41 a.5) ad 2 and ad 4; q.2 a.3c (= *Supp.* q.49 a.6c) and tit. and obj. 1; *Commentary on I Corinthians*, c.7 ad v.6 [329]; *ST* II–II q.154 a.8 ad 2; *De Malo* q.15 a.1c. For a much fuller treatment of Aquinas's sex ethics, see *Aquinas* ch. VII.2.

[22] All extra-marital sex (and even conditional assent {consensus} to it) is contrary to nature *in as much as (and because)* it is contrary to reason's requirements: e.g. *De Malo* q.15 a.1 ad 7.

[23] See *ST* I–II q.94 a.2c. In his treatment of sex ethics, Aquinas usually refers to the good of marriage, insofar as it is always at stake in the spouses' sexual activity, as the good of *fides*, i.e. of *mutual commitment in marriage*. The literal translation of *fides* would be faith(fulness), but in English this suggests merely absence of infidelity (i.e. of sexual relations with other persons), whereas Aquinas

Why are sex acts (seeking the orgasm of one or more of the parties) unreasonable unless marital? Implicit in Aquinas's often misunderstood[24] work is a rarely recognized train of thought, substantially as follows.

Marriage, in which a man and a woman would find their friendship and devotion to each other fulfilled in their procreation, nurture, protection, education, and moral formation of their children,[25] is an intrinsic, basic human good. Sexual intercourse between the spouses, provided it is authentically marital, actualizes and promotes the spouses' mutual commitment in marriage (their marital *fides*). But my sex act with my spouse will not be truly marital—and will not authentically actualize, and allow us in a non-illusory way to experience, our marriage—if I engage in it while I *would be willing* in some circumstance(s) to engage in a sex act of a non-marital kind—for example adultery, fornication, intentionally sterilized intercourse, solitary masturbation or mutual masturbation (for example sodomy), and so forth. To regard any of such types of sex act as morally acceptable is to regard one or more of them as something I might under some circumstances engage in, and this state of mind undermines the marital character of my sex acts with my spouse. In short, the complete *exclusion* of non-marital sex acts from the range of acceptable human options is a pre-condition for the truly marital character of any spouses' intercourse. Blindness or indifference to the inherent wrongness of non-marital sex acts renders non-marital the choosing and carrying out of even those actual sex acts which in all other respects are marital in kind.

Moreover, without the possibility of truly marital intercourse the good of marriage is seriously impaired. Any willingness to (counterfactually or actually) engage in non-marital sex radically undermines my marriage itself. For it disintegrates the intelligibility of my marriage; our sex acts no longer truly actualize and enable us authentically to experience our *marriage*; they are unhinged from the other aspects of our mutual commitment and project. And this unhinging or dis-integration threatens—runs contrary to—both of the goods inherent in the complex

---

explains (*Sent* IV d.31 q.1 a.2c and ad 3 (= *Supp.* q.49 a.2c and ad 3); *Commentary on I Cor.* c.7.1 ad v.2 [318]) that marital *fides* involves also, and primarily, a positive willingness to be maritally, including sexually, united (on a basis of mutuality and absolute equality in initiating or requesting intercourse).

[24] Thoroughly misunderstood and misrepresented in Noonan, *Contraception*; and Boswell, *Christianity, Social Tolerance, and Homosexuality*. Koppelman's view of Aquinas has (not unreasonably, but certainly unfortunately) been reliant upon these writers: see the longer version of his present essay: Koppelman, 'Is Marriage Inherently Heterosexual?'; and for a discussion of Noonan's and Boswell's misreadings, see essay 22, secs I–III.

[25] The marriage of a couple who have reason to believe that they are incapable of generating children is considered, once the basic lines of the argument are in place, below.

basic good of marriage:[26] not only the good of friendship and *fides* but also the good of procreation and of the children whose education etc. so depends on the context of a *good* marriage. *So* any kind of assent—even if conditional—to non-marital sex is unreasonable. (Indeed, all sexual immorality, including all willingness to treat it as a potentially acceptable option, is contrary to love-of-neighbour, that is, of children).[27] *And so* it is immoral, *and* out of line with human nature (and, Aquinas adds, with God's intentions about human conduct).[28]

This line of thought may seem complex when spelled out on the page. But it is no more than the articulation of married people's commonsense appreciation of the offensiveness of adultery and of being treated by one's spouse as a mere object of sexual relief, sexual servicing, de-personalized sex—'he/she doesn't love me, he/she is just using me/only wants me for my body [or: as a baby-maker]'.[29] The traditional sex ethic which, despite all backsliding, was fairly perspicuous to almost everyone until the acceptance by many people of divorce-for-remarriage and contraception began to obscure its coherence a few decades ago, is no more and no less than a drawing out of the implications of this same reasonable thought: the intending, giving, and/or receiving of pleasure in sex acts is reasonably respectful of and coherent with intelligible human goods *only* when those acts are fully expressive of and (so far as my willing goes) instantiations of the complex good of marriage. Acts of the kind that same-sex partners engage in (intended to culminate in orgasmic satisfaction by finger in

---

[26] Marriage is a complex but unified good in as much as its unitive goodness is inseparable from its procreative significance (even where procreation is *per accidens* impossible). Aquinas's train of thought sets out one way of understanding and acknowledging this inseparability.

[27] See *De Malo* q.15 a.2 ad 4; *Sent.* IV d.33 q.1 a.3 sol. 2 (= *Supp.* q.65 a.4c).

[28] Koppelman says that for Aquinas homosexual acts are uniquely monstrous. That is an exaggeration; for Aquinas, bestiality is a worse type of surrender to unreasonable, dis-integrated desire for pleasure, and rape and adultery are characteristically much worse in terms of injustice. Considered simply as sexually unreasonable, acts of sexual vice are, *other things being equal*, worse the more distant they are from the truly marital type of act: *Sent.* IV d.41 a.4 sol.3c; see also *De Malo* q.15 a.1c. Aquinas seems to be correct in thinking that homosexual sex acts are a type particularly distant from the marital: they are between persons who *could never be married*. (Indeed, this seems to be part of the reason why the word 'gay' was co-opted by the homosexual ideology.) A businessman copulating with a call-girl, though he is engaged in seriously wrongful sexual vice, can imagine himself being married to this woman, and engaging with her in behaviour of the same kind as spouses at some time in the future. But men committing or contemplating sex acts (even buggery) with each other cannot *rationally* think of those acts as acts of the kind Aquinas (rightly) considers the reproductive and marital kind. (See n. 14 above and text near n. 32 below.) Of course, in grading the gravity of *types* of sexual vice, Aquinas is not attempting to estimate the culpability of particular acts of particular persons, culpability which may sometimes be much diminished by passion that fetters freedom and/or by confusion of mind (e.g. ideology, fantasy) that obscures rational deliberation towards choice.

[29] On regarding one's wife as a baby-maker, see George and Bradley, 'Marriage and the Liberal Imagination' at 305 text and n. 19.

vagina, penis in mouth, etc., etc.) remain non-marital, and so unreasonable and wrong, when performed in like manner by a married couple.

Every married couple is sterile most of the time. Outside one or two remote tribes, that has always been well known, even when the limited periods of fertility in the female cycle were mislocated. Koppelman and Macedo absurdly think that *most of the time*, therefore, (a) the couple's genitals are not reproductive organs at all,[30] and (b) the couple's intercourse cannot be of a reproductive kind. The same line of thought also drives these writers towards the equally arbitrary conclusion that a man and a woman can never be biologically united—only sperm and egg can be biologically united! While in this reductivist, word-legislating mood, one might declare that sperm and egg unite only physically and only their pronuclei are *biologically* united. But it would be more realistic to acknowledge that the whole process of copulation, involving as it does the brains of the man and woman, their nerves, blood, vaginal and other secretions, and coordinated activity (such that conception is much less likely to result from rape) is biological through and through. The dualism embraced by Koppelman and Macedo[31] neatly shows how far humanness itself—the radical *unity* of body ('biology'), sense, emotion, reason, and will—becomes unintelligible once one loses one's grip on the way in which a marital sexual act, uniting *us*[32] in a *particular bodily* (and therefore biological) *way* can really *actualize*, express, and enable us truly to experience something as *intelligent and voluntary* as a freely chosen commitment to serving each other as friends in a form of life adapted to serving also (if fortune so provides) our children as the living embodiments and fruit peculiarly appropriate to our kind of (comm)union.[33]

Sexual acts which are marital are 'of the reproductive kind' because in willing such an act one wills sexual behaviour which is (a) the very same as causes generation (intended or unintended) in every case of human *sexual* reproduction, and (b) the very same as one would will if one were intending precisely sexual reproduction as a goal of a particular marital sexual act. This kind of act is a 'natural kind', in the morally relevant sense of 'natural', not (as Koppelman supposes) if and only if one is intending or attempting an *outcome*, viz. reproduction or procreation. Rather it is a distinct rational

---

[30] Koppelman sometimes, inconsistently, speaks as if they are not reproductive if and only if they belong to people who are completely sterile, e.g. 'a woman whose diseased uterus has been removed'.

[31] See also the response to Macedo on this point by George and Bradley, 'Marriage and the Liberal Imagination' at 311 n. 32.

[32] The organic unity which is instantiated in an act of the reproductive kind is not, as Macedo and Koppelman reductively imagine, the unity of penis and vagina. It is the unity of the persons in the intentional, consensual *act* of seminal emission in the woman's reproductive tract.

[33] See further George and Bradley, 'Marriage and the Liberal Imagination' at 304 text and n. 16.

kind—and therefore in the morally relevant sense a natural kind—because (i) in engaging in it one is intending a *marital* act, (ii) its being of the reproductive kind is a necessary though not sufficient condition of it being marital, and (iii) marriage is a rational and natural kind of institution. One's reason for action—one's rational motive—is precisely the complex good of *marriage*.

For: marriage is rational and natural primarily because it is the institution which physically, biologically, emotionally, and in every other practical way is peculiarly apt to promote suitably the reproduction of the couple by the generation, nurture, and education of ultimately mature offspring. And here we touch on another point of importance in understanding and evaluating the version of 'gay' ideology defended by Koppelman and Macedo. These writers claim that sex acts between persons of the same sex can be truly marital, and that to perform such acts two such persons can indeed marry each other. They want us to evaluate homosexual sex acts by focusing upon this sort of activity of this sort of couple. Koppelman adopts Sidney Callahan's claim that *when engaged in 'with a faithful partner'*, such same-sex sex acts 'produce...intense intimacy, bodily confirmation, mutual sanctification, and fulfilling happiness'. It seems rather careless of Koppelman to accept that 'mutual sanctification' is 'produced' by sex acts in a universe he proclaims to be 'disenchanted'. But more interesting is his failure to explain why this and the other effects allegedly 'produced' by sex acts[34] depend upon the faithfulness of one's partner, or partners,[35] and, I assume, upon one's own faithfulness.

The 'gay' ideology, even in the sanitized Koppelman/Macedo version, has no serious account whatever of why it makes sense to regard faithfulness—reservation of one's sex acts exclusively for one's spouse—as an intelligible, intelligent, and reasonable requirement. Only a small proportion of homosexual men who live as 'gays' seriously attempt anything even resembling marriage as a permanent commitment. Only a tiny proportion seriously attempt marital fidelity, the commitment to exclusiveness; the proportion who find that the attempt makes sense, in view of the other aspects of their 'gay identity', is even tinier.[36] Thus, even at the level of

---

[34] The idea that the value of sex must be in the desirable effects it produces is criticized by George and Bradley, who rightly understand the value of *marital intercourse* as more than merely instrumental, i.e. as intrinsic. As they point out, the view defended by Koppelman and Macedo 'presupposes that the point and value of sex can only be instrumental'. *Ibid.* at 304–5.

[35] Not yet disentangled from the Catholicism she is 'changing her mind' away from, Callahan just takes for granted that there will only be one partner. As we shall see, the assumption is groundless.

[36] e.g.: McWhirter and Mattison (both homosexual), *The Male Couple: How Relationships Develop*, 252–9, studied 156 male homosexual couples, most of whom once expected to have a sexually exclusive relationship, and found that only seven of these couples claimed to have succeeded; and none of these seven had been together for even five years. Kirk and Madsen (both homosexual), *After the*

behaviour—that is, even leaving aside its inherent sterility—gay 'marriage', precisely because it excludes or fails to embrace, and ultimately can make no sense of, the *commitment* utterly central to *marriage*, is a sham.

And this is no mere happenstance. The reason why marriage involves the commitment to permanence and exclusiveness in the spouses' sexual union is that, as an institution or form of life, it is fundamentally shaped by its dynamism towards, appropriateness for, and fulfilment in, the generation, nurture, and education of children who each can only have two parents and who are fittingly the primary responsibility (and object of devotion) of *those two parents*. Apart from this orientation towards children, the institution of marriage, characterized by marital *fides* (faithfulness), would make little or no sense. Given this orientation, the marital form of life does make good sense, and the marital sexual acts which actualize, express, and enable the spouses to experience that form of life make good sense, too.

Moreover, a man and a woman *who can engage in precisely the marital acts with precisely the same behaviour and intentions*, but who have reason to believe that in their case those very same acts will never result in children, can still opt for this *form of life* as one that makes good sense. Given the bodily, emotional, intellectual, and volitional complementarities with which that combination of factors we call human evolution[37] has equipped us as men and women, such a commitment can be reasonable as a participation in the good of marriage in which these infertile spouses, if well-intentioned, would wish to have participated more fully than they can.[38] By their model of fidelity within a relationship involving acts of the reproductive kind, these infertile marriages are, moreover, strongly supportive of marriage as a valuable social institution.

But same-sex partners cannot engage in acts of the reproductive kind, that is, in marital sexual intercourse. The permanent, exclusive

---

Ball: *How America will Conquer its Fear and Hatred of Gays in the '90s*, 302–7, 318–32 clearly set out the psychological causes *within* homosexual men which account for their promiscuity and failure to maintain stable or faithful relationships; they thus provide grounds for rejecting the oft-heard assertion that these phenomena result from society's failure to recognize 'gay' marriage. Readers should consult Kirk and Madsen, 280–356, for a detailed description of characteristic 'gay' lifestyles which gives descriptive and explanatory substance to, inter alia, the bare statistics earlier reported in Bell and Weinberg, *Homosexualities: A Study in Diversity among Men and Women*, 81–93, 308–9: among the 574 white male homosexuals studied, 97 per cent had already had at least three sexual partners, 75 per cent at least 100, and 28 per cent at least 1,000.

[37] Koppelman (like Strauss) has not fully, or at all, come to grips with the radically teleological character of contemporary 'Darwinian' biology's account of the molecular-biological genetic primordia, fundaments, or engine of evolution. But that, like the half-truth of the 'disenchantment' of the universe, is an issue with no bearing on the present argument.

[38] Those, however, who search out infertile spouses, choosing them *precisely for their infertility*, may well be manifesting the kind of contempt for the marital good which Philo Judaeus condemned in the rather confused passage from which Koppelman and Boswell quote some over-heated fragments.

commitment of marriage, which presupposes bodily union as the biological actuation of the multi-level (bodily, emotional, intellectual, and volitional) marital relationship, makes no sense for them. Of course, two, three, four, five, or any number of persons of the same sex can band together to raise a child or children. That may, in some circumstances, be a praiseworthy commitment. It has nothing to do with marriage. Koppelman and Macedo remain discreetly silent on the question why the same-sex 'marriage' they offer to defend is to be between two persons rather than three, four, five, or more, all engaging in sex acts 'faithfully' with each other. They are equally silent on the question why this group sex-partnership should remain constant in membership, rather than revolving like other partnerships.

The plain fact is that those who propound 'gay' ideology have no principled moral case to offer against (prudent and moderate) promiscuity, indeed the getting of orgasmic sexual pleasure in whatever friendly touch or welcoming orifice (human or otherwise) one may opportunely find it. In debate with opponents of their ideology, these proponents are fond of postulating an idealized (two-person, lifelong...) category of relationship—'gay marriage'—and of challenging their opponents to say how such a relationship differs from *marriage* at least where husband and wife know themselves to be infertile. As I have argued, the principal difference is very simple and fundamental: the artificially delimited (two-person, lifelong...) category named 'gay marriage' or 'same-sex marriage' corresponds to no intrinsic reason or set of reasons at all. It has few presentable counterparts in the real world outside the artifice of debate. *Marriage*, on the other hand, is the category of relationships, activities, satisfactions, and responsibilities which can be intelligently and reasonably chosen by a man and a woman, and adopted as their integral commitment, because the components of the category respond and correspond coherently to a complex of interlocking, complementary good reasons: the good of marriage. True and valid sexual morality is nothing more, and nothing less, than an unfolding of what is involved in understanding, promoting, and respecting that basic human good, and of the conditions for instantiating it in a real, non-illusory way—in the marital act.

NOTES

What is described in secs I and II as the standard modern position was more or less abandoned, widely in the western world, in the decade more or less immediately following the essay (which is an abridged version of 1994b, supplemented however by sec. V). One instance can stand for many: in December 2000, the European Union adopted a Charter of Fundamental Rights in which Art. 21 prohibits any discrimination on grounds of sexual orientation. It was a sound position, and its replacement by one in which criticisms of homosexual conduct or of public endorsement of such conduct are legally and/or socially penalized as offensive and unjust discrimination runs contrary not only to freedom of speech, association, and religion but, more importantly, to the rights of children and to the common good of political communities dependent in countless ways on the marital procreation of children and on their education in ways conducive to marriage.

† *State coercive jurisdiction does not extend to preventing strictly private immorality*...(p. 335). See *Aquinas* ch. VII; earlier, essay 5 at 93–4.

‡ *Evans v Romer*...(p. 345). In the Supreme Court of the United States, *Romer v Evans* 517 US 620 (1996) struck down the amendment to the Constitution of Colorado on the ground (as summarized by the court in *Lawrence v Texas*, n. 20 above) that that provision was 'born of animosity toward the class of persons affected' and also had no rational relation to a legitimate governmental purpose. The finding of animosity seems to have no other basis than the animosity of the majority Justices towards the provision, and the denial that there was any rational relation to a legitimate governmental purpose ignores the provision's doubtless primary purpose of protecting children from the influence of attitudes, doctrines, and openly proffered examples proclaiming the moral probity of homosexual conduct and the equal legitimacy of homosexual unions and familial relationships. The example of the UK's Equality Act 2010, and of its non-statutory antecedents, demonstrates that a general right not to be discriminated against on grounds of sexual orientation will commonly be taken—as so many Colorado electors anticipated and feared—to override or confine within unprecedentedly narrow bounds certain rights the exercise of which would be regarded by practising homosexuals as demeaning or offensive to them. Seriously impaired is the right to teach children in schools that reasonable and fair-minded people can hold that marriage is not morally open to or authentically possible for couples of the same sex, and that the related moral propositions defended in writings like this essay (and central to our civilization for many, many centuries) are sound.

What those traditions held, and these writings argue for, can be summed up, not quite unambiguously but with pragmatically sufficient clarity, in the conclusion: sex is for marriage. (That is the conclusion, in slogan form; it is not the form of the argument.) So the widespread adoption of libertine sexual mores, and the shaping of civil marriage law and customs and of conventions about sexual availability outside marriage, all make any particular restrictions on homosexual activities morally inconsistent and discriminatory. The unfairness, however, while real and quite deplorable, is in the public encouragement and facilitations accorded to heterosexual non-marital sexual activities, not in the restrictions on public encouragement or facilitation of activities which after all express more vividly than most the morally false and socially disastrous 'message' that sex is not for marriage.

22

SEX AND MARRIAGE: SOME MYTHS AND REASONS*

I

Aquinas organized his account of the morality of sexual relations around the good of marriage. The good of marriage is one of the basic human goods to which human choice and action are directed by the first principles of practical reason.[1] Sex acts[2] are immoral when they are 'against the good

---

* 1997d ('The Good of Marriage and the Morality of Sexual Relations: Some Philosophical and Historical Observations').

[1] *ST* I–II q.94 a.2c and *In Eth.* V.12 n. 4 [1019] list the *conjunctio maris et feminae* as a basic human good, and make it clear that here Aquinas has in mind the Roman law definition of marriage, which he quotes directly at the outset of his own early treatise on marriage, in *Sent.* IV d.26 q.1: 'the mating of man with woman, which we call "marriage"' {maris et feminae conjunctio, quam nos matrimonium appellamus}. References to Aquinas's works in this essay:

In Eth.   *Sententia Libri Ethicorum* (Commentary on Aristotle's *Nicomachean Ethics*) 1271–2. References (e.g. IX.7 n. 6 [1845]) are to the book, lectio, and paragraph number followed by a reference to the paragraph number in Raymundi M. Spiazzi OP (ed.), *S. Thomae Aquinatis In Decem Libros Ethicorum. Aristotelis ad Nicomachum Expositio*, Turin: Marietti 1949.

In Rom.   *Commentarium super Epistolam ad Romanos* (Commentary on Paul's Letter to the Romans). References (e.g. IX.7 n. 6 [1845]) are to the book, lectio, and biblical verse, followed by the paragraph number in Raphael Cai OP, *S. Thomae Aquinatis Super Epistolas S. Pauli Lectura*, 8th edn, Turin and Rome: Marietti 1951.

Mal.   *Quaestiones disputatae de Malo* (*De Malo*: Disputed Questions on Evil).

Quodl.   *Quaestiones de Quolibet* (Disputed [Debated] Quodlibetal [Random] Questions) 1256–9 (VII–XI) and 1269–72 (I–VI, XII).

ScG   *Summa contra Gentiles* (A Summary of Theology 'Against the Unbelievers') 1259–64/5. References are by book (I, II, III, IV) and paragraph number (n.)

Sent.   *Scriptum super Libros Sententiarum Petri Lombardiensis* (Commentary on the Sentences [Opinions or Positions of the Church Fathers] [Handbook of Theology] of Peter Lombard [c. 1155]) I, 1253–4; II, 1254–5; III, 1255–6; IV, 1256–7. References are by book (I, II, III, IV), distinction (d.), question (q.), article (a.), and sometimes to the response (solution) to a sub-question (sol.)

ST   *Summa Theologiae* (A Summary of Theology): I, 1265–8; I–II, 1271; II–II, 1271–2; III, 1272–3. References (e.g. I–II q.2 a.2c and ad 2) are to the four parts (first, first-of-the-second, second-of-the-second, third), question (q.), article (a.), corpus (c.) [i.e. the body of Aquinas's response], reply (ad 1, ad 2, etc.) to a particular, numbered objection (obj.1, obj.2, etc.), and/or to the provisional reply *sed contra* (s.c.)

Supp.   *Supplementum* (A Supplement to [or rather, a partial completion of] *ST*, posthumously and anonymously constructed from passages of *Sent.* IV)

Ver.   *Quaestiones Disputatae de Veritate* (*De Veritate*: Disputed [Debated] Questions on Truth).

[2] By 'sex act' (and '(have) sex' used synonymously with that phrase) I shall here always mean an act or sequence of performances engaged in with the intention or willingness that it secure orgasmic sexual satisfaction for one or more person doing or participating in the act. This is substantially the

of marriage',[3] and therefore unreasonable (and, in as much as unreasonable,[4] unnatural). Considered precisely as kinds of morally bad sex—rather than as, say, unjust (as rapes and some other morally bad sex acts obviously also are)—wrongful sex acts are more seriously immoral the 'more distant' they are from *marital* sexual intercourse.[5] Aquinas's account of what it is to act sexually 'against the good of marriage' leaves a good deal to be clarified. But he did deploy a line of thought that lawyers and philosophical theologians had articulated in the preceding century, and that brilliantly illuminates the ways in which sex acts, even when performed consensually between spouses, can be against the good of marriage and therefore unreasonable.

Germain Grisez's 1993 treatise on sex, marriage, and family life clarifies large tracts of sexual morality which Aquinas's account left more or less obscure. For it shows how various kinds of sex act, even when performed (for example as solitary masturbation, or homosexual sodomy)

concept employed also by Aquinas: see *ST* II–II q.154 a.4; Jordan, *The Invention of Sodomy in Christian Theology*, 156, is entirely mistaken in claiming that Aquinas has 'no other way of distinguishing the class of acts, pleasures, and sins as venereal' than by 'relation to the teleology of reproduction', and 'no category of the sexual apart from animal teleology'. Aquinas, like the moderns ('us') with whom Jordan is striving to contrast him, has a straightforward concept of sexual (= 'venereal') acts: those intended to arouse or experience sexual pleasure, viz. the kind of intense pleasure associated with orgasm—i.e. with the ejaculation of male or female seminal fluids: *ST* II–II q.152 a.1c and ad 4; q.154 a.4c and ad 2; *Sent.* IV d.33 q.3 a.1 ad 4 and ad 5; on female semen and orgasm see n. 115 below. Note that the definition I have given of 'sex act' is morally neutral: *morally good marital intercourse* is one kind of *sex act*. (And see *Aquinas*, ch. V.4 at n. 47.) The critique of my views offered by Ball, 'Moral Foundations for a Discourse on Same-Sex Marriage' at 1912–19, derails right from the start by groundlessly assuming that the equivalent definition of 'homosexual sex act' given in my 1994b at 1055 'contains its own built-in moral disapprobation'.

[3] This phrase (*contra bonum matrimonii*) is used in relation to adultery, including adultery with the spouse's consent (*ST* II–II q.154 a.8 ad 2 and ad 3; *Sent.* IV d.33 q.1 a.3 sol.1 (= *Supp.* q.65 a.3) ad 5). The concept is close to the surface in the discussion of many kinds of sexual misdeed in *ScG* III, c.122; see text and n. 115 below.

[4] Aquinas's moral arguments never run from 'natural' to 'therefore reasonable and right', but always from 'reasonable and right' to 'therefore natural'. As he says, 'moral precepts are in accord with {consequuntur} human nature *because* they are the requirements/prescriptions of natural reason {cum sint de dictamine rationis naturalis}': *Sent.* IV d.2 q.1 a.4 sol.1 ad 2; likewise, repeatedly, *ST* I–II q.71 a.2c (e.g. 'virtues...are in accordance with human nature just insofar as they are in line with reason; vices are against human nature just insofar as they are against the order or reasonableness'); also q.94 a.3 ad 2; q.18 a.5c; q.78 a.3c; II–II q.158 a.2 ad 4 ('the activity [of the capacity for anger] is natural to human beings just insofar as it is in accordance with reason; insofar as it is outside the order of reasonableness it is contrary to human nature'); *NLNR* 35–6. See also text and nn. 58–65 below.

[5] *Sent.* IV d.41 a.4 sol. c ('... secundum quod *magis distat* a matrimoniali concubitu'); see also *Mal.* q.15 a.1c. Koppelman's claim (56) that Aquinas regarded homosexual acts as 'uniquely monstrous' is false: see *ST* II–II q.154 a.12; *ScG* III, c.122; similarly mistaken is his claim (if he intends it, as the context suggests, to refer to degree of gravity) that Grisez holds that the considerations which show homosexual acts to be wrong '*equally* condemn other nonmarital sexual acts'. Grisez, *LCL* 654 (a page cited more than once by Koppelman) explicitly says that homosexual acts are generically 'more unreasonable' than fornication.

by unmarried people who have no intention of marrying, *violate the good of marriage.*[6]

In 1994 I published an essay which explored the reasons why 'Plato and Socrates, Xenophon, Aristotle, Musonius Rufus, and Plutarch, right at the heart of their reflections on the homoerotic culture around them, make the very deliberate and careful judgment that homosexual *conduct* (and indeed all extra-marital[7] sexual gratification) is radically incapable of participating in, actualizing, the common good of friendship.'[8] The essay then considered why homosexual conduct is 'never a valid, humanly acceptable choice and form of life' and is (rightly) 'repudiated as destructive of human character and relationships'. The primary reason I summarized thus:

it treats human sexual capacities in a way which is deeply hostile to the self-understanding of those members of the community who are willing to commit themselves to real marriage in the understanding that its sexual joys are not mere instruments or accompaniments to, or mere compensations for, the accomplishment of marriage's responsibilities, but rather enable the spouses to *actualize and experience* their intelligent commitment to share in those responsibilities, in that genuine self-giving.[9]

To emphasize the point, I added:

...the deliberate willingness to promote and engage in homosexual acts is, in fact, a standing denial of the intrinsic aptness of sexual intercourse to actualize and in that sense give expression to the exclusiveness and open-ended commitment of marriage as something good in itself.[10]

Thus, like Aquinas and Grisez, I argued that approval of homosexual and other non-marital sex acts is not simply non-marital, in the sense of being utterly incapable of consummating or actualizing the human good of marriage, but actually 'contrary to' or 'violative of' that good.[11]

---

[6] *LCL* 633, 649. Grisez's treatise is theological, but the relevant philosophical arguments and considerations can be distinguished and detached by careful analysis, and my own discussion in this essay is restricted to philosophical and historical considerations and method.
[7] In that essay I used 'extra-marital' to refer to all non-marital sex acts; in the present essay I shall use 'extra-marital' to refer to adulterous sex acts, a subclass of 'non-marital' sex acts.
[8] 1994b ('Law, Morality, and "Sexual Orientation"') at 1065.   [9] *Ibid.* at 1069.
[10] *Ibid.* at 1069–70.
[11] I also indicated that non-marital, including homosexual, sex acts are immoral because they violate inner integrity and entail preferring an illusory instantiation of a basic human good to a real instantiation of that or some other human good: *ibid.* at 1069. These elements of my position are developed further in Lee and George, 'What Sex Can Be: Self-Alienation, Illusion, or One-Flesh Unity'. I shall here say little or nothing more about them. But note that Koppelman's statement of the argument about disintegrity (Koppelman, 'Is Marriage Inherently Heterosexual?', text between nn. 143 and 144) misapprehends it.

Andrew Koppelman now offers a critique of Aquinas, Grisez, and me which overlooks this central argument entirely.[12] He constructs for Aquinas a sex ethics based on alleged principles—about respect for 'the natural order of things', or 'normality'—which are remote from those which Aquinas actually employs in his account of why some sex acts are morally unacceptable. He says (41) 'the fatal gap in [Aquinas's] argument...is his failure to show what human good will be frustrated by homosexual conduct', but he never mentions Aquinas's treatment of the good of marriage or Aquinas's thesis that morally bad sex is contrary to that good. Or my own similar thesis. Similarly, while quoting many snippets from Grisez, Koppelman neglects to mention Grisez's primary thesis and argument. He foists on Grisez and me an argument about sex and pleasure (and the 'experience machine'), an argument he constructs largely from bits and pieces of earlier philosophical writings (mostly of mine) in which sexual morality was not the issue. Like the scholars on whom he heavily relies—John Noonan and John Boswell—Koppelman is unaware that Aquinas's treatment of the radically different ways in which sex can be *for pleasure* sheds much light on the whole question of the good of marriage and the ways in which that good can be violated.[13]

A good many parts of Koppelman's essay I shall scarcely mention. No one need be detained by its reflections on the supposed incompatibility between evolution ('Darwin') and Aquinas's fifth argument for the existence of God;[14] or by its adoption of Ron Garet's home-made theology of sacramental grace; or by its fragmentary review of the psychological literature on the effects that choices to engage in homosexual conduct have on character, family,[15] and society; or by its creditably tentative re-run of

---

[12] 'Is Marriage Inherently Heterosexual?'; parenthetical numbers in this essay are to the pages of his article.

[13] When I wrote 1994b ('Law, Morality, and "Sexual Orientation"') I was by no means as keenly aware of the power of Aquinas's treatment of the good of marriage as I became in writing chapter V.4 of *Aquinas*.

[14] With Koppelman 71 at n. 94 compare the statement of Darwin's friend and colleague, the leading American botanist and evolutionist Asa Gray, in 1874: 'Let us recognize Darwin's great service to Natural Science in bringing back to it teleology; so that, instead of Morphology *versus* Teleology, we shall have Morphology wedded to Teleology.' And Darwin's response: 'What you say about Teleology pleases me especially, and I do not think any one else has ever noticed the point.' For the sources and illuminating discussion of related sources and issues, see Kass, 'Teleology and Darwin's *The Origin of Species*: Beyond Chance and Necessity?' at 97–8. [And see essay V.1 (2009c), sec. I.]

[15] Koppelman more than once cites Patterson, 'Children of Lesbian and Gay Parents' as his authority for stating that 'studies...have found' e.g. that 'children raised by same-sex couples develop just as well as...children of opposite-sex couples' (58 n. 34, 64 n. 66). The slenderness of the bases for this 'finding' is stated even in Patterson's own article at 1028–9 and 1036:

> systematic empirical study of these issues is just beginning....Studies in this area [sc. gay fathers] are still rather scarce....the preponderance of research to date has focussed on children who were born in the context of heterosexual marriages, whose parents divorced, and whose mothers

the manifestly sophistical argument that laws acknowledging or defining marriage as a relationship between a man and a woman[16] discriminate irrationally on grounds of sex.[17] One can, however, learn something from observing how comprehensively the traditional ethics of sexuality can be, and is, misstated by scholars who critique it in the name of more (Boswell and Koppelman) or less (Noonan) radical reform. In secs II and III I shall consider that critique. In sec. IV I shall sketch an argument re-stating the relationship between that traditional ethics of sexuality and the good of marriage. In sec. V I shall say something about same-sex imitations or caricatures of marriage.

II

In his immensely influential book *Contraception*, which manifests a familiarity with Aquinas's works far greater than Boswell's or Koppelman's, John Noonan claimed that for Aquinas it is a sin, 'at least venial', to seek pleasure in marital intercourse.[18]

---

have identified themselves as lesbians.... Two reports (McCandlish, 1987; Steckel, 1987) have focused on children born to lesbians in the context of ongoing lesbian relationships. Of [sic] the many other ways in which children might come to be brought up by lesbian or gay parents (e.g. through foster parenting, adoptive parenting, coparenting, or multiple parenting arrangements), no systematic research has yet appeared.... most [studies] compare children in divorced lesbian mother-headed families with children in divorced heterosexual mother-headed families.... A particularly notable weakness of existing research has been the tendency in most studies to compare development among children of a group of divorced lesbian mothers, many of whom are living with lesbian partners, to that among children of a group of divorced heterosexual mothers who are not currently living with heterosexual partners.

As was the case with divorce's now well-documented bad effects on children, it may take some decades for sociological research to catch up with realities which were always predictable and predicted by reflective and morally sensitive common sense.

[16] In this essay I shall not be considering what the law is or should be. For much information and good sense on those issues, see David Orgon Coolidge, 'Same-Sex Marriage? *Baehr v. Miike* and the Meaning of Marriage'.

[17] The sophism is easily detected once one realizes that 'discriminates on grounds of sex' is shorthand primarily for 'discriminates against women (and in favor of men) on the grounds that they are female, or against men (and in favor of women) on the grounds that they are male.' Of course, anti-discrimination laws characteristically embrace (sometimes justifiably) certain secondary forms of 'discrimination', viz. distinction between persons on the basis or grounds of certain characteristics (other than maleness or femaleness) which de facto are possessed only or disproportionately by males [or, as the case may be, females]. But even this secondary sense of 'discrimination on grounds of sex' still has nothing to do with distinguishing the relationship between husband and wife from all other forms of relationship on the ground that only a husband-wife relationship can be *marriage* (and that marriage deserves a kind and degree of legal support which other partnerships do not). Koppelman goes some way towards recognizing and conceding this in his remarks about 'the underlying purposes of sex-discrimination law' and in his evident unease in the face of the thought 'that discrimination against gays has nothing to do with sexism as such', in Koppelman, 'Three Arguments for Gay Rights' at 1662 and n. 113. Arguments that distinguishing marriage from heterosexual or homosexual concubinage is per se discriminating in favour of men are a sign of desperation.

[18] Noonan, *Contraception: A History of Its Treatment by the Catholic Theologians and Canonists*, 250 (the view that 'labeled the intention to seek pleasure in intercourse as venial... was held steadily

It is in fact quite clear that Aquinas thought it entirely reasonable to be interested in and motivated by the prospect of enjoying the pleasures of marital sexual intercourse.[19] Noonan is well aware of this. So he holds that Aquinas simply contradicts himself (within a couple of pages!) on the propriety of seeking sexual pleasure.[20] No such contradiction exists. The only text which Noonan cites to support his claim that Aquinas rejects sexual pleasure as a legitimate motive for marital intercourse is a text concerned, quite explicitly, with a rather different question: Is it wrong to make sexual pleasure one's *sole* motive in or for intercourse?[21] The answer is, Yes. But only after a careful explanation of what it means to make pleasure one's *exclusive* motive. In relation to intercourse between spouses, that means one or other of two kinds of thing, says Aquinas. At best, one is not interested in or concerned with anything about one's spouse other than what one would be concerned with in a prostitute or gigolo;[22] in other words, one's sexual activity is seeking, not to express affection for or commitment to the one person who is one's spouse, but to get pleasure. It is de-personalized, and de-maritalized. There is a worse kind of case: one is so concerned with pleasure alone that one *would be willing* to engage in intercourse with some other attractive and available person, even someone not one's spouse. In this case the pleasure-driven de-personalizing and

by... Thomas, *On the Sentences* 4.31.2.3'); 294 ('Why was it, according to Thomas, at least venial sin to seek pleasure?'); 295.

[19] See *Sent.* IV d.31 q.1 a.1 ad 1 (= *Supp.* q.49 a.1 ad 1): as hunger makes us interested in eating {ad excitandum ad comestionem}, so divine providence has attached pleasure to marital intercourse to interest us in engaging in generative types of act {ad excitandum ad actum...}; d.26 q.1 a.4 obj.5 and ad 5 (= *Supp.* q.41 a.4 obj.5 and ad 5); *Supp.* q.65 a.4 ad 3 (cf. *Sent.* IV d.33 q.1 a.3 sol.2 ad 3). Morally good marital intercourse shares with other sex acts the choice and purpose {propositum} of orgasmic pleasure {talem delectationem}: see *ST* II–II q.152 a.1c. See also *Ver.* q.25 a.5 ad 7: when what is rightly desired has been settled by reason [sc. intercourse between us as soon as appropriate, as an act of marital *fides*], then even though one's bodily appetite is aroused towards it there is nothing wrong with all that {tametsi sensualitas in id feratur, nullum erit peccatum}. Universally, 'part of the fullness of the morally good is that one is moved to the good [with which a particular act is concerned] not only by one's will but also by one's sense appetites, one's flesh:' I–II q.24 a.3c. And universally, 'it is natural to us as rational animals that our power of desiring {[vis] concupiscibilis} be drawn towards what is sensually enjoyable {in delectabile sensus} in line with reasonable order {secundum ordinem rationis}': *Mal.* q.4 a.2 ad 4 [or: ad 1].

[20] *Contraception*, 294 ('A contradiction existed between [Aquinas's] statement [*Sent.* 4.31.1.1] that God intends sexual pleasure to be an inducement and [his] statement [*Sent.* 4.31.2.3] that to act for sexual pleasure in marriage is evil.') Noonan offers to resolve the contradiction for Aquinas by suggesting that Aquinas should, on his own principles, abandon the first of these two [alleged] statements (which, Noonan oddly thinks, 'was a departure from Aristotelian principle')! (*Ibid.*)

[21] *Sent.* IV d.31 q.2 a.3 (= *Supp.* q.49 a.6): the question in issue is defined at the beginning of the article as to what extent it is sinful 'for someone to have intercourse with his wife, *not intending the [or: a] good of marriage* but ONLY pleasure [*solam delectationem*]'. The reference to pleasure being the sole motivation is repeated throughout the discussion (see objs. 1, 2, and 4), though occasional references (e.g. obj.3) to 'for the sake of pleasure' show that the latter phrase is, in this context, to be taken narrowly, as equivalent to 'for the sake only of pleasure, and without any interest in a marital good'.

[22] *Sent.* IV d.31 q.2 a.3 (= *Supp.* q.49 a.6) ad 1: 'nihil aliud in ea [sc. uxore] attendit quam quod in meretrice attenderet'.

de-maritalizing has gone so far that one's sex acts, even though they are in fact with one's spouse, are a kind of adultery, a serious violation of the good of marriage.

That is what Aquinas means by having sex precisely 'for the sake of pleasure', that is, *solely* for the sake of pleasure—for pleasure *alone*. His condemnation of such de-personalized and de-maritalized sex acts is completely compatible with his constant thesis that pleasure is a proper, indeed providentially appointed,[23] motive for engaging in marital intercourse. Moreover, Aquinas's objection to de-personalized sex has no exclusive connection with pleasure, and manifests no special suspicion of pleasure. For he makes it clear that there is the same kind of wrong— and venial or serious, depending on how far one's act is de-maritalized— whenever one's motive for engaging in intercourse is *solely* one's health[24] or *solely* 'cooling off', that is, the reduction of one's own temptations to extramarital sex.[25]

At the end of his main discussion of this kind of sexual immorality, Aquinas says that *in acts of such a kind*[26] one 'becomes "all flesh"'.[27] A sign of Noonan's far-reaching misunderstanding of Aquinas's entire account of sex is his remark (citing this passage) that Aquinas

treats Augustine as his teacher on the effects of sexual acts. He repeats the Augustinian epigram that in coitus man 'becomes all flesh'.[28]

Even in Augustine, however, the 'epigram' concerns not coitus (sexual intercourse), which might be morally good or bad, but *immoral* sex acts: in the relevant passage in Augustine the immorality is fornication (especially though not only as or with a prostitute); in Aquinas, as we have seen, it is having sex with one's spouse as if he or she were a prostitute. Aquinas is perfectly clear: an authentically marital act of sexual intercourse is an act which, so far from rendering the spouses 'all flesh', enhances their spiritual friendship with God.[29] Such a misreading bodes ill for Noonan's understanding of Aquinas's sex ethics—indeed, of the whole tradition's.

[23] See n. 19 above.
[24] *Sent.* IV d.31 q.2 a.2 (= *Supp.* q.49 a.5c) ad 4.   [25] *Ibid.*, ad 2.
[26] *Sent.* IV d.31 q.2 a.3 (= *Supp.* q.49 a.6c) ad 4: 'in illo actu'; *illo* ('that') refers back to the objection, which defines the kind(s) of act in question as having intercourse with one's spouse 'simply from sexual desire [or lust]' (*sola libidine*).
[27] *Contraception*, 254. The internal quotation, which Noonan does not identify, is a stock mediaeval paraphrase of Augustine, *Sermon* 162 (al. frag. 3 n. 2), *PL* 38 col. 887 ('sed simul totus homo dici possit quod caro sit'), reflecting on why St Paul in I Corinthians 6: 18 considers fornication to be a sin against one's own body.
[28] *Ibid.* (the citation to ad 3 is a slip for ad 4).
[29] *Sent.* IV d.26 q.1 a.4c (= *Supp.* q.41 a.4c), a text never cited by Noonan, though it is fundamental, and includes a treatment of precisely the same problem as the later 'all flesh' passage in *Supp.* 49, 6. The whole matter is clear enough already (about forty years before these writings of Aquinas) in the gloss on Lombard by Alexander of Hales (whose work influenced Aquinas), *Sent.* IV d.31

Noonan's mistakes about pleasure as a motive are tightly linked with a more important thesis—and a more profound mistake. Aquinas, he says,

is defending the proposition that only a procreative purpose excuses coitus.... Coitus is naturally ordained for procreation, and nothing else.[30]

Koppelman, too, claims that for Aquinas 'reproduction is... the only good that humans can pursue by the use of their sexual faculties' and desires for other goods are unnatural. But the very passage cited here by Noonan is sufficient to dispose of both Noonan's and Koppelman's claims. For it is in fact defending the contrary proposition: that marital intercourse is made right *not only* by the spouses' interest in the good of offspring (procreation) *but also*, and alternatively, by their interest in the good Aquinas calls *fides*—that is, by either of

those *two* goods of marriage which [unlike the third good of (Christian) marriage, *sacramentum*] concern the act of marital intercourse. And so, when spouses come together [sexually] in the hope of procreating children OR so that they may give each other what each is entitled to, which is a matter of *fides*, they are [each] completely free from wrongdoing.[31]

Indeed, in the same passage, Aquinas adds that if spouses have intercourse simply out of the natural impulse to have children, their act is morally 'imperfect unless it is further directed towards *some* marital good'.[32] Coitus, in other words, is naturally ordained for *marriage*, and nothing

---

para. 10f (in relation to the meritoriousness of the marital act): 'Though there is more *unity* in marital sexual intercourse than there is in fornication, there is no more *carnality*; so it is in deeds of lust, *and not in the marital act*, that "man is all flesh"' ('In opere coniugali maior est unio [than in fornication], quia unitas fidei et unitas sacramenti. Sed licet maior sit unitas, non tamen maior carnalitas; unde in opere libidinoso est homo totus caro, *non autem in opere matrimoniale*'). There is another passage where Aquinas employs the phrase 'totus homo caro efficitur': *Sent*. IV d.27 q.3 a.1 sol.1c (= *Supp*. q.66 a.1c). Here what 'makes one all flesh' is again not coition as such, still less authentically marital intercourse, but *concupiscentia*, the lust that incites someone to bigamy; that lust can be completely absent from those who are content with one wife and need not be present in those who legitimately remarry after the death of their spouse (see *Sent*. IV d.42 q.3 (= *Supp*. q.63) a.1c; in the special context of the mediaeval canon-law rules about restrictions on priestly ordination being considered in *Supp*. q.66 a.1, even a legitimate second marriage was, however, treated (i) as being defective as a sign of Christ's unity with his Church, and similarly (ii) as, *in the order of public signs*, suggestive of a lack of freedom from the lust which 'makes one all flesh', even if in fact in the given case no such lust were present).

[30] *Contraception*, 242, citing *Sent*. IV d.31 q.2 a.2 [*Supp*. q.49 a.5]. Jordan, *Invention of Sodomy*, 156 makes the same fundamental mistake, similarly associated with his own (similar) mistakes (143, 156) about Aquinas's views on intensity of sexual pleasure : see n. 52 below.

[31] *Sent*. IV d.31 q.2 a.2c [*Supp*. q.49 a.5c].

[32] *Supp*. q.49 a.1 ad 1. The preceding sentence, taken out of context, can be misread as asserting that marital intercourse must be directed, by actual or habitual intention, to offspring considered as pertaining to a marital good. But Aquinas says this only because he is considering the case of spouses who happen to be moved by the raw natural *reproductive instinct* {motus naturae}; these spouses, he is saying, will be acting to some extent wrongly unless they integrate their instinct with the intelligible, *marital* good of having and raising a child to be educated towards human fulfilment.

else; and marriage, as Thomas constantly teaches, is ordained for something—another particular marital good—besides procreation.[33]

What is this marital good, which Aquinas considers a good and sufficient motive for marital intercourse even when the marital good he calls offspring (*proles*: procreation) is not intended or possible? What is it, for example, that enables a married couple, as Aquinas says, to return 'with joy' (*laetantes*) to marital intercourse after a period of abstinence? It is the good known in the tradition which Aquinas is following as *fides*. That is the word for faith or fidelity, but Aquinas's explanations of it in the marital context make it plain that it cannot safely be translated 'fidelity'. For 'fidelity' in modern English signifies the real but negative good of not being unfaithful—of not committing adultery. But *fides* in Aquinas is also a motive. Indeed, in a sequence of passages partly overlooked and partly misunderstood by Noonan,[34] Aquinas indicates that it is the motive which is present in *every* genuinely marital act of intercourse, whereas other motives such as procreation are sometimes present and sometimes not.

---

[33] For a contemporary argument in the spirit of Aquinas that it is wrong for even married people to engage in sexual intercourse or other acts *purely* for the purpose of conceiving a child and apart from the good of marriage itself, see George and Bradley, 'Marriage and the Liberal Imagination' at 305 n. 19 (on Henry VIII).

[34] *Sent.* IV d.31 q.1 a.2 and q.2 a.2 (= *Supp.* q.49 a.2 and a.4). Citing the first of these two passages, Noonan, *Contraception*, 285, claims that Aquinas

says of 'matrimony'—*not of marital intercourse*—that... 'On the part of the act itself, it is good in its genus in that it falls on due matter; and thus there is set as a good of marriage fidelity, whereby a man approaches his own wife, and not another woman.' This analysis would seem to have been transferable to the act of intercourse. (*On the Sentences* 4.31.1.2 [= *Supp.* 49, 2]).

Indeed, the analysis is thus transferable. According to Noonan (*ibid.*), however, Aquinas (without ever discussing the matter) assumed that it was not transferable, that 'the analysis was not applicable to coitus'. But in reality, in *Supp.* q.49 a.4 (on the page after *Supp.* q.49 a.2) Aquinas asserts clearly that it is transferable—that the analysis of marital 'goods' applicable to marriage is precisely applicable to sexual intercourse and, when so applied, establishes why marital intercourse is decent, good, morally right, and meritorious. This second passage is dealing precisely with the question 'whether the marital act can be made completely right by *the aforesaid goods*', i.e. the marital goods identified in a.2 and discussed in a.2 and a.3. The *corpus* of the reply in a.4 answers, without equivocation, that 'the aforesaid goods'—i.e. the very ones named in a.2 (the article quoted by Noonan)—make the act good, i.e. entirely free from wrong . 'This is what *fides* and offspring do *in the marriage act* {in actu matrimonii}, *as indicated above* {ut ex dictis patet}.' 'Above', as editors agree, means a.2. So Noonan has not only overlooked a.4c but also misread a.2c, for he understood a.2c's phrase 'on the part of the act itself' to refer only to the act of marrying, whereas it in fact extended to the act of marital intercourse (although that act is not the primary topic of a.2, as it is of a.4). Surprisingly, a.4c is never cited in *Contraception*, which cites the almost adjacent articles preceding—q.49 a.1 (twice), a.2 (twice)—and the adjacent articles following—a.5 (four times), and a.6 (five times). The book even cites a.4 ad 3—the reply to the third objection in the article in question—a couple of inches from the decisive text. But that text—the subject-matter, the question, and the body of the response—is passed over in complete silence. So too is the immediately preceding article, a.3 which also teaches what Noonan is denying, viz. that for Aquinas *fides* is a good which pertains not only to marriage itself but also *ad usum matrimonii*, i.e. to the act of marital intercourse. And, as we have seen above, when he cites a.5 he claims it says the exact opposite ('only for procreation') of what it in fact says ('either for procreation or for *fides*').

Fides is the disposition and commitment of each of the spouses to 'cleave to {accedere}'[35]—precisely, to *be maritally* and thus *bodily united with*—the other and no other person.[36] Besides the negative commitment *not* to be maritally or in any other way sexually united to anyone other than one's spouse ('fidelity'),[37] *fides* even more basically includes a positive commitment and willingness, a reason *for* action.[38] This is nothing less than the key to understanding Aquinas's account of sexual morality. *Fides* is, indeed, the characteristic proximate object(ive) or 'appropriate matter about which {debita materia [circa quam]}' we are engaged when we choose to engage in marital intercourse, even on those occasions when we also have explicitly or implicitly the hope of procreating.[39] This positive *fides* is the willingness and commitment to belong to, and be united in mind *and body* with, one's spouse in the distinct form of *societas* and friendship[40] which we call marriage.[41]

This *societas* is a unique type of relationship; it is unified by its dual point {finis}: the procreation, nurture, and education of children, and the full

---

[35] *Accedere* has a wide range of meanings around 'approach' and 'adhere to', and importantly includes 'have sexual intercourse with' (e.g. as in fornication: I–II q.73 a.7c; *ScG* III, c.122 n.1 [2947]). Its meaning in respect of marital *fides* is clearly very closely analogous to its meaning in one of Aquinas's central theological propositions, viz. that it is by *fides* that one can adhere to {accedere} God (*Sent.* IV d.45 q.1 a.2 sol.1c (= *Supp.* 69 a.4c); *ST* I–II q.113 a.4c; II–II q.7 a.2); and it is virtually synonymous with the *adhaerere* by which man and woman leave their respective parents and 'cling/cleave to each other and become two in one flesh' (Genesis 2: 24; Matthew 19: 5): see *ST* II–II q.26 a.11c and ad 1 and ad s.c.[4].

[36] *Sent.* IV d.31 q.1 a.2c (= *Supp.* q.49 a.2c) (see n. 39 below); *In I Cor.* 7.1 ad v. 2 [318].

[37] In true, central-case marriage, this commitment is completely open-ended in the sense that it excludes any sexual act with anyone other than one's spouse during his or her whole lifetime.

[38] *Sent.* IV d.31 q.1 a.2 ad 3 (= *Supp.* q.49 a.2 ad 3): 'as the promise involved in marriage includes that each party will not go to {accedere ad} anyone else's bed, so too it includes this: that they *will give* each other due bodily cooperation in marital intercourse {quod sibi invicem debitum reddant} —and *this latter is the more basic* {principalius}, since it follows precisely from the mutual power which each confers on the other. And so each [of the two obligations, positive as well as negative] is a matter of *fides*.'

[39] *Sent.* IV d.31 q.1 a.2c (= *Supp.* q.49 a.2c): the act [of marital intercourse] is a morally good kind of act because it has an appropriate object, namely the *fides* by which a man cleaves to his wife and to no other woman [and a woman to her husband and no other man] {actus ... est bonus in genere ex hoc quod cadit supra debitam materiam; et sic est *fides*, per quam homo ad suam accedit, et non ad aliam} (for the translation of *supra debitam materiam* see *Sent.* II d.36 a.5c; *Mal.* q.2 a.4 ad 5 and ad 9, a.6c and a.7 ad 8, q.7 a.1c, and q.10 a.1c; *ST* I–II q.20 a.1 and a.2); and see *Sent.* IV d.31 q.1 a.1c and a.2c (= *Supp.* q.49 a.4c and a.5c), where what is said in *Sent.* IV d.31 q.1 a.2c (= *Supp.* q.49 a.2c) about the nature and good of *fides* in relation to marriage itself is shown to be equally and explicitly applicable to the 'marital act' of intercourse.

[40] *Sent.* IV d.41 q.1 a.1 sol.1c (= *Supp.* q.55 a.1c). *In Eth.* VIII. 12 nn. 18–24 [1719–24] explains in terms of friendship {amicitia} the whole justice, usefulness, pleasure {delectatio in actu generationis}, and delight {amicitia iucunda} in shared virtue which can be found in a good marriage with its division of complementary roles. *Sent.* IV d.33 q.1. a.1c (= *Supp.* q.65 a.1c) recalls this treatment when identifying *fides* as one of the two natural goods and ends of marriage. So *fides* is essentially marital friendship.

[41] *Sent.* IV d.33 q.1 a.1c and a.3 sol.3c (=*Supp.* q.65 a.1c and a.5c).

sharing of life in a home.[42] It is a companionship {societas} which should, Aquinas thinks, be

the greatest friendship, for they are united to each other not only in the act of bodily uniting in sexual intercourse {carnalis copulatio}, which even among lower animals creates a kind of delightful {suavis: sweet} *societas*, but also in mutual help {mutuum obsequium} in sharing together in the whole way of life of a household {ad totius domesticae conversationis consortium}.[43]

So, *fides* is a motive, a reason, *for* many cooperative acts intrinsic or incidental to a sharing in the 'whole life' of the marital household. As a rational *motive for* choosing to participate in an act of marital intercourse it is simply, we can say, the intended good of experiencing and in a particular way actualizing,[44] and enabling one's spouse to experience and in a particular way actualize, the good of marriage—of our marriage precisely as our being bound,[45] and belonging, to each other in *such* an exclusive and permanent

---

[42] *Sent*. IV d.27 q.1 a.1 sol.1c (= *Supp.* q.44 a.1c): marriage is oriented to 'some one thing {ad aliquod unum}', but the one thing is two things, each radically unifying and mutually reinforcing as, together, the point of marriage: *una generatio et educatio prolis* and *una vita domestica*. These two 'ends' of marriage define it, but there are other benefits intrinsic to it (other 'secondary' ends besides mutual help); one of these is the multiplication of friendship by non-incestuous marriages which link two families: *Sent*. IV d.40 (= *Supp.* q.54) a.3c. But the most important or intrinsic of these supplementary secondary ends or benefits is 'the healing of one's desires {remedium concupiscentiae}': d.33 q.2 a.1 (= *Supp.* q.67 a.1) ad 4. This is not a matter of simply providing sexual release; on the contrary, desires which are simply 'given an outlet' only grow in strength (*ST* II–II q.151 a.2 ad 2; a.3 ad 2; *Sent*. IV d.2 q.1 a.1 sol.2c; d.26 q.2 (= *Supp.* q.42) a.3 ad 4). Rather, and crucially, it is a matter of integrating sexual desire with reason, which is what one does when one chooses intercourse in order to actualize and experience the good of marriage, i.e. for the sake of begetting children and/or of marital *fides*. When sex is thus made marital by integration with the marital goods {bona matrimonii} it is 'healed' by being given intelligent meaning, and then the satisfaction it can give does 'restrain' the desire which now is directed by reason(s) {ratione ordinatur}: d.26 q.2 (= *Supp.* q.42) a. 3 ad 4. Desire so 'restrained' by integration with reason can issue in satisfaction (pleasure) of the most intense kind: *ST* I q.98 a.2 ad 3.

[43] *ScG* III, c.123 n.6 [2964]. On the tight link between conjugal friendship/love {amicitia}—the mutual love or even love affair {mutua amatio} between spouses—and that mutual help in life which is the marital benefit peculiar to the spouses, see *Sent*. IV d.26 q.2 (= *Supp.* q.42) a.2c; d.29 q.1 a.3 sol.2 (= *Supp.* q.47 a.4) ad 1. On the tight link between mutual help and the good of offspring (such that the former can be regarded as a secondary end implicit in the latter), see *Sent*. IV d.31 q.1 (= *Supp.* q.49) a.2 ad 1. On the love {dilectio} that properly exists between spouses—the strongest of all forms of love between human beings—see also II–II q.26 a.11c; *In Eph.* 5.9 ad v. 29 [328]. On marital intercourse (*understood always as a kind of continuation, expression, and experiencing of the common commitment to a shared and, where possible, procreative life*) as a cause of marital friendship, see *Sent*. IV d.41 a.1 sol.1c (= *Supp.* q.55 a.1c); as a cause of love {amor ex commixtione}, *ST* II–II q.154 a.9c; as a primary motive for the love between spouses, II–II q.26 a.11 ad s.c.[4]. For Aquinas's remarkable analysis of the passionate *effects* of love, an analysis implicitly but manifestly on the paradigm of spousal love as a fitting cause of marital intercourse, see I–II q.28 a.5c. On beauty as an appropriate occasion of sexual attraction which can appropriately lead to considering marriage; such marriages can be good ones (and outlast bodily beauty): III *Sent*. d.2 q.2 a.1 sol.1c.

[44] Note that to say that marital intercourse actualizes marriage does not imply that a marriage, having been consummated by such intercourse, cannot be very appropriately and amply actualized in many other ways as well.

[45] See *ScG* IV, c.78 n.5 [4123]: *fides*, by which man and wife are bound to each other {sibi invicem obligantur}.

cooperative relationship.[46] Each of us is entitled to the other's cooperation in such acts, provided there is no reason[47] for abstaining. So, truly marital intercourse is literally an act of justice, of giving each other what he or she can reasonably *expect* to be given.[48] And that does not prevent it being also an act of love.[49] It is an act which we can enter into with joy {laetantes};[50] the fact that it can give the greatest of all[51] bodily pleasures {delectatio intensissima} in no way makes it unreasonable;[52] there is nothing wrong at

[46] Because marriage is a type of relationship unified and specified by a single, basic human good, it makes sense even when one aspect of that complex good happens to be unattainable. So a man and a woman past the age of child-bearing can marry, and the integration of their sexual desires by the good of marital *fides* makes their marital sexual intercourse reasonable and morally good: *Sent.* IV d.34 a.2 (= *Supp.* q.58 a.1) ad 3.

[47] e.g. the health of either party: *Sent.* IV d.32 (= *Supp.* q.64) a.1 ad 1 and ad 2. Of course, the two-sided good of marriage itself provides many reasons, intelligible in themselves without invention, for spouses to abstain from sexual intercourse, e.g. when either of them is disinclined or unwell, or they lack the time or privacy appropriate, or when abstaining for a time will intensify mutual satisfaction, and so forth.

[48] *Sent.* IV d.26 q.1 (= *Supp.* q.41) a.4c; d.31 (= *Supp.* q.49) a.2 ad 2; see also d.38 q.1 a.3 sol.2 (= *Supp.* q.53 a.1) ad 3.

[49] The spouses' mutual commitment {pactio} which *fides* serves is properly a bond of love {vinculum amoris} (*In Is.* 7 ad v. 14 line 436); indeed 'spouse' is a word used to signify love (In *Matt.* 9 ad v. 15 [769]). Since *fides* is not merely negative but also positive, to speak of greater *fides* is to speak of greater love {fidelior amor}: see *ScG* III, c.123 n.,8 [2966]. See also n. 43 above.

[50] *In I Cor.* 7.1 ad v. 5 [325]. Note: this thought—that spouses who have been abstaining will return to marital intercourse with joy—is Aquinas's own contribution, not suggested by the text on which he is there commenting; for other sources of the thought see *ibid.*, ad v. 2 [319]; I–II q.105 a.4c (on Deuteronomy 24: 5).

[51] II–II q.152 a.1c; and see *Quodl.* XII q.13 a.1c; q.14 a. un. c [l. 53]. Note, incidentally, that Aquinas, appealing to the testimony of the eleventh-century Persian polymath Avicenna, takes it for granted that in marital intercourse the woman is not infrequently moved inwardly by orgasmic pleasure so vehemently that the neck of her womb temporarily opens up {ex delectatione, ut avicenna dicit, movetur et aperitur}: *Sent.* IV d.31 a.3 ex.

[52] II–II q.153 a.2 ad 2; *Sent.* IV d.26 q.1 a.3 ad 6 (= *Supp.* q.41 a.3 ad 6); d.31 q.2 a.1 ad 3 (= *Supp.* q.49 a.4 ad 3); I–II q.34 a.1 ad 1. Jordan, *The Invention of Sodomy*, 143 states that, for Aquinas, '[t]he present intensity of venereal pleasure is a penalty of the Fall (153.2 ad 2, ad 3)'; he then says (*ibid.*) that for Aquinas the vice of '*luxuria* is an excess of venereal pleasure'. The reader is thus invited to accept that Aquinas thinks the vice in morally bad sex is that it is too intensely pleasurable; indeed, the very last words (p. 176) of Jordan's book are: '"Sodomy" is the nervous refusal of theologians to understand how pleasure can survive the preaching of the Gospel.' But this is all wrong. Aquinas teaches quite plainly that no increase in the quantity or intensity of pleasure makes a kind of pleasurable act bad. Indeed, that is the unambiguous thesis of the first passage cited by Jordan (*ST* II–II q.153 a.2 ad 2):

the virtuous 'mean' [between too much and too little] is not a matter of quantity but of appropriateness to right reason. And so the abundance of pleasure given by reasonable sex acts is not contrary to the virtuous mean {et ideo abundantia delectationis quae est in actu venereo secundum rationis ordinato, non contrariatur medio virtutis}.

The 'penalty of the Fall' which Aquinas goes on to speak of in that passage and in the other passage (ad 3) cited by Jordan is precisely *not* that sex acts are now too intensely pleasurable, but that we now find it difficult to *integrate* or harmonize our sexual desires and pleasure with reason's moderation. And this 'moderation' is, again, not a matter of *less* (less intense) pleasure. Aquinas makes this as plain as could be in his full-dress treatment of the consequences of the Fall in *ST* I q.98 a.2 ad 3:

in the state of innocence [before the Fall] there would have been nothing of this kind [sc. the pleasure of coitus and the heat of desire] which would not have been moderated by reason—*not that there would have been less of these pleasures of the senses*, as some people claim (indeed, the sensory pleasure [of sex] would have been greater, in proportion to the greater purity of human

all with our welcoming assent to such pleasure in the marital act;[53] nor in our being motivated towards such an act just by the prospect of giving and sharing in that delight as token of our marital commitment.[54]

Once one sees that, for Aquinas, marital intercourse has an intelligible, rational point—the spouses' expression and actualization of their mutual commitment in marriage—one can readily see also that it followed inevitably, for Aquinas, that spouses act quite reasonably in seeking and taking pleasure in such intercourse. For throughout the whole order of things (as Aristotle had made abundantly clear)[55] we find that reasonable, morally decent action tends to be accompanied and certainly is perfected in pleasurable fulfilment {fruitio}.[56] Only when it is unhinged from consistency with practical reason's requirements does the pursuit of pleasure become morally defective.

III

The massive misunderstanding of Aquinas on sexual pleasure and on the goods which give reason for marital intercourse is tightly linked with another misunderstanding, which provides a primary and recurring theme of Koppelman's article. According to this misunderstanding or misreading (in Koppelman's version of it), Aquinas's sex ethics rests on the premise that one should not depart from 'the patterns laid down in nature' or 'what ordinarily and typically happens in nature' (32, 33); 'any departure from the natural order is a defiance of God's will' (32).

---

nature and the greater sensitivity of human bodies [before the Fall]), but rather that desire, being regulated by reason, would not have pursued this sort of pleasure in such disordered ways {ita inordinate}, and would not have clung to pleasure immoderately. *And when I say 'immoderately' I mean unreasonably* {praeter mensuram rationis}. For those who consume food 'with moderation' do not have less pleasure in eating than gluttons do; it's just that their desire is less fixated on that sort of pleasure. And this is in line with Augustine's thought that what was incompatible with the state of innocence was *not great quantities of pleasure* {magnitudinem delectationis} but rather the burning of lust, and confusion of mind and will {inquietudinem animi}.

That passage is from one of Aquinas's late works; in one of his earliest he maintains the same position: before the Fall damaged humankind's inner harmony of feelings with reason (see *ST* I–II q.82 a.2 ad 2; *In Rom.* 5. 3 ad v. 12 [416]), the pleasure given by sex acts would have been 'much less disproportionate to rational control [than now]', but simply in terms of pleasure {absolute} 'would have been *greater pleasure*': *Sent.* II d.20 q.1 a.2 ad 2. Jordan's misreading of *ST* II–II q.153 a.2 ad 2 goes further, for according to that very text, the fact that that *marital* intercourse is or can be *so intensely delightful* {abundantia delectationis} that it temporarily disables the spouses from thinking of spiritual matters {ad spiritualia consideranda} does *not* make it morally defective. See likewise Sent IV d.26 q.1 (= *Supp.* q.41) a.3 ad 6; q.2 a.1 (= *Supp.* q.49 a.4) ad 3.

[53] *Mal.* q.15 a.2 ad 17.   [54] See n. 19 above.
[55] Cf. Noonan's allusion to 'Aristotelean principle': see n. 20 above.
[56] See e.g. *ST* I–II q.31 a.1, a.3, a.7.

A teleological account of this kind appears to be the only way to account for Aquinas's conclusion elsewhere [that is, in *ST* II–II q.154 a.12] that homosexual intercourse is one of the worst vices of lust...(32)

Noonan, too, maintains that Aquinas's discussion of 'unnatural' sexual vice has assumptions which

are made explicit in [*ST* II–II q.154 a.12].... [T]he *order of reason is strikingly contrasted with the order of nature.* Nature is conceived in a special way as sacred and unchangeable. Fornication and adultery violate what 'is determined by right reason.' The sin against nature violates what is 'determined by nature.' Violation of this natural order is an affront to God, though 'no other person is injured.'... The *sharp distinction between acts that offend the natural order and acts that offend the rational order* goes back to a distinction in types of natural law.[57]

This thoroughly misrepresents Aquinas's understanding of (i) immorality [sin], (ii) sexual immorality (a subclass of immoralities), and (iii) 'unnatural vice' (a subclass of sexual immoralities). The very first words in Aquinas's treatment of sexual immoralities in *Summa Theologiae* are 'immorality [sin], in human acts, is that which is against the order of reason'.[58] The same point is made at the very beginning of his treatments of sexual immoralities in *Summa contra Gentiles*[59] and *De Malo*.[60] At the outset of his main treatise on sex and marriage he had already made the point, in terms of the requirements of 'natural reason' (explicitly contrasted with animal nature).[61] In *Summa Theologiae* Aquinas repeats the point again and again: 'it pertains to the very essence of sexual vice {luxuria} that it exceeds the order and way of reason';[62] 'the immorality of sexual vice {peccatum luxuriae} *consists in* this: that one is not using sexual pleasure in line with right reason {non secundum rectam rationem}'.[63] The vices against nature, which are Noonan's (and Koppelman's) concern, are introduced as the *very first category to exemplify being 'out of accord with right reason* {non convenire rationi rectae}'.[64]

In the article immediately before the one on which Noonan and Koppelman focus, Aquinas again repeats the point that in common with all other sexual vices, the vice *'called* against nature' is 'repugnant to right reason {repugnat rationi rectae}'.[65] Then he adds that this sort of sexual vice, 'over and above this [first-mentioned repugnancy to reason], is also repugnant to the natural order of sexual acts itself, the order appropriate

---

[57] *Contraception*, 239, 240 (emphasis added, here as elsewhere unless otherwise noted).
[58] *ST* II–II q.153 a.2c. See also n. 4 above.
[59] *ScG* III, c.122. Here the argument is not explicitly about the order of reason, but about what is 'contrary to human good', and thus implicitly but necessarily unreasonable.
[60] *Mal.* q.15 a.1c.   [61] *Sent.* IV d.26 q.1. a.1c and ad 1 (= *Supp.* q.41 a.1c and ad 1).
[62] *ST* II–II q.153 a.3c.   [63] II–II q.154 a.1c.   [64] *Ibid.*   [65] II–II q.154, a.11c.

to the human species {etiam, super hoc, repugnat ipsi ordini naturali venerei actus qui convenit humanae specie}'.[66] The essay which Noonan and Koppelman cite (they both ignore *all* the other texts I have cited here) also begins by taking for granted what has already been interminably asserted, that unnatural sexual vice is vice because it offends right reason; as Aquinas will observe, other types of sexual immorality 'transgress only what is in line with right reason—but presupposing natural foundations {principia}'.[67] Unnatural sexual vice transgresses, he says, not only the requirements of right reason in relation to sex but also those requirements' very 'presuppositions, determined by nature'.[68]

This idea—that setting aside the naturally given foundations or presuppositions of reasonable judgments about sex acts makes what is unreasonable particularly serious or far-reaching in its implications for character—is doubtless in need of further explanation. But the task of providing such a further explanation is not very urgent, since (as Noonan and Koppelman fail to observe) this whole article (q.154 a.12) is concerned, *not* with why unnatural vice is wrong—that was the subject of the previous article, unmentioned by our authors—but only with the comparative *gravity* of types of act already assumed to be wrong. As Grisez regularly makes clear in relation to his own work, factors which aggravate the wrongness of an immoral choice cannot be assumed to be factors which by themselves would be capable of making the choice immoral.[69]

Pursuing his mistaken view that Aquinas's sex ethics is founded on respect for given nature, rather than on respect for reason and the human goods to which reason directs our choosing, Noonan says that, according to Aquinas:

God, not neighbour, is offended by the sin [against nature]. This approach put enormous emphasis on the *givenness* of the act of insemination; the act was invested with a God-given quality not to be touched by rational control or manipulation.... [T]he act seemed to be assigned the absolute value of God.... [T]he only person injured by the sin was God.[70]

But in exactly the same passages in *De Malo*, as Noonan acknowledges forty pages later, Aquinas 'had based his case against lechery' [*luxuria*, sexual vice—certainly including homosexual and other acts popularly called 'unnatural vice'] 'on the ground that it impedes *the good of* offspring'.[71] And at the head of his little treatise on sex ethics in the *Summa contra Gentiles*

---

[66] Ibid.   [67] *ST* II–II q.154 a.12c.   [68] Ibid.
[69] See e.g. *LCL* 649, 658. Aquinas indicates this in other contexts: e.g. *ST* I–II q.20 a.5; q.73 a.8. Thus: what makes lying always wrong does not always make it gravely wrong: *ST* II–II q.110 aa.3–4.
[70] *Contraception*, 241, citing *Mal.* q.15 aa.2–3.   [71] Ibid., 279.

(in a chapter often cited by Noonan, and partially quoted by Koppelman), Aquinas puts the statement (never mentioned by Noonan or Koppelman) that 'God is *not offended* by us {non enim Deus a nobis offenditur} except when we act *contrary to our good*'.[72] Like it or not, Aquinas holds that *all* sexual immoralities {omnes corruptiones luxuriae} are 'contrary to [love of] neighbour'.[73] He does not dispute that simple fornication (not an 'unnatural vice') does 'no injury to' neighbour.[74] But he argues[75] that all sexual immoralities outside marriage are wrongs 'against neighbour' because 'against the good-of-generating-and-educating-offspring'. His thought, I believe, is that all sexual immoralities are *against marriage*, which (as he elsewhere argues explicitly)[76] is the only reasonable context for having and raising children. The way in which unnatural acts, which can never themselves lead to children, offend against children, is explored below,[77] when more of Aquinas's thought, overlooked by Noonan and Koppelman, has been set out.

Koppelman's dependence on Noonan comes to the surface in his quotation and adoption of the passage of *Contraception* which claims that Aquinas

> postulated as normal an act of coitus which led to generation. The norm was not derived from any statistical compilation. It was the product of intuition... Because the sexual act might be generative, and because generation was an important function, the theologian intuited that generation was the normal function.... [A]cts in which insemination was impossible... were unnatural;... acts in which insemination was possible and conception resulted... were natural and normal;... acts in which insemination was possible, but conception did not occur... were normal,[78] but accidentally different from the norm.[79]

No text of Aquinas is cited in support of this, and none could be.[80] Aquinas knew enough to know as well as we do that generation does *not* normally (that is, on most occasions) follow insemination.

---

[72] *ScG* III, c.122 n.2. In c.126 n.1 he adds that 'only those things that are opposed to reason are prohibited by divine law'.

[73] *Mal.* q.15 a.2 ad 4.   [74] *Ibid.*, obj.4.   [75] *Ibid.*, ad 4.

[76] e.g. *ScG* II, c.122 nn.6–8.   [77] See text at n. 112 below.

[78] The sense of the passage requires that this be regarded as a slip of the pen for 'natural'. Koppelman fails to see that the unamended train of thought (and the conclusion that there is an abnormal normality) makes no sense.

[79] *Contraception*, 243.

[80] Aquinas's reference to *per accidens* in *ScG* c.122, quoted on the preceding page of *Contraception*, has nothing to do with deviation from a statistical norm, or from a postulated or intuited (imagined!) norm according to which generation normally follows insemination. *Per accidens* is a phrase which gets its sense by contrast with *per se* or *secundum se*. In relation to human acts the fundamental and usual meaning of this contrast is: [1] intended v. not intended—it has nothing to do with what does happen or typically happens. In c.122 the reference is a little wider than intended/unintended, and includes also [2] what in the nature of things is *possible* or *not possible*. But it also retains the primary sense of: [1] what, in the plans and intentions of an acting person, is to be left as possible or made to be impossible. Thus, in the emission of seed into the female reproductive tract where it is to be intentionally sterilized by a contraceptive jelly, the impossibility or reduced possibility of generation

The other intellectual debt which Koppelman acknowledges in his critique of Aquinas is to John Boswell; Koppelman cannot imagine 'how Aquinas could answer' Boswell's 'devastating critique'.[81] And indeed it is not easy to reply to Boswell's account and critique of Aquinas: his incompetence and deviousness are so pervasive that one hardly knows where to begin. So I shall take just the main passage cited by Koppelman, a passage which is in fact the high-water mark of Boswell's critique.

That passage (found in Boswell at pp. 324–5, cited by Koppelman at p. 74) examines, apparently rather closely, a portion of the *Summa Theologiae* which concerns, not morality, but the nature and types of pleasure. Aquinas is asking whether some pleasures are unnatural. He answers that there are two immediately relevant senses of 'natural'. In the first of these senses, something is natural to human beings just in as much as it is *reasonable* (rationally appropriate), and unnatural insofar as it is unreasonable. Boswell interjects that 'it is very difficult to see how homosexuality violates "nature"' in this sense, since 'it was precisely the reason of man which proponents of gay sexuality had recently used to defend themselves' against the argument from natural design or 'the physical compulsions of procreation'.[82] His comment is absurd, since Aquinas was happy to use his own reason to evaluate allegedly rational arguments proposed by opponents, and does so about 10,000 times in the *Summa Theologiae* alone. By the end of the page which Boswell is considering, Aquinas will have made clear that he thinks the copulation of men with each other is 'contrary to human nature' in this first sense, that is, is unreasonable, so that the pleasure the sodomites take in it, being the pleasure of an unreasonable, morally wrong kind of act, is unnatural. Aquinas by then has also identified a second sense of 'natural' viz. what is sub-rational, common to irrational animals as well as human beings, and/or what is not obedient to reason[83] (like hunger, or sexual desire); in this second sense, human beings 'naturally' take pleasure in sex acts. Boswell, having foolishly said that this distinction of senses is a contradiction, claims that in pointing to the second sense of 'natural', Aquinas is 'here providing the only substantiation for the claim that homosexual acts are "unnatural"'.[84] In reality, Aquinas is not

is [1] not incidental {per accidens} but intrinsic/intended {secundum se} (even if, in a given case, by chance, generation does follow). Equally, in the emission of seed into the mouth, the impossibility of generation is [2] not incidental {per accidens} but intrinsic {secundum se}.

[81] (35) at n. 102. The three reviewers cited in that note display little or no interest in defending Aquinas, and there is no need to search the world for efforts to do so. Boswell's work collapses as soon as one looks at the texts he cites from Aquinas.

[82] *Christianity, Social Tolerance, and Homosexuality*, 324–5.

[83] Boswell *ibid.*, 325, misunderstands this as claiming (absurdly) that sex and food 'have nothing to do with thought'!

[84] *Ibid.*

370   PART SIX: MARRIAGE, JUSTICE, AND THE COMMON GOOD

here arguing for or 'substantiating' the claim at all; this portion of the work is not concerned to substantiate any claim in normative ethics. He is merely illustrating uses of the term 'natural', in order to classify pleasures; where the classification turns on the reasonableness or unreasonableness of certain kinds of act, the argument about reasonableness is to be sought elsewhere (for example in the passages I mention in the next section).

But we now reach the high point of Boswell's efforts. He reports that Aquinas's discussion of natural and unnatural pleasures concludes with 'the startling revelation following the second definition that homosexuality may in fact be quite "natural" to a given individual, in either sense of the word'! After quoting a sentence in which Aquinas says that what is *contrary* to human nature (in either sense) 'may become natural to a particular man, owing to some defect of nature in him'—which Boswell wholly misreads as conceding that what in *this* sense is natural to these defective people is *also* natural in the sense of reasonable for them—Boswell concludes his description of the passage:

Although it may not be 'natural' for humans in general to be homosexual, it is apparently [according to Aquinas] quite 'natural' for particular individuals.

He calls this a 'circumstantial etiology of homosexuality', helps himself to the premise that 'everything which is in any way "natural" has a purpose, and the purpose is good',[85] and concludes triumphantly:

Since both homosexuality and femaleness occur 'naturally' in some individuals, neither can be said to be inherently bad, and both must have an end. The *Summa* does not speculate on what the 'end' of homosexuality might be, but this is hardly surprising in light of the prejudices of the day. It would seem that Saint Thomas would have been constrained to admit that homosexual acts were 'appropriate' to those whom he considered 'naturally' homosexual.[86]

Here incompetence and deviousness are inextricably entangled. What Aquinas means by 'homosexual acts are natural to some people' is immediately evident from the parts of his paragraph which Boswell has completely hidden from his readers.[87] The kinds of 'defect' (or rather

---

[85] *Ibid.*, 327. Here Boswell is (or leaves his readers) blissfully unaware of the distinctions between metaphysical goodness (e.g. strength of the rapist-strangler's hands) and moral goodness, and between different senses of nature (not all explored in the passage he is considering). He overlooks Aquinas's view (quite coherent with the rest of Aquinas's work) that e.g. some people do and others do not have a 'natural inclination towards certain sins' (*ST* I–II q.78 a.3c), and that 'There is in us all a natural inclination towards what is appealing to bodily feelings *against* the good of practical reasonableness {contra bonum rationis}' (*Mal.* q.16 a.2c.).

[86] *Ibid.*, 327 and n. 87.

[87] Boswell's pages are decorated with extensive quotations of lengthy passages, in Latin. Here the quotation (both in English and Latin) is drastically truncated, for a reason which (as I am now

corruption {corruptio}) that make certain pleasures natural to some individuals can arise, says Aquinas, in different ways:

bodily defects/corruptions: e.g. sickness, as when sweet things taste bitter to people with a fever; or a bad physical constitution, as in the case of people who take pleasure in eating dirt or coal, etc.; or mental defects/corruptions, as in the case of men who, from habituation [or: convention/upbringing {propter consuetudinem}] take pleasure in *eating people*, or in *copulating with brute beasts or with other men*, or in other things of that sort, which are not in line with human nature.[88]

Had Boswell accurately reported what Aquinas is here saying, readers would have greeted with derision his claims that Aquinas's 'circumstantial etiology' of homosexuality gives Aquinas (or anyone!) rational ground to consider homosexual acts appropriate and good. For the very same 'etiology' would immediately give similar(ly good) ground for approval of cannibalism and bestiality.

Boswell completes his corrupt travesty of Aquinas a couple of pages later. He is now arguing that Aquinas's position on homosexual conduct was largely a result of 'the pressures of popular antipathy' but also contributed to later hostility to homosexuality. So he makes the following accusation:

Aquinas played to his audience not simply by calling on popular conceptions of 'nature' but also by linking homosexuality to behaviour which was certain to evoke reactions of horror and fear. He compared homosexual acts...with violent or disgusting acts of the most shocking type, like cannibalism, bestiality, [n. cite to *ST* II–II q.142 a.4 ad 3] or eating dirt.[89]

To keep concealed from the reader what he had kept hidden in the passage about 'circumstantial etiology' (when he was concerned more to co-opt Aquinas than to denounce him), Boswell is now citing not that earlier passage (with its undisclosed references to the unnatural pleasures of cannibalism, bestiality, eating dirt, and homosexual acts), but a passage hundreds of pages later, on the vices of surrender to pleasure. But Boswell lets slip his awareness of the earlier, suppressed passage: the reference to eating dirt occurs in the suppressed portion of that earlier passage, and *not* in the passage which he cites and quotes to show Aquinas's alleged crowd-pandering bigotry. And there is a further dishonesty in Boswell's accusation. As he knows perfectly well[90]—but conceals from all those readers who have not memorized, or are unready to consult, the *Nicomachean Ethics*—Aquinas

indicating) is obvious as soon as one looks at the sentence immediately following the one which Boswell quotes.

[88] *ST* I–II q.31 a.7c.   [89] *Christianity, Social Tolerance, and Homosexuality*, 329.
[90] See *ibid.*, 324 at n. 76, where Boswell states that 'the extent to which this discussion' [viz. I–II q.31 a.7—the passage whose content he partially concealed] 'is indebted to *Nicomachean Ethics* 7.5 is often overlooked by editors'.

takes his linking of cannibalism, bestiality, and homosexual acts (along with the reference to eating dirt) from Aristotle; the linkage conveys not the result of mediaeval popular prejudice but the opinion apparently[91] held by a great pagan philosopher in the midst of a homoerotic culture.

Aquinas's reasons for judging certain types of sex act wrongful neither depend upon nor even include the lines of argument which Koppelman, Noonan, and Boswell ascribe to him. His reasons are concerned rather with the preconditions for instantiating, and the ways of disrespecting, the good of marriage, viz. the way of life made intelligible and choiceworthy by its twin orientation towards the procreation, support, and education of children *and* the mutual support, *fides*, and *amicitia* of spouses who, at all levels of their being, are sexually complementary. How, then, is this good *violated* by non-marital sex acts, including even the sex acts of someone who perhaps could never marry?

IV

The answer to that question can begin by looking forward to Grisez's treatment of the same question. Grisez takes the vocabulary of his discussion largely from the Second Vatican Council's teaching on marriage. Speaking of acts of marital intercourse, the Council said:

Expressed in a manner which is truly human, these actions signify and foster that mutual self-giving by which spouses enrich each other with joyful and grateful hearts.[92]

The concept of self-giving, as used in this passage, is obviously closely related to Aquinas's concept of marital *fides* as a positive motive for bodily union in marital intercourse: devotedness to this unique spouse and commitment to this exclusive community and sharing of life intended to be ended only by death.[93] Accordingly, Aquinas's concept of 'giving *to each other* what is [sexually] due or appropriate {*sibi invicem* debitum reddere}' is

---

[91] See *NE* VII 1148b15–31; also *Pol.* I 1252a33–9, II 1262a32–9 (imperceptibly or evasively discussed in Nussbaum, 'Platonic Love and Colorado Law' at 1586 n. 307); see 1994b at 1061. Nussbaum's claim (at 1585; likewise 1589) that *NE* 1148b15–31 'was central in the dispute between Professor Finnis and me' is false; it was at all times Plato whose work and modern interpretation was of primary concern to me and central to my critique of Nussbaum's remarkable evidence in the trial of *Evans v Romer*, 63 Empl Prac Dec (CCH) ¶42, 719, ¶77, 940, 1993 WL 518586 (Colo. Dist. Ct., 14 December 1993); and see n. 109 below.

[92] *Gaudium et Spes* (Pastoral Constitution on the Church in the Modern World) (1965), 49.

[93] In John Paul II's encyclical, *Familiaris Consortio* (1982), sec. 32, this is spoken of as 'the total reciprocal self-giving of husband and wife'. This way of putting the matter is not too happy, since *total* self-giving is literally impossible; so 'total' must be explained as meaning no more (though no less) than a self-giving not impaired by any factor which ought not to be allowed to limit it. 'Total' thus adds nothing to the explanation of the factors that can wrongfully impair marital commitment or its expression in sexual acts[, though doubtless the word can be taken as recalling the whole set

substantially equivalent to Vatican II's concept of spouses mutually giving themselves in sexual intercourse as an expression and fostering of marital communion.[94]

In a sustained, penetrating argument of which Koppelman reports neither the principal conclusion nor all the premises, Grisez concludes that the good of marriage is violated not only by adultery (even when approved by the other spouse) and by a spouse's solitary masturbation (even when motivated by desire to avoid adultery), but also by all the intentional sexual acts of unmarried persons.[95] Among the argument's intermediate conclusions are the propositions defended now by Patrick Lee and Robert P. George,[96] about the masturbatory choice of self-disintegrity, and the fornicatory and sodomitic choice of an illusory intimacy and bodily communion. What I wish to explore here is the proposition proximate to Grisez's ultimate conclusion that choices of non-marital sex violate the good of marriage: the proposition that by such choices one 'damages the body's capacity for the marital act as an act of self-giving which constitutes a communion of bodily persons'.[97] It is this damage which makes such acts violative of the good of marriage.[98]

Whatever this damage to the body's capacity is, it is not, of course, a matter of physiological damage. Rather, it is a damage to the person as an integrated, acting being; it consists principally in that disposition of the will which is initiated by the choice to engage in an act of one or other of the kinds in question. It is a damage which can essentially[99] be eliminated by repentance (which can be formal—as for example in a religious context—or informal). So: to say that a choice 'damages the body's capacity for self-giving' is, I think, elliptical for: that choice deforms one's will in such a way that unless one reverses one's choice (repents), it disables one—precisely as a free, rational, sentient, *bodily* person—from engaging in a bodily act which would really express, actualize, foster, and enable one as a spouse to

---

of such factors and, indirectly, the radical character of reason's requirement that they all be excluded even from one's secret will (see at and after n. 104 below)].

[94] As Grisez notes: *LCL* 637 n. 166.

[95] *Ibid.*, 633, 649. Although Koppelman makes 28 citations to this volume, he fails to cite either of these key pages, though he cites e.g. 634 and 650.

[96] See n. 11 above.

[97] *LCL* 650. See also 654 on the same implication of sodomy (and equally of heterosexual activities within or outside marriage which are deliberately made not open to new life).

[98] For: 'to damage an intrinsic and necessary condition for attaining a good is to damage that good itself. Thus, masturbators violate the good of marital communion by violating the body's capacity for self-giving': *ibid.*, 650–1.

[99] I say 'essentially', because there can also be psychological effects which, not being simply in the will, but extending down into the sub-rational elements of the human make-up, may not be eliminated merely by the will's reversal in repentance.

experience the good of marriage and one's own commitment (self-giving) in marriage.

One can begin to understand this kind of deformity of the will, and its consequences for the capacities of the whole person, when one considers cases of the kind which interested Aquinas more, it seems, than any other aspect of sexual ethics—cases in which one or both of the spouses having sexual intercourse with each other can fail to integrate the act with the good of marriage, or can violate the good of marriage. The cases of obvious violation are those in which one or both of the spouses would be willing, or prefer, to be engaged in the act with someone else.[100] Such a spouse is *conditionally willing* to engage in this sex act with someone not his or her spouse. That is, *if* such another person were available and all the other conditions were in place, this spouse *would*—unless he or she had a change of mind—have sex with that other person.[101] (But such an alternative is not here and now available, so the spouse thus conditionally willing to commit adultery engages instead in intercourse with his or her spouse—perhaps even enthusiastically, in view of the pleasure or other benefits.)

Let us call such a conditional willingness to engage in extra- (that is, non-) marital sex acts *consent* to non-marital sex.[102]

People who attend carefully to the content of the willing in question easily understand that if one in this sort of way is consenting to non-marital sex, one *cannot* choose to engage in *marital* intercourse, that is, cannot make one's intercourse with one's spouse an expression of *fides*, commitment, self-giving. One may—as many actual adulterers do—*hope* to do so, but even if the intimacy with one's spouse gives one the illusion of marital communion, the experience remains illusory. And if one's spouse detects one's divided will, he or she can readily recognize, experientially, that one's participation in intercourse is non-marital (despite its having all the other characteristics of marital intercourse). In short: if one consents to engaging in extra-marital sex acts, one's choosing to engage in a sex act with one's spouse cannot succeed in being an actualizing of *marriage*. One's performances in moving towards one's own and/or one's spouse's orgasmic satisfaction are incapacitated from expressing marital commitment

---

[100] See text above at nn. 21–6 above.

[101] On conditional willing, see essay II.12 (1994a). The essential points explored and illustrated in that essay (in relation to many different types of eligible action) are (i) that the condition in conditional willing relates not to the willingness (which is actual, not merely possible or hypothetical) but to the proposal (course of action) chosen or consented to; and (ii) that a willingness to treat an option (not yet chosen) *as a serious option* is a state of willingness which in its moral significance is essentially equivalent to an actual *choice* of that proposal to do such-and-such if...

[102] Consent here is not to be understood as some momentary act of will, but as a disposition which (like other will acts) lasts in the will unless and until reversed by being repudiated (repented of, formally or informally).

because, by one's consent, one is (conditionally) willing to do the same kind of action with someone to whom one is not married. The only way one can restore one's capacity to express marital self-giving (commitment) by way of sexual intercourse is to negate—repent of—one's consent to any act of that kind.

We have been considering the consent to non-marital sex which may shape and divide the willingness of a married person, where the consent—conditional willingness—bears on that person's own actions in the (hypothetical) here and now:

(A) 'I am so keen on having sex now that if an attractive woman were available (and my wife were not here) I would have sex with her, right now.'

That was the kind of case Aquinas regularly discussed. But the consent which is the core of morally significant conditional willingness is just as real—just as capable of shaping and dividing one's will—if it bears on one's actions in some other possible circumstances.

(B) 'I'm not interested in having sex with anyone other than my husband right now, but if he goes off to war, I might well have sex with an attractive man.'

(C) 'While I'm married I'm not going to have extra-marital sex, but if I weren't married, I'd try to have sex with someone attractive once a week, to keep fit.'

Cases B and C, too, are forms of conditional willingness. 'If I were then and there interested, I would under certain circumstances choose to have non-marital sex.' The effect, the implication in the will of the person in question, is essentially the same as in Aquinas's case, case A.[103] If one seriously gives one's assent to any of the practical propositions A to C, one is *here and now approving and consenting* to sex acts *as* non-marital—one regards and consents to treating such non-marital acts as a reasonable option—and therefore, as long as so consenting, one is disabled from choosing to engage here and now in sexual intercourse with one's spouse *as* genuinely marital intercourse expressing and actualizing marital self-giving or commitment.[104]

---

[103] This essential identity of the objects (the intelligible content) of the different acts, by different persons, referred to in each of the type-cases, A, B, and C (and D and E below) respectively, is an implication of the universality or universalizability of the reasons for action (however specific) on which one's will—a rational faculty—proceeds in all its acts, notwithstanding that the action itself consented to, chosen, and done is always—or always would be, if and when done—a particular.

[104] Of course, the thought that any consensual and mutually pleasurable sex acts between adults are acceptable is not logically incompatible, in a straightforward way, with the thought that mutually pleasurable marital intercourse is also acceptable, indeed better, or with the thought that mutually pleasurable marital intercourse which succeeds in conceiving a child is even better.

What if one's state of mind is a version of C in which 'While I'm married I'm not going to have extra-marital sex...' is reinforced by '...because I think it's immoral for a married person to have extra-marital sex...'? Obviously one's will is then much less divided than A's or B's; one does not consent, even conditionally, to having non-marital sex of any kind while married, for one regards that as morally excluded. Still, one is willing to engage in sex acts outside marriage (for example one does not repent of having engaged in them before marriage, and/or is conditionally willing to engage in them non-maritally when one's spouse is dead and gone). So one's will, in willing intercourse with one's spouse, does remain divided, impure, motivated in part by something other than *fides*. What is true of A remains true here, albeit less extensively and intensively: one's performances in moving towards one's own and/or one's spouse's orgasmic satisfaction cannot express the exclusiveness of marital commitment and marital communion, because one is here and now (albeit conditionally) willing to do that sort of action for motives other than the expression of marital commitment.

Now consider cases where one's thought is turned explicitly to the conduct of other persons, and where one deliberately approves those persons' conduct:

(D) 'While I'm married I'm not going to have extra-marital sex. But I think it's quite OK for people who want to have *extra-marital* sex to do it...'

(E) 'While I'm married I'm not going to have extra-marital sex. But I think it's quite OK for unmarried people to get sexual satisfaction in any way they like, consistent with being fair to others...'

Cases D and E, too, are cases of conditional willingness. This is of course less obvious than in cases B and C. The bare thought that conduct X is permissible for people differently situated from me does not logically entail that I must have any interest, however tenuous and conditional, in doing X. But outside a legalistic morality of prohibitions and permissions, the thought 'It's OK for them' will convey the judgment that the conduct in question has some value. Moreover, the thinking is by a person who, like almost every adult, has some interest in orgasmic sexual satisfaction; indeed, this person is positively willing to engage in behaviour which culminates in such satisfaction, at least in marriage. So the thought that it is permissible and OK for certain other people to get such satisfaction by non-marital

---

The incompatibility only comes to light when one considers the conditions under which intercourse between spouses is genuinely *marital*, expressing and actualizing marital self-giving and commitment.

sex acts becomes deliberate approval, that is, a thought of the form: 'If I were in their situation, I would be willing to get sexual satisfaction by non-marital sex acts.'[105] As in cases B and C, the thought is: 'If I were then and there interested, I would under certain circumstances, and without having to violate or change any of my present moral beliefs, be prepared to choose to have non-marital sex.'[106] When that thought is conjoined with present interest in sexual activity and satisfaction, it constitutes a present, albeit conditional willingness which incapacitates one from willing sexual intercourse with one's spouse *as* genuinely marital intercourse.

Thus one's conscience's complete exclusion of non-marital sex acts from the range of acceptable and valuable human options is existentially, if not logically, a pre-condition for the truly marital character of one's intercourse as and with a spouse. Deliberate approval[107] of non-marital sex acts is among the states of mind (understanding and willingness) which damage one's capacity to choose and carry out *as marital* even those actual sex acts which in all other respects are marital in kind. It is a state of mind which, even in those people who are not interested in marrying, is contrary to, and violative of, the good of marriage.

And just as a cowardly weakling who would never try to kill anyone, yet deliberately approves of the killings of innocent people in a terrorist massacre, has a will which violates the good of life, so even a person of exclusively and irreversibly homosexual inclination[108] violates the good of marriage by consenting to (deliberately approving) non-marital sex

---

[105] This is true, even if (the thought of) being in that situation is at present quite repugnant to me in my condition and circumstances. Here the argument goes beyond, while following the trajectory of, Aquinas, *ST* I–II q.74 a.8.

[106] Since the condition, 'If I were then and there interested...', relates only to emotional disposition, there is still conditional willingness—consent—in the case where the person in D and E adds '...and if my wife died I'd probably give up sex...'. Even in the case where the agent's disposition not to have sex outside marriage seems more strictly volitional, i.e. based on reasons (e.g. 'Sex distracts me from my play-writing...'), the prioritizing is based on preferences which, not being required (or reasonably regarded as required) by reason, may be changed by choice. Where one has some interest in behaviour of some kind (e.g. behaviour inducing orgasmic sexual satisfaction), then, even if one's interest is at present trumped by some countervailing interest, one is conditionally willing to engage in acts involving that behaviour unless one regards those kinds of acts as excluded by reason (i.e. as immoral).

[107] On deliberate approval of others' acts (precisely as such—not merely in their beneficial effects or other morally accidental features) as a form of willing of such acts, see Grisez, *Christian Moral Principles*, 374, 376 (with the refinements and clarifications in ch. G.6–8); *LCL* 657 (ch. 9.E.4).

[108] It is worth noting, though nothing in this essay turns on it, that such a person would be one of a very small minority of those—themselves a very small proportion of the whole population—who 'have a homosexual orientation'. Consider the statistics given in research relied upon (for other purposes) by Koppelman, 'Three Arguments for Gay Rights' at 1665, viz. Edward O. Laumann et al., *Social Organization of Sexuality: Sexual Practices in the United States* (University of Chicago Press, 1994): Table 8.3A on p. 311 shows that (in the large, representative sample of the American population surveyed in 1992) only about 6 per cent of all men and 3 per cent of all women ever have any same-sex sex partner, and *of those who do*, fewer than 10 per cent have sex only with same-sex partners. The upshot is accurately summarized by the authors on p. 312:

acts such as solitary masturbation.[109] That is an implication of the logic of practical reason—the intelligible goods available to me for choice or rejection are human goods, good for anyone. Moreover, the 'wrongs of thought' of cowardly weaklings who will never kill (or homosexuals—or heterosexuals—who will never marry) rather rarely remain without impact on their own behaviour and on the thoughts and behaviour of other people. Such approval makes real killings of innocents more likely, and approval of non-marital sex acts contributes to the cultural climate in which actual marriages founder. The wrongness of such thoughts does not depend on any 'calculus' of consequences, of course, but should not be written off as of 'no practical concern' to others, still less as a motiveless imposition upon the consciences of people who are unmarried and perhaps unmarriageable.

since puberty, under 1 percent of all men (0.6 percent) have had sex only with other boys or men and never with a female partner.... Only 0.2 per cent of all women have had sex only with women.

So the overwhelming majority of homosexually oriented people are (like Keynes, Burgess, Maclean, Blunt, Stephen Spender, and numerous other figures in twentieth-century cultural, political, and literary history—and most of the 'gays and lesbians' studied in the sociological surveys relied upon by Koppelman: see n. 15 above) fully capable of heterosexual arousal and sex acts including marital intercourse. For some striking, if 'anecdotal' confirmation of this and other relevant realities mentioned in this essay, see Martin Duberman, 'Dr Sagarin and Mr Cory: The "Father" of the Homophile Movement', The Harvard Gay & Lesbian Review 4 (1997) 7–14.

[109] Koppelman (88) n. 150 buttresses his mistaken assumption that Grisez has a 'suspicion of bodily pleasures' by approvingly quoting the confession by Martha Nussbaum and Kenneth Dover that they cannot see any morally relevant difference between the senses (ways) in which swimming, hiking, and masturbating 'use the body for pleasure', and see nothing objectionable about any of them. Koppelman might have added that on the next page they seem to see nothing objectionable in 'nonmarital sex of many types'—*which* types they conspicuously fail to delimit even in principle: Nussbaum, 'Platonic Love and Colorado Law' at 1649, 1650. In the same article (at 1562 n. 176) they each express themselves unable to find any reference to masturbation in the passage (rightly taken by Nussbaum, elsewhere, to be of crucial importance in Plato's whole theory of human good) in Plato's *Gorgias* at 494 where Plato's Socrates obliges the tough sceptic Callicles to admit that there are bad pleasures, by getting him to think first of stimulating one's own body's lower (sc. genital) regions, and thence of a whole range of shameful acts including getting pleasure by being sodomized, 'and all those other shameful things besides'. Insensitivity to obvious differences among various ways in which one can use one's body in bodily activity, and to the fact that using the body to give orgasmic satisfaction (i) involves a focus on the desiring, experiencing self as subject and the body as instrument, and (ii) damagingly implicates one's capacity for giving bodily expression to marital commitment, results in literary/scholarly insensitivity to the sensitivity which Plato shares with countless others. On Nussbaum's shifting views (and explanations of those views) on the passage from the *Gorgias*, and on her reliability as a witness to ancient philosophy and modern scholarship on matters of sexuality, see 1994b at 1055–62; more fully, 1994d at 19–41; also George, '"Shameless Acts" Revisited: Some Questions for Martha Nussbaum'. On her Virginia L Rev article generally, see 1994b (Notre Dame J of Law, Ethics & Public Policy 9 (1995) 11) at 18–20 nn. 15–17. On Nussbaum and Dover as interpreters of Plato on sex and marriage, see the important Comment by R.E. Allen (whose outstanding capabilities as translator and philosophical commentator had been firmly attested by Nussbaum herself in commenting on vol. 1 of his Yale University Press translation of Plato: see the cover of the paperback edition of that volume), in *The Dialogues of Plato*, vol. 2 *The Symposium* (Yale University Press, 1991) at 46 n. 76, 99–102; on Plato's (and, it seems, Aristotle's) condemnation of homosexual sex acts, *ibid.*, 17–18, 46 n. 76, 74–7.

The argument I have been sketching is completed by turning back to consider the actually married, and the significance for good or evil of their states of mind. Without the possibility of *truly* marital intercourse the good of marriage is seriously impaired. Any willingness (no matter how conditional) to engage in non-marital sex undermines, radically even when not perceptibly,[110] one's marriage itself as a reality to be initiated, fostered, and preserved in and by clear-headed deliberation and the work of an alert and well-formed conscience. For it disintegrates the intelligibility of one's marriage: one's sex acts, understood from the inside (so to speak) as the bodily carrying out of choices each made in a certain state of mind (will), no longer truly actualize and make possible authentic experience of one's *marriage*; they are unhinged from the other aspects of the spouses' mutual marital commitment and project. And this unhinging or dis-integration threatens—runs contrary to—both of the goods inherent in the complex basic good of marriage:[111] not only the good of marital friendship and *fides* but also the good of procreation and of the children whose whole formation is so deeply benefited by the context of a *good* marriage. *So* any kind of assent—even if conditional—to non-marital sex is unreasonable. (Indeed, all sexual immorality, all wrong willing however conditional, is contrary to love of *neighbour*, perhaps most directly of children.[112]) And *because* it is unreasonable, it is immoral,[113] *and* therefore[114] out of line with human nature.

Koppelman quotes three fragments from Aquinas's *Summa contra Gentiles* III, c.122. He is right to find the apparent train of argument puzzling and unsatisfying. But he has overlooked the general movement

---

[110] Of course, in the real world of not too clear-headed people (all of us, to some extent), the disintegrative implications of some unintelligibility which renders an option (e.g. our being married while willing to perform non-marital sex acts) more or less incoherent are often muffled and/or postponed by other factors, such as convenience, individual or cultural inertia, etc. But ethics is concerned not with what happens to happen but with options as such, and the conditions under which they are or are not fully reasonable. As the late twentieth-century collapse of marriage suggests, irrationalities consented to, perhaps generations earlier, in individual wills (and the culture they shape) will very probably make themselves, sooner or later, rather extensively apparent in bad further effects.

[111] Marriage is a complex but unified good in as much as its goodness as unitive is inseparable from its goodness as procreative (even where procreation is *per accidens* impossible). Aquinas's train of thought about marital and non-marital sexual acts is one valid way of understanding and acknowledging this inseparability.

[112] See *Mal.* q.15 a.2 ad 4; *Sent.* IV d.33 q.1 a.3 sol.2 (= *Supp.* q.65 a.4c). In respect of children, at least, the violation of neighbour love is an offence against justice. It would therefore be entirely within the proper authority of law and government to e.g. withhold state or federal funding from any school which teaches that, say, masturbation is morally acceptable.

[113] To say that it is immoral does not mean that individuals who do acts of the relevant kind are subjectively morally culpable; their moral culpability may sometimes be much diminished by passion that fetters freedom and/or by confusion of mind (e.g. ideology, fantasy) that obscures rational deliberation towards choice. See *ST* I–II q.73 a.5c and a.6 ad 2.

[114] See n. 4 above.

380   PART SIX: MARRIAGE, JUSTICE, AND THE COMMON GOOD

of the chapter as a whole,[115] which points towards the necessity and goodness of the institution of marriage as the only acceptable framework for the generation and, ordinarily, the care of children. The succeeding three chapters explore the relationships between sex acts and marriage precisely as the maximal friendship {maxima amicitia} it needs to be if it is to be what it ought for children and their parents.[116]

But whether or not Aquinas did have it in mind, the train of thought I have sketched in this section (and earlier, much more briefly, in the essay to which Koppelman is responding)[117] establishes one important sense in which all non-marital sex acts, even by the unmarried uninterested in marriage, are contrary to the good of marriage because contrary to the self-giving in marital intercourse which is at the heart of marriage.

V

Near the heart of Koppelman's contentions is the claim[118] that there is no morally significant difference between the marriage of a sterile couple[119] and some committed liaison of two persons of the same sex who together

---

[115] And he has partly concealed that movement from himself and his readers by omitting from the first passage (73 at n. 99) a whole sentence that is a premise for that passage's penultimate sentence (beginning 'Therefore'!), and that introduces the theme with which the chapter is eventually dominantly concerned (and which simply disappears from Koppelman's account of it): the human need not just for generation or procreation but for *marriage*. The omitted sentence is (in the translation used by Koppelman):

But man's generative process would be frustrated unless it were followed by proper nutrition, because the offspring would not survive if proper nutrition were withheld.

The whole pages of c.122 which Koppelman ignores conclude that it is natural (in the defined sense: reasonable in view of human good) for a man to establish with a particular woman the lasting *societas* we call *matrimonium*, and that deliberate emission of semen (orgasm) outside marriage is contrary to human good and therefore wrong. (In reading *ScG* III, c.122 on emission of semen do not overlook the fact that Aquinas thought that in female sexual activity a kind of semen (albeit not a kind which is a biological component in generation) is pleasurably emitted in the female reproductive tract: see *Sent.* IV d.33 q.3 a.1c (quoted in n. 127 below) and ad 5; d.41 q.1 a.1 sol.4 ad 2; *Sent.* III d.3 q.5 a.1c; *ST* III q.31 a.5 ad 3.)

[116] What Aquinas says in *ScG* III, c.122, and the much fuller reflections on marriage and sexuality in the passages of his *Commentary on the Sentences* which I have mentioned, suggested to me the train of thought I have pursued in this section. Aquinas would have restated the argument of those passages if he had lived to write his projected treatment of marriage in Part III of the *Summa Theologiae*—a treatment to which he repeatedly refers the reader of the passages on sex in *ST* II–II q.154.

[117] See text at nn. 8–11 above.

[118] See (66), referring with approval to Stephen Macedo's claim that 'the homosexual couple is, in fact, the moral equivalent of the infertile heterosexual couple'. On (65) Koppelman claims that 'Grisez never explains the purported disanalogy between the gay couple and the heterosexual couple.... Finnis has attempted to fill this gap...' But in fact, everything I said was little more than a condensation of Grisez's treatment of precisely this question: *LCL* 634, 636, 651–4.

[119] That is, a man and a woman who can engage in marital intercourse (what Koppelman has to call 'penile-vaginal' intercourse) but who cannot thereby procreate (e.g. because the wife's tubes are irreversibly tied, or her uterus is missing).

engage in sex acts.[120] Any such claim is bound to fail, for reasons which I indicate in this section. One way of pointing to those reasons is this. The marriage of a sterile couple is true marriage, because they can intend and do together *all* that any married couple *need* intend and do to undertake, consummate, and live out a valid marriage. It cannot have the fullness that a fertile marriage can have, and in that respect is a secondary rather than a central-case instantiation of the good of marriage. But the committed liaison of two (why two?) persons of the same sex who together engage in sex acts is an artificially constructed type-case which is a secondary version of a central case radically different from the central case of marriage. Indeed, what is the central case of same-sex sexual relationships? Perhaps it is the anonymous bathhouse encounter, engaged in with a view to being repeated in another cubicle later that night. Perhaps it is a same-sex threesome or foursome between currently steady, committed friends. Who knows? What is clear is that in the account of sex and friendship which Koppelman offers there is *nothing* to show why a currently two-person same-sex liaison should have the exclusiveness-and-intended-permanence-in-commitment that is inherent in the idea of marriage (including the marriage of a sterile couple).

Every married couple is sterile most of the time.[121] Outside one or two remote tribes, that has always been well known, even when the limited periods of fertility in the female cycle were mislocated. Koppelman and Macedo absurdly think that *most of the time*, therefore, (a) the couple's genitals are not reproductive organs[122]—except perhaps in the sense that a dead man's *dead* heart 'is still a heart'! (76)—and (b) the couple's intercourse cannot be of a reproductive kind. The same line of thought also drives these writers towards the equally arbitrary conclusion[123] that

---

[120] The sex acts in question are generally referred to vaguely by Koppelman (e.g. 'sexual conduct' (2), 'sex' (2), 'pleasuring one another sexually' (62)), but sometimes more specifically ('anal or oral sex' (67)), and sometimes as 'sexual intercourse' (62, 93). 'Sexual intercourse', more properly speaking, is the kind of sex act which, today as always, is required in law to consummate a marriage, and persons of the same sex are simply incapable of engaging with each other in that kind of act.

[121] Koppelman greatly understates this when, in noting that 'normal women...are only capable of reproducing during a small part of their lives', he adds 'there is nothing abnormal about menstruation and menopause' (76 n. 105). For there is also nothing abnormal about the fact that ovulation occurs only about once a month, and the woman's capacitated ovum is capable of being fertilized for not more than about one day. Given the limited time that sperm can survive, the couple as such is fertile not more than four or five days in each more or less monthly cycle.

[122] See e.g. (66): 'A sterile person's genitals are no more suitable for generation than an unloaded gun is suitable for shooting.... [T]he only material aspect of reality that matters is whether the gun, *as it now is*, is in fact capable of killing' (emphasis added). Koppelman sometimes, inconsistently, speaks as if they are not reproductive if and only if they belong to people who are completely sterile e.g. 'a woman whose diseased uterus has been removed' (66).

[123] See (67) at n. 77: 'Macedo...could...still dispute that the spouses unite biologically...'. Koppelman defensively adds that Macedo 'could also concede that the biological union takes place, but deny that this union has intrinsic value'. The addition and envisaged concession are significant,

a man and a woman can never be biologically united—only sperm and egg can be biologically united! While in this reductivist, word-legislating mood, one might declare that sperm and egg unite only physically and only their pronuclei are *biologically* united. But it would be more realistic to acknowledge that the whole process of copulation, involving as it does the brains of the man and woman, their nerves, blood, vaginal and other secretions, and coordinated activity (such that conception is much less likely to result from rape) is biological through and through. The dualism embraced by Koppelman and Macedo[124] neatly shows how far humanness itself—the radical *unity* of body ('biology'), sense, emotion, reason, and will—becomes unintelligible once one loses one's grip on the way in which a marital sexual act, uniting *us*[125] in a *particular bodily* (and therefore biological) *way* can really *actualize*, express, and enable us truly to experience something as *intelligent and voluntary* as a freely chosen commitment to serving each other as complementary friends in a form of life adapted, by its permanence and exclusivity, to serving also (if fortune so provides) our children as the living embodiments and fruit peculiarly appropriate to our kind of (comm)union.[126]

Sexual acts which are marital are 'of the reproductive kind'[127] because in willing such an act one wills sexual behaviour which is intended

since the 'intrinsic value' of the biological union *in a genuinely marital act* is intrinsic not in the fallacious sense that value can be deduced from biological facts, nor in the ethically false sense that any biological union between a man and a woman is valuable or morally good, but in the logically and ethically valid sense that, by being a union of the reproductive kind, that union can be part of the instantiating of the intrinsic and basic human good (value) of marriage.

[124] See also the response to Macedo on this point by George and Bradley, 'Marriage and the Liberal Imagination' at 311 n. 32.

[125] The organic unity which is instantiated in an act of the reproductive kind is not so much the unity of penis and vagina (as my inexact wording in essay 21 n. 14, first part of last sentence, incautiously suggests) but rather the unity of the man and the woman—the unity which is consummated in their intentional, consensual act of uniting those genital organs in seminal emission/reception in the woman's reproductive tract.

[126] See further George and Bradley, 'Marriage and the Liberal Imagination' at 304 text and n. 16.

[127] In Aquinas, 'act of the generative type' is often the correct translation of *actus* [or *opus*] *generationis* (as used in the context of human sexual activity) . This is put beyond doubt by *Quodl.* XI q.9 a.2 ad 1:

old people are 'frigid' not in relation to the generative type of act, but in relation to the generation of offspring, and so since they can have sexual intercourse, their marriage is not dissolved {senes sunt frigidi non quidem ad actum generationis, sed ad generationem prolis, et ideo, cum possint carnaliter copulari, non solvitur matrimonium}.

For other passages in which *actus generationis* is being used as a kind of synonym for sexual intercourse of the behaviourally standard kind, and where actual generation seems entirely beside the question, see e.g. *Sent.* IV d.42 q.1 a.2c ('cognatio carnalis non contrahitur nisi per *actum generationis completum*; unde etiam affinitas non contrahitur nisi sit facta *conjunctio seminum*, ex qua *potest* sequi carnalis generatio;' *Sent.* IV d.32 q.1 a.5 sol.3c ('cum mulier habeat potestatem in corpus viri quantum ad actum generationis spectat, et e converso; tenetur unus alteri debitum reddere quocumque tempore et quacumque hora...'); *Sent.* IV d.33 q.3 a.1c ('virginitas...integritas quaedam est; unde per privationem corruptionis dicitur, quae in *actu generationis* accidit; ubi triplex corruptio est. Una corporalis tantum, in hoc quod claustra pudoris franguntur. Alia spiritualis et corporalis simul, ex hoc

as and is (a) the very same bodily and behaviour as causes generation (intended or unintended) in every case of human *sexual* reproduction, and (b) the very same as one would will if one were intending precisely sexual reproduction as a goal of a particular marital sexual act. This kind of act is a 'natural kind', in the morally relevant sense of 'natural', *not* (as Koppelman supposes)[128] if and only if one is intending or attempting to produce an *outcome*, viz. reproduction or procreation. Rather it is a distinct rational kind—and therefore in the morally relevant sense a natural kind—because (i) in engaging in it one is intending a *marital* act, (ii) its being of the reproductive kind is a necessary though not sufficient condition of it being marital, and (iii) marriage is a rational and natural kind of institution. One's reason for action—one's rational motive—is precisely the complex good of *marriage*.

For: marriage is rational and natural primarily because it is the institution which physically, biologically, emotionally, and in every other practical way is peculiarly apt to promote suitably the reproduction of the couple by the generation, nurture, and education of ultimately mature offspring. The version of 'gay' ideology defended by Koppelman, Macedo, and others who claim that sex acts between persons of the same sex can be truly marital, and that to perform such acts two such persons can indeed marry each other, suggests (without clearly affirming) that homosexual sex acts should be evaluated by focusing upon this sort of activity of this sort of couple. Koppelman adopts Sidney Callahan's claim that *when engaged in 'with a faithful partner'*, such same-sex sex acts 'produce... intense intimacy, bodily confirmation, mutual sanctification, and fulfilling happiness'. If it is a trifle careless of Koppelman to accept that 'mutual sanctification' is 'produced' by sex acts in a universe he proclaims to be 'disenchanted', much more interesting is his failure to explain why this and the other effects allegedly 'produced' by sex acts depend upon the faithfulness of one's partner, or partners,[129] and, I assume, upon one's own faithfulness.

---

quod per decisionem et motum seminis, in sensu delectatio generatur. Tertia est spiritualis tantum, ex hoc quod ratio huic delectationi se subjicit, in qua integritatem perdit quantum ad actum...') [Thus the significant and per se effects of this *actus generationis* do not include generation, but do include the pleasurable ejaculation and flow of semen, which is one of the reasons Aquinas gives, in this passage, for judging that intercourse is one way in which one's state of virginity is ended]. The very idea of a generative kind of act, or act per se apt for generation, is articulated—albeit not in those words—in e.g. *Mal.* q.15 a.2 ad 14 and *ScG* III, c.122 n.5.

[128] See Koppelman's discussion (especially around nn. 79 and 80) of what *outcomes* one can and cannot *intend* to produce with the unloaded gun whose wielding Koppelman vainly tries to analogize to marital intercourse.

[129] Not yet disentangled from the Catholic teaching on marriage she is 'changing her mind' away from, Callahan just *takes it for granted* that there is to be just one same-sex partner. (The same must be said of Paul Weithman in the article quoted and relied upon by Koppelman, 70 at n. 89; similarly Michael Perry as cited in n. 88.) The assumption has no rational ground. And see n. 136 below.

The fact is that 'gay' ideology, even in the sanitized Koppelman/Macedo version,[130] has no serious account whatever of why faithfulness—reservation of one's sex acts exclusively for one's spouse—is an intelligible, intelligent, and reasonable requirement. Only a small proportion of men who live as 'gays' seriously attempt anything even resembling marriage as a permanent commitment. Only a tiny proportion seriously attempt marital fidelity, the *commitment* to exclusiveness; the proportion who find that the attempt *makes sense*, in view of the other aspects of their 'gay identity', is even tinier.[131] Thus, even at the level of behaviour—that is, even leaving aside its inherent sterility—gay 'marriage', precisely because it excludes or fails to embrace and ultimately can make no sense of a *commitment* utterly central to *marriage*, is a sham.[132]

---

[130] Incompletely sanitized: for sometimes the veil of solemnity about 'same-sex marriage' slips, and the underlying, and more coherent, gay ideology peeps through: 'Why cannot sex at least sometimes be one more kind of harmless play?' (89). And see n. 132 below.

[131] See the surveys and discussions by homosexual sociologists and writers cited in Grisez, *Difficult Moral Questions*, 108, 110 (Q. 23 nn. 81–90). Koppelman, 'Three Arguments for Gay Rights' at 1665 approvingly reports research indicating that 'among couples together for more than 10 years, ... 30% of husbands ... and 94% of gay men reported at least one instance of nonmonogamy [sic: sc. sexual infidelity].' But he understates the contrast revealed by that research: of that 94 per cent, over 80 per cent had been unfaithful *during the twelve months prior to the research* (whereas only a minority of the unfaithful minority of husbands had been unfaithful in the same period), indicating that the infidelities of even long-term homosexual male couples are overwhelmingly more frequent. Blumstein and Schwartz, *American Couples*, 276. Blumstein and Schwartz soberly conclude (*ibid.*, 275) that for all homosexual couples, 'as the relationship goes on, *virtually all* gay men have other sexual partners'. Note also that when Blumstein and Scwhartz followed up their large cohort of couples eighteen months after the main survey, more than one in five of the lesbian couples had meanwhile broken up (compared with one in twenty of the married couples): *ibid.*, 308.

[132] The Fall 1997 issue of The Harvard Gay & Lesbian Review: A Quarterly Journal of Arts, Letters, & Sciences (vol. IV no. 4) has as its theme 'same-sex marriage' [SSM]. The Editor-in-Chief assembled five essays on the theme, and himself conducted a searching and sympathetic interview with a leading proponent, Andrew Sullivan. In his editorial he then says:

> The attempt to *sanitize SSM for tactical reasons* has resulted in a kind of studied silence on the subject of sex... [W]e end up soft-pedaling sex in favor of 'commitment.' And while the discussion of sex within marriage has been avoided, the discussion of non-marital and extra-marital sex has also largely been missing, at least in our 'official' pronouncements and lobbying efforts in Washington and Hawaii. And yet, in talking about an institution that most Americans define as fidelity to a single partner for a lifetime, how can we avoid discussing *sexual promiscuity and serial monogamy and the myriad ways that long-term gay couples have defined their relationships.*... Gabriel Rotello and Andrew Sullivan... have regarded SSM as a possible antidote to gay male promiscuity and wildness—which it may well be, though I think it's just as likely that gay marriages would liven up the institution as submit to its traditional rules (suits me fine). We also might examine just why we feel we need to sidestep the issues of sex and promiscuity and alternative partnering...(p. 4).

See likewise Gabriel Rotello, 'Creating a New Gay Culture; Balancing Fidelity and Freedom', Nation, 21 April 1997:

> The antimarriage sentiment in the gay and lesbian political world has abated in recent years, and the legalization of same-sex marriage is now an accepted focus of gay liberation. Yet... most advocates of same-sex marriage... are generally careful not to make the case for marriage, but simply for the *right* to marriage. This is undoubtedly good politics, since many if not most of the major gay and lesbian organizations that have signed on to the fight for same-sex marriage

And this reality is just what ethical reflection would lead one to expect. The reason why marriage requires not just 'a commitment to each other'[133] but commitment to permanence and exclusiveness in the spouses' sexual union is that, as a morally coherent institution or form of life, it is fundamentally shaped by its dynamism towards, appropriateness for, and fulfilment in, the generation, nurture, and education of children who each can only have two parents and who are fittingly the primary responsibility (and object of devotion) of *those two parents*. Apart from this orientation towards children, the institution of marriage, characterized by marital *fides* (faithfulness), would make little or no sense.[134] Given this orientation, the marital form of life does make good sense, and the marital sexual acts which actualize, express, and enable the spouses to experience that form of life make good sense, too.

Moreover, a man and a woman *who can engage in precisely the same marital acts with precisely the same behaviour and intentions*, but who have reason to believe that in their case those very same acts will never result in children, can still opt for this *form of life* as one that makes good sense. Given the multiple and profound bodily, emotional, intellectual, and volitional complementarities with which that combination of factors we call human evolution has equipped us as men and women, such a commitment can be reasonable[135] as a participation in the good of marriage which these infertile spouses can rightly wish to have instantiated more fully than they can. To repeat: they do really participate in it because they can make *every* commitment and can form and carry out *every* intention that any other married couple *need* make, form, and carry out in order to be validly married and to fulfil all their marital responsibilities. By their model of fidelity within a relationship involving acts of the reproductive kind

---

would instantly sign off at any suggestion that they were actually encouraging gay men and lesbians to marry. (Emphasis in original.)

[133] On the marriage-dissolving significance of the fact that many or even most American couples in recent years have married using their own home-made vows, which characteristically leave in shadow the vow of life-long union and replace it with some vow or affirmation of 'commitment', see Blankenhorn, 'I Do?'.

[134] Nussbaum and Dover ('Platonic Love and Colorado Law' at 1650–1) do not like 'Finnis' narrow definition of the marital relationship'—i.e. the definition that has been normative and central for our whole civilization (and not only ours)—but cannot agree even between themselves on a coherent alternative. Dover (speaking of himself in the third person) 'feels that deliberate joint procreation is qualitatively different from nonprocreative sex and that the latter is, so to speak, playing at procreation. (Play, however, may be very important.) He is therefore uneasy about the idea of homosexual marriage.'

[135] Those, however, who search out infertile spouses, choosing them precisely for their infertility, may well be manifesting the kind of contempt for the marital good which Philo Judaeus condemned in the rather confused passage from which Koppelman (64 at n. 61) and Boswell quote some over-heated fragments.

(and no other sex acts), these infertile marriages are, moreover, strongly supportive of marriage as a valuable social institution.

But same-sex partners cannot engage in acts of the reproductive kind, that is, in marital sexual intercourse. For them the permanent, exclusive commitment of marriage—in which bodily union in such acts is the biological actuation of the multi-level (bodily, emotional, intellectual, and volitional) marital relationship—is inexplicable. Of course, two, three, four, five, or any number of persons of the same sex can band together to raise a child or children. That may, in some circumstances, be a praiseworthy commitment. It has nothing to do with marriage. Koppelman and Macedo remain discreetly silent on the question why the same-sex 'marriage' they offer to defend is to be between two persons rather than three, four, five, or more, all engaging in sex acts 'faithfully' with each other. They are equally silent on the question why this group sex-partnership should remain constant in membership, rather than revolving like other partnerships. Koppelman devises an 'account of the good of marriage' by the easy-going procedure of asking us to 'consider the possibility that there is an intrinsic good pursued, distinct in kind from ordinary friendship or ordinary pleasure, but of which pleasure is a necessary component'—a good pursued by 'sexual activity' which 'as Paul Weithman has observed...could "constitute two people as a *social* unit..."'.[136] Should he not also have asked us to 'consider the possibility' that there is also an 'intrinsic good pursued' by the 'sexual activity' which 'constitutes three people' or 'one man and his dog' as 'social units'—or two people as a six-month 'social unit'? The list of possibilities to consider while we are devising 'accounts' or forms of 'marriage' has no real end.

Those who propound 'gay' ideology or theories of same-sex marriage or 'sexual activity' have no principled moral case to offer against (prudent and moderate) promiscuity, indeed the getting of orgasmic sexual pleasure in whatever friendly touch or welcoming orifice (human or otherwise) one may opportunely find it. In debate with opponents of their ideology or theories, some of these proponents are fond of postulating an idealized (two-person, lifelong...) category of relationship, and of challenging their opponents to say how relationships of such a (not too carefully delimited)

---

[136] Koppelman, 70. The good is said (*ibid.*) to be the good of marriage and the 'function or characteristic activity' of the postulated social unit is said to be 'to promote [these two people's] friendship and love through special acts of physical intimacy and tenderness'. As a prominent advocate of same-sex 'marriage' says:

> If the law of marriage can be seen as facilitating the opportunities of two people to live an emotional life that they find satisfactory—rather than imposing a view of proper relationships—the law ought to be able to achieve the same for units of more than two. (Chambers, 'What If? The Legal Consequences of Marriage and the Legal Needs of Lesbian and Gay Male Couples' at 490–1.)

kind differ from *marriage* at least where husband and wife know themselves to be infertile. As I have argued, the principal difference is simple and fundamental: the artificially delimited category named 'gay marriage' or 'same-sex marriage' corresponds to no intrinsic reason or set of reasons at all. When we realize that—and why—the core of marriage is *fides*, the stringently exclusive commitment whose rationale and implications for sexual activity's integrity, purity, and reasonableness were well understood by Aquinas, we realize that—and why—the world of same-sex partnerships (in the real world outside the artifice of debate) offers no genuine instantiations, equivalents, or counterparts to marriage, and so very few whole-hearted imitations.[137] *Marriage* is the coherent, stable category of relationships, activities, satisfactions, and responsibilities which can be intelligently and reasonably chosen by a man together with a woman, and adopted as their demanding mutual commitment and common good, because its components respond and correspond fully reasonably to that complex of interlocking, complementary good *reasons*.

Plato, Aristotle,[138] and other great philosophers, like the mass of ordinary participants in the tradition of civilized life, understand that complex as

[137] This is not to deny that some people try to make their sex acts with persons of the same sex acts of friendship, as I like Grisez, George, Lee, and Bradley have often said. Koppelman is indignant about a fragment he quotes (92 n. 163) from Grisez ('sexual intercourse is not chosen by sodomites in preference to conversation and mutually beneficial acts because it is the more expressive means of communicating good will and affection. Rather, it is chosen because it provides subjective satisfactions not otherwise available.') This claim, says Koppelman with approval, 'has struck many readers as a gross libel on many committed same-sex relationships'. But the real libel is Koppelman's claim that this fragment is 'all [Grisez] says in response to the argument that sodomitic sex may be a way of manifesting friendship and affection'. By slicing off the first words of the fragment ('However, just as with fornicators...') Koppelman not only leaves his readers to infer that Grisez has a bias against or blindspot about homosexuals, but also, more importantly, hides the fact that the deleted reference to fornicators is a reference back to Grisez's extended argument on the preceding pages (652–3) in response to an objector who asks: 'what if...the [fornicating] couple are interested, not in marital communion, but only in some other sort of real and intimate communion, such as friendship, which they presently enjoy and which their sexual intercourse nurtures by communicating good will, affection, and so on?' Grisez's reply begins by accepting that 'psychologically healthy couples who fornicate ordinarily do desire at least something of the experience of marital intimacy'; (652) and he explicitly says the same of the same-sex couple on the page (654) from which Koppelman quoted a fragment. Grisez's response to the objection proceeds with a careful argument to show why, seeing that 'precisely insofar as intercourse is not chosen for any aspect of [the good of marriage], it does not communicate anything definite by itself', and that it is indeed far less expressive than other modes of communication commonly used by friends, the true motive for choosing it is 'sexual desire and the pleasure of satisfying it'. Since I am not in this essay elaborating the arguments from self disintegrity and illusory good, I need not set out the whole argument (which begins on p. 649). Suffice it to underline that Grisez is not denying 'the experience of intimacy of the partners in sodomy' (653), but is giving reasons for *judging* that the experience 'cannot be the experience of any real unity between them'. A reasoned argument about what is real and what is illusory in what is granted to be an actual experience cannot be any kind of libel.

[138] 'Human beings are by nature more conjugal than political': *NE* VIII 1162a17–18. Nussbaum characteristically asserts that

> Marriage is mentioned only twice in the entirety of the *Nicomachean Ethics*: at 1123a1 as the occasion for an especially big party, and at 1165a18 as an occasion, like a funeral, to which one would want to invite one's relatives. ('Platonic Love and Colorado Law' at 1583 n. 294.)

constitutive of (the good of) marriage. And I have been arguing that true and valid sexual morality does no more, and no less, than unfold what is involved in understanding, promoting, and respecting (not violating) that basic human good, and what are the conditions for instantiating that common good of the two spouses in a real, non-illusory way, integrating all the levels of their human reality, in the marital act.

BIBLIOGRAPHY OF THE WORKS OF JOHN FINNIS

1962	a		'Developments in Judicial Jurisprudence', Adelaide L Rev 1: 317–37
	b		'The Immorality of the Deterrent', Adelaide Univ Mag: 47–61
1963			'Doves and Serpents', The Old Palace 38: 438–41
1967	a	I.17	'Reason and Passion: The Constitutional Dialectic of Free Speech and Obscenity', University of Pennyslvania L Rev 116: 222–43
	b	IV.8	'Blackstone's Theoretical Intentions', Natural L Forum 12: 63–83
	c		'Punishment and Pedagogy', The Oxford Review 5: 83–93
	d		'Review of Zelman Cowen, *Sir John Latham and Other Papers*', LQR 83: 289–90
1968	a	III.10	'Old and New in Hart's Philosophy of Punishment', The Oxford Review 8: 73–80
	b		'Constitutional Law', *Annual Survey of Commonwealth Law 1967* (Butterworth), 20–33, 71–98
	c		'Separation of Powers in the Australian Constitution', Adelaide L Rev 3: 159–77
	d		Review of Neville March Hunnings, *Film Censors and the Law*, LQR 84: 430–2
	e		'Natural Law in *Humanae vitae*', LQR 84: 467–71
	f		Review of H. Phillip Levy, *The Press Council*, LQR 84: 582
	g		'Law, Morality and Mind Control', Zenith (University Museum, Oxford) 6: 7–8
1969	a		'Constitutional Law', *Annual Survey of Commonwealth Law 1968* (Butterworth), 2–15, 32–49, 53–75, 98–114
	b		Review of Herbert L. Packer, *The Limits of the Criminal Sanction*, Oxford Magazine, 86 no. 1 (new series), 10–11
1970	a	I.6	'Reason, Authority and Friendship in Law and Morals', in Khanbai, Katz, and Pineau (eds), *Jowett Papers 1968–1969* (Oxford: Blackwell), 101–24
	b		'Natural Law and Unnatural Acts', Heythrop J 11: 365–87
	c		i. 'Abortion and Legal Rationality', Adelaide L Rev 3: 431–67
			ii. 'Three Schemes of Regulation', in Noonan (ed.), *The Morality of Abortion: Legal and Historical Perspectives* (HUP)
	d		'Constitutional Law', *Annual Survey of Commonwealth Law 1969* (Butterworth), 2–4, 27–34, 37–50, 65–81
	e		Review of H.B. Acton, *The Philosophy of Punishment*, Oxford Magazine, 87 (new series) (13 April)
	f		Review of Colin Howard, *Australian Constitutional Law*, LQR 86: 416–18

1971	a	IV.21	'Revolutions and Continuity of Law', in A.W.B. Simpson (ed.), *Oxford Essays in Jurisprudence: Second Series* (OUP), 44–76
	b		'The Abortion Act: What Has Changed?', Criminal L Rev: 3–12
	c		'Constitutional Law', *Annual Survey of Commonwealth Law 1970* (Butterworth), 2–4, 17–31, 33–42, 51–60
1972	a	III.11	'The Restoration of Retribution', Analysis 32: 131–5
	b	IV.18	'Some Professorial Fallacies about Rights', Adelaide L Rev 4: 377–88
	c		'The Value of the Human Person', Twentieth Century [Australia] 27: 126–37
	d		'Bentham et le droit naturel classique', Archives de Philosophie du Droit 17: 423–7
	e		'Constitutional Law', *Annual Survey of Commonwealth Law 1971* (Butterworth), 2–5, 11–25, 28–41
	f		'Meaning and Ambiguity in Punishment (and Penology)', Osgoode Hall LJ 10: 264–8
1973	a	III.3	Review of John Rawls, *A Theory of Justice* (1972), Oxford Magazine 90 no. 1 (new series) (26 January)
	b	III.18	'The Rights and Wrongs of Abortion: A Reply to Judith Jarvis Thomson', Philosophy & Public Affairs 2: 117–45
	c		'Constitutional Law', *Annual Survey of Commonwealth Law 1972* (Butterworth), 2–8, 23–56, 62–6
1974	a		'Constitutional Law', *Annual Survey of Commonwealth Law 1973* (Butterworth), 1–66
	b		'Commonwealth and Dependencies', in *Halsbury's Laws of England*, vol. 6 (4th edn, Butterworth), 315–601
	c		'Rights and Wrongs in Legal Responses to Population Growth', in J.N. Santamaria (ed.), *Man—How Will He Survive?* (Adelaide), 91–100
	d		Review of R.S. Gae, *The Bank Nationalisation Case and the Constitution*, Modern L Rev 37: 120
1975			'Constitutional Law', *Annual Survey of Commonwealth Law 1974* (Butterworth), 1–61
1976	a		'Constitutional Law', *Annual Survey of Commonwealth Law 1975* (Butterworth), 1–56
	b		Chapters 18–21 (with Germain Grisez), in R. Lawler, D.W. Wuerl, and T.C. Lawler (eds), *The Teaching of Christ* (Huntingdon, IN: OSV), 275–354
1977	a	I.3	'Scepticism, Self-refutation and the Good of Truth', in P.M. Hacker and J. Raz (eds), *Law, Morality and Society: Essays in Honour of H.L.A. Hart* (OUP), 247–67
	b		'Some Formal Remarks about "Custom"', in International Law Association, Report of the First Meeting [April 1977] on the Theory and Methodology of International Law, 14–21
1978	a		'Catholic Social Teaching: *Populorum Progressio* and After', Church Alert (SODEPAX Newsletter) 19: 2–9; also in James V. Schall (ed.), *Liberation Theology in Latin America* (San Francisco: Ignatius Press, 1982)

	b		'Conscience, Infallibility and Contraception', The Month 239: 410–17
	c		'Abortion: Legal Aspects of', in Warren T. Reich (ed.), *Encyclopedia of Bioethics* (New York: Free Press), 26–32
1979		V.18	'Catholic Faith and the World Order: Reflections on E.R. Norman', Clergy Rev 64: 309–18
1980	a		*Natural Law and Natural Rights* (OUP) (425 pp)
			Legge Naturali e Diritti Naturali (trans. Di Blasi) (Milan: Giappichelli, 1996)
			Ley Natural y Derechos Naturales (trans. C. Orrego) (Buenos Aires: Abeledo-Perrot, 2000)
			Prawo naturalne i uprawnienia naturalne (trans. Karolina Lossman) Klasycy Filozofii Prawa (Warsaw: Dom Wydawniczy ABC, 2001)
			自然法与自然权利 ([Mandarin] trans. Jiaojiao Dong, Yi Yang, Xiaohui Liang) (Beijing: 2004)
			Lei Natural e Direitos Naturais (trans. Leila Mendes) (Sao Leopoldo, Brazil: Editora Unisinos, 2007)
	b		'Reflections on an Essay in Christian Ethics: Part I: Authority in Morals', Clergy Rev 65: 51–7: 'Part II: Morals and Method', 87–93
	c	V.19	'The Natural Law, Objective Morality, and Vatican II', in William E. May (ed), *Principles of Catholic Moral Life* (Chicago: Franciscan Herald Press), 113–49
1981	a		[*British North America Acts: The Role of Parliament*: Report from the Foreign Affairs Committee, House of Commons Paper 1980–81 HC 42 (21 January) (87 pp)]
	b		'Observations de M J.M. Finnis' [on Georges Kalinowski's review of *Natural Law and Natural Rights*], Archives de Philosophie du Droit 26: 425–7
	c		[Foreign Affairs Committee, *Supplementary Report on the British North America Acts: The Role of Parliament*, House of Commons Paper 1980–81 HC 295 (15 April) (23 pp)]
	d		[Foreign Affairs Committee, *Third Report on the British North America Acts: The Role of Parliament*, House of Commons Paper 1981–82 HC 128 (22 December) (17 pp)]
	e		'Natural Law and the "Is"-"Ought" Question: An Invitation to Professor Veatch', Cath Lawyer 26: 266–77
1982	a		(with Germain Grisez) 'The Basic Principles of Natural Law: A Reply to Ralph McInerny', American J Juris 26: 21–31
	b		Review of Anthony Battaglia, *Towards a Reformulation of Natural Law*, Scottish J Theol 35: 555–6
1983	a		'The Responsibilities of the United Kingdom Parliament and Government under the Australian Constitution', Adelaide L Rev 9: 91–107
	b		*Fundamentals of Ethics* (OUP; Washington DC: Georgetown University Press) (163 pp)
	c		'Power to Enforce Treaties in Australia—The High Court goes Centralist?', Oxford J Legal St 3: 126–30

	d		'The Fundamental Themes of *Laborem Exercens*', in Paul L. Williams (ed.), *Catholic Social Thought and the Social Teaching of John Paul II* (Scranton: Northeast Books), 19–31
	e		['In Vitro Fertilisation: Morality and Public Policy', Evidence submitted by the Catholic Bishops' Joint Committee on Bio-ethical Issues to the [Warnock] Committee of Inquiry into Human Fertilisation and Embryology, May, 5–18]
1984	a	I.10	i. 'Practical Reasoning, Human Goods and the End of Man', Proc Am Cath Phil Ass 58: 23–36; also in ii. New Blackfriars 66 (1985) 438–51
	b	IV.2	'The Authority of Law in the Predicament of Contemporary Social Theory', J Law, Ethics & Pub Policy 1: 115–37
	c		['Response to the Warnock Report', submission to Secretary of State for Social Services by the Catholic Bishops' Joint Bioethics Committee on Bio-ethical Issues, December, 3–17]
	d		'IVF and the Catholic Tradition', The Month 246: 55–8
	e		'Reforming the Expanded External Affairs Power', in Report of the External Affairs Subcommittee to the Standing Committee of the Australian Constitutional Convention (September), 43–51
1985	a	III.1	'A Bill of Rights for Britain? The Moral of Contemporary Jurisprudence' (Maccabaean Lecture in Jurisprudence), Proc Brit Acad 71: 303–31
	b	IV.9	'On "Positivism" and "Legal-Rational Authority"', Oxford J Leg St 3: 74–90
	c	IV.13	'On "The Critical Legal Studies Movement"', American J Juris 30: 21–42; also in J. Bell and J. Eekelaar (eds), *Oxford Essays in Jurisprudence: Third Series* (OUP, 1987), 145–65
	d		'Morality and the Ministry of Defence' (review), The Tablet, 3 August, 804–5
	e		'Personal Integrity, Sexual Morality and Responsible Parenthood', Anthropos [now Anthropotes] 1: 43–55
1986	a		'The "Natural Law Tradition"', J Legal Ed 36: 492–5
	b		'The Laws of God, the Laws of Man and Reverence for Human Life', in R. Hittinger (ed.), *Linking the Human Life Issues* (Chicago: Regnery Books), 59–98
1987	a	I.9	'Natural Inclinations and Natural Rights: Deriving "Ought" from "Is" according to Aquinas', in L. Elders and K. Hedwig (eds), *Lex et Libertas: Freedom and Law according to St Thomas Aquinas* (Studi Tomistici 30, Libreria Editrice Vaticana), 43–55
	b	II.8	'The Act of the Person' *Persona Veritá e Morale*, atti del Congresso Internazionale di Teologia Morale, Rome 1986 (Rome: Cittá Nuova Editrice), 159–75
	c	III.2	'Legal Enforcement of Duties to Oneself: Kant v. Neo-Kantians', Columbia L Rev 87: 433–56
	d	IV.4	'On Positivism and the Foundations of Legal Authority: Comment', in Ruth Gavison (ed.), *Issues in Legal Philosophy: the Influence of H.L.A. Hart* (OUP), 62–75

	e	IV.12	'On Reason and Authority in Law's Empire', Law and Philosophy 6: 357–80
	f		Germain Grisez, Joseph Boyle, and John Finnis, 'Practical Principles, Moral Truth, and Ultimate Ends', American J Juris 32: 99–151 (also, with original table of contents restored, in 1991d)
	g		*Nuclear Deterrence, Morality and Realism* (with Joseph Boyle and Germain Grisez) (OUP) (429 pp)
	h		'Answers [to questions about nuclear and non-nuclear defence options]', in Oliver Ramsbottom (ed.), *Choices: Nuclear and Non-Nuclear Defence Options* (London: Brasseys' Defence Publishers), 219–34
	i		'The Claim of Absolutes', The Tablet 241: 364–6
	j		['On Human Infertility Services and Bioethical Research', response by the Catholic Bishops' Joint Committee on Bioethical Issues to the Department of Health and Social Security, June, 3–12]
1988	a	V.21	'The Consistent Ethic: A Philosophical Critique', in Thomas G. Fuechtmann (ed.), *Consistent Ethic of Life* (Kansas: Sheed & Ward), 140–81
	b	V.20	'Nuclear Deterrence, Christian Conscience, and the End of Christendom', New Oxford Rev [Berkeley, CA] July–August: 6–16
	c		'Goods are Meant for Everyone: Reflection on Encyclical *Sollicitudo Rei Socialis*', L'Osservatore Romano, weekly edn, 21 March, 21
	d		'"Faith and Morals": A Note', The Month 21/2: 563–7
	e		Germain Grisez, Joseph Boyle, John Finnis, and William E. May, '"Every Marital Act Ought to be Open to New Life": Toward a Clearer Understanding', The Thomist 52: 365–426, also in Grisez, Boyle, Finnis, and May, *The Teaching of Humanae Vitae: A Defense* (San Francisco: Ignatius Press); Italian trans. in Anthropotes 1: 73–122
	f		'Absolute Moral Norms: Their Ground, Force and Permanence', Anthropotes 2: 287–303
1989	a	II.5	'Persons and their Associations', Proc Aristotelian Soc, Supp. vol. 63: 267–74
	b	IV.3	'Law as Coordination', Ratio Juris 2: 97–104
	c	V.11	'On Creation and Ethics', Anthropotes 2: 197–206
	d		'La morale chrétienne et la guerre: entretien avec John Finnis', Catholica 13: 15–23
	e		'Russell Hittinger's Straw Man', Fellowship of Catholic Scholars Newsletter 12/2: 6–8 (corrigenda in following issue)
	f		'Nuclear Deterrence and Christian Vocation', New Blackfriars 70: 380–7
1990	a	I.12	'Aristotle, Aquinas, and Moral Absolutes', Catholica: International Quarterly Selection 12: 7–15; Spanish trans. by Carlos I. Massini-Correas in Persona y Derecho 28 (1993), and in

			A.G. Marques and J. Garcia-Huidobro (eds), *Razon y Praxis* (Valparaiso: Edeval, 1994), 319–36
	b	IV.16	'Allocating Risks and Suffering: Some Hidden Traps', Cleveland State L Rev 38: 193–207
	c		'Natural Law and Legal Reasoning', Cleveland State L Rev 38: 1–13
	d	IV.17	'Concluding Reflections', Cleveland State L Rev 38: 231–50
	e	V.16	'Conscience in the Letter to the Duke of Norfolk', in Ian Ker and Alan G. Hill (eds), *Newman after a Hundred Years* (OUP), 401–18
	f		Joseph Boyle, Germain Grisez, and John Finnis, 'Incoherence and Consequentialism (or Proportionalism)—A Rejoinder' American Cath Phil Q 64: 271–7
	g		'The Natural Moral Law and Faith', in Russell E. Smith (ed.), *The Twenty-Fifth Anniversary of Vatican II: A Look Back and a Look Ahead* (Braintree, MA: Pope John Center), 223–38; discussion (with Alasdair MacIntyre), 250–62
1991	a	II.9	'Object and Intention in Moral Judgments according to St Thomas Aquinas', The Thomist 55: 1–27; rev. version in J. Follon and J. McEvoy (eds), *Finalité et Intentionnalité: Doctrine Thomiste et Perspectives Modernes*, Bibliothèque Philosophique de Louvain No. 35 (Paris: J. Vrin, 1992), 127–48
	b	II.10	'Intention and Side-effects', in R.G. Frey and Christopher W. Morris (eds), *Liability and Responsibility: Essays in Law and Morals* (CUP), 32–64
	c		*Moral Absolutes: Tradition, Revision and Truth* (Washington DC: Catholic University of America Press) (115 pp) *Absolutos Morales: Tradición, Revisión y Verdad* (trans. Juan José García Norro) (Barcelona: Ediciones Internacionales Universitarias, EUNSA SA) *Gli assoluti morali: Tradizione, revisione & verità* (trans. Andrea Maria Maccarini) (Milan: Edizioni Ares, 1993)
	d		'Introduction', in John Finnis (ed.), *Natural Law*, vol. I (International Library of Essays in Law and Legal Theory, Schools 1.1) (Dartmouth: New York University Press), xi–xxiii
	e		'Introduction', in John Finnis (ed.), *Natural Law*, vol. II (International Library of Essays in Law and Legal Theory, Schools 1.2) (Dartmouth: Aldershot, Sydney), xi–xvi
	f		'A propos de la "valeur intrinsèque de la vie humaine"', Catholica 28: 15–21
	g		'Commonwealth and Dependencies', in *Halsbury's Laws of England*, vol. 6 re-issue (4th edn, London: Butterworth), 345–559
1992	a	I.14	'Natural Law and Legal Reasoning', in Robert P. George (ed.), *Natural Law Theory: Contemporary Essays* (OUP), 134–57
	b	III.7	'Commentary on Dummett and Weithman', in Brian Barry and Robert E. Goodin, *Free Movement: Ethical Issues in the Transnational Migration of People and of Money* (University Park, Pennsylvania: University of Pennsylvania Press), 203–10

	c	III.15	'Economics, Justice and the Value of Life: Concluding Remarks', in Luke Gormally (ed.), *Economics and the Dependent Elderly: Autonomy, Justice and Quality of Care* (CUP), 189–98
	d	V.9	*'Historical Consciousness' and Theological Foundations*, Etienne Gilson Lecture No. 15 (Toronto: Pontifical Institute of Mediaeval Studies) (32 pp)
	e	V.17	'On the Grace of Humility: A New Theological Reflection', The Allen Review 7: 4–7
1993	a	II.16/ III.19	'Abortion and Health Care Ethics', in Raanan Gillon (ed.), *Principles of Health Care Ethics* (Chichester: John Wiley), 547–57
	b		'The Legal Status of the Unborn Baby', Catholic Medical Quarterly 43: 5–11
	c	II.19	'*Bland*: Crossing the Rubicon?', LQR 109: 329–37
	d		'Theology and the Four Principles: A Roman Catholic View I' (with Anthony Fisher OP), in Raanon Gillon (ed.), *Principles of Health Care Ethics* (Chichester: John Wiley), 31–44
	e		'The "Value of Human Life" and "The Right to Death": Some Reflections on *Cruzan* and Ronald Dworkin', Southern Illinois University LJ 17: 559–71
1994	a	II.12	'On Conditional Intentions and Preparatory Intentions', in Luke Gormally (ed.), *Moral Truth and Moral Tradition: Essays in Honour of Peter Geach and Elizabeth Anscombe* (Dublin: Four Courts Press), 163–76
	b		'Law, Morality, and "Sexual Orientation"', Notre Dame L Rev 69: 1049–76; also, with additions, Notre Dame J Law, Ethics & Public Policy 9 (1995) 11–39
	c		'Liberalism and Natural Law Theory', Mercer L Rev 45: 687–704
	d		'"Shameless Acts" in Colorado: Abuse of Scholarship in Constitutional Cases', Academic Questions 7/4: 10–41
	e		Germain Grisez and John Finnis, 'Negative Moral Precepts Protect the Dignity of the Human Person', L'Osservatore Romano, English edn, 23 February
	f		'Beyond the Encyclical', The Tablet, 8 January, reprinted in John Wilkins (ed.), *Understanding Veritatis Splendor* (London: SPCK), 69–76
	g		Germain Grisez, John Finnis, and William E. May, 'Indissolubility, Divorce and Holy Communion', New Blackfriars 75 (June), 321–30
	h		'"Living Will" Legislation', in Luke Gormally (ed.), *Euthanasia, Clinical Practice and the Law* (London: Linacre Centre), 167–76
	i		'Unjust Laws in a Democratic Society: Some Philosophical and Theological Reflections', in Joseph Joblin and Réal Tremblay (eds), *I cattolici e la società pluralista: il caso delle leggi imperfette: atti del I Colloquio sui cattolici nella società pluralista: Roma, 9–12 Novembre 1994* (Bologna: ESP), 99–114
1995	a	II.11	'Intention in Tort Law', in David Owen (ed.), *Philosophical Foundations of Tort Law* (OUP), 229–48

	b	III.14	'A Philosophical Case against Euthanasia', 'The Fragile Case for Euthanasia: A Reply to John Harris', and 'Misunderstanding the Case against Euthanasia: Response to Harris's First Reply', in John Keown (ed.), *Euthanasia: Ethical, Legal and Clinical Perspectives* (CUP), 23–35, 46–55, 62–71
	c		'History of Philosophy of Law' (465–8), 'Problems in the Philosophy of Law' (468–72), 'Austin' (67), 'Defeasible' (181), 'Dworkin' (209–10), 'Grotius' (328), 'Hart' (334), 'Legal Positivism' (476–7), 'Legal Realism' (477), 'Natural Law' (606–7), 'Natural Rights' (607), in Ted Honderich (ed.), *Oxford Companion to Philosophy* (OUP)
1996	a	III.5	'Is Natural Law Theory Compatible with Limited Government?', in Robert P. George (ed.), *Natural Law, Liberalism, and Morality* (OUP), 1–26
	b	III.13	'The Ethics of War and Peace in the Catholic Natural Law Tradition', in Terry Nardin (ed.), *The Ethics of War and Peace* (Princeton University Press), 15–39
	c	IV.7	'The Truth in Legal Positivism', in Robert P. George (ed.), *The Autonomy of Law: Essays on Legal Positivism* (OUP), 195–214
	d		'Unjust Laws in a Democratic Society: Some Philosophical and Theological Reflections', Notre Dame L Rev 71: 595–604 (a revised version of 1994i)
	e	I.13	'Loi naturelle', in Monique Canto-Sperber (ed.), *Dictionnaire de Philosophie Morale* (Paris: Presses Universitaires de France), 862–8
1997	a		'Natural Law—Positive Law', in A. Lopez Trujillo, I. Herranz, and E. Sgreccia (eds), *'Evangelium Vitae' and Law* (Libreria Editrice Vaticana), 199–209
	b	I.15	'Commensuration and Public Reason', in Ruth Chang (ed.), *Incommensurability, Comparability and Practical Reasoning* (HUP), 215–33, 285–9
	c	III.21	'Law, Morality and "Sexual Orientation"', in John Corvino (ed.), *Same Sex: Debating the Ethics, Science, and Culture of Homosexuality* (Lanham: Rowman & Littlefield), 31–43
	d	III.22	'The Good of Marriage and the Morality of Sexual Relations: Some Philosophical and Historical Observations', Am J Juris 42: 97–134
1998	a	I.16	'Public Reason, Abortion and Cloning', Valparaiso Univ LR 32: 361–82
	b	III.16	'Euthanasia, Morality and Law', Loyola of Los Angeles L Rev 31: 1123–45
	c	V.3	'On the Practical Meaning of Secularism', Notre Dame L Rev 73: 491–515
	d		*Aquinas: Moral, Political, and Legal Theory* (OUP) (xxi + 385 pp)
	e		'Public Good: The Specifically Political Common Good in Aquinas', in Robert P. George (ed.), *Natural Law and Moral Inquiry* (Washington DC: Georgetown University Press), 174–209

	f		'Natural Law', in Edward Craig (ed.), *Routledge Encyclopaedia of Philosophy*, vol. 6 (London: Routledge), 685–90
1999	a	I.2	'Natural Law and the Ethics of Discourse', American J Juris 43: 53–73; also in Ratio Juris 12: 354–73
	b	III.12	'Retribution: Punishment's Formative Aim', American J Juris 44: 91–103
	c	IV.20	'The Fairy Tale's Moral', LQR 115: 170–5
	d	V.6	'The Catholic Church and Public Policy Debates in Western Liberal Societies: The Basis and Limits of Intellectual Engagement', in Luke Gormally (ed.), *Issues for a Catholic Bioethic* (London: Linacre Centre), 261–73
	e		'What is the Common Good, and Why does it Concern the Client's Lawyer?', South Texas L Rev 40: 41–53
2000	a	II.1	'The Priority of Persons', in Jeremy Horder (ed.), *Oxford Essays in Jurisprudence, Fourth Series* (OUP), 1–15
	b	II.17	'Some Fundamental Evils of Generating Human Embryos by Cloning', in Cosimo Marco Mazzoni (ed.), *Etica della Ricerca Biologica* (Florence: Leo S. Olschki Editore), 115–23; also in C.M. Mazzoni (ed.), *Ethics and Law in Biological Research* (The Hague, London: Martinus Nijhoff; Boston: Kluwer, 2002), 99–106
	c		'Abortion, Natural Law and Public Reason', in Robert P. George and Christopher Wolfe (eds), *Natural Law and Public Reason* (Washington DC: Georgetown University Press), 71–105
	d		'On the Incoherence of Legal Positivism', Notre Dame L Rev 75: 1597–611
	e		'God the Father', in Peter Newby (ed.), *Occasional Papers from the Millennium Conferences at the Oxford University Catholic Chaplaincy* No. 1 (Oxford), 24–6
2001	a	II.13	'"Direct" and "Indirect": A Reply to Critics of Our Action Theory' (with Germain Grisez and Joseph Boyle), The Thomist 65: 1–44
	b	III.6	'Virtue and the Constitution of the United States', Fordham L Rev 69: 1595–602
	c		'Reason, Faith and Homosexual Acts', Catholic Social Science Review 6: 61–9
2002	a	IV.5	'Natural Law: The Classical Tradition', in Jules Coleman and Scott Shapiro (eds), *The Oxford Handbook of Jurisprudence and Philosophy of Law* (OUP), 1–60
	b	V.22	'Secularism, the Root of the Culture of Death', in Luke Gormally (ed.), *Culture of Life—Culture of Death* (London: Linacre Centre)
	c		'Aquinas on *jus* and Hart on Rights: A Response', Rev of Politics 64: 407–10
	d		Patrick H. Martin and John Finnis, 'The Identity of "Anthony Rivers"', Recusant History 26: 39–74
	e		—— and —— 'Tyrwhitt of Kettleby, Part I: Goddard Tyrwhitt, Martyr, 1580', Recusant History 26: 301–13

2003	a	III.8	'Natural Law & the Re-making of Boundaries', in Allen Buchanan and Margaret Moore (eds), *States, Nations, and Boundaries: The Ethics of Making Boundaries* (CUP), 171–8
	b	IV.1	'Law and What I Truly Should Decide', American J Juris 48: 107–30
	c	V.10	'Saint Thomas More and the Crisis in Faith and Morals', The Priest 7/1: 10–15, 29–30
	d		'Secularism, Morality and Politics', L'Osservatore Romano, English edn, 29 January, 9
	e		'Shakespeare's Intercession for *Love's Martyr*' (with Patrick Martin), Times Literary Supplement, no. 5220, 18 April, 12–14
	f		'An Intrinsically Disordered Attraction', in John F. Harvey and Gerard V. Bradley (eds), *Same-Sex Attraction: A Parents' Guide* (South Bend: St Augustine's Press), 89–99
	g		'Nature and Natural Law in Contemporary Philosophical and Theological Debates: Some Observations', in Juan Correa and Elio Sgreccia (eds), *The Nature & Dignity of the Human Person as the Foundation of the Right to Life: The Challenges of Contemporary Culture* (Rome: Libreria Editrice Vaticana), 81–109
	h		Patrick H. Martin and John Finnis, 'Tyrwhitt of Kettleby, Part II: Robert Tyrwhitt, a Main Benefactor of John Gerard SJ, 1599–1605', Recusant History 27: 556–69
	i		—— and —— 'Thomas Thorpe, "W.S." and the Catholic Intelligencers', Elizabethan Literary Renaissance, 1–43
	j		—— and —— '*Caesar*, Succession, and the Chastisement of Rulers', Notre Dame L Rev 78: 1045–74
	k		'Commonwealth and Dependencies', in *Halsbury's Laws of England*, vol. 6 re-issue (4th edn, London: Butterworth), 409–518
	l		'Abortion for Cleft Palate: The Human Fertilisation and Embryology Act 1990', Sunday Telegraph, 7 December
	m		'An Oxford Play Festival in 1582' (with Patrick Martin), Notes & Queries 50: 391–4
2004	a	II.18	'Per un'etica dell'eguaglianza nel diritto alla vita: Un commento a Peter Singer', in Rosangela Barcaro and Paolo Becchi (eds), *Questioni Mortali: L'Attuale Dibattito sulla Morte Cerebrale e il Problema dei Trapianti* (Naples: Edizioni Scientifiche Italiane), 127–39
	b	IV.22	'Helping Enact Unjust Laws without Complicity in Injustice', American J Juris 49: 11–42
2005	a	I.1	'Foundations of Practical Reason Revisited', American J Juris 50: 109–32
	b	I.4	'Self-referential (or Performative) Inconsistency: Its Significance for Truth', Proceedings of the Catholic Philosophical Association 78: 13–21
	c	II.2	'"The Thing I Am": Personal Identity in Aquinas and Shakespeare', Social Philosophy & Policy 22: 250–82; also in Ellen Frankel Paul, Fred. D. Miller, and Jeffrey Paul (eds), *Personal Identity* (CUP), 250–82

	d	IV.6	'Philosophy of Law' (Chinese trans.), in Ouyang Kang (ed.), *The Map of Contemporary British and American Philosophy* (Beijing: Dangdai Yingmei Zhexue Ditu), 388–413
	e		'On "Public Reason"', in *O Racji Pulicznej* (Warsaw: Ius et Lex), 7–30 (Polish trans.), 33–56 (English original); <http://ssrn.com/abstract=955815>
	f		'Restricting Legalised Abortion is not Intrinsically Unjust', in Helen Watt (ed.), *Cooperation, Complicity & Conscience* (London: Linacre Centre), 209–45
	g		'A Vote Decisive for... a More Restrictive Law', in Helen Watt (ed.), *Cooperation, Complicity & Conscience* (London: Linacre Centre), 269–95
	h		'Aquinas' Moral, Political and Legal Philosophy', Stanford Encyclopedia of Philosophy; <http://plato.stanford.edu/entries/aquinas-moral-political/>
	i		Patrick H. Martin and John Finnis, 'Benedicam Dominum: Ben Jonson's Strange 1605 Inscription', Times Literary Supplement, 4 November, 12–13
	j		—— and —— 'The Secret Sharers: "Anthony Rivers" and the Appellant Controversy, 1601–2', Huntingdon Library Q 69/2: 195–238
2006	a	V.4	'Religion and State: Some Main Issues and Sources', American J Juris 51: 107–30
	b		'Observations for the Austral Conference to mark the 25th Anniversary of *Natural Law and Natural Rights*', Cuadernos de Extensión Jurídica (Universidad de los Andes) no. 13: 27–30
2007	a	III.9	'Nationality, Alienage and Constitutional Principle', LQR 123: 417–45
	b	IV.10	'On Hart's Ways: Law as Reason and as Fact', American J Juris 52: 25–53; also in Matthew Kramer and Claire Grant (eds), *The Legacy of H.L.A. Hart: Legal, Political & Moral Philosophy* (OUP, 2009), 1–27
	c		'Natural Law Theories of Law', Stanford Encyclopedia of Philosophy; <http://plato.stanford.edu/entries/natural-law-theories/>
2008	a	I.5/ II.7/V.8	'Reason, Revelation, Universality and Particularity in Ethics', AJJ 53: 23–48
	b	II.6	'Universality, Personal and Social Identity, and Law', address, Congresso Sul-Americano de Filosofia do Direito, Porto Alegre, Brazil, 4 October 2007; Oxford Legal Studies Research Paper 5; <http://ssrn.com/abstract=1094277>
	c	III.20	'Marriage: A Basic and Exigent Good', The Monist 91: 396–414
	d	[V.13]	'Grounds of Law & Legal Theory: A Response', Legal Theory 13: 315–44
	e		'Common Law Constraints: Whose Common Good Counts?', Oxford Legal Studies Research Paper 10; <http://ssrn.com/abstract_id=1100628>

	f		*Humanae Vitae*: A New Translation with Notes (London: Catholic Truth Society) (31 pp)
2009	a	II.3	'Anscombe's Essays', National Catholic Bioethics Q 9/1: 199–207
	b	IV.11	'H.L.A. Hart: A Twentieth Century Oxford Political Philosopher', American J Juris 54: 161–85
	c	V.1	'Does Free Exercise of Religion Deserve Constitutional Mention?', American J Juris 54: 41–66
	d	V.2	'Telling the Truth about God and Man in a Pluralist Society: Economy or Explication?', in Christopher Wolfe (ed.), *The Naked Public Square Revisited: Religion & Politics in the Twenty-First Century* (Wilmington: ISI Books), 111–25, 204–9
	e		'Endorsing Discrimination between Faiths: A Case of Extreme Speech?', in Ivan Hare and James Weinstein (eds), *Extreme Speech and Democracy* (OUP), 430–41
	f		'Discrimination between Religions: Some Thoughts on Reading Greenawalt's *Religion and the Constitution*', Constitutional Commentary 25: 265–71
	g		'Commonwealth', in *Halsbury's Laws of England*, vol. 13 (5th edn, London: LexisNexis), 471–589
	h		'Why Religious Liberty is a Special, Important and Limited Right', Notre Dame Legal Studies Paper 09–11; <http://ssrn.com/abstract=1392278>
	i		'The Lords' Eerie Swansong: A Note on *R (Purdy) v Director of Public Prosecutions*', Oxford Legal Studies Research Paper 31; <http://ssrn.com/abstract=1477281>
	j		'The Mental Capacity Act 2005: Some Ethical and Legal Issues', in Helen Watt (ed.), *Incapacity & Care: Controversies in Healthcare and Research* (London: Linacre Centre), 95–105
	k		'Debate over the Interpretation of *Dignitas personae*'s Teaching on Embryo Adoption', National Catholic Bioethics Q 9: 475–8
2010	a	II.14	'Directly Discriminatory Decisions: A Missed Opportunity', LQR 126: 491–6
	b		'Law as Idea, Ideal and Duty: A Comment on Simmonds, *Law as a Moral Idea*', Jurisprudence 1: 247–53

OTHER WORKS CITED

Abbott, Thomas Kingsmill (1883), *Kant's Theory of Ethics: Kant's Critique of Practical Reason and Other Works on the Theory of Ethics* (3rd edn, London: Longmans, Green)
Admiraal, Pieter V. (1988), 'Justifiable Euthanasia', Issues in Law & Med 3: 361
Allen, R.E. (1991), *The Dialogues of Plato*, vol. II, *The Symposium* (New Haven: Yale University Press)
Altman, Dennis (1986), *AIDS and the New Puritanism* (London: Pluto Press) (US edn, *AIDS in the Mind of America* (New York: Anchor Books)
Andrews, J.A. (1984), 'The European Jurisprudence of Human Rights', Maryland L Rev 43: 463–517
Anscombe, G.E.M. (1957), *Intention* (Oxford: Blackwell)
—— (1958), 'Modern Moral Philosophy', *Philosophy* 33 (1958), also in Anscombe (1981)
—— (1961), 'War and Murder', in *Nuclear Weapons and Christian Conscience* (ed. W. Stein) (London), also in Anscombe (1981)
—— (1976), 'On Frustration of the Majority by Fulfilment of the Majority's Will', Analysis 36: 161–8; also in Anscombe (1981) 123–9
—— (1981), *Ethics, Religion and Politics: Collected Philosophical Papers of G.E.M. Anscombe*, vol. 3 (Oxford: Blackwell, 1981)
Ball, Carlos A. (1997), 'Moral Foundations for a Discourse on Same-Sex Marriage: Looking Beyond Political Liberalism', Georgetown LJ 85: 1872–943
Barnes, Jonathan (1982), 'The Just War', in Norman Kretzmann, Anthony Kenny, and Jan Pinborg (eds), *The Cambridge History of Later Medieval Philosophy* (CUP), 773–82
Beatson, Jack (2004), 'Aliens, Friendly Aliens and Friendly Enemy Aliens', in J. Beatson and R. Zimmermann, *Jurists Uprooted: German-Speaking Émigré Lawyers in Twentieth-Century Britain* (OUP), 73–104
Beauchamp, Tom L. and Childress, James F. ([1979] 1989), *Principles of Biomedical Ethics* (3rd edn, New York: OUP)
Beck, L.W. (1969), *Foundations of the Metaphysics of Morals* (ed. R.P. Wolff) (Indianapolis: Bobbs Merrill)
Bell, Alan P. and Weinberg, Martin S. (1978), *Homosexualities: A Study in Diversity among Men and Women* (New York: Simon & Schuster)
Bennett, Jonathan (1966), 'Whatever the Consequences', Analysis 26: 83–102
Blankenhorn, David (1997), 'I Do?', First Things 77: 14–15
Blumstein, Philip and Schwartz, Pepper (1983), *American Couples* (New York: Morrow)
Boswell, John (1980), *Christianity, Social Tolerance, and Homosexuality* (Chicago: University of Chicago Press)
Boyle, Joseph M. (1984), 'Aquinas, Kant, and Donagan on Moral Principles', 58 New Scholasticism 58: 391–408
——, Grisez, Germain, and Finnis, J.M. (1990), 'Incoherence and Consequentialism (or Proportionalism)—A Rejoinder', Am Cath Phil Q 64: 271–7

Braine, David (1993), *The Human Person: Animal and Spirit* (London: Duckworth; Notre Dame: University of Notre Dame Press)
Brody, Baruch (1972), 'Thomson on Abortion', Philosophy & Public Affairs 1: 335–40
Canovan, Margaret (1996), *Nationhood & Political Theory* (Cheltenham: Edward Elgar)
Castañeda, H.-N. (1972), 'On the Problem of Formulating a Coherent Act-Utilitarianism', Analysis 32: 118–24
Catechism of the Catholic Church (rev. edn, 1997) (London: Geoffey Chapman)
Chambers, David L. (1996), 'What If? The Legal Consequences of Marriage and the Legal Needs of Lesbian and Gay Male Couples', Michigan L Rev 95: 447–91
Cohen, Marshall (ed.) (1984), *Ronald Dworkin and Contemporary Jurisprudence* (London: Duckworth)
Coolidge, David Orgon (1997), 'Same-Sex Marriage? *Baehr v. Miike* and the Meaning of Marriage', South Texas L Rev 38: 1–119
Daube, David (1965), *Collaboration with Tyranny in Rabbinic Law* (OUP)
—— (1972), 'The Linguistics of Suicide', Philosophy & Public Affairs 1: 387–437
Devlin, Patrick (1965), *The Enforcement of Morals* (OUP)
Dicey, A.V. ([1885] 1908), *Introduction to the Study of the Law of the Constitution* (1st edn, 1885), 239–40; (7th edn, 1908) (London: Macmillan)
Dorr, Donal (1989), 'Solidarity and Integral Human Development', in Gregory Baum and Robert Ellsberg (eds), *The Logic of Solidarity: Commentaries on Pope John Paul II's Encyclical On Social Concern* (Maryknoll: Orbis Books), 143–54
Dover, Kenneth G. (1978), *Greek Homosexuality* (HUP)
Dummett, Ann (1992), 'The Transnational Migration of People Seen from Within a Natural Law Tradition', in Brian Barry and Robert E. Goodin (eds), *Free Movement: Ethical Issues in the Transnational Migration of People and of Money* (University Park, PA: University of Pennsylvania Press), 169–80
Durkheim, Émile (1897), *Le Suicide: étude de sociologie* (Paris: F. Alcan)
Dworkin, Ronald (1977, 1978), *Taking Rights Seriously* (rev. edn with Reply to Critics) (HUP; London: Duckworth)
—— (1978), 'Liberalism', in Stuart Hampshire (ed.), *Public and Private Morality* (CUP), 113–43
—— (1978), 'Political Judges and the Rule of Law', Proc Brit Acad 44: 259–87
—— (1984), 'A Reply …' in Marshall Cohen (ed.), *Ronald Dworkin and Contemporary Jurisprudence* (London: Duckworth)
—— (1985), *A Matter of Principle* (HUP)
—— (1991), 'The Right to Death', New York Review of Books, 31 January, 14–17
—— (1993), *Life's Dominion: An Argument about Abortion, Euthanasia and Individual Freedom* (London: Harper Collins; HUP)
—— (1993), 'When Can a Doctor Kill?', *The Times* (London), 27 April, 16
—— (1996), *Freedom's Law: The Moral Reading of the American Constitution* (HUP; OUP)
—— (1996), 'Sex, Death, and the Courts', New York Review of Books, 8 August, 44
Edwards, Robert and Steptoe, Patrick (1981), *A Matter of Life: The Story of a Medical Breakthrough* (London: Sphere Books)
Festugière, A. J. (1978), *Deux Prédicateurs de l'Antiquité': Télès et Musonius* (Paris: Vrin)
Fisher, Anthony OP (1989), *IVF: The Critical Issues* (Melbourne: Collins Dove)
Fletcher, George P. (1984), 'Human Dignity as a Constitutional Value', U W Ontario L Rev 22: 171–82
Foot, Philippa (1967), 'The Problem of Abortion and the Doctrine of Double Effect', The Oxford Review 5: 5–15

—— (1985), 'Morality, Action and Outcome' in Ted Honderich (ed.), *Morality and Objectivity* (London: Routledge and Kegan Paul), 23–38
—— (1985), 'Utilitarianism and the Virtues', Mind 94: 196–209
Frankfurter, Felix (1955), 'Mr Justice Roberts', U Pa L Rev 104: 311–17
Freeborn, Dennis (1990), *From Old English to Standard English* (2nd edn, Toronto: University of Ottawa Press)
Friedman, L. and Israel, F.L. (eds) (1969), *The Justices of the United States Supreme Court 1789–1969*, iii
George, Robert P. (1988), 'Recent Criticism of Natural Law Theory', U Chicago L Rev 55: 1371–429
—— (1992), 'Does the "Incommensurability Thesis" Imperil Common Sense Moral Judgments?', AJJ 37: 182–95
—— (ed.) (1992), *Natural Law Theory: Contemporary Essays* (OUP)
—— (1993), *Making Men Moral: Civil Liberties and Public Morality* (OUP)
—— (1995), '"Shameless Acts" Revisited: Some Questions for Martha Nussbaum', Academic Questions 9: 24–42
—— (ed.) (1996), *The Autonomy of Law: Essays on Legal Positivism* (OUP)
—— (1999), *In Defence of Natural Law* (OUP)
—— and Gerard V. Bradley (1995), 'Marriage and the Liberal Imagination', Georgetown LJ 84: 301–20
Goff of Chieveley, Robert, Lord (1988), 'The Mental Element in the Crime of Murder', LQR 104: 30–59
Gormally, Luke (1992), 'The Aged: Non-Persons, Dignity and Justice', in Luke Gormally (ed.), *The Dependent Elderly: Autonomy, Justice and Quality of Care* (CUP), 181–8
Gregor, Mary (1963), *Laws of Freedom: A Study of Kant's Method of Applying the Categorical Imperative in the* Metaphysik der Sitten (Oxford: Blackwell)
Grisez, Germain (1970), *Abortion: The Myths, the Realities and the Arguments* (New York: Corpus Books)
—— (1970), 'Towards a Natural Law Ethics of Killing', AJJ 15: 64–96
—— (1975), *Beyond the New Theism: A Philosophy of Religion* (Notre Dame: University of Notre Dame Press)
—— (1978), 'Against Consequentialism', AJJ 23: 21–72
—— (1983), *Christian Moral Principles* (Chicago: Franciscan Herald Press)
—— (1990), 'Should Nutrition and Hydration be Provided to Permanently Comatose, and Other Mentally Disabled Persons?', Linacre Q, May, 30–43
—— (1993), *Living a Christian Life* (Quincy: Franciscan Press)
—— (1997), *Difficult Moral Questions* (Quincy: Franciscan Press)
—— and Boyle, Joseph M. (1979), *Life and Death with Liberty and Justice* (Notre Dame: University of Notre Dame Press)
Grotius, Hugo ([1625] 1925), *The Law of War and Peace* (trans. Francis W. Kelsey) (OUP)
Haksar, Vinit (1979), *Equality, Liberty, and Perfectionism* (OUP)
Hand, Learned (1958), *The Bill of Rights* (HUP)
Hare, R.M. (1972), 'Rules of War and Moral Reasoning', Philosophy & Public Affairs 1: 166–81
Harris, John (1985, 1992), *The Value of Life* (London: Routledge)
—— (1995), 'Euthanasia and the Value of Human Life', 'The Philosophical Case against the Philosophical Case against Euthanasia', 'Final Thoughts on Final Acts', in John Keown (ed.), *Euthanasia Examined: Ethical, Clinical and Legal Perspectives* (CUP), 6–22, 36–45, 56–61

Hart, H.L.A. (1968), *Punishment & Responsibility: Essays in the Philosophy of Law* (OUP)
—— (1972), 'Abortion Law Reform: The English Experience', Melbourne U LR 8: 388–411
—— (1973), 'Rawls on Liberty and Its Priority', U Chicago L Rev 40: 534–55
—— (2008), *Punishment & Responsibility: Essays in the Philosophy of Law* [1968] (2nd edn, with Introduction by John Gardner, OUP)
Hill, Thomas E. (1980), 'Humanity as an End in Itself', Ethics 91: 84–99
Hindley, Clifford and Cohen, David (1991), 'Debate: Law, Society and Homosexuality in Classical Athens', Past & Present 133: 167–83
Hobhouse, L.T. ([1911] 1964), *Liberalism* (OUP)
Hodgson, D.H. (1967), *Consequences of Utilitarianism* (OUP)
Hohfeld, Wesley N. (1923), *Fundamental Legal Conceptions as Applied in Judicial Reasoning* (ed. W.W. Cook) (New Haven: Yale University Press)
Holdsworth, William (1926), *History of English Law*, vol. ix (London: Methuen)
—— (1938), *History of English Law*, vols x, xi, xiii (London: Methuen)
Honoré, A.M. (1960), 'Rights of Exclusion and Immunities against Divesting', Tulane L Rev 34: 453–68
Hooper, Walter (2004), *C.S. Lewis. Collected Letters*, vol. II (London: Harper Collins)
John Paul II (1994), *Crossing the Threshold of Hope* (London: Jonathan Cape)
Jones, Ernest ([1953] [1961]1964), *The Life and Work of Sigmund Freud* (abridged edn, Harmondsworth: Penguin)
Jones, W.T. (1940), *Morality and Freedom in the Philosophy of Immanuel Kant* (OUP)
Jordan, Mark (1997), *The Invention of Sodomy in Christian Theology* (Chicago: University of Chicago Press)
Kant, Immanuel ([1780–81] [1924] [trans. 1930] 1963), *Lectures on Ethics* (trans. Louis Infield) (New York: Harper & Row; London: Methuen)
—— ([1781, 1787] [trans, 1929] 1965), *Critique of Pure Reason* (trans. Norman Kemp Smith) (London: Macmillan)
—— ([1784] 1963), *Idea for a Universal History from a Cosmopolitan Point of View*, in *Immanuel Kant on History* (ed. Lewis White Beck) (Indianapolis: Bobbs Merrill)
—— ([1785] 1956), *Groundwork of the Metaphysic of Morals (Grundlegung zur Metaphysik der Sitten)* (trans. H.J. Paton) (London: Routledge)
—— ([1785] 1976), *Critique of Practical Reason* (trans. Lewis White Beck) (Indianapolis: Bobbs Merrill)
—— ([1790] 1952), *Critique of Judgment* (trans. James Creed Meredith) (OUP)
—— ([1797] 1965), *The Metaphysical Elements of Justice* [Part I (*Rechtslehre*) of *The Metaphysics of Morals*] (trans. John Ladd) (Indianapolis: Hackett)
—— ([1797] 1964), *The Doctrine of Virtue: Part 2 of the Metaphysic of Morals, with the introduction to the Metaphysic of Morals and the preface to the Doctrine of Law* (trans. Mary Gregor) (New York: Harper)
—— ([1797] 1991), *The Metaphysics of Morals* (trans. Mary Gregor) (CUP)
Kass, Leon R. (1978), 'Teleology and Darwin's *The Origin of Species*: Beyond Chance and Necessity?', in Stuart F. Spicker (ed.), *Organism, Medicine, and Metaphysics: Essays in Honour of Hans Jonas* (Dordrecht and Boston: D. Reidel,) 97–120
Keizer, Bert (1996), *Dancing with Mister D: Notes on Life and Death* (London: Doubleday)
Kelly, George Armstrong (1969), *Idealism, Politics and History: Sources of Hegelian Thought* (CUP)
Kelly, J.M. (1984), *The Irish Constitution* (2nd edn, Dublin: Jurist Publications)
Kenny, John (1979), 'The Advantages of a Written Constitution incorporating a Bill of Rights', Northern Ireland LQ 30: 189–206

Keown, John (1988), *Abortion, Doctors and the Law: Some Aspects of the Legal Regulation of Abortion in England from 1803–1982* (CUP)
—— (1992), 'The Law and Practice of Euthanasia in The Netherlands', LQR 108: 51–78
—— (ed.) (1995), *Euthanasia Examined: Ethical, Clinical and Legal Perspectives* (CUP)
—— (2002), *Euthanasia, Ethics and Public Policy: An Argument against Legalisation* (CUP)
Kirk, Marshall and Madsen, Hunter (1989), *After the Ball: How America will Conquer its Fear and Hatred of Gays in the '90s* (London: Doubleday)
Kneale, William ([1967] 1969), 'The Responsibility of Criminals', in *The Philosophy of Punishment: A Collection of Papers* (ed. H.B. Acton) (London: Macmillan)
Koppelman, Andrew (1997), 'Is Marriage Inherently Heterosexual?', AJJ 42: 51–95
—— (1997), 'Three Arguments for Gay Rights', Michigan L Rev 95: 1636–67
Lang, Daniel (1969), *Casualties of War* (New York: McGraw Hill) = *Incident on Hill 192* (London: Pan Books, 1970)
Lee, Patrick and George, Robert P. (1997), 'What Sex Can Be: Self-Alienation, Illusion, or One-Flesh Unity', AJJ 42: 135–57
Legarre, Santiago (2007), 'The Historical Background of the Police Power', J Constitutional L 9: 745–96
Lewis, C.S. ([1943] 1978), *The Abolition of Man: or Reflections on Education with special reference to the teaching of English in the upper forms of schools* (London: Collins Fount Paperbacks)
—— (1945), *That Hideous Strength: A Modern Fairy-Tale for Grown-Ups* (London: Bodley Head)
Lucas, John R. (1966), *The Principles of Politics* (OUP)
—— (1995), 'The Restoration of Man', Theology 98: 445–56
Lutz, Cora E. (1947), 'Musonius Rufus "The Roman Socrates"', Yale Classical Studies 10: 3–147
MacCormick, Neil (1982), *Legal Right and Social Democracy: Essays in Legal and Political Philosophy* (OUP)
Macedo, Stephen (1990), *Liberal Virtues* (OUP)
—— (1993), 'The New Natural Lawyers', The Harvard Crimson, 29 October
—— (1995), 'Homosexuality and the Conservative Mind', Georgetown LJ 84: 261–300
—— (2001), 'Constitution, Civic Virtue, and Civil Society: Social Capital as Substantive Morality', Fordham L Rev 69: 1573–93.
Maguire, Daniel C. (1975), *Death by Choice* (New York: Schocken Books)
McCormick, Richard A. SJ (1981), *Notes on Moral Theology 1965 through 1980* (Lanham: University Press of America)
McWhirter, David P. and Mattison, Andrew W. (1984), *The Male Couple: How Relationships Develop* (Upper Saddle River, NJ: Prentice Hall)
Meldrum, Marcia (2005), 'The Ladder and the Clock: cancer pain and public policy at the end of the twentieth century', J Pain and Symptom Management 29: 41–54
Miller, Bradley W. (2008), 'Justification and Rights Limitation', in Grant Huscroft (ed.), *Expounding the Constitution: Essays in Constitutional Theory* (CUP), 93–116
Miller, David (2000), *Citizenship & National Identity* (Cambridge: Polity Press)
Morris, Herbert (1968), 'Persons and Punishment', The Monist 52: 475–501
Murphy, Jeffrie G. (1970), *Kant: The Philosophy of Right* (London: Macmillan; New York: St Martin's Press)
—— (1971), 'Three Mistakes about Retributivism', Analysis 31: 109–12
Nagel, Thomas ([1973] 1975), 'Rawls on Justice', in Norman Daniels, *Reading Rawls: Critical Studies on Rawls'* A Theory of Justice (New York: Basic Books)

New York State Task Force on Life and the Law (1994), *When Death Is Sought: Assisted Suicide and Euthanasia in the Medical Context* (New York)

Nietzsche, Freidrich ([1887] 1996), *On the Genealogy of Morals: A Polemic: By Way of Clarification and Supplement to My Last Book, Beyond Good and Evil* (trans. Douglas Smith) (OUP)

Noonan, John T. Jr. (1965, 1986), *Contraception: A History of Its Treatment by the Catholic Theologians and Canonists* (HUP)

—— (1970), 'An Almost Absolute Value in History', in *The Morality of Abortion* (ed. John T. Noonan, Jr.) (HUP)

Nussbaum, Martha C. (1994), 'Platonic Love and Colorado Law', Virginia L Rev 80: 1515–651

Ottaviani, Alfredo (Cardinal) (1954), *Compendium iuris publici ecclesiastici* (4th edn, Vatican: Vatican Polyglot Press)

Palmer, William (1832), *Origines Liturgicae* (OUP)

Patterson, Charlotte J. (1992), 'Children of Lesbian and Gay Parents', Child Development 63: 1025–42

Pijnenborg, Loes et al. (1993), 'Life-Terminating Acts Without Explicit Request', 341 Lancet 1196–99

Plummer, Charles (ed.) (1885), *The Governance of England, otherwise called The Difference Between an Absolute and a Limited Monarchy; by Sir John Fortescue* (OUP)

Pogge, Thomas W. (1989), *Realizing Rawls* (Ithaca: Cornell University Press)

Posner, Richard A. (1971), 'Killing or Wounding to Protect a Property Interest', J Law & Econ 14: 201–32

—— (1979) 'Utilitarianism, Economics, and Legal Theory', J Legal Studies 8: 103–40.

—— (1990), *The Problems of Jurisprudence* (HUP)

—— (1998), 'The Problematics of Moral and Legal Theory,' Harv L Rev 111: 1637–717

Price, Anthony (1989), *Love and Friendship in Plato and Aristotle* (OUP)

Radcliffe, Cyril, Viscount (1960), *The Law and Its Compass* (London: Faber)

Rawls, John (1971), *A Theory of Justice* (HUP)

—— (1980), 'Kantian Constructivism in Moral Theory', J of Philosophy 77: 515–72

—— (1985), 'Justice as Fairness; Political Not Metaphysical', Philosophy & Public Affairs 14: 223–51

Raz, Joseph (1982), 'Liberalism, Autonomy, and the Politics of Neutral Concern' in Peter A. French, Theodore E. Uehling, and Howard K. Wettstein (eds), *Midwest Studies in Philosophy*, vii (Minneapolis: Minnesota University Press), 89–120

—— (1986), *The Morality of Freedom* (OUP)

—— (1990), 'Facing Diversity: The Case of Epistemic Diversity', Philosophy & Public Affairs 19: 3–46

—— (1994), *Ethics in the Public Domain* (OUP)

—— (1998), 'Multiculturalism', Ratio Juris 11: 193–205

—— (2007), 'Human Rights Without Foundations', Oxford Legal Studies Research Paper No 14/2007, <http://ssrn.com/abstract=999874>

Regan, Augustine CSSR (1979), *Thou Shalt Not Kill* (Dublin: Mercier)

Reiss, Hans (1970), *Kant's Political Writings* (CUP)

Richards, David A.J. (1981), 'Rights and Autonomy', Ethics 92: 3–20

—— (1982), *Sex, Drugs, Death and the Law: An Essay on Human Rights and Over-Criminalization* (Totowa: Rowman & Littlefield)

—— (1987), 'Kantian Ethics and the Harm Principle: A Reply to John Finnis', Columbia L Rev 87: 457–71

Scott, James Brown (ed.) (1934), *Francisco de Vitoria and His Law of Nations* (OUP)
Scruton, Roger (1996), 'Not Mighty But Mundane', *The Times* (London), 30 May, 41
Shavelson, Lonny (1995), *A Chosen Death: The Dying Confront Assisted Suicide* (New York: Simon & Schuster)
Sidgwick, Henry ([1874], 1907), *The Methods of Ethics* (7th edn, London)
Smith, Christian and Sikkink, David (1999), 'Is Private Schooling Privatizing?', First Things (April): 16–20
Sommerville, Margaret R. (1995), *Sex and Subjection: Attitudes to Women in Early-Modern Society* (London: Arnold; New York: St Martin's Press)
Strauss, Leo (1953), *Natural Right and History* (Chicago: University of Chicago Press)
Suarez, Francisco SJ ([1612] 1944), *Selections from Three Works* (trans. Gwladys L. Williams et al.) (OUP)
Sutton, Agneta (1990), *Prenatal Diagnosis: Confronting the Ethical Issues* (London: Linacre Centre)
Taylor, Charles (2007), 'Sex and Christianity: How has the Moral Landscape Changed?', Commonweal 134/16 (28 September)
Teichman, Jenny (1985), 'The Definition of a Person', Philosophy 60: 175–85
Thomson, Judith Jarvis (1971), 'A Defense of Abortion', Philosophy & Public Affairs 1: 47–66
Tribe, Laurence H. (1978), *American Constitutional Law* (New York: Foundation Press)
Tuck, Richard (2003), 'The Making and Unmaking of Boundaries from a Natural Law Perspective', in Allen Buchanan and Margaret Moore (eds), *States, Nations and Boundaries: The Ethics of Making Boundaries* (CUP), 143–70
Twycross, Robert G. (1995), 'Where There is Hope, There is Life: A View from the Hospice', in Keown (ed.), *Euthanasia Examined: Ethical, Clinical and Legal Perspectives*, 141–68
Vattel, Emer de ([1758] 1916), *Le Droit des Gens, ou Principes de la Loi Naturelle, appliques a la Conduite et aux Affaires des Nations et des Souverains* (trans. Charles G. Fenwick) (Washington, DC: Carnegie Institution)
Vitoria, Francisco de ([1528–57] 1991), *Political Writings* (ed. A. Pagden and A. Lawrance) (CUP)
Vlastos, Gregory ([1973] 1981), *Platonic Studies* (Princeton: Princeton University Press)
—— (1991), *Socrates, Ironist and Moral Philosopher* (Ithaca: Cornell University Press)
Walton, Douglas (1992), *Slippery Slope Arguments* (OUP)
Ward, Keith (1972), *The Development of Kant's View of Ethics* (Oxford: Blackwell)
Webber, Grégoire (2010), *The Negotiable Constitution: On the Limitation of Rights* (CUP)
Weithman, Paul (1992), 'Natural Law, Solidarity and International Justice', in Brian Barry and Robert E. Goodin (eds), *Free Movement: Ethical Issues in the Transnational Migration of People and of Money* (University Park, PA: University of Pennsylvania Press), 181–202
Wertheimer, Roger (1971), 'Understanding the Abortion Argument', Philosophy & Public Affairs 1: 67–95
Wiggins, David (1976), 'Locke, Butler and the Stream of Consciousness: and Men as a Natural Kind', Philosophy 51: 131–58
Wittgenstein, Ludwig (1953), *Philosophical Investigations* (trans. G.E.M. Anscombe) (Oxford: Blackwell)
Wolff, Robert Paul (1970), *In Defense of Anarchism* (New York: Harper & Row)
—— (1973), *The Autonomy of Reason: A Commentary on Kant's Groundwork of the Metaphysic of Morals* (New York: Harper & Row)
Zalba, Marcellino SJ (1958), *Theologiae Moralis Compendium* (Madrid)

—— (1977), '"Nihil prohibet unius actus esse duos effectus" (*Summa theologica* 2–2, q.64, a.7) Numquid applicari potest principium in abortu therapeutico?', Atti del Congresso Internatiozionale (Rome-Naples, 17/24 April 1974), *Tommaso d'Aquino nel suo Settimo Centenario*, vol. 5, *L'Agire Morale* (Naples: Edizioni Domenicane Italiane), 557–68

Zander, Michael (1985), *A Bill of Rights?* (3rd edn, London: Sweet & Maxwell)

Zellner, Harold M. (1972), 'Utilitarianism and Derived Obligation', Analysis 32: 124–5

ACKNOWLEDGEMENTS

The following essays were originally published as indicated:

Essay 1: 'A Bill of Rights for Britain? The Moral of Contemporary Jurisprudence' (Maccabaean Lecture in Jurisprudence), Proceedings of the British Academy 71: 303–31

Essay 2: 'Legal Enforcement of Duties to Oneself: Kant v. Neo-Kantians', Columbia Law Review 87: 433–56

Essay 3: Review of John Rawls, *A Theory of Justice* (1972), Oxford Magazine 90 no. 1 (new series) (26 January)

Essay 5: 'Is Natural Law Theory Compatible with Limited Government?', in Robert P. George (ed.), *Natural Law, Liberalism, and Morality* (OUP, 1996), 1–26

Essay 6: 'Virtue and the Constitution of the United States', Fordham Law Review 69: 1595–602

Essay 7: 'Commentary on Dummett and Weithman', in Brian Barry and Robert E. Goodin, *Free Movement: Ethical Issues in the Transnational Migration of People and of Money* (University of Pennsylvania Press, 1992), 203–10

Essay 8: 'Natural Law & the Re-making of Boundaries', in Allen Buchanan and Margaret Moore (eds), *States, Nations, and Boundaries: The Ethics of Making Boundaries* (CUP, 2003), 171–8

Essay 9: 'Nationality, Alienage and Constitutional Principle', Law Quarterly Review (Sweet and Maxwell) 123: 417–45

Essay 10: 'Old and New in Hart's Philosophy of Punishment', The Oxford Review 8: 73–80

Essay 11: 'The Restoration of Retribution', Analysis 32: 131–5

Essay 12: 'Retribution: Punishment's Formative Aim', American Journal of Jurisprudence 44: 91–103

Essay 13: 'The Ethics of War and Peace in the Catholic Natural Law Tradition', in Terry Nardin (ed.), *The Ethics of War and Peace* (Princeton University Press, 1996), 15–39

Essay 14: 'A Philosophical Case against Euthanasia', 'The Fragile Case for Euthanasia: A Reply to John Harris', and 'Misunderstanding the Case against Euthanasia: Response to Harris's First Reply', in John Keown (ed.), *Euthanasia: Ethical, Legal and Clinical Perspectives* (CUP, 1995), 23–35, 46–55, 62–71

Essay 15: 'Economics, Justice and the Value of Life: Concluding Remarks', in Luke Gormally (ed.), *Economics and the Dependent Elderly: Autonomy, Justice and Quality of Care* (CUP, 1992), 189–98

Essay 16: 'Euthanasia, Morality and Law', Loyola of Los Angeles Law Review 31: 1123–45

Essay 18: 'The Rights and Wrongs of Abortion: A Reply to Judith Jarvis Thomson', Philosophy & Public Affairs 2: 117–45

Essay 19: 'Abortion and Health Care Ethics', in Raanan Gillon (ed.), *Principles of Health Care Ethics* (John Wiley, 1993), 547–57

Essay 20: 'Marriage: A Basic and Exigent Good', The Monist 91: 396–414

Essay 21: 'Law, Morality and "Sexual Orientation"', in John Corvino (ed.), *Same Sex: Debating the Ethics, Science, and Culture of Homosexuality* (Rowman & Littlefield, 1997), 31–43

Essay 22: 'The Good of Marriage and the Morality of Sexual Relations: Some Philosophical and Historical Observations', American Journal of Jurisprudence 42: 97–134

INDEX

Abbott, Chief Justice (Charles) II: 200, 204; IV: 341–2
Abbott, Thomas Kingsmill III: 55n, 64n
Abbott, Walter M IV: 52n; V: 173, 215n, 266
abduction I: 45n; IV: 11, 394
　explained IV: 1214
Abelard, Peter II: 245, 247; IV: 187n, 328n
abortion III: 15, 279, 282–312; V: 167, 172, 213, 221, 224, 266, 292, 296–7, 306–7, 340, 346–7, 352; and slavery I: 56–8; funding of II: 147, 171; V: 322–3; involvement in II: 170; III: 312–3; legalization of I: 56–8, 209, 256–7, 263–4, 267–74, 276; II: 27, 301; IV: 267n, 436–66; V: 70–2, 110, 121–3, 126, 315, 330–1; 'partial birth a.' II: 250, 252, 268
Abraham V: 86n, 240, 272n, 298
action, act-analysis I.8–14
absolutes, moral, *see* exceptionless
　includes investigations and reflections I: 19
　includes deliberation I: 1
　includes discussion I: 41, 50
Acton, John V: 209n
Adair, Douglas I: 282n
Admiraal, Peter III: 266
affirmative [v negative] moral rules I: 101–2, 189; III: 7, 119; IV: 15, 128, 141, 143, 366, 368, 370, 373; V: 7, 221–2, 267, 285, 293–4, 311–4, 317–22, 324–7
　cannot be absolute I: 226
aggregative theories of right and wrong I: 205, 209–11, 225, 229, 234, 242, 245, 254; III: 32, 196, 242–4, 248, 250; IV: 53–5, 61, 121–2, 356, 368, 371; V: 77
Albert, St. V: 150
Alcibiades IV: 159
Alexander of Hales III: 187, 359–60n
Alexy, Robert I: 85n
Alkire, Sabina I: 10–11, 28
Allen, R.E. I: 41n, 49n, 51n, 186n; III: 100–1, 378n
Alphonsus Liguori, St. V: 216n, 219, 221n
Altman, Denis III: 59n
altruism II: 110; III: 69; IV: 57–61, 68, 75
　not friendship I: 47n
Ames, J.B. I: 228n; II: 209n, 211
Amin, Idi II: 84
analogical reasoning IV.19
analogy, analogical terms IV: 395–6; V: 131
Anderson, Elizabeth S. I: 235n, 253n

Ando, T. I: 160n
Andrews, J.A. III: 30
Angas, George Fife II: xii
Angas, George French II: xi
anima mea non est ego I: 166; II: 40, 42; V: 330
Anscombe, G.E.M. (Elizabeth) embryonic life II: 291–2; friendship between strangers II: 129n; 'I' 93n; intention and double effect: 13–14, 76–7, 159, 189–93, 225n, 268n; III: 235, 296; IV: 236n; V: 366n; marriage and contraception V: 352, 355n, 358–9n, 362, 364–5; mystical value of human being I: 36; moral ought II: 74–5; proposal 3n; spirit 5–6, 8–9, 69–74; III: 4; state authority IV: 85–7; voting paradox III: 22n; IV: 54; *also* V: 116, 162
Anselm of Canterbury, St. V: 179n, 182
Aquinas, Thomas I: 14n; 'a liberal' V: 113 (*see also* affirmative v negative norms, central-case analysis, *ut in pluribus*)
　on 'act of generative kind' III: 326n, 382–3; IV: 135n; adjudication IV: 127–9; basic good of life I: 34; *beatitudo* and *beatitudo imperfecta* I: 162–72, 185; *bonum ex integra causa malum ex quocumque defectu* II: 172; connaturality I: 205; II: 73; conscience V: 10, 169, 171, 216, 218–20, 222; *consensus* II: 155–7, 231–2; created beings I: 96–7; deliberation as first *de seipso* I: 183; II: 50, 103; IV: 25; *determinatio* needed between reasonable options I: 230; IV: 149, 179, 181–2, 324; V: 318n; discourse opponents I: 44n; divine judgment II: 66; embryonic life II: 39n, 288; V: 307; epistemological principle: object-act-capacity-nature I: 179, 204; II: 7, 128n; IV: 317–8; ethics as practical I: 159; experience of self I: 135–6; II: 41; evil (problem of) V: 13n, 24, 197; first principle of practical reason I: 210; first principles I: 63–4; first principles and inclinations I: 39, 144–7, 150, 176–80, 183, 205; II: 59; first principles or basic reasons for action I: 28, 139, 148–50; IV: 53; V: 58, 120, 245, 268; four orders (and kinds of science) I: 200, 242; II: 36, 261n; IV: 94n, 166; V: 146, 151, 195; free choice and self-determination I: 214n; II: 42; IV: 110; freedom of will and choice II: 6,

Aquinas, Thomas (cont.)
71–2, 103; V: 183–4; friendship I: 112; IV: 432; global government III: 128–9; God V: 23–4, 28–9, 44, 144, 185–7, 226n, 301n; groups II: 95; IV: 214; *habitus* II: 10; harm I: 154; human acts v behaviour II: 133; humility V: 226–7, 230–1; identity and self-determination II: 36–43, 49–50; *imperium* II: 2, 154, 227; *in genere naturae* v *in genere moris* II: 164–9, 250–1; V: 160; 'intention' and 'choice' of 'objects' II: 149n, 151, 152–72, 239n, 245–7, 253n, 273n; IV: 463–5; V: 281, 367; *intrinsece mala* II: 151, 224; V: 298n; *Is v Ought* I: 7, 213n; justice I: 48n; justice and right I: 206; II: 214n; IV: 109–10; knowledge of historical causality V: 144–5, 150; laws' derivation and non-derivation from moral principles or beliefs I: 21; II: 1093; IV: 128, 149n, 177, 179; laws as propositions I: 19; II: 100; IV: 451n; law's alienated subjects I: 90, 108; law's positivity IV: 2n, 31, 76, 109–11, 160–1, 175–85, 323; *lex injusta* I: 209; III: 2–3; IV: 8n, 31, 181–2; limited, non-paternalist government I: 258; III: 10, 65, 83–5, 91; IV: 31, 135, 270; V: 49, 93–4, 112; love of neighbour as self I: 38; marriage as basic good and reason for action I: 154–5; III: 319n, 353n; marital *fides*, 'debt', and sex ethics II: 53–4; III: 110, 320–2, 345–7, 354–65, 372–6, 379–80; IV: 136, 272; V: 355; V: 356n; means as ends I: 180–1; II: 158–61, 201; IV: 238; moral absolutes (exceptionless negative moral norms) I: 188–97; III: 197; natural and eternal law V: 252; natural and positive law II: 102; natural because rational/reasonable I: 258–9; natural reasons accessible to non-believers (in revelation) I: 259, 265n; V: 3, 8, 115; nature and reason in morality III: 365–72; 'necessity knows no law' III: 202n; *per se* v *per accidens* II: 162–3; V: 186; person II: 10; *pietas* and patriotism II: 107; political and legal authority IV: 69; political theory III: 128–9; practical truth I: 170; *praeter intentionem* (side effect) II: 164, 171; V: 186, 341; property II: 120; IV: 145–6; prevalence of folly and evil I: 203; IV: 223n; principles, virtues, and moral norms I: 150–5, 181–2; III: 98; IV: 52, 460; V: 59, 77; promising V: 63; *prudentia* and ends I: 28–31, 173–86; punishment III: 159, 163–5, 173–6, 190; IV: 142–3, 147; V: 309–10; punishment of heretics V: 50n, 117–8; revelation, credibility, and pseudo-revelation V: 48, 83–4; rights IV: 116–7; 'secular' 331–2; self-defence (lethal) II: 188, 197; III: 117, 294, 299; V: 308–9, 367; self-refutation I: 46n, 70, 89–90; II: 37; V: 66n, 148; sex for pleasure (only) III: 358–65, 380n; sophists I: 52n; soul as form and act of body I: 35, 54; II: 34, 39; V: 66–7; *synderesis* I: 28–31, 139, 173, 175–6; territorial appropriation III: 130; types of government III: 83–4; IV: 149n; tyrannicide III: 204n; unity of virtues II: 46; war III: 186–8, 190.

Weaknesses in philosophy of I: 208; II: 10; V: 271; (*see also* I: 6, 60, 81, 98, 202; II: 67, 72, 256n, 264n; III: 310; IV: 9n, 10, 93, 157, 163, 208, 219, 328n, 334; V: 14, 140, 154, 361)

Arber, Edward V: 1
Archimedes IV: 331–2
Arendt, Hannah I: 189; IV: 369
Aristotelian
dictum about prudence I: 6
neo-Aristotelian reliance on nature not reason: I: 26
Aristotle (*and see* central-case analysis, focal meaning, nested ends, *orthos logos*, *phronêsis*, *spoudaios*)
on anthropology II: 36; ascent from family to *polis* II: 107, 126; IV: 214, 277; authority IV: 69; 'citizen' and citizenship III: 138n; IV: 240; crime and punishment III: 159, 163–4, 175; definitional Why? II: 82; IV: 23–4, 160; education I: 313, 315; embryology II: 292; ethics and political philosophy as practical reason I: 31, 129, 140, 208; final end of man I: 29, 143, 159–63, 165n, 166; IV: 51–2, 226n; friendship I: 40, 122, 306–7; II: 125; IV: 208, 312, 432; God I: 123, 170, 307; III: 220n; V: 28, 135, 193, 333, 336, 338; good as desirable I: 177n; historical causation V: 144–5; homosexual acts III: 99, 101, 323n, 336, 338, 371–2; identity of the *polis* across revolution IV: 430–1; individual ethics I: 48; insight (*nous*) IV: 124; *Is—Ought* (theoretical v practical) I: 78, 89n, 125, 202; V: 33; justice II: 214n; IV: 150, 337; knowledge of first principles I: 178n; V: 150; justice II: 214n; IV: 150, 337; law and rule of law III: 86; IV: 109, 149n, 157, 218–9, 316, 452n; marriage and sex I: 244n; II: 128; III: 88, 387–8; IV: 138, 272–3; V: 350; moral absolutes I: 187–94; III: 87n; V: 224; natural and legal right I: 201, 214n; III: 159; IV: 161, 176n, 180–2; object-act-capacity-nature: I: 26, 146, 204, 213n; II: 7, 94n; III: 89n; 'philosophy of human affairs' and social theory IV: 110, 214, 265, 318; V: 146; pleasure I: 36; III: 365; practical reasoning and intention II: 14, 160, 201n, 273; III: 186n;

INDEX

IV: 238, 465; V: 77; *praxis* v *poiêsis*
I: 240n; II: 104, 140; III: 93; prevalence
of error I: 265n; IV: 223n; property
IV: 145–6; sacrifice of identity I: 169;
self-refutation I: 65n, 70–1, 84, 133, 203;
V: 148; social contract III: 91–2; soul and
body I: 53n, 54; II: 34, 39, 67n; V: 67,
123; state paternalism IV: 135, 137, 270;
V: 107, 112, 118; truth and knowledge
I: 43–4n, 63, 97n; types of regime III: 83;
virtues I: 283n; weaknesses in I: 30,
59–60; IV: 75, 263 (*see also* I: 81, 90, 92,
138, 230, 303; III: 104n; IV: 9n, 10, 12,
76, 93, 234, 235, 259, 276, 321, 323, 355n;
V: 140, 227, 269, 273)
Armstrong, Robert V: 43n
Arrow, Kenneth II: 98n; IV: 54, 55n, 56
Ashbourne, Lord (Edward Gibson) II: 207
Ashley, Benedict II: 288n
Aspasius I: 192n,
Asquith, Lord Justice (Cyril) II: 228
assertion(s) I: 45, 77–9, 85, 93; II: 67, 111, 225;
III: 25; IV: 157, 227, 332, 368, 455; V: 149,
159, 164, 167, 173, 205, 372
athanatizein (immortalizing) I: 123; II: 75
atheism V: 1–2, 6–7, 13, 20, 31, 34, 45, 51n, 54,
60–1, 89, 95, 124, 178, 194, 332–4
Atkinson, G.M. II: 287n
Atkinson, Lord (John) III: 137n
Aubenque, Pierre I: 70n
Aubert, J.-M. IV: 187n; V: 253n
Augustine of Hippo, St.
on eternal and natural law IV: 127;
V: 216; on final reward and punishment
V: 368–9, 372–3, 374n, 375–7; on lying
I: 193; on marital good III: 100; on
peace and war III: 184, 185n, 188–9; on
Plato and revelation, V: 135; on private
punishment III: 191n; on self-refutation
I: 70–1, 135; V: 148; on sex acts and
pleasure III: 321, 359, 365; on two
cities I: 312; (*see also* III: 291, 321;
IV: 9n, 93, 218, 328n; V: 118, 205, 226n,
301n, 341)
Augustus, Caesar III: 108
Austin, J.L. II: 183n; IV: 258, 260n,
Austin, John I: 19; II: 177, 228n; III: 155;
IV: 10, 36, 40, 75, 99, 115–16, 162–3, 400
authority IV.2 & 4
Averroes III: 87n
Averroism
ethical I: 189, III: 87n; Latin I: 89–90
Avicenna III: 364n
Ayer, A.J. V: 130n

baby-making (*see also* IVF) III: 15, 276; V: 158,
213, 224
Bacon, Francis IV: 160; V: 1, 3, 13
Balthasar, *see* von Balthasar
Banner, Michael III: 250

Barker, Ernest II: 94n; IV: 189–90n, 196n,
202n, 205n, 430n
Barnes, Jonathan III: 187–8n
Barnett, Randy IV: 369
Barnhizer, David IV: 354n, 370–1
Bassey, Shirley II: 218n
Batiffol, Pierre V: 142
Baxter, E.L. III: 281n
Bayley, Justice (John) II: 200–2, 204;
IV: 345–6
beatitudo
imperfecta I: 29, 163–8; is
communal I: 167–8; *perfecta*
(*eudaimonia*) I: 149, 160–2, 165–71; V: 93,
228
Beatson, Jack III: 136n
Beauchamp, Tom L. III: 307n
Becanus, Martinus V: 212
Beccaria, Cesare I: 234
Beck, L.W. III: 55–6n, 58n, 63–4n, 69n
Becker, Carl V: 58n, 143–4
Becker, Ernest IV: 354n
Bede V: 189–91
Bell, Carlos A. III: 350n
Belmans, Theo G. I: 169n, II: 149n,
Benedict XVI II: 119, 124n; V: 40–1, 91–2, 289
Benedict, St. V: 225
Bennett, David III: 143n
Bennett, Jonathan III: 298n, 300
Bentham, Jeremy
utilitarian confusions I: 234, 305n; III: 154,
160, 234; IV: 53–4, 75; on definition
II: 82; on expository v censorial
jurisprudence V: 161, 165, 210;
on law IV: 1, 10, 12, 36, 99, 105, 108, 116,
160–2; V: 72; on oblique 'intention'
II: 242; III: 215; on responsibility
IV: 154; *see also* I: 6; II: 25, 189;
III: 168, 173; IV: 132, 147, 190n, 194n,
258; V: 223
Berger, René I: 287n, 291n
Berkeley, George II: 43
Bernard of Clairvaux, St. IV: 328
Bernardin, Joseph V: 291–327
Bertone, Tarcisio IV: 440n
Besant, Annie I: 279, 280n
Best, Justice (William) II: 202n
Bingham of Cornhill Lord (Thomas) III: 133n,
136n, 144–5n; V: 99n
Birkenhead, Lord (F.E. Smith) I: 68–70
Birks, P.B.H, IV: 401n
Bismarck, Otto von V: 209
Black, Justice (Hugo) I: 277, 292, 296; II: 28
Blackburn, Simon II: 74
Blackmun, Justice (Harry) II: 27n; III: 57n,
63n, 252n
Blackstone, William III: 12–13, 139n; IV: 10,
189–210, 320, 410
Blankenhorn, David III: 385n
Blumstein, Philip III: 384n

Blunt, Anthony III: 378n
Boccaccio, Giovanni II: 45–6, 57; III: 320
Bodenheimer, Edgar IV: 189–90n, 196n
Boethius II: 9, 29n
Bolt, Robert V: 169
Bonaventure, St. V: 222n
bonum ex integra causa, malum ex quocumque defectu II: 172; III: 187, 195–203; *also* II: 167
Boorstin, Daniel IV: 189n
Bork, Robert IV: 327, 331
Boswell, John III: 346, 350n, 356–7, 369–72, 385n
Bourke, Vernon I: 171n-2n; IV: 52n
Bouyer, Louis V: 64
Bowring, John II: 189
Boyle, Joseph M I: 33n, 45n, 66n, 70n, 73n, 84, 90, 153n, 154, 171, 195, 203n, 239n; II: 11, 13, 159n, 177n-8n, 183n, 191, 194n, 235n, 255n, 257n, 267n, 280n, 285n, 293, 302–12; III: 13–14, 66n, 97 , 243n, 250, 310, 357, 359n; V: 46n, 85–6, 96–101, 121, 149n, 150–1n, 186, 278, 303n, 316n, 340, 347n, 364
Bracton, Henry de IV: 191, 193
Bradlaugh, Charles I: 279, 280n,
Bradley, Gerard V. III: 345, 347–9n, 361n, 382n, 387n; V: 28
Brady, Paul IV: 373n
brain life, 'brain death' II.15, II.18–9
Braine, David II: 67n; III: 228n; V: 66
Brandeis, Justice (Louis) III: 63
Brandt, R.B. III: 290
Brasidas IV: 181
Breitel, Charles D. II: 27n
Brennan, Justice (William J.) I: 278, 294, 296, 297n; III: 246, 252n; V: 70
Brewer, Scott IV: 389–9, 392–6
Bridge, Lord (Nigel) II: 174–5n, 274n
Brock, Stephen C. II: 253n, 264n
Broderick, Patrick A. II: 224n
Brody, Baruch III: 303
Brooke, Lord Justice (Henry) II: 196n
Brown, Harold V: 277, 279
Brown, Louise II: 293–4
Brown, Peter R.L. I: 71n; V: 376n
Brown, Stephen II: 314, 318
Browne-Wilkinson, Lord (Nicolas) II: 313, 315; III: 133; IV: 398
Brubaker, Rogers IV: 225n
Buchler, Ira IV: 57n
Buchler, Justus I: 45n; IV: 394–5n
Buckley, Joseph I: 164
Budziszewski, J. V: 35n
Bullough, Edward I: 288–9, 320n
Burgess, Guy III: 378n
Burke, Edmund IV: 154
Burlamaqui, Jean Jacques IV: 197–8
Butler, Joseph I: 125; II: 43n; III: 225n; V: 54n
Butler-Sloss, Lady Justice (Elizabeth) II: 315
Byrne, Robert I: 276n

Caesar, Julius III: 98n, 204n
Cahn, Edmond I: 284n
'Caiaphas principle' I: 188–9; V: 287
Cairns, Robert B I: 278n
Cairo Declaration on Human Rights in Islam III: 149n; V: 39
Cajetan, Thomas de Vio I: 29n, 164n, 183n; II: 164n; IV: 52n
Calabresi, Guido I: 247n; IV: 346n, 350
Callahan, Sidney III: 349, 383
'Callicles' III: 105–6, 198
Callinan, Justice (Ian) III: 143–4n
Campbell, W.E. V: 165n, 167n
Canovan, Margaret III: 148n
Canto-Sperber, Monique I: 199n
capacities (*see also* epistemological principle)
 radical I: 35, 54–5, 272–3; II: 8, 67, 104–5, 286n, 297; III: 219–21, 225, 227–8, 238–40; V: 329, 336–7
Caputo, John V: 197n
Cartwright, J.P.W. II: 222n, 224n
Case, John V: 332, 334–6
cases (principal)
 A v Home Secretary (Belmarsh Prisoners' Case) III: 133, 135, 144–5, 149; IV: 15
 A, B & C v Ireland III: 43n
 A-G for Canada v Cain III: 136
 A-G's References (Nos 1 & 2 of 1979) II: 220
 Al Kateb v Godwin III: 143–4, 149
 Allen v Flood I: 226n; II: 207–8, 211, 219
 Anderton v Ryan III: 135n
 Bancoult (No. 2) IV: 18
 Begum, see R (Begum)
 Bird v Holbrook II: 202–4, 215, 226–7; IV: 344–5, 349–50
 Birmingham City Council v Equal Opportunities Commission II: 269–74
 Bland, Airedale NHS Trust v II: 311–2, 313–21, III: 213
 Bolam v Friern HMC II: 318
 Bradford (Mayor) v Pickles I: 226n; II: 207–8
 Bradlaugh, R v I: 279–81n
 Brown v Topeka Board of Education III: 42
 Burstyn v Wilson I: 285, 290, 292, 295n
 Byrn v NYC Health & Hospitals II: 27
 Calvin's Case III: 135
 Case of Proclamations III: 136
 Chahal v United Kingdom III: 45, 144–6
 Chaplinsky v New Hampshire I: 278, 284, 291
 Charkaoui v Canada III: 149n
 Compassion in Dying v Washington V: 74
 Conjoined Twins (Medical Treatment), Re A II: 196–7, 266–7
 Crofter Harris Tweed v Veitch I: 226n; II: 210, 219
 Croson, City of Richmond v IV: 370–1
 Cruzan v Director V: 76
 Cunliffe v Goodman II: 228–9
 Dred Scott v Sandford I: 275–6; II: 26–7; IV: 16, 153

Dudgeon v United Kingdom III: 27n, 29, 41n
Eisenstadt v Baird V: 70, 73
Factortame (No. 2) IV: 18
Frodl v Austria III: 44
Ginzburg v United States I: 277-8, 281n, 285n, 293-4, 296
Griswold v Connecticut III: 94n; V: 70
Hancock, R v II: 174n, 196
Handyside v United Kingdom III: 27n, 30n, 41n
Hardial Singh, ex p. III: 141, 143-4
Haughton v Smith III: 135n
Hicklin, R v I: 279
Hirst v United Kingdom, 30nm (No. 2) III: 41n, 44-5, 179
HJ (Iran) v Home Secretary III: 45, 332-3
Husseyn, R v II: 220
Ilott v Wilkes II: 199-202, 204, 226-7; IV: 341-2, 344-5
James v Eastleigh Borough Council II: 269-74
Januzi v Home Secretary III: 45
JFS (Governing Body), R (E) v, II: 269-75
Johnstone v Pedlar III: 137-8
Kesavananda v State of Kerala I: 68n
Kingsley International Pictures v Regents I: 277, 290, 292
Lawrence v Texas V: 95
Lonrho plc v Fayed I: 226n; II: 2, 41n18
Madzimbamuto v Lardner-Burke IV: 415n, 435
Mannai Investment v Eagle Star Life II: 9, 13, 31-2
McCawley v R I: 68n
Memoirs v Massachusetts I: 277, 288n, 293-7
Meyer v Nebraska V: 70-1
Mogul Steamship v McGregor, Gow II: 209
Moloney, R v II: 174n-5n, 196, 274n
New York Times v Sullivan I: 291-2
OBG v Allan II: 217-9
Paris Adult Theatre v Slaton I: 297
Pierce v Society of Sisters V: 70-1
Planned Parenthood v Casey I: 268; V: 73, 86, 95
Purdy see R (Purdy)
R (Begum) v Denbigh High School III: 3n; V: 98-9
R (Purdy) v DPP III: 46
Refah Partisi v Turkey V: 38-9
Roe v Wade I: 268-9n, 275-6; II: 27-8; III: 21, 23, 42; IV: 16, 324; V: 95
Romer v Evans IV: 16; V: 73
Roth v United States I: 277-81, 284n, 291n, 293
Saadi v Italy III: 45, 136, 145n
Şahin v Turkey V: 99
Sauvé v Canada (No. 2) III: 455
Shaw v DPP III: 28n
Tan Te Lam v Superintendent III: 141-2

Tuttle v Buck II: 211
United Zinc & Chemical v Britt II: 199; IV: 341
Vacco v Quill V: 71, 75
Washington v Glucksberg V: 71
Wheat Case IV: 12-13, 15
Winters v New York I: 292
Woollin, R v II: 196
Zadvydas v Davis III: 142-3, 149
Castañeda, Hector-Neri II: 222n; III: 290n
Castelli, Jim V: 326n
Catechism of the Catholic Church II: 197, 266; III: 173-4, 178n; V: 336n, 340-1
Catherine of Aragon V: 163-4, 170
Cattaneo, Mario A. IV: 407n, 409n
Cavanaugh, J.A. II: 267-8n
Cave, Viscount (George) III: 137n
Centi, T. II: 154n
central case analysis
    explained I: 109-13, 130-7; IV: 108-9, 160, 168, 235; illustrated I: 10, 118, 121, 123, 206, 259; II: 177, 179; III: 2, 183, 212-3, 317, 325, 347; IV: 36, 79-81, 126, 148, 155, 163, 167, 185, 241, 244, 250, 266, 271, 276, 289
'Cephalus' I: 313
certainty I: 130-7
Chadwick, Owen V: 57n, 58, 335
Chafee, Zechariah I: 282n
Chalcidius IV: 174n, 186n
Chamberlain, Neville IV: 256n
Chandos, John I: 289n
Chappell, Timothy I: 9, 100n, 102
Charlton, William V: 153n
Chaucer, Geoffrey III: 320
Childress, James F III: 307n
choice(s)
    free I: 5; lastingness of I: 36, 216-7; phenomenology of I: 223
Chrimes, S.B. IV: 409n
'christendom' V.20
Chroust, Anton-Hermann I: 71n
Churchill, Winston V: 275-6
Cicero, M. Tullius I: 71, 209; II: 5; III: 107, 191, 291; IV: 9n, 93, 157, 159, 177-8, 187, 193, 218-19; V: 3, 8, 265n
civic friendship (*philia politikê*) I: 112, 266-7; II: 125; IV: 50, 432, 434
civic virtue III.6
Clark, Justice (Tom C.) I: 295, 297n
Clark, Stephen R.L. I: 63n
Clark, William P. V: 277-8
Clarke, Samuel I: 125
Clerk, J.F. II: 210n
Clor, Harry M I: 269n
'cluster concepts', (*see also* central-case) IV: 77; V: 57
Cockburn, Alexander JE I: 279-80
Cohen, David III: 337n
Cohen, Lionel II: 228

Cohen, Marshall III: 26n, 31n, 32n, 36n;
    IV: 100n, 286n
coherence
    not sufficient for rationality I: 80
Coke, Edward III: 84n, 135; IV: 128
Coleman, Jules IV: 41–2, 44, 91, 105n, 112–15
Collingwood, R.G. IV: 232n
commensuration by reason I.14-I5; II: 144–5;
    IV: 360–4; *see also* incommensurability
common good I: 99–100, 168
complementarity of male and female I: 34;
    II: 105; III: 328
Comte, Auguste I: 47n; IV: 57n, 75
conceptual clarification II: 305
conditional intention II.12
Confucius III: 281
'connatural' knowledge II: 73;
    'non-conceptual' I: 205
connexio virtutum II: 46
conscience V.16; V: 169–70; *also* I: 116;
    V: 254–6
consensus and truth I: 42
consequentialism I: 13
'consistent ethic of life' V.21
contemplation I: 165, 169
contraception V.23; *also* I: 142, 279–80; II: 70n,
    265; III: 94, 281, 311, 324, 328; IV: 278;
    V: 158n, 272n, 297
conversion I: 60; II: 48, 52, 62–3, 76, 272;
    III: 4, 38, 328; IV: 274n; V: 91, 98, 111n, 117,
    177
Conzemius, V. V: 209n
Coolidge, David Orgon III: 357n
coordination, negative II: 85
    c. problems and solutions IV.2–3
'corporate personality' II: 81
corpore et anima unus II: 42
Cottier, Georges V: 255n
Craig, Thomas IV: 199–200
Cranmer, Thomas V: 164
'Critical Legal Studies Movement' IV.13 & 13,
    & IV: 327–32
Cropsey, Joseph I: 188n
Cross, Lord (Geoffrey) I: 318n
'culture' V: 138, 146
'culture of death' V: 328–31, 339
Cuomo, Mario III: 263
Curran, Charles E. V: 296–7n
Cuthbert, St. V: 189–92

Dalton, William J. V: 372
D'Arcy, Eric I: 171n; V: 209n
Darrow, Clarence V: 194
Darwin, Charles III: 350n, 356; V: 13, 17, 21–6
Daube, David II: 241n; III: 291–2n
Davidson, Donald II: 225n, 263
Davis, Henry II: 248,
Dawkins, Richard IV: 353–4; V: 6n, 23, 32
Dawson, Christopher V: 140

Decalogue (Ten Commandments) I: 152–4,
    190–2, 194; II: 149; III: 98; IV: 176, 460;
    V: 247–9, 260–8
Delhaye, Philippe IV: 187n; V: 215
deliberation, as action I: 1; and conscience
    I: 116; *de seipso/meipso* (about oneself)
    I:183–5; II: 50–2, 103; IV: 25; about ends (as
    well as means) I: 2, 28–32, 173–86
de Lubac, Henri IV: 52n; V: 58
democracy, democratic I: 53, 262–3, 266;
    II: 97, 400; III: 21–2, 40, 43, 44–5, 59, 77,
    95, 139, 147, 250; IV: 76, 170, 267, 322; V: 8,
    37–8, 40, 122; 'militant d.' V: 8, 38; 'People's
    D.' I: 275
Democritus IV: 188n
De Scala, Peter II: 232n
Descartes, René I: 66, 71, 84, 135; II: 5n, 78,
    268n
description, 'under a/the description' II: 76–7,
    189–91, 194, 255, 260, 274; *also* I: 76, 164–5,
    167, 170, 181, 207, 216, 258, 261–4; II: 13,
    137; V: 281, 374n
desirable, as perfective I: 29n
determinatio I: 22; II: 121; III: 3, 179, 331; IV: 2,
    12, 123, 128, 131–2, 140, 149, 161, 179, 181,
    309, 318; explained I: 208–9; II: 100–3, 106;
    IV: 182–4, 301–3, 314–5; of purely positive
    laws I: 22
deterrence, nuclear V.20; *also* V: 11–12; I: 188;
    II: 86–91; V: 125–6; and punishment III: 13,
    67, 91, 93, 154, 157–8, 173–4, 192
Devlin, Lord (Patrick) III: 27–9; IV: 270, 274,
    276, 277n
Dewey, John V: 17, 25–6, 32, 183
Diamond, J.J. II: 292n
Diana, Antonius V: 212n
Dias, R.W.M. IV: 378n
Dicey, A.V. III: 136
dignity II: 35; V: 51, 66–8, 338–9; *also* I: 35, 53;
    II: 320; IV: 170, 349–50; V: 49, 58, 68, 73,
    196–7, 247–8, 254–7, 259, 286, 315–6, 365
Dilthey, Wilhelm V: 144
Diplock, Lord (Kenneth) II: 210n; III: 20n,
    34–5n
'direct intention' II.13–14
'direction of intention' II: 187
discourse, discussion: ethics of I: 41–7, 50–5;
    internal (solitary) I: 52; metaphysics of II: 35
discrimination: anti-, new communism II: 126
disparagement, *see* insult
'diversity' III: 109; *also* II: 127; IV: 274
divorce III: 329
Dodd, C.H. V: 152n
Dodds, E.R. I: 49n
Döllinger, Ignaz von V: 209n
Donagan, Alan I: 153n, 227; III: 66n; V: 223
Donaldson, Lord (John) II: 174n
Donceel, Joseph II: 287–9
Donne, John III: 292n

Dorr, Donal III: 121; V: 272n
Dostoyevsky, Fydor II: 74
'double effect' II: 13
Douglas, Justice (William O.) I: 277, 292, 296, II: 28
Douglas, Mary I: 322–3
Dover, Kenneth III: 99n, 337, 385n
droit and *loi* I: 206
Dryer, Douglas P. III: 62n
dualism: body—soul, refuted I: 53–4; II: 8; *see also* '*anima mea*'
Duberman, Martin III: 378n
Duff, R.A. II: 174n, 189n, 199n
Duffy, Kevin V: 372
Dummett, Ann III: 116, 118–20
Dummett, Michael II: 74; V: 240, 242–3
Dunedin, Viscount (Murray, Andrew) II: 200n
Durkheim, Emile III: 292
duties to oneself III.2
Dworkin, Ronald I: 220–4; III.1 & 16 & III: 51–3; IV.12; *also* I: 189n, 229, 252n–3n, 298n, 301, 312n, 323n; II: 20–2, 33, 81–4, 86, 103, 108, 110–2, 117, 320; III: 3, 10–12, 14, 20–1, 23–6, 31, 35n, 36, 38n, 48, 95–6, 226n, 228–30, 245–6, 251n, 252, 254–5, 258–9, 261–3, 264n, 266, 268–9, 270; IV: 10–11, 13–14, 32n, 108n, 129, 163–4, 168, 170, 254n, 258, 266, 271n, 280–98, 302, 314, 319, 321, 328–30, 353–4, 360–1, 363, 381–4, 400, 401n; V: 18, 20, 30–1, 51, 71–3, 76, 85, 105, 107–8, 303

Economic Analysis of Law II: 203–6; IV.16
economics III: 242–3; IV: 337–40
Eddy, Mary Baker V: 56
Edgley, Roy I: 127n
Edward IV IV: 429
Edwards, R.G. II: 293–4, 298, 301; III: 280
Eekelaar, John IV: 245
Ehrensing, Rudolph II: 279n
Einstein, Albert V: 23n
Eisenhower, Dwight D. II: 242n
Eisgruber, Christopher L. V: 18, 20, 29–31, 86n, 95
Elders, Leo J. I: 144n
Elias, N. IV: 429n
Elizabeth I V: 91
Elizabeth II IV: 328
Ellenborough, Lord (Law, Edward) II: 202n; IV: 342–4
embryonic life II: 15–17
Empiricism I: 46n, 168–70; critique of I: 88; II: 9
Empiricus, Sextus I: 201
end: last e. of human beings I: 29, 147n, 159–72; basic ends I: 180; are usually also means I: 181; II.9, II.14
Endicott, Timothy IV: 28
Engberg-Pedersen, Troels I: 161

Engelhardt, Tristram V: 316n
Enlightenment I: 60n, 92; IV: 53; V: 118, 140, 143, 217, 372; confusion about value I: 26–7, 211; foundational mistakes of I: 59, 242; IV: 154; V: 152–3, 169, 183, 187, 287
'ensoulment' V: 109
Epictetus I: 141
Epicurus IV: 355n
epistemic conditions, 'under ideal e. c.' II: 101; V: 46–7
epistemological v. ontological I:147–8; II: 7
'e. principle' (object-act-capacity-nature) II: 7, 15
equality basic human I: 48; 'of esteem' III: 327
Erasmus, Desiderius V: 166
Escobar y Mendoza, Antonio V: 212n
Eser, Albin IV: 192n
Essex, Earl of (Robert Dudley) II: 41
ethics, ethical: not soundly distinguished from morality I: 48, 55–8, 92, 101; 'situation ethics' I: 51–2
eudaimonia I: 160–2
Euclid II: 54n
Eugenius IV V: 213n
Euripides IV: 148
European Convention on/Court of Human Rights (ECHR/ECtHR) III: 1–46, 140–1, 144–6; V: 38–9
euthanasia I: 56–8; II.18–19; III.14–16; V.22, V: 68
'evil not to be done for good' II: 143; V: 159–6
evolution III: 350, 356; V: 21–4, 26, 61, 136
exceptionless wrongs, norms, commitments I: 13, 101, 154, 187–98, 226–7; II: 196, 245–7, 252–3, 267; III: 7, 45, 86, 197–8, 200–3, 206, 234, 322; IV: 128, 173, 446, 460–1; V: 121, 172, 221, 224, 261–71, 296, 340, 351
'existential' II: 96
extremity: ethics of I: 187; III: 200–2

Fabro, Cornelio V: 58
'fact of pluralism' I: 42n
'fact v value', *see also* 'Is v Ought' I: 202
Factor, Regis A I: 203n; IV: 224–5n
Fahey, Michael V: 341
faith: as shaped by divine love help II: 52; fundamental option II: 52; V: 173; preambles to V: 162n
falasifa I: 198; III: 87n
family II: 127–8; *also* 123; f. wage III: 324
Fawcett, James III: 43n
feelings, discernment of II: 215
Felix, Marcus Minucius II: 231n
Festugière, A.J. III: 99n
Figgis, John Neville II: 99n
Filliucci, Vincenzo V: 212n
final: good or end I.10, I: 29

Finch, H.A. IV: 34n, 79
Finch, Henry IV: 191
Finlay, Viscount (Robert) III: 137n
Finnis, John I: 39n, 40, 154, 172, 195, 297n;
 II: 150n, 163n, 244n–5n, 267n; III: 59n, 97,
 145n, 243n, 337n, 372n, 380n; IV: 2n, 8n,
 71n, 108n, 166, 357–8, 362; V: 195, 224n,
 204n, 341–2n
Fisher, Anthony II: 289n–90n; III: 314
Fitzmaurice, Gerald III: 19n, 39n
Flannery, Kevin L. II: 254–6, 267n–8n; V: 341
flat earth: Enlightenment myth of I: 60n
Fleming, John G. II: 183n, 211n
Fletcher, George P. II: 176n, 182n, 185n;
 III: 61–2n, 64n
Fletcher, Joseph V: 316n
Flew, Anthony V: 23n
Flippen, Douglas I: 146n
focal meaning, *see* central case analysis
Fonda, Henry I: 284n, 301, 305
Foot, Philippa I: 30n, 115, 120–22, 123n,
 305–6; II: 14, 191; III: 32, 33n, 295, 296, 300
Ford, John C. V: 270n
Ford, Norman II: 289–90, 292n
Forsythe, Clark D. I: 257n; II: 28n
Forte, David IV: 372–3
Fortescue, John III: 84n; IV: 149n
four kinds of order and science (disciplined
 knowledge) I: 7, 200, 217–8
Franco, Francisco V: 275
Frankfurter, Justice (Felix) I: 277–8, 282n;
 III: 22n, 30n
Fraser, Russell II: 44n, 47n
Fredborg, K.M. IV: 187n
freedom: of choice I: 216; II: 4, 7; of speech,
 I.17–8; threatened I: 14
Freeman, Samuel II: 125n
Freud, Sigmund I: 116, 282n; III: 168
Freund, Julien IV: 34n
Fried, Charles IV: 171, 313
Friedberg, E.A. V: 222n
Friedman, L. III: 22
Friedmann, W. II: 27; IV: 189–90n, 196n, 221n
friendship I: 5, 40, 99; v. altruism I: 47n; types
 of, central case of I: 111–2; as condition of
 fruitful discourse I: 43; extends to strangers
 I: 15; a source of normativity I: 122, 129
Fuchs, Joseph II: 134n; V: 75, 115, 161, 287,
 296–7n, 299n, 341n, 360, 365
fulfilment (flourishing)
 integral human f., morality's master
 principle I: 5
Fulgentius, of Ruspe, St. V: 159
Fuller, Lon L. I: 63, 259; IV: 31, 64n, 170, 281,
 284, 324, 418, 419n

Gadamer, Hans-Georg I: 147n; V: 144n
Gaius II: 75, 102; III: 2–3; IV: 117, 183, 218
Gallagher, John V: 173

games: language game(s) I: 104, 123, 133;
 game theory IV.2 & 4
Gandhi, Ramchandra I: 74n
Gans, Chaim IV: 58–9n, 66, 69
Gardeil, Antoine V: 145n, 150n
Gardiner, Harold C. I: 288n
Gardner, John IV: 6n, 9n, 32, 36–7, 43–5, 188n,
 246n, 247
Garet, Ron III: 356
Garrigou-Lagrange, Reginald II: 155n
Garrow, David J. I: 269n; V: 70n
Gauthier, R.-A. I: 159n, 186n; IV: 180n
Gavison, Ruth IV: 74–5
Geach, Mary II: 69, 72, 75, 77; V: 352
Geach, Peter II: 40n, 43n, 233–4; IV: 53n;
 V: 355n, 374n
Gelasius I: 312
Gellius, Aulus IV: 187–8n
Gemelli, A. III: 298n
George, Robert P. I: 33n, 272n, 324n; II: 286n,
 292n, 310n, 313n; III: 87, 89n, 96–7, 324n,
 345, 347–9, 355n, 361n, 373, 378n, 382n,
 387n; IV: 120n, 135n; V: 72n
Gerber, Albert B. I: 288
Gerth, H. H. IV: 34n, 224n
Gessert, Robert V: 310n
Gey, Stephen I: 297n
Gibson, JB IV: 197n
Gierke, Otto von II: 94n, 99n; IV: 203n, 208
Gilby, T. G. II: 154n
Gill, S.T. V: xi, 14
Gilson, Etienne V: 141, 143
Gisborne, John IV: 274n
Gladstone, William V: 6–7, 209, 211
Glanvill, Ranulf de IV: 191, 320, 323
Gleeson, Chief Justice (Murray) III: 143n
Glover, Jonathan II: 281–2; V: 316n
God (*see also* atheism, religion,
 revelation) V: 21–5, 59–62, 80–3, 134,
 179–3, 197–8; active I: 169; providence
 V: 76–7; *also* V: 27, 57, 65, 74, 76–7, 184–6;
 triune V.15; vision (contemplation) of I: 159,
 170
Goff of Chieveley, Lord (Robert) II: 32n, 174n,
 182n, 212n, 270–1, 313–4, 316, 321; III: 215n;
 IV: 399–400
Goldberg, Justice (Arthur) V: 70n
Golden Rule I: 12, 59, 87, 101, 208, 210, 266;
 II: 183, 194, 213, 298; III: 119, 121, 124, 132,
 189, 195–6, 199–200, 218; IV: 15, 29, 101,
 253, 351; V: 59, 63, 159, 246, 296, 302, 315,
 317; explained I: 59n, 227, 247–53; III: 236;
 IV: 122
good(s) basic, good for anyone I: 4;
 desirable: I: 159; as to be pursued I: 3, 100;
 hierarchy or hierarchies among? I: 63, 80,
 140, 196, 244; intrinsic I: 4, 87–8; lists of
 basic I: 10–12, 140, 145, 213, 244n; III: 88;
 IV: 98; V: 245, 262, 270, 273; perfective I: 147

Gordley, James IV: 142
Gorer, Geoffrey I: 296n
Gormally, Luke II: 69; III: 249n, 250; V: 352
Gough, John W IV: 196n
Gousset, Thomas-Marie-Joseph V: 216n, 219–20n, 222
grace V: 231
Grant, C.K. I: 74n
Gratian IV: 174n; V: 222n
Gray, Asa III: 356n
Gray, John Chipman II: 27, 81n
Green, Leslie IV: 9n, 56n, 58–9n, 68n, 70n, 247
Greenawalt, Kent V: 51n
Gregor, Mary III: 55–7n, 61–2, 63n, 67n, 104n, 342n
Gregory IX V: 213n
Gregory XVI V: 158n, 218
Grice, H.P. (Paul) I: 74; IV: 395n
Griffin, James I: 245n
Griffin, Leslie C. IV: 446n
Grisez, Germain G. I: 28, 45n, 64n, 73n, 84, 90, 139–42, 146n, 152n–53n, 154, 169, 171–2, 195, 203n, 205n, 218n, 223n–4n, 239n, 272n; II: 3n, 8n, 11, 13, 52n, 66–7, 92n, 118n, 145n, 148n, 155n, 164n, 171n, 177n–8n, 235n, 243n–5n, 252, 254–67, 280n, 285n–9n, 293, 302–12; III: 13–14, 66n, 69n, 87, 97, 194n, 198, 243n, 247n, 249n, 289n, 294n, 296n, 297–8, 305, 310n, 313n, 339, 345, 354–6, 372–3, 377n, 380n, 387n; IV: 52n, 55n, 68n, 293n, 357, 359n; V: 23n, 46n, 60, 76n, 80n, 82n, 110n, 118–19, 123, 148–9, 150–1n, 153, 161n, 179n, 227, 268n, 278, 299–300n, 308n, 316n, 340, 346, 347n, 355n, 360, 364, 370–1
Grosseteste, Robert I: 192
Grotius, Hugo I: 6, 125; III: 131, 191n, 202n; IV: 95, 146n, 337
group existence and action II.4–5, II: 11
Grover, Robinson A. IV: 53n
Gula, Richard M. V: 139–40

Habermas, Jürgen I: 41n–6n, 48n, 50n–3n, 55–60, 61n; IV: 125; V: 99
habitus II: 10
Hailsham, Lord (Hogg, Quintin) II: 174n, 184n; III: 35
Haksar, Vinit III: 32n, 70n
Haldane, John V: 61, 69, 124
Hale, Lady (Brenda) II: 271; V: 99n
Hale, Matthew III: 12, 135n; IV: 191–2
Hallett, Garth L. II: 169n; V: 287
Halsbury, Lord (Hardinge, Stanley Giffard) II: 207–9n
Hamel, Edouard V: 140n, 259n, 261n
Hamilton, Alexander IV: 154
Hampshire, Stuart IV: 235–9, 255
Hampton, Jean V: 52n
Hand, Learned III: 22

Hannen, Lord (James) II: 209n
Hanson, Norwood IV: 394–5
Hardie, W.F.R. I: 110, 191
Hare, R.M. I: 128, 141, 198n, 312n, 323n, II: 281–4; III: 290, 291n
Hargrave, John Fletcher IV: 190n
Häring, Bernard II: 279n
Harlan, Justice (John Marshall) I: 277–8, 281n; V: 70
harm I: 154
Harman, Gilbert IV: 224n
Harrington, James IV: 321
Harris, John III: 211n, 223–41; V: 318n
Hart, H.L.A. IV.10 & 11; *see also* I: 35n, 62, 66n, 69, 92, 102, 104, 106–13; II: 14, 19–22, 30, 81–3, 85n, 99n, 110, 133n, 182n, 267n; III: 10, 48n, 153–60, 163–5, 168, 173, 176–7, 259n, 295; IV: 10–11, 27, 32n, 36–40, 44n, 47n, 50, 53n, 73, 74–5, 76n, 77–82, 87n, 106–8, 119–20, 126, 155n, 162–9, 185, 186n, 188–90n, 198–201, 211n, 221n, 229n, 289, 290n, 388n, 396, 410, 411n, 414, 415n, 416–21, 425–7, 429, 432–3; V: 32, 43, 105n
Hart, Jenifer (née Williams) IV: 257, 273
Harte, Colin IV: 447n, 449n, 455n, 459n, 463n, 466n
Hathaway, R. IV: 51n
Hazeltine, H.D. IV: 189–90n
Heaney, S.J. II: 288n
heaven (*see also beatitudo*) V: 199–202, 206, 249, 371
Hebblethwaite, Peter V: 173
Hegel, G.W.F. IV: 75, 93, 431; V: 144n, 153–4, 183
Hehir, J. Bryan V: 310n
Heidegger, Martin V: 183
Heisenberg, Werner V: 23n
Hekman, Susan J. IV: 79n
hell (*see also* punishment) V.24; V: 171–2, 177–8
Helsinki, Declaration of II: 296
Hemer, Colin J. V: 152n
Henderson, Lynn IV: 360n, 365n
Hengel, Martin V: 141
Henry IV IV: 408
Henry V IV: 408
Henry VI IV: 408
Henry VIII V: 163–4
Henson, Hensley V: 238
Heraclitus V: 143n
'hermeneutical circle' V: 263
Herschell, Farrer II: 207n
Heydon, Justice (J. Dyson) III: 143n
Heylbut, G. I: 192n
Hildick-Smith, Marion III: 249
Hill, Thomas E. III: 55n
Himes, Michael V: 140n
Hindley, Clifford III: 337n
Hintikka, Jaakko I: 135
Hippias of Elis IV: 160

Hippolytus, of Rome, St. V: 159
Hitler, Adolf II: 84
'historical consciousness' V.9
Hobbes, Thomas, on intention as dominant desire I: 23; II: 177, 228–9; on 'public reason' I: 13n, 275; *summum bonum* rejected I: 63; *also* I: 6, 26, 28, 43n, 59, 102, 120, 123n; IV: 10, 55–6, 83, 95–6, 97n, 98, 116, 134, 142, 160, 162, 169, 189n, 239, 255, 264–5; V: 4
Hobhouse, L.T. III: 66–7
Hodgson, D.H. III: 290n
Hoffman, Abbie I: 301
Hoffman, Justice (Julius) I: 301
Hoffmann, Lord (Leonard H.) I: 301; II: 31, 32n, 215n–19n, 318, 320–1; III: 148n; IV: 399–400; V: 99n
Hohfeld, Wesley, N. IV.18; *also* II: 30; III:123n, 137, 283–5, 302; IV: 11, 86, 115–16; V: 36, 90, 94
Holbrook, David I: 321
Holdsworth, William III: 135n; IV: 193
Holmes, G.L. II: 307n
Holmes, Justice (Oliver Wendell) I: 250; II: 199–201, 209n, 211–2; III: 22, 215, 252; IV: 142, 340–2; V: 32
Homer I: 118–19
Honoré, A.M. (Tony) II: 10, 29n, 83, 133n; IV: 166–7, IV: 376n, 409n
Hook, Sidney IV: 156
Hooker, Richard IV: 204, 208
Hooper, Walter III: 274n, 281n
Hope of Craighead, Lord (David) III: 45n, 63n; 144n; IV: 399–400
Hopkins, Gerard Manley V: 374n
Horrocks, John V: xi, 14
Hospers, John IV: 390, 394
Hovenden, John Eykyn IV: 190n, 194n
Howsepian, A.A. II: 286n
Hugh of St Victor IV: 186–7n; V: 115
Hughes, Gerard J. IV: 341n; V: 115, 224n, 258, 261, 262n, 263–4, 272, 280
human rights (*see also* rights) III.1–9
Humboldt, Wilhelm von III: 110, 115n
Hume, Basil V: 289n
Hume, David, denial of practical reason I: 22–3, 26, 33, 38, 234, 283; II: 129; IV: 4, 226n; V: 59, 69; on freedom of the press I: 310; 'genealogical' method I: 93; on *Is* v *Ought* I: 202, 242; IV: 10, 120n; V: 33; on miracles II: 72n; V: 9, 83, 137, 152; self-refuting IV: 131; V: 25, 130; on sympathy and morality I: 125–6, 128–9; *see also* IV: 154, 249, 255, 264, 337; V: 22, 141, 183 *also* I: 59–60, 102, 264; II: 38
Humean (Humeian), Humeanism on desire I: 161n; dogma that reason does not motivate I: 100; II: 4n; III: 320; IV: 252; empiricism I: 43n, 46n, 81; conception of reasons for action I: 96n, 125–9; idea of reason as slave of passion I: 22–3, 30n, 120n, 124; V: 73; misunderstanding of reason and will I: 1, 7, 22; IV: 162, 235, 239 (*see also* Korsgaard)
humility V.17
Hurst, G. II: 287n
Hürth, Francis V: 297n
Hutcheson, Francis IV: 337–8
Huxley, Aldous IV: 231

Iglesias, Teresa II: 284n
immigration II: 118–9; III.7–9; V: 12, 40
impartial spectator, of human arena I: 129
inclinations, and induction of basic reasons for action: I: 38–9, 144–7, 155
incommensurability (*see also* commensuration) I.15; of dimensions of judicial reasoning I: 222–5; of options (proposals for choice) I: 224–7; IV: 357, 360; V: 77
indeterminacy v under-determination I: 228
innate, practical knowledge and principles not strictly I: 177–8; but loosely I: 178–9
Innocent III V: 222n
Innocent XI V: 212
insight(s) I: 45n; into basic goods I: 2–3, 98, 204; non-inferential, non-deductive I: 2–3, 31, 45, 98, 147–8, 178, 204; supervenes on experience I: 2
insult II: 105; V: 30–1
integral directiveness of practical reason's first principles I: 12; human fulfilment I: 12–13, 159–72, 210; II: 122; V: 59
intention II.8–14, III: 213–8; V: 74–5, 158–60
internal attitude I: 108, 112
interpretation II: 32
intransitivity of action II: 10
'intuition' I: 60–1, 99, 148, 186; of feelings I: 237, 254; III: 50; 'of moral propositions' I: 138, 140, 194, 204; V: 264, 268–9; 'our intuitions' III: 368; IV: 35, 124, 422; V: 4
intuitionis: 'official' I: 113, 117, 237; unofficial I: 237, 254; III: 50
Irenaeus, St. V: 115, 247, 260n, 263n
Irwin, Terence I: 28–31, 39–40, 161n, 173–5, 183n; IV: 51n, 226
Is—Ought I.9: no valid inference: I: 50, 78, 126, 202, 206
Isaac V: 272n, 298n
Isaiah V: 203–4
Isaye, G. I: 45n, 72, 84
Isidore of Seville, St. IV: 187n
Islam III: 149; V: 6, 8, 38–41, 53–4, 91n, 96, 98–9
Israel, F.L. III: 22
ius gentium II: 101
IVF II.17, III.17

James I V: 5–7
James, William IV: 124n
Janssens, Louis V: 297n
Jefferson, Thomas I: 275n; V: 4

Jenkins, David V: 192n
Jenkins, Iredell I: 288n
Jensen, Joseph V: 264n
Jeremiah V: 135
Jerome, St. V: 56, 225, 331–2
Jerusalem, fall of V: 88, 142
Jesus of Nazareth V: 161–2; *also* III: 319n; V: 48, 50, 54n, 68, 74, 86, 88, 110–11, 116, 118, 125, 136–7, 141–2, 145, 166–8, 171, 175–8, 200–1, 203–6, 228, 230, 240–3, 245–9, 251–2, 253, 260, 262, 264–5, 267, 270, 273–4, 281, 286–9, 295, 300n, 301, 350, 368, 372, 375, 378; resurrection of, 191–2
John XXII I: 207
John XXIII III: 85, 193n; V: 173–4, 254n
John, the Evangelist, St. V: 204, 273
John Damascene, St. II: 163n; V: 159, 187n, 342
John Paul II (*see also* Wojtyla, Karol)
   contraception V: 355, 364–5; double effect II: 251; 'direct' killing V: 299, 341; ethic of life V: 297; exceptionless moral norms V: 281; faith as fundamental option II: 52n; final punishment III: 178n; hope of immortality V: 240–2; human dignity V: 250; 'imperfect laws' IV: 437–49; 'liberation' V: 242; nation II: 12, 123n; nuclear deterrence V: 290; marriage III: 100, 372n; on proportionalism II· 244n; III: 85; solidarity III: 123n; on repentance V: 172
Johnston, Harry III: 126
Jolif, J.-Y. I: 159n
Jones, Ernest I: 121n; III: 168n
Jones, W.T. III: 58n
Jones, William IV: 10, 209
Jonsen, A.R. V: 316n
Jordan, Mark III: 354n, 360n, 364n
Joseph, H.W.B. IV: 258, 274
Josephus V: 142n
Judas Iscariot II: 163n; V: 177, 186, 287
judgment: as prudence (practical reasonableness) I: 31; as bearer of truth I: 44–5, 91
judicial functions and reasoning IV.20
justice I: 47–50; needed in heaven I: 167; distributive III.4
Justinian II: 19, 300; III: 2n; IV: 187n, 218; V: 225–6

Kalinowski, Georges I: 78n
Kalven, Harry I: 279n, 281, 285n, 292n
Kant, Immanuel
   on autonomy III: 54–9; V: 73–4; carnal crimes against nature III: 16, 61–2, 64–6, 104n, 339, 342n; conscience III: 169; V: 60; dualism(s) II: 94; III: 68–70; IV: 136; kingdom of ends I: 245; III: 54–5; IV: 121; liberalism I: 264; IV: 178, 328; V: 183; marriage III: 104n, 342n; philosophy of moral law, right, and law I: 301; III: 10, 47–8, 53–71; IV: 111; punishment III: 161, 163–5; respect for humanity I: 211, 246n; III: 60, 64, 219; V: 246, 267, 270; universalizability and non-contradiction I: 141, 210, 236; III: 60; IV: 53, 97, 142, 164
   inadequate understanding of reason and human good and nature I: 5, 7, 12–13, 24–6, 28, 45n, 55, 59, 102, 128, 147n, 204, 236–7, 242; II: 129; III: 9, 320; IV: 4, 93, 98, 131, 239; V: 59; self-referential inconsistencies in V: 153, 155n
   Neo-Kantian I: 22n, 147n, 202; III: 64, 122; IV: 10, 75, 162, 166–7, 223–4; V: 22; *also* I: 287n; IV: 154, 333, 357; V: 4
Kantorowicz, Ernst H. IV: 410n
Kaplan, Fred I: 287–8n
Kaplow, Louis I: 249n
Kass, Leon R. III: 356n
Kauper, Paul G. I: 277n
Kavka, Gregory II: 233n
Keenan, James F, II: 236n
Keily, Bartholomew V: 305n
Keith, Harry II: 316
Keizer, Bert III: 261n
Kelly, George Armstrong III: 68n
Kelly, Gerald V: 297n
Kelley, J.M. III: 43n
Kelley, Patrick J. II: 211n, 215n; IV: 139 , 352n
Kelsen, Hans I: 19, 104–9, 112, 254, II: 24–7; III: 168; IV: 2–3, 12, 36, 40, 79, 99–100, 108, 112, 142, 162–3, 167–8, 186, 211n, 244n, 261, 263, 407n, 408–9, 411–17, 420–3, 426–7, 429n, 433
Kennedy, Duncan IV: 229n, 327–31
Kennedy, John F. II: 5
Kenny, Anthony I: 143n; II: 174n, 183n, 189n, 199n; III: 57n; V: 163n
Kenny, Justice (John) III: 43n
Keown, John I: 57n; II: 312n; III: 253–5n, 260n
Kerr, John II: 272–3
Ketley, M.A. III: 273n
Keynes, J.M. III: 378n
Kingsley, Charles V: 43
Kirk, Marshall III: 349–50n
Kis, Janos V: 103n, 105, 107–12
Kittel, Gerhard V: 261n
Kleinberg, Stanley III: 76–82
Kleinfeld, Andrew III: 256
Knauer, Peter V: 297n
Kneale, W.M. I: 71, 72n; III: 162
knowledge: as basic human good I: 2–5, 47, 62–5, 72–80, 139; is conceptual I: 205; of goods precedes adequate knowledge of nature I: 5; not innate: I: 148; order (epistemological) of coming to know natures I: 5; of possibilities, needed for understanding basic goods I: 5; practical I: 3; warranted, true belief I: 3

Knox, John II: 95n, 230n
koinōnia I: 48n, 123, 312
Koppelman, Andrew I: 297n; III: 326n, 345, 346–7n, 348–9, 350n, 351, 354n, 355–7, 360, 365–9, 372–3, 377–8n, 379–84, 385n, 386, 387n; V: 29
Kornhauser, Lewis IV: 348, 349n
Korsgaard, Christine I: 7, 23–7, 32–3, 101n; IV: 252
Kramer, Matthew I: 85n, 86–88, 91n
Kronman, Anthony I: 22; IV: 211–15, 217–19, 221–8, 315
Kuhn, Thomas IV: 33–4
Kuttner, Stephan IV: 174n, 187–8

Lacey, Nicola IV: 229n, 234, 236–7, 254n, 258–9n, 271n, 275, 278n; V: 32
Lactantius, I: 71n
Ladd, John III: 47n, 61n
Ladenson, Robert IV: 83n
Lafont, Ghislain I: 150n
Lagrange, J.M. V: 142
Lamennais, Hugues-Félicité-Robert de V: 158n
Landes, William M. II: 205–6
Lane, Lord Chief Justice (Geoffrey) II: 174–5n
Lang, Daniel III: 170
Langer, Suzanne I: 286n–8n, 290, 320n
Langholm, Odd V: 157n
langue v parole II: 67
Laplace, Pierre-Simon IV: 177
Larmore, Charles V: 51n
Latham, R.T.E. IV: 414n
Latourelle, René V: 142
Laumann, Edward O. III: 377n
law(s) IV.1–22; and 'bad man' I: 113; contradictory (inconsistent) laws I: 105–6; as cultural object and technique I: 219; foundation of rights (ratio iuris) I: 21n, and friendship I: 123; as means of social control I: 107–8; of nature I: 200; as part of moral life I: 123; primary and secondary rules I: 106–7; as reason for action I: 105; as social phenomenon I: 104–5, 108; sources of I: 19–21; universal propositions of practical reason: I: 19; IV: 449–50 (*see also* sources thesis)
Lawson, Penelope III: 273, 275
Lee, Patrick I: 39, 102, 151n, 154, 190n, 310, 313n; II: 312; III: 355n, 373, 387n; IV: 460; V: 187, 298n, 301n
legal positivism IV.1 & 4 & 7, IV: 99–109
legal reasoning I.14, IV.12–14, IV. 16–20
Legarre, Santiago III: 113n
Leibniz, G.W. II: 7n–8n, 155n; V: 153
Leiter, Brian IV: 32–3, 34n, 35–44, 105n, 112–15; V: 84, 195
Leo XIII II: 85, 126n; III: 186n; V: 253n
Lessius, Leonard V: 212n

Lewis, C.I. I: 72, 84,
Lewis, C.S. III: 16, 273–81
Lewis, David K. IV: 59n, 67n
'liberalism' I: 60–1n; V: 104–5, 113; 'political l.' I: 55–8
Lichtenberg, Judith IV: 366
Lindsay, A.D. IV: 259–60, 263
Line, Anne, St. I: 37; II: 54n
Line, Roger I: 37; II: 55n
Littleton, Thomas de III: 135
Livy IV: 321
Lloyd of Berwick, Lord (Anthony) IV: 398
Lloyd, Dennis IV: 380–1, 383
Locke, John I: 81, 102, 298; II: 38, 43; III: 191, 225n, 239; IV: 10, 12, 93, 95–8, 136, 142, 190n, 200, 208n, 320; V: 141
Lockhart, William B. I: 277n, 279n, 281n, 288n
Lockwood, Michael II: 279–85
Lombard, Peter I: 193; II: 165, 245, 247; III: 353n, 359; IV: 175
Lombardi, Joseph II: 257n
Lonergan, Bernard J.F. I: 71, 84, 88–9, 130n, 134, 137–40, 142, 143n, 168n, 288n; II: 135n, 258; IV: 396; V: 58n, 139–40, 143–8, 149n, 150–2, 155–6, 263n, 272n
Lottin, Odon I: 121; IV: 174n, 180
love: 'hath reason' I: 37–40; of neighbour as self I: 38n; II: 51
Lowry, Robert II: 315, 318
Luban, David IV: 357–69
Lucas, J. R. (John) III: 273n; IV: 378n
Lucas, Paul IV: 189n, 194n, 197–8n
Luce, D.H. I: 222n; IV: 56n, 60n, 68n, 359n
Luño, Angel Rodriguez IV: 440n
Luther, Martin II: 5; V: 164–5, 171
Lutz, Cora E. III: 99
Lycophron III: 92
lying: I: 50, 151; V: 164; and logic of assertion I: 74

MacCormick, Neil III: 37n; IV: 76n, 77, 163, 211n, 229n, 230, 235, 240, 248n, 390, 394
MacDonald, Margaret I: 74n
Macedo, Stephen III: 92n, 95n, 97–100, 102, 105–6, 110, 114, 326–7n, 340n, 342–3n, 348–9, 351, 380n, 381–2, 384, 386; V: 111n, 116
Machiavelli, Niccolò III: 199, 234; IV: 352; V: 76
Mackie, J.L. (John) I: 45n, 65–6n, 67–8, 71n, 74n, 81, 83, 85, 93n; IV: 133, 224n
Mackinolty, Chips III: 269n
MacIntyre, Alasdair I: 48n; IV: 372; V: 58
Maclean, Donald III: 378n
Macnaghten, Lord (Edward) II: 207n
Madison, James I: 283–4
Madsen, Hunter III: 349–50n
Magrath, C. Peter I: 296n

Maguire, Daniel III: 248n
Mahoney, John (Jack) II: 133n; V: 287
Maimonides, Moses V: 23
Maine, Henry III: 153
Maitland, F.W. II: 99n; IV: 320n
Malawi III: 125–7
Malcolm, Norman I: 73n
Mance, Lord (Jonathan) II: 272
Mandela, Nelson IV: 113
Manuel II, Paleologus V: 91
Marcel, Gabriel I: 210
Maritain, Jacques I: 205, 287n; II: 107n; V: 58, 78n, 243, 275, 285–6, 333
Marius, Richard V: 166
Marmor, Andrei IV: 246n
marriage III.20–22; IV: 135–8; a basic human good I: 9–10, 34, 155; III: 100; an action I: 9; III: 317
Marshall, Justice (Thurgood) III: 252n
Marsilius of Padua IV: 160
Martin, Christopher F.J. II: 43n
Martin, Patrick H. I: 36–7
Marx, Karl IV: 259–60, 332; V: 34, 237
Master, William V: 225, 229–30
Matthews, Gareth B. I: 70n
Matthews, Steven V: 1
Mattison, Andrew W. III: 349
May, William E. I: 154; V: 341
Mazzoni, C.M. II: 296
McAnany, Patrick D. I: 278n
McBrien, Richard P. V: 139–40
McClure, Robert C. I: 277n, 279n, 281n, 288n
McCormick, Richard II: 144–5, 147–9, 152n, 245n, 265; III: 248n; V: 261–2, 265n, 271–2, 287, 291n, 296n, 299–300n, 303–4n, 306n, 309–10n, 316n, 322n, 360n
McDowell, John H. I: 75n, 81, 186n,
McHugh, Justice (Michael) III: 143n
McInerny, Ralph I: 52–3n; V: 66–7n
McKim, Robert I: 234n
McKnight, Joseph W. IV: 189–90n, 194n, 198n
McKnight, Stephen A. V: 1
McMahan, Jeff II: 307–8, 310
McWhirter, David P. III: 349n
Medeiros, Humberto Sousa V: 291n
Medina, Bartolomé de IV: 52n
Meiklejohn, Alexander I: 282n
Meiland, Jack W. II: 222–4, 226
Melamed, Douglas I: 247n; IV: 346n
Mercken H. Paul F. I: 193n
metaphysics essential to ethics, political theory and law IV: 353; of freely chosen activity (discourse) I: 55, 217; II: 34–5; of persons I: 35, 53, 204; II: 66–7, 70, 93, 105, 283, 302, 307; IV: 142; see also I: 43n, 94, 172, 236; II: 7; III: 370n; IV: 155, 288, 328; V: 17, 42, 149
Meyer, Ben V: 141–2, 152–3

Mill, John Stuart I: 298–9, 304–9, 311n; II: 110n, 124, 126n; III: 2, 51n, 66–7n, 78, 115n; IV: 154, 259–60, 266, 276, 279, 385
Miller, David III: 45n, 148
Miller, Henry I: 287n, 289n
Miller, Jonathan I: 14, 321–3
Mills, C. Wright IV: 34n, 224n
Milton, John I: 13, 274n, 298–9, 309; IV: 385; V: 4
miracles (see also Hume) I: 275; II: 72n; V: 57n, 88–9, 116, 137, 142, 152–3, 167
Moleski, Martin I: 65n
Moline, John I: 165n
Montesquieu, Charles de IV: 12
Montgomery, George R. II: 8n
Moore, G.E. I: 74, 130
Moore, Michael II: 174n, 177n
moral: absolutes I.12; I: 13, 50–2; beliefs, diversity of I: 79; and action I: 115–8; evaluation I: 119–20; ideals I: 118; point of view I: 119; 'morality system' (Williams) I: 102–3; m. philosophy, modern I: 113–23; standards as second level of practical understanding I: 12, 31–2, 140–2, 148–9, 153–5; m. thought as rational thought I: 215
More, Thomas, St. V: 10, 118–19, 163–78, 368
Morris, Harry II: 40n
Morris, Herbert III: 177
Morris of Borth-y-Gest, Lord (John) IV: 435n
Morrison, J.S. I: 314n
Moses V: 136
Moya, Carlos J. II: 199n, 225n
Moya, Matthaeus de V: 212
Mugabe, Robert V: 199–201
Müller, Jan-Werner II: 107
Mulley, Graham III: 249
multi-culturalism (see also 'diversity') II: 12
Munby, James II: 316
Murphy, Jeffrie G. III: 61n, 161–4, 177
Murphy, Mark V: 193, 195–7
Murphy-O'Connor, Cormac II: 266n
Murray, John Courtney IV: 386n, 388n; V: 276, 282
Musonius Rufus I: 244n; II: 128; III: 88, 91, 100, 102, 323n, 338–40, 355; V: 350, 352
Mustill, Lord (Michael) II: 312–3, 315, 318, 320; III: 235n
Muzorewa, Abel V: 199n

Nagel, Thomas I: 259n, II: 84–5; III: 50n, 95n; V: 71, 72n
Namier, Lewis IV: 203n
Napoleon I IV: 395
Nash, John IV: 361
natural law I: 41, 144, 152, 177, 214; n.l. theory I: 199–21; theology of V.19
natures: knowledge of via capacities, acts, and their objects I: 5, 33, 147, 179, 204
Nero V: 203

nested ends and means II: 163
Newman, John Henry: V: 6–7, 9–10, 43, 46n, 54n, 60, 87, 152–3, 162n, 169, 204–5, 209–24
Newton, Isaac II: 8
Nicholls, Lord (Donald) II: 217n–19n; III: 144n
Nicolau, M. V: 153n
Nietzsche, Friedrich I: 22, 28, 41n, 49–51, 69, 88, 94, 96, 118; III: 9, 13, 167–78, 266–7; V: 33–4, 73–4, 183, 194, 197–8, 339
Nietzschian moral theory I: 118
Nigidius, P. IV: 187–8n
Noonan, John T. III: 294n, 298n, 320n, 346n, 356–61, 365n, 366–8, 372; V: 353n
Norman, E.R. V: 235–49
normativ(ity): as ought-knowledge I: 3; of theoretical reason I: 8; source of I: 98–9
Nozick, Robert I: 63, 169, 217; III: 80; IV: 53n, 266; V: 71n
Nussbaum, Martha I: 10–12, 28; III: 16, 99n, 323–4n, 372n, 378n, 385n, 387n

objective/ity: kinds of I: 134–5; certainty I: 130; moral I: 140; of principles I: 64; and truth I: 214; III: 25; of value judgments I: 202
offensiveness (*see also* insult) II: 117
O'Connell, Daniel P. IV: 407n
O'Connell, Timothy E. II: 133–5, 138, 150n; V: 160n, 257–8n, 261, 262n, 265–6n, 270–1n, 272
O'Connor, James V: 379
O'Connor, John IV: 441n
O'Connor, Justice (Sandra Day) III: 252n; IV: 371
Odo of Dour IV: 174n
Oecolampadius, Johannes V: 165
Olson, Eric II: 292n
omission II: 161
Origen V: 159
Orrego, Cristóbal IV: 262n, 275
Ortiz, Daniel IV: 327–32, 334
others: are like me in basic worth I: 4, 27, 47; III: 172; V: 67
Ottaviani, Alfred III: 191n
ought-knowledge I: 3, 99
Owen, G.E.L. I: 110

Pagden, Anthony III: 130–1n
Pannick, Lord (David) III: 44n
Parfit, Derek II: 150n; V: 305n
Parker, Isaac IV: 391–2
Pascal, Blaise I: 37, 313
passions (emotions): deflect practical reason I: 14, 47; reason's civil rule over I: 14, 211; support practical reason I: 14–15, 213
Passmore, John I: 66, 71n
paternalism II: 109; III: 10–11, 71, III.5; IV: 137n, 268, 270, 276; V: 105, 112, 117–8
Paton, G.W. IV: 189n, 378

patria: one's country II: 107, 118–9, 123; III: 290, 328; heavenly I: 167n
patriotism: I: 40, 253; II: 123, 126–7; IV: 258; V: 11; 'constitutional p.' II: 107
Patterson, Charlotte J. III: 356n
Patterson, Dennis IV: 44n
Paul, St. I: 96, 193, 258, 312; III: 353n, 359n; V: 10, 43, 45n, 115–16, 125, 131, 159–60, 169, 177, 200–1, 227–30, 247, 249, 263, 267n, 273, 302, 350, 372
Paul IV III: 103
Paul VI II: 128, 251; III: 121, 199n; V: 188n, 241–2, 244n, 246, 247n, 274, 299n, 341, 344–67, 371
Paul, James C.N. I: 130, 278n
Paulson, Stanley L. II: 24n
Pearce, Lord (Edward) IV: 435n
Pears, David II: 230n
Pearson, Lord (Colin) I: 318n
Peel, Robert II: 201n; IV: 341n
performative inconsistency, *see* self-refutation
Peirce, Charles Sanders I: 45; IV: 124, 130n, 394–5; V: 26
peoples II: 107
Pericles IV: 157
Perry, Michael III: 383n; V: 194, 197, 198n
person, personal identity I.5, II.1–2; defined II: 9, 98; metaphysics of I: 35; non-fungible I: 40
Peschke, K.-H. II: 153n; V: 75, 187n, 341n
Peter, St I: 258; V: 116, 125, 175, 203, 205–6, 287
Phillimore, Lord (Walter) III: 137n
Phillips of Worth Matravers, Lord (Nicholas) II: 271
Philo Judaeus III: 350n, 385n; V: 159, 187
Philosophers' Brief V: 71, 73
philosophy
    consistency with worth of philosophizing I: 81; of human affairs I: 63, 108
Pijnenborg, Loes III: 254n
Pildes, Richard N. I: 235n, 253n
Pinckaers, Servais II: 154n
Pink, T.L.M. II: 230n
Pius IX V: 218
Pius XI III: 100, 293n; V: 346
Pius XII II: 171n, 237, 249n, 251–2, 303, 306; III: 100–1, 193n, 195n, 199n, 293n, 308n, 310; V: 113, 160n, 215, 254n, 255, 299n, 310n, 341, 346
Planck, Max V: 23n
Plato
    on bad secularisms V: 57–9, 64, 66, 124, 333–4, 342; basic goods I: 161n; 'better to suffer wrong than do it' I: 241–2; III: 201; V: 267; Cave I: 94–7; II: 129; V: 133, 138; cooperation with God III: 9, 189; V: 44n, 133–4, 226–7, 230–1; family II: 13, 126n; friendship I: 41–53, 112; IV: 432; God's

existence and goodness V: 61, 187, 336, 338; good of truth I: 41–53, 63; *Gorgias* I: 41–53, 60; III: 103; IV: 93, 103, 125; law I: 108; IV: [51], 76, 157, 160; method in social theory IV: 80, 235, 265; natural law I: 201; III: 85n, 127; IV: 10, 76, 93, 124–5, 187; V: 33, 267; paternalism III: 27n; IV: 135, 270; V: 105–6, 112, 118; portrait of the philosopher I: 313–5; punishment III: 155, 157–8; V: 13; reason and passions I: 282; *Republic* I: 121IV: 134, 176; self-refutation I: 70, 83–4, 90–1; V: 148; sex ethics II: 128; III: 99–103, 323–4, 336, 338–41, 372n, 378n, 387–8; IV: 137n, 272–4; V: 350; soul II: 34, 40n; *see also* I: 81, 92, 188, 202, 208–9, 265n; II: 5, 38; III: 107, 186n; IV: 9n, 174, 225n, 234n, 258–60, 276, 279; V: 51, 135, 193, 273

play II: 151

Plutarch III: 99n, 102, 104n, 338–40, 342, 355; IV: 137

Pogge, Thomas III: 123–4n

Pollock, Frederick II: 209n; IV: 320n

pornography I.17, I.19

Porter, Jean II: 243n, 256–65; V: 76n, 340–1

positivity of law I: 208

Posner, Richard I: 234n; II: 203–6, 215, 226; III: 170, 242, 243n; IV: 9–10, 53n, 125, 172, 344–7, 349–50; V: 26n, 34

Possidius, St. V: 376

Postema, Gerald J. IV: 66, 73n, 87n, 108n

postmodern(ism) I: 46n, 94; II: 127; IV: 172, 327–34

Pound, Roscoe IV: 189n

Powell, Justice (Lewis) F I: 269n

practical reason I.1, I.6, I.8–11, I.14, IV.17

practical reasonableness: an architectonic basic human good (*bonum rationis*) I: 4, 34, 36, 172, 177, 183; V: 11; inner integrity, outer authenticity I: 14; requirements of II: 139

praxis I: 46, 207, 217, 240; II: 102; III: 93; IV: 283–5; V: 180, 205

Price, Anthony II: 44n, 46n; III: 99n, 103, 337–8n; V: 350

Price, David IV: 320, 321n, 323n, 324–5

Prichard, H.A. I: 237

principle(s): first principle of practical reason I: 29–30, 144–5; first principles of practical reason I: 9–12, 28, 144–50, 177–8, 205; general, of law I: 20; indemonstrable I: 147–8; induction of first principles directing to basic goods I: 5, 32–3, 148; master principle of morality I: 129, 210, 215; moral I: 208, 210, 215–6; of practical reasonableness I: 31–2, 140–2

Proclus IV: 188n

proposal for choice II: 11

propositions I: 65n; concepts and words have full meaning in I: 2; law as

IV.22 esp. 449–52 (*see also* assertion, self-refutation)

Prosser, William I: 226n

Protagoras I: 83

Proust, Marcel IV: 230, 251

prudence (*phronēsis, prudentia*, practical reasonableness); concerns ends as well as means I: 26, 173–86; connection with justice I; 120–1; measure of all virtues I: 121; needed in beatitude I: 167; not mere cleverness I: 121

public reason I.15–16, V.2, V.5; Rawlsian restrictions of I: 13, 55; V: 106, 138; straightforward sense I: 13, 58 (*see also* Rawls)

Pufendorf, Samuel von IV: 10, 95–6, 146n, 337

punishment III.10–12; IV: 83–4, 121, 142–4, 179, 381–4; V: 228, 310n, 370–1; capital V: 309

purity III: 387

Putnam, Hilary IV: 223

'pvs' II.18–19

Pythagoras IV: 188n

questioning, significance of V.7; V: 103

Quine, W.V. IV: 33–4, 41

Quinlan, Michael V: 289–90n

Quinton, A.M. I: 302; IV: 259–60, 263, 275

Radbruch, Gustav IV: 221

Radcliffe, Viscount (Cyril) III: 28

Rahner, Karl I: 89; V: 148, 149n, 155, 220–1, 224, 256, 270n, 272n, 373

Raiffa, H. I: 222n; IV: 56n, 60n, 66, 359n

Ramsey, Paul II: 147n; V: 296n, 299n, 304n, 310n

Raphael, D.D. II: 226n

'rational choice': ambiguity of phrase I: 218–9

rationality norms I: 8; V: 150–4

rationalization II: 13; V: 46

Rawls, John I.16 (*Political Liberalism*), III.3 (*Theory of Justice*); *see also* I: 13–14, 43n, 55, 57–9, 60n, 63, 96n, 141,189, 222; II: 12, 108, 123–7; III: 10, 48–51, 67n, 95 III: 92, 95, 121, 123–4n; IV: 57–8, 155–6n, 264–6; V: 4, 6–8, 11–12, 18, 48, 52–3, 71, 72n, 85n, 87, 113, 116, 138n

Raz, Joseph IV: 2n, 4–9, IV.2–3; *see also* I: 224n, 253; II: 33n, 81n, 112–7, 119n, 123–4n; III: 3, 37n , 50n, 68n, 70n, 95, 147, 148n, 168; IV: 2n, 27–8, 30n, 31, 38, 40, 42n, 100–1, 106n, 108n, 163–5, 169–70, 184, 185n, 188n, 235, 243, 246n, 247, 254n, 258–9, 261n, 278n, 284, 289n, 294–5n, 321n, 324, 414, 421–3, 430, 433; V: 18, 30, 63n, 72n, 105n, 107–8, 110, 111n

Reagan, Ronald V: 278, 280

reason(ing): as action I: 1, 127–8; is to be followed I: 8; judicial I: 221; legal I: 212–30; as motivating I: 22–4, 129; theoretical I: 40

reasonableness *see* prudence I: 128
reasons
　for action I: 1, 10, 212–3; basic I: 24–8,
　　213–6; 'instrumental' I: 22–3; and
　　law I: 105; 'internal' and external' I: 7
reductionism I: 218
reflection I: 52–2
Reformation, the V: 164–71
Regan, Augustine III: 193n; V: 309n
Reid, Elspeth II: 219n
Reid, Lord (James) IV: 400
Reid, Thomas II: 43n
Reiman, Jeffrey I: 256–7, 261n, 265n, 268n,
　272n, 273–6, 275n; V: 330–2
Reinhardt, Stephen III: 253, 256
Reiss, Hans III: 61
religion: basic human good of I: 59; V: 28–9,
　85–6n, 92, 117, 180–1; liberty V.4, V: 35–8,
　117–8, 158; 'natural religion' V: 27–30, 62,
　65, 217; and public reason V.2, V.5, V: 2–9,
　84–5, 116; and state V.1, V.4, V: 5–9
repentance III: 373
'respect nature' III: 104
ressentiment I: 118
retorsive argument, *see* self-refutation I: 65,
　135–7
revelation V.2, V.8; *also* V: 83–4, 102, 111,
　115–6, 175, 218
revolution IV: 8; legal effect III: 203–5; IV.21;
　IV: 2–3, 16–18, 118, 244–5
Rhonheimer, Martin II: 164n, 166n; V: 160n
Richard III II: 52
Richards, David A.J. III: 10, 48, 53–7, 58–9n,
　60, 63n, 66n, 290
Richardson, Alan V: 143
Richardson, Elliot V: 278
Richter, A.L. V: 222n
Rickman, H.P. V: 144n
rights: absolute I: 154, 211; logic of I: 206–7;
　IV.18, IV: 3
Riker, William IV: 54, 55n
Rinck, Hans-Justus IV: 189n, 196n, 209n
Roberts, Owen I: 278; III: 22–3
Roberts-Wray, Kenneth IV: 414n
Robinson, John A.T. V: 88, 152n
Rodger, Lord (Alan) III: 45n, 144n
Rolland, Romain IV: 251
Rolph, C.H. I: 296n
Roper, Margaret V: 163n
Rorty, Richard IV: 125, 331
Roskill, Lord (Eustace) II: 220n
Ross, Alf I: 66; IV: 415–17, 420–1, 423n,
　428–9
Ross, W.D. I: 71n, 237
Rotello, Gabriel III: 384–5n
Roth, Claus IV: 214n
Rousseau, Jean-Jacques I: 13, 275n,
　II: 126n; V: 4
Royce, Josiah I: 141, 210
Ruff, Wilfried II: 279n

Rule of Law III: 332
rules of law, explained II: 23–4
Russell, J.B. I: 60, 74n

Saeed, Abdullah V: 53
Saeed, Hassan V: 53
Sager, Lawrence G. V: 18, 20, 29–31, 86n, 95
Salaverri, J. V: 153n
Salmond, John IV: 376–7
Santamaria, B. A. III: 114n
Santayana, George I: 289n
sapientia I: 160n
Sartorius, Rolf IV: 47n, 72n, 74–87, 126n
Sartre, J.-P. I: 202; V: 183
Scalia, Justice (Antonin) IV: 153; V: 18n, 76
Scanlon, Thomas V: 71n
Scarman, Lord (Leslie) II: 174n, 220n;
　III: 23n, 30
scepticism I: 64–5, 70–80, 94, 130–7; critique
　of I: 201–4
Schauer, Frederick I: 297n; IV: 163
Scheffler, Samuel V: 304–5n
Schelling, Thomas IV: 59n
Schenk, Roy U. II: 279n
Schlesinger, Elliot V: 278–9
Schmitt, Charles B. V: 332n
Schnackenburg, R. V: 260n
Schneewind, J.B. I: 264n
Scholz, Franz V: 297n, 308–9n
Schüller, Bruno II: 144–8, 244n; IV: 75, 187n,
　261; V: 187n, 253, 265n, 287, 297n, 300n,
　304n
Schwartz, Pepper III: 384n
Scott, James Brown III: 191n
Scott, Lord Justice (Leslie) III: 34
Scott, Richard V: 99n
Scruton, Roger II: 92–8; III: 261n
Searle, John V: 339n
secularism v secularity V.3
Seifert, Josef II: 306
self-constitution II: 196
self-contradiction I: 85
self-evidence I: 64, 77, 133
self-referring laws IV: 230–1, 415–6
self-refutation (self-referential inconsistency,
　performative inconsistency) I.3–4;
　V: 148–9; *also* I: 45–7, 127–8, 133–7, 203;
　V: 32, 66n, 107, 144, 153; kinds of I: 65–8,
　81–2
Sellars, Wilfrid II: 222n
Semonche, John E. I: 285n
*semper sed non ad semper v semper et ad
　semper* I: 189
Sen, Amartya I: 10; IV: 56
Seneca III: 202n
sex ethics III.20–22; IV: 135–8; V.23
Sextus Empiricus IV: 355; V: 129
Shakespeare, William I: 36, 38
　All's Well that Ends Well II: 42, 44–8, 53,
　　55–62, 64; V: 334–5; *Anthony & Cleopatra*

INDEX

I: 31n; *As You Like It* II: 40n, 65, 334; *Hamlet* II: 38, 41n, 67, 104; *Henry IV, Part I* II: 63; *Henry V* II: 63; V: 335; *King John* V: 343; *King Lear* I: 33; V: 5n; *Measure for Measure* II: 57, 65; *The Merchant of Venice* II: 40; *A Midsummer Night's Dream* II: 39; III: 324; *Phoenix & Turtle* I: 36–7, 39–40; II: 54–5; *Richard III* II: 49–50, 52; V: 13; *Sonnet XI* IV: 272; *The Tempest* I: 35n
Shand, Lord (Alexander) II: 207n
Shapiro, Scott IV: 91n
Sharswood, George IV: 190n, 194n
Shavelson, Lonny III: 267
Shaw, Russell V: 161n
Shaw of Dunfermline, Lord (Thomas) III: 133n
Shearmur, Jeremy IV: 353–6
Sheehan, Duncan IV: 401n
Shelley, Percy Bysshe IV: 274n
Shewmon, Alan II: 307–9
Shils, E.A. IV: 34n, 79n
Shortt, Edward III: 116–17
side effects II.9–11, II.13–14
Sidgwick, Henry I: 30n, 198n, II: 182n, 212; III: 214–15; V: 74, 265n
Sikkink, David III: 114n
Simmonds, N.E. IV: 245, 250n
Simmons, A.J. IV: 72n
Simon, David II: 175n
Simon, Jürgen II: 300–1
Simon, Viscount (John) II: 210
Simon, Yves IV: 69
Simonds, Gavin III: 36n; IV: 268–9, 429n
Simpson, A.W. Brian IV: 16
Simpson, Peter I: 234n
Singer, Peter I: 57, II: 279n, 281–2, 302–12; V: 68
slavery: and penal servitude I: 59
Slough, M.C. I: 278n, 279n
Smart, J.J.C. V: 61, 69
Smith, Adam IV: 10, 337–40, 348, 352
Smith, Christian III: 114n
Smith, J.C. I: 217n
Smith, M.B.E. IV: 47n
Smith, Stephen W. V: 163n, 169
Smith, Sydney II: 199–202; IV: 342, 344
'social choice' theory IV. 2 & 3
social rules I: 107
social theory I: 205
Socrates I: 41, 43–4, 46, 47n, 49–50, 95, 115, 161n, 241–2, 313, II: 33; III: 4–5, 99–100, 157, 323n, 336–7, 355, 377n; IV: 76, 159–60, 186n, 225n, 226
Sokolowski, Robert II: 43n
Solidarity II: 125
Solon III: 102nm 339n
Sommerville, Margaret R. III: 320n
soul: form and act of body I: 35, 54
'sources thesis' (s. of law only social facts) I: 19
sovereignty: and limitation of self or successors I: 68–70

'speculative' knowledge I: 147n, 168–70
Spender, Stephen III: 378n
Spiazzi, R.M. I: 159n; III: 353n
Spicq, Ceslau V: 186n
Spinoza, Baruch II: 177; IV: 160
spirit(uality) II.3
spoudaios I: 108–13, 122–3, 143, 233n; IV: 80, 433
St. German (Germain), Christopher IV: 199, 200n, 208, 218
St. John-Stevas, Norman I: 279n
Stalin, Joseph II: 84; V: 58
'state of nature' I: 80, 200; IV: 55, 116
  and Blackstone IV: 198–200, 202, 207–9
Staudinger, Hugo V: 142n
Steptoe, Patrick II: 294n; III: 280n
Stevens, Justice (John Paul) III: 245–6
Stevens, Monica V: 170n
Stewart, Justice (Potter) I: 285n, 296
Stone, Julius IV: 376–7, 379–80
Stout, Robert III: 249–50
'stranger in the wilds' I: 15, 99; II: 129
Strauss, Leo I: 187–90; III: 86–7, 89n; IV: 225n; V: 152
Strawson, P.F. (Peter) I: 287n, 319, II: 92n–3n
Suárez, Francisco I: 6, 125, 177n; II: 291n; III: 185n, 188n, 190–2, 193–4, 195n, 198n, 200–1n, 203–4n, 206n; IV: 52n; V: 272, 374n
subjectivity II: 68
substantial change II: 287
sufficient reason, 'principle of' II: 7; V: 183–4
Sugarman, David IV: 274n
Sullivan, Andrew III: 384n
Sullivan, Francis A. V: 115
Sullivan, Thomas D. II: 183n
Sumner, Lord (Hamilton, John) II: 218–19n; III: 137n
survival: as aim I: 63
Sutton, Agneta III: 312n
Swadling, W. IV: 401n
Sylvester, David I: 289n
synderesis I: 28–30, 139, 163, 173, 175–6, 182, 194; V: 179

Tacitus, Publius Cornelius III: 184n
Taney, Roger B. II: 26n
Taylor, Charles III: 323n
Taylor, Gary II: 67–8; V: 335n
Taylor, Harriet IV: 279
Taylor, J. IV: 186n
Teichman, Jenny III: 239n
Teichmuller, Gustav I: 160n
Temple, William V: 243
'temporal' V: 92–3
Thierry of Chartres IV: 187n
Thomas, St. V: 60
Thomas, S. V: 93n
Thomism, Thomist I: 12
Thomson, Judith Jarvis I: 269–70; III: 15, 282–9, 292–3, 295n, 296–305; V: 71–2n, 331

Thucydides, II: 5; IV: 76
Tillyard, E.M.W. II: 46n
Tollefsen, Christopher I: 45n, 73n, 84n, 90, 100n, 203n, 239n; II: 177n, 286n, 292n; IV: 359; V: 149, 150–1n
Tooley, Michael II: 281–2, 287; V: 316n
Torralba, J.M. II: 69n
torts (delict), law of II.11; IV.16, IV: 138–40, 150–1
torture I: 102
transparency for I.8; II: 113; III: 25–6; IV: 255, 286
Tribonian IV: 117
truth I:5; V: 33–4
Tsikata, Fui IV: 429n
Tsikata, Tsatsu IV: 429n
Tubbs, J.W. IV: 149n
Tuck, Richard III: 125, 128–31
Tugwell, Simon IV: 180n
Turner, Stephen P. I: 203n; IV: 224–5n
Turrecremata, Johannes de V: 213n
Tushnet, Mark IV: 352n, 371–2
Twining, William IV: 232n
twinning II: 289–92, 296–7
Twycross, Robert III: 265–8n
Tynan, Kenneth I: 321n
Tyndale, William V: 165, 166–7

Ullmann-Margalit, Edna IV: 56–9n, 67n, 69
Ulpian II: 5; IV: 183, 218
Unger, Roberto M. I: 214; IV: 10, 123n, 299–319, 322, 324–5
usury V: 157–8
ut in pluribus v *ut in paucioribus* I: 189
utilitarian(ism) I: 141, 143

value: aspect of human flourishing I: 137; Lonerganian theory of I: 137–9, 143
'value-free' social science/theory I: 205–6; IV.1, IV.9, IV: 1–4, 7, 17, 106–9, 163–4, 232–5; V: 146
van Beeck, Franz Josef V: 309n
Van den Haag, Ernest I: 289n
Van Reit, Simone V: 84n
Vasquez, Gabriel I: 125; V: 212n
Vattel, Emmerich de III: 139n
Veatch, Henry I: 148n
Vendler, Zeno II: 93
Vermeersch, P. III: 298n
Villey, Michel I: 206–8
Vinogradoff, Paul IV: 409n
virtue I: 120, 150; dependent on rational norm: I: 151–2; end(s) of I: 175–6; to be found again in Kingdom I: 171; V: 288, 366, 371
Vitoria, Francisco de III: 130–1, 190–2, 194, 198n, 200–1n, 206n
Vlastos, Gregory III: 99n, 337
Voegelin, Eric I: 189, II: 14n, 126n; IV: 50n, 259, 278, 321n, 428, 431; V: 34, 58, 146n, 339

von Balthasar, Hans Urs V: 13, 64, 65n, 373–9
von Hildebrand, Dietrich I: 138
von Wright, Georg Henrik I: 130
Vorgrimler, Herbert V: 272n

Wade, F.C. II: 288n
Wade, H.W.R. IV: 415
Waffelaert, J. II: 254n
Walker, Lord (Justice) (Robert) II: 196n; III: 135n, 144n
Waller, Mark III: 23n
Walter, James II: 163n; V: 291n, 298–302n, 304n, 342
Walton, Douglas III: 213n
Walton, Lord (John) III: 211n, 213–16, 222n, 232–3, 262–4, 269, 277n; IV: 277n
Waluchow, W. J. IV: 164
war III.13
Ward, Alan II: 196n
Ward, Keith III: 58n
Warnock, G.J. I: 113–20
Warnock, Mary III: 21n
Washington, George V: 28
Waszink, J.H. IV: 187n
Watson, Lord (William) I: 226n; II: 207–8
Webber, Grégoire III: 45n
Weber, Max I: 22, 37, 202–3, 205–6; IV: 3, 33–4n, 76, 86, 163, 211–29
Wegemer, Gerard V: 163n, 169
Weinberg, Martin S. III: 350n
Weinberg, Stephen V: 194
Weinberger, Caspar V: 277–80
Weinrib, Ernest IV: 123, 163, 395n
Weinstein, Bill II: 81n
Weisheipl, James A. IV: 180n
Weithman, Paul III: 116, 121–2, 123–4n, 383n, 386
Wellman, Carl I: 72n
Wells, Deane II: 279n
Wenham, John V: 88n
Wertheimer, Roger III: 282n, 304
Wheare, K.C. IV: 414
White, Alan R. II: 174n, 199n, 315n
White, Justice (Byron) I: 295, 297n; III: 42n
Whitman, Walt IV: 330, 332–3
Wiggins, David I: 42n, 186n, 260n; II: 43n; III: 225; V: 46n
Wilberforce, Lord (Richard) I: 318n; IV: 256n
will: responsiveness to understood goods I: 1, 33, 38
William of Conches IV: 186–7n
William of Durham V: 189–92
William of Ockham I: 207; IV: 160; V: 150
Williams, Bernard I: 7, 92–7, 100n–1n, 102–3; II: 127–8, 129; III: 239n; IV: 251–3, 275; V: 135n, 305n
Williams, Glanville II: 174n–5n, 177, 182–7, 193, 228n; III: 215; V: 316n
Williams, Gwladys III: 131n
Wilson, George II: 71n

Winch, Peter IV: 211n
Winning, Thomas V: 119
Wishner, Julius I: 278n
Witherspoon, James I: 276n
Wittgenstein, Ludwig I: 71, 80n, 84, 104, 130–7, 142, 143n; II: 5–6, 71; III: 304; IV: 166
Wittich, Gunther IV: 214n
Wojtyla, Karol, (*see also* John Paul II) on action II: 136; on choice as lasting V: 78, 303n; II: 104; on nation II: 122–6, 128
Wolsey, Thomas I: 281
Wolff, Robert Paul III: 58n
Wood, Thomas IV: 191
Woolf, Harry III: 141–2
Wootton, Lady (Barbara) III: 156
Woozley, A.D. IV: 72n

words: bearers and manifestations of spirit I: 35
Wright, Benjamin Fletcher I: 284n
Wright, John, J. II: 118n, 123n
Wright, N.T. V: 192n
Wright, Thomas II: 41n, 44n

Xenophon III: 336–7, 340, 355; IV: 159

Yates, Simon II: 321n
Yowell, Maggie II: 108n

Zalba, Marcellino II: 254n; III: 295n, 298n, 310
Zander, Michael III: 19n
Zellner, Harold M III: 290n
Zeno IV: 428
Zipursky, Benjamin C. IV: 150–1n
Zwingli, Huldrych V: 165